by Edward Conlon

"The New York Police Department has, of course, inspired a huge variety of popular entertainments over the years, from genre novels to films to long-running TV shows. But *Blue Blood*, in terms of its ambition, its authenticity, and the power of its writing, is in a class by itself. Conlon is uniquely qualified to write about this giant yet famously insular tribe. . . . *Blue Blood* runs from the episodes of a cop's life to meditations on that life, from gun-in-hand assignments to mundane calls about vicious cats. Layered with Conlon's family history; allusions to St. Augustine and early police books; and his own views on department dysfunction, the war on drugs, and urban race relations, the book becomes a kind of rich ethnographic document. . . . The title is just right: Conlon bleeds policeman blue; 'the Job' to him is a Catholic-style calling, a vocation. . . . And the fact he's still on the job gives *Blue Blood* a charge and immediacy unlike any other police book I know."

—*The New York Times Book Review*

"Conlon stays alive to the humor and the sadness and the ironies of life even in the teeth of the city's everyday assault—bricks (and, once, a canned ham) thrown from rooftops, the festering bitterness of precinct-house feuds, the bizarro underworld of the midnight shift, the agony, both Dantean and Sisyphean, of sifting through the rubble of the World Trade Center. . . . Conlon has no ambitions as a whistle-blower or a hero—he's neither a Serpico nor a Supercop—and that keeps *Blue Blood* free of distortion and full of perspective."

—*Time*

"Conlon's look inside the NYPD is more chilling than even the most realistic cop dramas on TV. Short of getting recruited or mugged, you won't find a more up-close look at the NYPD than this gritty memoir. Harvard graduate and veteran cop Edward Conlon keeps the reader at his elbow from the time he takes his first steps in uniform to the day he earns his detective's shield. We hear the scratch and cackle of the police radio . . . We climb with him down reeking housing-project stairways, stepping over syringes and shell casings. This book is not for the fainthearted. . . . Conlon's account of the processing of a cop's corpse at a Ground Zero morgue is among the most graphic, heartbreaking images yet excavated from the 9/11 tragedy. . . . But there is also insight and humor. . . . His respect for cop life is palpable."

—*People*

continued . . .

"There are too many lame books about being a police officer written by people who haven't spent a single day in uniform or on the streets. *Blue Blood* is real, authentic, true. Beautiful and inspiring, terrifying and heartbreaking. It is a great book."   —James Frey

"There's stuff that will make your blood boil, juries and grand juries that let off defendants who've done everything but left a signed confession. And there's stuff that will make you sad, including Conlon's account of the days after 9/11. . . . *Blue Blood* is more than just a cop book. It's more than a provincial book about New York City. It's an intelligent examination of a swath of life most of us prefer to sweep under the carpet. If it were up to me, it would be mandatory pre-graduation reading for every college student who needs to learn that the real world isn't just an MTV show."

—*Milwaukee Journal-Sentinel*

"Conlon, Jesuit-educated and a Harvard graduate, examines his family's police background and the intense fraternity of cops. The fact that this book is written by a cop still on the job gives it much more urgency and immediacy than cop tales recollected in tranquility. And Conlon is a wonderful writer, street smart and poetic, arresting you with his deft turn of phrase. . . . Rapid-fire war stories capture the mania of Conlon's life as a cop, from his rookie days in public housing in 1995 to his current post as a detective in the South Bronx. Conlon characterizes being a cop as gaining entry into 'a drama as rich as Shakespeare.' Readers are lucky Conlon gives them a pass into his world."   —*Booklist* (starred review)

"A street-smart and hilarious memoir from Conlon who takes readers behind the squad-room door to reveal the inner life of New York's Finest. . . . Conlon's prose, buffed to a high sheen, mixes the rich and rowdy dialogue of police and 'perps' with department lore about legends like Eddie Egan and Frank Serpico, literary allusions, and overviews of daily routine that bristle with sharp observation. . . . It's all here: wayward crackhead informants, the roughhouse camaraderie of police units, precinct pettifogging . . . the haunting fear that a lying complaint by a civilian might derail a career, and, above all, the gravitational, 24/7 pull of 'the Job' with its 'wreckage and wonders.'"
—*Kirkus Reviews* (starred review)

continued . . .

"*Blue Blood* is a compelling autobiography as well as an insider's affectionate, unsentimental portrait of one of the most mysterious, mythologized, misunderstood institutions on the planet. For all of its factual richness, Conlon's story has the sense of inevitability and emotional power of a great novel."

—Jay McInerney

"This gripping account of his life in the NYPD by a Harvard-educated detective will evoke deserved comparisons to other true crime classics, like David Simon's *Homicide* and Kurt Eichenwald's *The Informant*. . . . He seamlessly weaves in family stories, autobiography, and a history of corruption and reform in the legendary police force, but the heart of the book is his compelling and detailed rendering of the daily grind of the average policeman, a refreshing antidote to car chases and running gunfights that are a staple of popular culture's depiction. There are dozens of fascinating supporting characters on both sides of the law, including pitiful addicts and career criminals hoping to become informants, devoted public servants, good bosses, and petty bureaucrats. . . . Even those with a more cynical view of the realities of police work will be impressed by the warts-and-all portrait Conlon provides, and his gifts as a writer will doubtless attract a wide audience."

—*Publishers Weekly* (starred review)

"It is difficult to imagine a more thorough immersion into the world of everyday copdom—with all its sudden excitements and excruciating procedural minutiae—than readers will find in *Blue Blood*. . . . Neither power-hungry nor bleeding-heart, Conlon lets his observations lead him to where they will. . . . [He] presents an array of colorful characters—resourceful cops, wily informants and elusive drug dealers—not so much for the color itself as to illustrate the tapestry of personalities a cop has to deal with . . . he admits us into a fascinating and frightening world that is never far from our own doorstep."

—*BookPage*

BLUE BLOOD

EDWARD CONLON

EBURY
PRESS

1 3 5 7 9 10 8 6 4 2

First published in 2010 by Ebury Press, an imprint of Ebury Publishing
A Random House Group company
First published in the USA by Riverhead Books in 2004
This edition published 2011

The Random House Group Limited Reg. No. 954009

Addresses for companies within the Random House Group can be found at
www.randomhouse.co.uk

A CIP catalogue record for this book is available from the British Library

The Random House Group Limited supports The Forest Stewardship
Council (FSC), the leading international forest certification organisation.
All our titles that are printed on Greenpeace approved FSC certified paper
carry the FSC logo. Our paper procurement policy can be found at
www.rbooks.co.uk/environment

Mixed Sources
Product group from well-managed
forests and other controlled sources
www.fsc.org Cert no. TT-COC-2139
© 1996 Forest Stewardship Council

Printed in the UK by CPI Cox & Wyman, Reading, RG1 8EX

ISBN 9780091940324

To buy books by your favourite authors and register for offers visit
www.rbooks.co.uk

For my mother, Elizabeth Trust Conlon

And in memory of Marc Deiter
1964–1993

All of this book is true, to the best of my memory, with these exceptions: certain names have been changed, as well as identifying characteristics of informants. The only conscious liberties taken are chronological, in the last two chapters, in that several of the cases took place after promotion rather than before.

For love of your love, let me tell of my wicked ways . . .

—ST. AUGUSTINE, *Confessions*

Enough. All right. This one time, this one time,
I'll let you ask about my affairs . . .

—MICHAEL CORLEONE, *The Godfather*

Unless asked, don't give opinions or volunteer information.

—from NYPD GUIDELINES FOR COURTROOM
TESTIMONY FOR THE POLICE OFFICER

ONE

As I took my first steps on patrol as a New York City police officer, heading out from the precinct onto East 156 Street toward the projects on Courtlandt Avenue in the South Bronx, a deep voice called out, "There's a new sheriff in town!" We had been told that people would know we were rookies by the shine on our leather gear and the dim, soft expressions on our faces—people can smell new cop like they smell new paint. When I grinned bashfully and turned toward the voice, I saw it was speaking to us, but not of us. It belonged to a tipsy derelict in an enormous Styrofoam cowboy hat, half-swaggering and half-staggering down the street. I thought of the NYPD Department Values, which begins, "In partnership with the community, we pledge to protect the lives and property . . ." During our time at the Academy, we would recite it every day in Gym, just as my high school track team would say a Hail Mary before a meet. The partnership with the community had not begun as expected, but it might be said that education is an adjustment of expectations, and although I was done at the Academy, my education had barely begun.

I was assigned to Police Service Area 7, which covered the public housing in five South Bronx precincts: the 40th, 41st, 42nd, 44th, and the 46th, with the heaviest concentration in the Four-O and Four-Two. Like the word "precinct," we used "PSA" to mean both our building and the area it served. On the first day, the PSA was hung with purple and black crepe bunting, for a cop from the command who had died of AIDS. We knew nothing beyond that fact, but as we waited in the muster room, a cop stormed in and began to yell at us: "I don't give a fuck what these assholes say, Mike was a good guy and a great cop, so if you hear different you can tell them to fuck themselves from me!" He left as abruptly as he arrived. We were bussed up to his wake, where we barely knew what to say, even to each other. Such was our introduction to the inner life of the precinct—good-hearted if sometimes misguided, bound by duty and tradition and semi-private heartbreak—into which most of us did not rush to insinuate ourselves, knowing it would find a place for us in time.

We were met with amusement or abuse, equally unexpected and unprovoked: a lieutenant might hold roll call and scream at us as if we were late with the rent, or a sergeant would begin by saying, "Thanks for stopping by." Some of the older cops watched over us and others looked down at us, and all of them told us how we'd missed out: on the greatest cops and the worst crime, and especially the Housing Police, "the best kept secret in the city." Three months before, New York City had three separate police departments— Housing, for the projects; Transit, for the subways; and the NYPD—which were then combined by Mayor Giuliani in April 1995, into one department of nearly forty thousand police. Even our new station house—a state-of-the-art cinder-block cube, with plenty of lockers and a gym in the basement—was seen as a kind of rebuke; it was as if the old PSA, which had comprised a few rooms in the basement of a project, and was prone to rat infestations and floods, told an awful truth that we were too late to learn. We'd never know anything but the NYPD, and it was a bigger, stiffer, colder job, as we'd find out when we called to take a day off, or were on patrol and needed to knock down a door. We were little players, late for the game.

They told us things we didn't need to hear, but often had no answer to what we asked:

Why do we call it the "four-to-twelve" shift, if it starts at three?

Why do we wear clip-on ties?

Where do we eat?

In fairness, the responses to these questions—"I don't know"; "To avoid strangulation"; and "Good luck!"—may not have been any different from what I'd answer now.

We were like the equipment we carried: dangerously new. I'd put on my blue polyester slacks and shirt; black boots; an equipment belt for holster and gun; two magazines, each holding fifteen rounds of 9-millimeter ammunition; radio, mace, handcuffs, flashlight. The equipment belt was snapped to the uniform belt with four "keepers." The bulletproof vest—"bullet resistant," technically—is made of two double panels of a synthetic material called Kevlar, inside a cloth carrier that holds it around your torso like a lead X-ray smock. One cop wrote phrases from the Bible on his, "Yea, though I walk in the valley of the Shadow of Death . . ." Other cops wrote their blood type. The vest showed in the neck of the summer shirt, which has short sleeves and an open collar, but if your T-shirt showed above that, some bosses would yell at you, or write you up, or make you change. The shield was pinned to the shirt with a kilt pin, over a black cardboard backing that held the nameplate on the bottom and medals on the top. Some cops' medals stacked up so high that the backing rose above their shoulders. The clips for the nameplates didn't hold, and someone found that the stoppers of crack vials worked better. They were not hard to find. I kept a prayer card to the Archangel Michael, patron saint of police, in my hat. The uniforms made us look alike, as intended, and since I said little, I didn't so much fit in as fade in.

We had a few weeks of field training, during which a cop named Vinnie Vargas led six of us around Melrose and Jackson Houses, adjoining projects a block away from the precinct. We worked as a group, at first—Paul Tannura, Matthew Goodman, Angel Suazo, Kim McLauren, Jose Velez, and myself— and then in threes, where McLauren, Velez, and I split off, and then with Velez alone. We wandered around, checking the parking lots and rooftops. Once a day, a sergeant or a lieutenant would raise us on the radio for the "scratch," to sign our memo books and tell us we were doing great or awful work, arbitrarily it seemed. A three-car collision occurred before my eyes, and the job took me five hours to complete, listing the license, registration, and insurance information, taking statements and diagramming the positions of each car and everyone in it. When I finally got it down, I felt like I could have learned calculus and French. There were three or four radio runs a day, mostly for domestic disputes and stuck elevators, though in the evenings we would hear gunshots. We would run toward them, holding on to our radios and nightsticks so they wouldn't fly out of our belts, and miss them so completely we were like kittens hunting a flashlight beam on the floor. In the precinct lunchroom one night, I heard shots and looked out the window to see two young men walking down the block toward me. We stared at each other and then, in unison, they pointed their thumbs back toward the projects.

I nodded and went back to eating. The gunshots came from the drug dealers, at war or at play, but to wean a team of rookies on drug collars is a tricky business, and Vinnie decided against it. While this decision was prudent, it allowed the rampant crack and heroin trade to take place unobserved all around us; the dealers could have had snowball fights with the stuff for all we'd have noticed. The beat cop in Melrose-Jackson was named Scott Mackay, and I liked the way he handled himself, friendly or forceful as the circumstances demanded. I told him I thought the post was a little on the slow side and he laughed at me.

When field training was over, we crowded around the board in the muster room to find out our assignments. Any of us could be a Project Community Officer (PCO), a beat cop assigned to a particular project, or on a Target Team, one of five or six cops assigned to a sergeant, moving from project to project every few months, or in a squad car. Squad was the most sought-after, in that you rode instead of walking, and it fit our expectations of a grown-up, cop-like, lights-and-sirens deal. But I had a city kid's indifference to cars— my driver's license was only a few months old—and most PCOs and Target Teams had either Friday and Saturday or Sunday and Monday off, while the three squads—day tours, four-to-twelves, and midnights—worked a rotating chart of five days on, two days off, five days on, three days off, five days on, two days off, and so on, so that your weekends fell on the weekend only a few times a year. I wanted PCO and I got it: Post 151, Morris Houses in Claremont Village, in the Four-Two. A few cops said, "You're in for it now. Watch yourself."

Claremont Village was one of the largest projects we covered, and it combined Morris, Butler, Webster, and Morrisania Houses. There were thirty buildings, each between sixteen and twenty-one stories tall, set around courtyards and playgrounds. Like most public housing in New York City, its design was inspired by the chilly optimism of the forward-thinkers of the mid-century. For them, the tall towers and wide plazas were "cities of the future" that would supplant the stacked rows of stuffed tenements where the poor had lived for the past century. From a certain distance, or at a certain angle, you could see what they were getting at: you could walk through the grounds beneath shady aisles of sycamore and maple, past tidy lawns and playgrounds teeming with children. There would be families having cookouts, old ladies reading Bibles on the benches, pensive pairs of men playing chess. Armies of groundskeepers and janitors, as well as plumbers, carpenters, painters, and elevator repairmen, were employed to keep up the physical plant. Inside, many people kept immaculate and well-appointed apartments, and even some hallways were clean and cared for, decorated for holidays as festively as a window at Macy's. But the semi-public spaces—the lobbies, halls, stairwells—were, more often than not, literal toilets. The debris of recreational annihilation was everywhere: condoms, crack vials, syringes, and shell casings; graffiti was cleaned constantly only to return at once, while bullet holes and scorch marks lasted longer. Multiple bodily functions took place in the elevators and rooftops, where you saw beer cans and smashed rum bottles amid pools of piss, piles of chicken bones beside heaps of shit. You learned not to lean against walls so roaches wouldn't nest in your clothes. More than ten thousand people lived there, by my estimate, and maybe three thousand of them made it a ghetto.

There were many bad neighborhoods in New York, but the South Bronx was a byword for "slum." There was no renaissance in its past, like Harlem, nor any signs of gentrification or renewal, as there were in parts of Brooklyn. "Fort Apache" was the nickname for the Four-One, just east of where I worked, though the Four-Two was used as the station house in the movie *Fort Apache, The Bronx*. Though the plotlines of interracial romance and police corruption were invented, the landscape of urban wasteland was not; "Fort Apache" was later known as "Little House on the Prairie," because so much of the area had burnt down. My uncle Gerry had been a firefighter in the South Bronx in the 1970s, and he told me that they were busier than the London fire department during the Blitz. In *Report from Engine Company 82,* the firefighter Dennis Smith wrote that they responded to as many false alarms as fires, and a man from his company was thrown from the truck and killed while responding to a false alarm pulled by a nine-year-old boy. A sign was put up on the call box, telling of the death and the danger of false alarms, but a false alarm was called in later the same day, from the same box, so they took the sign down.

I was born in the Bronx, but my family moved just north, to Yonkers, when I was little. I'd taken my father's old apartment in the Bronx seven years before, the "four rooms of gloom over an airshaft" where he'd grown up. It seemed like we owned the neighborhood: Uncle Eddie, a cop for thirty-three years, never left it, and Uncle Gerry's last fire house was three blocks away, across the street from Uncle Nick's office. Nick was a doctor who had married my father's sister, Theresa, a nurse. When I was a kid, when we drove through Kingsbridge, my father would point out where Joe Louis and Mike Quill had lived, but what I remember most about the Bronx then was the windows of the abandoned buildings a mile to the south. The City had covered them with decals, of curtains and shades with flower pots, to suggest that happy families dwelt within instead of junkies and ghosts. Though the official motto of the Bronx was ominous enough, *Ne cede malis*—"Do not give way to evil"—one writer suggested that it should be, "Get out, schmuck, get out!" Our official flower was the corpse flower, a massive jungle plant so named because its bloom smells like rotting flesh. It was cultivated for the first time in North America in the Bronx, in 1937, and the borough president decided the eight-foot-tall prick-shaped flowers (*Amorphophallus titanum*) would prove an apt symbol for our future growth. However, the corpse flower might go for thirty years between blooms, which stink and die within days. I still can't figure out what they were thinking.

For a long time, I kept to myself at work. I said hello to other cops but not much else. I always carried a book with me, slipping it under my vest or in a jacket pocket. When someone asked why, I'd say gravely, "You never know when nothing's gonna happen." Two other cops were assigned to Morris Houses, and six more to the other three projects that made up "the Village." Most of them tended to stick together on patrol. Though I took to walking by myself early on, when I didn't, I was with Angel Suazo and Osvaldo Rivera. We were all brand-new, and an odd threesome. Angel was Honduran, dark-skinned, and bald, an immigrant who had come here at the age of eighteen. His English was heavily accented and he was prone to saying things like "Cut me in half!" when he meant "Cut me a break!" He had been in the Army, and when I asked him what his assignment had been, he told me, "Communications." Angel was unflinchingly cheerful, and nothing could dent his good humor: he laughed as hard as the jokers did at the jokes about his driving a gypsy cab or the INS coming to take him away. He also had a nose like a bloodhound—he could smell someone smoking a joint a block away—and he had a surprising nimbleness to him: once, a sparrow flew into a bodega and he caught it with his hands, then let it fly out unharmed. Osvaldo was Puerto Rican, and from the South Bronx. He never took his hat off, and smoked twice as much as I did, which is to say like two chimneys. When we walked, he sometimes liked to sing and to do voices from kung-fu movies. He wouldn't say how old he was, called his wife constantly, and talked a lot about dogs. Though dogs weren't allowed in the projects, half the people seemed to have pit bulls, and half the pit bulls seemed to be named Tyson, so there were plenty who needed his advice. Though Osvaldo lived in a building where dogs weren't allowed, he owned an enormous German shepherd, which he would pack up into a duffel bag to take outside for walks. I asked him how the dog liked getting stuffed into a bag every day and he said he loved it—that he reacted like other dogs do when they see you pick up their leash. Both Angel and Osvaldo were serious family men and lived in the South Bronx. Whether from college liberalism or Irish sentiment, I had some measure of softness for the derelicts and delinquents of the neighborhood, but they had none, and their belief that these people should know better was good to hear.

In time, we took to each other, becoming a familiar sight around the projects: the black one, the brown one, the white one. Angel was quick to write tickets, I was quick to make arrests, and Osvaldo was quick to let us. I had started to learn Spanish the year before, but it fell to my partners to handle the rapid-fire and highly inflected dialects we heard—I would guess that our projects were slightly more black than Hispanic, with three white people that I knew of—and so my pidgin Spanish fell away. I did most of the paperwork, eagerly, as I wanted to master the Aided Cards, Complaints, Police Accident Reports, and Domestic Incident Reports that are the basic grammar of the NYPD. We did countless "vertical patrols," taking the elevator up to the top, then splitting up to check the roof, radios down, guns drawn, hats backward at night so there would be no reflection, creeping out to see whatever we might find. And then we would walk it down, taking separate stairwells but meeting on each floor. We ran into dogfights, blow jobs, and enough sleeping bums to fill a warehouse. At first, I was inclined to leave them unmolested, but I began to think if I had to step over someone every morning when I left my house, I might feel differently, and the working people in the projects deserved the same consideration. I would leave them alone when the weather was terrible, or if they were fastidiously clean or had a plausible story, like a fight with the wife, that argued for a temporary stay. In truth, the ones who stank to high heaven also got a pass, arrest-wise, though I'd throw them out of the building. We took a lot of people in for trespass, which prevented a lot of robberies, I'm sure, and maybe a few rapes and murders as well. The trespass collar is the Swiss Army knife of the beat cop, especially in the projects, where the City is the landlord. Anyone who doesn't have a good reason to be in a building probably has a bad one, and if you run into someone hanging out on a stairwell, the burden of proof falls on the mope.

We walked around and listened to the radio, with its scratchy hum of white noise and its string of coded calls and responses for lettered sectors and numbered posts, developing an ear for our own jobs, which a seasoned cop can hear, truly, in his sleep. "One-five-one, respond to a thirty-four on a female at one-four-five-eight Webster, four-Nora on the fourth, unknown weapons, advise when eighty-four . . ." And as we got to know the turf, the code might as well have been a telegram: "Ah, the Petersons again." Because the woman assaulted at 1458 Webster, #4N, calls every payday, because her boyfriend hits the rum and then he hits her. Or the woman's already called twice, today, and she perceives the assault in the minds of her upstairs neighbors, and no matter how much voodoo she sends at them, she can't block out their mental beams. The radio is constant and chaotic, a montage of stray details, awful and comic facts:

"Respond to a woman in a room cornered by a large rodent . . ."

"Supposed to be a one-year-old baby with its head split open . . ."

"The perp is a male Hispanic, white T-shirt, blue jeans, possible moustache, repeat, possible moustache, K . . ."

"K" meant a radio transmission is over, the way the military and just about everyone else says "over," and I don't know if the NYPD has any argument for the difference beside difference's sake.

"You okay, K?"

"A-OK, K."

"Okey-doke, K."

It is a code, after all, intended to mean nothing to most people. Codes, like good children, don't talk to strangers. The official terminology has a forced flatness, a clipped neutrality that keeps a lifted-pinky distance from lurid circumstance. I heard a dispatcher revise a job for the patrol car assigned: "Be advised, unit, that domestic dispute is now coming over as a severed limb." It was part of the general oddity of cop talk, its shotgun marriage of street slang and legalese. The raw talk of New Yorkers, criminals, victims, and cops themselves, was jury-rigged with the particularity of statutory phrases: "C/V states at T/P/O above perp called him a 'bitch-ass punk' and mooshed him, causing annoyance and alarm." The abbreviations are for "complainant/victim" and "time and place of occurrence"; to moosh is to shove in the face, and is almost more insulting than a slap (here, the form would be bitch-slap or pimp-slap) because of the suggestion that there is no need to inflict injury. Naturally, cops pick up a lot of criminal vocabulary, especially in the drug trade, where the criminal words for things are the only words there are; you can call it a deck, or you can call it a "glassine envelope of a white powdery substance . . . alleged and believed to be heroin." When crack was starting to be packaged in miniature heat-sealed plastic baggies the dealers called "slabs," the official and legal term which arose to characterize them was "slabs." It's what happens in language naturally, as common speech becomes acceptable usage, but to make a rule of this kind of exception would lead to indictments that read, ". . .to wit, defendant did possess one mad fat rock of *yayo.*"

Most often, though, the babel of the city just mixed with police jargon in striking ways, as we struggled to express ourselves with bits of hand-me-down language that didn't always fit. One would-be street lawyer protested what he took to be an "illegal search and seizure" of his cocaine by declaring it an "illegal circumcision." (Now that's a civil-rights nightmare for you, rogue mohels with guns.) A rookie cop I know had her own gift of phrase, once notifying the sergeant that a shooting victim had been "glazed by a bullet," though fortunately, he only suffered from "harasserations." And I overheard a cop recall, brightly, "Oh, sure, I was the first nonfatal shooting of 1994! In the keester!" The tone is intended to impress as exacting and detached, though the prefabricated phrases can sound cold-blooded and bombastic. When I hear cops refer to their "personal vehicle," I want to grab them and shout, "Say, 'my car,' dammit!"

If the NYPD is less and less a fraternity, it will remain a kind of ethnicity, because ethnicity is defined by language. An arrest is a collar, but also a pinch; a perp can be a skell or a mope, depending on whether he's a lowlife or a thug. A DOA is someone who's gone EOT, end of tour. One under, two under, ten under, is an accounting of collars, but in Transit, a "man under" is not under arrest but under a train. After a stabbing or a traffic accident, you'd hear over the air, "Is he likely?" It was short for "likely to die," and required the cop to make a crude wager of Likely or Not to summon Accident Investigations or a detective from the Squad to the scene. It gave many reports an unwarranted note of sarcasm: "Complainant states he was sleeping when his wife struck him with a two-by-four. Not likely." Perhaps because of its paramilitary nature, the department has a fondness for acronyms, which vary from the flatfootedly functional to the downright cool: TNT, for the Tactical Narcotics Teams of the mid-1980s, is still the street name for any kind of drug cop, though the units were disbanded years ago. The Robbery Apprehension Module took the place of the Robbery Identification Program, which broadened the range of the Senior Citizens Robbery Unit. And thus SCRU begat RIP, and RIP begat RAM, with a certain loss of panache. We were learning to talk the talk.

We were also learning to walk the walk. We'd walk out the front of the precinct, beneath the green lights that have marked police stations since Wall Street was a wall, and head out to post. We would stop by the management as soon as we got up there, either if a sector car rode us up, or more often, if we took the bus from 156th Street and Melrose up to Webster and 170th. Morris Houses had a manager who was almost as new there as its cops, but Ms. Brockington was a formidable lady who enjoined everyone around her to work as hard as she did, to help tenants or to hound them, according to need. Her secretary, Sarah DeBoissiere, had been at Morris Houses for over twenty years, and she was as hard and elegant as a malacca cane. She smoked long, thin cigarettes and wouldn't empty her ashtray so she could keep track of how many she'd had. She had assembled her own rogues' gallery of problem tenants, and she had the benefit of counsel of her fiancé, the legendary Detective Irwin "Silky" Silverman, who had caught killers for almost four decades before he lost his lawsuit to overturn the mandatory retirement age of sixty-three. The problem families at Morris Houses were well known and well established, sometimes for generations, and though they wrought spectacular havoc, they had been, until recently, virtually impossible to evict. One family of brothers, the sons of a South Carolina minister, were estimated to have committed more than fifteen hundred violent felonies, and their eventual removal was through the criminal-justice system rather than Housing Court. The Housing Authority had begun to press for evictions of tenants who committed crimes, or to negotiate the exclusion of individual family members—for example, if an old woman had a nephew dealing crack from her apartment, she would have to sign a stipulation saying he was not permitted to return—and it had begun to have an effect. After catching up with Ms. Brockington and Sarah, we'd sit down for a cup of coffee and the newspapers, and then head out for patrol.

The tenants themselves were organized, at least to a degree, at least on paper. I don't know how Morris Houses compared to other projects, but I would imagine that they were not the only ones where a few people were heroically dedicated to their communities, and where a few more helped when they could. Every building had a captain, though I didn't know most of them, and the honorific may as well have been kept on the shelf like an old Little League trophy. Others, like Curtis Johnson, swept and mopped their lobbies themselves, even though they were cleaned every day. About a third of our buildings had tenant patrols of some sort: a few people would sit in the lobbies around a bridge table, with a pad for visitors to sign in, and we had to stop by to sign in and check the building. A few buildings were watched over by old women who did not look up from their Bibles and - wouldn't unless the Holy Spirit entered the lobby. But others had real organizations, with a dozen or more tenants working tightly scheduled hours, and it had a definite effect, at least during the time of the watch, and if there was drug activity during their off-hours, they were at least able to let us know about it—quietly, always. Though the neighborhood had been improving, there was no guarantee that this would continue, and most members of the Resistance were wisely unwilling to declare themselves.

The neighborhood was one where children had to walk through three different brands of crack vials in the lobbies, and most people, young and old, - could tell the sound of gunshots from fireworks or a car backfiring: the hard, sharp crack, like a broomstick snapped cleanly in half. But because the shocks were somehow anticipated—you knew there would be bodies—the genuine surprise was how wholesome and ordinary many lives were there: the daily round of getting the kids ready for school and going to work, wondering if - they'll get another year's wear out of their car or winter coat. Life in the projects can be just like it is in suburbia, except it takes place on busier streets and in smaller rooms. Sometimes it's better, in the way that city life, when it's good, is better than anywhere else. Once, I went to the roof of a project and saw a hawk perched on the rail; always, you see the city in the near distance, its towers and spires studded with lights, both stately and slapdash, like the crazy geometry of rock crystal. There were many days when you felt sorry for people who worked inside.

And it was a revelation to see how many people in the South Bronx liked cops. In safe neighborhoods, a cop is part of the scenery, and mostly you don't have time to pay attention. Before I became one, I noticed cops like I noticed mailboxes, which is to say barely, unless I needed one. But on my beat, I noticed how people noticed me, and especially among certain classes of - people—older people, young kids, single women, people dressed for work or church—they looked at me with positive appreciation and relief. I was proof that tonight, on this walk home, no one was going to start with them. Sometimes, they expressed it, which was nice. The classic antagonism was with guys on the street, in groups, from the age of thirteen or fourteen on up to around twenty, or older if they were unemployed. Sometimes they were only going to make noise, sometimes they threatened to make more than noise, and I meant the opposite to them; I was a suggestion, a sign, that this wild night's not going to be, not as they hoped, not here. Sometimes they expressed themselves, too. There were those who saw us as their protectors, and those who saw us as their keepers, and both were right. Each group taught me how to be a cop.

Early on, I wanted to tell these pure strangers who would meet me with such strong feelings, whether grateful admiration or vein-bulging rage, "Hey, I just showed up here—relax! Maybe in a minute, or a year, you'll have a reason to love me or hate me, but as of now, you don't know me!" And I did remind people, with partial success, when they verged on losing control. But I began to understand the variety and potency of the guises in which I appeared to them—rookie cop, Irish cop, white cop, housing cop, ghetto cop, good cop or bad, stone-hearted or sympathetic or scared. It was like being a kind of celebrity, and it was hard to convince people that I was not like what was portrayed on TV, because I played still another role even as I explained it that I wasn't. I was not myself, but the latest cop, loaded with symbolism, and a loaded gun. For them, for now, I was the system.

· · ·

WHEN I JOINED THE NYPD IN 1995, IT WAS NEARLY FOUR times larger than the FBI and four-fifths the size of the total staff of the United Nations. There are more cops in New York than there are people in Beverly Hills. Most people think of a cop as a uniformed officer from a precinct, or a detective in a squad, but Patrol Services and the Detective Bureau are only two of nine in the NYPD. In addition to the seventy-six precincts, Patrol also includes School Safety, the volunteer Auxiliary Police, and the Special Operations Division, for Aviation, Harbor, Emergency Services, and Homeless Outreach. Detectives are assigned to two additional investigative bodies, Internal Affairs and the Organized Crime Control Bureau, the latter of which encompasses Narcotics, Auto Crime, and Vice. The Housing Police became the Housing Bureau, whereas the Transit Police was folded into the Transportation Bureau, which also includes Traffic Control, Highway Patrol, and the Mounted Unit. Personnel covers Applicant Investigation, the Police Academy, Medical Division, and Employee Management; Support Services has the Property Clerk, Fleet Services, Central Records, and Printing; and Criminal Justice runs Central Booking for each borough and serves as a liaison to the district attorneys, the courts, and the Mayor's Office. I doubt if one cop in ten could name each bureau at the beginning of his career, and even fewer could at the end.

In terms of hierarchy, the Job was only slightly less complex: the ranks from police officer to sergeant, to lieutenant and then captain, were determined through civil-service tests, and beyond that—deputy inspector, inspector, and four grades of chief, each gaining a star up to the four-star chief of department—the positions were appointed. Detectives were semi-appointed, in that the gold shield was generally given after eighteen months in what was classified as an investigative assignment, most often in Narcotics or a precinct detective squad. Though detectives did not outrank anyone, they alone took responsibility for a case or a crime scene, and this special autonomy led them to be seen as apart from the general chain of command.

As in most American cities, crime in New York had risen in the postwar decades, steadily or in great waves, and there was a deepening belief that no police department could do more than slow the tide. But the Giuliani Administration, then in its second year, had brought a new vigor to the NYPD, under Commissioner William Bratton and his three chief lieutenants, Jack Maple, John Timoney, and Louis Anemone. Previously, it was felt that the expense of police resources on people who hopped turnstiles or pissed in public when the mayhem had risen to such levels was foolish, to say the least. But the new approach held that killers and robbers are no more respectful of the little laws than the big ones, and stopping someone for smoking a joint allowed you to search them for weapons and run them for warrants. Many a cross-country career of rape and murder ended with a casual drink in New York. The frequency of these "stop-and-frisk" encounters also changed the culture of how criminals carried their weapons: in the 1980s and early '90s, many dealers would carry guns in their waistbands, and the decision to shoot someone—because he crossed into their territory, or he said something about their mother, or he looked at them funny, or just because—was a three-second decision. After Bratton, the dealers still had guns, but they were hidden under their beds or on rooftops, and the delay from impulse to act took five minutes or ten, allowing people to move and tempers to cool.

Just as revolutionary was the "Compstat" system, devised by Jack Maple, in which commanding officers were regularly called down to police headquarters to account for crime and arrest statistics. All were gathered in an auditorium as the data was projected on a large screen and examined in a forum that was often Inquisitional in tone:

"You've had robberies for the last four Fridays on the corner of 163rd and Tinton. Why don't you have a steady post there?

"You have three burglaries at the same address. How many parolees live there?"

"Your last three homicides are drug-related. Why haven't any search warrants been executed in your precinct for six months?"

As the last and least of police officers, my class was unaware of this revolution, which struck terror in the hearts of captains and chiefs. Compstat led to a slew of resignations and transfers for those who could neither deliver on improvements nor explain why they had not. It also gave them greater freedom to address their problems, and it effected a greater degree of cooperation between bureaus, as Patrol, Narcotics, and Detectives were obliged to share burdens and pursue solutions together. For ordinary cops, old and new, it meant that what we did would be noticed, with closer attention than ever before. We were also given to understand that each arrest counted, and that, in time, we might, too.

. . .

EARLY IN THE TOUR, THE COPS IN THE VILLAGE WOULD ASK each other, "You lookin'?"—which meant for a collar. Some cops never were; others, always. I was looking, almost all the time. In situations where an arrest was unavoidable, like a family assault where the perp was on the scene, a cop who wasn't looking usually could raise one who was, over the air, but - everyone got stuck sometimes. Cops collared for overtime, or for the pure pleasure of the hunt, or in the mostly-correct belief that their efforts would eventually be rewarded. The cops who didn't like to collar thought that the day was long enough as it was, or they were uncomfortable with the combative nature of court, or because since the merger of Housing with the NYPD, we processed our collars not at the PSA but at the local precinct, where we were not always welcome. We were extra work for their desk officers, who had to inspect and sign our paperwork and were responsible for our prisoners, should they get sick or claim abuse in the cells. Our bosses were supposed to sign the paperwork, but since we might only have one sergeant to cover housing cops in five precincts, they often couldn't come. Many of the DOs were famously irritable, and one was blind in one eye and deaf in one ear, right and left or left and right—I'd forget which—so if he wanted to see you or hear you, you had to jump from side to side.

And the process itself is laborious—if, for example, you arrested a man for hitting his girlfriend with a tire iron, and then found a crack vial in his pocket, the paperwork would include a Domestic Incident Report, for follow-up visits by the domestic violence officer; a "61," or complaint, which describes the offense, perp, and victim; and an Aided Card, which contains information on the victim and what medical attention she received, which are assigned numbers from the Complaint Index and Aided and Accident Index. The Aided number goes on the 61, and the 61 and Aided numbers both go on the On-Line Booking Sheet (OLBS), which provides more detailed information on the perp, and has to be handwritten, then entered into the computer, which generates an arrest number. You would have to type two vouchers, both of which have serial numbers that have to be entered on the 61 and the OLBS, for the tire iron and the cocaine, affix a lead seal to the tire iron and put the crack vial in a narcotics envelope in the presence of the desk officer, writing your name, shield number, and the date across the seal. A Request for Lab Exam (Controlled Substance and "Marihuana," in the NYPD spelling) is also filled out and attached to the envelope. You would run a warrant check on the computer, take three sets of fingerprints (city, state, and federal), each of which has to be signed by the cop and the perp, then bring the perp up to the squad to be debriefed by detectives, who ask if he knows about and is willing to talk about other crimes.

Generally, detectives investigate specific past crimes, and the interrogation aims for a confession or other inculpatory statement. The classic interrogation, in which the detectives sweet-talk, bluff, and browbeat the perp into an admission of guilt, is seldom a part of what a patrol cop does. Patrol responds to all manner of events—drug sales, disturbances, lost children—and debriefings seek to elicit information on broader criminal activity. Some offenses—many sex crimes, most domestic violence—take place outside of any larger criminal context, due to their spontaneous or solitary nature; wife-beaters don't usually join a wife-beaters' club, and rapists don't have a union. But most robberies and all drug sales are committed by members of felony society, from suppliers to fences, and all manner of partners in crime. They know people, know things. And with every arrest, you take the time to persuade them to share that knowledge.

The prisoner is then searched again (he's been searched twice before, at the scene and at the precinct) and delivered to Bronx Central Booking, at Criminal Court, where he waits in a holding cell until he's arraigned before a judge. At CB, you photograph your prisoner, attach one picture to the OLBS and another to a Prisoner Movement slip, and have the prisoner examined by EMS, interviewed by the Criminal Justice Agency for his bail application, and searched again before he's in the system, out of your hands. You would then see an assistant district attorney to write up and swear to a document that is also called a complaint. The victim also must appear, unless he or she is hospitalized or some other extreme circumstance presents itself, or the case is dropped. The entire process usually takes six to eight hours, though it - could easily be twice that, if a prisoner was sick, a computer went down, or there was a backlog at Central Booking or the Complaint Room.

The paperwork, procedure, and personnel add up to bureaucracy, which is famously wasteful or a necessary evil, sometimes both. Sometimes it reaches a nuanced complexity that is itself somehow sublime, like a martial art. Once I arrested a sixteen-year-old for burglary, whose recent birthday permitted him to be charged as an adult. Several months earlier, when he was fifteen, he'd stolen the keys to his elderly neighbor's apartment, and he helped himself to her belongings when he saw fit, sometimes with the coerced complicity of her ten-year-old grandson. The grandmother had made dozens of calls to the police, who were only able to file Lost Property or Petit Larceny reports and never had probable cause for an arrest. She had even gone to her congressman to demand an end to the reign of terror by the little boy downstairs. Finally, she caught him, held him at knifepoint until we arrived, and presented us with the perp, and her house key, recovered from his pocket. I charged him with Burglary, Criminal Possession of Stolen Property, and Possession of Burglar's Tools, to wit, the previously stolen key. The ADA reduced the charge to Attempted Burglary, and wanted me to re-arrest him as a juvenile, charge him with Petit Larceny for the theft of the key, and present him with a Juvenile Appearance Ticket at his arraignment in Criminal Court, as an adult, and release him on his own recognizance to his mother for the simultaneous Family Court case. Now, you're thinking, simple enough, but does he get the same arrest number for the adult and juvenile charges? Can he be in the system with two different arrest numbers, or since they're different jurisdictions, is the conflict irrelevant? To put it mildly, the ADA and the supervisor at Central Booking disagreed, and I was sent back and forth between them—"The District Attorney has the case now, we're the ones who decide"; "You're a police officer, and I'm a lieutenant, and you'll do what I tell you if you like getting a paycheck"—for several hours, diverted by a search in Family Court for missing forms for the juvenile arrest. When I called my sergeant to ask what to do, he laughed and said, "That's a good one! Let me know what they decide, maybe it'll be on the lieutenant's test." I know a decision was made, because I did go home at the end of that day, but God help me if I can remember what it was.

When you arrest someone, it's like a blind date. You spend a few hours with a stranger, a few feet apart, saying, "Tell me about yourself." You ask,

"How much do you weigh?" and, "Are you a gang member? Really! Which one?" So maybe I haven't been on a blind date for a while. But you do hold hands, for a few minutes, as you take prints, rolling each fingertip individually, then four fingers together, flat, and the thumb, flat, at the bottom of the card. Three cards for adults, four for juveniles. You coat a plastic plank lightly with ink, rolling it from a pad, then take each finger—"Relax!"—and roll it, on the plank and then on the card. A lot of people try to help you, rolling the fingers themselves, which usually smudges the impression; sometimes that's their intent. Crackheads often don't have usable prints, with fingers burnt smooth from gripping the red-hot glass pipe. Junkies, coming down, can go into a whole-body cramp, and have hands as stiff as lobster claws. Perps collared for robbery or assault might have bruised, swollen, and bloody fingers. You try to be gentle, and you wear latex gloves.

When you print a perp, you're close to him, and because you're close, you're vulnerable. You take off the cuffs, and you put your gun in a locker. Once, I was printing a guy as he found out he was not getting a summons, but instead going through the system. He'd been shouting abuse at the desk officer—an excellent way to prolong your imprisonment—in a routine street-guy, trash-talking way, when he was told, in effect, that he faced another twenty-odd hours in lock-up instead of less than one. And he became enraged, screaming curses and threats, and I wondered if he'd make a run at the desk, or worse, at me. But I was holding his hands and could feel them, how they were limp and loose as if he lay in a hot bath, as if his body was indifferent to the hatred in his voice. So I went on printing as he went on shouting, each of us concentrating at the task at hand.

· · ·

IN TIME, MY CLASS OF FORTY OR SO COPS BEGAN TO MAKE names for ourselves at the precinct, as workers or weirdos, or as passing casualties of circumstance. A perp flipped out on one of us, putting the cop's head through a window in the precinct; two cops made an off-duty drug collar at a bar, when a man offered them peyote; another cop fired a round when a homeless man surprised her on a roof landing. News of goof-ups or great collars were eagerly circulated, and nicknames began to stick: Smiley, Wimpy, Stix. If I had made a name for myself, no one told me. During one roll call, as names were called and duties assigned—a regular post might be changed to guard a DOA or a hospitalized prisoner, to fill a seat in the sector car, or to drive the boss—I felt bad for one poor guy, who was plainly deaf or AWOL as the lieutenant bellowed his name, without reply:

"Coyne!"

"Coyne!"

"Coyne, where the fuck are you!"

As the curses and shouts escalated, I was looking down, blithely writing in my memo book, until I felt the lieutenant's breath: "What the fuck is wrong with you, Coyne! Do you need to have your fucking head examined? Is this some kind of fucking game?"

"Um, I'm Conlon, not Coyne, sir."

The lieutenant snarled and turned away, as if I'd put one over on him. Bobby Coyne was another tall, skinny, quiet Irish guy, and our loose resemblance gave the advantage of invisibility. Osvaldo had something of a similar experience, though it was far more disturbing. One day, he received a notification from Internal Affairs, ordering him to appear downtown in six weeks, with an attorney present. When he called to ask what it was about, he was refused an answer, presumably due to the sensitivity of the investigation. He had to sweat it out, waiting sleeplessly for the date, and when he finally went down, it emerged that they had sent for the wrong man. Another cop with the same name was wanted for questioning in the "Dirty Thirty" corruption scandal that had broken not too long before.

That kind of event seasons and shapes a cop, colors his view of the Job from the inside, its bureaucracy and office politics, what it wants and how it treats its own. My outlook on the interior life of the NYPD was from a peaceful and largely positive remove, in that I thought a great deal of a lot of the bosses and very little of just a few, but I knew that the worst I could expect from the latter was a random tongue-lashing or a boring assignment for the night. For that matter, I was largely unsupervised—the forty or so PCOs ostensibly had a sergeant, but there were so many of us, working different times in different precincts, that I didn't even know who my sergeant was. When a cop makes an arrest, a sergeant is supposed to be called to the scene, but at first I didn't know that, and later I felt I knew what I was doing, and often enough, no sergeant could be found. The Job for me took place not in the precinct but on the street, and it was the public dimension of police work that held my interest and inspired my confidence. An irritable lieutenant made me more nervous than checking a rooftop alone at midnight. I preferred the outhouse to the house.

And since I tended not to work with cops who were senior in rank or experience, I learned to take the initiative and make decisions on patrol, quickly developing a rhythm and a style, a sense for when to step up or step back, as the situation required. Good cops are method actors, in that they make a controlled use of their emotions, from empathy or anger, depending on whether the scene to be played is a conflict with a crowd or persuading an Emotionally Disturbed Person (EDP) to go to the hospital. Once, a woman called to say that her son, a well-built schizophrenic, had gone off his medication, and I was able to cajole him into the ambulance, saying that I believed him when he said his medicine didn't work, but only the doctor could change it, and he didn't want his mother to worry, did he? As he walked out, his mother clutched my arm and said, "Thank you, Officer, thank you so much, this is the first time he went without fighting the cops!"

The police work of action, of confrontation and force, the roundhouse punches and high-speed chases, is what makes both the movies and the news—and, now and then, means everything in real life, our real life, too. But what you say and how you say it comes into play far more often than anything you do with your stick or gun, and can prevent the need for them. If you talk a good game, you're halfway there. A talker can do things, or undo them: I know cops who have talked would-be suicides from rooftops, and who have convinced raving gunmen to release child hostages. More often, you talk people into talking, only talking, instead of screaming and waving a knife. There are fighting words and the opposite, passwords that most people seem to have, some topic or tone that cuts them short or brings them down, reaches them through reason, decency, or shame. I once watched an eight-year-old boy silence a foul-mouthed drunk in a pizza parlor, by barking at him like a colonel: "Hey! There's ladies here!"

You also have to listen. You believe most people when they call you, because the help they need is obvious—they're hurt or sick, or they've had something stolen. And you encourage them to talk, so they can ventilate, or rant themselves through to some vital detail (my favorite witness: "He was tall! Five-ten! Maybe even five-twelve!"), or, sometimes, to give themselves enough rope. When a robbery victim told Angel, Osvaldo, and me that three white men in white suits broke into her apartment, locked her in the bathroom, and made off with her cigarettes, I felt I had to question her further before I put out an APB for the Bee Gees. Her English was poor and a great set of dentures floated in her mouth, like she was sucking on a lump of ice.

When I first suggested an ambulance come, she shook her head no. "Sometimes you don't know if you're hurt right away, the shock of it and all, it's best to be safe and check. Are you under any kind of treatment right now, do you take any medicine?"

She nodded. "For the voices."

You have to ask. The quality of information you get is only as good as you demand, vetted through repetition and playback, prodded along for further detail, probed for the soft spots in the story like dry rot in a wall. You learned to pitch your questions. You didn't ask, "Do you have a gun in the house?" because in perp-logic, an honest denial is appropriate because it's not his gun, he's only holding it. You'd ask, "Is there a gun in the house?" or better yet, "Where's the gun?" The built-in presumption saved time: if you ran a warrant check for someone with a common name like Jose Gonzalez, and there was a hit for a Jose Gonzalez of 123 Broadway, you wouldn't ask, "Did you ever live on Broadway?" but "When did you move from 123?"

For all that, you should still expect to get it wrong sometimes. Or for it to get you wrong. When I went to testify for the Grand Jury after a rape collar, I was greeted by the ADA with the eight words I least wanted to hear: "You know he has an identical twin, right?"

I wanted to shout then, but I didn't. Maybe I should have, for the practice. You have to be ready to shout, or at least show your teeth. On most jobs, I rarely came on strong at first, so I'd have something in reserve, to raise the ante, and in the daily confrontations with groups loitering in the lobbies or in front of my buildings, there was plenty of rehearsal for each manner, hard and soft. I never made an empty threat and I never let anyone make one to me: if someone said they were going to hurt me, no matter how unimpressive the speaker or the speech, they would wind up in handcuffs or I'd wind up with a profound apology. Though I never had to do much more than push someone against a wall, I gained an understanding of the old-time cops who broadcast a message of respect with a nightstick. When you walked a beat like mine, the perps got a quick sense of how much they could get away with, which was as much as you let them. Moreover, when you let things like that slide, you're "setting up the next cop," who may be less capable of handling a perp who's now willing to take it to the next level. You couldn't let a perp "hook" you, taking the bait and blowing up over his remarks about your race, your mother, or your putative boyfriend, because when you lose control, you risk losing everything, and the law and the Job will turn on a dime from ally to enemy. And even with your allies, you had to be careful: a cop from my class arrested a perp, who then threatened to kill him, and then re-ported it at our command. It was probably nothing, he thought, but he de-cided to be safe and at least put it on record. Once formal notice was made to the Job, however, an exhaustive series of countermeasures ensued: there were meetings and debriefings and directives as the Intelligence Division assessed the threat, after which the cop was moved to another post. Had that hap-pened to me, I would have seen it as a defeat—it would be the perp's post again, and mine no longer.

And it was becoming mine. The appeal of patrol is its spontaneity and va-riety, reacting to the rhythms of the street, with its long lulls and sudden con-vulsions, of pick-up jobs and radio runs that propel you into action, or interaction; into a foot pursuit, a dispute, a birth. No other post was as busy—I might answer a dozen or more jobs a day—and I had finally begun to mas-ter the territory, learning the players and the plays. I worked with Leo, the super at Morris, in putting up floodlights in a few areas favored by nighttime dealers. One day we had to check all the elevator cars for contraband, and a maintenance guy showed us how to surf the elevators, riding atop them as they shot up hundreds of feet through the shafts. Whenever I collared up, I went upstairs to the Squad at the Four-Two, to ask the detectives if they were looking for anyone in the Village. The detectives welcomed with open arms any rookie who wanted to do their work for them—except for Howie "the Hump" Denton, a cigar-chomping First Grader, who would make a show of taking the burglary or robbery complaint I gave him, crumpling it up, and bouncing it off my head—"Thanks, kid, mark this closed"—before looking at it, and I was like a mascot for two partners, Donovan and Duarte, who'd hand me a polaroid of a perp and say, "Go get 'em, tiger!"

Sometimes I got 'em, and sometimes they got me. The first ten-year-old rape victim I interviewed, I had to camouflage what I felt, and I don't think I succeeded. When you interview the victim of a sex crime, you have to be spe-cific. You ask, "Did he put his penis in your vagina? Did he wear a condom?" Any anxiety on your part communicates to the victim, and it can make them more ashamed, less trusting in you and hence less safe. You can't flinch, even when you ask a little girl, "Do you know if anything came out of his penis?" The second ten-year-old rape victim I interviewed, I didn't have time to feel anything: I had to get the description of the perp over the air, collect infor-mation on the victim, an adult relative, the paramedic, and the hospital, di-rect the sealing-off of the crime scene (one elevator, the fourth- through eighth-floor stairs, where he led her at knifepoint), and brief the succession of detectives and superior officers as they arrived. An old family friend, Inspector Thomas Mullen, responded that afternoon, and I was proud of the casual confidence with which he asked me, "Whaddaya got, Eddie?" But when it was over, I only thought about going home.

"Whaddaya got?" That's what the boss asks when he arrives at the scene, to make a decision or review one you've made. You gotta have a story, as they say. You tell him, I got a dispute, a matched pair of bloody noses, a shaky ID on a chain snatch. I got a lady with a stopped-up toilet who thinks I'm gonna help mop the bathroom. I got an order of protection that says I have to throw the husband out of the house, but he has custody of the three kids because she's a junkie and they have nowhere to go. I have twenty-seven facts in front of me, too many and not enough, in a broken heap like they fell off the back of a truck that left yesterday. I have a mini-mob beating a man bloody. *Pardon me, mob, but why?* Because he tried to lure an eight-year-old boy down the alley, to tell him special secrets. *All right then, mob, hold off a bit, let's talk to the boy.* The boy is found, he says it wasn't him, it was his friend Jose, who left, without a last name or address. . . . The beaten man refuses to press charges, just wants to go home, less a half-pint of blood, a few teeth, and now that he notices, his watch. *All right, mob, your work is done here, now you can go chase Frankenstein into the burning windmill.* Whaddaya got? I got nothing, Sarge, and plenty of it. Good work, Officer, I knew you had it in you.

You may only have seconds to take stock, to make a nearly instantaneous appraisal of a jumble of allegations, injuries, insults, histories, and relationships between neighbors, brothers, lovers, ex-lovers, lovers again, with roots of enmity as tangled and deep as those between Balkan tribes. You say, "No, I just need to know what happened *today*. . . ." The outpouring of stories can move like a horse race, a hectic and headlong jostling for position, but all moving in the same direction, toward the same finish. Or it can end up like a four-car crash at an intersection, where all the drivers sped up to lay triumphant claim to the right of way. Brawls often conclude with such a profusion of contradictory stories that you simply take the losers to the hospital and the winners to jail. Legally, the difference between harassment, for which you cannot make an arrest unless it happens in your presence, and assault, is whether or not there is an injury or "substantial pain." Certain bodily grievances are tough calls: a bruise, a gash, a good lump is clear evidence of an assault, but I've surveyed people with a flashlight, trying to find a scratch as if it were a dirt road on a map—"There it is—no, there!"—and had to come up with kind words to inform the victim that she hasn't suffered enough.

When a woman named Tonya called, she seemed to qualify squarely on the side of assault. She was surrounded by female relatives who let out a steady stream of consolations and curses, all attesting to her assailant's history of violence. His name was George, and he was the father of her baby girl. Tonya moved stiffly and was covered with scuffs and scratches, and her earlobe was notched from where an earring had been pulled out. I asked her about it, and she said, "Oh, that's old," and looking closer, I saw that it was, as were many of the marks on her. But then she lifted up her pant leg and showed a fresh red scrape that covered most of the kneecap, and the course was clear. I asked for a detailed description, and got one: "He's about five-eight and two hundred pounds, a lotta muscles and a bald head. Gonna take a lot of you cops to lock him up, 'cause he on parole for armed robbery and he say he ain't goin' back for nothin'!"

"Does he have a weapon now?"

"Wouldn't be surprised."

We set out to canvass the neighborhood. When Angel spotted him on the street, I called him over. He was as described, not an enormous man but a substantial one.

"You George?" I asked, and he said that he was, in a clear, precise diction that was unusual for the street. He'd spent his time well upstate. I asked if he'd fought with Tonya and he laughed, with mild embarrassment, as if he'd found out they'd awakened the neighbor's baby.

"Yeah, we did argue, over some stupid little thing."

"Tell you what, take a walk with us up there, let's straighten it out."

The only thing to be straightened out was the "confirmatory identification," a procedural nicety for which I was glad to have his innocent cooperation. His complete lack of concern was puzzling, and suggested that either her story or his mind was plenty shaky. Upstairs, Tonya made the ID, I discreetly put my location and condition—"Holding one"—over the air and asked George for a lengthy, time-killing version of events, as if there was more to be discussed. But even when plentiful reinforcements arrived, and his alarm became demonstrable as he caught on to what was happening, we wanted to talk. We wanted him in handcuffs, but we would talk. Given his strength and the dimensions of the cinder-block hallway where we were gathered, no one wanted a brawl. And he didn't fight, but he didn't give up, pulling back as someone tried, gently, to take his arm, and he began to shake, and to bellow, "I did not hit her!" and "I am not going back to prison!" We were tempted to believe both statements, but managed to coax him into restraints, though he continued to shout, calling for neighbors to find other friends, his sisters, to let us know what was really going on.

As we put him in the car, George told us that Tonya was a crackhead, that he had custody of their infant daughter, that he was angry at her because she left the baby alone, that her marks were from a fight she had yesterday, that many people saw her attack him earlier that day, and saw how he never raised a hand. One woman, who looked like a crackhead, said she'd fought Tonya last night; a man, who didn't, said he'd seen George endure Tonya's beating without protest. Denise, another baby-mother—George had two daughters, each a few months old—whom he referred to as his fiancée, stood by him, shaking her head in disapproval of Tonya. But I still had a complainant, an ID, a fresh injury, and no choice. And when George admitted he "might have knocked her down," I didn't feel bad about taking him in.

At the precinct, he was still convinced he could convince me: "She's *wrong,* man, I'm telling you, you know she's *wrong!*" I told him, "Look, she's the mother of your kid, you roughed her up, and you know that's wrong. If she's a crackhead, you shouldn't leave the baby with her. I hear what you're saying, but she's hurt and says you did it, so there's nothing I can do. You got a story—tell your lawyer, tell the judge, you'll probably be all right." He nodded. George underwent profound changes in manner as his thoughts strayed wildly from dark reveries of injustice, where his voice would drop an octave ("She's *wrong!*") to civil, smart, and likable reason, to soft-voiced and agile menace, where you couldn't tell if he was putting on a mask or dropping one: "I did *time,* man, time. I know people who rob every day, I know people sell guns, sell machine guns. I know people, sell you a grenade, man, I could help you out. . . ."

I was interested. I told him so. But I didn't want to get greedy, let the balance tip from buyer to seller. I knew if he meant it, he'd say it more than once, and for it to work, he'd have to be willing to keep talking when he wasn't wearing my handcuffs. So I treated him with consideration—"You got change? I'll get you a soda"—told him what to expect (seeing a judge within twenty-four hours; time served, probably, on the assault), and continued to process the arrest. As he predicted, Tonya dropped the charges, and she even came down to Central Booking to take George home. ("It isn't right what he did, but he takes care of the baby, we'll work it out. . . .") He was elated as he left, telling me, "I'm gonna get you a gun collar!" I laughed as he turned away, and said, "Give me your number," watching to see his reaction. He hesitated, then turned and gave me his beeper number. "I'm telling you," he said.

. . .

THERE ARE ARRESTS THAT COPS HOPE AND TRAIN FOR LIKE athletes, and in this felony Olympics, collars for homicides, pattern crimes, and drugs by the kilo are considered gold medals. They used to call it "the Door," and if your name was on the bottom of an On-Line Booking Sheet for the Son of Sam or the French Connection dealers, it would open for you. Sometimes you can almost hear the lock click open: on a routine car stop or hallway patdown, you can feel that this perp will take you more places than the Commissioner would, even if you married his daughter. But the likelihood that things will go wrong with arrests seems to escalate with their importance: a baroque legal system, combined with the whims of chance, provides an inexhaustible source of misadventure. You feel like a diver on the platform who has just noticed that all the judges are Russian.

There had been a number of sexual assaults on elderly women who had been followed into their buildings and taken at knifepoint into the stairwells. A sketch was circulated, of a Hispanic man in his mid-twenties, with short dark hair and a slight moustache. Ten percent of the neighborhood might have matched the description, except for the fact that the rapist was supposed to have striking green eyes. There had been numerous panicked sightings, most of them entirely without value, but when a number of calls came over about a suspicious person lurking on the 12th, 15th, then 16th floor of the building where the last rape had occurred, Osvaldo and I ran there. In the lobby, two people claimed to have seen him, but when we began to speak to a third, the first two disappeared. The last witness said the man was banging on an apartment door on the 16th floor. We called for backup, and Osvaldo stayed to freeze the lobby while I went upstairs.

The elevator was crowded as we started up, thinning out as it stopped on each floor. After two young guys got out, the older man next to me said, "Those are the ones who robbed me last month." I felt like I'd been slapped: how many empty stairwells I'd walked, how many hours on rooftops I'd waited, watching for the bad guys, to have this sudden embarrassment of riches thrust upon me. But the older man insisted that he hadn't reported it then and didn't want to now, and I didn't push him like I might have, as the elevator reached the 16th floor.

At the apartment, a young woman told me, "My mom's not here, but this guy was just banging on the door, asking for her. I don't know him, I said she wasn't here, and he tried to get in, he turned the knob and pushed." She thought she had seen him before, in passing; her mother, whose name was Barbara, was similar in type to the other victims. Another neighbor, who had followed me to the door—she had called 911—was horrified to hear the story: she knew that the man used to go out with another woman on the floor, but she had called only because she'd seen him standing in a stairwell with a strange look on his face. We had a male Hispanic in his twenties with a moustache, who was familiar with the building, wandering around, acting bizarrely, and attempting to enter the apartment of an older woman. It looked better than good.

I went downstairs to get Osvaldo, and when a sector arrived I asked those cops to freeze the lobby. We went up for a vertical patrol, and when we reached the 16th floor, we came upon a man in the hallway. We walked toward him and he walked away, a little faster, though there was nowhere to go—"Hold on, boss, slow down"—and he broke into a run, and as we tackled him, he began to scream, "Barbara! Barbara! I love you! Help me! Someone get a video! They didn't identify themselves as a police officer! Help!" He got something into his mouth and chewed it, and we got him down but for a long time we couldn't get any further. We wrestled with him for what seemed like ages, he was limber and strong and sweat-soaked, slippery as a live fish; we tried to get him to spit out what he had in his mouth—it turned out to be cocaine wrapped in a dollar bill—and at one point, Osvaldo and I actually took a break, sitting on him, looking at each other and catching our breath. When we finally cuffed him up, his hands and mouth were bloody. He looked just like the police sketch, with the distinctive green eyes. We later found out that his ex-girlfriend, who lived on that floor, had thrown him out on the day of the last attack. When Sgt. O'Hagan arrived, he looked at him, and then he looked at us, and smiled. "It's him. Definitely. You got 'im." Visions of medals and promotions danced in my imagination, sustaining me through the long night ahead.

At the precinct, he collapsed, and he told the paramedics he'd ingested three grams of cocaine, half while he lurked in the stairs, half in the dollar bill while we wrestled him. At the hospital, his heart rate was 220 beats per minute, and they made him drink an electrolyte solution and eat activated charcoal, which made him drool black. He was handcuffed to the cot in the ER, while the midnight pageant of medical catastrophes were brought in: one Emotionally Disturbed Person, who bit clean through his tongue, clipping it into a precise impression of his upper teeth. Another EDP, an enormous drunk picked up from the streets, floating in and out of consciousness, writhed and thrashed as a little Filipino nurse tried to draw blood: "Now I prick you! Now I just prick you!" An old man threw up and another prisoner-patient, handcuffed to the cot next to him, kindly handed him the closest receptacle he could find—a plastic pitcher half-filled with urine, which splashed back as he vomited and made him vomit more. And a beautiful teenage Spanish girl, who had choked on cotton candy hours before at a carnival. Her problem was long gone, as were her once-worried friends, but she had been told to remain for examination. She was more than a little embarrassed.

"Well, I hope we all learned an important lesson about chewing our food."

"Shut up."

But she soon went home, and I was left with the wretched strangers. We'd made the arrest eight hours into the tour, and I waited with him at the hospital for another nine, and only then did I begin the arrest processing. I'd worked almost around the clock before Special Victims called to say that my perp had already been taken in for a line-up and had not been identified. In my mind, I began to rehearse the arguments: they were elderly victims, traumatized, maybe with bad eyesight . . . but it was pointless. In this kind of case, without an ID, there was often nothing to go on. And then, suddenly, I hated him. Throughout our ordeal, I'd felt nothing toward him, no contempt or anger, even when I fought with him, even though I believed he had done hideous, brutal things. Suddenly, I hated him, because he had changed; he was no longer a trophy, a magnificent and malignant catch, but some random asshole who had stolen an entire day of my life. He asked me mildly what he was being charged with and I told him. His tone was pouty when he responded, "Criminal trespass, isn't that a little harsh, Officer?"

I just looked at him, but it must have been expressive. "Sorry," he said, turning away. You can't cry for every crime victim you come across; you can't even cry for the awful ones, not if you want to work for twenty years, and often the way to catch someone is to want to, very much. A few days later, I saw him on the street, and he said hello. I didn't. A few days after that, he beat up his girlfriend again, then disappeared. There weren't any more rapes.

· · ·

WHAT CAN YOU SAY? MOST OF THE TIME, IN THE END, YOU say 90-X, 90-Y, or 90-Z. These radio codes give dispositions, meaning unfounded, unnecessary, or gone on arrival. The terse dispatch of them—"You can X that, Central"—can reduce an epic to a letter, scraping it clean of context, all the drama and the decisions. My uncle Eddie had been a cop for over three decades, and when I first looked at his memo books, I was surprised at how little they said, given the zany color of his stories. The jumpy, crabbed notations of "all normal" and "nothing to report" were barely less vivid than the occasional mention of a parking ticket issued or "three under arrest—burglary." But in time, I came to appreciate the telegraphic brevity of the codes, which allowed me to finish stories I barely knew how to start.

Angel and I once went to a 10-10, a possible crime, in this case a "dangerous animal condition." The complainant was a woman on the 19th floor of one of my buildings, and a familiar caller. A stout, opinionated lady in her early fifties, she claimed to be the frequent victim of espionage on the part of her cable company, the Housing Authority, and several less terrestrial bodies, against which she protected herself by covering the walls and ceilings of her entire apartment with tinfoil. I sometimes wondered if it was a cop who had recommended it, to buy a few weeks' peace while she busied herself with the defenses. I know it wasn't a fireman, because the foil, which was tattooed all over with pentagrams, covered a thick layer of crisp and dry newspaper, mostly department-store circulars for men's underwear.

"I need you to get rid of my cat, it attacked me, it's crazy, it changed. I can't have it here, it used to be so wonderful, it's a mystical cat, you know, a Jewish cat. I tried everything, petting it, feeding it, throwing boiling water at it—nothing works, nothing!"

It was five in the afternoon, and our options were limited. Her son was with her, a large, shambling man in his early thirties who kept a weary and sheepish distance, meeting my eyes briefly when I looked to him, then shrugging and shifting aside. It was too late in the day to call the ASPCA for a pick-up. I doubted the cat was dangerous as much as I doubted the cat was Jewish, but the last thing I was going to do was call Emergency Services. When you call out the SWAT team for a kitten, other cops tend to bring it up now and then—one guy couldn't talk on the radio for months without hearing meows in the background. She rambled on, "I would have called Augie to take it out, you know, Augie's in the Mafia, he'd kill anyone for me, but he can't do it now, he can't, and the cat's in my bedroom and I can't go in. . . ."

I began to tell her that the best thing to do was to confine the cat in another room and leave it alone, while I would make an appointment with the ASPCA to take it off her hands the next day. She would have none of it, and with one hand on a hip and the other slicing the air she let me know she had dealt with my type before: "You will take care of this now or I will call the Housing Authority! I will call your captain! I will call Jim Jensen at Channel Seven News! I will call Eyewitness News! Yes, I'm calling now, give me Eyewitness News!"

As she marched to the phone to punch random numbers, I sidled over to the son and said, "Listen, why don't you shut it in another room?" He looked at me weakly, and his mother hung up the phone. "My son," she hissed with dry distaste, "is mentally ill." Silly me. Silly all of us.

Though I had decided our course by then, I thought I'd check the cat, to make sure it was in fact safe enough to remain in the apartment overnight. When I opened the door to the woman's bedroom, I saw a small white cat lying on the bed. A brown patch of fur on its head did look something like a yarmulke, but otherwise neither its religious affiliation nor its menace was obvious. When I took a step toward it, however, the transformation was profound: the back arched, the ears flattened, the eyes narrowed, and it seethed and spat like a cobra on crack. This lady didn't need a cop, she needed an exorcist. I withdrew and closed the door.

"Okay," I said. "The cat has to go."

From there, mother and son became my loyal aides-de-camp in the campaign that followed. A large piece of plywood was set up in the hallway to block access to the living room, and all doors were shut except for those to the mother's room and a smaller, spare room beside it. The first phase would be to isolate and contain the cat in a secure area, and the second phase . . . the second phase would certainly commence when the first phase was brought to a successful conclusion. Angel kept mother and son stationed behind the barrier as I put on my gloves, picked up a broom, and reentered the bedroom. Again, the cat bared its teeth and swiped with its paws, coiling up on the bed to prepare for a leap, but as I came closer it bolted for the radiator, and the merry chase began: the cat dashed to the top of the cabinet and then to the radiator, and then under it, and then under the bed, paused to turn and fight, meeting the broom and tearing at it as I tried to herd it out to the door. Again and again, it would bolt and then turn and fight, and hiss and spit, its lithe swiftness as amazing as its hatred. Once more it fled between cabinet and bed before it charged me and I fell back, swinging the broom, before it dodged and sped into the hall. But before the cries of acclaim could erupt from behind the barrier, the mother and son fell back, too, as the cat raced to them, leaping up and over the plywood as they dropped it, and pursuing them into the living room, where the field of battle was greatly enlarged.

"Get back! Get back! I've got it!"

I picked up the barrier again and sent them behind it, and once more engaged the cat: its rage, speed, claws, and teeth against my broom, my paramilitary training, and a chorus of meows on the radio echoing in my head. Here, it had the couch, chairs, cabinets, and shelves, a windowsill with heavy drapes, and an entire kitchen for its guerrilla maneuvers, and it made use of all of them in its rounds of flight and fight. As I fought on without success, my supporters were galvanized, and the woman cheered me on and brainstormed: "I know! Fire! We'll burn him out! All animals are afraid of fire!"

"Don't you dare! Angel! Stop her!" I shouted, but as I swept the cat from beneath the drapes, he darted for the kitchen, and after reconnoitering atop the refrigerator, he dove to the floor and under the stove. I paused to think and to breathe. As far as I saw it, we were still in Phase One.

"Still out on that ten-ten, unit?" came the call over the radio.

"Still out, Central."

Clearly, there was need for further revision of our strategy. The barriers were changed again, so that they led to the open door of the apartment. Once out, I figured, all of us—cat, crazies, Angel, and myself—would return to our better natures, and resume our lives on some kind of normal footing. Also, I didn't care anymore. So I returned to the kitchen and lifted up the stove, where the cat, writhing beneath, had become coated with the grease of a decade of breakfast bacon and Easter hams. The broom seemed to hold no more terrors for the cat, and I wielded it less adeptly as I also had to hold up the stove. I had to escalate, and I gave it a few blasts of mace—the old kind, which was a kind of weak cousin to tear gas—and though it had no apparent effect on the cat, it drove me, choking, outside into the hall. As I gasped for breath, I saw with my reddened eyes the woman leap across the living room with a great cooking pot stuffed with blazing newspapers, the flames reflecting off the foil walls.

"All animals are afraid of fire!" she shrieked, and I bellowed "No!" and raced back inside. Angel ran in to take her outside, and though I stamped the pot out before the fire engulfed the apartment, I was now doubly choked by the acrid bite of tear gas and the unfurling plumes of smoke, which set off the fire alarms throughout the floor. Neighbors began to step out of their apartments to investigate. I sent them back inside.

"It's all right, folks—the police are here, everything's in hand, nothing to worry about."

I was humbled and a little worried—if help arrived, I would have much to explain—but the woman was delighted. She called the police twice a week, and usually got a couple of guys who walked away a minute later, muttering about straitjackets; here, a hero had arisen who brought down forces of destruction that might well be commensurate with her perception of the threat. I had turned the place into Beirut, and she couldn't be more grateful. I opened the windows until the air cleared, and I almost toppled the stove to sweep the cat out from its refuge. Ignoring the open door, it bolted over the barrier and fled back into the bedroom. There, it darted between bed and radiator again, as if to show that the learning curve for both cat and cop remained flat, before it took off for the window, and slipped outside to the ledge. And then, I had a revelation: a vicious cat could not be put up for adoption. No matter the provocation, the cat would have no day in court; my nemesis had no future beyond being drugged, bagged, and caged before being put down. I moved forward without thought, but as if guided by some mysterious force. As I put my hands on the window, the cat scrambled to turn and come at me, but lost its footing and dropped from sight. The woman called the precinct for weeks afterward, demanding to talk to the captain to tell him what great work I had done. But when the desk officer asked me what had happened, I just shrugged and repeated what I'd told the dispatcher when she asked about the job:

"Still out, on that ten-ten, unit?"

"Make that a ninety-Z, Central."

The technical term for that kind of event is "clusterfuck," and whenever I began to feel I had a handle on the Job, some cluster would break out, reminding me of how much I was unready for. The novelty of knocking on a door and calling out "Police! Open up!" had passed—*Yeah, I mean me!*—and I was comfortable on post, answering jobs, learning more faces and names. And in time, as I ran into cluster after cluster, I began to see them not as testimonials to how much I had to learn, but as proof that I never would get it all. And that was the better wisdom, because when a cop thinks there is nothing left to see, he may not take the trouble to keep his eyes open.

• • •

FOR THE MOST PART, THE TIME YOU SPEND WITH PEOPLE you tend to like and respect occurs when they're at a very low point in their lives: they've just been robbed, or are having severe chest pains, or their husband is dead in the back bedroom. You are less the bearer of bad news than the proof of it. More often, you become bound up in lives that are dismal and messy: junkies who take too much, EDPs who won't take anything for their pains. As you make the acquaintance of their broken minds and ruined bodies, you reluctantly invade their privacy, and you must vigilantly protect your own.

It can be troubling to be so intimate with these random strangers. And not just with criminals, though you see more of a person searching drug dealers ("Lift 'em. Arright, turn around and spread 'em.") than you ever wished. There are matter-of-factly named "lift jobs," for the elderly or ailing who have fallen down. I did one for a man who weighed more than 300 pounds, with two-thirds of it on the hips and legs, which were massively swollen and corrugated like Godzilla's. He wore a short nightshirt with no underwear, and his bladder control was chancy at best. His condition was the result of having been told he had cirrhosis of the liver years before and saying, "Hell, I'm still gonna have a drink now and then." Do you help him? Of course, you lift him up. Do you feel for him? *All right then, move along now, nothing to see here, move along.*

It was near the end of tour, and I was headed back to the precinct when an Aided case came over the air. Aideds are among the most frequent jobs, usually entailing an escort of EMS to the scene of an illness or injury. When Osvaldo, Angel, and I arrived in the apartment, I could tell from the smell why someone had called. Walking down the hall, past numerous, spacious rooms, the rank, ripe odor of a body grew stronger, and when an expressionless sixteen-year-old girl directed me to the last bedroom, I was thrown less by the sight of the still, frail old Puerto Rican woman in bed than by that of the four EMTs working around her. Two were crying.

The old woman was naked, lying face-down, stuck to plastic sheets, and her body made a crackling sound when she was unpeeled from them. She had once been a hefty woman, but she looked now less slimmed-down than deflated: her breasts were empty, pressed against her chest, and the bones of her hips and thighs were plainly visible, draped by loose, lifeless skin. Maggots crawled on her, inch-worming along, popping off like broken watch springs. There was rodent excrement in the bed with her, and examining her legs, one EMT said, after a horrified intake of breath, "Those are rat bites! Whoever did this to her should go to jail!"

The old woman let out a breathy moan as she was rolled over, feeling pain wherever her body was alive. And that's why the EMTs, who see dead children and bodies in pieces as a matter of course, were brought to tears. This woman was dying, was in fact dead in lesser percentages, as maggots do not eat live tissue. And she didn't live alone. I turned away and went to talk to the teenage girl: "Who takes care of this lady?"

"Well," she huffed, in a long-suffering tone, "I'm the one who does most of the work."

"Who lives here? How old are they?"

"Me and my sister and my grandmother. My sister's twenty-three but she's out now. I'm the one who does most of the work."

"Can you tell me why you didn't feed her?"

"She said she wasn't hungry."

"Why didn't you call a doctor?"

"I'm the one that did."

"Before now, why didn't you call?"

"My mom said not to."

Her mother lived in another part of the city. I told her to call her mother and tell her to go to the hospital. I asked how they lived, and she said her grandmother got checks, and her sister cashed them to run the household. I called a sergeant over and explained the situation in a rapid, dazed manner that made him look at me, carefully, before we all went downstairs. Ordinarily, EMS prefers to have a relative ride with the Aided, but when the teenager approached the ambulance, the no-longer-crying EMT told her, curtly, "You want to visit Grandma? Take the bus."

Back at the precinct, it took a while to figure out how to write the complaint, aside from descriptions of rat bites and maggots. The girl was too young to be charged. And the offense was not clear; while there are many laws regarding the care of children, the elderly are less explicitly protected. I found a misdemeanor called "endangering the welfare of an incompetent adult," and named the adult sister and the mother as perpetrators. The sergeant pointed out that there were checks coming in, so "investigate larceny" was added. And that, I realized without satisfaction, explained the family's nearly homicidal neglect. The old woman was the keystone of a tidy edifice of subsidies: a large apartment, Social Security, welfare for the teenage girl. If she went to a hospital or nursing home, all these benefits would vanish from their pockets. People talk about living from paycheck to paycheck; this family almost let a woman die that way.

I found out later that detectives made arrests at the hospital. I was also told that the two sisters sometimes visited their grandmother in the nursing home where she was later sent, and were trying, without success, to bring her back home. Another cop's mother worked there, and he told me, "And the old lady, she's kind of nasty herself."

Sometimes, the victims are less sympathetic than the offenders. When a woman called to say that her thirteen-year-old son had locked her out of her house for hours, Osvaldo and I responded, and we told her we couldn't knock down the door unless there was an emergency. She would have to pay for it, and we would have to wait until it was fixed. For more than an hour, we knocked, reasoned and threatened, fiddled with the locks. She had obtained a Family Court warrant that allowed her to call the police whenever she couldn't control her son, and we would bring both parties to court, or the child to an overnight facility if court was not in session. It was a responsible act, on her part, but one of few, it seemed. We had ample time to find out about the family.

"Is there someone he isn't mad at, who could talk to him, get him to open the door?"

"Oh, he's not mad at me," she said. I let it go.

"Maybe a friend from school?"

"I been tellin' him to go to school since last year," she said, adding that he stopped because the other kids beat him up. Asked why, she said that he wore makeup and women's clothes. Osvaldo went to get a coat hanger, to see if he could work the chain off. The woman went on about her troubles, how the boy's father had left her, how she worked, how the boy stayed out till dawn, how all kinds of adult men called him. She paused a moment, as if she'd just remembered, and said, "I had a three-year-old, she died. She was pretty." She paused again, and said, "I wish that faggot never was born."

Osvaldo got the door open. The thirteen-year-old, a light-skinned black boy with hair dyed a sunny yellow, was asleep. He seemed genuinely asleep, and I hesitated, unwilling to take him to kiddie jail for being a sound sleeper. But he admitted that he heard us, pounding and shouting through the afternoon, and I told him to get some things together, that he was going to court in the morning. I saw by his bedside a list of about twenty names, all male, and all but a few with beeper rather than phone numbers. His mother showed us the warrant, then picked up a skimpy pair of gold satin shorts, held them up to her substantial waist, and said, "Who wears these? Not me!"

What friendly or fatherly advice was there to offer? *I didn't peddle my ass when I was thirteen years old, young man, and now I have a cushy civil-service job. . . .* We drove downtown without saying much, and I haven't seen him since.

Another time, as I stood outside the management office, I saw that a middle-aged woman was staring at me, in the throes of indecision about whether to approach. I went over to her and asked if I could help. "My husband, he beats me, he beats me very bad." I pressed her for details, telling her how even if I couldn't make an arrest, she could get an order of protection, but she brushed me aside: "No, no, that's all no good. My daughter, she says she's just gonna get somebody to take care of him."

I told her that if he was beaten, he'd probably take it out on her anyway, and again, she saw I didn't get it: "I don't mean beat him up, I mean, *take care* of him. You know!" She raised her eyebrows, like she was letting me in on a sweet deal. "What do you think?"

"Lady, you noticed I'm wearing a blue hat, badge, the rest? That I'm a cop? And you want to know what I think about having your husband killed?"

We parted before she could ask me to quote a price, each convinced that the other had only a flimsy grasp of reality. A few hours later, I responded to a call of a "violent domestic dispute," and a cop named Anna Ramirez backed me up. A middle-aged man answered the door and allowed us in. He was in his underwear and seemed at ease, showing us around with a cavalier smirk. He was large and strong, and had a corrupt and military air, as if he were some tropical Presidente for Life. I didn't like him, and Anna hated him. There was no one else in the apartment, but as we left, I noticed the woman's picture on the wall. She was trying to win our argument, I think, saying, "Look at him. Look. If this one ended up dead, would you really come after me?"

The dead are commonplace for cops, and the sight of bodies never troubled me much, even from the beginning. My first murder was an awful one—an old man, on the floor in a hiked-up flannel nightshirt, who had been strangled, stabbed, and beaten, his arms bent into unnatural angles like chicken wings, and though I felt sorry for him, I wasn't unduly troubled. Sometimes homicide victims have a peaceful expression, while deaths from natural causes can appear as horrific as the worst crime scenes: one elderly diabetic fell down, and apparently tried to crawl to the phone as he died of cardiac arrest. It looked like he had been picked up and smashed around the room: his face was contorted and his body was bruised all over; there were bloody handprints on the wall and long, slashing smears of blood and shit on the floor. The stillness of the dead transfixes me, reminding me that nothing living doesn't move, not the deepest sleeper or a cat on the prowl, poised to leap. There is always some rhythm, some tremble or shift, that betrays animation. Only when that goes do they become motionless as photographs, as stones, and their meaning, like their movement, is only in what they inspire in those around them.

One old man lived alone, and died crumpled on the floor in the little alley between the bed and the wall, wearing a dirty shirt and no pants. His room was small and cluttered, and all his clothes were in old suitcases, or stacked beside them, as if he were packing for a long trip. There were two televisions, one old, one brand-new. A manic kitten darted amid the piles of clothes and rubbish around the body. Because he lived alone, we had to search for valuables, in the presence of a sergeant, and voucher them at the precinct. We found his discharge papers, false teeth, and stacks of pornography. The other cops left and I stayed. It was my turn to sit on the DOA, waiting for the ME to have a look, then the morgue crew to take him away. A man knocked at the door and said, "I took care of him, I'm his stepson. He wanted me to have the TV."

I told him to get some proof, and until then he should take the kitten. He left and I turned on the television. Less than an hour later, he returned, with a lady friend. Both were roaring drunk, and demanded in unison, "We loved him! *We* was his *family!* Let's have that TV!"

I closed the door on them and sat back down. There was a phone call. I waited, then picked it up, hoping that whatever friends or family he had, whoever cared for him, would not learn of his death by accident, from a stranger.

"Is Mr. Jones at home?"

"No, he isn't."

"Is this . . . Mrs. Jones?"

"No." But thanks for asking.

"When will he be available?"

"No time soon."

"When should I call back?"

"Can I ask who this is?"

"Mr. Jones had recently expressed an interest in our low-cost insurance policies, and . . ."

"He's not interested."

"And who, may I ask, is this?"

"The police. Mr. Jones is dead, that's why I'm here."

"Well, do you think—?"

"Dead."

"There may be some—"

"Dead, dead, dead. He's stuck to the floor six feet away from me, guy, no sale."

"Have you considered whether you have all the coverage you need, Officer?"

I hung up and went back to watching television.

TWO

One night on patrol, I went to an Aided case, a medical call for help. A woman's ankles had begun to bleed and would not stop, because of collapsed veins, she told me. She was in her early thirties and had nine children. Her feet bled like stigmata, as if there were no cause but grief. Her children ranged in age from newborn to young teens, in color from dark to pale, and together they looked more like a United Nations assembly than one little country. The ambulance took a long time to come, so my partner that day—an older cop whose steady partner was out—and I passed the time by talking with the kids, who gathered around us. A boy of eight or nine was mesmerized by us, by the sight of our blue uniforms, our cuffs and guns.

"Lemme see the handcuffs, lemme try," he said. I handcuffed him— rear-cuffed, as per *Patrol Guide,* Section 114-08—and gave him the key. He tensed up for a moment, planning his strategy, then twisted himself around mightily before collapsing in a spasm on the floor, where he flopped about like a fish on a dock. The key went flying. I picked it up and handed it back.

"I bet you twenty dollars you can't get out in one minute."

"Three minutes," came back the immediate counteroffer. I checked my wallet: I had a twenty-dollar bill, plus a couple of singles. I planned to give him a buck for the effort.

"Go ahead, three minutes."

He sat down on the ground, drew his legs through his cuffed hands, bent his wrists perpendicular, and unlocked the cuffs. He had two minutes and forty seconds to spare.

"Want me to do it again?"

"No, I want you to shut up."

The ambulance had come, and I handed him the money, suddenly realizing that I could now afford exactly one slice of pizza for dinner. He careened around the apartment, holding the prize aloft like a pennant, followed by his pack of siblings. We left, but he ran out into the hall after us, telling me his mother wanted him to give it back. He offered the money far more matter-of-factly than I would have managed at his age, rounding out a two-minute circuit of rags to riches to rags. And though I've never been much of a gambler, I wasn't about to welsh on whatever his name was, the plucky little waif who'd taken me for a ride.

"No, a bet's a bet. Tell your mother the police said you had to," I said, and he was content that there would be no more argument. The reality of the win now seemed to set something off in him, and he attached himself to me, determined to unburden himself of all his knowledge before I got to the elevator. Random pronouncements left him with such a rising and urgent rhythm that they took on the fervor of prophecy:

"I'm gonna ride in a limousine . . .ž

"You better watch your back out there!

"Do you read the Bible? It says the world is gonna end pretty soon. Do you believe it's gonna end? I do!

"The guy who sells crack in the lobby, his name is Roscoe, I can watch him and you can lock him up—and then you can come over for dinner!"

For days after, the older cop could not look at me without laughing. "You're gone," he said. "You're done." He was right, though he had no idea how right. Like my great-grandfather Paddy the Cop, I was gambling on job time. Taking after my uncle Eddie the Cop, I helped a poor kid out with a little cash, no matter if it was the last thing I'd intended. And as for a resemblance to my father, I may have to reach a bit—though I did gain an informant—but I put on my hat, and walked out into the evening, and was swept up in quiet awe at how this Job and this City can pull you in with its wreckage and wonders, unsatisfied with only one lifetime.

· · ·

WHEN I WAS A TEENAGER, I STAYED OVER AT A FRIEND'S
house in Brooklyn. His grandfather, who had briefly served as police commissioner, lived with the family. The Commissioner was a massive and shad-
owed form in the corner, still as a statue, like a stone Buddha in an ancient
temple lost to the jungle. He seemed old enough to know anything, and so I
asked him if he knew my great-grandfather Sgt. Patrick Brown, who joined
the NYPD a few years after Brooklyn joined the City, and who retired at the
onset of the Second World War.

"Sure I knew Pat Brown," he said, stirring. "He used to carry the bag on
Atlantic Avenue."

As my mother said when I dutifully reported this to her, "They were different times, back then." The whiff of Capone-era rascality delighted me, in
fact, much more than had I been told that he was straight and upright as a
flagpole. I knew good cops all too well, and to have the other kind—at a safe
distance—offered novelty and contrast, the glamour and danger of bootleg
whiskey. When I became a cop and began to think about it again, I wasn't
proud—though it would be an exaggeration to say it kept me awake at night.
Now, the memory is a curiosity, so remote from my own life that it has the
discreteness of an object, like the "come-alongs" my father once showed me.
They were wrist restraints, also called "nippers," and cops carried them
through the 1950s. Made of a short length of chain between two T-bars, they
worked like handcuffs, except you had to hold on to them, and their coiled
weight, dull steel gleam, and imagined history made them satisfying to look
at and feel and wonder about. You wrapped them around one wrist and
twisted, and though it left a perp one free hand, you could snap the bone in
a second. Come-alongs depended on a cop's control. They could do what
good or harm you wanted, as long as you kept your grip.

I'd bet that many cops now wouldn't even know that a bagman collects
money, as an intermediary between the underworld and the upper—it is becoming a fragment of obsolete criminal slang, like "yegg" for safecracker or
"betty" for picklock. For us, "the bag" is the uniform. Almost all I know
about my great-grandfather is summed up in that simple, double-edged
phrase, "the bag." He spent thirty-three years on the job, mostly in uniform.
The six years he lived afterward were occupied in the operation of a horse
room in New Jersey. The transition from law enforcement to the sporting

world, I am told, was not abrupt. Pictures of him show a handsome man, well-fed and well-tailored, a figure of overripe charm with a note of elegant menace. He looked like the kind of character played in movies by Brian Dennehy or Charles Durning, winningly fleshy, light on his feet, and quick with his hands. He seemed determined that his appearance reflect his place in the world, and if his attire was a little flashy but of good quality, bespeaking both gentleman and gangster, then it may have described him more truthfully than he intended. In fact, after he retired to the horse room, where bets were collected and paid as the teletype hammered out news from the track, the progression from crooked cop to upstanding criminal could be viewed as a step in the right direction, at least in terms of appearances.

When Patrick Augustine Brown was appointed to the New York City Police Department on June 8, 1907, he was obliged to purchase two bags, for summer and winter. The summer uniform consisted of a gray helmet, white gloves, a dark single-breasted tunic with a white leather belt, and trousers with a white stripe on the side. For winter, there were a blue helmet and greatcoat, with a double row of brass buttons. In better neighborhoods, the uniform was a thing of splendor, a fit garment for a figure of respect, and in poor neighborhoods it could make cops stand out like redcoats in a forest of angry Indians. At the time, hoodlums would wait on top of buildings and push the chimneys down on passing cops (although generally the noise gave the patrolman a chance to run), or overwhelm them and stuff them into coal boxes. These assaults were directed at the bag itself; at the dignity of office—though it could be argued that the other kind of bag represented just as pernicious a threat.

In his book *Low Life,* Luc Sante says the patrolman's lot at the turn of the century was "a choice between starvation and extortion," and Pat Brown did not go hungry. At his retirement dinner in 1940, the menu told of roast spring chicken with chestnut stuffing, rissole potatoes and "bisquit tortoni." Though Brown retired as a sergeant, his dinner was attended by a number of inspectors and the Honorable William O'Dwyer, district attorney of Kings County, former cop and mayor-to-be. O'Dwyer had worked with Brown years before, and both careers testified to the fact that New York was a place where you - could go as far as you liked, and maybe farther than you should. Or maybe it suggested that, at its worst, America offered a choice between evils.

O'Dwyer, a thoughtful, large-hearted man, was an Irish immigrant with the common touch. His goodwill and good fortune, his rise from Ellis Island to Gracie Mansion, made him an epitome of New World promise, and his canny but easygoing pragmatism made him a New York natural. "Lots of - people would have us believe this town is loaded with thugs, racketeers, gamblers," he said. "I said it's a friendly city. It's been friendly to me." O'Dwyer's friendliness extended to a pre-election meeting with gangster Frank Costello, and his decidedly incomplete success in the prosecution of Murder, Incorporated, nearly led to his own indictment. When a police-corruption scandal erupted involving a Brooklyn gambler named Harry Gross, Mayor O'Dwyer was hastily appointed Ambassador O'Dwyer and he finished his government service in Mexico City. O'Dwyer had an indisputable personal decency and a record of genuine achievement, but in his later years, in his retirement in the Southwest, he felt obliged to inform acquaintances that he was not, in fact, a fugitive.

Because Pat Brown left his wife and three children in near-poverty, he does not share in the amber glow of nostalgia in family memory. He married Catherine Moran on June 10, 1908, within a year of joining the NYPD. His former occupation is listed as "clerk." I don't know whether he delayed marriage until he secured his new job, or she fell for the young patrolman in his gray helmet and wing collar. They moved to 42 Butler Street, in Carroll Gardens, on the day of their marriage, and every few years they shifted to some other pleasantly middle-class row house in sedately striving neighborhoods like Bensonhurst and Borough Park. They had my grandmother Anne, then Jack, and then Eleanor, and then there is a change of address, in 1926, to 1 Prospect Park West, a massive and stately apartment building beside Grand Army Plaza that would suggest a dramatic upswing of fortune—an inheritance, or a stock windfall—but if there was, Pat Brown did not share it. It was rumored that his sister Nellie, with whom they shared a house in Borough Park, inspired the breakup of the marriage. In the family legend, Nellie was a horrible woman—she buried three husbands and two children, because "God didn't want her and the Devil wouldn't take her"—who whispered to Pat that his wife "had visitors" while he was at work. There had been much more money than there should have been, and then suddenly, for his wife and children, there was very little indeed. My grandmother was finishing grade school when her parents separated, and plans to send her to an expensive Catholic boarding school on Long Island were put aside. Catherine found such work as she was able to, and when her children were grown—or considered themselves grown, as Eleanor married at sixteen—she would "tour the family," staying with relatives when a child was born, making herself quietly useful, and then moving on, so as not to be too much of a burden.

After Anne married, her mother lived with her. Neither Jack nor Eleanor had anything to do with their father again, and they lived strange and saddening half-lives, one leaving her husband and children forever, the other dwindling and drifting and dying young.

Pat Brown paid occasional visits to my grandmother, which she bore out of duty rather than love. My mother's older sister, Ann Daly, recalls that when she was a little girl, he would "haunt us, two or three times a year. My mother would be cold to him but polite. He'd visit for maybe fifteen minutes. My grandmother would go to another room. I hid under the table." She remembers him from below, the perspective of an anxious child: a diamond pinky ring on a manicured hand ("He had polished nails, but my grandmother didn't"), stout legs in a chalk-striped suit, black shoes with white spats—ominous, glamorous, and incomplete. He would never be completed for his descendants, never known in full.

"Everyone loved him but his family," Ann told me. "Even my father loved him—he knew he was a lot of baloney, a b.s. artist, everything was 'big time' and 'big money.' But he thought he was a wonderful guy, funny, generous, everything—and he'd ask my mother what the matter was. But she didn't want anything to do with him. Pat Brown bent over backwards for your grandmother—he didn't care about Jack and Eleanor—but she would have closed the door on him. He wasn't invited to my mother's wedding, September 22, 1929. Her brother Jack gave her away.

"He always had big, flashy cars—Cadillacs, I think—and his clothes, well, I wonder who his tailor was, because he wore nothing off the rack. He had to pay something like twelve dollars a month in support, which he did without question. That was about it, though. I remember in the thirties, he took my sister Dolores and me to a precinct Christmas party, it was for the poor children in the neighborhood."

My mother's recollection of Pat Brown is more vague and less critical. She barely knew her grandmother Catherine, who died in February 1941, after catching a cold when she went to see her son Jack off to the Army. A few months later, Pat Brown married a woman named Margaret Cramer—he never divorced Catherine, and had to wait to remarry if he intended to remain a Catholic—and there seems to have been a mild thaw in his relations with what was left of his family. In any case, he did make some effort to see more of them, and it was not prevented. Margaret grew especially fond of my mother. Where Ann Daly viewed Pat Brown through her mother and grandmother, as a man who wronged them by leaving, and wronged them again by coming back, my mother had Margaret to frame and filter the view. And since Margaret was so kind and decent, my mother believed that Pat Brown must have had those qualities too in some measure, at least in theory. Even so, when my mother spoke of him, her tone was restrained and avoiding rather than affectionate. He seems to have struck her as a man who showed the wear of a lifetime spent not going home after work, with the broad, brisk gestures of affability that appeal more to bartenders and waitresses than to young children. He died when she was eight, and she remembers him, without much certainty, as being partial to scotch and steak—my grandmother died when I was seven, and while I don't remember what she would have ordered in a restaurant, my memories of her are vivid and warm.

My mother remained close to Margaret, and I remember visiting her as a child—she was a sweet old lady in Bay Ridge, who was related in some way that I didn't understand. Her apartment was spacious and immaculate and looked like nothing had moved in thirty years. There was a dish of peppermint candy on a coffee table that stuck together into one big glom of sweets, so you had to wrestle it to break off a piece. That was fun, but there was nothing else for children there. After Pat died in 1946, Margaret married a retired inspector named John Sullivan, who also was recently widowed. Both couples had been good friends and childless. Sullivan lived only a few years longer, and so Margaret, who must have feared becoming an old maid, ended up a widow twice over, in a fairly short time. Margaret once told my mother that my father reminded her of Pat Brown; that he was a big man, handsome, and good company. When my mother told me, she made the kind of face she'd make if she had to eat the grubby, sticky candy, adding with some emphasis that she never saw any resemblance. She even said that Inspector Sullivan was a little more like him. Sullivan, of all people, her step-grandmother's second husband. She put the compliment aside, like an unwanted gift.

This private antipathy colored their view of Pat Brown as a public servant: the distance allowed the family to look at his life as a cop from a cold distance, an aerial view without detail or context. Sonny Grosso, one of the heroes of the French Connection case, once told me that even a lousy cop does more good than an ordinary person, in spite of himself—even if he stands there like a scarecrow, he can stop fights and robberies and make old ladies feel safe. Pat Brown received no such benefit of the doubt: unaware of any of his accomplishments, indifferent to whatever explanations he might have offered for his choices, his family knew little of him and liked less. Had he stuck around, his days at work would have been the talk of the dinner table, and his troubles and jokes, his feats and foibles, would have been cherished threads woven into the family lore. And his gambling life, taking money from bookmakers and then becoming one himself, would likely have been glossed over, or else recast as a kind of quaint and rather comic, olden-time malarkey, as if he made moonshine in the bathtub. The world of corner bookies survived the era of the speakeasy, but both have an air of nostalgia; when you imagine them, it is in sepia tones, with a jazz soundtrack, more redolent of period charm than positive menace. Like most New Yorkers, my family did not believe that a glass of beer or a game of cards imperiled their souls, and there was something ugly and silly about those who insisted that they did. The prevalence of betting and drinking when both were banned—Ann Daly said that it seemed that "every empty garage had a teletype," and "you got knocked over by the runners going down the street" as they delivered their slips—led to an increase in cynicism about law enforcement, but since that was the kind of enforcement the public seemed to want, the arrangement struck many as pragmatic rather than hypocritical. The fact of the matter was that Pat Brown was not respected at home, and so his career in the station house and the street was viewed with derision. His personal life shaped his public appearance, and those who were inclined to condemn him were amply accommodated.

The divide between his work and his life, or rather the way he broke apart the pieces of his life, was an arrangement that allowed most memories of him to fall through the gaps. He was said to frequent a bar called McLaughlin's on Flatbush Avenue, and to be friends with the undertaker Austin Moran. How many years have passed since Moran was a name to drop, or "the crowd at McLaughlin's" was rich in meaning? McLaughlin's may have been a favorite of cops, judges, gamblers, or Brooklyn Dodgers, or some combination of all of these—my aunt said it was "supposed to be a classy place, full of politicians." Moran, I would guess, was a figure of middle-class respectability, as successful funeral directors tend to be, friendly with professionals and priests. Ann Daly recalls Pat Brown as prominent in Catholic laymen's groups, and as she is devout herself—her daughter Patty is a nun—she held his own devotion against him: his practice and his profession were glaringly distinct. Maybe most people loved Pat Brown unless he gave them reason not to, but those who thought better of him have little to say now. You gotta have a story, and he never told us his.

On the single index card that constitutes Pat Brown's entire surviving NYPD record, it states that he was punished three times and praised once, all in his early years. On February 29, 1908, he "failed to make report of ambulance case," and one week later, he was cited for being "absent from post and in restaurant," for which he lost five days' pay. The next year, in September, he "did not properly patrol," and lost another day. (Ninety years later, my command discipline for "improper patrol" cost me three days, so maybe the Job's toughened up since then.) All three reprimands are in the same handwriting, which suggests that he was not a favorite of a particular sergeant or lieutenant. In October 1912, he stopped a runaway horse, for which he received a medal for Excellent Police Duty. The next three decades of service were unremarked upon.

If Pat Brown was troubled by anything in his life, there is no evidence of it. Though he did not see his children Jack and Eleanor, apparently by mutual agreement, his visits to his daughter Anne bespoke some confidence in a fuller restoration of relations. He lived at the St. George Hotel, the most fashionable in Brooklyn at the time, the seasonal residence of many of the Dodgers. Park Slope was nearby, as was McLaughlin's, on Flatbush and Atlantic—*He used to carry the bag on Atlantic Avenue. . . .*His horse room may have been up and running before he retired, perhaps in Jersey, perhaps closer. He took to frequenting the Copacabana, where he was known as "Paddy the Cop," and he was friends with the comedian Joe E. Brown. He would die in January 1946, a few days after his old friend O'Dwyer was inaugurated as mayor.

When *The Brooklyn Eagle* broke the Harry Gross story in 1949, "Thank God your grandfather isn't alive" became the household refrain. His partner in the horse room was sent to prison. The details of Pat Brown that survive in family memory are few and fragmentary, like the debris in a hit-and-run accident. I know that his parents survived the potato famine, which emptied Ireland of a quarter of its population; when he went to work in 1907, more than two million people a day went to nickelodeons, and when he retired in 1940, the Manhattan Project was under way. Because corruption was pervasive in certain eras, it can seem odd to observe that the prisons were filled and refilled, by and large, with people who belonged there. And year after year, cops died fighting the same gangsters who made their peace with the politicians. I know a little about how Pat Brown was a bad cop, but I don't know how he was a good one; if he saved lives or took them, delivered babies or calmed angry crowds. There is that one decorated act of bravery, but I don't know much more about him than the horse. Did he sleep well at night, dreaming of showgirls on his mattress full of money? Or did he sweat like O'Dwyer, and try to do good with one hand while the other strained against the come-alongs held by the gangsters in Brooklyn? I don't think - people change, too often or too deeply, but many are quick to adapt. Like his old friend O'Dwyer, Pat Brown escaped judgment but paid with his reputation, escaping fond and common remembrance as well.

. . .

I THINK MY PARENTS WERE MEANT FOR EACH OTHER NOT because theirs was an especially happy marriage—though it was—but because they met through an undertaker called Charlie Le Chance. The name of the man had a peculiar music, vaudevillian but haunting, and he lived up to its billing. Le Chance, a friend of my father's, worked as a freelancer for several funeral homes, and he either owned or had easy access to a hearse. There must have been a shortage of cars in my father's circle in the Bronx during the fifties and early sixties, because the hearse saw a lot of social mileage. I heard a lot of Charlie Le Chance stories, and they all featured a corpse in the back seat. Either Charlie's passenger would casually examine the back to find a post-mortem chaperone, or a friend would be given a lift somewhere, and told not to mind the cargo. After the friend's protests were dismissed— "You're the one who asked for the ride, pal"—Charlie would announce that he had a quick errand to run, and when he hopped out of the car, his return would be mysteriously delayed. The passenger would wait uncomfortably as the minutes passed, perhaps glancing back, and wonder if it was his imagination when he heard the body bag slowly unzip. The punch line can be imagined. In any case, Charlie was my parents' matchmaker, and since he - could bring together the living and the dead, I think of their marriage as almost an arranged one.

My mother's name was Elizabeth Trust, and she was known as Betty. Betty Trust is not a musical name but it has an evocative flair, as sweet and warm and homey as a cake. Le Chance met her at a wedding, through another undertaker she was dating at the time. I don't know if it was an all-undertaker affair, though more than one guest probably wondered where the flowers came from. When my mother broke up with her undertaker, she later told me, Charlie saw an opportunity for himself, having formed a wishful impression from the few facts he knew of her. "I was studying psychology, and had spent the summer in Europe," she explained. "He assumed that 'Free Love' was next." When it became clear that she was not the girl for him, he thought immediately of my father. He told each of them what he had in mind, and both seemed amenable to a meeting. It was not an obvious pairing, at least not for my mother, but then again, Le Chance was my father's friend.

My father was fifteen years older than my mother, approaching forty as she had just passed twenty. They were old-fashioned and good-hearted - people, both the most intellectually ambitious of their families, but at ease with those who were not. As an FBI agent and a doctoral student in psychology, probing the underworld and the unconscious, they must have had a touch of the exotic about them, though exoticism in the working-class Irish world—or half-Irish, in my mother's case—was a large enough category, and could have included missing Mass or liking opera or living alone in Manhattan. Each had been engaged before: my father for several years, to a woman who kept postponing the date—in part, I was told, because my Uncle Gerry, a somewhat feral teenager, would join them in the new household. My mother broke off an engagement to a man who expected a more traditional wife than she was willing to become. My mother's undertaker followed, and my father must have begun to wonder if he'd meet his own undertaker before he met his wife.

My father dropped by to see her at Columbia University, where she was studying, and they went out for coffee. It was the late fall of 1960, an era that is harder to picture than those that preceded and followed: hair was still short, but the more current men had stopped wearing hats, as President Kennedy would, at his inauguration a few months ahead. My father kept his hat—always—and it covered gray hair. He wore a trench coat, stood six-foot-two, and weighed just over two hundred pounds (I have his FBI files, and these facts were noted). When he met my mother on campus, the other students probably would have guessed she was meeting an uncle before they suspected a date. The political temper of Columbia was earnest and liberal, with pro- and anti-Communist factions, and though I am sure the campus supported Kennedy over Nixon in great numbers, many would have preferred Adlai Stevenson to either. My father admired Kennedy, on the strength of his war record and as an epochal advance for Irish Americans, though he disapproved of his playboy lifestyle, which even then was something of an open secret. He voted for Nixon, perhaps following the inclination of Cardinal Spellman, who was said to be furious at the prospect of losing his position as First Catholic. My mother voted for Kennedy. As a subject for contention, I don't think presidential politics would have divided them any more than the fact that one was from the Bronx, the other from Brooklyn.

They weren't the kind of people who argued over these things any more than they were the kind who settled arguments by arm wrestling. It certainly - wouldn't come up on a first date.

Their first, proper dinner date was on the evening of December 15, at the Commuter's Cafe, on Church Street in downtown Manhattan. The restaurant was owned by a close friend of my father's, an Austrian immigrant named Joe Tretter, and two of his brothers. The choice was shrewd: the food was good, the price was right, and they would be treated with extreme consideration. My father would be comfortable and confident there, unlike anywhere else respectable enough to bring a date. To walk into a good restaurant, exchange pleasantries with the maitre d', look at the menu, and order food—forget about wine—would have been an unnatural act, as alien to my father as flamenco or the Japanese tea ceremony. For many working-class New Yorkers, the most commonplace aspects of city life—restaurants, taxis, nightclubs—were as familiarly unreal as movies, and while you saw them every day, to find yourself in one could be traumatic. It may seem odd that headwaiters inspired more fear in my father than hijackers, but it doesn't now, to me—you're afraid of what you don't know. The date went well enough, until the plane crash.

There were two plane crashes, in fact, or two planes that collided in midair, over Brooklyn, killing one hundred and twenty-nine people in the air and six more on the ground. One little boy lived for a day, after falling from the sky into a snow bank. At the Bureau, they call this kind of event a "special," and the term can cover anything from a kidnapping to a jailbreak. Agents are pulled from their normal assignments to work on the incident. My father was working on railroad thefts and on my mother, though not necessarily in that order, but both had to be left alone for the moment. One special preempted another. He dropped her off at home and went to the crash site.

For the next several months, they went out once a week and regularly spoke on the phone. My mother thought he was a good man and enjoyed his company, but the relationship just seemed to amble along. When he picked her up for their next Saturday-night date, she told him that they had something important to talk about. As they drove, she told him that they should break it off—he was a nice guy, but things didn't seem to be going anywhere.

"Oh," he said. "I was going to ask you to marry me."

My mother reconsidered her assessment of their progress, and told him she'd have to think it over. After she decided in the affirmative, she told her mother, Anne, who in turn told her husband, Bill, "We're going to have a wedding in the family." Bill assumed that it was his son, and said, "That dumb kid, he doesn't have a nickel to his name, what is he getting married for?" Anne corrected him: "No, it's Betty who's getting married." And Bill said, "To who?" My mother said it was the most impulsive thing she'd ever done, and it was all the more telling in that her life was not exactly lived on a whim. And so what Le Chance began, choice finished.

. . .

THEY WERE DIFFERENT TIMES, BACK THEN. IN 1961, THERE WAS more time—so it seems now—for everything. There was less variety in how things turned out: more people got married sooner and stayed married longer. As my mother explains it, to be engaged meant something less than it does today: it meant you might get married, and you'd decide as you went along, and wouldn't date other people in the meantime. In that sense, it was a faster and less formal arrangement, which is not how I think of life then, when marriage was the substance and purpose of most women's lives. It was a given, as the draft was for men, and if it scared you during the haircut and physical, you were proud of yourself when all the fuss was over. To worry about it too much, or to try to escape, was either a weakness or a luxury, and my parents' backgrounds discouraged both.

My father met my mother's parents, and they got on well—he was as much their contemporary as hers. That he had a fine mind, a good heart, and a sense of humor would have been quickly apparent, and the fact that he was a gentleman—and a large, armed one at that—would have made them feel sure that their daughter would be safe with him. They liked him a great deal as a man, but his job and his background gave him no natural advantage in their sympathies.

The term "Irish cop" didn't have the same sentimental pull for the Trusts, in sum or in its parts, as it did for the Conlons. The Trusts were more Catholic than Irish, beyond even the obvious ethnic math of a match between Bill Trust and the former Anne Brown. St. Patrick's Day was not a landmark on the calendar, and bagpipes did not stir any deep feelings of ancestral glory and strife. Union jobs and the civil service did not earn the nearly cultish devotion they did on the Conlon side. The Browns came over after the Famine of the late 1840s; it had been three generations since anyone had spoken with a brogue. As for the police, they were to be respected, always, but the Irish cop they knew best was no hero to them, as Pat Brown had a long career in the NYPD but a short one as a husband. Despite the fact that my father was a very different man, I wonder if to my mother, or to her mother, he felt like a throwback sometimes. They were past that, and things got better all the time.

The Trusts were more American than the Conlons, in that sense, more comfortable and more optimistic. My mother was the third of four children—Ann, Dolores, Betty, Bill. Her two sisters married businessmen, and her brother became one. The roll call of the five Conlons read down from the FBI, the NYPD, the Transit Authority, nursing, and the New York City Fire Department. It surprised me when my mother told me that her family didn't have any more money than my father's—her father was a bookkeeper for an oil company, his was a laborer for the phone company—though both had remained employed through the Depression. Both my parents loved their families, but my father's childhood seemed one of confinement and loss, whereas my mother's was of warmth and safety. Their lives were differently lit: the six Trusts had a bright apartment in Flatbush, Brooklyn, where I can picture the family in the parlor, listening to Fred Allen on the radio. The seven Conlons lived in four small rooms at the back of a building on Kingsbridge Avenue in the Bronx, on the first floor over the alley. Sometimes an extra uncle took the kitchen floor. In the summer, the kids slept on the fire escape. They ate greasy legs of mutton and drank milk from jelly jars. My mother's family fussed over birthdays and took vacations every summer; my father's did neither. Later on, when we did celebrate his birthday, he accepted the custom with a dutiful confusion, as if he'd landed in Hawaii and we'd garlanded his neck with flowers. He'd raise his glass and say, "Happy Birthday, everybody." When I picture each childhood, my mother's has the genial formality of a sitcom from the 1950s, with amusing dilemmas resolved in twenty-six minutes; my father's is like a newsreel from the 1930s, set against a backdrop of breadlines and war.

My father's young life, which seems as remote to me as the war in which he fought, was related as a succession of sad facts and funny stories. He was the oldest in his family, and his parents had been dead for decades; all I knew of him was from his tales. But I knew my mother's parents, and her sisters' memories reached further back than hers. Her life was more lifelike to me, less a series of allegories than transparent memories without a moral, even, but also without a beginning or an end.

"Joe Daly would take us to see the Dodgers at Ebbets Field, and he'd always look so sharp in his porkpie hat . . ."

"When I was a little girl, you could ride the subway alone, even when you were eight years old, and they had wicker seats and windows that opened . . ."

"When we had a party, we'd gather around the piano and my mother would play . . ."

As I remember her, my grandmother Anne wore short-sleeved dresses and had large, freckled arms that shuddered rhythmically when she laughed and erratically when she didn't. She wore a gold charm bracelet, which also shook, and narrow glasses on a chain. At our house, she played a dinky electric organ, coaxing out "East Side, West Side" and "Give My Regards to Broadway" in a sweet, nostalgic wheeze. She and my grandfather joked and played cards and drank red-white-and-gold cans of Rheingold beer, which was made in Brooklyn, and which you had to open with a "church key." Their accents were old Brooklyn, and they sometimes said "terlet" and "erl" for "toilet" and "oil." I can't remember Anne being unhappy with us, or even ever being unhappy.

The blessedly ordinary life my mother led was her mother's doing, for the most part. Anne Brown had come from a broken home, and so she made hers rigorously whole. At one time, Anne thought about becoming a lawyer, but she decided to stay in with her children. And though she was a talented musician as well, she only played at church and home. Her mother Catherine lived with her after Anne married, though she died when my mother was two. Anne's brother, Jack, moved in after the war. Her younger sister, Eleanor, had a husband, who was also in the service, and three children. Eleanor patiently awaited victory and homecoming and then packed up and left, asking for nothing and offering less; more than half a century passed without a word from her. I'd heard of fathers who "went out for a pack of cigarettes and never came back," but I'd never heard of mothers doing that. "The war was hard on families," my mother said, tactfully.

My great-uncle Jack was in show business for a while. He was a crooner in the thirties, singing sentimental ballads in the low, smooth style suitable for radio broadcast at the time. He was as handsome as a leading man, athletic and elegant, with fine, strong features. In one photograph, he shares a studio microphone with a brunette wearing white flowers in her hair. The brunette is as white as the flowers, with wide, dark lips, and she looks at the camera. Jack is tan, darker than the Cuban-style shirt he wears, his hair is slicked back to show a widow's peak, and he looks down at the sheet of music. Her mouth is open, as if to sing "Ahh!" and his is half-closed, as if to sing

"Ooh!" The sheet he holds is folded in thirds, and the only part of the title you can read is ER KNOW. Maybe it was "You'll Never Know." In the late thirties, Jack was married to a piano player named Marie, and they played the big nightclubs in Manhattan. When Marie became pregnant, Jack went into a fugue state and disappeared for six weeks, until he was found, emaciated, wandering in a bus station. Marie stood by him for years, until she discovered him with company in their hotel room; when she told my mother about it, more than fifty years later, the shock was so fresh and the telling so elliptical that my mother suspected it was something beyond ordinary adultery. I felt the same way, when Marie told me, because when she reached the climax, she halted and said she couldn't, wouldn't *ever* say what she had seen. But Marie was a professional entertainer, after all, and perhaps it was better to leave it at that: *You'll never know . . .ž* After Marie left him, Jack took to drinking and declined from singer to singing waiter to waiter, and that's when he moved in with his sister Anne. He died a few years later.

My mother's young life strikes me as rich in every way except anecdote, which seems to need a degree of misadventure to thrive. As a teenager, she was bitten by a dog and had to suffer through the course of rabies vaccination, sixteen shots in the stomach. Aside from that, her life varied between things she liked and things she loved, and the majority fell into the latter category. She liked her neighborhood and she loved school; she loved her friends, she loved her family, and she loved her Church. Religion made her good, and it made her happy as well; it was a like a walled garden, where you were sheltered as you grew.

The Trust family had its share of calamity, to be sure, but even when it struck them, it seemed that they were shielded by some hidden and benevolent hand. From the 1950s on, at the end of every summer they went to the Pocono mountains for two weeks, first to a little bungalow colony in a town called Matamoros, and then to a hotel called Locust Grove. The other guests were like them, mostly Irish and Catholic and from Brooklyn, working-class and white-collar, for whom vacations were as new and American as highways. They sat, they swam, they played cards, then went for walks and began again. Every few minutes, someone would say, "Ah, what a delightful breeze," or, "Smell that country air!" My grandparents put plastic shields on their noses, or zinc oxide, or both; my mother avoided the sun as much as she could. She could get sunburn from a flashbulb. She liked the country better than the beach—the sun was less severe, and you didn't get sand in everything. When they swam, they went to the Delaware River, which by August is gentle, slow, and brown as tea, and you can walk across it in many places. Trees lean in over the banks, and you can put blankets down on the grass.

In the summer of 1955, the Delaware flooded. Heavy rains brought flash floods, and the river rose and swept its banks, taking from them houses, couches, horses, coffins. From the ridge in Matamoros where the Trusts were, they saw the flotilla pass by, a waterborne catalog of what people once had, like in the tornado scene in *The Wizard of Oz*. The ridge itself had been cut off from the land, and the river gained wildly in its new course. Trees and tons of earth were torn up, and the water was half-mud and trash-ridden, running fast and hungry. The Trusts were atop their diminishing sliver of land, waiting with a rowboat to see if they would be forced to flee. Within hours, they'd gone from vacationers to refugees. I wonder if they thought that if they reached the sea, they might row back to Brooklyn.

The water rose, and with it came the decision to leave. The family boarded the boat, a hectic chorus of afterthought and advice: "You sit there!"

"Not there—there!"

"Is everyone here?"

"Gently! Gently!"

The boat was filled with canned food, jars of water, blankets wrapped in plastic bags, wallets, purses, money, and jewelry—all they could not bear to part with that would not kill them on their trip. As they put in, my mother was looking into their bag of provisions, when she leapt out and ran back to the house—

"Betty! Wait!"

"Betty! What is it!"

"Betty! Come back, you little—!"

"Bill!"

Moments later, she emerged from the house, and ran back to the boat. She took her place again and set the bag down as the boat eased into the water. I try to imagine that moment when the force of nature and the force of family met, and which promised the greater violence. She was asked to explain her actions.

"It's Friday," she said.

Asked again for clarification, she reminded them of the ban of meat on Fridays.

"We took the wrong soup. We had chicken noodle, so I had to go back in the house to get the tomato."

If there had been a priest in the boat, he might have thrown her overboard, but as it was, her response was the only one that could not be gainsaid. I'm sure there was some comment, but what was even the risk of death next to the commandment of God? Circumstance did not permit further discussion. They set out upon the waters, then, and were spared the wrath of the flood, finding instead sanctuary on the far shores of the land, where they prospered and multiplied.

· · ·

MY FATHER HAD A RIVER IN HIS CHILDHOOD, TOO, AND A mother. His mother's name was Delia Laffey, though on some documents it was Della, and her age was a mystery as well. Delia was from County Mayo, twenty-odd miles away from the village where William O'Dwyer was born. Mayo, in the northwest of Ireland, is craggy and windswept, and the people were especially poor and Gaelic-speaking, which, in certain quarters, meant they were especially Irish. My grandmother came over as an indentured servant, just after the First World War, and on postcards she wrote home, the name is spelled Laife and Laffe before becoming Laffey, the Irish spelling suffering the same Anglo alchemy as that of her fellow immigrants from Naples or Kiev. No numbered address is given, only the family name in a village—more of a crossroads, really—that is alternately spelled Mohollogy and Mocollogan, a point on a map modified by place names almost as obscure: Tuam, Shrule, Ballinrobe, Mayo. Whatever shape the words took, Delia never had a problem making herself understood.

The river was the Hudson, dirty but still beautiful, gray as a battleship and as massive, flanked on its western shore by the tawny cliffs of the Palisades. Fifty Delawares could flow through its course. The sea washes up into it from the harbor with the tide, and over from the Harlem River, which is a tidal channel, flowing back and forth between the Hudson and the Long Island Sound. The Harlem River changes directions every six hours, running between Hell Gate and Spuyten Duyvil, Dutch for "Spit on the Devil" or "In Spite of the Devil," each a tribute to the treachery of its currents. When my father was eleven or twelve, he and his friends had a little rowboat they played with, below Spuyten Duyvil, in the stretch between the rock face with a huge "C" painted on it, for Columbia University, and the railroad bridge that marked the edge of the Hudson. Inwood Hill Park is on one side, and wild land along the railroad tracks on the other, and the boys could imagine they were the pirates who had worked the river through their grandfathers' days, or the Indians whose arrowheads still littered the hills of Inwood.

I don't know how my grandmother Delia found out about the boat; whether my father mentioned it innocently, or his brother Eddie did out of revenge for not being taken along. I don't know how well the boys could swim, if at all. Delia was from a part of Ireland where the fishermen could not, and their sweaters were knit in patterns to show which village they were from, so that their drowned bodies could be claimed if they ever washed ashore. She could have knit a "231st Street and Kingsbridge Avenue" sweater for my father, or she could have forbidden him to go boating. On the day the boys had planned the next river outing, she confined him to the house, leaving him to brood heavily on the injustice of it all. His mood did not lighten that evening, when he learned that the boat had capsized and two of his friends had drowned. My father was swept away, too, in wonder and dread, at the luck that mixed like the waters where the rivers met, pulling some under until their breath left them, sparing others to walk home to their mothers in the summer night. Delia must have seemed to have some power of fate in her, awesome in its love, awful in its cost.

My father also had a summer vacation, once. It was around the time that Delia sent him upstate with the Colored Orphans League, as I remember him calling the organization. The Boy Scouts were known as a Protestant group, and in her reckoning, he was better off as a white rarity than a Catholic one. Regardless, he had gone away grudgingly, and wanted only to go home. He was sent there with two vast cardboard suitcases of clothing that weighed more than he did; his mother anticipated that he would not spend much time doing laundry. She was right, my father told me: one suitcase remained unopened and the other was barely unpacked. I don't suppose he sweated much: he spent most of his time as the scorekeeper when the other kids played basketball or baseball. On the bus trip back to the Bronx, he watched the alien greenery of the countryside give way to asphalt and brick, the heat and crowds of the city, the thrill of home. When he arrived back at his apartment, he dragged his suitcases up the stairs and eagerly banged on the door.

But instead of the familiar, foreign voice of his mother, the consoling brogue to which he was more accustomed than to his own accent, the people inside spoke a different language entirely. A Sicilian family lived there, and the exotic sounds and smells made the shock of his displacement all the more acute. *"Little boy, those people, they move . . ."*

Down the stairs he went, weak in the knees from his luggage and loss, and he sat down on the sidewalk, crying. For all I know—and all he knew—he would have stayed there until he died of hunger among his clean clothes. But another Italian passed by, a vegetable and fruit vendor in his horse-drawn cart, and asked him what was the matter.

"Little boy, don't cry. You come with me, maybe we find them. . . ."

And so my father got up beside the vendor and wiped his nose, and put his belongings with the lettuce and potatoes and strange things he'd never seen before, like eggplant and artichokes, and watched the streets anxiously as the horse shambled along. Their progress was painfully slow as they moved through the route, but the novelty of the horse ride and the revival of hope distracted him from his plight. And they had ridden less than half a mile before he saw his brother Eddie in the street, playing handball with a group of kids, new to him but clearly friends.

"Hey, Eddie! Where do we live?"

Eddie was in the middle of the game, and pointed to a five-story apartment house of tan brick, with the name "Vanity Court" painted on the transom. My father blurted out his thanks, grabbed his bags, and ran inside to pound on the door. When Delia answered, his rage and relief took over him, and he complained senselessly through his tears. She laughed and kissed him, and said, "Ahh, Johnny, we knew ye'd find us."

Today, she would have been arrested. We might be doubly stunned, as my father was, by her apparent lack of feeling and her cold confidence in her son. But Delia had sailed to America in her teens; she knew no one, and she would never see her parents again. I don't know if she expected to. Sacrifice was ordinary, and survival was its sometime reward. In Mayo, the famine was especially harsh, and memories of it were recent and fierce. When my parents visited her village, in the 1970s, they looked up the family records in the church and found that after Delia's grandparents lost two children named - Thomas and Bridget, they named their next two children Thomas and Bridget. You could see it as a commemoration and a forgetting at once. You moved on. Ireland then was both the Old World and the Third World, an economy in which sentimentality had little place. For my father, who was American-born, the divide between generations was compounded by culture, and he learned in time not to quarrel with it. Then again, she might have left a note.

A woman like my grandmother takes a war in stride. When Delia suspected it was coming, in the late thirties, she went to see Edward Flynn. Known as Boss Flynn, he had run the Bronx Democratic Party since the early twenties, as no one before or since. He represented machine politics not only at its most effective but its most progressive; he was one of the three or four men responsible, more than anyone else, for the election of Franklin Delano Roosevelt as President, and he remained an influential advisor and back-room champion of the New Deal. Delia went to see him to pursue an appointment to West Point for my father, reckoning shrewdly that his education would amount to a kind of deferment, and that the Army would be more thrifty with the lives of its new elites than with those of ordinary enlisted men. I don't know how she got in; Boss Flynn was atypical of those in his position in both his reputation for honesty and his inaccessibility—he was a lawyer, a cool-headed strategist rather than the smiling *padrone* handing out holiday turkeys. In any case, she did not secure the appointment, though I am impressed by the presumption of an immigrant woman demanding the best for her son, and by a politics that took immigrant women into account.

When she made decisions about her children, Delia was as hard and canny as Flynn, deploying her resources where they were needed most and - could best succeed. I don't wonder why she never asked, "Well, if you can't take my Johnny at West Point, what about my Eddie?" Eddie had attended a series of high schools, and was asked to leave one because he rode a motor-cycle down the halls. His education was exclusively in Catholic institutions, in the apt belief that he needed the discipline, and the rest of the kids followed suit. My father, she felt, could go it alone among the pagans. As he recalled his grammar-school graduation from St. John's, when the Monsi-gnor read the list of graduates and which high school they would attend—Cardinal Hayes, Fordham Prep, All Hallows for the boys; Sacred Heart, St. Catherine's, Mount St. Ursula for the girls—the announcement of "Conlon" and "De Witt Clinton" was intoned like an obituary. The Monsignor did not shake his hand. My father did well at Clinton, and he graduated early; Delia had been right, no matter if it was little comfort at the time.

She was right about the war, too. When the Japanese attacked Pearl Har-bor, my father was enrolled at Manhattan College. In October 1943, he en-listed in the Marines. He went through boot camp at Camp Lejeune and Officer Candidates School, and was duly appointed second lieutenant. He continued his training and his education for the next year while stationed in Pennsylvania, before being moved to Los Angeles, in preparation for ship-ping out to the Pacific theater. Then Delia fell ill, with what was eventually diagnosed as liver cancer. She found this news extremely irritating, as she - didn't drink, and thought the neighbors would whisper that she was a secret tippler. Around Christmas of 1944, my father received word that she had days to live. His superiors were sympathetic, but unmoved: no leaves were to be granted. Despondent, he found himself in the Officers' Club one night, where he met a Catholic chaplain. He confided in him, and as the details came out, the priest stopped him—he had been assigned to St. John's in Kingsbridge, he said, and he knew Delia. He told my father not to lose hope, and that he would be in touch. Within days, my father's leave was arranged, and he was home when his mother died, on New Year's Day, 1945. His unit shipped out without him, to what would become the battle of Tarawa. His OCS class suffered the highest casualty rate in the history of the Marine Corps. Delia had saved him, again. And then she moved on, again, beyond where he could find her on a horse-drawn cart, much farther than she had gone in her first emigration.

. . .

MY FATHER MARRIED MY MOTHER BECAUSE HE LIKED HER life, I think, and hoped to have a family that fate would treat more like hers than his own. Often enough, when he got a call from a relative, it was because there was trouble to be sorted out: someone needed a job or was in jail. When she got a call, it was because someone wanted to know if she could bring a casserole to a christening. For her, marriage would be a great continuation of life, remaking for herself what she had known in childhood. For him, it would be a change: if they moved while a son was away at summer camp, she would let the child know. When the river rose, it would bear them to safety, and take neither them nor their friends down to the bottom. They would pack the right soup. As for war, they would have to trust in God, as - everyone would, but He seemed to show special favor to Betty Trust.

My father's hopes were rewarded: they had nearly thirty years together, and five children, and even through the end of their years, they would take walks in the evening, holding hands. All the while, history happened: the *Daily News* headlines for each of our births tells of a million-dollar jewel heist at the Hotel Pierre (for Marianne); the ejection of a Cuban spy (for Stephen); a strike on the Long Island Rail Road (for Regina); a two-million-dollar drug raid (for me); and for Johnny, the oldest, on November 23, 1963, PRESIDENT IS SLAIN. My father spent his spare time reading about history, and he knew it well enough to keep it out of the house.

My parents didn't always agree, but I can remember only one argument between them, when he wanted us to get in the car before she was finished cleaning up the kitchen. It might have lasted two minutes, and their voices were barely raised. My father could aggravate her with his devotion to garage-sale bargains, and with his near-fanatic habit of book-buying, which at one point inflicted structural damage on the house. My mother had enough trouble keeping order with five kids, but she said, "I'd like him to lose some weight, and to try going to the library instead of the bookstore for a while. But he doesn't drink, smoke, gamble, or cheat, so how can I give him a hard time?" When you don't make many mistakes—or when whole worlds of mishap are closed to you—you begin life better than if you were rich.

I can say they were meant for each other, regardless of fate or Le Chance, because they matched. Not only in that they were loving and loyal to each other, a true union in what they worked for and believed in, but because she was tireless and giving, running the house and pushing him to do things he - wouldn't have done on his own—which is to say, anything beyond sitting in his easy chair and reading. He brought the strange gift of his history, the sad facts and funny stories, the talent for wonder at the wild, wide life outside what little we thought we knew. Every marriage is a mixed marriage, joining two pasts for a new possibility. And one superstition was observed at their wedding, no matter if they were unaware of it. He was old, and she was new. The borrowed part was time, as all time is. The blue was in the blood.

THREE

Whenever I ran into George on the street, he told me things. The information was always good, but never quite useful. He confirmed things I knew, told me about witnesses to assaults and robberies who wouldn't come forward. He had an eye out for my gun collar: "There's a guy, he's in the park sometimes? He carries a nine. When he's with his girl, she's got the piece, in a knapsack." All right, that's some guy, known associate of some girl. Got it, ten-four. I paged him once or twice, and the call was never returned. Still, I knew there was more to come.

A month after I arrested him for his fight with Tonya, George slapped another teenage girl around, leaving her with a swollen cheek. She had argued with him, telling him some bad news about one of his baby-mothers, and he was furious because he believed her, or didn't, I forget which. "I don't know his last name," she said, and I told her not to worry, as I filled out the complaint, writing his vital statistics from memory. George lay low for a while, knowing I was looking for him. When the girl told me she had decided against pressing charges, I went to the record store where he worked—his brother, who was on parole for murder, owned the store—and left word that he wasn't wanted anymore. The next day, after roll call, a cop at the desk called me over and said, "There's some perp on the line, he wants to talk to you." George wanted to know for certain that he was in the clear, and after I reassured him that he was, he thanked me profusely. On the street, he was even more friendly and eager to provide. George played both sides, comfortably and well.

And then something happened at the record store. It was a successful business and a legitimate one, in that they made a lot of money selling a lot of records. But I'd bet that drug money started the place and moved through it, and that it served as a kind of information clearinghouse for serious gangsters, who planned and bragged of robberies, looked for crew and targets for new jobs. One evening, near closing time, when the staff and the last few customers were readying to leave, a man walked up to the glass door and fired five or six shots inside. No one was hit, no one was even cut by the rain of broken glass. The sloppy botch of it left it unclear who the intended victim was, and there was the usual chaos of conflicting statements—a dark-skinned man with dreadlocks, or short hair, was seen walking away, and running, into a black Lexus, a white Mercedes—and a tenor of cordial noncooperation. A dozen cops responded, a large crowd gathered, and I quietly took George aside. He told me, "We don't know what's up, but we're gonna find out. People gotta take care of business, but this was not right. There was women here, coulda been hurt. There's things I gotta check, I'll let you know."

That was the real pleasure of being a beat cop, the local authority and the free agency, to find things out and follow them where they led. I knew the seventeen red-brick towers of Morris Houses as well as anyone on my side of the fence, and when other cops were looking for someone from there, they were put in touch with me. A fire marshall asked me to help him collect an arsonist. Manhattan detectives showed me blurry video stills from a jewelry store stickup and I could tell them the guy wasn't around, I'd been to the apartment the other week for an Aided case. A detective in Staten Island was looking for a guy known as "Man" who had stabbed his girlfriend and thrown her puppy out the window; I'd locked him up for beating up a deaf kid, and was hunting him for assaulting another girl in his building. Child Welfare called me because one of their workers had been harassed by a man named Larry during the investigation of a case of child neglect, and I was quick to interrupt, "That would be Crazy Larry." He sometimes dated an enormous drunk woman who had loose custody of her niece's children, and when they were on the outs, he would leave threatening notes under her door. He had somehow obtained stationery from Bronx Lebanon Hospital, but the woman was able to discern that the crude scrawls of "You got the AIDS, Bitch! Fuck you, You got the Clapp!" were not the diagnosis of a qualified physician. In fact, I was there for the removal of the children, early one Sunday afternoon, when the woman's brother tried to wake her, pinching her nose and covering her mouth till she came to, pitching and bucking like a Brahma bull—she'd risen and fallen early that day, on fortified wine—and the caseworker walked past the three smiling children in playpens to examine the refrigerator and its solitary container of sour milk, when there was a furious pounding on the door. I inquired, "Who is it?"

The reply came: "This is the police! Who are you?"

I said, "This is the police! Who are you? Crazy Larry?"

"No, I'm the police, you're Crazy Larry!"

"No, you're Crazy Larry, I'm the police!"

"Police!"

"Crazy Larry!"

"Police!"

"Larry!"

In the end, I think I won the point, because he left first. Moreover, although we both get checks from the City, I still wear a blue uniform while he yells at fire hydrants on 169th Street and Washington Avenue. But I became known as the go-to guy of the Village, and because I didn't talk much except to mumble a number-heavy answer to a question—"Thirty-six-oh-three Third, Five Boy, yeah, I know, kid's wanted for a shooting, twelve-sixty Webster"— one cop took to calling me "Rain Man." Was it any wonder that I looked forward to work every day?

On Sunday mornings at my girlfriend's, I barely spoke, knowing the new week began in hours, and I felt the gleeful fear you get in the belly as the roller coaster idles at the crest before the first big drop. Once, I had a dream about work that drifted into a scene where someone was pounding furiously on my apartment door, and as I woke, I realized that the pounding was my own heartbeat. The crash course unexpectedly accelerated, after a year, when Osvaldo was transferred to another project and then Angel began coaching the NYPD soccer team, which meant that he mostly worked days. I was by myself most of the time afterward, and though a car would back me on heavy jobs, the routine pick-ups and run-ins had to be handled alone. I could make of them what I would, mountain or molehill.

One evening, I was called to an unbelievably petty domestic dispute. The woman was smug and derisive, the man looked like he was about to cry. They had argued, and then he'd taken a bunch of her videotapes and destroyed them. There was an irritating consensus to their positions: she demanded that I arrest him, and he demanded it, too, saying yes, he took the tapes, and yes, he destroyed them, because he hated her, and yes, most definitely, I should arrest him. While I usually didn't hesitate to make an arrest—I once locked up a woman who was eight months pregnant for robbery—she was such a bitch and he was such a baby that it became clear that I was not brought in to solve a problem but to join one. At the same time, I had two misdemeanors—Petit Larceny and Criminal Mischief—arising from a Domestic Incident, which, in the aftermath of the O. J. Simpson case, was treated by the Job with an inflexible severity. I took him in, not incorrectly but not without embarrassment, and I was glad that the DO didn't grill me on the details of the collar.

When the perp provided me with the details, I felt even worse. They had fought, and then she'd told him that she'd had an abortion, in the way she might have said she'd thrown away a box of candy he gave her. She'd been six months pregnant. When I called her later for additional information, she confirmed his account, telling the story in a rushed, victorious tone which might as well have ended with her saying, *Gotcha last!* I felt terrible for him, and I bought him soda and candy as we finished up, acting as much like his butler as his captor. He had a bench warrant in Manhattan for fare-beating, it turned out, and so I had to take him downtown from the Bronx. Hours had passed since the arrest, and when I dropped him off, he reached out with his cuffs for a kind of handshake and said, "You been good to me. I know a guy with a lot of guns in his house, I want to tell you about it . . ." I shook his hand and took his number.

I was clueless about how to obtain a search warrant, still less how to execute one. Suffice it to say at this point that it requires many hours of investigative and procedural labor, and the application itself must be approved by a captain even before you take it to a DA, and then to a judge. I met my guy a few days later, walked him in, and got it done. When I returned to the precinct, warrant in hand, and found the Special Operations lieutenant and the sergeant from the PSA's gun squad—it was acronymmed "FIST," for Firearms Interception . . . Something . . . Team—they were equally amazed by the wrongness of method and rightness of result, as if I'd gone to the Supreme Court and gotten a parking ticket dismissed. My guy—he wasn't even registered as an informant yet, which was one of many missed steps—was brought back in and grilled by both bosses. His story was as detailed and plausible as it had been before: he met a man he knew as "Bird," a street acquaintance of many years, who'd told him he had guns to sell. Bird had brought my guy to his apartment, which was the second building down from the southeast corner of College Avenue and East 170th Street, and taken him up to the third floor, into the second apartment to the left of the stairs, and in which there were a dozen semiautomatic and two automatic weapons, in the bedroom closet, inside a Pampers box. He said the reason he was doing all this was to thank me, and because he didn't like guns—his brother had been shot and killed. We put him in a van with tinted windows and he pointed out the building as we drove by; a Hispanic cop in plainclothes checked the inside and found everything to be as described. The cop also said the building was a cesspool, a hive of crime. They wanted to send them both back, together, but my guy began to stammer and shake; he thought Bird would know it was him. When they asked him to go back on his own, the fear spread through him like a fever, and he sweated and quaked, nearly in tears, telling me that he had no idea he was in for all of this. Other cops told me to watch it, that he was a perp at heart, and perps live to hurt cops. He did have a decades-old rap sheet, mostly for little things like stealing hubcaps, although Bird must have shared the cops' opinion to some degree, as he showed him the guns for a reason. But I didn't believe the other cops: I thought some perps lived to get high, and others lived to steal money, and others lived to show women why they ought to be afraid of them. And while I believed that most would prefer to see me get hurt if it meant I wouldn't catch them, I didn't think this guy, especially, would take such elaborate pains to just make me look like a jackass. But time would tell, wouldn't it?

When we readied to hit the door, we kept my guy in the precinct, so that if he was playing us, he wouldn't be able to call Bird to warn him. He seemed to shrink into the couch in the lunchroom, nearly catatonic. Twenty-odd cops were deployed in their various roles, and I drove the gun sergeant, a somber man with arms that were bigger than my legs, and who had never spoken to me before—all rookies and even most cops were invisible to him, aside from those who worked with him on his hunt. As we rode toward our destination, it was as if we were old friends; when we drew close, forming a line with the other cars, he quieted down, breathing deeply, and his intensity of focus had the torque of a diving fighter plane and the stillness of prayer. "There is nothing like this," he said. "Nothing." I believed him. We drove to the front and leapt from the cars, raced inside the building and up the stairs, and someone handed him a battering ram and with one swing he sent the door flying from the hinges, and he charged in, shouting, "Police! Get down! Don't move!" And

I was right beside him, gun in hand, bellowing as the rooms of the apartment opened up to us like conquered cities.

"Down! Down! Down!"

"Cuffs! Cuffs!"

"Hands! Lemme see your hands!"

"Clear!"

"Get down!"

We were inside for seconds before the dismay set in. There were women and children, and a few heavyset men in their underwear whose bellies shook as they raised their hands so high it looked like they were grabbing for God. There was supposed to be one young man and his girlfriend; the kitchen was supposed to be to the left, and there was supposed to be one bedroom, not three. Everyone was handcuffed and brought outside, and from the outset, the lieutenant took a pacifying tone, explaining that we had a warrant and what we had to look for. There were no protests, and a few tears. I searched the back bedroom, starting with the closet, which was packed from top to bottom. I found a Christmas tree, the good china, a dildo. I had never seen as many roaches in my life. I sweated through my T-shirt, vest, and even my blue nylon raid jacket, soaking it as if I'd been swimming. As a matter of course, we checked the entire apartment, and found nothing. The head of the household was one of the heavyset men; he was an EMT, recently retired, with a heart condition. He told us, "You could have hit any other apartment in this building and got a drug dealer." With abject apologies, we withdrew. My guy had been released from the precinct as soon as we hit the door, and apparently he fled at a gallop. I never saw him again, and never learned what kind of mistake I'd made. A few other cops patted me on the back and said, "They can't knock you for trying," but for the gun sergeant, I receded back into invisibility. I stripped off my wet clothing and returned to the paperwork, registering the informant. When the Special Ops lieutenant told me I had to pick a code name for the informant, I chose "Hindenburg." He didn't object.

As General Custer might have said, it was quite a learning experience. Afterward, I had mixed feelings about moving on to the next step. When I first came on the Job, I was hell-bent on getting my detective shield as soon as possible: complex and far-ranging investigations were what I was made for, I felt, not to mention the most exciting and rewarding part of the Job. But the best detectives were just that because they had years of street experience behind them, and the more I saw on patrol, with its daily wonders and horrors, the more I knew how far I had to go. I had a "hook"—once known as a "rabbi," a high-ranking officer I could call on for a favor—in my parents' friend Inspector Mullen, but I thought I'd better stay put for a while, and grow in the Job. The gun sergeant was right, there was nothing like it, that feeling when you're about to hit a door, but the feeling afterward, when I knew we were wrong, was distinctive as well. And there was a family on College Avenue who had their own feelings on the matter.

You can do it right and get it wrong, I knew, and I had no expectations that I'd leave that experience behind me, as a cop, no matter how long I was on the Job. One afternoon, a call came in for the sexual assault of a mentally retarded woman, who said she had been gang-raped by staff and residents at the group home where she lived. There was a sluggish chaos to the scene, as if the weight of the allegation made the littleness and lateness of what we - could do all the more trivial. A plump young black woman with a heart-shaped face sat on the couch in her boyfriend's apartment, neatly dressed, surrounded by EMTs. She was in her late twenties, with the nervous smile of a schoolgirl at a piano recital. Her boyfriend, a wiry Puerto Rican man, had a rigid grin, and spoke in the roundabout affirmations of a drunk at a reunion: "I will always take care of her, she can stay with me, she wants to stay with me." I had asked him what happened. I asked him when she got there, and he began, "I will always take care of her. . . ." I took her aside and asked if she was raped, and she said yes. She said that she had since bathed and changed her clothes. The actions were typical of rape victims, but destructive of evidence. We left for the hospital.

We sat in the crowded emergency room, amid its flea market of trauma and disease. For a few minutes at a time, I was able to bring her into an examining room. When asked what happened, she shook her head, and said nothing. "But you were raped?" I asked again, and she nodded. I began the dismal catechism: "Did he put his penis in your vagina?" She nodded.

"Did he put his penis in your mouth?" She shook her head, no.

"Did he do anything else? Did he hit you or take anything from you?"

Again, no.

"And you didn't want to have sex?" She nodded.

"Did you tell him you didn't want to?" She nodded again.

"Did you try to stop him? Did you try to run, or fight him, or yell for help?"

She said she did none of these things. How did she tell him she didn't want to have sex with him? "I told him I didn't want to."

"How many times? Once, more than once?"

"One time."

"And did anyone else do anything to you, was anyone else there when this happened to you?" They were alone, in her room.

"And do you know the man who did this?" She did. She gave his name, Roberto. I asked her how she knew him, and she said they both lived in the same group home.

The entire landscape of the facts had changed, like a beach swept away by a storm. The new contours of events left the old maps useless. I didn't know how the first allegations of gang rape, which the EMT had relayed to me, had been made. If the young woman was revising a gang rape to a date rape, the case might be lost. For most people, there is no easy transit between the territories of lies and truthfulness. If you're coming from one place, it's hard to believe you've been anywhere else. I had trouble asking her if she was retarded. Though I have managed to find the detachment to interview children about the vilest details of sexual assault without squeamishness—it gets easier with practice—to ask this young woman her IQ seemed like an insult: *Exactly how dumb are you?*

"Why do you live there, in the home?"

"Because my mother died."

"How long have you lived there?"

"Not too long."

"How long? A week, a month, a year, more?"

"A month."

"Your mother died a month ago?" She assented, and I said, "I'm sorry. Where did you live before? Here, in New York?"

She nodded, but when I asked where in the city she lived, she made the same face, mute with pain, as when I asked her to tell me about the rape, as if her old address was not just forgotten but successfully repressed. "Manhattan, the Bronx, Brooklyn, Queens?"

"Brooklyn."

"All right. Maybe it was Flatbush, Bed-Stuy, Canarsie . . ."

She confirmed that it was Flatbush, and I marshaled these particulars for the report. We waited a few hours, but there was no gynecologist available, so we were sent to another hospital. It was against the law to turn away rape victims, but the preferable course; the nurse apologized but said that we were expected, and the young woman would be seen immediately. I called for a car, and the victim seemed excited by the ride, looking around at the instruments and lights. At the next hospital, I stayed with her until they began the physical exam. She yipped like a puppy when blood was drawn.

Outside, I met a staff member from the group home. I didn't much like him. Though the initial allegations had been set aside, the home itself seemed tainted, still, in its failure to protect her even if its employees had committed no offense. He was a delegate of the crime scene. And he readily accepted her claims except for one: "The only thing that bothers me is her saying it happened at the home. Supervision is very good. I think it's highly probable that something did happen, but that it took place somewhere else." His version, unsolicited and abridged, was free of institutional liability.

I asked about the perpetrator, Roberto, and was met with a confused look. After some discussion, we concluded that it was an Alberto we were after: he had been her boyfriend, and he had recently been pressuring her for sex, even though she had broken up with him.

"She was sexually active?"

"Yes, she is. She uses birth control. Retarded people have rights, too. Our residents, they're adults, and can do whatever adults enjoy doing."

Something in the way he said it left me with the impression that there was lots of adult enjoyment going on there, and an image of the group home as Playboy Mansion idled uncomfortably in my mind. When the woman came out from the exam, she reacted with alarm at the sight of the staff member. "I don't want to go back there," she said. I assured her that it would not happen, and when two detectives from Special Victims arrived, they took her aside for a private interview. The administrator of the group home then entered the hospital, along with two more employees. My first impression was that she was organizing a counterattack. That was my second impression, too, when she announced, "I think all this is about her wanting to move in with her new boyfriend."

The flat-out dismissal of her story was startling. I didn't argue, partly because I was surprised, but mostly because her certainty, however ugly, cut through all the muddy misinformation. I wanted to be sure of things, too. I remarked that the woman might still need time to get used to the place, so soon after her mother's death. "Soon after what?" the administrator asked.

"Her mother's death."

"Her mother died when she was a child."

"How long has she been with you?"

"For years, since she was a young teenager."

"She didn't live in Brooklyn with her mother till recently?" Her mother and Brooklyn were inventions. My questions to her were leading, I knew— she'd picked Brooklyn from a menu of choices—but if she hadn't been drawn out to tell me what happened, she wouldn't have spoken at all. Without her story, we had nothing, and I was certain there was something there.

But when the doctor and the detectives had all concluded their interviews, there were still more revisions. The rape allegations were dropped entirely, and she now said only that Alberto had molested her. The medical findings were inconclusive. One detective reminded me that whatever sympathy I might feel for this woman, the perpetrator was also retarded, and if we were to move forward on her allegations, we would appear for him like a bad dream as he ate dinner or watched TV, hauling him off in handcuffs for a night—at least—in a cell. "We can't go forward with this," he said. "It's an unstable story. You can't put a retarded boy through all that with a story that isn't stable."

I went to talk with the young woman again, asking her the same questions she'd been asked all day, which somehow meant something different to her each time they were put to her. She had the same flighty, schoolgirl manner, with eager smiles alternating with pursed, apprehensive frowns. I asked her if Alberto put his penis in her, and she said no, and I asked her if Alberto put his hands in her, and she said yes. I offered to get her a drink or some candy, but she declined. "You must be getting tired of all these questions, over and over," I said. She smiled and nodded.

"You remember before, when I asked you if Alberto put his penis in you, and you said yes? And now you said no? Can you tell me why, did you not understand?"

The smile left her as she looked at me, plaintively, as I led her out. "Come on, now, it's time to go home," the administrator said. The woman began to tremble, then to cry.

"It's all right, honey, nobody's gonna make you do anything—" and I was about to say, "that you don't want to do," which I had told her before, but instead said, "that isn't right." She cried and she looked at me; she may not have told me the truth, but she knew that my promise would be broken as well.

The administrator was her legal custodian and had the right to compel her to return. I pointed out that there was a core of consistency in her claims some kind of abuse had occurred, that her bathing and washing her clothes were telling, that if the police could do little, for now, the group home had to do more, at least in keeping Alberto away from her. The administrator concurred, and the detective also agreed I would rewrite the rape complaint as "Investigate sexual abuse," for follow-up by the precinct squad. And the young woman cried now like a motherless child, sobbing with such force that she could barely catch her breath, wailing she didn't want to go, she wouldn't. The administrator and the staffer led her away, not without kindness, but with a cool finality because nothing she could say would change a thing.

. . .

I MADE MY FIRST CONFESSION WHEN I WAS SEVEN YEARS old. Though I don't remember what I said, I suspect it wasn't even half the story. The other kids talked about making things up, so as not to disappoint the priest, but I never would have done that. The confessional was of the old, highly cinematic variety: a dark and curtained booth, walled to separate the priest from the penitent child. When you walked in to kneel on the velvet bench, a little grille slid open with a whoosh and a click, like a secret passage in a haunted mansion, prompting you to speak: *Bless me, Father, for I have sinned . . . this is my first confession*. Later on, you would say that it has been ten days or one month or twenty years since your last time, but this was the first, which is why I wanted to make an impression. The terror of the encounter was eased by the grandeur of what was promised: full pardon from God, and the assurance that the priest could not tell anyone what we did, ever, not even if he was tortured by Russians. I had a hard time coming up with things to say, knowing that, all in all, I was a good boy—I think I owned up to fighting with my brother, not cleaning my room, and the like, which were suggested examples of age-appropriate offenses—and also that I had some real grasp of true sin; of hate and greed and self-pity. My experience of these may have been more in thought than in deed—though I may have been genuinely enraged at being sent to bed when I wanted to watch TV, I didn't burn the house down—but my inability to confess was only partly because I couldn't find the words. Had I known them, I would have been just as reluctant to speak. I couldn't say that I'd wished my sister was dead when she broke my toy, even if I'd taken it back as soon as I'd thought it. And so when I confessed, I felt good and clean and new not only because I had been pardoned for the little things I had done, but also because I had escaped the ordeal with my real sins safely locked away, where they belonged.

A few pages into his *Confessions,* St. Augustine says that no one is without sin, even a newborn child. Because he is not only talking about Original Sin, he is ready to be ridiculed—"Was it a sin to cry when I wanted to feed at the breast?"—but he nonetheless holds that "if babies are innocent, it is not through the lack of will to do harm, but the lack of strength." Unlike most saints, Augustine was also a father, and the icy bite of the perception seems unsentimental rather than unloving. Babies strike out and scream not only for what they need, but for all that they want, whether food, attention, a lit candle, or a sharp knife. With children, this absence of judgment and control springs from natural limitation rather than any moral shortcoming, but it shows that sin is something missing, and that it can be seen in human nature from the beginning. And often we do not know what is missing until we look for it and find that it is not there.

At home, my first real confession came six years later, when I was thirteen. The teenage conflicts with my father were yet to come, and even within my family, I was thought of as truthful, more quick to come clean than the others when the five of us skulked around a broken cookie jar. I could be depended on to admit what I had done. I would confess, but not inform, and I don't recall ever being especially pressed to do so. But in a sense, all children are informants for their fathers—though perhaps the comparison would only occur to a cop—in that what they do and how they think tells a father things, which he would bear in mind to meet whatever trials or mysteries lay ahead. My father knew that I would make mistakes that he never would, and encounter possibilities that he could only imagine; that I would be the cause of many troubles, and that I would have to help him find their cure. I wonder if he had any ulterior motive when he told me—apropos of what, a war story, a history lesson, nothing?—that it was a rarity for anyone to hold up under a sustained interrogation. Almost no one holds out, he said, and it was not long after he told me this that he proved it.

In the winter when I was in eighth grade, there was a tremendous blizzard, and I went out with a few friends early in the evening to enjoy it. We did so by making heavy, wet snowballs, heaving them at random houses in the neighborhood, and then running like hell. One highly satisfying shot walloped a glass front door, prompting an unexpectedly rapid response from the man who lived there. We scattered: I ran with another boy named Joey Quinn, and as the man drove up on us we split again, and the man caught me. He then returned me to my house, where my father thanked him and said he would deal with it. To give some indication of how my luck was running at that point, after a brief conversation it emerged that the man was not only a police officer but that he worked in the same precinct as Uncle Eddie.

He left, satisfied that justice would be done. I offered up terrified denials of having thrown the snowball, as I had done on the ride home, but for some reason the line of questioning was exclusively directed to the identity of the boy with me. I said I couldn't tell, I wouldn't, and my father took me downstairs to the basement. He had never hit me, and he didn't then, but there was something significant and dreadful in the transit. My mother was alarmed, calling out, "John . . ." The syllable carried every meaning, as if to speak his name should remind him who he was, which was a good man who did not lose control, no matter the provocation. But he was also an interrogator by trade, and downstairs we went. It did not take long. His voice was cold and concentrated, with a force that seemed all the greater for being held in check, like the surging of a river at the head of a dam.

"Give . . . me . . . his . . . name!"

"Joey Quinn . . . but we didn't do it!"

The speed of my surrender astonished me as much as the defiance of my lie. There was another call from my mother—"John!"—which brought it all to an end. The glass was not broken—there were no damages to be paid, only order to be restored—and so it went no further. My punishment was sufficient, I think, when I heard my father tell the man in a tone that was modest but final, "I know Eddie. He's an honest boy, and he wouldn't lie."

And though the glass did not shatter, my friendships did. My father was disappointed to hear Mr. Quinn's testy denial that *his* son could *ever* do such a thing, though in truth, Joey was a bit of a thug. Those boys and a few others made much of it for a month or two, yelling insults and cutting me out of their circle. To my shame, I knew that this exclusion was only slightly more vehement than others I had known in the past, when I had joined in the derision of whoever was the outcast for the season. I knew also that in time, if I took my lumps, I'd be let back in. But when time did pass—not much time, but it didn't pass quickly—I didn't want back in. Had any of them been walked down to the basement, I was sure, names would have been supplied as well as Social Security numbers, not to mention a complete confession of - every snowball ever thrown. We were in the eighth grade, and would go on to different high schools the next year. Most of my friends would attend Catholic schools in Westchester County, whereas I was going to Manhattan, and if I accepted the prospect of change with equanimity before the winter, afterward I positively looked forward to it. Somehow the finality with which I discarded my friends now seems colder than their playground swinishness. But as I look back, I note both that the role of the informant presents itself to those in need of escape, and that a confession, even if its candor is not complete, can take you much farther than you expected to go.

. . .

BEFORE YOU HAD A CONFESSION, YOU HAD TO HAVE A COMplaint. For cops, there was never any shortage of complaints, formal and otherwise: the crime reports we wrote were called complaints, and when the DA wrote up a charge, it was called a complaint, and when a civilian accused a cop of wrongdoing, it was also a complaint. We complained among ourselves, about bad food, hurting feet, lousy bosses, long hours, and little money. We complained about the sun and the rain. We did have a lot to complain about, within the Job and without, but some cops seemed to lose the power of speech altogether, except for complaining. And most of the others tried to stay away from "hairbags," as they were called, not so much because the complainers were wrong about anything in particular, but because you - didn't want to be persuaded of the larger point of view. It was tempting sometimes, though, because if you listened to the neighborhood, the news was rarely good, at least when it was talking to you.

At the same time, I was becoming friendlier with the cops at the command. For the most part, we got along in the house, and on the street, I knew I could depend on them. I didn't hang out much, aside from the occasional Christmas party or racket, as benefits are called, but in general I became less standoffish. I was known as a collar guy, dependable on the street, and the bosses treated me well. They even finally learned to tell me apart from Coyne. I was offered a spot on one of the Target Teams, but I turned it down. I still liked my post, and it seemed that in those groups, there was always one cop who annoyed the hell out of everyone else. But I was starting to itch for something more, and I admired the plainclothes teams, Anti-Crime and SNEU, the Street Narcotics Enforcement Unit, whom I'd sometimes see sweep through the project and come up with a heavy stash or a gun. I was mostly self-taught, which you have to be, if you want to learn how to handle yourself on the street, but there were a lot of cops in the command who played at an entirely different level, with perspectives and moves that were well beyond my own. Still, while I waited for the next step, I would take things as far as I could. And when you took that approach, things could move faster than you expected.

At first glance, and occasionally even after some thought, it could appear that the worst of the neighborhood *was* the neighborhood. Though the obvious signs of the ghetto were painfully plain, the subtler attributes were equally depressing. One day it struck me, as I looked around for a newspaper, that there were only three or four places around the Village that carried them, and I doubted if they sold a hundred copies of the *Post* and the *News* a day, and half as many Spanish-language papers. The *Times* was not found at all. At a rough but generous estimate, 2 percent of the neighborhood read a daily paper. You saw what happened when people got used to not paying for things: though the hospital was a block away, people called for ambulances constantly when they had 99-degree temperatures or mild diarrhea; or worse, they claimed to have chest pains or difficulty breathing because they needed prescription refills, and didn't want to walk to the pharmacy or wait in line. The ride cost them nothing, so they'd take it every time.

Whenever there was an attempt at physical improvements to the projects, it usually reflected a Charlie Brownish determination that this time—*this time!*—things couldn't be smashed or burnt so easily or so often. Good old Charlie Brown: after a spate of fires, the Housing Authority repainted every single stairway with fireproof paint. All the talk about the fires led some - people to set even more, proving that the paint was not as fireproof as advertised. Was the paint even fire-retardant? No matter—to make a difference it would have to be shit-retardant and bullet-retardant, or maybe just retard-retardant. The Housing Authority then stripped the hallways down to the bare concrete and cinder block, which became saturated with urine and graffiti, neither of which couldn't be mopped away. If you needed to get onto the elevator for an emergency on the eighteenth floor—a robbery, or a violent dispute—you often risked riot by telling people they had to wait for the next elevator. I did take some pleasure on one downward trip, with a DOA. The gurney was too long for the elevator, and it was stood up; the bagged body was on its feet, just out of sight of the doors. When we stopped on a floor, midway, a man stepped toward us and I said, "Sorry, you'll have to get the next one." He made the spit-face and the spit-sound—*Ptuh!*—because nobody was going to tell *him* what to do, and he strode inside. He met the corpse, face to face, and fell silent. His deliberately reversed footsteps had the quality of mime: *Here I am, leaving.* "Thanks for your cooperation, and have a nice day."

As a cop, I took some consolation from the fact that when people did wrong things, they did them the wrong way, too—nearly thoughtlessly, with the lazy malice of a chain snatch, or the drunken impulse of a punch. If the bad guys put much thought into what they were doing, we'd be hard pressed to catch most of them. And so when I responded to a "possible shooting," I felt it was one of the more sinister incidents I'd run across: an eighty-year-old Jamaican man heard a knock at his door, and when he opened it, he felt a slight resistance, and then he heard a pop and felt a sting in his hand. The elevator was directly in front of his apartment, and he saw the elevator door close as he opened his own. He had to think for a while, he told me, but he came to believe that he'd been shot in the hand—there was a pockmark in the flesh between forefinger and thumb, which an X-ray later proved to be a pellet. But while the crime itself resulted in relatively minor injury, the scene revealed a perpetrator of some elegance and real evil: the light bulb was unscrewed in the elevator, and a length of string dangled from the doorknob. The perp had waited in the dark, with the string attached to the pellet gun, so that when the door opened, it pulled the trigger. The old man believed it to be a boy in the building named Hassan, a hulking and I thought doltish teenager, who'd threatened him after he'd told him not to hang out in the lobby, smoking blunts and leaving garbage. The crime did show an adolescent delight in whiz-kid plots and gadgetry, but there was also a cold-blooded calculation, and several aspects—the choice of victim, the staging of the trap so that the victim would participate and the perp could watch—were so disturbing that I felt there was more to come, from Hassan or whoever it might be, and that his future efforts would be felt beyond the Village, long after I left.

Old people told me how beautiful the projects had been when the buildings were new and people were proud to live there. And while there was something forlorn about those whose ideal of civilized living was the public housing of the South Bronx, circa 1960, it was perhaps sadder still to consider the eye of the beholders, myself included, and what they now beheld. For those immigrants, whether from Kingston, the Carolinas, San Juan, or even Harlem, Morris Houses was a new world of elevators and refrigerators and mowed lawns, a cherished opportunity and a respected trust. And so when - people from the neighborhood took it upon themselves to demand a restoration of dignity and decency to their surroundings, I was glad to work for them as hard as I could.

In one of my worst buildings, two women decided to set up a tenant patrol. The building had half a dozen crack spots and was the scene of a recent rape and murder; it was a place that belonged to the bad guys. Chief among them was a family named Bodie, whose apartment had seen occasional shootings, constant drug sales, and the death of a child who'd overdosed on crack, eating it from the table where it was being packaged. I knew the eldest son, Alvin, who was alleged to be the worst of the bunch, and, strangely enough, he liked me; early on, I'd walked into him buying heroin on the street, and because I could only grab the seller, he thought I'd given him a break. Also, his mother was ailing, which brought me to his house a number of times with EMS, and he appreciated how I treated her. (The mother was also the reason management was unable to evict the family.) Alvin held no menace for me: he was in his late twenties, scrawny and a little stooped; I knew he was a junkie and I'd heard he had AIDS. I felt that sooner or later I'd catch him at something, or turn him to work for me, and if he was the worst the building could offer, the odds were not so daunting.

The two women who constituted the new tenant patrol were not to be easily dissuaded, either. Both were middle-aged black ladies, though the resemblance ended there. Ms. Smith was proper and devout, and her conversational style was one of gentle persuasion. Ms. Cunningham hit you like an A train. I'd had a brief confrontation with her once before, after I'd written her son a summons, I think for Disorderly Conduct, and she'd come at me bellowing, "Why you gotta harass my son, who's minding his own business! Mm! If you cops went out to catch the rapists and killers like you go to bother my child, then this would be a lot better neighborhood!" It was a classic project-mama harangue, delivered in the timeless and full-throated black-lady gospel voice whose dug-in defiance is a beautiful thing when directed against injustice and a huge pain in the neck when it's directed against you. "It's just a ticket, lady, he deserved it and he's getting it." But somewhere along the line, Ms. Cunningham decided that I was the least of her problems, or maybe not the problem at all, and we worked well together.

Ms. Smith and Ms. Cunningham sat together, almost every night, without any help from the other tenants. I'd stop by two or three times, if I could, and do a vertical, top to bottom, or just wait with them. Anyone who didn't want to sign the visitor's log got an earful from Ms. Cunningham, and if that - wasn't enough, a 911 call that brought me over. If she complained about a tenant, they'd better watch their step. While many tenant groups worked with the police, usually in a somewhat clandestine way, Ms. Cunningham and I had an openly declared alliance, which reflected her own fearlessness more than any faith in me. She told me about a girl who'd let her pit bull loose in the playground, and the next time I saw the girl, I wrote my first and only unleashed-dog summons. It was difficult to see any immediate effect on the building, but the effect on us lightened the heart. Though I knew several of the crack spots beforehand, Ms. Cunningham told me about the rest of them, and I sometimes stood guard in front of their doors. It was not what you'd call interesting work, as such, but it felt important, and it pointed out a lesson of the peculiar value of patrol: when in doubt, don't just do something, stand there.

As I stood, I watched. When I saw certain children, I wondered how much time it would take to tell if they'd grow into the next generations of Cunninghams or of Bodies. The day after I locked up a man for beating his wife, I saw his two daughters in the street. They were perhaps six and eight years old, and they clung playfully to my hands like a favorite uncle as they asked, "Where's Daddy?"

I knew that some Mafia mothers told the kids, "Daddy's away at college" when their husbands were guests of the state, but I could neither think of a fairy tale to tell them nor see the point of telling it. "He's in jail," I said.

Neither stopped hanging from me, but the older one took a peevish tone, as if I'd said there'd be no dessert until she finished her dinner: "He didn't kill nobody."

"No, he didn't. But he treated your mom bad."

The little one did an uncanny imitation of her immigrant mom: "Oh! He a no-good man, he a no-good man!" And then the older one asked, "When can we come see him, tonight?"

"No."

"Can we see him without permission?"

"No, you cannot," I said. I patted their heads and they ran off to play. Whenever I'd run into them, they'd rush over to greet me. The last thing I wanted was to trouble them, but I was struck by how untroubled they seemed to be.

My own troubles were becoming clear, at least in type. While certain incidents bothered me for a while because of the misery I'd seen, like the maggot lady, or because of the mistakes that I'd made, like Operation Hindenburg, I'd take what I could from them and move on. But certain kinds of encounters were becoming more common, and more tiresome. While it was rare that I didn't feel safe on the street—even when I've faced off against hostile crowds, I've known that help, in droves, is moments away, and I'd usually be more concerned with someone getting hurt racing to help me, if the background noise on my radio sounded like the fall of Saigon. Almost all the people I've fought with, hard, were trying to get away. It was the little things that got to me, and the little things had a knack for getting bigger.

The issue was "Quality of Life," one of the cornerstones of the crime-fighting policy of the new regime at the NYPD. The theory was that if you ignored all the other forms of low-grade disorder that formed the backdrop of inner-city life, the center-stage crimes like robberies and shootings tended to thrive. The practice meant nearly ceaseless confrontations with people hanging out, whether they were relaxing on a Friday night after a hard week of work, or did so as a way of life. The groups that loitered in the lobbies and in front of the buildings provoked perennial complaints from management and the tenant patrols. Sometimes they were just noisy and messy, leaving beer bottles and blunts all over, and often enough selling drugs was the pastime if not the purpose of the congregation. While many people called 911 to report drug sales or a gun merely to get cops to clear out some loud teenagers, others were as crankily suspicious of their neighbors as any white bigot from the sticks, and could not conceive of any innocent meeting of a few friends with a free hour. One man in Manhattan had recently been charged with manslaughter, after a cop was killed racing to the scene of the "shots fired" he routinely and falsely called in to clear his stoop of rowdies. But for every gun run that proved unfounded, there were many others that went unreported, and the irony was that, on my beat, even when the calls were false, they tended to become true, if the buildings were neglected.

In the process of working for a better quality of life for a neighborhood, the quality of life for a cop usually went downhill for a long time before its theoretical ascent. When I worked alone, the dynamic changed: I got better but the Job got bigger, and the cornerboys were more likely to step up to one cop than two. As I learned the beat and the beat learned me, the warning called out over the dice game changed from "The cops are here!" to "That cop is here!" (One kid called me "Cuco," a Puerto Rican word for "bogeyman," which I took as a compliment when I finally found out what it meant.) Often it went smoothly, but it never stopped, and I sounded like the bartender at last call, "You don't have to go home, but you can't stay here." They came back and I cleared them out; they iterated and I reiterated. I was a glorified hall monitor, and it was often hard to see the glorification. The paradox of these petty run-ins was that the power of the cop increased as the stakes grew less. As long as the offense was a violation, it was completely within my discretion, as a matter of statute, whether or not to issue a summons. In the event of an assault or a theft, the facts and the law dictated my actions; in the event of three or more persons gathered together in a public place who refused a lawful order to disperse—one of the seven subsections of Disorderly Conduct—the person decided what I'd do. I was constantly amazed by how many people talked me into arresting them.

If I saw a bunch of guys on a bench with their boom box and beers, I'd stroll over to them, taking into account how late it was and how loud they were, which would determine whether I'd say, "What's up, guys?" or "You gotta keep it down, guys," or "That's it, you guys gotta break out, we got complaints." But what I wanted most was a reaction, offering my blue uniform as a litmus test, to see how they saw me, which is to say, how they saw the rules. Would we both bend them together, showing enough respect to earn a little give? Sometimes I'd pass by and I'd get an almost friendly acknowledgment, especially when they realized the party wasn't necessarily over, and sometimes I'd get a catcall after that, as I was walking away, and sometimes I took it for a weak little joke that wasn't worth a response, but other times, the challenge was unmistakable, and then impossible to ignore.

"What the fuck are you gonna do about it?"

For as long as there has been an NYPD, every cop has had to answer that question, and always—at least at first—alone. In Pat Brown's early days, he would have beaten the cobblestones with his locust-wood nightstick to summon aid, while cops of Uncle Eddie's era might have had to find a callbox. Although I had instant access to faster backup, the moment would be as it was for them, and the answer would have to be the same, too: *Whatever I have to.*

For cops, respect is seen as the foundation of safety. While individual circumstances were always open to interpretation, rudeness or even overfamiliarity can be seen as an opening to physical threat. When people start to scream at you, their loss of control can escalate into violence. And whatever has to be said, whether in anger or in need, should be said from at least five feet away. No one is going to point a finger in my face, or step up, chest to chest, as if they're protesting a call to the umpire, thinking the technical lack of contact will keep them from being thrown out of the game. Drunks often want to shake your hand, and so do ordinary people on occasion, if you've returned their runaway daughter or decided not to write them a ticket, and though I'll return the gesture for the latter, it's never without a flicker of awareness for what could come next, now that someone has a grip on my hand. In the balance between preparedness and paranoia, the more lopsided confrontations can be the more dangerous, especially when older people, young teenagers, and women in general need to be separated or stopped. If you have to get physical with someone with whom your upbringing forbids you to be rough, your concern is with your dignity rather than your safety, and both are put at risk. In one of my buildings, a cop was slashed in the face by a woman with a razor. I knew them both, and wondered if his vigilance was less because she was a female, if only because I suspected mine would have been.

In some ways, the cop code and the ghetto code reflected each other in a fun-house mirror. Respect was everything, though on the streets, it meant so much that it meant nearly nothing. It should mean a kind of esteem or at least an equal regard—*R-E-S-P-E-C-T, find out what it means to me*—looking eye-to-eye at someone, if not up. When a drug dealer told me I was all right, that I treated him with respect, I had to laugh. What did that mean, that I didn't slap him around on sight? I would nod at people, good or bad, when I walked, but for the bad guys it was a way of saying I'm out here, watching you. Maybe they misunderstood me. In the ghetto code, respect could mean fear, as in I won't attack you because you're bigger than me, or it could suggest some small consideration, as in I'll sleep with your girlfriend but I won't feel her up in front of you. But while respect was reduced to some tiny and temporary relief from contempt, perceptions of disrespect—the infamous "dis"—could be seen all around, in the nuances of a word or gesture, even a glance, provoking violent and sometimes lethal reaction. And the ghetto could be a world of three-dimensional, three-hundred-sixty-degree insult, where no one had enough so they ruined what they had, and then came looking for yours. Here, you moved up as others fought their way to the bottom. You had to *represent,* it was said, and often people did it too well.

Rap music has its roots in the Bronx, in the 1970s, with DJ Kool Herc and Afrika Bambaataa, and though gangsta rap started as a West Coast style, it is heard—and felt—here, too. A musical style became a personal stance, for the last man standing. The civics lesson of gangsta rap is of feral individualism, where desperate claims to fame rest on girls, guns, and gold. While the music's embrace of drug dealers and pimps is widely and wearily decried, to describe gangsta rap as a new low in the culture is, at best, half true. In the lyrics and the police reports, thug life is a litany of petty slights that lead to brutal slaughter, but it is also the story of the Trojan War. Ten years of siege and suffering began with an insult to Paris and continued through an insult to Achilles, inspired by gods you wouldn't trust with your wallet or your sister. "I sing of arms and the man" might sound a loftier note than the nigga-trigger rhymes of Tupac Shakur, but the spirit is often the same. We might not like it, but it's not as if we've never seen it before.

Once, someone hit me with a brick from a rooftop. Glancingly, off the arm, and it barely left a mark. I wondered whether they considered it a hit or a miss, and then wondered if I really wanted to know. There was a hideous litany of assaults on cops, some fatal, that had gone unpunished: in the Five-O, PO Vincent Giudice responded to a violent domestic dispute, in which a man with a long arrest record was beating his girlfriend. He threw a mirror that cut Giudice's femoral artery, and he bled to death. The perp was convicted only of a misdemeanor assault on his girlfriend. There was no conviction for the attempted assassination of a captain named Joseph Plavnick, who was shot as he stood outside the Four-Six precinct; or for the shooter of Capt. Timothy Galvin, of Bronx Narcotics, who supervised a search warrant at the apartment of a black nationalist, where a cache of weapons was recovered. The subject wasn't home at the time, but when he returned, he shot Capt. Galvin in the face, and later claimed that he mistook him for a burglar. After the verdict, one juror was quoted as saying that Galvin "got what he deserved."

From twenty stories up, bottles, eggs, and blocks of ice can cause immense harm, and this kind of "airmail" has missed me by a few feet or less, more times than I'd like to count. A canned ham once, too, which would have made me one very pissed-off ghost. It's hard not to take that kind of thing personally, and I keep a piece of that brick on my desk. Sometimes I thought of mounting it on a plaque that said PRESENTED TO POLICE OFFICER EDWARD CONLON BY THE PEOPLE OF 420 EAST 169 STREET, IN APPRECIATION FOR HIS DEDICATED SERVICE. But it would have been wrong, for any number of reasons. First, because it wasn't true—I knew good people in that building, including Mr. Ferguson, a retired Housing cop who sat tenant patrol. And maybe more important, because it's a bad way to think, to imagine that it was a message from the people, that there was an "everybody" out there, unappreciative of my work or even looking to hurt me. Many people were unappreciative, and, too plainly, there was at least one person who thought it a joke or better to see me die, but there is no such thing as "everybody," anywhere. The way I worked as a cop was to know the basics, trust my instincts, and make it up as I went along. I had to be careful that it didn't make me up as I went along, too.

• • •

FROM THE EARLIEST DAYS, THE PUBLIC HAD A MIXED VIEW of the Department, a melange of derision for the loafers who hid in taverns and admiration for the stalwarts who kept peace on the street corners. The middle classes tended to hold them in more favorable regard than did the poor. Through the 1880s, most cops were Irish, as were most criminals, and it was only later that ethnicity compounded with economics to exacerbate tensions between the police and the poor. In general, popular support of the police department reflected that of the administration they served, for whom they provided a strong arm and a public face. Problems in the government were most visible in the police department, and it was often the test case for experimental medicines for the larger body politic. Municipal housecleaning often began and ended there.

As a result, the police viewed their lot with pride and resentment, with the latter predominating. In the view of one historian, the rank and file "had little faith in their leadership and little pride in their calling," and "faced with an impossible task, they responded with less than total dedication." Police stations also served as lodging houses for vagrants and transients, exposing cops to all kinds of communicable diseases. Although they were paid somewhat better than the laborers at the time, and enjoyed benefits such as paid vacations and a pension, they worked an arduous and complex schedule, and even when they were off duty, they had to be available in the event of a riot or other emergency. A schedule for Monday through Thursday for a patrolman, beginning at six a.m., would include two hours of patrol, five hours of reserve, five hours of patrol, six hours of reserve, then six hours of patrol—twenty-four hours of work, on the first day. After twelve hours at home, on Tuesday, he'd come back at six in the evening for six hours of patrol. From midnight Tuesday through eight a.m. Wednesday he could go home again, followed by five hours of patrol, eleven hours of reserve, and six hours of patrol again from the next midnight. Thursday at six a.m. brought twelve hours at home, followed by six hours of patrol, six hours in reserve, and you were then back again at 0600, to begin the four-day chart again. The insularity of police culture derives in part from this schedule, in which the police tended to socialize with one another during their free hours, few and odd as they were. Station houses were so called because the cops effectively lived there.

Alone on patrol, sometimes far from their precincts, without means of communication, the patrolman had to be able to defend himself. The 1870s saw an increase in crime, including attacks on police. Though patrolmen - could carry firearms, some did not, relying instead on their nightsticks and their reputation. Violence was simply a far more common currency at the time: it was largely acceptable for husbands to hit their wives, parents to hit their children, bosses to hit their employees. The Irish hit everyone, and, for them, the fistfight had an almost conversational quality. Sholem Aleichem, the "Yiddish Mark Twain" and Bronx immigrant whose tales became the basis for *Fiddler on the Roof,* had a character in one story explain it: "They have a habit of fighting in the street. Not that they want to kill you, knock your eye out, or push a few teeth down your throat like they do here. God forbid! They fight just for fun. They roll up their sleeves and slug away to see who beats who. . . ."

The vagaries of the criminal-justice system, which allowed politically connected criminals to go free while sometimes jailing complainants, if they - could not guarantee their appearance on the witness stand, encouraged a degree of street justice. When Cornelius Willems was a rookie at the turn of the century, as he recounts in his memoir, *Behind the Green Lights,* he brought in two perps and their victim from a robbery. The perps were untouched; the victim, bloody. The sergeant berated Willems, "Look at the condition of this poor fellow and not a mark on these two bums!" He ordered two patrolmen to return the perps to the street for a moment, to balance the scales. Thirty years later, Willems reflected, "In a lecture I once stated, with perfect truth, that I had beaten up hundreds of hardened criminals . . . I've forced confessions—with fist, blackjack, and hose—from men who would have continued to rob and kill if I hadn't made them talk. The hardened criminal knows only one language, and laughs at the detective who tries any other."

Confessions were obtained through beatings or other coercion, known as the "third degree," and the practice was a matter of public knowledge and, generally speaking, heartfelt approval. Even the reformers didn't object to bad guys getting beaten, but rather the careless extravagance with which certain cops used their nightsticks. One cop even clouted former President Ulysses Grant, when he was part of a crowd pressing in to watch a fire. When a reporter pointed out what he had done, the patrolman nearly fainted, but Grant lodged no complaint.

As it happened, the police were punished for everything but serious wrongdoing. Civil-service protections made prosecution for brutality or graft an elaborate and lengthy process, and the political will to achieve them was spasmodic at best. But patrolmen nonetheless saw themselves as hostage to myriad regulations, peculiarly contrived and arbitrarily enforced, as if the police department had created a make-believe world of order to compensate for the larger corruption of city government and the chaos of the streets. The cop who accepted a payoff to leave a gambling house alone would rarely face sanction, while one who took momentary shelter from a snowstorm could lose a week's pay. Patrolmen were supervised by roundsmen, so named because they walked counterclockwise from post to post, and the roundsmen were evaluated by how many complaints they issued. Patrolmen were punished if a store on their post was vandalized, or if they were observed in social conversation with a passerby. One cop lost a day's pay for failing to report a dead cat on his post. They were expected to be investigators, social workers, bouncers, and soldiers, but they were often treated like errant schoolboys.

These contradictions led many New York City police officers to develop a decidedly ironic point of view. Then as now, the distance between the loftiness of the ideals that we embodied and the smallness of so much else—the bosses, the newspapers, the politicians, the people, and, often enough, us—could make your head spin. And you needed your head, sometimes, though not for what you thought. We had a captain who would watch us race to gun runs and ask us afterward why we weren't wearing our hats. I might spend hours on a frozen rooftop, watching below, and when a sergeant raised me for the scratch, he would reach out and feel my shield, to see if it was cold to the touch. Whenever I hear denunciations of police power, in solemn editorials or in routine street static, I have to laugh a little. I think of the Transit cop's line, "You want to know what my job is like? Go to your garage, piss in the corner, and stand there for eight hours." Or I think about how when we are sick at home, we have to call in for permission to leave the house, and call again when we return. Or better yet, I don't dwell on it at all; as we like to say to bosses when we screw up, "Yeah, but Sarge, you've said so yourself—they don't pay us enough to think." More than anything else, this mind-bending knot of paradox explains the vaunted "blue wall of silence"—it's not so much that cops don't want to talk, it's that they can barely begin to explain.

. . .

GEORGE DID TELL ME ABOUT THE RECORD STORE, HAVING gotten my attention in the usual way—by beating a woman. This time, Danielle called: the night before, George had knocked her down, shoved her against a wall, and confined her in a bedroom when she threatened to call the police. He'd slept at the door of the room, on the floor, to prevent her escape. The next morning, he'd gone out and brought back breakfast, made her a bath, and then walked her to her mother's house, where she called the cops. She cried and could barely walk, and though there was no visible injury, I -

could charge an assault on the basis of "substantial pain," as well as unlawful imprisonment, another misdemeanor. I left as the ambulance arrived, and I told the EMTs to stop by the record store on the way to the hospital.

"We got another problem," I said, returning George's greeting and asking him to step outside the shop. He stiffened, like he was immersed in cold water, and began his rebuttal, as edgily eloquent as the last time: Yes, they argued but no, he didn't hit her—"Did you see a mark, a single mark on her?"—and if he shoved her once, it's because she said she'd have him arrested if he ever left her. A cop witnessed that, we have to find him. And he has a letter, in which she makes that threat, we have to find it. I have to find them for him, he says, now. As I cuffed him, Tonya approached to offer him her sympathy and support, knowing that her turn to take him in had come round again.

I reminded him, "George, what I gotta do now is bring you in, I have no choice, like last time, and maybe like last time it'll work out . . ." He shrugged his acceptance as the ambulance pulled up. I got the nod from Danielle, and we left for the precinct.

Once there, he saw the cop who had witnessed his argument with Danielle the afternoon before. George had flagged him down for a "clothes job," an escort to their apartment for him to remove his belongings. The cop told me he'd heard Danielle say she'd get him sent back to prison if he left her, but the two then decided to try to work things out. "Looks like they didn't," said the cop. George looked to see my reaction, and I told him that whether he had good reasons to beat her or bad ones, it didn't matter to me. "I got things to tell you," he said.

For a year or so, it had been procedure to debrief every prisoner who came into the precinct. Most perps wouldn't talk, and many were as blankly ignorant of the local underworld as they were of Vatican intrigue. The Squad asks, "Do you have information about robberies, homicides, guns, arson, hate crimes, chop shops, terrorism?" I've had people say, "Chop-chop? What chop-chop?" You'd also get perps who would offer dirt on the order of "Psst! John Gotti runs the Mafia!" and expect to walk on a gun collar. When George's turn came, he said, "Yes, yes, yes, yes, no, yes, and what was the last one?"

My prisoner was the Rosetta stone to scores of violent felonies, past and planned. People approached him to do hits and robberies every week. The narcotics king of Atlanta wanted to open nightclubs in the city, for dancing and dealing, and he asked George to run them. A robbery, at a bodega, tonight, hours from now; he knew the two guys who planned it, what kind of gun they'd carry, why they picked it, how they knew that the owner's brother, a pockmarked Dominican, carried a .357, and how he was the one to watch, to take out if he moved. One of the guys had robbed a meat market a few months ago, with two other guys. They got five thousand dollars, with at least a grand in food stamps, which they moved through a Chinese restaurant. The shoot-up at the record store was a hit on a guy named True, but since True made his living robbing drug dealers and numbers spots, and had testified against another drug gang at trial, and was messing with some gangster's girlfriend, George hadn't narrowed down who ordered it. He knew about another planned hit on a Brazilian man, a witness in a state case. He wouldn't say more.

It was as if George spread a deck before him and asked the detective to pick a card, any card, but only one. The detective chose the robbery planned for tonight. It was a natural choice: the bodega was in the precinct, and the detective handled robberies. The exchange to be made, help for help, was remarkably frank, brisk, and businesslike. George knew that Danny and Bebe planned the robbery, where Danny lived, and where the bodega was. If a robbery occurred and arrests were made quickly, it would be good; if it could be prevented, it would be better. Either result should be enough to secure his freedom. While it seemed shabby, and even dangerous, to bargain Danielle's distress against the safety of a grocery store, it was just that, a bargain. What was left unmentioned was that George would, in all likelihood, be freed by the judge at his arraignment. Danielle's case was weak, even terminal, with a police witness to her threats and no visible injury. George would have a problem with his parole officer, but that decision would wait until this case was adjudicated, and if history served as a guide, the charges might well be dropped. But George was back in the cage now, and he'd do what he needed to get out of it. It was a line of thought we encouraged.

Calls were made, hours passed. George told me that he had no problem giving up people who weren't close friends and who were going to hurt - people. He had hurt people himself, and while it didn't keep him up at night, he thought it a better thing if people didn't get hurt during jobs. It was a thin and abstract pity, as if his victims were the victims of an earthquake in Chile, and his efforts at moral understanding had a rote, calisthenic quality: "You think, what if it's your brother, your girl who gets shot in a holdup, how would you feel?" What bothered him was that he had information of great value and had to spend it on freedom that should be had on the cheap: "I'm in here on bullshit, I know that, Danielle, she *wrong*. I'm not gonna say all I know, I'll give up Danny and Bebe, that's it, that's a *lot*. What if they grab me with a gun sometime, what am I gonna have left to give?" I told him I was sure he'd manage, and he didn't disagree.

The detective ran Danny's address on a computer program that lists every criminal who has used that address. None of the resident perps were named Danny, and none matched the description of eighteen-year-old male Hispanic, five-eight and slightly built. For his own safety, the detective was reluctant to wait in the store without knowing whom to expect, and while George sounded believable, the detective wanted more before he spent the rest of his day on an as yet nonexistent crime. It was after dark now, and the bodega was only open for a few more hours. There was a brief burst of rain. There were countless reasons for the robbery not to happen then: a hangover, a date, the flu, an argument, a bad horoscope, or an arrest. The next night was Halloween, when they could even wear masks without attracting notice. The detective passed the information to Bronx Robbery, and was told in turn that they couldn't find any open cases that matched the meat-market robbery as George described it. The detective sent us on our way.

The password had been spoken, but the gates remained shut. I hadn't quite expected that, and neither did George. Because the information was untested, of indeterminate use, whatever reciprocal favor he was to receive would have to wait. At Central Booking, I put him in the holding cell; he was back with the losers, with their foul smells and sad stories, their tough-guy sneers and choked-back sobs. George leaned close to me and whispered that he wanted to talk.

"About the Brazilian?" I asked.

"About the Brazilian," he said. I loved that part, it was just like the movies. As they say, this is no job for a grown-up.

It was getting late as I went to the Complaint Room, where Danielle was waiting. An ADA told me the caseload was backed up, she would have to come back in the morning to sign the complaint, and if my defendant wanted to make statements, I should take him up to the detectives in the video room. Danielle was amenable to returning, so I thanked her, made sure she got carfare from Victim Services, and went back to the cells.

Upstairs in video, things went badly. It was nearly midnight, and everyone was tired. The detective didn't know me, he didn't know George, and the debriefing began in the irritatingly standard form: "Do you know anything about chop shops . . ." The detective asked George about his most recent arrest, and took an instant dislike to him when he began, "The bitch lied!" And George seemed determined to justify his contempt. When he was asked why he had spent almost ten years in prison, he responded with a lack of hesitation that sounded almost like pride: "I robbed a place. The man tried to grab my gun. I shot him."

"When you say 'the man,' was it someone who was with you?"

"I mean the victim."

I was frustrated with the detective. I was peddling a murder conspiracy, and he was supposed to be in the market. This was no time to act like a human being. But before things could deteriorate further, two detectives from Bronx Robbery arrived, with note pads and cell phones. Their people had staked out the bodega, from a car parked outside, and awaited more detail on the perps. When the car called back to say the bodega had closed without incident, the detectives concentrated instead on the meat-market robbery. Did it happen in April or June? Of the three perps, were any arrested? Who had the guns, were any shots fired? There were four or five robberies that matched their initial, rough outline, and they began to narrow it down. When they left, after midnight, they said they would tell the DA and his parole officer about his assistance, if he wanted. We had good faith on both sides, satisfaction on neither. It was time to go, and I took George back downstairs to the cells. Since I'd have to come back early in the morning with Danielle to swear out the complaint, I knew we could start it all again, and the thought was exhausting even as it brought relief.

Danielle arrived at court in the morning looking fresh and rested, and she remained resolute in her desire to press charges. She walked with a limp, and said that she was told at the hospital that she needed some kind of surgery on her hip. I asked if it was from what George had done to her, and she shrugged, but added that "they'd been telling me to have it for a while." I asked if the doctors had told her whether George had contributed to her condition, and if so how much, but she only shrugged again. When the ADA was ready for the case, I told her the story, then brought in Danielle to tell it again. When they were finished, I was taken aback at the vehemence of the ADA's reaction. "Did you see that poor woman? I've never seen such fear!" she said. "I really want to put this guy away!" She had tears in her eyes.

Ordinarily, I would have been delighted. Time after time, I'd brought in assault cases, from domestic violence more often than not, and seen them dealt down to next-to-nothing. Sometimes you respect the compromise, and sometimes you can't. At last, I'd met a blazing champion of the downtrodden, and it couldn't have happened at a worse time. My peculiar mix of motives—I wanted something from George, so I needed something for him—made me uneasy, but I genuinely felt her reaction was naive and awry. Danielle seemed justifiably angry, but not really afraid. He hurt her, but how much? He shoved her, and trapped her in a room overnight. It was fitting that he spent the night in jail for it, and it would be prudent to provide her with an order of protection, which would allow her to send him back to jail if he so much as raised an eyebrow at her. After a woman from Victim Services had interviewed Danielle, she'd told me, "She doesn't seem afraid of him. She wants him in jail because she thinks he should be there." And then there were her threats, made in front of the cop and, it was alleged, in writing. There are times when your heart breaks for people; this wasn't one of them.

After Danielle signed the complaint, the supervising DA sent me back to the video room, where I met with another detective. He reacted to the story as I hoped, saying we had to move, immediately, and do whatever possible to get to the Brazilian. I took George back upstairs. The night had taken its toll. He'd barely slept or eaten, and his mood swung between sullen resentment and dazed despair: "I don't care, I'll do time, I can do it, I did ten years, man, I know what it is . . . this is bullshit, it's bullshit what Danielle did, and it's bullshit that I gave up a robbery, a robbery that my friend did, and I'm still here. . . ." He agreed to talk and refused to, talking in crazy circles, saying he didn't care, he'd go back to jail, or he'd never go back because he - didn't do anything. Once, he broke down, crying with his face in his hands, and I thought we'd lost him. We moved between paying him sympathetic attention and allowing moments of privacy; we fed him, let him call his sister to talk. "Think about your children!" I said. Let me tell you, we were ruthless. He came around, and told us what he knew.

The Brazilian was playing both sides, with the dealer and the law; how exactly, George didn't know. He didn't know if the Brazilian had testified or was scheduled to, if he was an informant or just suspected of thinking about turning. He said he didn't know the man in prison who had commissioned the hit, but the fee would be six thousand dollars, half on agreement, half on completion, and he knew the name and address of the Brazilian. He'd seen a video shot as a kind of prospectus for the hit: footage of the man's block, his building, his apartment. In the last ten seconds, the Brazilian appears, stumbling into the frame as he happens to come out of his home, then smiles and waves at the camera. All this he knew, he said, because he was asked to do the hit. Throughout the afternoon and into the evening, we made the deal. Calls went back and forth between cops and prosecutors, word went up the chains of command; bureau chiefs were consulted. The DA wanted the Brazilian's name, to run it through city, state, and federal databases to see if he was a registered informant, to check with the U.S. Attorney and the other DAs to find out if he was a witness in a case. We were determined to prevent a murder, but the DA, in particular, was terrified of another one, whose headline would read: DA FREES PAROLEE, GIRLFRIEND SLAIN. He asked me about the case, and I told him George hit a woman every month. It wasn't ferocious violence, it was shoving and slapping, never even a punch, but it was habitual. He had Danielle brought back in to see her for himself.

George would not give up the name without a promise from the DA that he would be out, today. The DA said he needed the name, to make sure the information was good. George said he wouldn't give up his friend, who had relayed the order from the man in prison, but that he could show them the tape when he got out, and maybe get them the gun for the hit. The DA said it should be enough, if the name checked out. George gave up the first name, which was all he remembered: Kari. The detectives left to start calling.

I sat with him for a while, as he mused aloud: "I think about these hits - people want me to do, and I wonder . . . I always say, 'I'll think about it, let me think,' then tell them, 'Nah, it don't feel right.' I'm not into that anymore, even though it's good for people to think I am. Like this hit in the Heights they asked me to do? That guy, I could walk up to him and he'd be no more. No more . . . ."

I didn't ask him why so many people were under the impression that he was a contract killer. Somehow I didn't think most record-store clerks get that kind of offer.

The calls went back and forth: "DEA has a Bosnian named Kiri, wants to know if it's your guy."

"FBI has a Corio, from Naples."

"Naples, Florida, or Naples, Italy? Never mind, forget it, but keep taking anything close, Brazilian Kari might be Jamaican Kelly after how many guys are passing along the name. . . ."

By sundown, there had been no confirmation, but after George repeated his information on the robberies and the record-store shooting, there was little doubt about his credibility. The DA agreed to let him out that night, in exchange for the address, with the stipulation that George would accept the terms of the order of protection, enter a batterer's program, and agree to bring them the videotape the next morning. George gave the address in Manhattan, 325 West 57th, and in a few minutes, DEA agents were on a cell phone from a car. There was no such address. How tall is the building? Is there an awning, a light? George was surprised, and described an apartment house. Maybe it was East 57th? Ten minutes later, they called back. The building didn't match, it wasn't even residential. Was it on a two-way street? No? Then it isn't on 57th. "We'll call you back." The DA prodded George for details. He remembered a CVS on the corner. The DA called information, asked for the locations of CVS stores in Manhattan. Bleecker Street, Eighth Avenue. "Give me Eighth Avenue." He called and asked for the cross street. "Fifty-eighth? Thanks!" He called the DEA, and when they called back, they were in front of 325 West 58th Street, a building like George had described. They would call back in a minute, they said, after they went to the apartment.

It was almost half an hour when they called. No one was home, but neighbors confirmed that a Brazilian lived there, and several said he was a drug dealer. They had a name. The Manhattan DA confirmed that he was a defendant in a drug case, resulting from a search warrant executed at his house. And he wasn't the witness of a kidnapping but the victim of one, though those who had released him clearly had had second thoughts afterward. He didn't sound like a very good man, but thanks to George, he would be a living one, at least for a little longer.

George would go back to the cells for an hour, then see a judge and be released. "I keep getting pulled out of there and put back, people are gonna put things together," he complained. The detective told him, "You'll think of something to say." He said nothing, nodding as he left.

Later on, the detective told me that George had delivered the videotape, as agreed. In fact, the hit was supposed to have taken place that night, but the killers were spooked by the DEA presence. The Brazilian was in police custody. There was also news of True, the intended target at the record-store shooting, who had been shot six times. He was alive, but he wasn't talking to police. And Danielle had decided to drop the charges.

Every week or so, I'd run into George on the street, and we'd say hello. I liked him, as far as it went. The feeling was as mutual as it could be, I think; as it can be between two people who wouldn't hesitate to shoot each other. As hit man and cop, the odds of this occurring were less remote than they might be otherwise. Semi-retired hit man, pseudo-retired hit man, it didn't matter. Anyway, we'd both be around, and I was sure we'd be talking.

. . .

THESE CHANCE ENCOUNTERS ALONG FAMILIAR PATHS OF-fered a glimpse of where the Job might lead—to a higher stage, where the stakes were urgent and the players elite, as our gathered forces improvised with a killer to save a life. Other meetings pointed toward a lower road, dull and degraded, and one such meeting took place hours after another cop took his last steps altogether. On a midnight tour in May 1997, cops in Chelsea re-sponded to a robbery in progress. A masked gunman had broken into the apartment of a wealthy garment manufacturer, where he tied up the man and his girlfriend. The girlfriend managed to free herself and call for help, and PO Anthony Sanchez and his partner responded, splitting up between the stairs and the fire escape to seal off the robber's exit. Sanchez met him in the stairwell and was shot in the head and back. He died at the scene. He was thirty years old, married, with two young children. The bottomless shame of it, the poisonous waste, worsened with the arrest of the perp, a failed stock-broker with a cocaine habit named Scott Schneiderman, because his intended victim had been his father. Whether he was dissatisfied with his allowance or wanted to rush his inheritance, he had destroyed the Sanchez family in an as-sault on his own kin.

And so I wore a mourning band, a slip of black elastic that covers the em-blem of the City on the shield, when I took my post the next morning. For a while, I watched drug spots, without success. At around six in the evening, I got a job for a Missing Person. Such cases overwhelmingly involve teenage girls who are out with their boyfriends, or husbands who later turn up with a hangover or lipstick on the collar. But unless I could prove something like that within an hour or so, to make certain that this missing person wouldn't turn up in the East River, I would have to make it an official case and go back to the base for at least two hours of paperwork and phone calls, making no-tifications to the precinct, the Missing Persons Squad, Operations, Transit, and the Port Authority.

When I arrived at the apartment, a painfully sincere woman told me that her fifteen-year-old son hadn't come home. Though I tried to point out that a teenager who isn't even late for dinner yet isn't necessarily a police emer-gency, she protested that her son was an angel who practically ran home from school every day to get a start on his homework. In response to my other questions, she sobbed that they hadn't fought, that he didn't have a girlfriend, and that she had never had any prior occasion to call the police. I was disinclined to believe her, but I felt for her genuine tears, and I didn't want to risk the worst—and by that I mean getting jammed up myself, in part because that's how cops think, but also because whatever had happened or would happen to the boy was out of my hands. One of the ironies of handling an ordinary Missing Person case is that you only look for the person before he or she is declared missing. And so I took a picture of the boy, instructed his mother to call 911 again if he returned, and set out to check the usual haunts. After the playground, the schoolyard, and the busier corners, I went to the Community Center, where the gym was crowded with basketball players. I walked along the sidelines, hoping to spot my kid. And then one of the ballplayers ran up in front of me and started yelling, "Get out of here! You can't come in here, this is our place! Get out!"

I stopped, glared at him, and told him to get out of the way. He stepped back a pace but went on shouting: "Cops can't come in here! Leave us alone, get out!" I thought about locking him up, and I had a solid disorderly conduct and even a plausible misdemeanor—obstructing government administration—but mostly I had a loudmouthed jackass who was keeping me from doing my jackass job. And it hooked me a little, the out-of-the-blue, fact-free rudeness of it, the doubly deluded posturing as victim of the Man and hero of the 'Hood. And it was in part because I was starting to lose my temper that I didn't lock him up, after I stepped up to him and he stepped back, which in our impending dogfight was a sign of submission as distinct as a lowered tail. I continued to canvass the gym before hitting the streets again. Although it was probably the better way to handle it, I was bothered by how much it bothered me. He had a familiar look to him, and if I was setting up the next cop, that cop would most likely be me. That was the mixed blessing of a beat: you got second chances with people, and they got them with you.

After an hour had passed, I went back to check the apartment to see if the boy had returned. He had, of course, and when I began to lecture him about consideration for his mother, he said, "I'm fifteen years old, and she calls the cops every time I go to my friend's house after school." I looked at her and she turned away. I gave back the job: "Mark that a 91, Central, missing returned." The code meant "condition corrected," but it didn't feel like what had been wrong was in any way righted.

Not for the first time, I began to suspect that this is what my father would have warned me against. But how could he begin to convey the maddening circularity of patrol, the daily diet of bullshit, the smallness of people and the grandeur of their demands? The danger was not in corruption but corrosion. I stewed: *They call it the beat for what it does, not what it is—it beats you down . . . for all that, I take home seventy-five dollars a day . . .žand I did go home, unlike Anthony Sanchez.* Such was the drift of my thoughts as the sun set and then the skies opened, dousing my self-pity with cold, blind rain.

After I was soaked to the skin, a sector car came by and I hopped into the back. Some beat cops rode like that fairly often, if their post was slow, or to back up the sector, if we had only one car to cover the precinct, but I liked walking by myself. The cops in the car were Chris Meyer, who was a couple of classes ahead of me, and John Timpanaro, who was in the class behind me. As was typical for cops who were no longer quite so new, I didn't really know Timpanaro; it was as if I was a second-grader, and while I knew most of third grade, the first grade was a blur of babies, indistinguishable to anyone but their mothers. I sat quietly in the back as they talked about the Job, bitching about the bosses and laughing at the gossip. We drove around for a few hours, and the downpour seemed to drown out the complaints. As the tour wound down, the rain stopped, and the radio woke up again for a domestic dispute. The three of us responded.

A crowd of teenagers had already gathered at the building, immediately back in position after having been deprived of hours of hang-out time. There had been frequent complaints of dogfights there, and two guys in the crowd had pit bulls. In the past, they had told me that they didn't fight their dogs, they just "faced" them, holding them on the leash as they strained to attack, snapping and barking, inches apart. While I didn't expect them to know that they verged on violation of the animal-cruelty statute, an unclassified misdemeanor in the State Agricultural Law, I thought it shouldn't be such a stretch for them to realize that they were a nuisance, especially late at night. It was the kind of rebuke I had to make daily, often to hostile incomprehension, whether a man decided to relieve himself beside a busy playground or a woman lit her cigarette in an elevator packed with children. "You can't tell me what to do," I'd hear, and,"But there's no sign. . . ." I knew others in the crowd, and they knew me, and they knew that when I told them to leave, I meant it.

"All right, that's it, no hanging out in front of the building," I called out, and we went upstairs to the job. A couple had fought, or rather a wife had taken out her frustrations on her husband, who had called us to calm her down. And it was an actual, legal husband, with a real job as a union electrician. In this neighborhood, working husbands were a small and respectably eccentric fraternity, like the Freemasons. Though he was somewhat the worse for wear, he insisted he didn't want his wife arrested, and so we calmed her down, wrote our report, and went back out. The group hadn't moved.

"Let's go!" I called out. "Everybody move! You don't, you get locked up!"

The teenagers looked at each other, reading the cues from those inclined to stay and those beginning to go, until the momentum built among the latter and the groups began to walk off. And then a few guys turned back and started to mouth off. One in particular seemed to have a lot on his mind, and he broadcast his opinions of the police with some volume. The general theme was that as individuals, we were pathetic cowards of dubious manhood, but together, we were worse than the Gestapo. I recognized him from the basketball courts, that afternoon. We started to walk toward him and he backed away, going on as he went about how it was a great thing when the people took matters into their own hands, and the cops got what was coming to them. We walked a little faster, hoping to gain before he broke into a run, when he bellowed, "And that's why your buddy got scraped last night!" And then he turned and ran, with us hard after him, as the crowd let out a cheer.

A few inches of rain had fallen in the past hours, and the ground was a sea of mud. The terrain didn't favor him any more than it did us, and in fact he fell down as we chased him, though he recovered quickly. But I knew we were no match for the skinny young guy in his "felony fliers," loaded down as we were in our equipment and heavy boots. He fled across the lawns of one project, across the street to the projects on the other side, ducking out of sight behind a building and heading toward the next street beyond. Timpanaro proved to be a great sprinter, however, and held his pace, with Meyer following gamely. I slowed to a jog, figuring that he might double back, because he was more likely to live in the projects on Webster or Washington Avenue than in the tenements by the park, where he was now headed. And so I was less surprised than he was as he rounded the corner, almost running into me, and I was close on his heels as he fled back toward the crowd. We skidded though the wet lawns until he hit a fence which he could not clear, and he went down into the mud, with me on top of him. As Timpanaro and Meyer joined us, the crowd moved forward, yelling and jeering, but I was too winded to notice. "Okay, okay, you got me," he said, as I cuffed him up. *No shit,* I thought, *we got you.*

The crowd was getting jacked up and ugly, so we hauled the perp back to the car. I looked at them: for one girl, I'd collared a gang leader who had threatened to shoot her; for others, I'd been in their houses, trying to help when their mothers were sick or their brothers had disappeared. They were rooting for this criminal, who had taken such pride and pleasure in the death of a young cop. When we got back to the precinct, I realized that I'd been to the perp's house as well: his brother had called after his ex-girlfriend had threatened him on the phone. The perp reclined on the couch as I took the report and explained the procedure for obtaining an order of protection, and had even called the girlfriend to tell her to lay off. Why did he hate cops so much, and why did I care? As I checked his record, I found some clue—he was a crack dealer—and as I wrote out the summons for Disorderly Conduct, he recovered his perp composure. He paced in the cell, saying he wouldn't let us plant drugs on him, that he would sue us for what we'd done. All of us were muddy messes, and he had a lump on his head, and he demanded to go to the hospital. I told him he could go if he wanted, in handcuffs, now, or I - could wait for the warrant check, give him his ticket, and send him on his way. He said he'd wait. As I saw it, I couldn't really charge him with Resisting Arrest, though he deserved a night in jail, because running isn't resisting. Moreover, I was just as glad to go home. The tour had ended, Timpanaro and Meyer had gone, and once the warrant check came back, I cut him loose, suspecting, however, that I hadn't heard the last of it.

Some months later, I was called down to Internal Affairs. The interview was routine and, in fact, anticipated, as Meyer, Timpanaro, and I were notified at the same time. They don't advise you of the allegations beforehand, nor do they inform you of their findings afterward, unless you are charged. Two detectives interviewed me in "good cop, bad cop" style, though the vaguely embarrassed tone of the younger one may not have been purely tactical. I certainly was embarrassed to be there. I did note for the record that management later told me that my accuser had been banned from the Housing Authority for dealing drugs, and that his family had signed a stipulation that permitted them to keep their apartment as long as he stayed away. The man claimed we beat him, which was expected, but he also alleged that I had robbed him of his jewelry. As we left, Timpanaro said, "So that's why you've been sporting that four-fingered gold THUG 4 LIFE ring."

"Hey, I gotta have something to show for this."

While I appreciated the necessity of process, just as I do for audits and root canals, it didn't mean I had to enjoy it at the time. In any case, I heard nothing afterward, which I had to assume was to the good. When I was called down to the Civilian Complaint Review Board, I felt I had rounded out my education. Again, I had only been told to bring my memo book for a particular date, but since I was assigned to a "conditions car" that day, to look for arrests and summonses, instead of a full page of entries for building checks and jobs, it said little beyond "exterior patrol." The investigator was a pleasant young guy who appeared to be straight out of college, who shook my hand, turned on a tape recorder, and asked whether I had choked a child, nine months before. At IAB, I had been nervous and angry, appalled that the lies of some random criminal would leave a permanent mark on my record; here, I was simply intrigued. It was not my habit to choke children, and I was curious about how it was construed that I had. Specifically, it was claimed that two kids were play-fighting in front of one building, when a cop of my general description mistook it for a real fight, and used excessive force in breaking it up.

"How about that!" I said. Most of this investigator's interviews consisted of gruff, defensive, one-syllable denials, I was sure, much as mine had been at IAB, but at CCRB, I was a cheerful participant, as if we were playing a game of Clue. I told him what I did in general and on that day, and said that breaking up fights between kids was routine. While I might not recall one instance from almost a year before if I'd only had to yell at them, I thought I would remember if I'd had to use force, however slight. "Can you help me out here? Were they black, white, Spanish?" If he'd asked to hypnotize me, I might have consented; as it was, we were equally confused, which was not the worst situation to be in. He told me he would talk to the complainant again, and might have to put my picture in a photo array for her—my mug shot among five others, in the standard form—which I found a bit offensive. The interview ended, and when he turned off the tape recorder, we both saw there was no tape inside. We shook hands and I left. Some six months later, I received a letter from CCRB, informing me that I had been "exonerated," in that I was the officer in question and had used force in the event, but that my actions were appropriate. Yeah, whatever.

Veteran cops often warned us, "If you're out there as an aggressive cop, sooner or later you're gonna get jammed up." Sometimes the implication was to expect punishment as much as reward for your efforts; sometimes it only meant, "Watch your back." Another one said to me, "The way you're going, you're gonna be burnt out in five years." When I first got on the job, those remarks struck me as embittered and exaggerated; now, they were beginning to make sense. I had to make sure that the last comment wasn't true, at least—I only had two years on patrol, and I was already starting to get a little crisp around the edges.

After the night with Timpanaro and Meyer, I had two weeks off. I needed it. In the NYPD, the pay is bad but we get more time off than Frenchmen. On my first day back, I left Sunday dinner at my mother's house for the four-to-twelve, and I filled in a sector with another cop from my class, Gina Fredericks. Right after roll call, we responded to a job for an EDP in one of my buildings. An elderly woman told us her grandson had drunk a bottle of liniment—she showed it to us; the liquid was thick and pink as shampoo—before he began to break the furniture and talk to God. We wrestled him all over the bedroom, knocking over the bed, and when Gina blasted him with mace, he licked his lips as if it was whipped cream. After we finally subdued him, we both went out for the rest of the day with line-of-duty injuries. I had been back at work for an hour, and I was off again. *Vive la France!*

As my third summer in the Village approached, the weather was getting hot again. One sweltering afternoon, an Aided case came over for a pregnant woman in front of a building. When I got there, I saw it was Tonya, sitting on the curb, about to deliver another one of George's children. She hugged her belly and moaned, surrounded by neighbors. I didn't know what to tell her, to sit or stand or walk, so I said, "It's okay, take it easy!" The ambulance was long in coming, and people began to complain about the police: "They don't do *nothin'!* They *never* around!" I put a second call in for the ambulance, and a third, and then George walked by, eating an ice cream cone. He stopped to watch, at the edge of the crowd, with an expression of idle curiosity. Tonya was about to give birth to his child, literally in the gutter, and she might have been a stranger, or even a strange dog, about to drop a litter of pups. I'd heard that when a cop delivers a baby—in a cab, on the street, wherever—the mother often names it after him. Would I deliver my informant's child, and would he be named after me, or at least code-named? Were there special forms to be filled out, or notifications to be made? A woman began to complain about the police again, and I snapped at her, "The police *are* here, lady, whaddaya want me to do, carry her to the hospital on my back?" George finished his ice cream cone and shook his head. "Man, this is one hot day!" he said, and then he walked away. *I have much to learn from him,* I thought, and when the ambulance came and took Tonya, not long after, I walked away, too. It was time.

FOUR

When I was in the Academy, a detective came in to give us a talk about trouble. For years he had worked undercover in organized crime and narcotics, to great effect and at visible cost. Pacing the stage and chopping the air with his hands, he warned us of hot-blooded crackheads and cold-blooded dealers and how each could kill us, and speaking of blood, how the random prick of a junkie's needle could leave us dead from AIDS in a few miserable years. He couldn't have been more alarming if he had a flashing light on his head, and sometimes I thought the Job put people like him out in front of us to say, "Are you sure about this? You better be—it's your last chance!" The near-paranoia of his tone, warranted as it was by the assignment, bumped up a notch—for all of us—when he told us how his undercover career came to an end: a fellow cop gave him up. "I don't care what you did before, if you used drugs, stole cars, whatever it was—maybe you can use it to become a better cop," he said. "But you're cops now, and a cop who does any of that is a piece of shit."

The last epithet silenced the room. Had we been inclined to speak, I doubt that anyone would have argued with either the harshness of the line, or its finality. But it made me wonder about what pasts were gathered around me, what winding roads had been taken to this place—and whether they would straighten out entirely for all of us, from this point onward. My own path had taken a few odd turns along the way. Whenever I'd dwell upon my great-grandfather's litany of sins, suspected and certain, I could imagine old Pat Brown cutting me short: "At least I never got arrested." Though I never thought of myself as a symptom of declining standards in the NYPD, if they - didn't allow people with criminal records to join, I wouldn't be here. *They were different times, back then.*

The detective was on to something when he said our juvenile delinquencies could be transformed in maturity, whether it meant a deeper understanding for those who had done wrong, or a more discerning eye for how wrong is done. One cop I later worked with told me, "When I was a kid, my mother found weed in my pants pockets when she did the laundry. I told her that I was holding it for a friend. Now, I know it's the lamest line in the world, but it's really what happened—God's honest truth! So when I hear it, I have to think twice, because I know it's bullshit ninety-nine times out of a hundred, but it did happen to me." Another told me that a cop in his precinct had a true gift for spotting stolen cars because, as a teenager, he was responsible for a few of them.

Arthur Niederhoffer, an NYPD lieutenant who became a distinguished sociologist, observed of his former colleagues that "the more maladjusted tend to be more satisfied with their work than the less maladjusted." There was a lot to consider in the phrase, from the coppish cynicism in the formulation—none of us are "the better adjusted," only "the less maladjusted"—to the loop-the-loop logic of unhappiness lending the only hope of happiness here, and vice versa. How do you see yourself, and what should you wish for, if the dark clouds are drawn to the silver lining? I wondered how it could effect screening, or even recruitment: *Are you irritable and withdrawn? Do you have trouble sleeping, or maintaining relationships? You may be just crazy enough for the NYPD!* As for myself, I was troubled enough to believe I might one day be a detective.

The idea that you could benefit from beginning on the wrong foot, or at least profit from having made a few missteps along the way, is not new: the reformed sinner is at once the most typical and the most powerful character in our culture, whether in religious terms or those of self-improvement, with the newly thin, sober, solvent, or self-esteeming among the traditionally born-again. Counselors for addicts and ex-convicts routinely work their way up from the ranks of their clients; no one else can command the authority, or extend the empathy, of a veteran among veterans. We admire the self-made more than those who have it all from the get-go, and we'd rather hear about a roundabout journey, full of setbacks and pitfalls, than the express trip from good to better. As St. Augustine prayed, before he found his calling, *Make me holy, Lord, but not yet.*

While most of us are moved by stories of people who find religion in prison, few look as kindly on those who happen upon their redemption in the police department, whether during or after their term of employment. Movie-hero cops are almost always rule-benders but rarely lawbreakers; in real life, when bad cops confess to how and why they crossed the line, the audience—myself included—tends to be dubious of their sincerity and unhurried to forgive. Hackneyed stories of the "slippery slope" that leads the innocent rookie from the proverbial free cup of coffee to the all-out, two-fisted, steal-a-hot-stove take are part of our training, and in the past, especially, there was no shortage of little seductions and large pressures to accommodate the freewheeling style of the City. But the reverse has been true as well: some of us have slipped up the slope, or scaled it, less from serious crime than from lives low in purpose or prospects, which we sometimes stooped to fit. And while the history of policing has seen unimaginable changes in what we do and how we do it, from the rattle watch of New Amsterdam to the SWAT teams, DNA tests, and digital fingerprints of today, the stories of individual police officers are no less miraculous in the distance traveled and the directions taken.

. . .

IF MY FIRST EXPERIENCES WITH POLICE OFFICERS OUTSIDE my immediate family foretold any contributions I might make to the NYPD, it would be as a source of arrest overtime. One night in my senior year of high school, I went out with my best friend, a Hispanic immigrant I'll call Eddie. Spring was approaching, and so was graduation, if we needed reasons to be spirited and stupid—and we went to a club in lower Manhattan. While we waited to get in, a bouncer walked along the line and told a number of people to leave. When he approached us, Eddie got the same non-invitation. We walked away without protest—democracy is as alien to New York nightclubs as it is to North Korea—and though it took me about a half a minute to see the rule of thumb at work, Eddie had it figured out in an instant: nonwhites should pursue nightlife elsewhere. So we did, heading back to the neighborhood in upper Manhattan where he lived. I'll shorten the story to say that our fiery mood increased with the consumption of flammable liquids, and our new dedication to the cause of breaking down barriers was commemorated by my shattering the plate-glass window of a Greek diner. And then we ran away.

We got about a block before an unmarked police car rolled up on us, and two plainclothesmen jumped out. I froze and raised my hands, as ordered. Eddie danced a little, stepping up to protest and deny—we hadn't done anything, they couldn't stop us, and so on (a speech I've heard many times as a cop, never from the innocent)—talking fast, and with his hands. The cops talked with their hands, too, popping him in the face a few times. I was untouched. My instinct to freeze had been instilled by years of education by my father: do what you're told; do not argue with cops; do not say anything at all, in fact, except that your uncle is Chief McNulty—which was not, strictly or loosely speaking, true. We were charged with Criminal Mischief, and since our arresting officers were Transit cops, we were taken to an underground precinct. The rumble of the trains lent the cells a feel of steerage, as if we had been shanghaied, along with the other mutts, skells, and drooling lunatics, to the bottom of a cargo hold bound for Shithead Island. Since I was more afraid of my father than the cops, I waited it out, without calling home or dropping the name of my newly adopted uncle. We were released at dawn the next day, and I had a track meet in the morning. Still charged with adrenaline, I showed off my handcuff marks and set a school record in the quarter mile. My teammates were impressed, and none were rude enough to point out that if I'd run as well the night before, I wouldn't have been arrested. In truth, I don't remember how much it worried me at the time: trouble then meant trouble with my father, for wanting to stay out late or not doing chores. Justice would not be rougher in the streets than at home. Whatever his warnings about the gravity of a criminal record, I knew that an eighteen-year-old who broke a window would not be cast out of society altogether. I had a court date six weeks later, and a family vacation in between. The family vacation scared the hell out of me.

The court date was set for the day after we were to return from our first real trip, on a plane, to a foreign place. My mother had finagled a package deal to the Bahamas, where seven of us—Mom, Dad, Johnny, Eddie, Regina, Stephen, and Marianne—would share two rooms for the week for around five hundred dollars. The trip was carefully orchestrated and long anticipated, and I'm not sure how my mother managed to persuade my father to spend money on a trip to a faraway beach. We were budgeted for one meal a day, and we carried the rest of our provisions in two enormous suitcases—perhaps the same ones my father had taken to summer camp—that were filled with tuna fish, peanuts, and Tang, the orange-flavored drink powder famously marketed as the beverage of astronauts. The moon for them was not as far as the Bahamas were for us, nor as hazardous. I had been stupid, but I was not suicidal, and I was not about to confine myself on an island with my father for a week-long discussion of what was wrong with me.

Although for most of my life I have gotten along quite well with my brothers and sisters, at the time they had the burden of being relatives, and so were not my first choice of company. Steve, my thirteen-year-old brother, was a different story altogether—I loathed him. He was finicky and complaining and disinclined to movement, preferring to spend his time reading and watching television, except when in pursuit of that which both consumed and provided his energies: Coca-Cola. When he didn't have it, he wanted it, and his increasingly devious thoughts were more and more directed against moments when he might find himself without it. For Steve, it was still made with cocaine: he had secret caches of soda, like a guerrilla army has its buried rifles, or a squirrel its nuts. Cans and cases were hidden under his bed, in his closet, and even underground, in the yard.

At the airport, he set off the metal detector. Though my father would have been angrier had his youngest son turned out to be the more conventional kind of coke smuggler, this was embarrassment enough. Cans were produced from pant legs and shirtsleeves, to the amusement of security. Though my father often attempted to ease difficulties by mentioning the fact that he was an FBI agent, he did not do so then. The flight was otherwise uneventful, and the trip turned out to be a mix of the advertised tropical pleasures and typical family strains. The days at the beach were beautiful, and we swam for hours, fortified by tuna and Tang. In the little room we shared, my brother bounced off the walls when he found that his beloved refreshment was a gift America had given the world. On the last morning, my sister Regina determined to take home as dark a tan as possible. Another tourist advised her to use baby oil, and a few hours later, she was loaded on the plane in a wheelchair, shivering beneath her blankets, sun-poisoned and in shock. When we were back in New York that night, and the last empty suitcase had been unloaded from the station wagon, I somewhat offhandedly broached the subject that had been on my mind but, thank God, not yet his: "Dad, are you going to work tomorrow?"

I could see how he half-consciously registered that something was afoot, but he brushed it aside as he headed toward the bathroom.

"Of course I'm going to work tomorrow, it's Monday, I work every Monday."

"Because, uh, I was wondering if you could go to court with me. . . ."

The story then poured out of me, and my father asked why I hadn't called him from the cells. I said I didn't want to bother him, or to spoil the vacation. I think he said, "You've spoiled it now," but we both knew that wasn't true—the vacation was over; it was my life that was ruined. He asked a few questions and made a few statements. His voice hit me like a gale. What he said had the force of reason and rage together, and because I'd never heard him shout before, it was as if he'd saved it all up for that moment. I would have confessed to anything, but I had already done so, and it was best for me to be quiet then.

The next day, when his manner returned to a more familiar low-boil anger, he was no longer interested in my opinions. We went to court with my co-defendant, Eddie, and his father, as well as Mr. DiMichele, a favorite teacher, and the grown men all greeted each other with plentiful apologies and thanks. Eddie's father spoke little English, and though Mr. DiMichele had coached numerous national debating champs, he was there more or less as a stage prop, to attest to our bright futures and blameless pasts. Eddie and I were to sit quietly, in visible contrition. The arena was my father's, to do whatever he could. He could do everything, it seemed, and though I was relieved that the drama was ending, I was enthralled by his performance. Though the conversation was largely out of earshot, he was quick to elicit the educational background of the assistant district attorney—she went to Fordham Law, did she, why, he did too!—and her father, it appeared, was also an acquaintance from the NYPD. And then he re-created the crime, for the judge and the ADA, moving like a dancer to show Eddie and me pushing and pulling back, play-fighting, and the inadvertent smash of the poor man's window, for which he would be reimbursed immediately, of course. The case was Adjourned in Contemplation of Dismissal, which meant that if we stayed out of trouble for six months, the charges would be dropped. It was a fair sentence for a first offense and a minor crime, probably no different from what we would have gotten without the pantomime and the belabored name-droppings. In the course of twelve hours, I had seen my father transformed into a thunder god and then a Tammany shyster, and each shift brought its own revelation.

As with the case of St. Augustine, however, there was a certain interval between revelation and reform. A month or so later, I broke another window.

Or rather, one was broken with me. I went to a Jesuit high school called Regis, on the Upper East Side of Manhattan, which drew students from neighborhoods ranging from Scarsdale to Bedford-Stuyvesant. Occasionally, friction would arise between us and kids from Yorkville, the neighborhood to the east, where there were still a dozen bars where German or Hungarian was spoken, as well as the remains of an Irish neighborhood. My friends and I met some of our local counterparts one night at a bar, and somewhere along the way, a few words and then a few punches were exchanged. Though the matter was soon settled, some of us took the radical step of calling it a night. One of our side had been a friend of mine since the beginning of our freshman year, and I'd felt a certain guilty closeness to him: we were from similar backgrounds and nearby parishes, and both of our mothers had become ill with ovarian tumors at the same time. Though my mother had been told to prepare for the worst, her condition proved to be benign and readily operable, whereas my friend's mother had died. Afterward, he became a kind of willfully innocent kid, and I believe that night was his first at a bar. The first skirmish sent him rushing to his father's car, which was parked in front, and his sudden departure was interpreted by our rivals as an attempt to bring in reinforcements. The bar emptied into the street, and a couple of them pounded on the car and prevented it from leaving, and someone punched him and someone else said, "Your mother!" and the combination more or less did him in. I tried to break it up and calm them down, but I might as well have tried to make my case with geometry proofs. Another one of their gang, unfortunately a much larger person, happened by, and I wound up fighting with him. We each threw a punch and then he grappled me around the middle, pushing me back. Behind me was a beauty parlor with eight-foot-tall plate-glass windows. I shattered it with my back, then raised my hands as the glass rained down, and one shard pierced the center of the palm of my right hand. Alarms sounded and the street cleared as the flashing lights of patrol cars approached. I ran, with a couple of other guys, and as the cops pulled over and stepped out, one said, "This guy's covered with blood," and I responded, "My uncle's Chief McNulty, and I have to go to the hospital." The cop asked, "What hospital do you want to go to?"

That particular dust-up sidelined me, and I was able to avoid trouble for a while. The median nerve of my right hand had been severed, and even after extensive physical therapy, the hand remained somewhat stiff and numb, scarred from knuckle to wrist. My father tried to take some comfort in my presumed disability: "Well, it's your shooting hand, so if there's a draft, I guess you're safe. And at least it'll keep you out of the police department."

So much for that prophecy. I was hard to predict, which may have been a great part of my father's frustrations with me. I defied his expectations, high and low: I would be going to Harvard in the fall, but with an arrest record; I won the city championship in the half mile, and would become a pack-a-day smoker. My avowed interest in becoming a writer was similarly troublesome; while no one who read as my father did had anything less than respect for authors, as a livelihood, writing required too much luck. My father's sense of caution was so profound that he once warned me about speeding, in a canoe. He suggested teaching, publishing, speechwriting, and advertising; any salaried approximation of what I wanted to do. My ambitions were less confusing than conflicting to him, I think. He was a great junk collector who also despised the fact that I smoked; nonetheless, when he came across a brass ashtray in the shape of a horsefly at a garage sale—with wings that moved!—he bought it for me.

Likewise, our family ate for free at our uncles' restaurant at the World Trade Center, and for years, birthdays, anniversaries, and every other special occasion that merited a meal outside the house took place there. We ate nowhere else that had metal utensils. When the World Trade Center opened, it was desperate for tenants, and my father got the uncles an extraordinary twenty-year lease. There were three uncles—Joe, Herman, and Victor—and three businesses: a bar called the Trade Inn, a coffee shop, and a restaurant called the Commuter's Cafe. The Tretters were Austrian immigrants, and the three who owned the restaurant weren't really uncles; a fourth brother, Nick, a doctor, had married my father's sister, Theresa, a nurse. Their meeting was a coincidence, their romance a secret, and their wedding a surprise, at least to my father. Theresa broke the news to him the day before, by way of a request for assistance with Nick's citizenship papers. Joe and my father had been close friends since the 1950s, when Joe had owned another restaurant downtown, also called Commuter's, where my parents had their wedding reception. When Nick and Theresa married, Joe and my father vowed to remain friends, family notwithstanding. My father took a fee for the lease, but soon afterward, he felt that the volume and variety of requests—the calls about a cook's drunk-driving arrest, a job for a waitress's nephew, a complaint about an inspection—suggested that the half-blood, half-money ambiguity of the relationship promised a lifetime of mutual resentment. He decided to set forth a rule that he would do what he could for them, as he saw fit, without charge, and that he and his own would eat, *gratis,* in perpetuity.

From high school onward, I had an open tab at the restaurant, which was a dangerous thing for a young man. My father's work and my uncles' generosity translated into regular feasts of shrimp cocktail, Wiener schnitzel, and imported beer for my friends. I felt like a tycoon. If these visits became excessively frequent, or just excessive—*This round's on me, boys, and try the veal, it's excellent. Hey, could you believe that Latin test?*—my father would be quietly informed. My father didn't drink, and he struggled more to contain his disapproval of alcohol than his desire for it, and in any other circumstance it would have brought on a stern and lengthy speech. But at the Commuter's, my extravagance was his revenge, and he could only offer a few casual and half-smiling words, "Be careful . . . be polite . . . and don't forget to tip."

As Senator Daniel Patrick Moynihan observed, "Harvard men were to be checked. Fordham men were to do the checking." Though he was talking about government service in the 1950s, it was also true in the Conlon house. When I arrived at college that fall, my first scuffle showed I hadn't learned much since the spring. Again, a friend for whom fistfights were as foreign as bullfights found himself being roughed up, completely unprovoked—this time by the most substantial resident of a ten-man suite that was hosting a Halloween party. Ten-man suite! I was always bad at math. I quickly emerged as the silver medalist in that conflict, though my being knocked cold apparently didn't dissuade my opponent from continuing to swing away. But the pain lasted for only a day or two, whereas the college needled me for months, as they conducted a bizarre and exhaustive investigation with a special subcommittee, and finally concluded that I was somehow at fault. I was placed on disciplinary probation for the rest of the year. Thereafter, out of disgust at the college more than anything else, I did try to stay out of fights, with mixed but increasing success.

What struck me at the time—aside from enormous, drunken thugs—was the rarity of physical confrontation for the young men around me. For some football players and other jocks, brawls were ordinary enough, but I would guess that three-quarters of the rest hadn't been in a fight since the third grade. At home, I knew people for whom most Saturday nights brought a few rounds of beers and a few rounds of punches, and they often felt the former more than the latter the next morning. Having learned the two essential drawbacks of fighting—bodily harm and litigation—I began to take the position I hold now: that it is to be avoided until it truly can't be, and that on most occasions you can give people enough room and reasons to agree with you. But my altercations had given me a reputation, which was neither very comfortable nor deserved (my record had not seen many recent additions to the win column): that I was a useful person to look for in the event of trouble. A female friend who found herself followed by a pervert and a male friend who had been threatened with a beating each came looking for me. I had to spend several weeks, almost without interruption, with another friend who was being stalked by a boyfriend, who threatened persuasively that he would kill her. (He was a genuine villain and went to prison several years later for molesting children.) She had to move from room to room in various dormitories to stay hidden, and I escorted her to classes. There was one little scrap with the stalker, but he was neither a big man nor a brave one, and he left quickly. Neither the college nor the courts were any use—one judge urged them to reconcile, because they were "such an attractive couple," and if the college took any position at all, it is probably noted in the minutes of one of its subcommittees. For me, violence was a language that I wasn't fluent in, but I knew enough to get by in the places where it was spoken.

As a cop, I wouldn't exaggerate the value of being reckless or quick to fight, young or not, and I would recommend even less the kind of wildness that I definitely enjoyed back then. I lost some fights when justice was on my side, and I won others when it wasn't, and the lessons to be drawn from them are not ones I'd like to teach. I made plenty of trouble for myself for no other reason than because I was good at it, more or less. Every now and then, some friend will reminisce about some evening that I had forgotten and which I neither regret nor wish to explain in a job interview. "Remember the lady who complained about the noise at the party, from the apartment behind the yard?" it begins, and from there it goes on to the pith helmet, the catapult, and the herring. I wish I could say that the evening had been the germ of some later innovation, the development of a device to control crowds of unruly sailors or to counteract fish piracy, but it would be a big, fat lie. Education has a point, but experience doesn't have to.

Although I'm sometimes tempted to view old misdemeanors as a necessary link in a chain that led to my present job, if there was some force of fate or anything else at work, I did not see it. Whatever I did as a young man - could have prepared me for a life on either side of the cell bars, and I now know firsthand which side I prefer. There is something to be said—everything, by some lights—in that preference, that choice, which has to be made daily, for what you want to do and be. I don't see how I've changed, but I can feel it sometimes, not as a chain of necessity but like the escape rope a convict would make in his cell, handmade from the scraps of his mean and small surroundings, a lifeline from old ways to new.

· · ·

IT WAS A STRANGE THING TO HEAR HOW PEOPLE COULDN'T believe Eddie Conlon had died. He was my uncle, and I was named after him. At his wake, a man on the other side of the family said, "When I first heard, I thought it was you." The implication was that he wouldn't have been surprised—or would have been less so, at any rate—had disaster struck any of my brothers or sisters or cousins. It was the fall of 1988, and employment had eluded me for several months. I was a scholarship kid, but school had been out for a year and a half, and, in terms of my prospects, my coin was still in the air. I wasn't out robbing banks, but my teenage years were over in a numerical sense only, as if I'd found a good accountant who could keep the deductions going. If bets were taken on whether, in ten years, I would have some extra money in my pocket or I might be asking for yours, the odds would have favored the latter. But if becoming a criminal was highly unlikely, becoming a cop was completely unreal. If there were two Eddie Conlons, there was one "Eddie the Cop," and the line had ended there. For me, cops were still people you ran from. It was an adult line of work, in several ways. Cops were firm and fair and mad at you, a lot of the time, for good reason. Cops were fathers.

I had never seen Uncle Eddie in uniform. And while he embodied the Job for me, in his steadiness, his thick skin, and the pleasure he took in the raw comedy of street life, I knew next to nothing about him as a New York City police officer. I couldn't imagine him saluting without rolling his eyes and winking at you afterward. I have a hard time picturing him writing reports or tickets, let alone chasing anyone, although he did all three—the last at least once, when he tore his knee for his efforts. In a way, his old-time coppishness contradicts much of the daily reality of the police life I know: he worked from the gut—and it was a considerable gut—in a way that is increasingly rare amid the technologies and bureaucracies of today. For that matter, Eddie was less of a father to me than a kind of counter-father, offering boat rides instead of assigning chores.

Eddie was heavyset, easygoing, and outgoing, and he seemed to have the stolid permanence of the civil service, or of the apartment he'd lived in for fifty years. When he made a change, it was a big one. His death devastated my father. It had been a long time between deaths for his family, and this first breach of his generation was not only early but out of order. As the oldest, my father must have felt guilty and lucky at once, the survivor who could not afford to die. The two of them had shared a bed until they left home, and as adults they still spoke every day. When two days had passed without hearing from him, my father went with my older brother John to check the apartment in Kingsbridge in which the family had grown up and which Eddie had never left. They found him there. He had recently been diagnosed with prostate cancer and had died of a heart attack, not long after their last conversation. I didn't see my father shed a tear—I never did—but later I watched him say, quietly and to no one, "The poor kid, he died alone."

Don't we all, though, I thought, even at the time. And that aspect of his death never struck me as especially sad. My father had urged Eddie to marry his girlfriend, Susan, whom he had been seeing for as long as I could remember, not least because he could leave her his pension, which was probably the only argument that carried weight. Eddie had only recently retired, after having worked to nearly the maximum age allowed by law. You might call it a superstition among cops if it wasn't so commonplace; the guys who do "twenty and out," leaving on the first day of full pension eligibility, die happily of boredom in Florida in their dotage, whereas lifers in the NYPD are just that, gone soon after they go. But Eddie was not a sentimental man, nor likely to change his life when it had suited him for so long. Maybe when you start life sharing a bed, you want to finish it with a little more elbow room. Eddie lived as he pleased, without regret. But my father and Eddie had faced most hard things together, and maybe that was what he was talking about.

My father and Eddie were true partners, complementary in type and in temperament. One planned, one improvised; one saved for you, one emptied his pockets; one got the calls when your career was in jeopardy, the other when a sunny Saturday afternoon was going to waste. Within the family, they tended to fall into a kind of "good cop, bad cop" routine: my father would urge you to take things more seriously, while Eddie would convince you, in fewer words, to lighten up. When my father told stories about the odd jobs he'd worked during the Depression, delivering newspapers or helping the super, he cast himself as a plucky orphan who was glad for the chance to earn his gruel. Eddie once worked as a "mutt" for Western Union, delivering telegrams for three dollars a day or some such starvation wage. When we chimed in, as if it were one of my father's stories, "But that was a lot of money for the time, right, Uncle Eddie?" he replied, "It was lousy money for the time." He carried a sack of telegrams through Harlem, trudging up and down the tenement stairs, until one day he decided he'd had enough, and threw the entire bag into the river and went home. And if we had any doubts as to whether the story had a message or moral like one of my father's, he put them to rest: "What do they expect from me for three bucks a day, I'm gonna climb up six flights of stairs just to give some poor bastard his draft notice?"

If you ask any cop what his partner means to him, or what's best about him, or why he is his partner, the reply will almost always be, "I can depend on him." You have each other's back. For my father, he could depend on Eddie in all the usual ways, but he could also depend on him for surprise, for some relief in laughter. After their parents died, Eddie and my father raised their younger sister and brothers, and continued in that role at home throughout their careers. My father was the image of a G-man: tall and prematurely silver-haired, with a trench coat and fedora, a profile in sternness and probity that masked a playful curiosity and a devious sense of humor. Eddie also might have been sent from central casting, if the picture was set in a coal mine or on the docks: he was shorter and heavier, with a perennial crew cut, a pug nose, and a quick, skeptical smile that could seem devilish beneath his broad V of an eyebrow. Eddie was a patrolman for most of his life: twenty-eight years as a non-cop, thirty-three years as a cop, less than two years as a retired cop. He was "Eddie the Cop" to many, himself maybe not least. And for Eddie, the Job, the family, and the neighborhood ran together, whether loosely twined or tightly knotted. My father's interests, however, strayed beyond the dominion of the Bronx Irish, the familiar parishes and precincts—strayed beyond, and sometimes fled from them, though never without the exile's bittersweet regret for the loss of the hoary certainties. He also kept a door open to the old world, an escape hatch, should the newer, wider world go to hell. Eddie set his course early and stuck to it, stiff-arming his way through any setbacks.

The setbacks came soon enough: as a youngster, Eddie would "walk a beat" in front of the family's apartment, carrying half a broom handle on a thong as his nightstick. One day, a man walking past stopped to watch him, then opened up a conversation.

"Hey, kid, whatcha doin'?"

Eddie told him he was on patrol.

"That's your billy club? Lemme see it—"

Eddie handed it over, only to get it back across his jaw, breaking the bone.

My grandmother dragged him from the hospital to the precinct, where the incident was duly reported. As my father recalled it—Eddie never told me the story—they were again beaten to the punch, so to speak. The man's girlfriend had a brother who was a detective, and expecting some repercussion from the assault, had already filed a complaint. My uncle was charged with carrying a concealed weapon, a violation of the Sullivan Law. His admiration for the cops brought him a criminal record.

When Eddie later applied to become a police officer, that record presented a problem, which was resolved in part because my father, already an FBI agent, had the authority to persuade the Department that the record was at odds with the truth. (Eddie and I filled out identical forms, in 1952 and 1994, to explain our arrest records.) And even though I accept this version of the anecdote, I wonder about the details of the encounter that have been lost not just to time but in the retelling, as simple, pointed stories are more likely to survive the natural selection of family lore. Maybe the man remembered Eddie as having egged his car some previous Halloween, or maybe some exchange occurred along the lines of the man jokingly saying he might want to keep the stick, and Eddie suggesting where he could shove it. Eddie sometimes gave advice like that.

Like his namesake, he prepared for his life as a peacekeeper by being a troublemaker, only more so. He ran away at the age of sixteen to join the merchant marine, and he spent some time in the brig after knocking out a superior officer. The incident was typical of the kind of broad farce that Eddie ordinarily thrived on: he had a habit of sleeping with his eyes open (which I did also, when I was younger) and one day, while he was in bed, his boss ordered him to hop to it and do some job. When Eddie's response was an expression of peaceful indifference, and perhaps a snore, his superior grabbed him to show he wouldn't tolerate such insubordination, whereupon Eddie woke up and flattened him. When my father was in the Marine Corps, in 1945, he received a letter from his brother Joe relating that, while on leave, Eddie had made some qualified progress toward entering his chosen profession: "By the way, Eddie and Dave are still doing crazy things. Their last escapade was to rent cop uniforms, they rented them for a week for five dollars. They went up to Yonkers and White Plains impressing girls with them. It really was quite funny. Eddie would go into a bar and have a beer, then Dave would come in with Mike Mikanko handcuffed to him and say to Eddie, 'What am I gonna do with this prisoner?' Then they would have a beer before they took the prisoner to the station house. Mike would just stand there with that dopey expression on his face. The uniforms are turned in now so don't say anything to Dad he doesn't know." Eddie's apparent belief that the way to a woman's heart is through prisoners and beer may explain why he never married.

But once he became a real cop—a dream come true, at the expense of a gag—that role fell from his repertoire. The theme of the impostor ran through my uncle's relentless practical jokes, and in a letter to my father during the war, he wrote, "I met a nice girl in the U.S.O., she comes from Texas. I told her I came from Arizona, we get along pretty well." Of course, there was far more to Eddie than his jokes, and his other signal qualities—his generosity, his devotion, and his love of the macabre—are all in evidence in the same letter, written from San Juan in 1943. He sends money for my father's college graduation ring and money for his mother, with the stipulation that she spend it on herself. He promises he will buy a suit and have his picture taken for her, and he offers to pick up cigarettes for his father, since they are six cents a pack. He also gives assurances that he is going to church, and describes at length the bodies he's seen in glass coffins in the cathedral, as well as that of "Ponce De Lon, the fellow who was looking for the water of youth."

Eddie spent his life on the water, from his adolescence in the Merchant Marine to his leisure hours on his outboard motorboats, the first named after my cousin Maureen and the second after my sister Marianne, the first- and last-born in my generation of cousins. Though he started out in precincts in upper Manhattan and the South Bronx, in the Three-Four and Four-One, he spent the largest part of his career, from 1961 to 1975, in the coveted Harbor Unit, on patrol in the waters of the city. If my view of his cop life on land is somewhat hazy, on the water it is completely lost in fog, and even now I'm not sure what cops in Harbor do for eight hours and thirty-five minutes a day. In Eddie's NYPD files, I found a few letters of thanks from people he helped after their boats capsized, and in one of my father's scrapbooks— Eddie favored the scrap heap over the scrapbook—I discovered a *Daily News* clipping, from July 19, 1965:

SHOWER AIR CONDITIONS
THE CITY

A violent thunderstorm which struck the metropolitan area yesterday afternoon drove temperatures down 8 degrees in one hour, knocked out power in five sections of Staten Island and flooded the Belt Parkway in Brooklyn for three miles.

In Coney Island an 8-year-old boy was struck by a piece of masonry knocked off a building by lightning. A 24-foot sea skiff . . . owned and operated by Joseph Derrico, 53, of 2132 LaFontaine Ave., Bronx, exploded and burned off the northwest end of Hart Island at 2:45 p.m.

Derrico, who was alone on the craft, said he was in the rear and that the explosion occurred up front. He thought it must have been caused by lightning. He leaped overboard and was picked up by a police launch.

Patrolmen Edward Conlon and Charles Bengston, in another police launch, saw Derrico jump and went aboard the burning craft to make sure no one else was aboard. They suffered minor burns and smoke poisoning. Derrico was unhurt.

Cops are awarded medals for this kind of incident, and deservedly so. But since we have to write up these exploits ourselves for commendations, Eddie would have been disinclined to bother, out of both laziness and modesty. *Why would I want everybody to know that I jumped onto a burning boat, when the guy on it already had the sense to jump off?* It happened, and no real harm was done, so why dwell on it? When he told the story at the bar, or to his nieces and nephews, he could embellish it with pirates and sharks. Such stories were not for medals or to impress bosses, but for a few laughs before you went back to sea.

In Harbor, these rescues are not only of the living. Every year around tax time in April, the winter jumpers become the spring floaters; the holiday suicides undergo a bodily sea change in the warming water and rise to the surface, as if prompted by second thoughts when the days grow bright and long again. Eddie liked to wander around on Hart Island in the Sound, which has been the city's Potter's Field since the Civil War. The unknown and unclaimed dead are buried there by prisoners from Rikers Island. When my family went out on his boat, we would sometimes pass by the flat and green haunch of land, where bones fell from the little dirt bluffs around the shoreline.

Those years when Eddie was in Harbor were tumultuous ones for the City and the Job. Narcotics flooded the streets and crime surged, and racial tensions and civil unrest broke out into violence, while he sat it out on Launch #13, maneuvering through the swells. When the City nearly went bankrupt in the mid-seventies, he returned to shore, to the Four-Seven, in the north-central Bronx, a neighborhood that changed from the old trio of Irish-Italian-Jewish to West Indian during his time there. Though he finished his career on land, I still think of him as a helmsman, as much at ease in the ebb and flow of street life as he was on the tides, a steady little vessel in the great, mercurial element. He was never a "collar man," but he took care of what came his way, whether it was an armed robbery or a family dispute. He often drove his lieutenant, Eddie Donovan, who became a close friend. Donovan told me a story about a time they were parked outside a nursing school on a winter night, having a cup of coffee. There was an abandoned car beside them, and when a sleepy derelict stirred within the car, it startled them. A nun then came out from the school to tell them to drive the man off, complaining that he was a loud drunk and an obnoxious panhandler. Donovan told me, "Eddie then gave the nun a lecture on Christian charity that made her blush. By the end, she went back inside and brought the man blankets, and Eddie gave him five bucks out of his own pocket. Things like that were continuous with Eddie, he was such an easy touch for people who were down on their luck. When he had the cells, he would sometimes add his own money for the prisoner meals, so they could get something decent."

For Eddie, to be a cop was to have a lot of fun and do a little good. If you missed out on either, shame on you. Because his pleasures and his labors were so simple and so long-standing—in the same apartment, in the same job, with his free time spent in his boat and the bar around the corner—his theater of identity served a purpose; he was a kind of reverse Walter Mitty, supplying daydreams to lives that needed a jolt or a twist. Eddie's sense of play came from a denial of the seriousness of things, a view of fate that says, *Don't kid a kidder,* as the polite version of the saying goes. At his wake, there were stories that began, "I never knew he wasn't a lion tamer," and others that ended, "And it was only when the plane landed that I realized he didn't have a pilot's license." They went on for two days at the funeral parlor on Broadway in Kingsbridge, told by patrolmen and officers of high rank, guys from the boatyard with names like "Pinkie," and people from the neighborhood, then and now. But even when the stories were told, by men red-eyed with laughter and grief at once, they often had a "you had to be there" quality that was pronounced even for the circumstance. Eddie was the subject of stories more often than the teller of them, an actor who improvised for the moment. He had a talent for making things up as he went along, and he had come to a full stop.

At St. John's Church, across the street from Vanity Court, six officers in dress blues carried out Eddie's coffin, snapping a final, white-gloved salute as he left for Gate of Heaven to join his parents. It was an Inspector's Funeral, and many cops would argue that he died in the line of duty, in his way, passing away so soon after serving so long. His commanding officer, Inspector - Thomas Mullen, was there in uniform, lending the ceremony an air of purpose and belonging, as if Eddie had at long last been promoted after decades on patrol. Mullen lived in the neighborhood and was a friend of my parents'. When Mullen was a patrolman, my father introduced him to his friends, and Mullen in turn looked out for Eddie the Cop. Mullen later went to Bronx Narcotics, and he helped me get there, when it was in Eddie's old precinct, the old Four-One, the "Fort Apache" of legend. At the time, I thought that if I'd died then—had my other uncle been right—I don't think the other messengers or copy-machine operators I had worked with could have mustered up much of a send-off.

But the NYPD had not yet entered my thoughts as a possibility of livelihood, still less a life. It was a private world, like that of Eddie's apartment— which hadn't been painted since the New Deal, and probably hadn't been cleaned since the Kennedy Administration—and it intrigued me mostly because I wasn't allowed inside, rather than because of any obvious allure of its own. Within weeks, however, I was living in Vanity Court, and the Conlons would continue on Kingsbridge Avenue for another decade. But if the Job - didn't appear to be the life for me, at least not then, it became increasingly clear that I had to find what was, or would be. I had enough of my father in me to know that it was time to move on.

And I had enough of Eddie in me to go where I wanted, indifferent to reproach and immune to regret. Near the end of his life, at some family dinner for Easter or Thanksgiving, we were all watching old Super-8 movies from the '60s and '70s that had been transferred to videotape. The jumpiness of the hand-held camera gave the old footage an accidental vitality, as if the juice, the tempo of those days, could barely be contained on film. My uncle had no children and little time remaining, which would incline most people to a retrospective mood. But he stayed on a couch on the far side of the room, indifferent to the fishing trips and First Communion parties that had enlivened the past decades. I went over to him and sat down, asking if he wanted to watch the tape. "Nah," he said, a look of calm bemusement on his face. "I never look back."

• • •

MY FATHER KNEW THAT HISTORY NOT ONLY REPEATED IT-self, but often spoke louder the second time around. Strange as it seems now, I looked up to cops more than he did. Not all of my friends' fathers were cops, but a number were: Rich Ferrari, Mike Gilchrist, and Brian O'Connor all had cops for fathers, and there were other men like Inspector Mullen in the neighborhood. Beneath the surface of the uniform, I saw a uniform sub-stance, strong and caring and fair, if not always welcome when you were out with your friends. FBI agents don't wear uniforms, and my father's job was often not like theirs, though the difference was more pronounced in the past. My father had been a police officer briefly, after the war, though I don't think he spent a day on patrol. He took a leave of absence after the Academy to go to law school. In his scrapbook, I found a clipping from the July 2, 1948, *Journal-American* of his graduating class, which expresses a sense of nearly ra-diant patriotism and achingly local hope. The caption quotes from the address delivered by Commissioner Arthur W. Wallender, who "ordered the new policemen to 'use rough tactics with criminals and kindness with the general public.'" My father is somewhere amid the sea of faces in the photograph—all men, all veterans, and mostly white, though with more black faces than might be expected—whose diverging horizons draw the eye back like the crosses of Arlington Cemetery. But its broadcast of a great, collective "Attaboy!" is under-cut by my memory of my father's ambivalence. Wallender would resign in a few years, driven out by the Harry Gross scandal, as would his boss, the ex-cop and friend of the family Mayor William O'Dwyer. As my father told it, the Job was a kind of safety net, and he had just begun to climb the ladder: "I was a veteran, a Marine lieutenant—acting captain, for a while," a college gradu-ate for whom the GI Bill offered still more opportunity, in a city and country and a time of promise as none other in history. He could do better than the NYPD, he felt, and ambitious men in the police department faced their own peculiar risks: "People would tell me, 'With your background, we'll get you on the Commissioner's Squad, no problem—you'll get rich!'" He wanted no part of it. My father had many friends in the NYPD—a few retired cops have told me, with some vehemence, that my father was the only FBI agent they ever got along with—but he felt it was not the place for him.

The NYPD was a more human institution than the FBI, for better and worse; more varied in its actors and aims. The NYPD was subject to the pressures and compromises of local politics, whereas the FBI was led by a man who, regardless of his other qualities, had led an independent and professional organization for decades. Nonetheless, there was ample room in the field of play for honorable men, and because those men were the ones I knew, their characters reflected the character of the Job. The stories of villainous police officers that sometimes appeared in the newspapers were seen as rarities, and their portrayals in movies and TV were silly cartoons. Men like Pat Brown were figures from a distant and long-dead age. And so when Eddie's old friend Davey—his partner in crime from the impostor prank that Uncle Joe had described in his letter—came over to the house after the wake and reminisced about his time on the Job, he brightened our dark days with some very strange light.

Davey was wiry and fair, in a checked tweed blazer and a Bavarian-style hat, with a narrow brim and a jaunty green feather. I noticed the hat because he wore it indoors, but also because I'd heard he'd killed a lot of Germans during the war—he was highly decorated, and even captured a U-boat—and I was tempted to check the lining for a Nazi scalp. Davey had availed himself generously of the spoils of war, which was apparently a habit he'd picked up in childhood: his mother was the Democratic district leader who likely arranged my grandmother's audience with Boss Flynn, and she and Davey were the caretakers of various historical sites. My father told me that they sold many of the beds that George Washington was said to have slept in, several times over. As Davey sat in our living room, slight and quick as a ferret, he told cop stories of such plain and unapologetic corruption that any comment by my father would have been pointless, like taking a cannibal to task for his table manners. On television, when a crooked cop spoke of his misdeeds, it was usually in a haltingly pious, broken-backed apology, a confession from the bowels of shame. By contrast, Davey was the cat, as he might have put it himself, who ate the canary.

My father told me that Davey once led cops from Internal Affairs in a high-speed pursuit, which led to his tossing a load of guns off the George Washington Bridge. I don't know if he heard it third- or fourth-hand, if Eddie told him, or if Davey said so himself, still less what truth or embellishment accompanied the source. When I read a few articles from the summer of 1958, there was no doubt that much had been left unsaid; the question was whether they even told of another escapade entirely. The *Daily News* broke the story:

POLICEMAN HELD IN PISTOL THEFTS
6 TAKEN FROM PROPERTY CLERK IN BRONX—
SPECIAL SQUAD TRACES MISSING ARMS

A Bronx policeman was held on $7,500 bail yesterday on charges of stealing six pistols from the Bronx office of the Police Department property clerk. He was also charged with possessing two other weapons stolen from a policeman's locker in 1955.

Patrolman David . . .žwas arrested Thursday after a three-week investigation by a special police detail. The police said that [Davey] who has been on the force eleven years, had traded the six pistols to a Yonkers dealer for merchandise, money, and two other pistols. In addition, the investigators said, two pistols stolen from a policeman's locker at the Bathgate Avenue station were found among thirteen unregistered weapons in [his] possession. . . .ž

Two days later, the *Times* ran an update:

2 ARE ARRAIGNED IN POLICE ROBBERY

With the arrest of two more cops, however, the gun dealer in Yonkers reconsidered his identification of Davey, who apparently bore a strong resemblance to one of them. And three days later, the *Times* reported that this doubt had borne fruit:

PATROLMAN CLEARED OF STEALING PISTOLS

Though Davey still faced charges relating to the theft of guns from another cop's locker, his luck held, and within two weeks, it was all sorted out:

POLICE THEFT JURY INDICTS 2, CLEARS ONE

They had a witness and a lot of guns, and then they had nothing. Now, especially, I would have loved to hear how Davey beat the case, but it also seems rude, like pestering a magician to explain a trick.

In ordinary police procedurals, a clever sleuth finds the culprit, as his unerring instinct guides him through a maze of obstacles. In Davey's version, there was something of this, too, in form if not content. "It happened on the Upper West Side, an old lady kicked the bucket," began one account, as he settled into his easy chair, the children gathering around him on the floor. "She was a junkie, it turns out, there's more of them like that than you'd think. The sergeant called me in to help search the place, which was a wreck—piles of magazines, stacks of laundry, books up to the ceiling." When someone dies alone, the police have to search the scene to secure valuables, safeguarding them until the next of kin can be located. "These other cops were sick of it, ripping through her old underwear and coming up with morphine—what a disgrace, the old bitch!—when something told me to take a look up on the top shelf of the bookcase. It was a thick medical book, and I climbed up and opened it. It was a fake book, with a pocket inside, and there was thirty thousand dollars in cash!" Davey sat back and smiled modestly, as if he were Sherlock Holmes discovering the Duchess's necklace in the maid's pantry. I don't remember if he smoked a pipe, but when I imagine him now, that impression grows stronger. "After that, they always called me in for DOAs. I always knew where the money was."

In Davey's chronicles of larceny, he was a figure of canny aplomb, favored by fortune and making the most of his luck. For most of his career, he was a motorcycle cop: "A lot of times in a car wreck, people get knocked right out of their shoes," he went on. "Now there was one wreck where a priest was killed, thrown clean from his car, and he's lying dead in his socks. You know how well priests dress, and I found the shoes, they were better than anything I'd ever seen, and brand-new. And wouldn't you know, they were my size, exactly! I thought, is this a sign from God, or is this a sign from God! When the sergeant came to the scene, he asked where the shoes were, and I said, 'You know, Sarge, how a lot of times in a car wreck . . .'"

I didn't want to brood over what Davey might have prayed for, or how his prayers were answered. There was much to take in. St. Augustine said that evil was not a phenomenon in and of itself, but an absence of good, much like cold and dark have no physical reality beyond the absence of light and heat. And yet you could see this creeping nothingness, like an eclipse. Was there something more than something missing in this man, who came to the wake to tell funny stories about robbing corpses? He had no fear, no shame, and not enough money, plainly and in no particular order. Maybe he did only lack things, as if he had a hole in his pocket that he kept on trying to fill.

But why did we welcome him, even in our home? Again, I thought it better to listen now, and think about it later. I knew from my father that Dave and Eddie were friends from childhood, but they had never worked together. Though I don't doubt my uncle's integrity—I doubt if he even would have liked the stories—he knew Dave well and long and remained fond of him. And so we listened with some trepidation when Dave began a story that cast them both as police officers, when the uniforms they wore weren't rented. "I had a partner who thought he could ride a motorcycle better than me, poor man. One night we decided to have a race in Central Park," he commenced, and then proceeded to recount the curves and straightaways as the two men flew through the park, with Davey allowing his partner to stay close enough to appear to be competitive. Then, rounding a turn into a transverse, the man tried to take the lead, and collided head-on with a taxi. "The driver was an old Jew, he came out crying, 'My God! I've killed a policeman! Oy vey! Vat vill I do?'" Davey knew that that the accident wasn't that bad—he'd get no new shoes that night—and took the driver aside. "I tell him, 'He's not dead, my friend, but this is very serious business. If you do exactly as I tell you, you might make it through this all right.' Now I happen to know there's a problem with this kind of motorcycle, a manufacturing defect—there's a weakness in the front struts and they sometimes give out. I says, 'Now try to remember, and be very clear. Did you see, as my partner and I were driving along at a moderate rate of speed—slowly, even better, you saw us drive slowly—when you saw the front of his motorcycle buckle down. . . .' And he says, 'Ya, ya, I can see that, I remember, that is exactly how it happened. . . .'"

His partner suffered a broken leg and was brought to a hospital on Fifth Avenue ("a very boola-boola joint," in Davey's phrase), which distressed the partner in its way as much as the injury. At that point, Davey called Eddie and apprised him of what had developed. That night, Eddie went to the hospital and announced that he was a police surgeon and would require a stethoscope and surgical gown. So costumed, he clamored for a nurse to escort him to the cop's room, where he viewed his patient with alarm and dismissed her: "My God! What kind of hospital are you running here, anyway!" He lit a cigarette and ominously reviewed the chart. After a period of study, he took his cigarette and placed it between the man's toes, which protruded from the end of his cast. Putting on the stethoscope, he listened to the man's pulse, in his chest first ("Mmmm, not good"), then moving on to his head ("Brain waves very weak"), and leg, newly plastered and smoking from the toes: "No, no, no. Officer, I don't know what these quacks told you, but this leg has to come off, toot-sweet." With fierce dispatch, he tossed the chart away, collected his cigarette, and marched out of the room. The terrorized cop called his wife, who raced to the hospital and had the car waiting as he hobbled out to escape. For my uncle, at least, the Job came with great benefits.

For Dave, however, the story had a bittersweet ending: "The motorcycle company paid out sixty thousand dollars for the accident, split between my partner and the old Jew. Did I see a nickel of it? No, I did not!"

The first shock was that these things happened; the second was that we learned of them in what was more a boast than a confession; the third, far longer in coming, was that we didn't even hold it against him. Davey's tales were a kind gesture, in their awful way, making us laugh as we prepared for a burial. And it was not the first time he had done such a thing for my father. In the first days of 1952, when he and Eddie buried their father, Davey came to the funeral. Their mother had been dead for seven years by then, and their youngest brother, Gerry, was eleven years old. What a winter it must have seemed, to be orphans and parents at once. Requiem means rest, but not for them; as they left the church, all the hymns and prayers, the promises of God in a dead language, faded in their ears. They would have mustered on the cold, familiar sidewalk in their black ties and fedoras, smoking cigarettes, as they readied to leave for the cold, familiar fields of the cemetery. And then Davey arrived, in uniform on his motorcycle, at the head of a delegation of cops on bikes, helmets gleaming and engines roaring, in formation at the head of the cortege. They led the hearse and the line of cars northward through the city streets, as other cars pulled aside to let them pass, and the drivers must have wondered which dignitary had died and deserved such splendid ceremony. They did not stop at the city line but drove on, commanding the highways until they reached the place called Gate of Heaven and saw my grandfather home. And so my father must have been glad that Davey had been there then, as he was now, and glad he had not seen much of him in the intervening years, and gladder still that it was not his place to judge.

• • •

IF DAVEY SHOWED ME THE KIND OF COP THAT MY FATHER feared, a few months later, one of my closest friends provided a dramatic counterpoint, offering the Job such talent and heart that it hardly knew what to do with it. And when Mike Kelly took up his beat in Spanish Harlem, my father was angrier with him than he ever could have been with Davey. Mike Kelly had gone to Regis with me, and then on to Williams College. After graduation, he worked for the Chase Manhattan Bank, and seemed destined for a steady ascent through the white-collar world of the city. Which, as my father saw it, was as it should be. Our families were close: my parents looked on Mike as a son, and I was at the Kellys' in Brooklyn with their seven children almost as often as at my own house.

My father had a particular fondness for Mike, not just as a surrogate son but almost as a surrogate self—the resemblance between them was stronger, in many ways, than it was between my father and me. Mike even had a younger brother, Pat, who also became a cop, and he reminded me of my Uncle Eddie. Both Mike and my father were strivers, with a seriousness of purpose and a self-sufficiency that I lacked; from an early age, the Kelly boys worked as teamsters during the summer, covering the cost of their education and helping with household expenses. Both were readers, especially of history. Now that I think back, both had the quality that Father Callahan, our sophomore-year Latin teacher, tried to describe when he talked about "pious Aeneas," who founded Rome after the defeat of Troy. By piety, he didn't mean its modern sense of something fussy and narrow, an almost fearful clinging to old conventions, but a steadiness and strength that came from its roots in the past. Aeneas was a man who carried the stones of the old city until he found the place to build the new. When it turned out that, for Mike, the new city would be Spanish Harlem, it wasn't exactly what my father had in mind. Mike received no offers to get rich by joining the Commissioner's Squad, but that's not what mattered most to my father. The move was not only against common sense—to leave a bank for a beat when you have loans to pay off—but a violation of something deeper, a derailment of our progress in America that was closer to a crime against nature than a bad career choice. From the hardscrabble West of Ireland to the docks of Hell's Kitchen, to the apartments in the Bronx and then our house in Yonkers, where we moved when I was young, the generational trend in the Conlon and Kelly families had been to move up and out. For Mike to choose as he did, he might as well have announced that he was going back to Ballinrobe, to tend a few sheep and dig potatoes with a stick. For months, my father was mad, and I had to hear about it. "If you have any influence with your poor friend Mike Kelly," he would begin, as if I could have talked Mike out of it, even if I'd wanted to.

For one thing, I thought it was funny, in the way it's funny when any of your friends does something stupid. For another, Mike was happier than I'd ever seen him. At the bank, he looked as if he was going gray from within, but the Job brought out a sense of fervor and mission. In the Academy, he was somewhat self-conscious, and glad that no one had heard of Williams College, one of the "little Ivies," to spare himself the questions and complaints of his classmates, who by and large would have taken the same position as my father. Given that he was a twenty-four-year-old Irish kid from Brooklyn, the gap between him and the other rookies was not exactly un-bridgeable, but there were moments when he slipped up. One day in law class, the teacher asked him to explain the Fourth Amendment, and since he was dozing or daydreaming, his response was unguardedly good:

"The right of the people to be secure in their persons and their homes, their papers and effects, shall not be abridged, except . . ." As he rattled off the text, he noticed that the rest of the class was staring at him. "And shit like that," he concluded.

Mike graduated first in his class of two thousand, which gave him his choice of precincts. A cousin was a lieutenant in the Two-Three, which covered 96th to 116th Street, from Fifth Avenue east to the river. It was a bad neighborhood, except for the lower extremity, which touched on the Upper East Side and the yuppies—a term that was new at the time, and the group to which Mike might otherwise have belonged—and the remnants of an Italian enclave at the northeast edge, which I called Very Little Italy. It was a good choice, for Mike: bad enough to keep him busy but not unrelievedly poor, and, for him, the closest bad neighborhood in Manhattan, the center of the world as we knew it. Mike worked steady day tours, which allowed him to go to school at night for a master's in criminal justice at John Jay College. Day tours—the second platoon of three, following the midnights and leading to the four-to-twelves—are usually the slowest, in terms of crime, but the most engaged with the neighborhood, at its most benign and routine. School opens and lets out, the streets are full of *mamis* on their errands. Men who work have left for work, and the men who don't aren't up until at least mid-way through the tour. More than at any other time of day, you see the people who are happy to see a cop, and with Mike, their expectations were fulfilled. After his tour ended, he volunteered at a community center called the Oasis, tutoring and playing basketball with the kids. Although the stories he liked to tell were not action-movie arrests but adventures in absurdity—"Did I ever tell you about the time I nabbed the infamous cheese bandit of 103rd Street?"—Mike's belief in the white knighthood of the Job never abated.

That belief was what Mike was most afraid of losing, I think—I never heard him talk about his personal safety, as a real concern that lasted beyond a few moments of danger, fighting an EDP, facing a volatile domestic dispute, and so on. The threat was to his faith in the Job—what the Job meant, as a whole; what it would do to him, and with him, in the event of some crisis. And the crises we read about usually came in the form of racism or corruption. In a sense, he expected to encounter them in the NYPD not because it was an especially crooked or racist institution, but because these evils were part of the human condition, and to be a cop meant you would experience humanity at a level of skinned-alive intensity. The fact that a Brooklyn neighbor was one of the cops involved in the "Buddy Boys" scandal, which involved a ring of drug-dealing thieves and became a book by journalist Mike McAlary, didn't make him rest any easier. But the fact remains that he never saw any corruption, never saw a cop take a nickel or even heard of any who did.

Racism was another matter, not nearly as simple, and if what he saw - wasn't enough to shake his faith, there was much to challenge his reason. Mike was from a part of Brooklyn that had reconvened from other parts that had "turned"—turned bad, or turned black, which to the shame of liberals and the bitter delight of bigots often meant the same thing. But in the aftermath of racially charged killings in Bensonhurst and Howard Beach, the attitude of simply being fair in how you dealt with people, and figuring it out as you went along, didn't seem to be quite enough, either. After Mike went to the Two-Three, he was sometimes partnered with an old-timer who used racial slurs almost as if they were punctuation marks. Mike didn't like it, and tried to explain why the best he could—which, in a rookie-veteran partnership, is somewhat like an altar boy preaching to the Pope. In most ways, the old-timer was a plainly decent guy, and his treatment of people was respectful, no matter if it masked an abstract contempt. On the street, or responding to a job, he handled matters with the amiable pragmatism of the veteran city cop, and face to face, he was an effective public servant. But once they retreated to the car, it was all color commentary, so to speak: "Would you believe how these niggers . . ." and "It reminds me of the time this spic . . ." Suffice it to say that they agreed to disagree, Mike being a fair guy who figured it out as he went along. And then came a day that made it all the more confusing. Mike was at court or on vacation—not on patrol, in any case—when his partner went into a burning building, alone, and saved an elderly black woman. Mike was never able to reconcile his partner's constant and audible prejudice with his act of color-blind heroism. In the old-timer's case, the divorce between word and deed was wide enough that there's at least one black person who is grateful he worked as a cop.

Mike's own call to arms came at an unexpected time and place as well. He was in his apartment with his fiancée, Tara, in the Bay Ridge section of Brooklyn, which was mostly middle-class Irish and Italian. Late one night, Mike and Tara were awakened by a loud disturbance on the street, and when it became clear that they would not sleep again soon, Mike took a look out the window. From his third-floor room, he could make out five or six white guys surrounding a Hispanic man on the street, closing in on him, then stepping back as he brandished a screwdriver. Mike shouted at them to knock it off, and when they didn't, he threw water at them, which sometimes works on dogs. It was the summer of the riots in Washington Heights, which Mike had been sent to: three nights of burning and looting after a cop killed a drug dealer who was trying to kill him. Mike dreaded the thought of Bay Ridge joining Howard Beach and Bensonhurst on the martyrs' trail, of riot duty at work followed by protests at home, of having to push past the Reverend Al Sharpton and the cameras to get to his dinner. Whether the Hispanic man was right or wrong, whether he was coming home from the job he worked at for a hundred hours a week—turning screws, I suppose—or whether the white guys caught him stealing hubcaps, it didn't much matter—or it - wouldn't, as Washington Heights had proved. And so Mike picked up his badge and gun, told Tara to call 911, grabbed the first piece of clothing at hand, and headed down to the street. As soon as he entered the fray, he stopped it cold. It might have been the badge, and it was more likely the gun, but it was even more probable that what shocked the combatants into détente was the fact that Mike was wearing Tara's nightgown.

When you see a statue of Justice, remember: she usually carries a sword but she always wears a dress. Though Tara's message to 911—"Mexicans . . . screwdrivers . . . Sharpton . . . *and tell Michael that I love him!*"—may not have been entirely lucid, the situation must have been powerfully confusing to the responding officers. Mike shouted that he was a cop, but he wasn't the only one shouting:

"Put your hands up!"

"Put the gun down!"

"Don't move! Don't move! *Don't move!*"

One cop approached Mike, grabbed his outstretched hand—which still held the gun—and it went off. Mayhem broke out, briefly, but Mike gave up his gun and assumed the position. The other cops moved in, and they put - everyone against the wall till the collective blood pressure went down. The bullet had gone through an apartment window across the street, but everything was spared except a pane of glass and the peace of mind of the old woman who lived there. The duty captain arrived—a rotating assignment for precinct commanders, covering the borough—in time for Mike to recover his composure if not his pants. When a cop shoots his gun, either punishment or praise is allotted, as a matter of course: either you get a medal or you lose time, from a loss of vacation days to a potential prison sentence. In this case, which entailed an accidental bad thing happening during a good deed brought about in a deeply weird manner, no easy judgment was available, and so Mike was simply told not to do it again. Sometimes, Justice wears a blindfold because she'd rather not know. And so the city held together, that night and for many to follow, with our many warring tribes gathered in enforced harmony beneath the soft skirts of Patrolman Kelly.

My father couldn't remain mad at Mike for long, and as it happened, things got better at home for me, too, not least because I left it, weeks after Eddie's death. My father eased up on me; maybe he'd lost some of his fight, as if part of him had gone into the ground with Eddie, or—as I prefer to think—because he kept something of Eddie with him. Things between us had never been terrible, in retrospect, but after I left home, they were positively good. When I was in high school, he once threatened to throw me out of the house—at the same time, I threatened to leave—and though neither of us threatened lightly, it came to nothing, when tempers cooled, and my father asked me to stay "for your mother's sake." After Eddie's death, he realized that what time we had together would not be well spent on lectures, which never had much of an effect on me anyway. We would not be partners, as he had been with Eddie, but he would have to trust me to find my place in the world. It would not be far away, or long in coming: within a month, I moved into Eddie's apartment in Vanity Court and found a real job. It wasn't as a cop—in a sense it was the opposite—but now I see it as taking a step back, readying myself for the big jump. From the time of the wake, I began to realize that the NYPD, which could employ Davey, Mike Kelly, and Inspector Mullen, not to mention Uncle Eddie, offered entry into a drama as rich as any in Shakespeare. And I didn't want to hear the story as much as I wanted to tell it, and I didn't want to tell the story as much as I wanted to join it.

• • •

A FEW WEEKS AFTER UNCLE EDDIE DIED, MY COUSIN SISTER Patricia Daly, O.P. (aka "Patty the Nun"), offered me an extra ticket to a big fund-raising dinner. Not one to turn down a free meal, I went, and I met a friend of hers, a Jesuit priest named James Joyce, who introduced me to a friend of his named Janet Storti, who ran a small social-service agency in Brooklyn called Consultants for Criminal Justice Alternatives. The position of Court Liaison was available—it had been most recently filled by Meyer Lansky's nephew, but I wasn't to make too much of that—which involved meeting indicted or convicted felons, writing up their life stories, and proposing alternatives to prison, usually some combination of community service, counseling, education, and job training. Though the undertaking would have pleased my predecessor's uncle more than mine, my father was more than content that I had a job of any kind. And so it was by a chance meeting, a few words, and a handshake, amid echoes of Irish writers and Jewish gangsters, that I started on the road to the Job.

Consultants for Criminal Justice Alternatives was a mouthful to say, and it suggested something massive and shadowy, as if what we did took place in an outbuilding on the grounds of the Rand Corporation. There were as many people employed there, in fact, as there were words in the title, which was shortened to CCJA. There was Janet the boss; Sheryl the secretary; Liz and Louis and me, who had different titles but did the same thing. When a defendant in a criminal case cannot afford a lawyer—which in New York City is in the vast majority of instances—they are represented by the Legal Aid Society or a private attorney, paid by the state, from a list known as the 18B panel. We worked for 18B, and other defendants were referred to us by judges who knew us—usually in cases in which they were inclined to give a defendant a break, and wanted us to give them a reason to do so. We handled fewer than eighty cases a year, and as there were some fifteen thousand felony indictments annually in Brooklyn at the time, we had the luxury of choice. As one defense lawyer told me—he was also a Jesuit priest—"After you get your third baby-killer in a row, you don't want to go to work anymore." We were engaged on behalf of people whose guilt was not in doubt but whose futures, hopefully, were; we would try to cut a deal for the deserving. The idea was a good one, however slight its effect on the raw volume of cases in the system, and as I saw it, it worked—though there were surprises in our successes and our failures.

My first case was my best case, and my hardest. It involved a great kid who became a bona-fide bad guy, quite suddenly, but who looked as if he - could be turned around again. Jack was "a rare case with a real chance," as I later told the court, precisely the kind of defendant we should be fighting for. His case was also, on the face of it, a loser: Jack had been arrested three times for robbery within a year, all of them "wolf-pack"-style muggings, in which a group of teenagers had roughed up another teenager and taken a hat or a chain or a radio. Jack had pled to a misdemeanor on the first case; the second two were still open. After the third arrest, his mother wouldn't bail him out, and he was sent to Spofford, the juvenile jail in the South Bronx, where he had been for a few months before I got the case. He was fifteen years old. Judges tend to feel in these cases that the defendant hasn't been getting the message, and a stronger one has to be sent. They are right.

Until the year before, Jack had been a good athlete and an excellent student, popular with adults and other kids. At his parish grammar school in Bushwick, St. Barbara's, he had led the youth group, and he'd been selected as a delegate to Washington for a conference sponsored by the Kennedy Center. From there, he'd attended a special junior high school, in which all students were required to pass an entrance examination, and his mother, Maria, proudly showed me the trophies he'd won at graduation, for English, Science, Physical Education, and Community Service. Both his science teacher and the assistant principal raved to me about Jack, and they even went to visit him at Spofford—the only time I've ever heard of teachers making jail visits, before or since.

This transition from honor student to inmate was occasioned by three events, in the span of a few months: his family left Bushwick for Brighton Beach, a better neighborhood but a move that left St. Barbara's behind, along with his teachers, counselors, and friends; his special junior high school was superseded by a huge, chaotic, and gang-infested high school in Manhattan; and a reunion with his long-absent father took place just before the father's death from AIDS. "I changed," Jack said. At home, he became withdrawn and argumentative, eating little and sleeping often. At his new school, his grades were poor and he began to cut class. He also hung around with a wild bunch of kids who called themselves "the Decepticons," and he got into fights. Two months after Maria had a heart attack, Jack and a few other Decepticons took someone's radio, and he was arrested again.

When I first met Jack, it was painful to witness his nostalgia, especially when it was so well-earned. He was a fifteen-year-old kid in prison coveralls, talking about his trip to the Kennedy Center and how the hotel had "HBO and rugs and everything." He was handsome and well-built, with an openness to his expression that usually doesn't last long in jail. He was at once a regular kid—his mother described his interests, before things changed, as "weights, basketball, and girls . . . he spent a lot of time smiling in the mirror," and a special kid, personable, articulate, and bright. He knew what he had going for him, and he knew what he was up against.

Jail proved to be just the place for Jack. He picked up a lot of his old, good habits, and his new teachers and counselors began to repeat the accolades I'd heard before. His social worker told me, "It's a good thing he was in here. It shook him up—he feels he let a lot of people down." His dormitory supervisor was even more enthusiastic: "He's a beautiful kid, a great kid. Of all the kids I've seen come through here, and I've seen a lot of them, Jack is one of the best. He has tremendous, tremendous potential." Everyone I spoke to thought Jack could readjust to life outside, as long as he was provided with a significant degree of structure; I wanted to make sure the structure wasn't made of cinder block and barbed wire.

I found a residential school in upstate New York for "gifted but troubled youth," which would have been ideal, as Jack excelled in both categories. I got him admitted to the school and found a way to pay for its fifty-thousand-per-year tuition. I amassed statistics, showing that the juvenile prison system was not only significantly more expensive, but utterly disastrous for kids like Jack: for fifteen-year-old urban minorities with multiple violent crimes, the recidivism rate was over 90 percent. At the school, where Jack's record was not regarded as abnormally or unworkably grave, the recidivism rate was under 15 percent, and three-quarters of their graduates went on to college. If they listened to me, I would argue, Jack would be saved, and if they didn't, he was doomed. I had convinced myself, at least.

In my report, I wrote about the Decepticons, the gang Jack had joined in Manhattan. The childishness of it struck me—they were named after the villains in a cartoon called *The Transformers,* in which cars and trucks turned into missile-shooting robots—and I thought the silly juvenility of it all would show that we were hardly dealing with Murder, Inc. On the day of the sentencing, the front page of the Metro section of *The New York Times* led with the headline A GANG GIVES A NAME TO STUDENTS' FEAR: DECEPTICONS. The article said that the gang was organized so loosely that no one quite knew who or where they were, and this anonymity helped feed the legend of its menace in city high schools. As I entered the courtroom, I felt a little sick.

The judge had many shortcomings, but alas, he wasn't illiterate. He had read the *Times.* He read my report, too, but his interpretation of it wasn't mine. "So you're saying, because he's bright, he shouldn't be held responsible? Because his home is a good one, he shouldn't do time? These are arguments *for* a prison sentence, not the opposite." He asked me if I had anything to say, and, heart in my throat, I made a stammering, angry speech. I didn't insult or provoke him, I think, but in truth I don't recall exactly what I said. The judge sentenced Jack to two to six years in the maximum-security version of juvenile prison. I felt nauseated. Jack looked sad but stoic. "It's all right, Mr. Conlon," he said, touching my arm. "Thanks for everything. You gonna be okay?"

After Jack, I kept my distance from my clients. The cases tended to fall into two categories: people like Jack, who had led ordinary and even good lives that fell apart in a short period or through a single act, and found themselves as far away from the familiar as if they'd swum into a rip tide. These sudden derailments were easier to work with than those in the other category—those of the non-starters, who seemed to have been doomed from the outset, and who arguably deserved a break from the system, since they had never had a break in life. For some of these, the debate was chiefly over what kind of cage they should be in, as when I visited a guy named Dwayne at the prison hospital at Rikers Island. He believed he needed his sneakers in order to breathe, and he had a habit of exposing himself and assaulting interviewers. He had been picked up in the subway for carrying a Molotov cocktail, and CCJA hoped to put him in a hospital instead of prison.

Or Frank, a cheerful, chubby, and middle-aged Italian man with the mind of an eight-year-old brat and the body of his great-grandfather, and whose heart disease, diabetes, and hypertension required a dozen medications that didn't mix well with lithium and mixed worse with crack. Frank had tried to make off with a refrigerator from a construction site. Because of his lifelong history of such offenses, he was in jail, where his chances for survival were slim. There are places for mentally ill people, and places for addicts, and places for the physically ill, but I could find only one for all three, and they didn't want him because, years before, he'd set a fire in another institution—after, he told me, he had been raped. Arsonists aren't welcome anywhere. But if I could get him admitted to Kings County Hospital, and then transferred to a state hospital, he could be evaluated and placed from there. I went to court and offered to take him in myself.

"Okay," said the judge, and he released the big lunatic into my custody. Frank was like a two-hundred-and-fifty-pound puppy, not nearly ready to be let off the leash, which I wished I had thought to bring. He wore oversized hospital pants that kept falling down. I called Mike Kelly, who was a rookie cop then, and he picked us up. Frank liked Mike. He liked lots of things—me, crack, and other people's refrigerators—and he gabbed away as we sat in the emergency room of the massive gothic red-brick hospital, amid the survivors of car wrecks and gunshots, and howling schizophrenics who made Frank look as grounded as Harry Truman. After five or six hours, Frank was seen by the attending psychiatrist, who asked him if he wanted to hurt himself or anyone else, and whether he heard voices. Frank was feeling quite chipper at that point and said so, after which the doctor promptly dismissed him. It was not what was supposed to happen, and I protested to the doctor, explaining my predicament and insisting that Frank's moment of clarity was no reason to disparage his first-rate résumé as a loon—which was the only thing keeping him out of jail, and alive. I couldn't call the cops—he'd committed no new crime—and I had no real power to make him wait with me overnight and then surrender to the judge. The doctor was unimpressed, even as Frank's pants fell down again. We would have to try again later, with another doctor. In the meantime, we decided to take him shopping for pants.

Thus began a long night for the three of us. At a department store on Flatbush Avenue, Frank tried to put things in his new pockets even as security followed us in a man-to-man defense. At a McDonald's, Frank said he wanted to drop by to see an old girlfriend—not to worry, he tried to assure us, he'd just meet us later. Back at the hospital, we were told to wait until the morning, when we could again make our pitch to the day staff. There, Frank helped us stay awake by engaging his brother John in a lively debate, notwithstanding the fact that John had been dead for fifteen years. Frank stared fixedly at a spot on the wall as he said, "No, Johnny, you know I never did that, it didn't happen!" and "Yeah, I know, I miss you, too!" as Mike and I gazed at him with weary dread. Then he turned to us and grinned: "Had ya goin', didn't I?" Yes he did, we had to admit, and we persuaded him that the quality of his performance was such that it would be wrong to deprive the next doctor of it. And so when morning came, it was Frank's ability to act crazy—and perhaps Mike's and my appearance of losing our grip as well—that won his admission to the hospital, and our final freedom.

It's hardly worth mentioning that there is no formal training for this kind of work. The massive, interconnected systems of cops, courts, and corrections, physical and mental health care, social service, community service, and educational facilities, public and private, religious and secular, would take a lifetime to learn, or you could just wing it. Although I'd had a mother who was a psychologist, a father who was an FBI agent, and a brother in law school, each of whom was consulted constantly, the responsibilities to which I was entrusted now seem laughably large. I had been an English major, with a postgraduate résumé that included messenger, elevator operator, and guy at the copy machine. Now, I argued in court; I visited jails, and homes that were worse; I learned to ask women how many fathers their children had without embarrassment or accusation, questions which would have been fighting words where I came from. This was in the late 1980s, when New York City was breaking its homicide records, and I would walk into neighborhoods that led the city in that statistic—Bedford-Stuyvesant, Brownsville, East New York. Once I asked a cop for directions in East New York, a precinct where there were one hundred and twenty homicides in one year, and he looked at me, shaking his head, and said, "You go three blocks that way, if they don't kill you first." My clients included a three-hundred-pound Czech Gypsy crackhead, whose father kept weeping on my shoulder while trying to stuff fifties in my pocket, and a charming little girl gangster, who used to go to church and announce that various relatives had died, to take up collections. I had a woman who'd put a butter knife through her boyfriend's heart, men who killed each other barehanded in street brawls, a thirteen-year-old who had thought the gun didn't work.

The thirteen-year-old was named Dondre, and he stood just under five feet tall and weighed less than a hundred pounds. He was at once an ordinary child and a working criminal: he had an imaginary friend and loved to watch Saturday-morning cartoons; he sold crack, carried a gun, and at the age of eleven had been discovered hiding in the ceiling of a bank, after closing. He lived with his grandmother, and his best friend, named Kataun, was her boyfriend's grandson, making them "cousins." Dondre's father was unknown, and his mother's rap sheet listed burglary, assault, arson, and other generally masculine felonies, as if she was trying to be two bad parents at once. One Saturday, after a morning of cartoons, Dondre and Kataun went out and bought a forty-ounce bottle of malt liquor, which they shared, after which they played with the gun Dondre had recently bought—he was told it contained three "dead" bullets, which wouldn't discharge—and they began to horse around, wrestling in the hallway outside Kataun's apartment. When Kataun got him in a headlock and wouldn't let him loose, Dondre took out his gun and put it to Kataun's head and pulled the trigger, once—*Click!*—twice—*Click!*—and a third time, which covered the wall with Kataun's head. Dondre ran to his own house and went to sleep for a long time. Odd details of that case have stayed with me: for some reason, I was more irked by the fact that Dondre, who looked like he was eight years old, was buying beer than that he was selling crack. And I was struck by the conversation with

Kataun's gently sorrowing grandfather, who remained with Dondre's grand-mother afterward, and from whom I hoped to obtain some statement of support for our claim that it was neither an adult nor an intentional act. Instead, he told me, without anger but with deep conviction, that he hoped Dondre would be charged with murder and remain in prison. But what I remember most about that case was talking to Dondre's grandmother in her favorite chair in the living room, a stack of paperback books on one side of her and a bottle of brandy on the other, and how she was reading the spy novels of John le Carré. I wondered what she made of them—their chess-game of subterfuge and betrayal in foreign capitals, their patterned world of clever rules and lofty purpose—and how it all appeared from an easy chair in a housing project in Brooklyn, amid dead bullets that came to life and living children lost forever.

What I did not see was the crime. CCJA rarely disputed the facts of a case—even for Dondre, who we argued should be sentenced as a juvenile—and our remoteness from the violence in which we trafficked could give it the blandness of a statistic, like a bad report card. The closest I came to the reality of a killing was when I happened across a crime-scene photo showing a young man who had nearly been decapitated, his spine completely severed and his head loose on his neck like a chopped-down tree. My client in this case was a hapless little old man named Cecil, an immigrant from the tiny island of Montserrat in the West Indies, and the cause of his clienthood was his stepson Keith, the youngest of his wife's five children from a previous marriage. The first four had grown up on the island, and in America they were distinguished and professional people—teacher, banker, and so on—whereas Keith, who had grown up in Brooklyn, had become a crackhead and subjected his mother and Cecil to years of terror, breaking in, beating them, and stealing everything in sight, including wedding rings and wedding pictures. One night, after Keith begged for hours to be let in the apartment for a shower, his mother relented and opened the door, and once in, he blew up, shouting threats and tearing the phone from the wall. Cecil picked up a kitchen knife and took one swing at him, which connected with a force that, in photographic retrospect, was amazing to consider. Initially, both Cecil and his wife argued that Keith was to blame for his own death; it was what cops sometimes call a "public-service homicide." But during the year that it took to litigate the case, his wife had a change of heart and a change of story, out of natural remorse and pressure from her other children. Keith was now a blameless angel whom Cecil had murdered in cold blood. When she made dinner, she would set a place for Keith but not for Cecil, who lost his job as a dishwasher and sank into a depression, responding to most questions by muttering, "I would not be able to say." For Cecil, the bloody reality of his act was offset by the surrounding circumstances, and although the jury found him guilty of manslaughter, he was sentenced to probation on the condition that he go back to Montserrat.

But there were other cases which no past wrong or present optimism - could explain, crimes which I hoped I would never begin to understand. One night I worked late in the office and got a call from Rikers Island, from a woman who was on trial for killing her infant. (My phone number must have been on the wall of the murderesses' washroom.) I told her that I might have been able to do something before she went to trial, or could perhaps do something after, if she were found guilty, but that I had little to offer innocent people, as such. She was a lost, lonely person with a sweet voice, and, as the trial went on, her calls became increasingly friendly, and we spoke less about the case, which had to do, sketchily, with a baby and a bathtub, and which she insisted was an accident. One day, her lawyer called, an Indian man with an accent so heavy that I could barely understand him. The verdict was guilty, he said, because the prosecution was able to show that the water in the tub had been heated on the stove. I had been chatting with a woman who had boiled her baby to death. She called, half an hour later, when I was still a little dizzy from the revelation, and I said abruptly that I would not be able to do anything for her. As when I became a cop, I found myself entwined in lives I - could barely imagine, and I wondered if theirs were the better for it, or how mine, in time, would be the worse.

• • •

SOME OF MY COP FRIENDS DIDN'T THINK MUCH OF WHAT I did at CCJA, but others respected it, whether because they took a larger view of the system, or because I told them the stories, or just for my sake. As I said, my father liked my job primarily because it was a job, but also because he saw that I was taken with it, how it drove and stretched me. There was no obvious next step in sight: I had no interest in leaving the field for an administrative position, and since I got to play lawyer without the burden of law school, or the awful caseload—numerical and moral—of real defense attorneys, pursuing a degree made little sense. And so it came as something of a surprise when my father mentioned, offhandedly one afternoon, that I might think about becoming an FBI agent. It happened not long before he died.

We were outside in the yard, on a warm afternoon. I think I might have nodded, or said, "Hey, yeah, maybe." I had begun to take a zealous interest in La Cosa Nostra, and I had a fair command of its history in America. I thought of his angry reaction when Mike Kelly joined the NYPD, and I wondered if his suggestion implied that he thought things were looking down for me, or up. Given all that had passed between us, the adolescent storms and the recent years of grace, the remark struck me as a gift: you could do what I did, and it would be good. He also told me that when he'd worked on the docks, loading freight, he knew that some of the men there would sew razor blades into their caps. When a cop approached one of them, he would take off his hat, feigning humility, and then swipe it across the cop's eyes to blind him. Later on, as an agent on the waterfront, when my father confronted a man who took off his hat—"Geez, Officer, what's the problem?"—he knew to step back, gun out, and tell him to drop it. Because he had seen it before, he would see it again. That's what he thought I should know.

There is a scene in *The Godfather* when Don Corleone tells his son Michael how the other families will come after him. The Don has survived a shooting, but he is in semi-retirement, having handed down power to the son whom he hoped would do better. He tells him he is not ashamed of his own life, that he felt he had done what was necessary, but that Michael had gone to college, and might have been "Senator Corleone . . . Governor Corleone . . . I don't know. . . ." He mutters and meanders when he talks, but he makes himself clear. There is no sense that Michael shares his regret, though he will later on. All he says is, "I know, Pop. I know."

Until the very end, when my father spoke of his career, it was often with a distinct note of remorse; though he was proud of his service in the Bureau, he began to question whether he would have been equally proud had he stayed there for ten years, or fifteen, or twenty, instead of the twenty-eight he was permitted before mandatory retirement at the age of fifty-five. When he retired, the eldest of his five children was fifteen years old and the youngest was seven. He made another deeply cautious choice by becoming a security consultant for Con Edison, which supplied power to New York City and was as close to the civil service as any job there was. He declined the opportunity to become head of security there because he would have had to be available twenty-four hours a day, rather than be a deft, daylight fixer of such problems as arose. Because his responsibilities came so early and heavily, the cultivation of opportunities for their own sake—whether for financial or intellectual rewards—had an air of vanity about them, of selfish pride. And during the time when he expected to live a long life, to endure with the thrifty eternity of the civil service, it troubled him. But when he began to suspect he was going to die, soon, and for no reason in particular, the fact that he lived well and had loved his life restored his perspective like the clouds breaking below the North Star to a sailor lost at sea.

In 1991, the last year of his life, my father had a minor prostate operation in the month of March. It was a routine and successful procedure, after which he walked out of the hospital and resumed work without impediment. But something entered his mind in the next few months, lightly at first, but then with the grip of a premonition. He had always been in good health, and I can't even remember him having a cold, though when he did suffer some physical ailment—a cut on his finger that turned septic, say—he made an uncharacteristic fuss. By June he believed that he was going to die, and though he maintained a dignified skepticism on the outside, the increasing strength of his belief led him to consult five different doctors in the week before it proved true. The last referral was on Friday, to a company psychiatrist, who prescribed valium despite his protest that he was not depressed: *No, I like my job, I love my wife and kids, my life is good—I just think I'm going to die.* On Saturday afternoon, he sat on his red fake-leather easy chair in the living room, watching television as my mother was in the kitchen putting the house together and planning the remainder of the day—the Mullery boy's graduation party, then five o'clock Mass, then a drive to the Poconos, where they would spend the weekend. There was something in his manner that made my mother ask, "John, do you want to skip the party?" And he said, "Yeah, Betty, why don't we?" After a little while in the kitchen, she came in to look at him and said, "We could go to Mass in Pennsylvania in the morning," and he said that might be a good idea. A few minutes later, she returned and looked at him again, and asked, "John, do you want me to call an ambulance?" And he said, "Yeah, Betty, I think maybe you should. . . ." She held him as he dozed off, and he never woke up again.

At the funeral, I gave my father's eulogy, and I had secretly arranged for my friend John Rowland, a Transit cop, to play the bagpipes outside the church. As we followed the coffin down the aisle, the organ played "Jerusalem" and the bells pealed, as the drone of the pipes rose from the street. John played the "The Minstrel Boy," because it was a sad, Irish song:

The minstrel boy to the war has gone,
In the ranks of death you'll find him.
His father's sword he has girded on
And his wild harp slung beside him . . .ž

And then he played the Marine Corps Hymn, which my father loved, and then "Going Home," because that was the usual way it was done. I thought I had done well by my father. There were over a thousand people there, and I saw none who were not weeping. I hugged Uncle Gerry on the sidewalk, and he shook his head and smiled.

"There's nothing like the pipes to get you. I love them, I could hear them all day."

I nodded, as I loved them too.

"One thing about your father, though. He couldn't stand the bagpipes, I never knew why. Well, go figure, you can't please everybody."

• • •

THREE AND A HALF YEARS LATER, THERE WAS SOME DEBATE over whether I was in the picture. After the first row, and maybe the second, the faces began to dissolve into the grid of dots. The caption above the photo in *Newsday* read NEW, BUT TRUE BLUE, and it told how we were the last class of Housing cops to be appointed, as the long-rumored merge of Housing, Transit, and the NYPD would take effect in April. We had our hands over our hearts as we were sworn in as officers, in the auditorium of the Police Academy. My brother John said that he couldn't see me there, and it did take some imagination to make me out in the third row, where individual features blended into the background. If my family had doubts about whether I was there, they were utterly mystified as to why; I wasn't sure myself, but it felt right. My circumstances were different from those of my father, when the *Journal-American* snapped the picture of his class, with their hands on their hearts, forty-seven years before, but my reasons were fairly similar: I needed a job, and I thought I might like this one. A couple of days later, a friend called to say, "Hey, I saw your picture in the paper!" It had to be true, though it didn't seem so at the time.

The Academy was to last six months. There was a moment a few days in—the first several were spent in an auditorium, filling out forms—when the guy next to me, Kenny Wade, whispered, "How do you spell 'deceased'?" I pointed to my form, where I had written it, though he was already looking at it anyway, as I was looking at his. Everyone was watching how everyone else filled out the forms, as if knowing the Social Security number and next-of-kin of our neighbors could spare us from failure. As it happened, this particular answer was the same for Kenny and me, and the flash of affinity was a consolation. We had dead fathers, and that connection was more apparent than any other in the auditorium, where four hundred individual responses to the term "business attire" suggested that business ranged from ditch digger to pimp: jeans, T-shirts and work boots, and pajama-like suits of pumpkin and purple. To look around was to learn what "motley" meant.

Some of the instructors made a show of drill-sergeant bark and bravado, making public examples of those of us who returned late from lunch or otherwise showed a lack of seriousness. I wondered if it would have been faster for them to pick out the biggest guy in the room and knock him flat. There were questions from the audience that might have warranted it:

"I have a twenty-six-inch neck. Do they have a uniform for me?"

"I expect to get a lot bigger from working out; should I buy a uniform for my size now, or for the size I expect to be?"

"I had stuff to do during lunch. Mind if I pop out for half an hour and grab a quick bite?"

In the past, cops who were recruited for long-term undercover assignments skipped the Academy altogether, so that the NYPD sensibility wouldn't rub off on them. The risk seemed minimal, as far as I was concerned. In the months before I was sworn in, I had told only two people that I was going to become a cop: Mike Kelly's brother Pat, who reminded me of my Uncle Eddie and therefore seemed like the most typical cop I could imagine, and John Driscoll, my smartest friend. Pat thought it was hilarious, and John thought it was good, and their opinions showed at least that I had chosen my confidences well, as there were few other endorsements when the decision became known. One friend called it "the worst career move since Rudolf Hess parachuted into Scotland." Though my brother Steve was intrigued, the rest of my family thought it was awful, that it would be dull and depressing work.

Initially, they were right: even before the Academy, I had to make repeated three-hour subway trips to Queens for my background investigation, bringing in heaps of paper to explain my career so far. When I brought in my college diploma, my investigator made me return with my high school transcript, to make sure I was educationally qualified. When I brought in my passport, he told me I didn't need it, and then changed his mind later, making me spend another day bringing it out. I took to bringing in information by the boxload—when he asked for taxes, he got all the receipts, too—which deterred further interrogations along those lines. I had to explain my criminal record, which no one made too much fuss over. As I had no license, there was no driving record that needed explanation—unlike the recruit in the next cubicle over, who defended one summons by saying, "That was the time I sneezed and missed the stop sign."

But these tedious chores, necessary or not, became bearable when you viewed them as halting steps toward the destination. A lot of the Academy was degrading, or at least recalled a degree of humiliatingly close regulation that I could barely remember from childhood. The day would begin on the muster deck, the open roof where we would form into companies for drill and inspection. Strangers would denounce you for the quality of your shoe shine or haircut. When actual cops walked past you on the stairs, someone had to call, "Make way, recruits! Make way!" signaling us to press to the side to let them pass. Our gray polyester uniforms made us look like Cub Scouts. Discipline was enforced through demerit cards, or "Star Cards," and administered in the dreaded Room 512, where General Patton himself would have been berated for the quality of his posture and salute. Stairways were specifically designated UP or DOWN, and there were lanes painted in the halls. Seats were always assigned, as were the places we stood in for Gym. After Gym, a hundred men would stand in line for the three working showers, nearer to each other's sounds and smells than we would have liked, but preferable to the course chosen by the stinking shy-guys who skipped the showers altogether. On that note, I discovered that the Department employs men for what has to be one of the most awful jobs in the world, and though I don't know the formal title, "piss inspector" describes it plainly enough. For drug screening, we had to fill a bottle at a urinal with a slanted mirror at the top, so the piss inspector could tell it was produced from the genuine article. Those who were afflicted with "stage fright" were given coffee, water, and all the time they needed—some lasted through the night, I was told—so that it could be ascertained that the delay was prompted by embarrassment over what was in the pants and not what was in the bloodstream. One guy in my company failed, a postal worker who had left his old job "because of the stress." The drug test was given the day after St. Patrick's Day, and I wondered if it was a coincidence.

My classmates in Company #95-04 were older than I'd expected—a third of us were my age, thirty, and above—slightly more white than black and Hispanic, and substantially more male than female. The youngest was a twenty-year-old guy named Kris Cataldo, who rarely spoke, and the oldest was the once and future postal worker. By and large, we were an earnest and studious group, who had been mechanics and teachers and toll takers before, married as often as not, sometimes with several children. I got along best with two white guys from Long Island, Wade and Breitfeller, and two black guys from Queens, Ford and Casey, and though we sometimes talked about going out after work, we never did. I was surprised when I asked Ford to go to lunch one day and all the other black people in the company came, too, but if we had any kind of social life together outside the Academy, I never heard about it, and our old friends and other responsibilities claimed our free hours. We never called each other by our first names. A number of instructors went on about the importance of keeping our old, civilian friends, so that we had a wider and healthier perspective on life, and wouldn't live completely within the Job. We seemed to have weathered that danger.

During training, we were force-fed massive amounts of technical detail, some of it powerfully moral and logical, some microscopically petty. I worked far harder than I did in college, copying out homework assignments on loose-leaf each day for each class, in proper 49 format. This was one:

POLICE DEPARTMENT
CITY OF NEW YORK

May 24, 1995

FROM: PPO Edward Conlon CO#95-04
TO: Sgt. Alvarado
SUBJECT: Homework, Lesson #63

1. State the rules regarding Environmental Control Board "Notice of Violation and Hearing" summons and return locations.

    ECB, 1250 Broadway, 7th Floor, NYC 10001 for
        a. Food vendor regulations
        b. General vendor

c. Health code violations
d. Public health law
e. Noise code violations
f. Sanitation provisions
g. Air code provisions

2. State rules regarding an incident where there are both ECB and Criminal Court offenses.

A Universal Appearance Ticket can be issued for summonsable Administrative Code offenses not covered by list at Desk.

3. State the provisions of the Canine Waste Law, Unleashed Dog Law, and Unnecessary Noise Law.

a. Any person who owns, possesses, or controls a dog must remove feces from public area.
b. Dog in public place must be on leash no longer than six feet.
c. 1. Involving sound reproduction device:
   Seize and write voucher.
   2. Not involving sound reproduction device:
   Attempt to correct, write, advise Desk Officer.

5. Apply the general procedure regarding the "Notice of Violation and Hearing."

a. Inform violator of offense.
   1. No enforcement v. blind in Canine Waste Law
   2. Discretion in re elderly/handicapped
b. Request proof of ID and residence
   1. Escort offender to Station House if proof refused or dubious
c. Separate Notice of V & H for each offense
   1. Complete captions in block letters, ballpoint pen
d. Insert violation code, section of law, mail-in and maximum penalties on Notice as determined from Common ECB Offenses at Desk
e. Make notice returnable to ECB, 1250 B'way, 7th Fl, NY NY 10001
   1. If food/property removed, make return date 21 days on next business day
   2. If none removed, return date 30-37 days
f. Violator gets pink copy
g. Arrest log entries
h. Entry on certification of summonses served

      i. White (ECB) copy: precinct of occurrence
        Yellow & cardboard: retain with certification
      j. If violator cannot be ID'd, confer with Desk Officer
      k. Effect arrest only when criminal sanctions committed in addition to
        ECB violations (Civil jurisdiction only.)

6. For your information.

  Edward Conlon
  Probationary Police Officer

I notice in that homework assignment, which only in part discussed dogshit, I skip from number three to number five, and I suspect that I put one over on the otherwise vigilant Sgt. Alvarado. Though the Academy felt like an odd combination of kindergarten and boot camp, I was nonetheless buoyed by a sense of mission, a heart-lightening hope that I was becoming part of something unexpectedly strong and large and good. My instructors were excellent, on a par with any I'd had in college in terms of their dedication to the subject and to their students. Sgt. Alvarado, our immediate supervisor and Police Science instructor, was a forbidding man, at least initially. He had a rabbinical devotion to the *Patrol Guide,* the four-inch-thick manual of procedures for everything from how to handle Emotionally Disturbed Persons (EDPs) to the dates when short-sleeved shirts were authorized, with exceptions for specified temperatures and the discretionary power of commanding officers to alter same. Sgt. Alvarado told us he kept separate folders of Revision Notices and Interim Orders, even when they became obsolete, so that he - could observe the evolution of NYPD thought on matters like tow-truck notifications. It was up to him to impart the procedure for every phenomenon the police officer is likely to encounter: the sick, the lost, the crazy, the dead, cars, traffic, accidents, dogs, bombs, crowds, missing persons, runaways, juvenile delinquents, domestic disputes, gangs, arrests, hospitalized prisoners, community policing, investigations, tactics, victims, complaints, complainants, civilian complaints, corruption, and the storage and disposal of found and seized property, from drugs and cash to body parts—as well as the forms and formalities by which the Department governed itself; its structure, protocol, conduct, and discipline; times and charts of tours of duty, overtime, night differential, off-duty employment; the kinds and terms of sick leave, military leave, terminal leave, bereavement leave, and death benefits; uniform and equipment regulations and maintenance, radio codes, and all manner of in-house record-keeping. As such, Sgt. Alvarado was the man for the job, and we learned everything. He was especially severe at first, as if he were breaking horses, and then increasingly open and easy as we learned our paces and marks. He began to display a surreptitious sense of humor, asking us, during the lesson on civilian complaints, what was the one word cops use with the public that gets them in trouble most. We shouted out in unison, "Asshole, sir!" He nodded and smiled.

PO Rickard, a young Housing cop who taught us Law—constitutional law, case law, criminal law, and procedural law—was equally methodical and fervently enthusiastic, and she tried to convey the seriousness of the material while making it fun, with occasionally unintentional success. In the "justification" lesson, which outlined when a police officer could use deadly force, she ran through scenarios where shots might be fired: "What if you hear a burglar alarm, and you see a guy running down the street with a television?"

"No."

"What if he sees you and says, 'Let me go, or I drop the TV'?"

"No."

"What if he pulls a gun, and is gonna shoot a little girl if you don't let him go?"

"Yes."

"All right, forget about the burglar. What if the little girl comes up to you with her old, sick dog, and says, 'Please, officer, I need you to put him down!'"

There was a pause, and a few mumbled negatives.

"It's the sickest, oldest three-legged dog, howling in pain, and she begs you to please put it out of its misery. . . ."

A few votes shifted to the affirmative, and then Rickard tried to pull the rest of us in.

"What if she's a little blind girl, and she comes tapping up to you with a cane, and . . ."

Breitfeller interjected, "Since she's a blind girl, couldn't you just yell 'Bang!' and tell her it was dead?"

Sgt. Solosky, who taught us Social Science, would open, close, and interrupt classes with the motto "Remember, we're the good guys!" and the ringing phrase rose to mean whatever it needed, whether the curriculum covered bias crimes or poverty. Our instruction on discrimination was no different from what would have been taught at a liberal-arts college, but Solosky's street-corner regularity and surpassing decency stripped even the touchiest subjects of controversy. He asked the black students what they thought of the way black people use what's called the "N-word," and got the widest-ranging and most civil debate I've ever heard on the subject. The one person who thought it was unobjectionable to use in a casual, friendly way was my friend Casey—he'd call me a "crazy nigger" in conversation—and he surprised me later as well, when he had to do a presentation on an ethnic group. He chose the Irish, and announced that their favorite food, drink, and music were corned beef, whiskey, and bagpipes. I began to wonder if he'd missed the lesson on stereotypes, and then he concluded, "I know all of this because my grandmother told me, and she's from Wexford, in Ireland." We listened to Sgt. Solosky because he was a good talker, but also because he told us things we hoped we'd never learn but knew we might. Once such lesson had been imparted to him, some eight years before, when an accident of roll-call assignments put a rookie named Eddie Byrne on his post, guarding a witness in a drug-related homicide. Four men crept up behind him and shot him in the head. Sgt. Solosky could keep things light because he had seen things that were not.

For each of the three academic classes, we had to fill out biographical forms with education, work and military experience, languages, and other special skills. I had written where I had gone to college in a cramped scrawl, and the best guess for what it said would have been "Howard." Sgt. Alvarado and PO Rickard must have wondered why I'd gone to a historically black school, but Sgt. Solosky interrupted himself in the middle of class to say, "Hey, wait a minute! Conlon, there's a rumor going around that you went to Harvard! Didja?"

I made a derisive sound. "Not lately, Sarge."

After class, I approached him and apologized, saying I didn't mean to mislead him but I preferred to keep that quiet. He slapped me on the shoulder and said, "Don't worry, Conlon, it's nothing to be ashamed of."

The Academy also got us in shape. In one book I read, a cop recalls being told in his Academy Gym class during the 1920s, "We've studied the various physical-culture systems of England, of Sweden, even of Japan, and we think our course here combines the best features of each." The Anglo-Swedish elements seem to have been dropped since, and, for us, Gym combined running and calisthenics with self-defense, first aid, and CPR. Our instructor was Detective Washington, who had taught there for most of his career. He was a superb athlete and a black belt, and he sought to hone our survival skills by providing all kinds of so-far-unimagined motivations:

"You know what's gonna happen if you get killed on the Job—if you're too fat to run up to the thirtieth floor of the Polo Grounds projects on a gun run, and you're gasping for breath on the fifth, too wiped out to do anything but throw up, you can't even lift your arms, forget about remembering this wrist hammer-lock we learned today—and *Bam!* You are done! And everybody's gonna be sad for a while, and the Mayor and the PC will go to your funeral, and a few months, a year later, your partner, your *best friend,* the one who said he'd look out for you, he's gonna be looking out for your *wife!* He calls to see how she's feeling, and he's the only one who understands, and the next thing you know, they're on the beach together in Martinique! Martinique! My favorite place in the world, and they're gonna be drinking mai tais and daiquiris and saying, 'Should we have another?' and 'Yeah, why not!' because you're paying for it! They're living *fat* on your pension money there, and speaking of fat, you're gonna look down and say, 'Shit, she's looking good, why couldn't she lose those fifteen pounds for me! She does it for him, and not for me!' So do yourself a favor and stay in shape, and remember what I'm teaching you today so your partner can buy his own mai tais for his own fat wife. . . ."

Each of our instructors stressed that his or her subject was the most important part of the Job—that if we didn't know the *Patrol Guide,* we were finished, or if we didn't know the law, or how to deal with people, or how to defend ourselves, or drive, or shoot, we might as well go home now—and all these things were true in their way. We were force-fed acronyms to help us remember mandatory memo-book inserts (DICES: Domestic Violence, Auto Identification, Corruption, EDPs, Spanish phrases), circumstances when you - couldn't carry a gun (FAVOR: Family court as a respondent, Alcohol, Vacation, Off-duty employment, and, of course, "R"), the felonies for which a juvenile could be charged as a Juvenile Offender (MARK ABRAMS: Murder, Arson, Robbery 1, Kidnapping, Assault 1, Burglary 1, Rape 1, Aggravated Sexual Abuse 1, Manslaughter, Sodomy 1). We did role-plays, acting out good guys and bad in family fights, car stops, drug sales. We took a class trip to the morgue, and though no one embarrassed him- or herself amid the filed corpses, most of us thought the smell stayed on us for a few days afterward. We were appointed to the New York City Housing Police, but Housing merged with Transit and the NYPD in April of 1995, so we would graduate as NYPD. No one seemed to care. As the months passed, the mood became less autocratic, but we were both exhausted and increasingly anxious to get out. During one lesson—I believe it was on authorization dates for tire chains—Breitfeller, Wade, and I took turns banging our heads on the wall to pass the time. I got in trouble once, or near-trouble, after our schedule changed and I went to Meal while the rest of the company went to Gym. My absence was immediately reported, and an investigation commenced, with a thorough examination of my background and disciplinary record. I returned from a pleasant fifty minutes with a cheeseburger and the newspapers to meet the Integrity Control Officer, who had a death-in-the-family look in his face.

"Where were you?"

"Lunch?"

"Where were you supposed to be?"

"Not lunch?"

To be AWOL is a serious matter, but as he led me up to Room 512, he had a hard time keeping a straight face. He asked, "Where did you go to school again?" He also mentioned that if I had been inclined to rob a bank, the Police Academy would have provided a wonderful alibi. In Room 512, another lieutenant looked at me, my record, the report of the incident, and said, "Oh, get the hell out of here."

When I did—when we all did—it was on a bright and warm afternoon in June, and we quick-stepped to Frank Sinatra's "New York, New York." Three blue columns poured into the auditorium from the entrances, stage right and stage left, and the production had far more Broadway flair than military pomp, as if the reigning spirit of good-natured wiseguy had finally transcended the bureaucratic weight of the Department. Mayor Giuliani spoke, as did Commissioner Bratton and several others, and I don't remember what anyone said except Sinatra, who belted out, *I want to be a part of it, make a brand-new start of it, in old New York!* That much was true for me, and I laughed to think of the aptness of the old standard, sung by the mob-guy wannabe whose heart was in so many places, both right and wrong. *You got a problem with that, pal? I didn't think so. . . .* We stood in our new dress uniforms, and saluted with our white gloves, then took them off and tossed them up, and they filled the air like a flock of birds.

FIVE

The Street Narcotics Enforcement Unit and Anti-Crime were considered the elite teams of the precinct, each a local version of the citywide Narcotics Division and Street Crime Unit. The SNEU sergeant, Tom Messer, had told me that if another spot opened up, he'd like me to work for him. "I told the captain, I need you since you know how to get search warrants," he said, and I don't think he was kidding, but with Messer, it was hard to tell sometimes. Messer was a legend at the precinct. He spoke his mind indifferent to rank, above him or below, and there was a perennial debate among the cops as to whether he was crazy or only acting. One recent story had it that Messer had been working behind the desk while another cop was about to eat lunch, when a woman came in screaming that she wanted to make a Civilian Complaint. Messer listened to her thoughtfully and said, "Those are very serious charges, Ma'am. Tell you what—I'll give you a choice: I'll take the complaint, or I'll give you this nice cheeseburger." Messer handed her the cop's lunch and she walked out of the precinct. Someone else told me that when Messer was a cop, he saw a drug dealer counting a fat wad of cash and asked him, "Want to double your money?" Before the dealer could reply, Messer took the wad, tore it in half, and handed it back to him. I knew better than to ask him if either story was true. When Messer left SNEU for another assignment, most of his cops went with him, and there were only three holdovers from the old unit: Kris Cataldo, from my Academy class, who picked up the nickname "Stix" because he was a distance runner; Alicia Hall; and Sammy Maldonado.

When Sgt. Mike Carroll took over the unit, I asked him if I could join. I liked him: he was bright and driven, with an attitude that had a nice balance of enthusiasm and sarcasm. On patrol, I'd had one experience with him, when I'd asked him how to handle complaints about a man who was selling fireworks to kids in one of my projects. Carroll had been a cop in Housing, and whether it gave him a belief that procedure was dispensable, or that the dignity of a police officer should be, his remedy was to send me in there "undercover." He cobbled together some ridiculous getup—I believe it was an Army coat and a Con Edison helmet, worn over my uniform—and dispatched me to the apartment. I suppose I should have been grateful that there wasn't an Avon Lady costume around. It felt like I was pledging a fraternity, and the people didn't even open the door, but it apparently showed Carroll that I had the right stuff.

For the first few days, Stix, Alicia, and Sammy were somewhere else, in training or on vacation, and so Sgt. Carroll and I took the lay of the land together, driving around the public housing of the five South Bronx precincts covered by PSA-7. It was mostly new territory for me. At my old post, I'd rarely driven, because even when they gave us a car, it made me realize that while walking the four-by-five-block grid of the Village got dull after a couple of years, driving went stale in minutes: up Webster, down Washington, up Park, down Third, One-Six-Eight to One-Seven-One. We called the route "the Claremont Village 500." Sgt. Carroll and I drove around the major projects in the Four-O: Mitchell Houses, Millbrook Houses, along One-Three-Seven Street, and then Patterson and Mott Haven, the adjacent low-rise and high-rises around One-Four-Three, and then Betances, with its smaller, scattered buildings in the upper 140s, from Willis to St. Ann's Avenue, then Adams-St. Mary's, along Westchester, and Melrose-Jackson, by the PSA, from One-Five-Three to One-Five-Eight, from Courtlandt to Morris. The numbered streets made it easy, as the evens went east, the odds west—with a few exceptions—and I began to memorize the avenues: Lincoln, Alexander, Willis, Brook, St. Ann's, Cypress, and Jackson, west to east along One-Three-Seven, gave me LAW BAC Jackson, with the second A for St. Ann's, and I didn't include Brown Place, a three-block street between Brook and Willis, since I remembered it anyway, because Jose Velez from field training lived there, and we'd hung out one night on his stoop and had a few beers. Learning the buildings—which ones had roof alarms, or exits in the back, or working locks on the front doors—would come in time.

Just after midnight one night, Sgt. Carroll and I went to the roof of 169 Cypress, in Millbrook, and looked out over the grounds, the familiar red-brick towers and wide green lawns. A few young men loitered in a lobby, and a fat man sat alone on a bench along the pathway, but otherwise it was desolate, unusually so for a night in the city, as we eased into the summer heat. "Quiet tonight," Sgt. Carroll said. I waited a beat and added, "Too quiet," because that was the line that usually follows in war movies, which was a bad idea: seconds later, three or four shots were fired, and the rounds passed just over our heads. We hit the deck, a decent impulse and yet a pathetic one, as if we could have dodged the bullets. We laughed nervously as we crept back inside the building.

To have a boss, and especially to drive one, was a novelty. On patrol, most of the sergeants had regular drivers, and the assignment was prized to the degree that the sergeant was; as a driver (a "chauffeur," technically, though only the very old bosses or the slightly delusional ones used the term), you tended to work less but to see more, as you made the rounds of beat cops and sector cars to raise them for the scratch, and to respond to heavy jobs, complicated jobs, or arrests. You had to call a boss for a Missing, or before you could force entry into an apartment where you heard a brawl going on inside, or if you couldn't make head nor tail of a situation. As with any partner, you had to pass the eight hours and thirty-five minutes of the tour sitting eighteen inches away from each other, and if there was a lack of sympathy or shortage of small talk, the time crawled by. But even if there was no mismatch between cop and boss, there could be for the rest of the precinct: some drivers saw themselves as junior supervisors, and others saw themselves as lobbyists for the rank and file. Usually, a kind of lopsided fraternity developed, and if their respective personalities and experiences fit the big brother–kid brother roles, a partnership as strong as any might be formed. Sgt. Poplaski was "Pops" to Richie Henderson, and Sgt. O'Hagan was "Hagie" to Joey Castaldo, but it was some time before Sgt. Carroll became "Mike" for me, and usually only off-duty even then. I was at least as old as any sergeant in the command, but most had ten or more years on the Job, and their experience as much as their rank earned my respect.

I liked my boss, and I was ready to try out my new partners. Partners in a squad car could almost seem married, in their devotions and divisions, in the conversations they could pick up from months before, as if they had never stopped talking. The two-cop team became customary when the patrol car came into use, and this accident of technology led to what now seems the natural arrangement: wolves run in packs, cattle in herds, cops as partners. When long-term partners broke up, that was the term people used—"Didja hear, Mike and Joe broke up!"—and it was spoken in the sorrowing, fretful tones usually reserved for news of divorce. Partners faced the street together, and the sheer size and variety of what they encountered intensified their bond. With a partner at your back, you were free to think about the street, the radio runs, and the pick-ups; to look outward and ahead.

On a team—or in a squad, or in a unit, which SNEU was, though we called it a team—it was different from patrol. In a team of one sergeant and five cops, one and eight, one and ten, the odds were better when you faced the street, but the perspective was different as well. We usually worked in vans, not cars, and so the social model was not marriage but a family, or a pack of kids with a single parent. The teams didn't chase the radio, taking what came to them, but instead largely picked their own targets—drugs for SNEU, stolen cars or guns for Anti-Crime. As much as cops can, they engaged the world on their terms. But in deciding those terms, there was a lot of talking among themselves, and of themselves. In the precinct, or driving around in the van, as much attention was focused inside as out: there was always someone complaining that they had to go to the bathroom every half hour or had missed a meal, or making everyone else complain because they had just gone on a protein-shake diet and they were stinking up the place. Even if the boss was a dictator, there was always a rowdy democracy to a unit, if not concerning when or where they worked, then at least how. If the police department was a paramilitary organization, as we were frequently reminded, the units stressed the "para."

I kept quiet at first, but keeping to myself was out of the question. After I joined Stix, Sammy, and Alicia in SNEU, Tony Marcano and Orville Reid, who had been partners before, came onto the team. We got along well enough, but there were disparate personalities in play, and, in terms of background, we were like an updated version of a unit in a World War II movie— Orville, or "OV," the strong-minded Jamaican Christian; Stix, the cagey, quiet Italian kid from upstate; Tony, the down-to-earth Puerto Rican guy from the

South Bronx; Sammy, also Puerto Rican, even-tempered, modest, and older; Alicia, the princessy but tough-as-nails black woman; and me, whatever the hell I was. In real terms, I was the newest guy there: Stix and I had the least time on, but he had been in the unit for six months already; Orville and Tony had occasionally worked with the unit when Messer was the boss. Moreover, everyone else knew the Four-O: Stix had worked in Betances and Mott-Pat, as had Sammy and Alicia, and Tony and Orville had been beat cops in Melrose-Jackson.

If I didn't have the least to offer, I certainly had the most to learn. When Orville said later, "You should have a game already when you come to SNEU. You're not supposed to come here with nothing, expect us to teach you," he wasn't talking about me, but I kept my mouth shut anyway.

A SNEU team makes arrests for "observation sales," and the way it works is by dividing into an observation post, or "OP," and a catch car. One or two of us go to the OP—if you're in it, you're "doing ops"—on a rooftop or in a vacant apartment to watch a "set," or drug operation. The set might be one teenager standing on a corner with one pocket full of crack and another full of cash. Or it could be an organization of complexity, with lookouts, managers, money men, steerers to guide customers, and pitchers for the hand-to-hand transactions. The dealers might send out phantom or dummy buyers, who appear to have bought narcotics but have not, to see if they're stopped. There were systems of such intricate subterfuge that you'd think their purpose was to deliver canisters of microfilm from double agents to covert operatives instead of ten-dollar bags of junk to junkies. We would watch, and give descriptions of buyers for the catch car to pick up, a few blocks away, on a radio frequency dedicated to point-to-point communication within a range of a few blocks.

As the catch car, we usually had a van, and though we preferred an unmarked van to the blue-and-white, in reality we were so well known it made little difference. Once you got the description, or "scrip," and the buyers' direction of flight, you moved toward them, allowing a distance from the set, but not too much, or else you'd lose radio contact, or they'd get home—in neighborhoods like this, you didn't have to travel far for hard drugs. Sometimes they'd run, and sometimes they'd fight, and sometimes they'd toss the drugs, and sometimes they'd eat them when they saw you coming. You'd want a scrip with something distinctive, something beyond the "white T-shirt, blue jeans" of warm weather, "black jacket, blue jeans" of cold. You didn't want "Male, walking three pit bulls." You were glad to hear hot pink or lime green, T-shirts with legible writing on them, "Female in purple-and-yellow track suit, with a Cat-in-the-Hat hat, riding a tiny bicycle." For crackheads as much as any other species, protective coloration was a successful evolutionary strategy.

When we had a handful of buyers, we'd move in on the sellers. Most of the spots that we hit were well-established, patronized and pursued on a regular basis. Others would pop up and disappear, as a player for a day picked a spot for the day, sizing up his prospects with an expert or rookie eye. You might drive around, to see who was out, the faces at the places, the traffic pattern of steady customers and usual suspects. Sometimes you felt like the man on the catwalks over the casino floor, scanning the tables for the sharps and card-counters, looking out for luck that's too good to be true. Other times you felt that you were in a nature program, some *National Geographic* special on the felony ecology of the streets.

Though I'd watched from an OP before on my post, I had little experience with a catch team, which may have explained my limited success with drug collars in the Village. Generally, if you were looking, you would do verticals until you ran into someone with drugs on them. If I saw a sale, sixteen floors or twenty floors below, it was unlikely that I would get down in time even to get the seller. I stumbled into most of the decent collars, like when I watched a playground from a rooftop for a few hours before I gave up and came down, then walked into a guy smoking a blunt whose knapsack was filled with bundles of crack and heroin. My eyesight was less than perfect, and I wore glasses at night; staring for a long period of time through binoculars gave me a headache. Tony rarely went up into an OP, and Alicia almost never did. Stix, Sammy, and Orville went up most often, and Orville, especially, had an eye that approached genius. Orville could survey a crowded playground and say, "The guy in the green shorts has it in his right pocket."

On our first day out, we watched a building in Mott Haven from a school across a street. I was with Sgt. Carroll in an OP in the gym, peering through the window to see who made thirty-second visits to the lobby. If drug dealers ever hired consultants to find the best defense against arrest for observation sales, they'd probably recommend this kind of set: a dealer in a lobby with a locked front door and the stash nearby, usually in the stairwell, concealed in a light fixture or over a doorjamb. Any change in the variables—if they kept stash on them, or if the front door was broken, or if we had the key—made an arrest more likely, but in general we couldn't take them for sale, as we rarely saw the transaction inside. We could pick off buyer after buyer, rattling off the scrips for the in-and-outs, and stopping them to ask what they were doing in the building. If they had no answer or a false one—"Um, I watched a movie at Maria's house, I forget her last name, and where the apartment is,"—after we'd seen them spend less than a minute in the building, we got to search them. But once we hit the lobby—creeping up, then rushing in, maybe when the door opened for someone to leave, hoping that an unfriendly neighbor wouldn't blow us up on purpose, or that a friendly neighbor might betray us by their astonished look or questions—if they didn't live in the building, the most we could charge them with was trespass.

A young Hispanic guy worked the door, in a white shirt and black tie, greeting customers like the maitre d' of a restaurant. After filling the van with buyers, we moved in and grabbed him, and though he wasn't holding drugs, he had several hundred dollars in small bills. The maitre d' was a great explainer, unfailingly polite, maintaining a patient and sympathetic tone as he attempted to correct our benighted delusion that he was a drug dealer. It was as if he understood that we were limited people presented with ambiguous circumstances, and he could hardly fault us for coming to foolish conclusions. At the precinct, his explanations were endlessly elastic, and we asked more and more questions just to see how far he could stretch: no, he didn't live in the building, but his aunt did, and he waited in the lobby because he - didn't think she was home, and he let in those people because they knocked, of course, and it was the civil thing to do. Why did they all turn up with heroin in their pockets? He had no idea, but he had some of the cash because he had just been paid, from his job as a stock boy in Manhattan, and yes, it was more than a week's pay, but the rest was from his wife's baby shower, and he had to buy a crib. . . .ž

Sgt. Carroll laughed in his face. I didn't believe him, either, but there were times when I found myself wavering—not because of his technique as a liar, though it was excellent, but from the sincerity that welled up in his voice when he talked about his wife and baby, and how he could never, ever have anything to do with drugs because of them. It wasn't my first drug collar any more than it was the first lie I'd heard, but it always amazed me to witness the passion and nerve that addicts brought to their falsehoods, though they often lacked skill. Once, a huge woman bellowed at me as I took a crack vial from her open hand, "You planted that there!" It reminded me of the Richard Pryor line about a man whose wife catches him in bed with another woman,

"Who are you going to believe, me or your lying eyes?" My perp followed up with an unassailable truth, as she lifted up her shirt: "You can't take me to jail, I don't got no bra—look!"

But we charged the maitre d' with sale, arguing that the pattern of conversation and movement, the recovery of cash and identical product—in this case, heroin stamped AIRBORNE—from all of the buyers, gave us probable cause for the charge. It was certainly true that he was the seller—he even admitted it, months later, when I saw him again in the precinct after another arrest—and it should have appeared so to most people, in most places, but as a sale case in the Bronx, it was dead on arrival. No transaction was witnessed, no contraband was recovered from the defendant, and inference alone, no matter how obvious, would not warrant prosecution. He was out the next day, and if he did have an aunt in the building, not even the trespass charge would stick. That bothered me a little, not because I had any vested interest in whether the maitre d' spent ten minutes in jail or ten years, but because it meant our work meant nothing, or we didn't, and all the hours of labor and risk were for our benefit alone. The gap between what we did and what it meant seemed to widen, though the work engaged us enough that we didn't bother dwelling on the big picture.

Within the team, that kind of arrest occasioned a frequent debate over "splitting collars." If three perps were collared for robbery, of course, one cop would take the arrest, but if two cops saw two people trespassing in a building, they sometimes tried to split it up into one for each. The pressure for "activity," specifically arrests and summonses, was always on the increase. On my beat, I didn't like writing summonses, and I eventually stopped writing parking and moving violations altogether, but since I made a lot of arrests, the bosses never minded. Since crime was rampant, it seemed ridiculous and even dangerous to take a day's pay out of someone's pockets because they parked in a Housing lot without a sticker, or their registration had expired last week. The people who had cars tended to be the people who had real jobs, and I wanted to keep them on my side. But other cops had slower beats, and others worked in sectors where they raced from job to job, and some were simply lazy, and for them a month or two could easily pass without an arrest and twenty summonses, which was a rough average of what was expected. As Compstat pressures increased, those cops could have days off denied them, or have their weekend switched to Tuesday and Wednesday, or be transferred to another post or even out of the precinct. Quotas were illegal, but the Job needed some concrete measurement of performance, and so the Job usually won the argument.

As SNEU was an arrest-oriented unit, the problems were slightly different. We were all eager to collar, on most days, and so our concern was to keep the numbers roughly equal, both for the activity and the overtime. If Orville had five for the month but Sammy had none, Sammy was up. But in a maitre d' situation, you could say either you had five misdemeanors and one felony, with one arresting officer, or you had six misdemeanors, with six A/O's. After arraignment, you would have six misdemeanors, regardless, so the decision rested on whether you wanted the felony statistic, which benefited one cop, the sergeant, and even the captain, in some tiny increment, or for every cop to get a collar. When a team worked together, taking their time and evenly distributing the labor of paperwork, fingerprints, vouchers, and prisoner search and transport, the time passed quickly and the quality of work was better. If one person took all the collars for that day, the rest of the team would help, certainly, but not in quite the same way, all the time, and each piece might not be done precisely as the A/O wanted. More to the point, the non-arresting officers might be sent home to save on overtime. Alone, your paperwork for six collars could be overwhelming, late in the day, if one of the perps got sick or went crazy, or a computer broke down, or a DO started to scream at you that your prisoners were in the precinct too long. For us cops, it was better to split things up, as much as possible; for them—the boss, the precinct, and in some thin and theoretical way, society—it was better to wrap everything into one case.

I wasn't sure whether I was us or them. Carroll was them, certainly, but he wanted the felony for the catch-of-the day satisfaction more than anything else, the pride of taking out a set to throw to the lawyers and say, "We got 'em. Now, it's up to you." I agreed with him, but I wasn't going to go against the team. I couldn't say, "Felonies are more fun, guys!" and I couldn't say, "Our purpose is to drive out the scourge of narcotics that has bedeviled Three-Eight-Three East One-Four-Three since they piled up twenty-one stories of cinder block and sheetrock and stuck a fucking junkie in every fourth apartment." And I couldn't tell Carroll, "Who are you kidding? We'll work hard, and we'll get our numbers, but why go crazy when we're not backed up by the DA or anybody else?" When Messer was the boss, he was less involved in the street operations, often covering the desk or supervising patrol while the team picked up bodies. When they were ready to go, they would raise him on the radio to head into the Four-O, and he would take care of whatever was necessary to process the arrests. Carroll was in the mix, as much as any of us, sneaking up into an OP or rolling around with perps on the street. It was a change, and change did not always go smoothly.

. . .

WE WENT OUT TO COLLAR ALMOST EVERY DAY, EXCEPT WHEN we had court, training, or some other contingency, or when the boss was out, in which case we would fill in patrol cars or take footposts. Sometimes they let us work together in a van, but technically we weren't supposed to mount a SNEU operation without a supervisor. For some reason, however, setting up to pick off trespass collars was not considered SNEU work, and if we came in with a van full of prisoners, no one complained. If something went wrong—an injury, an escape, or anything that invited scrutiny—we would have been in trouble, so when Carroll was out, they mostly stuck us on patrol. And I'd had enough of patrol to last me for a while.

The change from a beat to SNEU was exhilarating. For one thing, you only dealt with criminals. There were no more domestic disputes, EDPs, or DOAs, the morass of negotiable and non-negotiable difficulties people had with their neighbors or boyfriends or stepchildren. On patrol, you dealt with the fluid whole of peoples' lives, but usually when the tide was going out: - people who had the cops called on them weren't happy to see you; people who called the cops didn't call when they were having a good time. In SNEU, all I did was catch sellers of crack and heroin, and catch their customers to show they sold it. The rest of their lives, the parts unaffected by coca- or opiate-based products, was none of my business. Patrol was politics, but narcotics was pure technique.

There were rules like in chess, percentages like in poker, moves like in schoolyard ball. We called dealers "players." When we drove around to set up, early in the tour, we'd read the street, looking at who moved and who stood still, the solitaries and small groups, their reactions and relations to one another. Most people occupy their environment blithely, with only a slack and occasional awareness of their surroundings. A store window or a noisy garbage truck might distract them for a moment, and they might look around before crossing the street, but the ordinary pedestrian is a poster child for daydreams and tunnel vision. Not so in the narcotics trade, where the body language of buyer and seller alike reads of outward focus, a taut awareness of opportunity and threat. There are distinctive addict walks, such as the prowler, who might be new to the spot or sussing out an operation that has shifted to a more favorable corner. His pace is slow and his progress is roundabout; he wanders, floating around like a flake of ash above a fire, looking out, alert for the deal. The addict on a "mission walk" moves with double-quick footsteps, leaning forward, as if against a strong wind, so as not to waste an extra second of his wasted life. Many players have a way of carrying themselves, a body language that is as plainly open or closed as a hand. They have a watchfulness, a containment, a false repose like a cat sunning itself on a windowsill, eyes half-closed but ready to pounce. Attention must be paid, and we had to outspend them.

A street set operates through an odd combination of aggressive marketing and strategic defense, with simultaneous needs to broadcast and deny its function. The young man on the park bench needs to look like a high school senior from thirty yards but has to show he's a merchant at three, to have the drugs near enough for convenience but far enough away to be out of his "custody and control" should he be stopped. If he's holding the drugs, he has to have an escape route, through a hole in the fence, to an alley, to the building where his grandmother lives. The kid on the bench is a kid on a bench regardless, and it takes time for his context to prove him to be anything more. You watch who he watches, who approaches him. And as you do, figures emerge from the flow of street life as coordinates on a grid, as pins on a map.

Say you have a street with three young guys on the corner by the bodega, a couple with a baby in a carriage by the stoop, old men with brown-bagged brandy bottles by the vacant lot. A man on a bicycle moves in a slow lazy slalom, up and down the street. The cornerboys are the obvious pick, but I have to wait. A buyer is easier to recognize, and his arrival on the set sends a signal, a vibration like a willing fly landing in the spiderweb. The buyer is the bellwether and bait, who draws the players out and makes them work, prompts them into visible display.

The buyer walks past the old men at the lot, the family on the stoop, to the cornerboys, as I thought. One cornerboy takes the buyer aside and palms his cash, the second stands still, watching up and down the block, the third goes to the family on the stoop, has a word with the woman with the baby. The woman steps inside the lobby for a few seconds—thank God, I think, the stash isn't in the carriage—returns and hands the cornerboy something, and he meets up with Player #1 and buyer, handing off the product. The buyer walks away, retracing his route. The man on the bicycle follows him, slowly.

I put the buyer over the air: "Hispanic male, red cap, blue Tommy Hilfiger jacket, blue jeans, south on Willis. . . . Be advised, you got a lookout on a bike, white T-shirt, blue jeans, black bike, tailing him to see if he gets picked up, let him run a couple of blocks if you can. . . ."

Now I have a three-player set, with Mama and Cornerboys #1 and #3 down cold. The buyer should be taken, the lookout only observed, for now. Mama's short time in the building tells me the stash isn't in an apartment, but either on her person or right in the lobby, in a mailbox or a crack in the wall. Player #2 is the one to watch, to see if he's the manager or a lookout, up a rank from them or down. His position will become clear, through watching the group dynamic, the choreography of who stands where, who talks and who listens, who tells the jokes and who laughs, who's the one who runs to the bodega for the chips and soda. Until he participates in the exchanges, taking money or product, he's legally safe from arrest for an observation sale. If he's a manager, he's the one we want, to try to turn, moving up the organization; if he's a smart manager, touching neither cash nor stash, he's the one we're least likely to get. In a sense, we both want the spot to get busy: with more buyers, they're less likely to get away, popping into a nearby building before we can grab them, and the players will be less wary as they get greedy, bringing out more product, paying more heed to the customer and less to us. The manager might have to step in and lend an incriminating hand. When the spot is slow, the cops and the players both have to be patient.

Even when nothing happens, there is much to interpret: are they out of product, and will they re-up within ten minutes or an hour? Are they "raised," afraid we're around, and if so, is it because they saw our van, or one of us creeping into the corner building to peer over the roofline, or is it because three patrol cars raced by, to the robbery a few blocks away? Did they turn away the last customer because he wanted credit, or because they thought he was an undercover cop, and were they right? Is it worth waiting, is it worth watching?

Watching isn't always easy. I've spent hours on tar rooftops, crouched down till my legs cramp, sweating, shivering, wiping the rain from my binoculars every ten seconds. There have been times when I've forgotten to look down before I kneel by the ledge, and seen piles of dog shit, broken glass, or syringes beside me. On one rooftop, there was an ornate Victorian bird cage, five feet tall, bell-shaped and made of brass. Chained to it, still on a rotten leather leash, was the skeleton of a pit bull. You walk up dirty stairs to a dirty roof to watch a dirty street. At night, even the light is dirty, as the sodium-vapor streetlights give off a muddy yellow haze. But when it's happening, sometimes, you realize how perfect your concentration is, you feel the cool, neutral thrill of being completely submerged in your task. And when it's not, you can still be caught up in the beauty of the view, the hallucinatory strangeness or the small, random graces of the landscape:

An incinerator chimney shoots out a lash of black smoke, which loops into a lariat before dissolving into the grimy sky.

"Gray livery cab, buyer in back seat, passenger side, possible white with white sleeves, U-turning now to the left . . ."

A soap bubble, then two, then dozens rise up in front of me, iridescent, shimmering in their uncertainty, floating up to be lost in the blue sky. There is a child, two floors below me, as rapt at the view above as I am with the view below.

"Arright, we got one, he's beelining to the player, they just popped into the lobby . . . now he's out—that's fast, he must have the stash on him. Arright, buyer's walking off, now—hold on, he's just kind of idling across the street—it's not an I-got-my-rock walk, I don't think he got done. Stand by . . ."

A man stands on another tenement roof, whirling an orange flag, making it snap like a towel. His flock of pigeons takes flight from the coop with a whoosh like a gust of wind, spiraling out in broadening arcs, the smoky gray of their backs as they bank out, the silver-white of their bellies as they circle in, rising up all the while.

"Player's walking off, he sent the last two away, he's out, he's raised, I don't know, but—*Go! Go! Go! Go!* Hit the set!"

When you hit a set, there is always a charge of adrenaline, arising from the jungle-war vagaries in your knowledge of the terrain and the determination of your adversary. There are elusive ones, explosive ones, and lots of sitting ducks. Some dealers opt for a businesslike capitulation, aware that it's the way to go through the process with the least fuss. Others, especially lobby dealers with access to an apartment upstairs, tend to make a mad dash for freedom. In brief, it could be a surrender as slow and dignified as Lee at Appomattox, or it could be bedlam, a roil of running, struggling bodies, and airborne stash. When you can't count the evidence at the scene, you at least have to control it, the hundreds of dollars in small bills, fistfuls of crack slabs, loose decks and bundles of dope, and you jam it in your pockets like a handful of ball bearings, when there might be a crowd screaming, or perps for whom the fight-or-flight reflex is not a simple either-or proposition.

The smarter dealers carry nothing on them, but you await information from the OP, sometimes with distaste that verges on dread: "It's in his sock—"

"It's in the cast on his right hand—"

"It's in his cheek—sorry, guy, the other cheek, check between 'em. I mean it's in his ass, you copy?"

There was nothing quite like watching someone sniff a bag of dope that was fresh from a dealer's ass. Stash could be hidden under a bottle cap or in a potato-chip bag, strewn amid the liberality of non-criminal trash. It could be wedged in a light fixture in a hall, or tucked inside the bumper of a car; in a magnetic key case, stuck to the iron bolt beneath a park bench, or on a string, taped to the wall and dangling down the garbage-disposal chute. It was the last part of the game—the triathlon, or pentathlon, plus or minus one—of a SNEU op: Watch and Catch; Chase and Search; Fight and Find.

No day passed without some little adventure or eccentric encounter that made us wonder, or made us laugh. Or in my case, that brought up something to keep in mind for the next time: to check the player for keys, to see if one fit a mailbox; to pull a buyer around a corner or into a lobby, to limit public attention to the stop; or to check for the stash inside of the hat brim, or behind the leather brand patch on the waist of the jeans, or under the tongue of the sneakers. It was Stix, I think, who picked out a kid in the park and said he had just hit someone off. I stopped him and searched him, coming up with nothing, and then Stix said, "Open up and smile," and he grimaced to expose a dozen black-topped crack vials that filled his mouth like rotten teeth. Tony once pulled product out of one guy's ear, like a magician.

There was one spot we'd hit that we called The Hole, a huge, abandoned factory where they sold heroin. It occupied a large corner lot, and they pitched from each side of the building, through a blocked-up front door on one side, and at a sidewalk-level gap in the wall below a loading dock on the other. Until recently, the South Bronx had been full of such buildings, burntout and falling down, with a shell-shocked look, like the war was over and the other side won. Inside, it was more like a haunted house, with vast, dark, high-ceilinged rooms where your footsteps would startle pigeons and rats into sudden flight, and vice versa; if you walked up the stairs, they'd creak and give ominously; if you walked down them to the basement, the growling of pit bulls would stop you in your tracks. You might find a half-dozen junkies sprawled out on the floor, moaning a little, or moving a little, but there was something wrong with how they shifted, or made sounds, or - didn't, as if they were in intensive care and someone had turned off all the machines. The Hole was run by a crew from down the block, and the junkies bought from them and sold for them, and the healthy, happy fatness of the dealers stood out as they hovered on the corner to supervise or to bring in new supplies to their cadaverous charges. On Saturdays, a busload of white Christians would park there, handing out sandwiches and pamphlets, and the dealers and junkies gathered around to blend in with them. The half-dead and the overfed mingled with the well-scrubbed missionaries, eating free baloney and talking about Jesus as they peddled their dope. When we'd hit the set, all of them looked at us like we were Cossacks.

We had spirit, and we had standards. There was plenty to do in the Four-O, and we didn't have to scavenge for collars. We didn't bother with marijuana, and we rarely took the buyers just for trespass, as it didn't seem sporting—if they beat us, they beat us. The dealers didn't catch that break, of course, and taking them in for trespass gave us the opportunity for a more thorough search at the precinct. And like most cops when they had a little time on, we left bums alone, mostly out of sympathy, mostly for ourselves—what good was done by taking a street guy off the street for a day, having to pick through six layers of year-old underwear for a slab of crack, while he's hacking up hepatitis all over you, and his feet are giving off a stink that could capsize a ship? A police officer was supposed to use Discretion—*a little D*—and if we laid claim to a larger measure than we were entitled to, no one complained:

"Hey, Tony, you get the guy in the black leather? Is he a hit?"

"Mmm, we got 'em, OV, but this is a D. Heavy D."

"How heavy?"

"He puked."

"Ten-four. Let me know when you're 98, we got more."

· · ·

AS WE FUSED TOGETHER AS A TEAM, OUR GROWING DEVO-tion to the idea of all-for-one, one-for-all did not always work to our practical advantage. Some variation of this conversation seemed to take place daily:

"I'm going to get something to eat."

"Where you going?"

"Chinese."

"Could you pick me up a slice from Giovanni's?"

"And could you stop by McDonald's?"

"Could you wait half an hour, and I'll go with you?"

"Me, too, except in an hour, and I don't want Chinese, I wanna sit down, for Spanish."

"You know what, forget it, I'm not hungry anymore."

But God forbid if you just went out and grabbed something. Then the accusations would fly, in tones that insinuated a form of adultery: "You ate, - didn't you? *You ate!* Admit it!"

"How'd you get there?"

"I bet you took Brook Avenue, motherfucker, 'cause it's a one-way street."

"One-way streets are all you take. . . ."

In response to our cockeyed communism, Carroll became a kind of mock-democrat. He'd ask us where we wanted to work, and the team would offer suggestions:

"Let's do Mitchell—one-seven-five Alex."

"How about Melrose-Jackson, maybe three-oh-five-oh Park?"

"Or Betances."

"Betances, yeah, one-four-eight and Brook."

And Carroll would listen judiciously and say, "All right, good. So . . . let's go set up for Mott-Pat." In general, Stix, Orville, and Alicia felt more strongly that the team should decide how we worked, whereas Tony, Sammy, and I tended to think Carroll would run the show, as a matter of reality if not natural right. As Tony put it, "Shit rolls downhill." He had a talent for summing things up.

At first, SNEU was a uniformed unit, and over the years, it had gone back and forth between plainclothes and "the bag." Inspector Mullen told me that a few years ago, when he was the CO of the Four-Seven, it was considered a radical step to let the cops in the OP wear NYPD windbreakers over their regular uniforms, which was not exactly deep cover. Plainclothes still had a Serpico-era stigma of corruption, but the more immediate concern was that when you had precinct-level units like SNEU and Crime in the mix with Narcotics, Street Crime, and whoever else was out there, there was a greater chance for mishap if cops failed to recognize one another. As the precinct units were presumed to be less experienced, they were the risk that was reduced. In the bag, you were less effective—sometimes, slipping into an OP while in uniform was impossible—but in plainclothes, there was greater institutional liability. When something went wrong, everyone went back in the bag, regardless of whether the issue was related to uniforms, but as the incident faded from memory and efficiency again became the priority, we slipped back into our own clothes. The cycles went round and round, every few years.

When we started, only the cops in the OP wore plainclothes. Usually, we'd decide among ourselves, in the locker room, but it happened now and then that we all came down in plainclothes, or uniform. Carroll would look at us with hapless aggravation, and we'd shrug—no one can play dumb like a bunch of cops. Some of the guys, like Orville, didn't care whether they were in the bag, but I did—you could get in to the precinct a little later and stroll in to roll call, and you were more comfortable outside without the uniform, especially in the heat. After the regimentation of patrol, from shoeshine inspections to assigned meal times, plainclothes felt grown-up and professional. I grew the white-guy-in-Narcotics goatee, which appeared to be mandatory. But when we all showed up in plainclothes, it was often with an agenda, as we hoped that Carroll would just say, "Oh, the hell with it, let's just go like we are." Eventually, we worked in plainclothes all the time.

Once, we tried to pull that same trick with a tour change, starting at seven in the morning on the last one, instead of at ten. I didn't think we'd get away with it, but since Tony had broken his leg playing football, the menshevik faction was short a vote, next to the bolsheviks. Sgt. Carroll saw through it immediately, partly because he'd heard we'd all come down to roll call in uniform. And he wasn't pleased, to say the least, though he never pushed me to tell him about it, which inspired some relief and greater respect. We got along well, and I went to his house for his son's christening—sorry guys, I never told you—but whether you looked at it as part of the laws of gravity or those of loyalty, the first bond was among partners, cop to cop. The friction with Sgt. Carroll was petty and infrequent, and though I sometimes missed the independence of working alone, I came to see each of my partners as a great asset to the team.

Tony looked black and had an Italian name. He was from the heart of the South Bronx, near Charlotte Street, where presidents since Carter had come to witness the wastelands of the inner city. More than any of us, Tony knew how rough it was out there, and how much worse it had been, and how funny it could be sometimes. Once, we drove past kids playing in an inflatable pool on the sidewalk, leaping and splashing around the gutter, and he said, "Ain't you living ghetto-fabulous." A lot of the team's in-jokes came from Tony, the double- and triple-aged ironies of us and them. When you'd get up from a scrap with a perp, he'd ask, "You ah-ite?" and you'd say, "I'm ah-ite, yo.'" When Sgt. Carroll's wife was pregnant, Tony got us to inquire after her health by asking: "How yo' baby-mother? How she feelin'? How yo' baby-moms?"

Orville also had a way with words, although whether it was Jamaican or just Orvillean was hard to tell sometimes. A scrip from OV might go, "He's got a blue shirt and pants, they're like space pants, I don't know, he's got some kind of space-ass pants on. All right, Space-Ass is getting in a car and going south. . . ." Where someone else might say "John Doe," he would use "Joe Neckbone," as in, "It's not the kind of gun you get from Joe Neckbone on One-Five-Three and Melrose." And once we locked up a guy for buying crack who began to cry, saying he'd never been arrested before, he was only getting it for a girl he liked. "So what's the moral of the story?" Orville asked. "Don't trade crack for ass."

Orville was also one of the more driven guys in the group, quick to say what was on his mind. In contrast, nothing got under Sammy's skin. Sammy was the oldest of us, the father of four children and a sergeant in the Marine reserves, so that the pitch and roll of team life bothered him least. Sammy had an unassuming way about him, and in plainclothes, he could go anywhere without being made for a cop. Part of this had to do with his stature; as we liked to put it, Tony was Puerto Rican but Sammy was "Short-a-Rican."

In the Academy, Stix was even quieter that I was, but he seemed to have gotten over it, at least within the team. The underlying idea behind his jokes was a pretense of innocent confusion, whether his own or that he caused in others. If a squad car was in the way of our ops, he would get on the radio and pretend to be the desk officer, calling them back to the base: "Ten-two, unit, come on in a minute. . . ." At the precinct one day, in the arrest processing room—a small room in the back, with two cells, a long table for cops to do paperwork, and a fingerprint area—we collared a perp named Trujillo, and Stix subjected his name to ever more inventive mispronunciations, at increasing volume levels: "Which one a you is . . . Trilogy? Yeah, Trilogy, step up, you heard me, I got work to do!"

"Hey, Tally-ho, step out of the cell, we gotta search ya, hop to it!"

"Hey, True Jello! Yeah, you—True Jello! You know who I'm talking to, what's your address!"

There was just enough sincerity in his voice to make it work. He was particular, about his hair and about bathrooms and especially about what he ate. He was a healthy eater, favoring salads and pasta and sliced turkey, and mostly, he would bring food from his girlfriend Anna's deli. If he got South

Bronx pizza, he would scrape the sauce and cheese off it, because he only ate homemade. He would grill you about what you ate as if it were a matter of national security:

"What you get?"

"A hero, sausage and peppers."

"How was it?"

"Arright."

"Arright? Just arright, not good, not bad?"

"Yeah, pretty much—it was arright."

"Would you say it was—"

"Fine, it was great, it was incredible, it was the best fucking thing I ever ate."

"Yeah? Really? That good?"

In contrast, Alicia often maintained a shrewd aloofness toward work. She didn't drive, and she only took misdemeanors, because she didn't like going to court—for every felony, at least one officer had to testify in the Grand Jury, and those cases were more likely to go to trial, though few ever did. While we waited in the van, she would sit in the back and read, which some of the other guys found irksome, although I didn't—probably because I did a lot of reading, too. When she finished her own book or magazine, she'd ransack my bag to see what I had. Because Alicia was petite and female, perps sometimes thought they could get over on her, which was a mistake. On the street, Alicia was as tough as anyone. Tony did an impression of a perp with Alicia's hands around his neck—"*The—drugs—are—in—my— pocket!*"—as he rolled his eyes and gasped. I never saw that, but I did see that when perps even cursed at her, they were quick to apologize. Alicia was black and Puerto Rican, "a swirl," as Orville would say, or "black and brown, like a Doberman." She was married, with two kids, and one of them would be dropped off at the precinct now and then, and it was a wonderful thing to watch her help him with his homework, tender and patient, and see the contrast between home life, job life, and street life, and how it demanded a different person to meet each.

The natural bonds of police work made us closer, even as the inevitable strains pushed us away from the rest of the precinct. For example, the precinct had only two unmarked vans, and often one or both would be out of service. Our chief competition for vehicles was Anti-Crime, whom we viewed as equals, but we sometimes got the feeling that the favor was not returned. Their boss, Tommy Clark, was one of the guys whose medal rack stretched above his shoulder, and his cops were also a talented and dedicated crew—

Eddie Wynne, Jimmy Rizzi, Richie Hyde, Anna Ramirez, Rob Knapp, Nefti Cruz. We were scheduled for alternating weeks of four-to-twelves and ten-to-sixes to reduce the overlap, but it didn't always work out. One day, as we brought a van full of prisoners to Central Booking, we got a series of calls to return the van to the base. We couldn't, at first, and then we weren't much inclined to hurry, and then we found out that one of our perps had active TB. We'd spent the last couple of hours breathing the same cubic feet of air. When we returned to the precinct, we all climbed out of the van wearing surgical masks, tossed Crime the keys, and said, "It's all yours." They didn't think it was as funny as we did, but as Sgt. Carroll liked to remind us, "We're here to make collars, not friends."

The stronger bond came from what happened in the street. We all knew that if there was a scrap, the whole team was there for it, as far as it had to go. That trust could make you feel extravagantly wealthy, but it was also the minimum wage you needed to work: if a cop demonstrated a too-acute instinct for self-preservation during a brawl—"Go get 'em, guys, I'll find backup!"—many cops refused to work with him or her again, and their requests were usually honored. At least as often, there were situations that arose that required a common read on things, when everyone's instincts jibed to say, "This one's a little weird, let's do it by the book," or, "This one's a lot weird—let's keep walking, like it never happened." Let's call them hypotheticals.

What if you tossed a guy and came up with a crack stem or a little weed? You didn't want it, or him, and you also didn't want to bother with the vouchering and the rest of the paperwork. What if you just threw it out, and told him to watch his step? On the good side, you'd get a guy who owed you, and he might give you some useful information down the line, and you could get back to doing your real work. On the bad side, you had just destroyed evidence, and if it came up and you denied it, you'd have committed perjury.

What if you found drugs in the back seat of the van, or a squad car? What you were supposed to do was notify the desk officer, and the previous operator would get a Command Discipline for his failure to search the vehicle. Maybe he would get a "Warn and Admonish," or maybe he would lose time, depending on his record, or his relationship with the CO or the lieutenant assigned as Integrity Control Officer. Since squad cars often transported someone else's prisoners, it seemed especially unfair for them to take the hit, when it was the arresting officer's fault for not searching the perp. What kept you from throwing the drugs down the sewer was the fear that they were planted by Internal Affairs, who could hit you with charges relating to the destruction of evidence and possibly perjury, again, if you were questioned and your answers were cute. You tried to guess what was going on by what you found and where you found it—if there was a little slab wedged under a seat belt, it could well have been there for weeks, but if there was a bundle of dope in the middle of the seat, it was a harder call. If the previous driver was still around, you might suggest he look again before he "officially" turned in the keys, but if he had already left, you had to make a decision.

What if you had three or four perps in the van when you rolled up on a dealer, and there was a rumble? The driver of the van has to stay with the prisoners; they are his responsibility, without exception. But who would stay inside a car when his partners were in trouble on the street? What would it matter if all the junkies in the world went free, if it kept your partner from getting hurt? And what if, when the dealer was subdued, you returned to the van to see that there was a little more room in the back seat, with a crowd gathered, laughing? Do you put it over the air, making official notification of escaped prisoners, that will cost at least the cops in the van their spot in the unit, plus a ten- or twenty-day hit? Or will you just pack everyone up and start looking? And if you still don't find them, what do you do? Hope that they aren't collared by a cop without a clue, and that you didn't scratch your shield number on your cuffs? What kind of trouble are you willing to get in to stay out of trouble?

What if you grabbed a lady for buying heroin, and she started moaning and yelling about how sick she was? A lot of people develop sudden illnesses when they're in cuffs, and you do not treat them as if they were relatives who said they weren't feeling well. What if you put her in the van, and she started screaming, "I got AIDS! I got mental problems! I got diarrhea! Take me to the hospital, now!" And what if you knew she was telling the truth about the third ailment, because she stood up on the seat while still rear-cuffed, dropped her drawers and unloosed a fetid green stream into her hands, which she flung toward the front? And the cops dove from the van like it was being shelled, and when they stood outside and watched her, she began to grind her massive, bare cheeks against the windows, pumping out sewage as she moved, smearing it across the windows until you couldn't see inside? Would you take that collar, or decide that maybe cops should have the power to pardon, like presidents and kings, and offer horrified amnesty on the spot?

As I said, these are hypotheticals, and I won't say whether any of them happened to us. I won't even say what I would have done, or defend the merits of any decision, excepting, perhaps, the diarrhea attack, where I would have not only let the lady go, but then poured gasoline onto the van and lit a match. But I will say, at least, that narcotics has been a very funny business for a very long time.

• • •

ALMOST EVERYTHING SAID ABOUT DRUGS IS AT LEAST HALF true. Drug laws are unfair, because vastly disproportionate numbers of black men are incarcerated, while white drug use is considerably larger; the drug laws are reasonable, because the effects of drugs are far more destructive within poor communities. It is hypocritical for us to police the drug-supplying nations, because America's appetite for drugs is their reason for being; we have to go after evil foreign drug lords who have enslaved innocent Americans. Addiction is a disease, and we are wrong to rely on a legal remedy for a medical condition; drug use is a choice, and we have to hold people responsible for their actions. The War on Drugs is a failure. The War on Drugs is a success.

From a police perspective, narcotics falls under the category of vice offenses, which traditionally included gambling, prostitution, and alcohol. No aspect of policing has had as troubled a history as vice enforcement: these were crimes that did pay, often extremely well, and the reasons for prohibition are more abstract than for crimes against persons or property, a distinction that has often undermined public support. In New York, criminal possession of a controlled substance in the seventh degree—for up to five vials of crack, or seven glassines of heroin, give or take—is a class-A misdemeanor, punishable by a maximum sentence of one year in jail. So is assault in the third degree, which differs from felony assault by a lack of "serious" injury or the use of a weapon. And it is hard to argue that beating someone up is just as bad as putting cocaine up your nose. Even when large numbers of people are doing large amounts of cocaine—which tends to drive up the assault rate—couldn't we just punish the assaults in and of themselves, and treat the addiction as a sickness instead of a sin?

Although heroin and cocaine are so contagious that they sell themselves, major epidemics of drug abuse have always been sponsored by organizations of extraordinary dedication and ruthlessness. Long before the Mafia, the Colombian cartels, and the Burmese warlords, there was the British East India Company, against which the first War on Drugs was lost. In the two

Opium Wars of the mid–nineteenth century, the Chinese fought the British to prevent them from smuggling opium into China, which it had done since the late 1700s, to improve the balance of trade. Though there were other issues behind the conflict, the bald fact of the matter is that the British created the largest intentional outbreak of a disease in human history: one third of the Chinese were regular users, and half of those were "sots," hopeless, useless, and nearly lifeless. The Chinese were forced to cede Hong Kong after the first war, in 1842, and to legalize the drug after the second, in 1860. After the British victories, the Americans and the French negotiated their own trade agreements, though the British continued to dominate the market.

By the late nineteenth century, the problems of addiction became a widespread concern in the West, which found outlet in the usual forums of public debate and popular culture. Sherlock Holmes was a great detective, but he probably wouldn't have worked out too well in SNEU. In one story, he defends his use of cocaine to a worried and skeptical Dr. Watson, claiming that the drug provides a worthy diversion when his mind is not stimulated by a case. Cocaine had been hailed as a wonder drug by many eminent figures of the late nineteenth century, among them Sigmund Freud, whose essay "Über Coca" was a "hymn of praise." Cocaine-infused drinks such as Celery Cola, Dope Cola, and most famously Coca-Cola, were touted by the Temperance movement as healthy and stimulating alternatives to alcohol. Cocaine was recommended for treatment of a range of ailments, from sinus trouble to morphine addiction.

Opiate abuse had been commonplace in America at least since the Civil War. Morphine was prescribed primarily for depression, insomnia, and pain, and secondarily for just about everything else, from nymphomania to hiccups. Though the opium dens became locally notorious in the Chinatowns of New York and San Francisco, the typical addict was a middle-class white female whose habit developed from medical treatment rather than recreational use, like the tranquilized housewives of a century later. Americans were avid consumers of the patent medicines marketed with Barnumesque fraudulence and flair, and it was only after the Pure Food and Drug Act of 1906 that people realized that so-called cures for opiate and cocaine addiction were often loaded with opiates and cocaine. At the turn of the century, it was estimated that there were 200,000 cocaine addicts and 250,000 opiate addicts, an overlapping population that may have included one American out of every 250.

Domestic control of drugs began in 1914 with the Harrison Act, and it gathered force through the 1920s with further restrictions and the establishment of a Federal Bureau of Narcotics. Almost immediately, the addict population shifted, from female to male, medical to recreational, and the modern profile of the drug user emerged, of a marginal and transient young man in the city. For the most part, drugs were of a piece with the down-and-out world of the pool hall and the flophouse. They circulated through the traditional vice rackets, at the lower-end bars and brothels, where they were dominated by the same gangsters: Arnold Rothstein was a financier of the opiate trade in the 1920s, which primarily came from legal manufacturers on the continent, and Lucky Luciano's first arrest was for selling heroin.

Somewhat astoundingly, the federal interdiction effort was quite successful by the 1930s. The first head of the Bureau of Narcotics was ousted after it emerged that his son, an attorney, had represented Rothstein on a tax case, and his son-in-law had borrowed money from the gangster. Harry Anslinger then led the agency for the next three decades, and though he is now generally regarded as an empty suit, his first ten years saw a marked decline in the shipment and use of drugs. Opium and cocaine virtually disappeared, and heroin became increasingly more diluted, expensive, and difficult to obtain. By the Second World War, the United States could claim near-total victory over drug use and trafficking, however short-lived.

The Cold War inadvertently set the stage for the return of narcotics, in devastating strength. For the most part, the Mafia had been bitter enemies of Mussolini, and several men who would become leaders of the American underworld, such Joe Bonanno, were driven into exile by the Fascists. During the Allied Occupation, many of the local mafiosi were returned to power by the Americans, who were in need of a leadership that was equally free of Fascist and Communist taint. This resurrection of the Sicilian Mafia coincided with the deportation of some four hundred gangsters, including Lucky Luciano, who introduced their local counterparts to the lucrative narcotics trade. The Sicilians often worked with Corsican gangsters in Marseilles, where the "French Connection" soon supplied 85 to 90 percent of the heroin that arrived in the United States. The French government did little to discourage it: de Gaulle was delighted to thwart American policy, and the problem of addiction was not significant in France at the time. More sinister was the fact that the narcotics trade helped finance French military and intelligence efforts in its about-to-be former colonies, especially in Indochina, where the "Golden Triangle" was the world's great opiate producer, along with the "Golden Crescent" of the Near East, from Turkey to Pakistan.

After the war, heroin use was largely confined to a few, narrow subcultures—among jazz musicians, most famously—from which it spread, like a rumor or a fad, in a geometric progression. The drug was seen as part of a lifestyle that opted out of the mainstream, whether as a protest against the specific exclusion of blacks from postwar opportunity, or as part of the larger, looser cynicism of the counterculture. Some junkies started because they were shut out of society, others because they didn't want to join it, and still others because they believed it explained how Charlie Parker played or Billie Holiday sang. Whether the pipe dream appealed to them or the American dream didn't, once people started, their original reasons didn't matter. As heroin spread through the larger black community, especially in the northern ghettoes, the price went up and the quality went down, even as the addict population exploded. Property crimes skyrocketed to pay for habits, and then violent crimes followed, not only in the competition between dealers, but also disciplinary and debt-collecting functions of the gangs. By the 1960s, changes in the welfare system had accelerated the already extraordinary chaos of the ghettoes, in its disastrous effects on patterns of marriage and work, which remain the two greatest bulwarks against criminality. Heroin created thousands of rich killers and millions of derelicts, whores, and thieves. In short, it created crime as we know it.

In a sense, heroin was one of many white appropriations of black culture, following the same routes of imitation as the blues and hip-hop. But if heroin moved up from the ghetto, cocaine reached down from the white upper classes, offering a mass-market taste of glamour, like designer jeans. Through the mid-eighties, most media coverage of cocaine had an envious quality, as if the chief problem with the party favor of Hollywood parties and Studio 54 was that it was too expensive. Though official anti-drug rhetoric had been fairly constant for decades, it was only in 1986, after the death of basketball star Len Bias, and after crack began to burn through the cities, that action backed up the words. Until then, there was little attention paid to cocaine at the federal level: in 1985, of the hundred agents in the New York office of the DEA, only ten were assigned to cocaine cases, and in South Florida, where the drug had become a seven-billion-dollar industry, the DEA had to have a bake sale to raise money. In other words, until fairly recently, the war on drugs was remarkable for its lack of troops and ammunition, though the casualties certainly abounded.

The modern cocaine business began when George Jung met Carlos Lehder in federal prison, in 1974. Jung, who was from a white, working-class New England background, had developed a sophisticated marijuana business, in which he bought drugs by the ton in Mexico and flew them all over the country in small planes. Carlos Lehder was a car thief from Colombia, who would join with Pablo Escobar and the Ochoa family to form the Medellín cartel. Jung had a hippie's soft-minded indulgence toward drug use, believing it to be kind of harmless and sort of a civil right, whereas the fanatical Lehder saw cocaine as the atomic bomb he was going to drop on America. Cocaine, which had been smuggled by the pound, now began to enter the country by the ton, and the Colombians introduced a degree of violence to the trade that would have made the Mafia blanch. Cops were killed by the hundreds in Medellín, and entire families were murdered, sometimes by the "necktie" method, in which the throat was cut and the tongue pulled out to dangle down the chest. Sometime in the early 1980s, someone invented crack, and business got even bigger than anyone could have imagined.

Cocaine used to cost as much as the best champagne, but crack made the price drop to that of a pack of cigarettes. People fought to buy it and sell it, with more and bigger guns that they sometimes shot without even looking. By the early 1990s, the New York City annual homicide rate had passed two thousand, of which half were estimated to be drug-related. Crack ravaged entire neighborhoods and seemed to claim as many women as men; heroin took a lot of fathers, and now crack took mothers, too. If heroin made the streets unsafe, crack killed people who hadn't even left their homes, and mothers in the ghettoes practiced a kind of fire drill, sending the kids under their beds or into the bathtub at the sound of gunfire. Even as the crack epidemic started to level off, the Colombians began to produce heroin of exceptional quality.

We're not back where we started, by any means, but quitting time—for addict, dealer, cop—is nowhere in sight. Certain countries that used to produce narcotics—Turkey—seemed to have kicked the habit, although others—Burma, Colombia—have picked up the slack. Here, many of the kinds of people who used to take drugs fairly casually in the late 1970s—maybe a third of teenagers, almost half the armed forces—don't use them in anywhere near those numbers. In New York, the expansion of the Narcotics Division was as much a bulwark of Giuliani's crime-fighting strategy as Compstat and the "Broken Windows" theory, though rarely as celebrated, and the eight years of his administration saw the murder rate drop by nearly two-thirds and violent crime by half. As always, most of the money for drugs comes from the suburbs, but most of the blood is shed in the city streets. While some people complain that there are too many people in prison, and others think that there aren't enough, the fact of the matter is that if you got rid of narcotics, you could send half of the cops in this city home. Until then, we take it a day at a time.

And every day, we got to pick: crack or dope, dope or crack. Overall, I'd say I came to prefer dope. It was an acquired taste. Maybe because the players seemed more reachable, as the street dealers at dope spots were often junkies themselves, with a half a mind to clean up and get out, while the hand-to-hands at crack spots were mostly hard-rock younger guys, out to fuck the world and make a buck. Crackheads themselves were rarely trusted with the stash, or even to stand still and look out for the cops. For the most part, they were figures from a famine, bone-thin and filthy. Months in that life took years from their lives, with thirty-year-olds who could pass for fifty, burnt-out almost literally, with a red-hot core of desperation beneath a dead, charred surface. Junkies were a little more human, for a little while longer. Heroin is far purer than it has been in the past, and a lot of junkies snorted it, instead of shooting it, which decreased the risk of disease and also seemed to slow the forward momentum of addiction. They had a longer ride to the bottom, though for all I've run into, the habit gradually slid from being a part of their life to becoming the point of it. But the terminal junkies are even more awful, to me, because they have none of the trapped-rat frenzy of the crackhead, possessing instead a fatal calm, as if they are keeping their eyes open as they drown. When you collar them, they can have a look of confirmed and somehow contented self-hatred, as if the world is doing to them what they expect and deserve. Maybe I didn't prefer heroin, after all.

There is something authentically tragic about addicts, in the way the wreckage of their lives is both freely chosen and somehow fated. They are both casualties of a condition that is believed to have a genetic component, and committed collaborators in their own downfall. They deserve pity, always, and often they inspire contempt. We collared one crackhead, bumping into him by accident as he stood in a lobby counting out a handful of vials. He was a street peddler who sold clothing, and he had about eighty dollars in his pocket. He had the shrink-wrapped look that crackheads get, as if his skin was two sizes too small. He moaned and wept for his infant child, who would starve without his support, he told us. Yes, he acknowledged, the baby lived with the mother, but he was the provider. They were only about ten blocks away, in a playground, and so we drove to meet them. The mother was a pretty and well-dressed woman, though her soccer-mom demeanor was heightened by the contrast with her handcuffed spouse. We called her over, and her look of mild confusion became one of mild dismay as she saw our back-seat passenger. She didn't look surprised and didn't ask questions. He took out his wad of cash, peeled off three dollars and handed it to me to give her. "You gotta be kidding me," I said. "You give me all this father-of-the-year shit, just to throw her three bucks?"

"C'mon," he said. "When you get out of Central Booking, you're hungry, you want some real McDonald's or something."

I gave him back the three dollars and took the wad for the mother. "The Number Two Special, two cheeseburgers and fries, is $2.99," I told him. "It's what I get, and it's all you can afford." For an addict, the priorities are never unclear.

For dealers, the pull of the drug trade is obviously financial, but most make surprisingly little money. The economics—call it crackanomics, or smackanomics—generate vast amounts of money, but it is rarely shared with the front-line pitchers. After talking to one dealer I arrested, I worked it out that he sold three-dollar vials of crack and made five dollars for every twenty he sold. Though he usually averaged around fifteen vials an hour, the day we grabbed him had been slow—all told, he'd worked four hours for fifteen dollars. His proceeds, which were confiscated, were less than the minimum wage.

"Do you realize you'd make more with a paper route?" I asked. He shrugged. He'd had a job at Blockbuster, once, but he stopped going because his shirt was dirty and he didn't have a chance to wash it. His father was in prison for drug sales, and he'd sold since he was thirteen, he told me, as if it was a habit he was unable to break.

Because the "victims" of drug sales literally line up to pay for the privilege, the dealers sometimes don't have the forthright menace of violent felons. In the movies, there are a lot of drug-dealer villains, but the characters usually have to slap their girlfriends around or kill a lot of cops to heighten the dramatic point of their bad-guyness. While life has provided art with plenty of rough stuff to imitate, some people have argued that it need not be so bloody; that the violence generated by the drug trade would disappear upon legalization. In other words, we can't eliminate the drug business, but we might try improving it. The usual analogy offered is that of Prohibition, which shifted the liquor industry from an aspect of hospitality to an engine of organized crime. But for history to repeat itself in this case would be more wishful than anything else; after the repeal of Prohibition, the Mob not only moved on but grew even richer, larger, and more destructive. In SNEU, it seemed that the illegality of narcotics was precisely what drew the sellers:

most players had rap sheets for robbery or theft before settling on the more lucrative and "less illegal" world of drug sales, and many remained committed to a diversified life of crime. The perps were perps before they became dealers, and the question they asked—and answered—was not whether to commit a crime, but what kind of crime to commit. Amid all the heavy weather of the issues, it was surprisingly easy to make out the bad guys.

And if I had any doubts, the dealers were good enough to spell it out for me. Heroin is stamped with a brand name on the little wax-paper envelopes in which the drug is packaged. This practice gives a glimpse not only of a corporate structure, when the same brands appear in different locations, but also of a corporate imagination, showing what they believe their product should mean to their market. Some convey the blandly generic aspiration of quality that you might find on brands of corn flakes or detergent: First Class, President, Original, Amazing, and Amazed, though the last was more distinctive, as it was illustrated with a picture of a baby gazing at his enormous penis. I liked the politeness of Thank You, the impoliteness of Fuck You, and the surliness of No Joke, because it suggested a certain lack of self-esteem. Others invoked a racier allure, but the gimmick is so hackneyed in regular ads that the genuinely illicit thrills of No Limit, Poison Ivy, or Knockout invoke the mock-illicit thrill of ads for perfume or fat-free ice cream. Topical references are common, from the flat-out copyright infringement of DKNY or Ford, to movie tag-lines like Show Me the Money. But the best brand names are the literal ones, which announce without apology the bad things to come: 911, 25 to Life, Undertaker. There is the suicidal candor to Lethal Injection and Virus, a forthright finality to OD. There is a truth in advertising here that few products can match.

• • •

EACH OF US PUT TOGETHER A LITTLE KIT, OF BETTER THINGS and extra things, like handcuffs, knives, Leatherman tools, a smaller, more powerful flashlight than standard issue, antibacterial soap, latex gloves, and batting gloves, whose thin leather allowed for a better search. I had several sets of binoculars from my father—he was a collector of potentially useful devices, like telescopes and barometers—and we went through them all. *You got eyes?* Yeah, I got eyes. They would get beat up on the street and dropped in the van, and one eye would lose focus, and then both, but even so, it seemed an honorable end to them. They were large and unwieldy, however, and since I couldn't move in plainclothes as well as Sammy or Orville could, the additional tip of the binocular case would have made me look like I was on safari. But when subtlety is not an option, banality can be, and so I'd dawdle over to an OP in uniform with the binoculars in a Dunkin' Donuts bag, so that my presence did not draw any great interest. We made do with what we had.

We also made do with each other. I could talk to Alicia about books. I went back with Stix to our first days on the Job. Anyone could get along with Sammy. Orville and I usually wanted to push things, to stay out longer and take more bodies. Tony and I were hungry for guns, for mix-it-up adventures like hitting the Hole. Sgt. Carroll and I were determined to move up in the game, to get search warrants. Our idiosyncrasies also were duly noted. Orville and Tony didn't like dogs, Alicia didn't take attitude, Stix had a dread of roaches, and Sammy drove like Grandma Moses. I wasn't big on heights. In a sneaker-conscious environment, I had ratty old white canvas high-tops, the like of which most of us hadn't seen since childhood. I ate big sloppy sandwiches that I had to hold with both hands, usually with gobs of hot sauce. I stuffed my old paperwork into the bottom of my locker, which Tony regarded with horror. I tended to show up for work at the last minute, or a minute or two later.

Though we were a tight group, we didn't go out together. Everyone was married or had a steady girlfriend, with plenty of friends outside of the Job, and to keep each other company for fifty or sixty hours a week was enough. If the four-to-twelve shift went out for a beer, a couple of times over the summer Orville and Sammy might stop by for one, and Tony, Sgt. Carroll, and I for a few more, but Stix and Alicia wouldn't go at all. But that was the extent of it. Other cops were close, off duty and on, like the Bike team, with Sgt. Steve O'Hagan, Scott "Smacky" Mackay, Tommy "Stretch" Dolan, George "Chicky" Mendez, Steve "Sprinkles" Vergeli, Andy Bielawski, and later, Joey Castaldo and Joe Barongi. And they went out often, for a beer or to go golfing, even sometimes for vacations. As cops, they were at least as good as we were, at least at first, in part because the players somehow couldn't take a cop on a bike seriously—in the summer, they wore polo shirts and shorts, and in general there was something innocent and playful and time-killing about a guy on a bike. It seemed less like a vehicle than a toy, as if they patrolled on pogo sticks. But when they hit a set, they could move in like the cavalry.

So could we. One morning as we drove to get breakfast, we passed a player as he hit off three or four junkies in a park, on One-Four-Six and College, plain as day, one after the other, with a deft, practiced hand like a black-jack dealer over a green felt table: *Hit me!* It was so near and so clear that it set off an animal instinct in us—*Fetch!*—and when we swerved in and jumped out, it seemed like we dropped on them from above. The junkies tried to run and the player tried to fight and the drugs sailed up into the air, but in a moment, we had it all wrapped up. A day's work was done in half a minute, with a solid catch: six or seven bundles of dope, a few bodies, a dealer who glared at us, muttering threats. It wasn't the French Connection, but it was good, quick work. We hadn't seen that spot before, and we didn't again, and that was a fine feeling, since it was across the street from Mother Teresa's convent. Cops make collars, DAs make cases, the bad guys go away, and the neighborhood gets better. That's how it's supposed to work.

When we brought them in to the precinct, a few of us felt another pang, nearly as deep: "Couldn't this have waited until we ate?" Aren't the dealers like mosquitoes, and in the South Bronx it's an endless, sweltering summer, with plenty of rain? None of us had any regrets, but we did wonder whether we might have swatted them just as well on a full stomach as an empty one. After a few days, when other cops looked at the spot, intrigued by our stories of easy pickings, one of them yelled at us, only half-joking, "What the hell did you guys do! You killed the spot!" It was as if we'd not only caught the biggest fish, but drained the pond afterward. In a narrow view of things, a cop who steadily delivers a couple of misdemeanors will never have a problem with the bosses about productivity. Cops used to call the practice of picking off an apple with a care for the cart "angeling," and in Pat Brown's day, gangsters supplied cops with "friendly collars" for gambling raids, so the brass could claim success and move on. On patrol, where you spend your time putting out fires and preventing them, in kitchens and on street corners, you could be a great cop with little "activity" to show for it, and so angeling in some form had its ass-covering value. But in a specialized unit like SNEU, the point was to make collars that meant something. Of course, that wasn't entirely up to us.

Once, we took a dealer for trespass. We knew him and had watched him run his spot, stepping into a building to direct junkie traffic to another player in the lobby. He had left when we hit the set, but we picked him up a few blocks away, and though he had no contraband, he also claimed that he - hadn't been inside the building. As I said, the trespass collar is the Swiss Army knife of the beat cop, but a device with so many uses can sometimes be misapplied. In response, the Bronx DA developed a protocol for trespass arrests, an affidavit that required you to fill in blanks about what you asked and what was answered, where the person did reside, what explanation was offered for their presence, and what you did to check the story. The purpose was to lock in the elements of the crime and to screen out shaky arrests by cops who were too literal-minded—"If you live on the third floor, what are you doing on the eighth?" But for certain ADAs, the form seemed to inspire an equally senseless rigidity of interpretation. For my collar that day, the ADA inquired, "Did you ask him if he knew anyone in the building, if he was visiting anyone?"

"No, I didn't. He denied being there."

"Well, why couldn't he be visiting people there?"

"He was. He was visiting lots of people, to sell them drugs."

"Then why didn't you charge him with sale?"

"We didn't have enough to go on. All we had was the trespass."

"For trespass, you have to ask him if he has a reason to be there."

"No, I don't. I have to find out why he's there. Not even that—if he doesn't live there, he has to tell me why he's there. If he lies to me, I don't have to help him come up with another story."

"On the affidavit, you have to fill out—"

"The affidavit isn't the law. It's a handy way to spell out a charge. It's a useful tool, unlike yourself." Actually, I only thought the last bit, I didn't say it.

"I'd better get my supervisor."

"Okey-doke."

But the exchange I had with the supervisor was even more weirdly circular. She tried to undermine the case in ways I'd never imagined.

"Where was he in the building?"

"He went into the lobby."

"Did you arrest him there?"

"No, when we hit the set, he was gone. We took him a block or two away."

"So you never actually saw him *inside* the building."

"I saw him go through the front door."

"Right, but you didn't see him inside?"

"The door leads to 'inside,' it's where they keep it, inside the building."

"You didn't see him—"

"Maybe you should talk to my supervisor."

Sgt. Carroll had the pleasure of the rest of the conversation, which continued in the science-fiction vein: "You're right, we saw him *go* inside, but not *while* he was inside. He could have vaporized."

Once it was conceded that the door did not lead to another dimension, the line of argument shifted. As I watched Sgt. Carroll, his sense of humor did not leave him altogether, but it took him to places he did not expect to go. We had been together in the OP, and his conversation picked up where mine left off: "He went in and out a lot, all afternoon."

He pursed his lips, nodding.

"Maybe ten seconds here, half a minute there."

There was an ill-concealed sarcasm in his voice, as he conceded, "You're right, it wasn't very long at all."

There was another pause, after which I knew the talk would not go on for long.

"I see. Are you telling me that someone has to be in a building for a certain amount of time before they're trespassing? Can you tell me, as a matter of law, how much time we need? Two minutes? Ten? I'd like to be able to clock it, if that's what we need, and to let the other cops know."

Of course, the trespass "time limit" was pure fabrication—the law says to trespass is to unlawfully "enter or remain" in a premises—but the charges were nonetheless dropped. The collar was a misdemeanor, and it was hard to think of anything that could matter less to any of us—perp, cops, ADA—but the indifference did rankle. Alicia asked me, "And you care about this because . . .?" The answer was partly and simply having a stiff neck, but I also knew that if I didn't fight for my cases, no one else would, and not caring was an easy habit to fall into. When they taught us boxing or judo takedowns in the Academy, they told us, "As you practice, you will play," meaning that if you dog it now in the gym, you're more likely to come up short in the street. And physical and verbal self-defense are not so far removed in mind-set, deriving from an ability to think on your feet and act as you are trained.

"Ya gotta ah-tic-ya-late," we were told, and if you were asked why you stopped someone, you can't say "because they looked funny," unless you can spell out the funniness, the heavy clothing in warm weather, the way they circled the block, their nervous reaction to your arrival. What might begin as pure instinct has to stand as hard argument. The skill of articulation lay in balance of detail and clarity: if you left too much out, it could seem evasive or dishonest, but if you supplied an overabundance of information, the story might be simply incoherent. Anyone would rather handle a simple situation than a complicated one—there is a turn-of-the-century story of a patrolman dragging a dead horse from Kosciusko Street over to Smith Street, so his report would have fewer spelling errors—and in SNEU, the language of each complaint for an observation sale was virtually identical: "At T/P/O Perp #1 did exchange small objects for US Currency from Perps #2 & #3." Perp #2 and Perp #3 might have acted in concert with Perp #1, to exchange small objects for US Currency with Perps #4, #5, and #6, and you would also list what money and drugs were recovered from each, but the language was the same because the situation was the same. No matter if the set was as simple as a cheese-line, or it worked with the many-sided misdirection of the Statue of Liberty play in a football scrimmage, the essential act was a hand-to-hand transaction. The entire criminal-justice system functions as an editorial process, as a story is refined, supported, and checked from the complainant to the cop, to the sergeant and maybe the lieutenant, and then to the ADA, and then to the judge, and sometimes to a jury.

For all that, in the Bronx, they rarely indicted for an observation sale, unless there were four or five buyers, with stash and cash recovered from the dealer as well. If you caught two buyers and the dealer, but he had no drugs, you didn't have a case. Or if you missed the buyers and just grabbed the seller, they only charged misdemeanor possession, even if he had felony weight several times over. They did prosecute with vigor if the perp had prior felony convictions, but that suggested that the perp's past rather than your efforts mattered. My sister-in-law, Beth Brennan, was an ADA in Manhattan, and she was amazed to hear it, and cops who came from other boroughs often found themselves in bewildered confrontations with Bronx ADAs: "I saw the one guy hand the other guy drugs, I saw him take the money, I got them both, what do you mean you're dropping it?" The labor of articulation seemed futile when your word meant so little.

In response, most cops tried to speak up for each other, on duty and off. There were rackets for Sgt. O'Hagan, who had two autistic kids, and Sgt. Kelly, who had triplets with cerebral palsy. There was a funeral for Sgt. Poplaski's boy Frankie, who had a heart condition. There was another funeral for Sgt. Walker Fitzgerald, from the Four-Two. Walker had always been a cool-headed and lighthearted leader in the field, and had looked out for me in his precinct when I was there with a collar. He laughed more than most cops do, but he also was a rising star on the Job, graduating first in his class and gliding through promotional tests. One night in Queens, he was in a car accident, and when he pulled over, a block away, he was jumped and killed. Sordid speculations found their way into the press: Hadn't he been coming from a strip club? Hadn't he "fled from the scene of an accident"? What was he doing in that neighborhood? For cops, the presumption of innocence is a rarity, not a right, and Walker would never get to tell his side of the story. I thought of other questions: wasn't he a murder victim, and a police officer, and a young man with a bright future? The Mayor and the Police Commissioner didn't go to the wake, which was held at the same funeral home where my father's was. I shook his brother Eddie's hand at the casket, where he stood in his dress uniform with an honor guard from his own precinct, Midtown South. He had a fixed smile and a faraway look.

Some days I laughed at how easy it could be: once, we wrapped up a set with five collars, when there were six of us on the team. I didn't take a collar, though I wanted one. As the rest of the team processed, I went up to the second floor of the Four-O and watched the project across the street, at 215 Alexander Avenue. I saw a crackhead pop in and out of the building, and I slipped out after him. I loped down the street, cut into the lot next to St. Jerome's, and grabbed him. I walked him back to the precinct and put him with the rest of the prisoners. "Now we got six," I said. On other days, you were reminded how hard it might go, like when Tony and I took a guy the size of both of us and put him over the hood of a car, and I thought, *Shit, I thought crack's supposed to make you skinny.* As we tried to connect two sets of cuffs behind his back, the perp only then seemed to realize that he was being arrested, and he lifted us up like boats on a tide. Tony and I looked at each other, knowing that we had seconds before he would toss us aside, and locked the cuffs tight. For months, we hit a dope spot run by a guy named Lamont, taking bundles of heroin weekly and in one nice grab, over a thousand dollars in cash. Though we were little more than an aggravation to him—he was always released, usually without bail—the aggravation did mount, and after I collared him the second time, he told me, "You're making this personal, you're costing me. You watch your back out there, something might happen." Lamont had a few bullet holes in him and I didn't doubt he gave better than he got. At the time, I thought his threat meant that he'd say he was paying me, or I was robbing him, but later I realized he intended something else.

One under, two under, three under. Orville once watched a dealer as the guy bounced a spaldeen off a wall, hitting people off as he whiled away the afternoon. When Orville grabbed him, he searched him all over without finding the stash until he squeezed the pink rubber ball, and a slit opened up to reveal the drugs inside. Richie Hyde from Crime saw four junkies in a car, looking out as one of them hid something under the hood. He stopped the car and went through the engine block without finding anything, until one of the junkies admitted what he had done: he had a container of clean urine warming below the fan belt, so they could provide body-temperature drug-free specimens for their parole officer. One day with Bike, we did a car stop. I checked under the seat and felt something heavy in a brown paper bag. I pulled it out and looked inside, but it was a different kind of weapon than the one I expected. "Ugh," I said, "Look at this," and handed it over to one of the other guys. He reached inside and pulled out a dildo, crusty and stained, heavy as a lead pipe. We all looked at him, horrified. "Why don't you head in and wash your hands?"

We ran, fell, and got up again. Once, I chased a guy on a bicycle, and be-cause he had to turn as he saw me I gained on him, and I could see him pump down on the pedals with all his dead weight, but I gained even as he started to pick up speed, and I knew he was thinking, *If he catches me when I'm on wheels, it's time to give it up. . . .* As he rounded the corner I closed in to a few feet away, until I hit an oil slick and my feet flew out from under me. My radio, nightstick, and ass bounced in three different directions over the pave-ment. It was a good spill, I knew, because the crowd winced instead of laugh-ing. Of course, my partners laughed. Our entertainment didn't depend on seeing each other trip, but it helped. I watched from an OP as they prepared to hit the lobby of 175 Alex, creeping along the wall in the dark, toward the railed stairs and the locked front door, which meant they would have to leap over on cue as someone left the building. When I gave the signal, it was like watching a herd of wildebeest charge across a river, losing the unfit to the current and the crocs.

We didn't develop a herd mentality as much as a hive mentality, instantly known to each other by temperament and task, but a droning, indistinguish-able whole to an outside observer. That's probably what it sounded like, too, if you heard us argue over which diner to go to for breakfast:

"We can't go there, I saw five roaches. Let's go to the other place."

"By the clinic? That place is full of junkies, the Number Two special comes with methadone."

"Well, I'm not going where you want, I heard a cop got a bloody Band-Aid in his BLT."

"It was an honest mistake. What do you think the 'B' stands for in BLT?"

Whenever I got a minute with a perp, taking him to the bathroom or for a drink of water, I tried to talk. I'd say, "You don't have to talk to me, but don't lie to me, either. You can save us both some time." Some cops say that you can get anyone to talk, and I'd at least agree that if you can get them to say anything, you can get them to give a little more. But if the perp had been through the system a few times, we couldn't threaten credibly with long prison sentences, and we were also limited in how much time we could devote to each collar. Moreover, the detective from the Squad who interrogates a suspect is looking for any kind of useful admission—if a robbery suspect says, "I was there, but I didn't do anything," he might have effectively owned up to the crime. A detective may only need a moment of cooperation to get what he needs, the utterance of a self-defeating half-truth, and as such the range of persuasive methods is wide. You can threaten the perp with the flames of hell, or promise him candy; you can offer friendship or cash; you can lie about having fingerprints or the confession of accomplices, or whatever pledges or threats it takes to reach that moment of capitulation. You're not even looking for a one-night stand, you're looking for the quickest of quickies, standing up, with your clothes on, and you have no intention of staying friends later. At SNEU, we were looking for a more serious relationship; we didn't need confessions, we needed collaborators, and for the perp to stop and realize, a day or two later, "Wait a second, there was no hidden camera in that crack vial!" would not have done us any good.

Still, there was need of persuasion, even if what you were after was a straightforward, businesslike bargain instead of a heat-of-passion surrender. You had to make the perp concentrate on the moment, and then on the future, and how you could work together to change them. You wheedle, enlighten, repeat. I've heard the sum of these techniques referred to as "jerkology." When I first tried to flip Maria, who was collared for selling heroin, the first ten minutes brought nothing. She was a hard-core junkie, an operator with such mileage on her that the first word that came to me when I saw her was "survivor," though it should have been the last. She didn't look just dirty but dusty, as if she'd been left in the attic, and she had ulcerated limbs as if someone had taken bites out of them. On being questioned about whether she knew anyone who had guns or was doing robberies, she offered a bored denial, and when she was asked about the heroin spot where she worked, she just shook her head. I knew she had done state time, and I knew a bit about the spot she worked—the brands, the players, the hours. Debriefings are like poker, even though it's clear that you're the better player, with the better hand. It's also unlike poker, in that if you play well, you both win.

"Maria, there's only one way you can make this go away, right? It's through us, right? Talking, helping us out? It's not through your boss, JJ. We know him, too. Today, he was hanging out on the corner while you were running your ass ragged, taking money, handing out bags of dope. And you're in cuffs, while he's home, watching *Oprah*. Yeah, Maria, it's four o'clock already! You moved a couple hundred decks this morning for JJ—ten bucks each, that's a couple grand. How much did he pay you, fifty bucks? Or did he just throw a couple of bags your way? Is he gonna send a lawyer down for you, is he gonna water your plants while you're away?"

But she didn't reply. I asked her about prison, and she said she didn't like it much. She still owed time for parole, and if she was convicted, she'd have to do that time before she started what she earned today. She knew that, she told me, but she told me nothing else. My mistake with Maria was to keep pitching appeals to her freedom. She was an addict, whose life was a closed circuit of having it and needing it, and nothing I could say would affect her truly solitary confinement. But she'd been talking, and I wanted to keep her talking. I asked if she had kids. She flinched, and asked for another cigarette. She nodded.

I changed the subject back to her dealing that day, describing customers, lookouts, and so on, authoritative blather to lead her to believe we had her down. Then I asked her what her kids' names were. As she said them— "Fernando and Lucy . . ."—it was as if she were watching them sleep. She breathed deeply, and softly began, "JJ keeps it in the corner building, on the second floor, the first door on the right. He brings enough for the day, from a stash house in the middle of the block." At that moment, I felt like I had jerkologically arrived.

. . .

SUMMER PASSED. A NEWS STORY BROKE ABOUT A HAITIAN man who claimed to have been sodomized by a cop with a plunger in a precinct in Brooklyn. A lot of cops didn't believe it because they couldn't imagine it; in their worst, what-if-he-killed-my-mother nightmares, they could picture killing someone but not—*ever*—that. I didn't recall ever having seen a plunger in the precinct, but the rumor was that the Job had henceforth banned them. I remember talking to a friend, a veteran homicide detective, and we lowered our voices to say we suspected the accusation was true. Autumn passed. On a Sunday in November, we had to come in for an overtime shift for "CPR" training at Fordham University, short for "Courtesy, Professionalism, and Respect." We heard lectures and were sent in groups to classrooms, where we met with people from the neighborhood, all of whom were eminently decent and respectable except for a teenager so snot-nosed and rotten that we suspected he was a plant: "I hate cops! They *stoo*-pid!" We had to say our names and how much time we had on, and Stix and I, who had less than three years, decided to amplify things a bit—"PO Cataldo, PSA-7, six years on the Job," "PO Conlon, PSA-7, I got, oh, six and a half years on"—as if to bolster our credibility, though we had no intention of doing anything but sitting there and shutting up. When we returned to the auditorium, an announcement was made: PO Edward Fitzgerald, brother of the late Sgt. Walker Fitzgerald, had committed suicide hours after a family memorial service.

As it got colder, we visited Housing management offices for keys to vacant apartments, so we could set up OPs protected from the weather. We slipped into buildings, leaped out of vans. Old people and working people thanked us on the sly, while the perps shouted that we were crackers and faggots. If a lookout took off on foot from us, leaving his bike, we made sure it found its way to a needy child in a nearby neighborhood—"Hey, kid, want a bike?"—and community relations thus moved forward on both fronts. We called it the "Bicycle Relocation Program. We saw dope called Stingray, Passion, and Independence Day. I look at my memo book and see that I collared Benita H, three blue slabs right front pocket; Miguel V, eight glassines, Samuel T, nineteen black-top vials. I don't remember Benita or Miguel, but I remember Samuel, because he fought Orville and me in the lobby of 3050 Park Avenue. My note says "MOS injured," for Member of the Service, but I - couldn't remember at first who it was—it was Orville, who got conked in the head. After you catch your breath, you get up and keep going.

And then Sgt. Carroll did just that. After we had worked together for six or seven months, he was promoted to lieutenant. For the ranks of sergeant, lieutenant, and captain, there is a civil-service test, and the grade, along with experience and several lesser factors, provides you with a list number. The Job promotes people in groups, moving down the list. Sgt. Carroll hoped that his promotion would be delayed, at least until after the holidays, so that he would keep his old schedule, rather than show up in a new place, where he would be just the man to fill in on the midnight for Christmas Eve. I also like to think that he liked us. But before Christmas came, he was gone.

Again, we were reshuffled back to patrol, sometimes together, mostly not. Sgt. O'Hagan grabbed us when he could, to work with Bike. We filled in for random footposts, sectors and conditions cars, and my memo book is filled with now-meaningless headings for assigned radio numbers, meal times, posts, and jobs. The notes from jobs are hardly more vivid: "Cabbie slash," and "Abusive, threatening one week, unknown if taking meds," and "It's my brother's jacket." Another one came to me, but only after some thought: "Known perp, asked c/v for $ . . .ᶻgrabbed all $20 . . .ᶻshows crowbar. C/V . . . says fuck it . . .ᶻperp turns, tries to stab, block with crowbar, clean thru right hand. Unknown flight." One four-to-twelve, I worked with a cop named Steve Carroll, and we had seventeen jobs, all of them ridiculous. The last came over as an EDP, called in by a man who said his wife was on drugs. The apartment had the blasting-radiator project heat that forces many people to keep their windows open through the winter, and on one wall there was a poster with a poem in Spanish entitled "My Son," illustrated with a drawing of a toddler pulling on his foreskin. An amiable man greeted us and showed us a drowsy woman watching TV, a baby sleeping peacefully in the bedroom, and another, younger woman, in shorty-shorts, cleaning the kitchen. "Who's she?" I asked Steve. "Um, let's call her the au pair," he said, as he tried to write it up, though none of them spoke English. Because the job was an EDP, the sergeant and his driver arrived, and an ambulance with two EMTs, but they didn't speak Spanish either, and so another set of cops were called to translate. I wondered how many hundreds of dollars per minute it cost the City. The woman on the couch casually admitted that she did smoke crack, but that had been hours before, and she'd been lounging around ever since. All of them lived there—husband, wife, girlfriend, kid—and happily, too, as far as she was concerned, because the "au pair" pitched in around the house when the wife was on the pipe. The husband felt there was no particular emergency but he wanted to send her away, preferably to the hospital but to jail if necessary, because he wanted the apartment. One of the cops remembered that he had been locked up before, when he claimed his wife had a gun to expedite her move. The wife agreed to go to the hospital, and the eight public servants went home. On Christmas Eve, I walked my old beat in the Village.

We had been pretty good that year, we felt, and hoped that Santa would bring us a nice, new boss. I don't know how much influence we had in the selection; certainly, we were a productive unit, and our commanding officer, Deputy Inspector Cavanagh, wanted to make sure we so remained. Rumor of who we wanted would have reached upward, but it hardly would have been the weightiest concern. And so when we heard that we were getting Sgt. Tommy Carrano, it was a relief. Carrano was the least bossy of bosses, acting as if his sergeant stripes were a kind of accident, like a birthmark, that let him sign our paperwork and give us days off. If we wanted to take a break, it was fine, and if we wanted to work, it was fine, too, and since we were a driven group, we wanted to work most of the time anyway. Sgt. Carrano was as regular a guy as you could ask for: he played on the precinct hockey team and in a rock band at home, and since SNEU was something in between a contact sport and a pick-up jam session, he fit right in.

We got used to having a good time again. We lumbered after perps through snowbanks and down icy sidewalks. We picked new spots. Stix caught a guy on a bike after a six-block foot pursuit. Carrano tackled a dealer with a cast on his arm and mashed it; fortunately, it was a prop, a fake for concealing the stash. For a while, we diverted ourselves by giving *Cosmopolitan* quizzes to each other, and then to the perps:

"If you could be any kind of animal, what would it be?"

"Now use three adjectives to describe it."

"What's your favorite color, and why?"

"If you were in the desert, would you rather take a quick shower or a long bath?"

"Bear in mind, the desert question is a sex question."

"Shut up! Don't ruin it!"

We oohed and ahhed like psychiatrists as they told us they liked tigers because they were tough or green because it was like money. I think the animal question was how you see yourself, and the color question was more or less the same thing, and the desert question was how you liked to have sex. As we filled up the van, the old perps quizzed the new perps, and giggled with us at the answers: "So, you like black panthers, 'cause they're all mysterious, huh? Yeah, right!" As we dropped them off at Central Booking, we'd call out, "Thank you for being arrested by PSA-7 SNEU. Is there anything you'd recommend for next time?" Most of them laughed, and some said that though we were the nicest cops who'd ever collared them, they hoped we didn't catch them again.

But Sgt. Carrano had put in for a transfer to a unit in midtown, so he could commute in on the train. Though his move could take months, we knew his was a short-term posting, and as it happened, we had him for six weeks. We were beginning to feel a little orphaned, and to chafe at the precariousness of the arrangement. We had been lucky with bosses, but who knew how long that would hold? Not surprisingly, the best bosses, like Clark and O'Hagan, already had their own teams and wouldn't leave them. Most of the bosses who had steady tours, like days or four-to-twelves, were used to the schedule and had arranged their lives around it, whether they were going back to school, working a second job, or taking care of the kids while the wife worked in the day. We were glad to hear that Sgt. Pat Kelly was thinking about taking over the unit. Kelly was on the midnights, and he was genuinely beloved there. There was a rumor that the fix was in, that Sgt. Spinelli from Admin had even called Kelly's wife, Vicki, to sell him on the change, and that her reaction was favorable. That almost sounded like a dirty trick, calling the wife, but I was glad Spinelli did it. The midnight guys began to curse at us when we saw them, which was a good sign. We had a feeling it would work out just right.

SIX

Everyone always asks, "Is it like how it is on TV?" There are more cop shows than any other kind, and more are set in New York than in any other place: *Car 54, Where Are You?* and *Naked City, Kojak* and *Barney Miller, Law & Order* and *NYPD Blue*. To watch a cop show with a cop can be a joyless experience, as they scold like Sunday school teachers at each departure from the facts as they know them. But most people seem eager to know the degree of realism in these shows, which always seemed to me beside the point, as my colleagues Batman, Superman, and Spider-Man would likely agree. In the national dream life of movies and television, the good guys and bad guys do battle in our heads, much as they did in our childhood reveries. And while gangsters might learn how to be gangsters by watching *The Godfather,* there are tests designed specifically to screen out Academy candidates who've grown up on too much cops-and-robbers TV. But I didn't want to be a cop when I was a kid; my disappointments had nothing to do with expectations shaped by Hollywood. When I watch a police drama, I like what they get wrong as much as what they get right, especially if the story is drawn from the headlines or history. I watch them for what I can use. The best movies are like the kind of daydreams you have during a long roll call, of rescues and revelations that are unlikely to happen on this tour of duty, but that aren't out of the question. You have to remember as much as you have to imagine: this could be the day that could change you.

On October 7, 1961, Roger Maris, Sonny Grosso, and Eddie Egan each had a day that would change him. Maris hit a home run in the ninth inning to win Game Three of the World Series for the Yankees, and Egan and Grosso, two detectives in the Narcotics Division, were so elated that they went out on the town, despite having worked for the past twenty-seven hours. They went to the Copacabana, where Egan had an eye for the coat-check girl, but their attentions were soon distracted by a large party across the room. Egan and Grosso recognized several of them as Mob-connected dope dealers and gamblers, although the center of their attentions, the big shot, was a new face. They watched him for a while from inside the club, and then from outside, and then they followed him as he stopped in Little Italy, where he switched cars, until finally, at six in the morning, he crossed the bridge to Brooklyn. As the sun rose, he went into a little luncheonette and opened it up for business. How did this guy from a greasy spoon on the wrong side of the river get to be the man to see at the Copa?

That is how the French Connection case began, perhaps the most celebrated investigation in NYPD history, as related by a fine book and a great movie. Egan and Grosso were classic cop partners: Egan, known as "Bullets" or "Popeye," was an Irish street kid, outgoing, hard-charging, skirt-chasing, strongly built with a bit of a belly, ruddy and fair. He never knew his father and his mother died young. Before he joined the NYPD, he was in the Marines, and he might have made the Yankees if an injury hadn't ended his baseball career. Sonny Grosso was known as "Cloudy" because he kept an eye on the down side. He was disciplined and reserved, a black belt, tall and thin, with dark hair, dark eyes, and olive skin. His father died young, too, but he became the teenage man of the house for his mother and three sisters, with a courtly manner and old-fashioned beliefs. Sonny hated drugs because he could see how they were changing his old neighborhood, in East Harlem; Popeye hated them after four junkies beat his six-year-old niece to a pulp after she walked in on them robbing the piggy-bank in her bedroom. Both hit the NYPD running, and Popeye got his shield a year after he joined. They teamed up in Narcotics in 1959.

When Sonny and Popeye made the man from the luncheonette as Patsy Fuca, they were excited. Fuca was the nephew of Angelo Tuminaro, who had been a major Mafia heroin dealer since the 1930s and a fugitive since 1960, when he skipped bail before the federal drug trial that sent mob boss Vito Genovese to prison for the rest of his life. A task force of NYPD detectives and federal agents was assembled. Sonny and Popeye set up surveillance from the X-ray room of the hospital across the street from the luncheonette, where they became familiar to Fuca as the medical technicians who stopped by for coffee. They obtained wiretaps on the phones there and at Fuca's house, where they pieced together his aspiration to take over his uncle's role as the New York Mafia's conduit for Marseilles heroin. They also realized that Fuca was aware of surveillance in the area, so Sonny arranged for Vice to raid a nearby numbers joint as a diversion. When Fuca's wife ordered curtains for their house, Sonny and Popeye intercepted the delivery van and donned UPS costumes, so they could get a look inside. Popeye got a girlfriend a job in a bar that Fuca frequented. There were a lot of those funny little things you notice when you get inside someone's life, but mostly, there was waiting. October passed, and then November, and then December. New York was running out of dope. Any junkie could tell you there was a "panic" on the street. Sonny and Popeye had a pretty good grip on what was happening, lacking only the Frenchmen and the heroin.

On December 21, in France, Jacques Angelvin, the debonair host of a TV show called *Paris Club,* announced that he was taking a trip to the United States. Angelvin was short on cash and unsteady in his prospects, and I picture him as a cross between a poor man's Johnny Carson and a poor man's Hugh Hefner. Through the nightclubs, he came to know a Corsican gangster named François Scaglia, a pimp, kidnapper, and drug dealer with underworld interests throughout the Mediterranean. Scaglia offered Angelvin ten thousand dollars to take a car with him on his trip, a 1960 Buick Invicta, which had 112 pounds of nearly pure heroin concealed in the rocker panels, on the sides of the chassis below the doors. Angelvin probably didn't know precisely what his errand was—he once took the car out for a spin in Paris, to Scaglia's horror—but he knew that his employer was not in the grocery business. Scaglia and another veteran heroin broker named Jean Jehan, a striking figure in his mid-sixties who stood six-foot-four and favored homburgs and white spats, would meet him in New York and manage the exchange with Fuca.

The movie *The French Connection* is perversely gripping in its depiction of the grueling dullness of a surveillance. In Narcotics today, there are all kinds of sophisticated technologies for collecting information, while undercovers and informants penetrate deeply into criminal organizations—sometimes it almost seems unfair. But the French Connection was a SNEU case: aside from the two wiretaps, it was all shoe leather and peeking around corners. There were hours and hours of tails: standing on sidewalks in nine-degree weather, pretending to make a phone call or window-shop while Frog #1 had coffee or Frog #2 tried to pick up a waitress after his fifth cognac. The cops stamped their feet and choked down dirty-water hot dogs and cold coffee in styrofoam cups, hoping they wouldn't get the runs the moment before the briefcase was exchanged for the car keys. It wasn't even like a ten-day poker game, it was a ten-day poker hand, raising and staying and raising again. The Frogs enjoyed the city, walking for miles and then doubling back; getting in cars, driving, stopping, switching; trying to spot the cops, or shake them, or simply exhaust them. The scene in the movie where Popeye and one of the Frogs do an elaborate dance in the subway, stepping on the train, then off, then on, until the Frog is on and Popeye is off, and he tips his hat as the train pulls away—that happened. The famous pursuit of the elevated train - didn't—Sonny and Popeye had to beat a train to the next stop, but the train was underground. Sonny and Popeye did seize the Invicta, and Sonny noticed on the shipping declaration that the car was to be 112 pounds lighter on the return trip to France—an economy on Angelvin's part, through which he hoped to save thirty-three dollars. But they didn't give the car back with the dope, of course—it had already been removed—and the ending of the case is slower, stranger, and more compelling than the screen version.

After nearly four months of surveillance, there was a certain amount of tension in the task force. Popeye got in a fistfight with a federal agent. Though all involved were determined to succeed, of course, several would not have been unhappy to see the cocksure Popeye fail. When they finally made their move, taking Scaglia, Angelvin, and another Frenchman—Jehan escaped—then executing a search warrant at Fuca's father's house, where twelve pounds of heroin, several machine guns, and a grenade were recovered, it looked like a success. But the numbers didn't add up, and Sonny and Popeye continued to look until they found a steamer trunk in the basement of 1171 Bryant Avenue, in the Bronx, where Fuca's brother Anthony lived. It was labeled A. FUCA, #5C, and it contained eighty-eight pounds of heroin. The problem was that Anthony had been arrested with his brother and father, and he hadn't made bail. They could voucher the drugs, but the collar might not stick—the Manhattan DA had passed on the case, in fact, though Brooklyn prosecuted—and they wanted a body to go with it, whether it was An-

thony Fuca or anyone else. The first phase, on Fuca alone, had taken three exhaustive months, and the still more intensive second phase, on Fuca and the
Frenchmen, had taken another ten days. And then Sonny and Popeye had to
sit in the basement of 1171 Bryant for almost another month. They got a little
punchy. Because they couldn't tell anyone who they were or why they were
there, a variety of people drew their own, nearly lethal conclusions. Days and
weeks passed, as Popeye, Sonny, and the others sat quiet in the dark, shotguns on their laps. After a time, one man became convinced that the red light
on the furnace was a man smoking a cigarette; on another occasion, when the
superintendent karate-chopped a wooden plank, he was very nearly shot.
There was a painter working on the building who became obsessed with the
sinister men in the basement—he didn't believe their story that they were on
a burglary stakeout; he didn't believe they were cops at all, and they didn't
take great pains to correct him. But his constant calls to the authorities
brought visits from beat cops, the Department of Sanitation, and even a raid
from the 41st Precinct Squad, which had near-disastrous results. Finally, they
arranged for Anthony Fuca's bail to be lowered, and he was released. On
Saturday, February 19, Sonny was the best man at a wedding, wearing
a tuxedo at St. Patrick's Cathedral, when he got a call from Popeye: *Get
back, this is it.* Sonny skipped the reception and came back to collar Fuca in
black tie.

A great investigation became a legendary one: 112 pounds of heroin
seemed like a diamond as big as the Ritz. In the NYPD at the time, there were
only 200 cops assigned to the Narcotics Division, and there were sixty federal
drug agents assigned to New York. The size of the pot, relative to the scale of
the game, broke the bank in a way that has subsequently been impossible to
duplicate. Popeye and Sonny essentially confiscated one month's supply of
heroin for the entire country. That one collar could almost make you believe,
not altogether foolishly, that we could stop crime as we were getting to know
it. The movie gets so much right: the feel of police work, the easy camaraderie and the well-stacked chips on the shoulder; the deep moral passion of
it and the pure joy of the game. I get a charge from imagining the nightlife
of a hot-shot cop in New York in 1961, when you'd put on your porkpie hat
and go out to the Copa for a couple of rye and gingers. What couldn't be
done? *And the Yankees win! And the Yankees win!* The case that began with a
home run ended with two, in Brooklyn and the Bronx, and inspired the best
cop movie ever, which reverberated back in the real world by helping push

the French government into shutting down the Connection. Popeye and Sonny aimed high, pushed hard, and won bigger than they'd ever imagined, but there were times—maybe most of the time—when it looked like it was heading straight down the drain. Always, always, there was the edge of doubt: Do we move in, and blow it? Do we wait, and miss it? If we pull back, can we pick them up again? How long will the Feds give us to let this play out? How long will our boss? The wiretaps will expire, and then the search warrants, and maybe the next time, the judge will say, "You guys again? I heard it before, forget about it." And the Feds will roll their eyes the next time the cops come up with something, and the PD will yawn the next time Narco has a caper, and Sonny and Popeye—well, if someone wanted to make a movie about them, it would be more along the lines of the Keystone Kops. Almost forty years later, Sonny told me that when he and Popeye chased the subway, screeching and dodging through midtown traffic, trying to beat the shuttle from Grand Central to Times Square, his dismay grew acute. "Whaddaya think?" he asked. Popeye smiled as he looked over at him and said, "I think Paul Newman's gonna play me and Ben Gazzara's gonna play you."

• • •

WE DIDN'T THINK AS BIG AS POPEYE, BUT WHEN SGT. PAT Kelly took over SNEU, we couldn't be small anymore. We were never especially petty, but on the team, there were frequent external aggravations, such as doing without vehicles or being sent out on footposts, and occasional internal ones, like griping over who was quick to grab a collar, or who was slow to help with yours. As it was often intense work, and we could be intense people, the frustrations could grow beyond their proper proportions, and a lesson in perspective had its value. Pat Kelly, or PK, was ours, and he - didn't need words to teach it.

PK was in his mid-thirties, amiable and unassuming. He was a little softer around the middle and thinner on top than he might have liked, but when he described himself as "the fat, bald guy" he made it sound like a good thing to be. He had almost fifteen years on the Job, and he became a detective before he made sergeant. He was shot once, in the leg, during a pursuit. He was an extremely capable cop whose management style was extremely low-key. He'd say, "You guys know what you're doing," but he didn't have to repeat himself if he made some alteration to our plans. He called you "laddo," as if he were old and you were young.

PK had been working midnights, a tour with some heavy activity on the early end, followed by hours of down time. You finish at almost eight in the morning. I got the feeling he spent many hours looking at the night sky, thinking about things. PK and his wife, Vicki, had four little boys—Paulie, Dominic, Sean, and Brendan—and the first three were triplets with cerebral palsy, in varying degrees of severity. Paulie was in a wheelchair, Dominic was in braces, and Sean was on crutches. Together, they had undergone dozens of operations, progressing steadily but painfully, until the previous September, when Paulie had died suddenly from a respiratory infection. After years of daily struggles that would have been beyond the endurance of most of us, PK suffered a loss that was past what we could begin to understand. You wouldn't have known it to look at him.

PK made it impossible to be small about things. He never came in without a smile on his face, never complained about any of his problems, never hesitated to help another cop. Amid the martinets and bureaucrats scattered through the upper ranks, it was easy to forget that PK was our boss, but only because our admiration for him was so deeply felt that rank was immaterial. The less he asked of us, the more we offered. SNEU had always been a cliquish group, but now we became positively cultish. Because of his family situation, PK needed to change his tours frequently or take days off. When that happened, the desk would put us in uniform and send us out to foot-posts—often, it seemed, with a certain glee. But we would all change our tours to work with him, regardless of the instability it brought to our own lives, and we would rush the desk to try and get off when he wasn't there. People began to call us "the Manson family."

Everything got better with PK, even the food. We started going to breakfast at a diner called Stacy's, or the Locust, in Port Morris, the industrial spit of land on the bottom of the Bronx, east of the Bruckner. There was some consternation about bumping up the average expense of breakfast from around four dollars to six, but the consensus came to favor two bucks as the price of freedom from methadone and roaches. Stacy and her brother John, who ran the place, always saved newspapers for us and remembered what we liked. They opened up at five in the morning and closed twelve hours later, but if we came by when the door was locked and all the seats were up on the tables, they took us in and fed us. Often, I sat at the counter to read the papers while the rest of the guys took tables, until Tony noticed that my seat offered a better view of Stacy, and the rest of them jammed around the counter. We ate better and so we felt better, all around.

We chased people through alleys, hopped fences, and ran along rooftops, more sure in our paces. We watched, rolled in, and packed them up. We saw cops at the Four-O as much as we saw those in our own command. And there, we saw the new classes of cops look at us with curiosity and admiration, as they shined their shoes and readied for roll-call inspections, while we walked past in our street clothes and goatees, acknowledging the desk with brief nods. We were serious about work, about SNEU and PK; otherwise, we cracked each other up, all the time.

We also made some progress with our vehicle problem. Every other week, we worked ten-to-sixes, which began at nine-thirty in the morning, although the Warrant team didn't finish with the vans until eleven or noon, or sometimes later. We could catch up on paperwork, get something to eat, or hang around and bullshit, each of which had its attractions but none of which required half a day. Moreover, the sight of a bunch of cops doing nothing was an aggravation to the desk officer. If we didn't sign the Interrupted Patrol Log, we could get in trouble, and if the duty captain looked in to see we'd been there for hours, he could get in trouble. As some DOs seemed to think that whatever cops did in the street was merely the crude raw material that was made useful and true by the art of administration, several of them developed a distaste for us that they did not conceal. If enough time passed without hope of a vehicle, we would set up nearby on foot, but it was less safe and less effective, as it required stopping to walk every prisoner back to the house. And so we started to use my car.

Most cops don't use their cars on patrol because they couldn't afford to total them—in the event of an accident, the insurance situation would be a mess—or out of a prima donna belief that police cars should be supplied by the police department. But PK told me that there was a form you could fill out to get approval to use your own car on duty. I had a 1980 Oldsmobile Omega, blue as a whale but not quite as big, which hearkened back to other family vehicles, generally large and near-derelict, with names like the Gray Ghost and the African Queen. Patrol cars have four-digit numbers—"9786, can you eighty-five 9222 at One-Four-Nine and Third?"—and in Housing, the term "Triple-O" meant "out of operation." My car was christened Nine Triple-O. The interior of the roof was covered with mock-velvet cloth, affixed to the frame with a foam adhesive that had long since dried out; when I drove, the cloth billowed and the foam flaked, swirling around the car like snow in a paperweight. Alicia wouldn't ride in it. After a while, I yanked out the cloth and scraped off the foam, so the interior was bare, rusted metal. Alicia still wouldn't ride in it.

Triple-O was a great car to have, because it fit in the neighborhood, and because I frankly didn't care what happened to it. One night, when Tony and I transported prisoners in the van up to the Five-Two, there was a vehicle pursuit that went on for over an hour. The car went from local streets to highways, from the Bronx to Westchester, and then to the Bronx streets again, speeding past us with its caravan of cars in tow. There were more than a few reasons why we couldn't join in: we had perps; the van was unmarked—it - didn't even have a working horn, let alone a red light; we were on overtime; and there were plenty of cops involved. But a vehicle pursuit is just too much fun to miss altogether, and we kept close, as if our faces were pressed against the glass. Once the car passed, Tony said, "I bet I know where he goes!" We took off in a different direction and parked by a corner, where the pursuit flew by, and then he picked two or three more streets, anticipating precisely where the chase led. If we had Triple-O, I thought, we could have rammed the hell out of it, and the car would have gotten an Inspector's Funeral. Alas, it runs to this day, though without glory.

For all our burgeoning confidence, we didn't forget how the street could outmatch us at any moment. Once, we worked a set on One-Five-Six Street, and I had to pick up a guy in the middle of the block, between Courtlandt and Morris. I stepped out from the corner and walked toward him, approaching within about thirty feet before he made me. He was a big man, well over six-foot-four, and he was built like a sack of clams, thick all over and bottom-heavy. He moved like one, too, dragging one leg behind him and propping up his bulk with a cane. When he saw me, he froze, and I could see him think, which I expected, and then I saw the result of his thought, which I did not. We're trained to say, "Police! Don't move!" and it was as if he took the injunction to mean "Move slowly!"—he practically made a three-point turn to reverse his course, and I just started laughing. I could have caught him if I was wearing cement shoes. He had over a hundred pounds on me, not to mention his cane, so I didn't go in lightly, in spite of everything. I stepped up and put him in a headlock with one arm as I tried to control the flailing cane with the other. I wound up for a roundhouse punch but it seemed to go wide—I felt it connect, though it had no effect on his bucking and heaving. And it was then that I saw that I had help from PK, who was taking him down from the other side, and we put him on the street and cuffed him. When we caught our breath, I noticed the red welt that began to rise from PK's temple.

"Did that asshole whack you with his cane?" I asked.

"Um, no, actually, it was you."

"Oh. Sorry."

"It's all right, laddo."

"I guess this would be a bad time to ask for next weekend off. . . ."

In retrospect, I can think of a lot of bosses who deserved a wallop in the head, and I regret all the more that I wasted a free shot on PK.

· · ·

AS EVERYTHING WAS GOING SO WELL, THE NEXT CHANGE IN the unit didn't appear, at first, to be such a stroke of fortune; on this Job, it always seemed that your opportunities to move arose when you were content to stay, but when you were in a hurry to leave, all the doors were closed. The Job had begun to rotate SNEU cops through Narcotics, and Sgt. Spinelli told me that I was being sent there in appreciation of my work, which was nice to hear, though it was also true that Stix, Tony, and Orville had pointedly announced that they had no interest in going. I don't know whether the idea was to train cops from SNEU, or share intelligence, or just make it more likely for us to recognize one another in the street. There were three teams for each module, with a sergeant for each team and a lieutenant for each module, and three modules for each precinct, plus a school team, which totaled some ninety cops in Narcotics for the Four-O, in addition to the SNEU teams from Housing and the precinct—more than half as many in one precinct as there had been for the whole city during the French Connection case. We bumped into Narcotics teams often, and they always had the right to play through. If nothing else, having friends there would make the reminder of our second-class status less pointed and more polite.

And when I found out that the assignment would only be for thirty days, there was little doubt that it was the right thing to do. Traditionally, there had been two ways to get a detective shield, which is purely appointive: you might make a great collar—The Door, they called it—and the chief or the Commissioner will whisper, "Where do you want to go, kid?" as the flashbulbs pop at the press conference. More often, you would work for eighteen months in what was classified as an investigative assignment. In the past, most cops would work their way up in a precinct, from a beat to a team like Anti-Crime, and then go upstairs to the Squad, where you'd work for eighteen months as a "white shield" before promotion to gold. But after the merge, Housing didn't have their own detectives anymore, and the Squads stopped taking white shields. There was also Applicant Investigations, which interviewed recruits and was more of a clerical position, and Internal Affairs, which—to put it mildly—was not what I wanted to do. Most cops grudgingly respected the need for IA, but it had only recently been separated from Inspections, which primarily investigates smaller, procedural violations, and the impression remained that they'd swarm all over a precinct looking for thugs and grafters and leave with a raft of complaints for wearing white socks and signing out in blue ink instead of black. Finally, there was Narcotics, which expanded considerably in the late 1990s, and offered work as an investigator or as an undercover. For women and minorities, especially, undercover work offered a fast track to the shield, as you needed only two years of experience to go there, whereas you usually needed at least five years for a "career path" transfer. Since then, Warrants has also expanded, and the Squads have reopened to cops, but at the time, Narcotics was the only way to a detective shield, and I found myself with the rare opportunity to be able to test a new assignment before signing on.

The shift from making drug collars in the Four-O to making drug collars in the Four-O, was not, as you might expect, such a radical one. There was a scattering of connections: Bea Moore and Hector Nolasco were from PSA-7; John Reilly's best friend, Angelo Ricci, was also from 7; Eddie Engel knew Mike Shea, from my neighborhood; Jack Keane was a friend of my brother Steve's; and Rob Richardson knew PK from PSA-8, in the north Bronx. Cops are often cautious around each other, as you never knew if the new kid was going to be a pain in the office or a liability in the street, but almost as soon as I arrived, it was as if there was a great choral mutter of "This guy's all right." It had come over "the wire," as the grapevine used to be called, and I checked out OK. The rest of the crew, Vicky and Jenny, Carlos, Nefti and EB, Marty, Adam, Abe and Dex, Janet and George, were all good cops and a pleasure to be around. I was assigned to Sgt. DeNaro, but I also went out with Sgts. Turner and O'Brien, all solid bosses who reported to Lt. Zerbo. The name sounded like a villain in a James Bond movie—"Ahh, pleased to meet you, Mr. Bond," "The pleasure is yours, Lt. Zerbo"—and he was only slightly less intimidating. He had almost thirty years on the Job, but he was still the first one to charge through the door on a search warrant. When I walked into the office, he yelled, "Jesus! What the fuck did they stick me with another Housing guy for?" So much for Courtesy, Professionalism, and Respect.

But I knew the sets we worked, the players and the brands, the layouts of the buildings and the streets, and it was good to know that I could move up to the next level without anyone even much noticing how new I was. Teams went out for B&B (Buy and Bust) twice a week, hitting eight or ten sets, with catch cars tailing the undercovers to pick up the sellers immediately after each buy, and "ghosts," who followed the undercovers on foot, at a distance, reporting their progress and watching their backs. It was a rapid and systematic way of working: hit or miss, you moved on to the next set in fifteen minutes. While SNEU stuck to crack and heroin, Narcotics scooped up everything: marijuana, methadone, pills. They were more methodical and less discriminating, and their cases stuck—the evidence included marked money, drugs vouchered by the undercover, as well as his or her firsthand testimony. The undercovers were miked for the boss to hear, and he or she directed the field team over the radios; unless you drove the boss, you received your information secondhand. That never presented any tactical impediment, but the remove sometimes made me feel less involved in the action, and the division of labor between investigators and undercovers was not the case with SNEU. The rest of the week, the investigators mostly worked on "kites," or complaints about drug sales phoned in to 911 or the Mayor's Hotline that - couldn't be handled by patrol. If someone called to say drugs were sold in an apartment, cops from a squad car couldn't just walk in to take a look. Investigators would observe the location, and undercovers or informants would be sent to make buy attempts, and a report called a DD5, the standard detective's memo, would be typed up after each effort. The kite would be closed after arrests were made, or after it was found that they weren't selling, at least not to strangers. A good percentage of kites were nonsense, called in out of boredom or spite, or against neighbors who were noisy, messy addicts but not dealers. I had no kites assigned to me, so I went out with a B&B team for most days.

In SNEU, we would spend hours on a set: a peek first, and then a surreptitious trip to the OP, walking over from several blocks away, and then the patient wait for buyers or sellers or both. Often, we recovered larger stashes, spending time searching the vicinity of the sale for where the drugs were concealed, whereas Narcotics had their case when they had their collar—the pre-recorded ten-dollar bill, the two slabs of crack—and they moved faster.

In SNEU, you were more invested in your collar, so to speak, whether in watching or catching or both; the arresting officer in Narcotics—who was always an investigator—would simply be the one who collected the body, after the transaction by the undercover and at the direction of the boss. If someone else on the team made the physical apprehension, the relation between cop and criminal might be only on paper. But Narcotics was also serious and professional in ways that we were not. The Job was committed to their work: they had money to spend to buy drugs and guns and to hire informants; they were supplied with equipment, transmitters and recorders and surveillance devices; they didn't have to use their own cars. For them, word might come in, late in the day, that everyone had to suit up for a case takedown; for us, the news flash was more likely that we had to get in the bag to write tickets. As a temp in Narcotics, I got a month closer to my shield, and I got a glimpse of the next step. It was a good place to go, and I was in no rush to get there.

When I got back, the guys asked me, "How was it?"

I brushed them aside: "Listen, I'd like to tell you guys, I really would, but this is need-to-know stuff, and why sugarcoat it? You people do not need to know."

• • •

BUT THE URGE TO MOVE ON, OR AT LEAST MOVE UP, WAS IN all of us. While I was away, an informant had presented herself at the precinct, announcing that she wanted to work. She had known a cop named Paul Callahan from PSA-7, who had since moved on to Narcotics. Callahan seemed to have more informants than Kennedys have cousins, and most of them were a bit on the odd side; more than once, some shady figure would creep out of an alley and whisper, "Pssst! Tell Paul to call me!" We joked about them all living together in the Callahan Compound, making dinner, buying each other Christmas presents, and taking trips to Great Adventure. This particular CI, or "Confidential Informant," was a crackhead who didn't like the way one dealer had treated her, so she decided she'd turn him in "for the mood of it." When she came into the precinct one day, someone called out, "Conlon, your girlfriend's here," and she said, "He don't want this twisted ass." Actually, she was working for Tony, and he didn't want her twisted ass either, but the name stuck, and so Operation Twisted Ass was born.

Operation Twisted Ass was, among other things, a lesson in why Operation Hindenburg ended up the way it did. Twisted Ass was officially registered as an informant, for one, and Callahan could attest to her credibility. She didn't have a complete name for her dealer, but she did know that he lived with his girlfriend in a project on Park Avenue. With the address and apartment number, we could run it through the Housing Authority, and confirm, at least, that the tenant of record was a woman of the right age and race, and we could get a blueprint of the floor to ascertain that the layout was as described—there would be no after-the-fact corrections along the lines of, "Come to think about it, it was apartment #14G, not H." We took our time, sending her back to describe the door in detail, its markings and position. We knew that the subject had a tattoo that said "Shadow," and that he was sitting on a gun and a lot of crack.

The moment before you execute a search warrant is heavy with anticipation, a cross between opening a present and defusing a bomb. We hit the apartment at dawn, with the Emergency Services Unit taking the door. ESU is our SWAT team, with responsibilities that include shooting wild dogs with tranquilizer darts and rescuing people trapped in elevators. "When a cop needs a cop," the saying goes, "he calls ESU." They take a door with a ram or a kind of jack, which pops it out from the frame, and then charge in with ballistic shields, helmets, heavy vests, and shotguns. It makes an impression. The man with the shadow tattoo was roused by the noise and got out of bed to greet them. Once ESU cleared the apartment, I guarded him in the hallway where he stood, blinking sleepily in his underwear, as Tony and PK searched the place. They found sixty slabs of crack, some money, rounds of ammunition, a fake Rolex, and a big cake of crack on a dinner plate, ready to be cut. When they wrapped it in plastic to take it down to the precinct, it looked like leftovers from a picnic. Shadow didn't talk to us, but we had made it through the door, we felt, in more ways than one.

We continued to work on Lamont's heroin set, around 305 East 153rd Street, which dominated the dope in Melrose Houses. They were affiliated with two brothers, known as Satan and Loochi—short for Lucifer—who controlled most of the narcotics in those projects. Lately, we had heard a lot of machine-gun fire at night, and one evening, someone had targeted us with a red laser pointer, which could have been a kid playing or someone aiming a gun. I'd heard Lamont had withdrawn from the street-level hand-to-hands, so we'd hadn't collared him recently. Moreover, since his grandmother lived in the building, we couldn't even pick him up for trespass. We had to content ourselves with hacking away at the edges of the operation, but there was plenty to do there, regardless.

One night we picked up a dealer after five or six sales. A second player had worked with him, in the lobby, but he'd escaped. It was a decent grab, though a little low on stash. Since they had access to several apartments on lower floors, we had limited expectations of finding much in a public area, but we searched anyway. I worked my way up to the third floor and found an unlocked janitor's closet. It was full of trash, and a mouse dove down through a crack in the wall, which sent me back a couple of steps. There was also a plastic garbage bag full of clothing. Homeless people often have caches of possessions hidden in such places, but when I opened it, the clothes were for a teenager, smaller and cleaner than was likely for a street person. I didn't have gloves, and as I felt through the top few garments, I half-hoped to find nothing, which would give me reason to stop the search. But when I pulled out a pair of overalls, two .38 caliber bullets dropped out and bounced on the floor like dice. I thought, Damn. Now I'm gonna hafta spend half an hour groping through mouse shit. When I put the bag down on the floor, it made a clank.

I dumped out the clothes and found a submachine gun, a MAC-11. I went over the air: "PK, come on up to the third floor, the slop sink."

"You got someone?"

"I got something."

"Ten-four."

PK and the other guys gathered around, with the near-reverent hush that falls on cops around such hardware: *Look at this, look at this. It could have been aimed at us.*

PK said, "All right, I guess we'd better go through the rest of the building."

I said, "Hold on a minute, let's finish off this one first."

PK paused and leaned into the closet. "You're right, laddo. There's another one."

On the floor was another gun, a silver Smith & Wesson 9-millimeter with a black grip.

"Okay, then, I guess we ought to put on gloves."

In another closet, we recovered a long-barreled Colt .45, which wouldn't have looked out of place in the hand of Wyatt Earp. We picked up a box with 120 decks of heroin (worth twelve hundred dollars, and probably less than one day's supply), boxes of ammunition, and then a plastic bag containing almost 100 rounds for an AK-47, copper-jacketed and each over two inches long, coming to a long, sharp, conical point like a dunce cap. The AK-47—the one that got away—would send these bullets out at over 1,200 feet per second, passing through my vest with barely a pause. We packed it all up and went in to the Four-O, where my Narcotics team was in with collars as well. They gathered around to see our arsenal, all the more amazed that it had been collected from somewhere open to anyone who bothered to look.

We had opened up another door.

• • •

WE HAD OFTEN WORKED WITH OTHER COPS, SUCH AS BIKE, when we were short of people or vehicles, or when a set was especially busy. Sometimes a beat cop would hook up with us, if he was looking for a collar. PK's reputation was well known, and we were earning ours as well, as a team that made things happen. There was a growing list of people who wanted to join us, though we were more or less content to keep things as they were. One exception was that of John Timpanaro, who was working six-to-twos so he could finish college at St. John's in Queens, and he took to jumping in with us on our four-to-twelve weeks. He fit in, not so much because he was like us, but because he was unlike anyone we'd ever met.

John was boisterous and buoyant, a natural on patrol who would always stop for a pick-up basketball game with local kids. He was Italian—*Hunnid percent, half Sicilian, half Na-bolly-tahn*—and while he could talk like Tony Soprano, he planned to go to graduate school. He was an athlete, talented and disciplined at once: he had been a competitive bodybuilder, wrestler, and skier. His blond hair and blue eyes made him look more like a lifeguard in Malibu than a Bronx cop, and his nickname on his old post was "Baywatch." John had made some great collars, including a fugitive from a bank robbery who had been featured on *America's Most Wanted*. I thought of him as a shit-magnet, with the perverse admiration cops have for people with a talent for bumping into bad guys. Several bosses had picked him to be their regular - driver, and he'd had to plead to be allowed to work alone, to go out and collar and learn the business of police work. When he finished college, he was ready to concentrate harder on the Job, willing to work the long and changing hours that come with dedication to collars. He was a serious cop, but his effect on us was like laughing gas.

"Look at him," Tony said. "He's so damn cute!"

If there was a joke behind his jokes, it was that he loved the world and it loved him back, madly, and he sometimes wasn't sure if either he or the world was kidding. He offered sexual favors to PK and he'd tell Alicia that he was in love with her husband, with whom he played on the precinct basketball team: "With all due respect, Alicia, if you don't want Big Ed anymore, I gotta have him. He's gotta be hung like a butternut squash." When we were in the van and he'd see a girl on the street, he'd say, "That's it, no fooling around anymore—out come the guns." And then he'd roll up his sleeve and hang an arm out, flexing a biceps. "The poor girl, she doesn't stand a chance. . . ." He could make his pectorals jump independently, as if he had exploding breast implants. "Look at this, I'm on fire here!" was his refrain. He was always on fire: if he went out to a club, he was on fire; if he walked down Webster Avenue, he was on fire; if he stood alone in a phone booth, he was on fire. We took to calling him "GQ."

It's not as if we didn't have a good time before John began to jump in with SNEU, but I remember the jokes from that time better; they may not have been any funnier, or funny at all, but they stick with me like songs. There was a rumor that another cop we knew was trying to get off the Job with a psychiatric disability. He had stayed home, AWOL, and when the bosses called, his girlfriend claimed that he couldn't talk because he was curled up on the floor in a fetal position: "He can't come to the phone, he's in a ball." That became our catchphrase for the casual psychosis of work, the strange reactions to stranger demands, and summed up everything:

"You wanna get something to eat?"

"Sorry, I didn't hear you, I'm in a ball."

"Hey, OV, when you stopped that guy, did he have anything on him?"

"Nah, I didn't get around to it, I was in a ball."

"What did you do last weekend?"

"Nothing, really, I was in a ball."

We didn't joke like Bike, who busted on each others' mothers and wives, but there was an ethnic tinge to the mix-it-up. Our affection and respect for each other—so we kept telling ourselves—gave us permission to treat each other to torrents of abuse on the most personal level, and because we were a mixed group—Puerto Rican, Short-a-Rican, Jamaican, black, Italian, and Irish—our conversations were a gorgeous mosaic of insult. The frame of reference veered between the ghetto and the trailer park, regardless of which of our ancestral islands was reputed to have produced car thieves, spliff fiends, mafiosi, or drunken terrorists. Stix seemed to get it coming and going, as an Italian with what might be called a Roman nose—

"This nose, in my family, it goes a long way back."

"It goes a long way forward, too."

"I'm saying there's a lot of history there."

"Geography, too."

And as a guy from upstate, he also got the white-trash jokes, the parking tickets for your house, rebel flag on the pick-up, not having sex with your sister until you're engaged kind of thing. Stix got all of that, which suited me, the other white guy in the unit—just fine. Moreover, I was not above stirring it up a little myself:

"Hey, Stix, what's this in your memo book: '98 to 52 Pct with eight PRs'?"

"What's the matter, what do you think it means?"

"Eight PRs—why do you have to say you took eight Puerto Ricans to the 52?"

"It means 'prisoners.'"

"Hey, Tony, Sammy, Alicia, listen to this—Alicia, you only have to half-listen—does PR mean Puerto Rican or prisoner?"

"Listen, you people—"

"'You people!' Did you hear him? Whaddaya mean, 'you people'—why don't you come right out and say it!"

With the memory of PK's loss of a child so fresh, the fact that we were having such fun took on a kind of moral dimension. No one would have been so bold as to compare what we offered to what he had lost, but when we made him laugh we were proud of ourselves. And we looked to make him proud, too. We looked forward to coming in to work, and at the start of the tour, you'd hear talk around the office that was not typical of the civil service, as we'd let slip what we'd done on our own, off duty:

"Driving in, I saw Luther out on One-Five-Three, they're pumping there."

"Yeah, I saw 'em. Also, on One-Five-Seven and Elton, the usual crew."

"The fat kid?"

"Nah, it was a new chick."

"'Cause I saw the fat kid over on Melrose, but he wasn't holding, I don't think, I watched him for a while. . . ."

While there were still plenty of drugs in the Four-O, it was getting crowded with cops, and we decided to expand our horizons. Two partners who had the Four-Six conditions car, Chris Hickson and Rob Dressler, said they had a guy who wanted to work for us, a street guy, a junkie. We took a ride up to the neighborhood and liked what we saw. The Four-Six was north and west of us, in a neighborhood called University Heights, which extended from west of Webster Avenue to the Harlem River, above the Cross Bronx Expressway and below Fordham Road. Unlike the rest of the Bronx, which was a flat, glacial plain, the terrain was hilly and the streets broke from the grid, angling and curving over the lay of the land. But if the neighborhood caught a break during the Ice Age, recent history had been less kind. Homicides were twice that of the adjacent precincts to the north and east. For dope fiends, and hence for drug cops, the Four-Six was God's country. In the four or five blocks around the intersection of Tremont and University avenues, there were more than a dozen dope spots, and almost as many for crack. Washington Heights, across the river in Manhattan, had been the center of the East Coast cocaine trade from the mid-eighties onward; when the NYPD cracked down in force, some of the traffic had moved across the river to the Bronx. They got a lot of Jersey junkies, who crossed the bridge, at first, for fun. Charlie had been one of them.

Charlie was tall and lanky, with long hair and a scraggly beard like a hippie Jesus. He had been on the street for two years, and he made his living—such as it was—as a steerer, an intermediary between the suburban addicts and the dealers who were wary of white people. They had no worries about Charlie; they knew him, for one thing, and there was no mistaking him for anything but what he was. He slept in the dirt and he stank like a corpse. I asked him, "How often do you get high?"

He told me that he shot eight to ten bags of dope a day, but added, "I - haven't been high in years." It was a medicine, like insulin, that kept him from getting sick, and the pleasure it had once offered was a distant and mocking memory.

When he wasn't at the extremes of stupefaction or desperation, Charlie's intelligence and decency were plain to see, and sad to consider. He was quick to learn and eager to please, and he came to look forward to seeing us, as much for the company as the cash. Charlie had been locked up plenty of times before, and even though he thought a lot of them were bullshit collars by bullshit guys—"C'mon, all I had was a needle and some empties!"—he nonetheless looked up to cops. His father was on the Job, a lieutenant in a small city in another state. At the moment, they weren't talking, though Charlie called home now and then and talked to his mother. She kept some hope for him, and would not close the door, figuratively at least. He'd mention his mother with love in his voice, and his father with respect, but he usually wouldn't talk about them for long.

For the past year or so, he'd lived on a wooded median strip above the Cross Bronx Expressway, a hundred feet in from the street, with a few other, more transient addicts who'd set up an encampment, with blankets on cardboard, and heaped and battered possessions—a radio, paperback books, a winter jacket—that surrounded their little hideaway like flotsam from a shipwreck. Farther away, at the stone ledge over the highway, was their shooting gallery, with beer bottles and empty glassines littered over the bare rock, and I wondered sometimes whether it was the cliff's edge that drew them there, or the sight of traffic, the thousands of people going heedlessly home, as if it was a daily and natural thing, because they could. You knew that you were close to the camp—"Charlie's Gardens," as we called it—mostly because of the smell, which was like nothing I'd ever encountered before. It was a rotten-meat smell and a sour chemical smell, pungent and pervasive, and it held in the ground, even after a heavy rain, as if the earth had not just been polluted but defiled for the ages. I know that it was my imagination, but I thought I could smell the place on my sneakers, even after I left there, the first time, and when I got back to the precinct, I threw them out and went home in my uniform boots.

I told Charlie that street sets were fine, but that we didn't really need anyone to help us find them. We were happy to hear whatever he had to tell us, but what we wanted was to find apartments where they sold, to get search warrants. Charlie said that he knew a teenage kid named Justin who sold crack, mostly, in white-top vials, with a sideline of five-dollar half-bags of dope. Justin lived in the apartment down the hall, but his mother wouldn't let him sell there—it was his girlfriend's place that he dealt from, as her family had no such objections. Charlie thought the dope was garbage, and so he didn't go there, except in emergencies. He was an authority on the subject, and it seemed that the vintages and blends of heroin were as distinctive as those of wine—there was purity, of course, but there seemed also to be varied qualities to the cut—and when someone wanted to introduce a new brand, they tested it out for free on Charlie, as the junkie's junkie. Charlie wasn't into crack, really, but he was a Renaissance addict, and he'd be happy to go there, too.

Justin lived in a project, but the Housing Authority had leased it to a private company, with whom we had to confer for lobby keys and tenant information. In general, we were cautious about speaking with civilians about the particulars of an investigation, as you never knew whether the janitor or secretary or administrator had a son or girlfriend or cousin who might wind up in the crosshairs, still less who might broadcast the information in the coffee room, or even be on the payroll of the bad guys outright. But at this company, we had an "in," a woman named Yvonne, who had enthusiastically helped Dressler and Hickson with identifying drug dealers, who not by coincidence happened to be problem tenants. Whenever we went there, in fact, the problem was not access but exit, as Yvonne was a cop buff in general and fond of me in particular. When that became apparent, Timpanaro, especially, was happy to intervene. "No, Eddie doesn't have a girlfriend," he volunteered. "And to be frank with you, Yvonne, I don't want to tell tales out of school, but I think he's a little lonely, looking for a good woman to help him settle down." Whenever we needed something from the office, I took to waiting in the car. John would bring her out to see me.

Such were the unexpected hazards of my first warrant for SNEU. I had to make excuses for my romantic availability, and I had to not throw up when I went looking for my informant. I learned the actual investigative preparations for a warrant, the computer checks for kites and collars in the building through the NYPD "NITRO" computer system; the background checks on the tenants—one arrest, on a previous warrant, for possession with intent to sell; the tenant research through the phone company or Con Ed; the "claim" of the apartment through the Drug Enforcement Coordination System, or DECS, which is a central registry for people and places that are the subjects of city, state, and federal investigations, to make sure we don't step on each other. I had to do reconnaissance on the building, so that I'd see that it was as described, in layout and detail, and count the number and kind of locks on the door. I also had to get Charlie in there to buy drugs, preferably three times within a ten-day time frame, and to find out if there were children, old - people, dogs, guns, fortifications, or traps in the apartment, not to mention where the drugs were. When it was done, I had to bring him in to the DA to write up an affidavit, which would be sworn before a judge.

Under ordinary circumstances, it was a fair amount of work as well as risk—you had to meet the Confidential Informant (CI) often, and you never knew who might notice—but several particular problems presented themselves with Charlie. As a stone junkie, he had a shelf-life of only a few hours before he would go into withdrawal and its attendant sweats and nausea. We'd have to take care of business in the course of the morning—if they were busy at court, and told us to come back after lunch, we were done for. And in sending him after the white-tops, I seemed to have turned him into a crackhead.

"Didja get in there?"

"Ohyeahyeahyeahyeah, oh, boy yeah,"

That disturbed me—it wasn't as if Charlie's life wasn't in the toilet anyway, but he didn't need me to help him flush. When we went to court, I told him to clean himself up before we went in, and though I was impressed with the results, the grimaces of the ADA and the judge suggested that, at best, his hygiene was only relatively improved. That may have worked in our favor, however, as they moved us through with some haste, and Charlie performed admirably, testifying in crisp detail of the times and takes of each visit. I gave him twenty bucks and took my warrant back to the precinct.

Again, we met in the muster room for the "tac" plan, plotting out the times and contingencies, listing the assignments for who would watch the windows, freeze the lobby, and wait in a car to race to the hospital, if necessary. Though the drill was becoming a little more familiar, the exhilaration—the tension and the hope—did not fade. We had a captain from the Borough with us, and, of course, Yvonne, who would secure the apartment after we finished; ESU would take the door, and EMS would wait outside, on call. The particular configuration of the building required that we approach it from behind, slipping down an alley to scale a wall, then cutting in through the back door. We ran upstairs and I pointed out the door for ESU, then stepped back as they hit it with the ram. In retrospect, I have to give the Housing Authority credit for the sturdiness of the door, although I was not grateful at the moment: they hit it, and hit it, and hit it, and then set up the jack. Time does not pass quickly when you wait like that, but I could have sworn it was several minutes before we stepped over the threshold.

It looked right, as we rushed inside, the kitchen to the right, the living room, the bedrooms on the left, and there were three people in handcuffs, face-down on the floor. But I felt a spike of dismay as I looked down on them, a middle-aged husband and wife, and a young girl, thirteen or fourteen years old, it seemed, slim and pony-tailed; it was the right place, maybe, but it was the wrong time, as there was no sign of Justin. I bent down to the girl to look closer, to say that it was all right, we would look around and move on, when I saw that it was a guy. I asked him his name and he said, "Justin." I beamed at PK and gave him the thumbs-up: *Laddo!*

There were three more people in the apartment, and foil-wrapped packets of cocaine, and dozens of pre-cut foil squares to package more; we got some weed, and a ledger of transactions, crudely scrawled columns of accounts for guys named Mikey and Murder. Where the white-top crack was, I had no idea. The apartment was big and messy, and it would take a long time to search thoroughly. I found a big garbage bag full of stuffed animals, at least fifty of them. I looked at the teddies and duckies and tore one open before putting it aside, out of embarrassment. Yvonne was thrilled with the action, and she stepped in and seized a bunny, tearing off its head like a wolverine: "We gotta look here! It could be anywhere!" She disemboweled several little creatures before she was gently reminded that only police officers could search, and the remnants of the menagerie survived. It wasn't spectacular, but it was solid, and the captain shook our hands. We'd done it, he said, smiling, and he added, "Again."

At the precinct, I figured I had the best shot at the father. The mother's English was chancy and Justin was cockily—and correctly—betting that his age would allow him to walk on the charges; when I interrogated him, he listened as if I were a telemarketer offering a new, low-cost long-distance plan. The father offered weepy protests of all-encompassing household innocence, but when I told him an undercover had bought from his apartment, he changed tack, claiming Justin sold drugs, but he couldn't stop him. His daughter liked Justin, but he was so afraid! He also had other children, younger ones. He wasn't well, you know, he had his blood pressure to think about. I didn't begin the interview with a very high opinion of him, but at the end, I thought that if he were a roach, I would have stepped on him. And he was a roach. I said something like this to him, only a little louder:

"You let this five-foot-three, hundred-pound, sixteen-year-old fuck with a smirk and a ponytail bang your underage daughter? You let him broadcast to every junkie and crackhead around to come to your house to get happy? This is the choice you've made, as a father? This is what you're telling me? And you're not going to tell me where he gets it, or where it is, because you're scared of him? And you have other kids? Guess what, shithead, I'm gonna make sure they don't grow up with you. I'm gonna take your kids away."

He held his head in his hands and blubbered: "They already took my kids away!"

Since his face was still downcast, I looked over to Tony, still furious but holding back a laugh: *Oh, well, never mind then. Wait, no, I'll double-take them away!* Tony took him back to the cells, and when he returned, he said, "Shit, I would have confessed."

Some weeks later, I browsed through the inch-thick stack of paperwork for the eviction proceedings. Yvonne had sent it to me, as I would have to testify about the arrest. Idly, I looked back at the earlier criminal history of the family—they'd been locked up after another warrant, in an apartment around the corner. I read about how an undercover had been steered there, and the father had sold him heroin. A Narcotics team had done the warrant, and they'd recovered a respectable stash of dope. I sat up as I read where they'd found it, and thought maybe Yvonne wasn't such as lunatic after all: the drugs had been hidden inside a stuffed animal.

. . .

WHEN YOU SIGN UP AN INFORMANT, YOU OFFER A NEW LEAF, a new life, an appeal to the better angels in their nature. When an informant signs, however, he sees it as a deal with the devil, and though he'll take his cash or freedom for now, he knows that one day he'll have to pack for the warm weather. The informant is constantly renegotiating the contract in his head, considering his options and opportunities. I don't remember what I knew about Melvin Jones when he called the house when I was young— *"Daaaah! It's your informant!"*—but obviously I knew what he did. I don't remember many calls afterward. Maybe my father had decided that work and home should maintain their distance, or maybe their business would conclude soon after. My mother remembers Melvin's South Carolina courtliness and manners: "How are you, Miz Betty, is everything all right? I'm glad to hear that! Is Mister John available?" Melvin had worked as an informant for my father since the mid-fifties, supplementing his on-the-book work as a truck driver, and presumably supplanting his off-the-book activities as a thief.

In their respective capacities, both Melvin and my father were assigned to Thefts from Interstate Shipment, which centered on the movement of freight on the West Side, from the docks to the streets and the rails. It was the landscape of *On the Waterfront,* the Hudson piers and the walk-up tenements of Hell's Kitchen, of water towers and pigeon coops and fire escapes hung with laundry. Even in the fifties, the old Irish laborers and gangsters watched as the city became more modern and corporate, and generally less interested in their abilities and their demands. Honest work became less physical, and the dishonest kind became more vicious and less local, as the airports began to compete with the docks, and the ships found new ports in Jersey. Marlon Brando's *I coulda binna contenda* speech spoke for any number of guys who saw their best chances pass, whether at an odd, introspective moment or after long conversations with a radical priest. Brando's character, Terry Malloy, wanted to be a boxer but wound up as union muscle; as he realized how the gangsters betrayed him, he struggled to convince himself that his break from them wasn't a betrayal as well. He couldn't think of himself as an informant, a role which no culture respects but the Irish particularly despised, from the traitor-ridden centuries of revolt against England, and even farther back, to Spy Wednesday, when Judas collected his silver from the Pharisees, for passing along a tip. I don't know if Melvin Jones suffered any torments of conscience when he changed sides on the waterfront, but he knew what the costs might be, should the shift in his allegiances become known.

Melvin Jones had first been arrested by another agent, who was nearly ninety when I spoke to him. The agent pressed me not to use his name, lest his old enemies come to seek him out, professing humility with a razor beneath the hat brim. But when the agent moved to another assignment, Melvin stayed to work for my father. When Melvin saw merchandise diverted from the ships or the trucks, or heard of plans to do so, he let my father know. My father made collars and Melvin made money. When I read through some of those cases, I was surprised at how penny-ante many of them were, especially at first—a case of pet food here, two boxes of ladies' coats there. The complete arrest reports were not made available to me, but I wasn't desperate to learn the details. Had the ladies' coats traveled to the city from Buffalo or Albany instead of Newark or Paris or China, their disappearance would have been a matter for the local precinct instead of the FBI.

At the same time, I knew that my father much preferred the work to his previous assignment in Communist surveillance, if only because it was more fun to play cops and robbers than spy-versus-spy. He told me how they set up a reverse sting at a pawn shop, buying stolen property to identify the thieves. Once, when he had to make an arrest, he found himself without a partner and without a gun—details which didn't seem worth interrupting the story for, at the time—and he followed the man down the block to stop him. Though my father was six-foot-two and averaged around two hundred and fifty pounds, he said that his perp towered over him. He stuck his fist in the pocket of his trench coat and extended a finger: *FBI! Get your hands up or I'll put one right in your back!* He saw the man tense up, deciding, before he obeyed. As the two walked back to the pawn shop, passersby stopped to give their opinions:

"What did he do wrong!"

"What's the matter with you, let him go!"

"We're watching you, there better not be any police brutality!"

I'm sure my father was tempted to take his hand out of his pocket and wave his finger at them, but such satisfactions are better postponed. It's also the part of the story you leave out of the official reports.

After the ships stopped coming in to the West Side docks, there was less work for Melvin, and for my father, too, at least in Hell's Kitchen. Melvin's only other arrest was for getting picked up in a stolen car, in the late 1960s, in Washington Heights. Because Melvin was not the most successful criminal, I'd suspect that the long stretch without arrests meant that he stayed out of trouble generally, and he stuck to driving and whatever else he picked up on the side. It was in the 1970s when he and my father had occasion to speak again at length.

On September 17, 1974, a thirty-year-old Yonkers police officer named Harold Woods stopped by a supermarket on his way to work for the midnight shift. He picked up a pack of cigarettes and quart of milk, and as he walked up to the checkout line he saw that the clerk looked afraid. "Are you okay?" he asked. "I'm a cop. Is there a problem?" And then one of the two men who were robbing the store stepped out and shot him in the face. Woods died five days later. He had a wife and three children.

Not long after, Melvin overheard a conversation in a bar in Harlem, where a man said that he had "wasted this dude upstate." I don't know if Melvin read the papers or otherwise knew of the killing, but he'd been in the business long enough to know there would be a reward. Did Melvin know a first name, full name, nickname, or an address? Or did agents or cops pay a visit to the bartender, and urge him to rack his memory for further details about the man who sat in that stool, that night? The case was further complicated because it was split between three different jurisdictions: a federal informant gave up New York City perps for a Yonkers homicide. With NYPD detectives and Yonkers cops, my father cruised the streets of Harlem, hunting the men. After a four-day stakeout, they picked up one perp in Harlem, at his girlfriend's apartment, and the other was arrested weeks later, in New Orleans. Both men were convicted and sentenced to death, though the sentences were later commuted to life in prison.

Of all my father's cases, I am proudest of his role in the Woods homicide. I spoke with the detective lieutenant from Harlem, Herman Kluge, and he told me that without my father, this case might well have remained unsolved. Robbery-homicides can be among the most difficult to break: the perps were not local, there was no relationship between them and their victims, and eyewitness testimony is often of little value. The perps were prepared to kill but had not apparently planned to, in that Woods's arrival was by chance. It was by chance, too, that Melvin came upon the information, but it became relevant because my father had built a relationship for nearly two decades. There was trust there, at least enough of it, and there was ten thousand dollars. As the saying goes: How does a fish get caught? *He opens his mouth. . . .ž*

Melvin took the cash and bought a social club in the Bronx, at 1822 Carter Avenue, a block east of Webster and Tremont. My mother told me that my father had to fight for Melvin's reward money, but it didn't buy happiness for him. In a later set of police reports, I read that Melvin had all kinds of problems. Though he was selling marijuana and taking bets at the club, he owed a lot of money. He owed money to the landlord, he owed money to his partner, he owed money to a certain Vito Ambrosiano, from whom he leased the cigarette machine, juke box, and pool table. Without intending any offense to Mr. Ambrosiano, the vending machine business in New York City at that point in history was not considered entirely reputable. Melvin even owed money to his bummy barback, Shorty. The police had occasional reason to visit: in June of 1977, Melvin was at the club when he was hit in the head with a bottle and robbed of a shotgun, a radio, and five bottles of whiskey. Not long afterward, he had a dispute with an employee, during which he was again struck in the head with a blunt object. There was a report that a man named Johnny Eagles was interested in taking over the club: Johnny Eagles drove a white Lincoln Continental and had gambling arrests going back to 1946, and he'd menaced a cop with a gun in 1974. For all his problems, Melvin was untroubled on the afternoon of January 18, 1978, because he - didn't even look up from his game of solitaire when someone walked up behind him and shot him once in the back of the head with a .38.

Melvin was fifty-eight years old, clean-shaven, with dark skin and "full teeth." He was six feet and one inch tall and weighed two hundred and fifteen pounds. He wore a brown turtleneck, gray trousers, black dress socks, and brown construction boots. His widow, Beverly, could provide no relevant information. Shorty claimed to have left the club at noon. Johnny Eagles was never found, though I don't know how hard they looked. The Four-Six probably saw fifty or sixty homicides that year, and twice as many shootings, and thousands of robberies, burglaries, and other felonies. I haven't read enough homicide files from the 1970s to know whether the effort made for Melvin was casual, typical, or exhaustive. Several reports describe neighborhood canvasses for Eagles's white Lincoln Continental, all with negative results. They are the kind of thing you bang out, just to have something in the file. No mention is made of Melvin's public testimony in the Woods case, and reprisal by associates of the imprisoned cop-killers doesn't appear to have been considered as a theory. There were people who would have killed him, on principle, had they discovered how he came across the windfall that bought him the club.

Melvin was executed as he played cards, unaware of what was about to happen, which is generally not the style of stick-up man or even a jealous husband, who usually wants a word with the victim before the trigger is pulled. Melvin could have known the other man in the club as a customer or friend, and thought he didn't need to watch his back more carefully than his cards. Then again, maybe the jukebox was playing and he didn't hear anyone enter. You can't even rule out robbery, because you don't know what was missing if you didn't know what was there before. Melvin was broke all the time anyway, and he could have lost the last cash in the register, playing solitaire against himself.

My father would retire a little over a year after Melvin was killed, and he had moved to another assignment, doing liaison work with Scotland Yard. I'm sure that my father said a prayer for Melvin, though my mother doesn't recall that he was especially saddened or surprised by the news. She doesn't recall him making any particular effort to see what happened in the investigation, or to offer assistance. As far as my informants went, I'd have taken more trouble with Charlie than George the hit man, but I don't know if I'd have done much beyond telling the case detective what they'd done for me. My father would have had sympathy for Melvin's good intentions but no illusions about his bad habits. Melvin was a human being who offered service in the course of justice, no matter if that service was unwilling at the beginning and accidental at the end. Did he help himself along the way, or did he hurt anyone else? We all have our vocations, and we all have our mysteries. Not all of us find religion over the wandering years, but sooner or later, - everybody gets to meet God.

• • •

AT THE BEST OF TIMES, YOU FELT THAT YOU COULD GO ON forever, with bigger cases and better collars, and the Job would ask only how they could help. You'd think, "Who could touch us? Who would want to?" And then you'd catch yourself, because you knew the answer: Just about anybody, any time. In June, John asked PK about joining us as a permanent member of the team. PK asked us what we thought, and after we all agreed, he worked out the post change in Admin. The next day, we received word that SNEU would cease operations, as such, for the indefinite future.

That spring, it was believed that four serial rapists were at large in the Bronx. The first had strangled one victim on the roof of the project called Twin Parks, in the Four-Six, a vast maze of a building where Larry Davis had lived. Davis was a psychopath who made his living robbing drug dealers, and he was wanted for four murders when he shot six cops who had come to arrest him. Davis's acquittal on six counts of attempted murder—and three out of four of the other killings—helped make famous the term "Bronx Jury." Two other men, one Hispanic, one West Indian, according to their descriptions, were believed to have committed attacks on middle-aged women in the Five-Two, breaking into their apartments through fire escapes. The last was not least: the perpetrator of Citywide Rape Pattern #6 had raped and robbed fifty-one women, at gunpoint, over several years, from upper Manhattan to lower Westchester but mostly in the Bronx. Our Anti-Crime team had already been shifted to steady midnights because of it, and then further redeployed by assigning several of them on foot in uniform. They still made some collars, but their productivity did, of course, decline; the inspector who ran the Borough then summoned Sgt. Clark to his office and informed him that he wanted ten felonies per month, per cop, which would have been impossible without any restrictions whatsoever. Clark quit, and the rest of the team followed. The rapists didn't. In June, a Task Force of more than a hundred cops was dedicated to the condition, for Street Crime–style saturation of target areas throughout the borough. Each command was asked for a team of cops, and we were volunteered.

We would work from nine-thirty at night until six in the morning. One team had Monday and Tuesday off, the other Wednesday and Thursday. PK, Tony, Orville, and Sammy were on one team, and Alicia, John, and I were on the other. I was fuming; I was out the day the teams were decided, and I saw it as the short end of the stick, day-wise and PK-wise. It effectively meant that I only had one full day off—Wednesday—as you'd work through dawn on Tuesday and have to come back for Thursday evening. I had just started to date a girl—not Yvonne, thank you—and had hopes of seeing her more often than for an occasional breakfast. It was the full flush of summer, and it was the custom of my countrymen to find outdoor places near water on weekends, which would not be possible for me. I partnered with John, and I explained that it was nothing personal, but that he could expect me to be in a bad mood for the rest of my career.

"I gotta tell you, pal, I'm glad to have you here," I told him, "but I think you're an idiot for staying. This is a raw deal. You just got in, no one would hold it against you if you waited. We'll get back to the regular shit sometime, and you can join SNEU again then."

"Nah, I can't. I've wanted to work with PK and you guys for a while, and I can't back out on the first day, at the first bump in the road. Let's see what we can make of it, it might be all right."

DNA had been recovered from many of the victims, but the wanted poster showed a masked man; we knew his genetic code but he could pass us in the street without notice. We would get him, but only when we got him. Sometimes it appeared that the rapist had followed women home from a bar or a club; in other cases, the point of interception appeared to be accidental. There were targets of opportunity as well as victims picked out of crowds; there were older ones, younger ones, taller and shorter ones, of differing physical builds, and he had attacked two and even three women at a time. He wore a mask and carried a gun, and he took money and jewelry. One night, John and I were assigned to a quiet neighborhood of single-family houses, and we drove until we found the site of one attack, a vacant lot. We got out of the car and walked through it, staggering through the shoulder-high weeds and ankle-twisting nests of briars, the angry greenery of the city ground returned to seed. The earth was rocky and divoted, and I was thinking that it would have been hard to find a less hospitable place, when I remembered that the rape had taken place in February. Had she cried for help, no one would have heard. I wondered if the misery of the surroundings was part of the pleasure he took, or if his concentration was such that he wouldn't notice if he was inside a burning building. Another crime scene was as public as this one was isolated, behind a housing project along Westchester Avenue, a major street with the elevated train tracks overhead. This assault was in the summer, on a Friday around midnight: the three young women were leaving the building for a party, and he forced them outside, through the back door. The project was one of several around a courtyard with benches; a playground was a few yards to the side; there would have been people outside, in the summer, and it was brightly lit. He herded them to a patch of lawn behind the building, where a fenced-in rock ledge separated the grounds from Westchester Avenue below. Above them, the trains passed, and beneath them, the buses, cabs, and cars rolled along; twenty feet away, there were hundreds of neighbors who talked, watched television, and slept. The three women were raped and robbed beside a vast, oblivious audience; had they screamed, they might have escaped, or summoned aid in droves, or died.

Though I wasn't glad to be there, the neighborhood was delighted to see us. In the streets, there was a gratitude I'd never experienced before in such forthright manner and volume. Passersby practically applauded when they saw us, and even those we stopped to question often thanked us and wished us luck in the hunt. After each, we had to fill out forms called "250s," or "Stop and Frisk," which were designed to cast a wide net around just such pattern crimes, to see if any names turned up with a telling familiarity. Each night began with a roll call for the gathered forces of Street Crime, Narcotics, Special Victims, and patrol, and in the beginning, various chiefs and inspectors gave speeches about the urgency of our mission, and how they believed in us. They gave us new cars and let us ride.

We drove and watched. A week passed, and then another. One night, John and I had a post in the Four-Three, in Soundview, where there had been a concentration of attacks. Just after midnight, we did a vertical in a housing project, checking the roof, the stairwell, and the terraces. On one floor, we found a padlocked terrace with a broken window, narrow and shoulder-level, a foot high by two feet wide. We looked in, and saw a sleeping derelict. We extracted him, ordering him out at gunpoint through the window, each of us taking an arm once he was halfway out, then handcuffed him, searched him, and tried to get him to admit if there was anyone else still on the terrace. Satisfied that his answers were as good as we would get, I went through the window to see if there was anything—specifically, a ski mask, a gun, or jewelry—to connect him with the crimes. The pane had been shattered, and the frame was edged with shards of glass like shark's teeth. I clambered in as well as I could, with John holding up my legs, wheelbarrowing me in to the ominous dark. There was nothing there, beyond a soggy couch littered with pizza boxes and crack vials, and I crawled back out. We took the man in for trespassing, but mostly to talk.

On the street, John started with him: "You know what we're taking you in for! You know what you did! Where's the ski mask?"

I turned away so neither he nor John could read my face. This guy was no more the rapist than he was Josef Mengele or Judge Crater. There were bluffs, and there were bluffs: *Give me three cards, and I'll raise you fifty.* "Sorry sir, this is the craps table." The man mumbled sleepily in denial.

John charged ahead, undaunted: "You know who he is, don't you, guy? Give it up!"

And then the perp looked away uneasily, stammering, "Well, you know . . . I don't know if, I don't want to say, you know . . ." My pulse quickened. This would be an interesting conversation. We called for a car and took him in.

The man knew what we wanted; everyone in the neighborhood did. We talked at length and at leisure, to put him at ease and build up some trust. He sort of had a wife and he did have kids, and they lived with his mother in a nearby project. He lived there, too, now and then, when he wasn't on a crack binge, but that happened as often as he could afford. He thought he knew the man, after an odd exchange some time before, which had stayed with him. He was peddling some stereo equipment he had come by—we didn't ask— when an acquaintance from the neighborhood struck up a conversation, the key parts of which went as follows:

"That ain't makin' money."

"Don't I know."

"What I do, is I rob bitches and then I fuck 'em."

"Oh—that ain't me, man."

Even at the time, he said, the remark disturbed him powerfully, and later he came to believe that the man was the rapist. When I inquired why he - hadn't told the cops before—there was a twenty-thousand-dollar reward for his capture—he said that no one had asked him. Moreover, he had another problem, in that he couldn't remember the man's name. After strenuous recollection, he could only say that he had a funny first name, and a common last name.

"How do you mean funny, African-funny? Muslim-funny?"

"Nah, not like that—it was a little funny, though."

As far as he could recall, the guy had been locked up before, but not for rape or anything noteworthy. He thought that he sold drugs, and when I pressed him for the brand, he thought it might have been red-tops. We were reaching, I knew, and I knew that for most people—let alone a mind as ill-used as his—the strain to recall could break down the boundary between memory and fantasy. But from a fragment such as "red-top crack vials," there would be a string of perps on the NITRO database; from an address, there would be several systems that would provide names of robbers and rapists. He did remember where the man's mother lived, and from that slender fact alone, an investigation could begin.

We talked for a long time, and when a detective from Special Victims arrived, we told him what we knew before leaving them alone for another interview. Special Victims had doubtless received vast amounts of that kind of low-grade but tantalizing information. The detective was intrigued, but if he had any deeper feelings, he did not betray them. He'd look into it, he said, and if it panned out, he'd let us know. I was excited by it, and so was the crackhead, and what struck me was that we all cared a great deal about it, and in almost the same way. This man was a criminal, too—a nuisance from afar, a tragedy up close, to the wife and children who lived with his mother— but in relation to the rapist, he was a concerned member of the community. John and I imagined our gold shields, and maybe our collar imagined enough crack to fill a pipe the size of the Holland Tunnel, but, ambitions aside, we both wanted the man gone: we wanted the mothers and sisters and daughters of this troubled neighborhood to walk the streets unafraid. It was us—all of us, the cops and the street—against him. I gave the crackhead my beeper and work numbers, and I took down the address where he lived when he was not lost to the pipe. I told him that I would not only make sure he got the reward, if it led to an arrest, but I would put twenty dollars in his hand the minute he came up with the name. We were both determined to continue our partnership. Weeks later, I even wrote to him, but by that time, we had already returned to PSA-7 SNEU. I thought sometimes about going to look for him again, but my resolve thinned as other responsibilities piled up, and time went on.

When the rapist was caught, the following April, I read that his name was Isaac Jones—funny first name, common last—and I wonder about it to this day. Was there anything to the story? How thorough was the detective in running down the names? Did the crackhead get the right building? Did Jones give another address in his prior arrests, to spare his mother aggravation from the Housing Authority? Jones was caught when his girlfriend tried to pawn jewelry that the store owner recognized from a police flyer. She admitted that she knew it was stolen but said she had no idea about the rapes. Jones was from Soundview, the neighborhood in question. He was sentenced to many lifetimes in prison, and I don't know if he had committed other robberies and rapes between that summer and the next April, but much would have been different, for all of the cops in the city, had our chance meeting led quickly to an arrest.

Back at PSA-7, Deputy Inspector Cavanagh said to me, as I brought him a bottle of single-malt scotch, "You know, when they told the Inspector that they want him to give up his best guys, he actually understood it to mean that we should give up our best guys. What am I supposed to do without a SNEU team?" He gave me a hapless shrug. Our return was as abrupt as our departure had been, as joyous as our exit had been dismal. The scotch didn't count as a bribe, I figured, since it was after the fact, but if it had occurred to me that it could have gotten us our weekends back, I'd have given him a truckload of it. We were back in business.

. . .

AUGUST WAS A GOOD MONTH FOR US. WE HOPPED BACK AND forth between the Four-O and the Four-Six, picking up bodies a dozen at a time. Our numbers crept up, to twenty and thirty and forty collars, a third of them felonies. Thirty would have been respectable, and forty excellent, and more than that would have raised questions as to why we hadn't been doing better all along. We wondered what we should shoot for, heading as we were toward a record-breaking month, and PK said, "Well, Roger Maris's record was sixty-one." And why not? Weren't we the Boys of Summer?

The farther we reached, the more we grasped. We started taking bikes out, which let even Stix and John cruise around with a degree of anonymity. To beat the lookouts on well-guarded sets, we'd hail livery cabs to roll up on them, popping out from feet away on startled dealers. Once, we grabbed a junkie who was driving a dry-cleaning truck, which we borrowed for the rest of the afternoon—if my car, Triple-O, was low-profile, the truck was perfect cover. PK asked over the radio, "What's up with the green van? When did we get that?"

There was a pause before someone responded, "Uh, what van, boss?"

"Ten-four."

There was no mistaking what we did for anything vast or grand; our collars and cases didn't lead us to Mexican generals or offshore bank accounts, let alone the French Connection. We were little scrappers who worked some rough ground, and sometimes left it a little more level than when we'd begun. But we sometimes found a place in the larger scheme of things: a joint NYPD and federal task force called "HIDTA," for High Intensity Drug Trafficking Area, was working on a case against our friends Lamont, Satan, and Loochi. Various detectives and agents would call, or come by with pictures, and we'd fill them in on background, associates, and the like. We worked most often with Mike Donnelly, who had been a detective in the Four-Seven and had known Uncle Eddie: "Sure, heavyset guy, worked midnights, always reading?" Some of the Feds had Southern or Midwestern accents, and it was fun to take them through the projects, looking for perps, walking them through the pissed-on and bullet-pocked halls and the stairwells, pointing out the stash spots in the cable boxes, fire extinguishers, and trash disposal chutes. You could see the looks on their faces: *This is what you guys do, every day? Here?* Some of them didn't seem all that comfortable. We were the Indian scouts for their cavalry, sniffing the air and saying, *No perp-hunt today, HIDTA-sabe, heap big rain come. SNEU go to Stacy's, eat meat loaf special. Yum-yum!*

Every day, Satan and Loochi's crew might commit a hundred felonies. When we caught them, they'd sneer and laugh at us, bragging that street-smart guys like them could run circles around clueless country boys such as ourselves, and we'd say, "You got a point there. Lemme know if those cuffs are too tight." In a funny way, we had a similar view of the Feds: If we had the savvy, why did they have all the success? We locked them up, over and over; but HIDTA locked them up just once; when they took their case down, Luther, Lamont, Satan, Loochi, and a dozen others pled to sentences of fifteen and twenty years to life. It wasn't that we thought we were the best team, so why weren't we winning; it was more like we were a great team, so why weren't we really in the game?

In the Four-O, we worked sometimes with Hector Berdecia. He was the gang officer, a newly created position, and I'd check in with him and share information. Hector had been a cop when the CO of the Four-O, Capt. Shortell, had been a sergeant; as Shortell rose in rank and moved through commands, he took Hector with him. Good cops make their bosses look good, and Hector was a one-man beauty school. He made things happen: whenever a cop collared some semi-derelict or little wiseguy who decided he wanted to talk his way out of a problem by offering up where his best friend had the crack or his uncle hid the gun, Hector stepped in. Hector was generous with credit, and that helped his various joint operations go smoothly. While we paid informants out of pocket and drove Triple-O, Hector had federal grant money and a car from the DEA.

Hector's talent for diplomacy only took him so far, sometimes. He once told me, furious, about how a Narcotics team stole one of his warrants—my old team, in fact. After they'd done the entry and a large amount of heroin was recovered, their captain announced they were taking the collars. Narcotics did their own search-warrant entries, which we preferred to ESU; they did "dynamic" entries, taking the door, then rushing in to prevent the drugs from going down the toilet. ESU's was a defensive entry, methodically clearing each room from behind ballistic shields, one by one, for maximum safety. From the street to the door, they were a highly visible and relatively slow-moving deployment, and I sometimes wondered if we'd do any worse with a marching column of bagpipers from the Emerald Society. Then again, ESU would take the door, cuff the perps, and go home, whereas we were in competition with Narcotics, working the same territory, for the same purpose. Hector could have called Capt. Shortell to square things away, but one of the reasons for their long partnership, I'm guessing, was that he didn't call him at home too often to complain.

That was always the dilemma: you could reach out for help to Narcotics or HIDTA, who had the experience and resources to develop a case properly, but you risked losing control altogether. Maybe the whole team could go out with them once or twice, for a warrant or a canvass, and maybe one or two of us could work with them for a longer period, through the course of the investigation. But it would be in effect a "ride-along," as the back-seat tour of patrol arranged for reporters and community leaders is called. And though there is far greater cooperation now, within the NYPD and between agencies, the division of credit isn't always the model of congeniality. One collar goes to one cop, regardless of how many others watched, chased, fought, or otherwise worked to get it, and every boss on the Job knew the difference between going to Compstat with a formidable array of arrest statistics as opposed to a lovely album of thank-you notes.

And so when PK told me that SNEU guidelines required that informants be handed over to Narcotics, after one search warrant, I dutifully made a call to the Four-Six Narcotics module about Charlie, while plotting sabotage all the while. Before the rape detail, I had gingerly broached the matter of hygiene with him, one night before I was to pick him up in Triple-O: "Don't take this the wrong way, Charlie, but you gotta clean yourself up when I get you tomorrow. You're a little ripe."

"Nah, it's all right. I know it, I know where I live."

And to my surprise, when I met him the next morning, he'd bathed and found clean clothes. In general, his range varied from stinking a little less than usual to stinking a lot more, and in my car, I averaged around two spray cans of Lysol per week. To be fair, there were several weeks when a foul odor seemed to hang about the car, which John blamed on the cream in my coffee that spilled on the mats, curdling in the summer heat. That theory was demolished when Sammy found a doggie bag from a long-forgotten dinner in the back seat, and the very act of dislodging it unleashed such a rancid cloud that I had to race around for blocks with all the windows open before it could be dispelled. But when I'd arranged for Charlie to come to the precinct to talk with two cops from Narcotics, no such sanitary preparations were undertaken; he was at his outer range, stink-wise, and the interview was brief.

"Well," said PK, "Narcotics had been notified, so I guess we're in the clear."

The Four-Six was a great hunting ground, not least because it was the first place where we began to lock up white people in any numbers. PK called them "strays," and they wandered around like lost dogs. Everywhere we had previously worked had white populations that were virtually microscopic. There was a slight overrepresentation of white arrests, of lost-in-time locals and the suburban addicts who commuted for a fix, but that part of the South Bronx was generally off-limits to white strangers. It was a double-reverse racism, as the dealers refused to collaborate in white suicide, while growing rich on the suffering of their like-colored neighbors. In the Four-Six, however, there was a spillover of the old white Heights trade; the dealers welcomed them, and so did we.

For us, there is a house brand of bullshit that black cops have to take when they lock up black people, and another brand for when they lock up white - people, and the same for white cops locking up white, black, or brown, and so too for Hispanic cops—not to mention what female cops go through, when accused of harboring hidden agendas. If you lock up someone who looks like you, you're a race-traitor; if you lock up someone who doesn't, you're a racist. In the end, the color of your skin doesn't matter but the thickness of it does. Sometimes, we gave out scrips not by color but by counterpart on the team; there were no blacks or Hispanics, but instances of a "Male Orville, blue shirt and jeans, Yankee cap, south on Elton," or "Male Sammy, that's a male Sammy, north on University toward Tremont."

We enjoyed the contingent of white faces—for what you might call diversity grounds, in part, but also because so often they were so easy, from the street to the station house. Many even came when you called them. The strays seemed to have less of a lower-middle ground of "functional addiction" than black and Hispanic addicts, whether because their survival skills - weren't there, or their families cut them off faster; there was no slippery slope of decline but a sheer drop-off, and the whites we collared either looked entirely normal and healthy at first glance, or like poster children for Skid Row. For many people, being arrested is an aggravation on the order of getting a flat tire—you see them put on a pair of handcuffs like you'd put on a pair of socks. For others, it is a trauma comparable to a death in the family. Many whites fell into the latter category, and it was a pleasure to collar them: they were so obedient and polite, they'd fill out their own paperwork if you asked. We'd get excited by the sight of a white face on the street, thinking an easy pinch was on the horizon. "Fifty bucks says it's a nun, in plainclothes," I'd say, spoiling the fun. I could do this because, as I'd tell my partners in a grave whisper: *I know white people. I know what makes them tick.*

Even better, it set off a competition between Stix and John and me, for who could lock up more Irish and Italians, respectively. The competition came to be known as Wopstat, as I called it, though they seemed to feel it was Mickstat. When we'd stop two white guys, they would stare at us, perplexed, as we asked for their names and listened as if it were a lottery drawing:

"McCarthy."

"Shit!" I'd say, as Stix and John high-fived each other. "Hold on a second, you—what's your name?"

"Russo."

"Yes!"

"All right, one and one, let's get back in the van."

Once, we locked up a Cuban guy, or rather, a Cuban who, under interrogation, admitted to some remote Irish and Italian ancestry, a grandfather who was half-and-half, which confused him to no end at the precinct:

"Whose collar is the Italian guy?"

"Hey, Irish, step out, we gotta print ya."

"Seamus—yeah, you, tell me your address."

"Hold on a second, Vito, you can make that phone call in a minute."

Mickstat and Wopstat each picked up a number through our informants in the Four-Six. Charlie had a "partner" named Tommy, another homeless guy who knew of our arrangement and hoped to work for us as well. Tommy was also in his late thirties, shorter and darker and generally less imposing than Charlie, who had a kind of wild hillbilly look from his life outdoors. Tommy had also lately migrated from the Heights after it was locked down. Like Charlie, Tommy steered white junkies to the dealers, but he made more money panhandling during rush hour, by the side of the entrance ramp that led from the Major Deegan to the Cross Bronx Expressway, when the traffic moved ten feet a minute. He told me he had a severe circulatory problem with his legs, which manifested itself in a rather showy limp, and as he stood at the roadside with a sign that said, "Homeless, Hungry, AIDS," he was a pitiful sight.

Tommy once confided in me, "Don't take this the wrong way, but Charlie got real down when you guys weren't around for a while. It's like he missed you. Me, this life—I mean, it's not like I wanted to do this when I grew up, but I always been a street kid. Not Charlie. He goes a little crazy sometimes, he'll rip off stashes from dealers, you know, not rob 'em–rob 'em, but peep out where they hide the shit and sneak back and take it later. Here, you do that if you want to die. Charlie was like a small-town guy—high school jock, lots of girls, nice car, all that shit. For Christ's sake, his old man's a cop! Anyway, you guys mean a lot to him."

Charlie and Tommy had moved from the median strip to beneath one of the great stone arches of a bridge that led to Manhattan. The hideaway was at the crest of a ridge that rose north from Yankee Stadium, on a wooded slope between the Harlem River and the neighborhoods of Highbridge and University Heights. You had to climb an eight-foot fence and then scramble across the loose and rocky soil of the hill, cutting over and then climbing back up like a ski slope. At the fence, there were signs of primitive religion: for weeks, the body of a three-foot-long snake was threaded through the steel mesh like a garland; for days, it was joined by a chicken carcass, plump as a pom-pom, with greasy white feathers, and neatly decapitated. Under the bridge, their encampment had a stone-age simplicity, with its humble and soiled basics of bedding, food, and fire; you could picture a cave painting of primeval Charlie and Tommy in animal skins, bringing down a mastodon with flint-tipped syringes. But what brought us to the woods was scarcely more complex than what kept them there; in our way, we were hunter-gatherers, too.

Charlie bought drugs. We gave him money. We didn't give him money for drugs, but that's where it went. In the sixties and seventies, it was said to be common for cops in Narcotics to give their informants drugs directly, throwing them a bag or two from a seizure. Though the practice was plainly illegal and fraught with risk, morally, I didn't see the problem. The payment in cash instead of drugs was a necessary legality, but, in human terms, nothing more: if Charlie didn't stick a needle in his arm ten times a day, I wouldn't be talking to him. If he wanted to get well—and I hoped he would—I would help him. Until then, I would take advantage of what he knew to do my job. For me, there was a concrete benefit in the relationship, but I wasn't sure whether the same held true for Charlie. He and Tommy both told us about young dealers who sometimes beat and robbed them for fun. Before, he wouldn't have pressed charges out of fear of both cops and crooks; ironically, our new availability made the idea of reporting a crime still less attractive, should it expose our relationship. He liked us, and he trusted us, but he needed the dealers.

All of us collected old clothes to give them, and John even gave Charlie a Walkman radio he had lying around. He had always been deferential to me, out of respect for the badge and recognition that I was in my way his employer, and he became increasingly grateful. There were moments of equality and familiarity between us, as if we'd met at a bar or a ball game, but they always had an undercurrent of the pathetic; we were the same age, from similar backgrounds, but not even everyone on the team could bring themselves to shake his hand. Once, when I drove him to court to get a search warrant, he changed the radio till he found a song he liked (Supertramp's "Breakfast in America": *Could we have kippers for breakfast, Mummy dear, Mummy dear . . .*) which annoyed me at first—Hey, it's my car, and that band sucks!—when I realized how long it had been since he'd looked for a song on the radio, and what it meant to him. It was in the casual and conversational—the remarks on how he liked my leather jacket, because it's hard to find a plain one, without zippers or buckles or a fancy cut, or how he used to drive a Mustang, years ago—that the gap between us yawned. I reminded him of his life before drugs, with its glories, such as 1980 Oldsmobiles and sleeping indoors. It occurred to me that these visits, when I sought him out for information or to take him to court, had something of the affectionate but awkward quality of a divorced dad picking up his kid every other weekend. The streets had custody of him, but I had visitation rights. And while our relationship may have consoled and inspired him for a few hours a week, my job was not to reform him and his heart was not in reform.

For me, the most routinely nerve-wracking part of work occurred during brief periods of time with Charlie. There were a lot of confrontations that I remember with some dread, but they were haphazard and scattered, and they struck with the randomness of fate. I trusted my partners, my ability, and my luck. But with Charlie, there were built-in moments of potentially lethal exposure, every time we met, stepping into the precinct or out of court. I might stop by the bridge on the way to work to ask who was on the street, and where the stash was hidden. When we'd head up to the Four-Six, we might see Charlie on the street; passing by, we might honk the horn and yell at another car—"Can't you drive?"—to get his attention without acknowledging it, and meet in the woods. If we ran into other forest junkies, we'd play tough-guy cops: "You got anything on you? I toss you and find something, you're under. Go ahead, now, move." They were glad to be clear of us, and they wouldn't have any stories about the nice guys who came to talk to Charlie. We were more careful than he was, until the day when he left the precinct through the front door, in his hurry and indifference. The precinct was some two miles from his turf, but he passed a woman he knew from the street, a crackhead, and he thought she recognized him. It didn't matter if she hated dealers and loved cops, or loved Charlie: it was information she could use, and that glimpse of him was like finding a ten-dollar bill on the sidewalk. Maybe a twenty! If she was out of money, she could say to a player, *Listen, I got something to tell you, but you gotta front me. . . .* For days, Charlie was in a panic, and his panic, like his elation, sorrow, ambivalence, and every other emotion, was treated with the same medication. He shook more, he smelled worse, and his extended sentences were not prizes of clarity and grammar. But the shock may have served a purpose: he told me that he'd talked with his mother, and he was ready to go into rehab.

"That's great, Charlie. When do you want to go?"

"Soon, today maybe. No, tomorrow."

"You want a ride home?"

He thought a minute. "Nah, I think I'll take the bus, get my head together. I could use the bus fare, though, if it wouldn't be a problem."

"You got it. Tomorrow morning, you want to go for one last warrant?"

There were two places where we were working on warrants. At one, the dealer lived in a first-floor apartment on University and sold from the lobby. If he ran out, he'd go back in to re-up, or if an established customer—say, Charlie—went there early enough, he could knock on his door and get done. After one buy, however, Charlie hadn't managed to catch him in more sales from the apartment. We worked a lot at adjoining buildings on Nelson Avenue, a block over from University, which sold four different brands of dope—Checkmate, Shotgun, Brainstorm, and Fugitive—as well as cocaine and crack. Charlie had got done in an apartment there the day before, and he made two more buys in quick succession. The next morning, we went in for the warrant.

With Charlie, we obtained "sight warrants," the weakest of the three types of information used to establish probable cause. Generally speaking, the Bronx DA wanted three "looks" within a ten-day period if there were only drugs present, and they preferred additional corroboration, such as an identified subject with a criminal history, the complaints of neighbors, or other arrests in the building for the same kind of narcotics. Another approach is through "controlled buys," in which an informant is sent in with marked money, and the drugs purchased are field-tested and vouchered, a method that improves the quality of evidence a step beyond the say-so. In most instances, two buys were required for a judge to issue a warrant. Finally, through the firsthand testimony of undercovers, whether buys or observations, one visit was sufficient. A variety of other factors had their weight, such as the cops' familiarity with the target location, and the past credibility of the informant. Where one judge or DA saw a bright line of probable cause that we crossed twice over, another saw shadows and doubt. But you never know what's on the other side of the door until you look, do you?

Judges varied in their thoroughness. Some simply looked over the affidavit prepared by the ADA, which recounted the details of each transaction, and asked the cop and the informant if it was accurate; others grilled each of us for an extended period. With the warrant on Nelson, it was the former style, and we moved quickly—all of us motivated, perhaps, by Charlie's deterioration and its attendant odor. In the rush, I didn't do the recon the night before. The building was Perp Central, and difficult to enter without being made; in such instances, you might visit in uniform, in a marked car, to suggest a general visit rather than a specific purpose. Another trick was for the informant to mark the door in some subtle way, or draw graffiti on the frame; with Charlie, especially in his state, it was not possible to expect him to hold on to a pen for couple of hours. In any case, we got the warrant without having seen the door.

When I did see the door, the next night, it was as if it had been slammed in my face. It was where it was supposed to be, on the second floor, the second apartment to the right of the stairs, but instead of being marked 2D, say, it was marked 24. In housing projects and in many other buildings, the floor is numbered and the apartment is lettered, but it is hardly a universal system. The apartments in this building were badly marked, and the most visible door marking on the floor had simply an A. What I suspect had happened was that Charlie had seen the A, assumed it was 2A, and counted over to 2D. He had also said the door was brown, while to me, the paint looked not-so-brownish, though in a certain light, maybe, you could . . .no, it was lime green. The paint was fresh, so the color difference could be accounted for, but the warrant said we could knock down the door marked 2D, and there was no such apartment in the building. Legally, that stopped things flat. Further, it meant our claim of the apartment through the Drug Enforcement Coordinating System (DECS) was meaningless—naturally, no one else had a case in a nonexistent apartment—and indeed, the real address had already been claimed by Narcotics, who had done a warrant several months earlier. I talked to the case officer, who said they didn't get anything out of it at the time, but he was glad to hear it would be worth starting up again.

When I told PK, I made a couple of half-assed arguments, thinking aloud as much as talking with him, trying to come up with a way to pull it off. That kind of perseverance is a good thing, sometimes. I didn't let little things like walls get in my way when I wanted to get somewhere. When Mike Donnelly came to the precinct, Tony told him, "Eddie doesn't take 'No' for an answer. He's the most determined one on the team, when it comes to it." I was proud of that, but John tended to remark on the flip side of the characteristic: "You're *gabbados*. It means thickheaded, you don't listen." With PK, I had to listen; we all did, mostly because of his very lack of argument. He didn't give orders, because he didn't have to; we knew that he did every good thing that he could for us, and every tough break was equally shared. He smiled a little and listened, and said, "It's a shame, laddo. We'll all have to be more careful next time." When my hot air cooled a little, he said, "OK, so let's go out."

. . .

BECAUSE IT WAS PLAIN THAT I HADN'T QUITE REACHED THE peak of the learning curve, it was interesting to see how much I had mastered, or at least what now came with thoughtless habit: the attitude on a stop, the thoroughness of a search, or phrasing the question, "When was the last time you were locked up?" instead of "Were you ever arrested?" John had certainly been a capable cop before he joined SNEU, but there were aspects of work than only came with practice, like what to look for in an OP, or guarding your speech around perps. As the van filled up, you put the perps in the back seat and turned up the stereo, but not so high that you couldn't hear your radio. You had hours to kill, sitting there in the van, driving, sitting again, and so naturally you talked to your partner. But you didn't talk about work—you didn't want them to pick up useful details about how we operated, where the OP was, or whether someone told us about the dealer, which could lead them to guess who might have, correctly or not—and you didn't talk about your personal life, either. You couldn't say your wife's name, or complain about the commute this morning, because it might tell them where you lived. Although few perps would make serious use of that information, many would take advantage of stray personal details in the short term, calling from the cells, "How's your wife? You know, Jenny, your wife?" And so you have to bullshit about nothing in particular: TV, girls, cars, the joke of the day, the more stupid the better. It had a morally uplifting effect on the perps, I thought, as they shifted in their cuffs in the back seat, listening to two cops argue for hours over who farted. They had to wonder: *These are the guys that caught me?*

Other lessons were common cop lessons, hardly unique to SNEU. One day, John and Stix were on bikes when we worked One-Five-Seven and Elton, and Stix got a flat. He went back to the precinct to fix it, while John stayed out to catch bodies alone. The OP gave out a body, and John went after him. This was a body indeed: two hundred and seventy-five pounds of it, stacked up six feet and three inches, which found work in the evenings guarding the door of a strip joint. John came in aggressively and put him on the wall, but when the bouncer saw that John was alone, he stepped out and faced off. John's eye was drawn to his right fist, which both held the dope and sought to meet his face. John put him down in the street: his radio slipped out of reach, while the perp threw the dope down a sewer. A crowd drew near, neither to help nor to harm, and John and the perp locked into each other, the perp swinging for John's face, while John massaged the perp's head against the curb. John was able to reach his radio, yelling for backup; the perp was cuffed, and ESU retrieved the dope from the sewer.

In the cells, the perp fumed, in disbelief that he hadn't been able to take him: "I woulda kicked that guy's ass if he wasn't on steroids."

"Yeah, you had your chance. Look who's spitting tough juice now," John responded.

Far more unnerving to John was an early appearance in Grand Jury. A Grand Jury is composed of sixteen to twenty-three people, impaneled for several weeks to vote on indictments in felony cases. Defense counsel is not present, and the standard of proof is the same as it is for an arrest; for the most part, they mechanically affirm mechanical accounts of collars, and it is dull work. Testimony for observation sales generally begins with the cop in the OP saying he saw the buyer and seller make an exchange, and ends with the apprehending officer saying he made an arrest based on directions from the OP. Sometimes, a juror might ask a question like, "Were you using binoculars?" One panel that I appeared before several times had a man who asked that for each case—he'd found a good thing to say, and he stuck with it. More often, they said nothing, and the tedium of the panel was usually so pronounced that I expected someone to ask one day, "Yes, Officer, I have a question. What's a five-letter word for 'bedspread'?"

The DA asks, you answer; you should know what's coming, and so should they. It goes like this:

"Good morning, Officer."

"Good morning."

"Would you please state your name, rank, and command for the record?"

"Police Officer Edward Conlon, shield number nine-eight-seven-six, Police Service Area Seven, Housing Bureau."

"Officer, I'd like to direct your attention to events which occurred on or about August 15, 1998, at approximately two-fifteen in the afternoon, at the corner of One Hundred and Fifty-seventh Street and Elton Avenue, in the county of the Bronx. What, if anything, did you do then?"

"I was working as a New York City police officer, in the Street Narcotics Enforcement Unit of PSA-Seven, in an observation post. I observed the defendant for a period of one hour, during which he made exchanges of small objects for United States currency with numerous individuals."

"All right, Officer, and then what happened?"

"I transmitted the information to the field team on point-to-point radio."

"Thank you, Officer. If no one has any questions, you can go."

Grand Jury is easy, but it is still public speaking, which makes me a little nervous. I was slightly more nervous, during the first case that I had with John, as the ADA ambushed me with all kinds of odd questions—not only rudely co-opting the binocular question from the poor man in the back, but following up with a pop quiz: What was their power of magnification? There had been no preparation for the testimony, which is not unusual for such a formulaic appearance, but it is received wisdom among trial lawyers that you do not ask a question to which you do not know the answer. This was somewhere between a game show and a fraternity hazing. As it happened, I knew the specifications of the binoculars, but then he asked me, "How did you recognize the voice of Officer Timpanaro over the radio?"

It stumped me. What the hell did it mean? Were we supposed to be trained in voice-recognition techniques? Was he after something metaphysical: Does another person ever *really* know someone else? Is there something particular about Timpanaro and broadcasting: *Sir, as you are well aware, Officer Timpanaro is one of the most beloved entertainers of our generation.* I think I said, "Umm, because I work with him?"

John followed me, and returned several minutes later, pale and stunned, looking like Frank Costello before the Senate Subcommittee on Organized Crime, stammering denials to Bobby Kennedy. When the binocular question came, I think he even took the Fifth. He expected to go in and say, "Based on a radio transmission by Officer Conlon, I arrested the defendant. I took ten glassines of heroin from his right pants pocket, a hundred dollars from his left." God Bless America, and Good Night. Boy, was he was pissed at me. And it was only the memory of him telling Yvonne not to give up, to keep on trying to win my heart, that gave me the courage to laugh in his face. And then we went back out.

Out was always good. It was summer in the Bronx: new songs from San Juan and old ones from Santo Domingo blared from the bodegas and the gypsy cabs; the "icey-man" made his rounds with his little white cart that said HELADO, filling a cup with shavings from a sweating block of ice, then squirting it with mango, coco, or cherry syrup; laundry hung from the lines strung across the alleys, as if to proclaim, "Our drawers are clean. Are yours?" There were some women you wished wore more clothes, and some you wished wore fewer, and others who had it just right.

We cowboyed it a little bit. When we drove to the Four-Six, PK once blanched to see John and Stix skitching on the back of a bus—on bikes, holding on to the back bumper for a tow uphill. I found that if I worked alone in my car, no one looked at me twice in the neighborhood. I chased a guy over the bridge into Manhattan, if "chase" is the word for a pursuit that coursed along at three miles an hour. The man had a mastiff in the back seat, a dog that was almost as big as I was. When the rest of the team got there, I had the perp in cuffs. Tony and OV would have preferred to stop a man with a live shark in the back, and the rest of the team was in no hurry to become pet food either. The dog seemed friendly enough, though, and we were stuck with it, so I got in the passenger seat and told the perp to drive back to the Four-Six, adding, "If this dog bites me, I'm gonna shoot you both." The dog laid his chin on my shoulder during the ride. We rushed the perp out with a Desk Appearance Ticket, so he could go home with his pet.

Cops don't do this kind of work alone, or at least they shouldn't. I did, sometimes, even off-duty, checking out spots on the way home from a night in the city, especially if I was well dressed. At midnight, a solo stray in jacket and tie would attract notice in the neighborhood, but he'd be made as a Wall Street junkie readying for a binge. I'd rub my eyes bloodshot, and stagger a little. In truth, I was more concerned about being stopped by a cop than a perp. But I could walk into a building we were looking at for a warrant, see the layout of the hallway, the marks on the door, and then look at the roof, to see where the windows faced, over which airshaft and alley, and whether there was a fire escape. Orville or Sammy might be able to look while we were working, but no secondhand report would give me the detail and certainty I'd have if I saw it myself. One night, I went out with a few friends, one of whom had the use of the company limousine. At the end of the evening, the car drove uptown, dropping people off, and as there were no other Bronx residents in our party, I was left as the last passenger. The driver had an English accent, "Where can I take you, sir?" *Home, James, by way of Junkie Town. . . .*

One night, Stix and I walked up University, checking things out. It had looked a little slow, and when the same black van with tinted windows makes too many trips up the street, whatever's out won't stay out long. PK and the rest of the team followed from a distance. "See what turns up," said PK. We were both scruffy-looking, skinny white guys, looking around for drug dealers; there were two possible explanations for our stroll through the neighborhood, and we decided to see if the players would fall for the other one. Slipping into a lobby, we stuck our radios down the fronts of our pants; we had big, loose shirts on, which covered vests and guns. Stix was breezily confident, enjoying it as the practical joke it was—in a certain sense, working undercover is the ultimate practical joke—whereas I was nervous as an understudy thrust onstage for opening night. What were my lines? What was my motivation? Why was my dressing room so small? Still, I thought that the combination of nerve and neurosis could work on our side, and we stepped out.

No one was out for Marlboro or Audi, or for Turbo or Checkmate or Brainstorm. The West Hell Cartel no longer used 1669 and 1675, and the rest of the street looked clean of players. Up the block, by the bodega on Tremont, there was a crew on the corner, easy to make. We walked up and stopped, walked again and stopped to consult each other: they would see us coming, desperate and lost. We waited under the bodega awning, in the light, nattering audibly as out-of-town dope nerds: "No, you ask!"

"No, you! It's your turn!"

"I asked last time!"

And a guy from the crowd sauntered over: "What you want?"

"Heroin," said Stix brightly. "We want to get some heroin. You got any?"

Look, Ma, I finished all my vegetables. Can I have some heroin now, please? It was slightly surreal, but also perfect. Stix didn't play ghetto, because he couldn't—*"Got D, yo? Anybody holding the D?"*—would have come out of his mouth like Charlton Heston reciting from the collected works of Snoop Dogg.

He stared at us, taking it in. He was not, by the look of him, any deep thinker: *Could we be cops? Has the NYPD sunk so low? Don't they teach them anything?*

"I don't know, maybe," he said. "How much you want?"

He was on the fence, and I spoke up: "We want a bundle."

If he doubted we were worth the trouble for a ten-dollar bag, a hundred-dollar bundle might tip the balance. He went back to the crew at the corner and consulted with them before returning.

"Give me the money first."

"No."

"Lemme have the money, I'll get it for you. You gotta front it."

I think we had twelve dollars between us. I spoke up again, heatedly: "Forget about it, let's go down the street for Miracle or Macho, we don't need this shit, fuck this! This guy don't want our money, somebody else does." We walked up the street, and got about fifty yards before the dealer called us back.

"C'mon, I got ya."

Waving us to follow, he stepped into the building. 1815 University has a narrow, iron-gated courtyard, with the lobby door recessed in the back. We followed into the dim corridor and inside the building. We didn't look back at the crew, milling at the gate, with whom the player had consulted after each step. Again, the player asked for money, and again, we refused, and he walked upstairs, promising to return. I weighed my options, which seemed to be to take the drugs and then blast him with mace, or to take the drugs and punch him in the head. Stix and I looked at each other, in quiet unease. I forget if we giggled. Another player drifted in from the street.

And then the team rushed in. They took the player and put him against the wall, and I tapped Stix and we grabbed the wall, whispering to OV to search us. The first player was nowhere to be found. Three of us left the building in cuffs, and when we were out, Stix and I were loud in our protests: "What happened? We were half a minute from a collar! Why'd you come in?"

PK told us, "The rest of the crew was coming in after you. They were gonna rob you." I thought, So? A robbery collar would have been all the better!—which, in retrospect, was a fearsome indicator of our level of enthusiasm that summer. The next night, we gave it another try—this time, Stix and I even took out our shoelaces, as if they'd been removed after a night in the cells, and wrote up arrest paperwork for ourselves. I made mine for an Italian guy, of course, and Stix's perp was Irish, though had the dealer looked closely, it would have said I lived at 12 Junkie Lane. A player on a bike circled around us, intrigued, disinclined to do us but all the while peppering us with questions like "Where's your car parked?" He even touched my shoulder to see if I had on a vest, though he felt the wrong spot. "Nah, nah, nah . . ." he said, "I don't know nothin' about dope around here. . . ."

We'd get him next time.

After the warrant that we didn't execute, I wondered whether I'd see Charlie again, to tell him what had happened. He seemed to be coming closer to a move, a change in his life. Though he'd yessed me a little on the door markings, I could hardly beat him up over it—it was my responsibility, for one, but also he'd been trying to come to terms with the idea that his suicide on the installment plan might be fast-forwarded by a .38 behind the ear. I found Tommy first, and he said Charlie was in a bad way. He also told me about another inside spot, as well as the players on the street that day. When I handed Tommy some money, he held up his hands and said, "C'mon, Eddie, you don't have to, it's okay." I said, "It's all right, you guys work, you take risks for us, you should get paid." He took the money, but he shook his head.

"Don't take this the wrong way, but I feel a little funny, since you guys pay out of your own pockets. Do you know how much we make out here, panhandling, during rush hour?"

"No, how much?"

"About a dollar a minute."

"Oh."

I didn't take my money back, but I saw his point: Charlie and Tommy made more money than us. I should have realized that earlier, as the math was not complicated—we took home less than a hundred dollars a day, while their habits were at least that. I tried not to dwell on the fact that, economically, a New York City police officer was a notch down from a bum.

When I did find Charlie, he said he was sorry about the warrant. He had an abased and abstracted look, as if his career as a junkie hadn't been going all that well, and the informant's life might not be quite the thing, either: maybe it was time to clean up and go into rehab. But the next time he called home, to tell his mother that this time, this time was finally it, that he was ready to go into the hospital and start living again, his father answered the phone and told him that his mother had died, days ago, and hung up. The funeral was already over.

By the end of August, we had sixty-five collars. We got twenty-two in two days, hitting One-Five-Seven and Elton, for blue-top vials of crack, China White, and Eazy Money, and Bike worked with us on one of those days as well, taking a dozen collars more. It killed the spot. OV watched from the projects, I watched from the senior citizens building, giving out bodies as they moved west to Melrose, east to Third, north to One-Six-One, south to One-Four-Nine. We caught them in vans, cars, bikes, and on foot:

"Is he a hit?"

"He's a hit."

"Good, I got another one for ya. . . ."

At the end of our Roger Maris month, PK wrote in the margins of our collar book, "Roger who?"

Narcotics was picking people up in great numbers. By that time, Inspector Mullen was at Bronx Narcotics. I told him about our month, and he said to bring everyone up for a talk. We packed into the van and rode up to his office, then gathered around his desk as if it were a campfire. "I need people," he said, and we leaned in to hear more. We said we all wanted to work together, as a team. He said that at first, he'd probably have to mix us up with veteran detectives until we knew what we were doing. We looked at one another and murmured assent. It was like all your best friends from high school getting a scholarship to the same college. We were going to be OK.

In early September, it was PK's son Paulie's first anniversary. The team bought PK a mass card. I handed it to him at the end of the day, and he smiled and nodded, and walked quickly to his car.

SEVEN

I t was Inspector Mullen who told me about the glass toilet. One of the airport squads uses it for drug mules, forcing them to sit until the co-caine or heroin-filled condoms they've swallowed on distant shores reappear here, at the journey's end. The device so fascinated me that I was afraid to ask him for details about how it worked—was there a safety or a trigger-lock on the flusher, to prevent destruction of evidence?—because my interest was so avid that I thought it might disturb him. But I also didn't want to know more about the glass toilet because the way I imagined it, it had be-come the perfect symbol of police work, and I didn't want facts to spoil my fantasy. You picked people from crowds, took them aside, and waited to see what came out. Every cop was a bowl keeper, in his way, in possession of tools and techniques for the inspection of what people had deep inside them; each tour of duty was a reminder that innocence and guilt can leave an equally foul odor. You realized that to work beside the bowl could be awful enough, but it was better than being on it, or in it. It made you appreciate that a good life is full of decorous separations, from its own parts and from other - people, so that its intimate functions, moments of weakness, occasions of sin, could pass on and be forgotten.

I'd become used to a kind of double life, or at least two jobs, apart from each other and largely out of sight. I thought of the arrangement in terms of privacy rather than secrecy, though the edges blurred, and it had been that way from the beginning, when my family and most of my friends had no idea that I was about to go into the Academy. Like many cops, I was reluctant to tell strangers or new acquaintances what I did, and was irked when non-cop friends would preemptively announce it, to a girl in a bar or whoever else, because it brought out strange reactions in people. Most were enthusiastic in some manner, but sometimes you got the feeling that if they'd met a comedian, they'd demand to hear something funny. You also met gun nuts and other ostensible supporters, who were disappointed that my mastery of firearms didn't extend far beyond the ability to make mine go *Bang!* A lot of people asked me if I'd ever killed anyone, and a few asked, "Do you see much corruption?" I wondered if those people asked newlyweds if they'd cheated on each other yet. And those were the ones who liked the police.

At a Christmas party, I was pointed out to someone's date, who tried to corner me on the subject of parking tickets, a perennial conversational hazard for off-duty cops. My usual tactic of measured agreement—Yes, some cops are petty, but sometimes it's because the sergeant ordered them to be, and Yes, of course you should fight the ticket if you didn't deserve it—did nothing to deter his harangue.

"You know, in alternate-side parking in Manhattan, there's just no place to put your car sometimes, and—"

"You're right, it's a shame."

"Yeah, but what you do is—"

"I don't write tickets, and I don't work in Manhattan."

"But *still,* what you have to do about the parking below 59th Street, is—"

I ducked him and he followed me, and again, until I turned and barked at him: "Listen, guy, what do you do for a for a living?"

"I'm a chef."

"Fine, next time I get a bad meal at a restaurant, I'll call you at home on your day off."

The fact of the matter is that most cops lead double lives of some kind, of high contrast if not outright contradiction. At the most ordinary level, there are the cops who commute daily between suburban order and ghetto mayhem, or who at least have a home that is some kind of refuge from the streets. That was how it was for my father, who spent nine-to-five with the bad guys, nights and weekends with the wife and kids. Conversely, the steadiness and definition of the Job, with its rules, traditions, and diffuse base of blue-collar Catholicism, provided a workaday counterbalance to many cops' off-duty worlds, whether they were twice-divorced loners at the bar or in other straits of familial chaos. In some way, that was the situation of Pat Brown, as a crooked cop and a man-about-town. Just about the only exception I can think of was Uncle Eddie, in Harbor, who spent his days hanging out with cops on a boat, and then went home to hang out on his boat, often with cops. Sometimes it must have felt like it wasn't like working at all; at others, it must have seemed that he spent his whole life on overtime. But for most cops, there is a split of some kind, a distance if not a discord, between public and private, their passions and pastimes.

I was no different. As a cop, I worked out of love and for the money, as I had when I was a freelance writer, always hoping that there was enough of each not to force a choice between the two. I hadn't done much writing since. And so when I was asked to write a magazine piece about being a cop, and then a few more, I was glad for the opportunity to pick it up again, but I was insistent that it be published under another name. I was still new, and while I didn't want to lay claim to any larger experience than I'd earned, I also didn't want to be dismissed as a rookie, or worse, someone who'd gone on the Job as a stunt or for a story. I didn't want to speak for other cops, but rather to portray the Job as I'd known it and let that speak for itself. When I described some adventure or encounter on patrol, my partners' roles were related in a narrowly factual manner; I didn't want cops to have to second-guess me, to wonder if they were under a kind of surveillance. No one in any occupation likes the idea that they are being observed unawares, and cops have a particular aversion to it, as they are used to conflict on the streets and criticism in the press. With your partners, at least, you should be able to depend on a measure of reflexive support.

The fact of the matter is that all cops exist in a state of mild infraction. Their memo books aren't up to date, or they don't have the new insert for Spanish Phrases or Domestic Disputes, or their shoes aren't shined, or their socks are white, or they stopped to eat or cash a check without putting it over the air, or they signed out a little early, or they left their hat in the car when they went to a job. It was only recently that I learned that you can get a Command Discipline for reading the newspaper in a patrol car, an offense for which I'd be serving life without parole if I'd been caught each time I'd committed it. No one is completely by-the-book, because our book is the *Patrol Guide,* which not only maps out every turn in the bureaucratic labyrinth but is self-described as "flexible," which could be read cynically to mean that even if you followed every step, you could still get jammed up if things - didn't work out, because you could have done it differently. Everyone knows this, from cop to commissioner, and if you work hard and in good faith, in compliance with the basics, the best you can hope for is that the trouble you get in won't be too frequent or too deep. You were probably breaking some kind of rule just by showing up, it seemed, and this general understanding that the less said the better is yet another basis for the "blue wall of silence."

I was careful, but not paranoid. I wasn't a CIA agent or a Soviet spy, but a more-or-less-contented witness to the daily travails of big-city police work. I had permission to write from the Deputy Commissioner of Public Information, Marilyn Mode, and the commanding officer of that office, Inspector Michael Collins. Mode and Collins both read the first piece, but only Collins the later ones. My initial fear that they would see the articles as a public-relations opportunity—"Give us something on bicycle summonses, the Mayor's all over it this week"—was baseless, though Inspector Collins did point out several typos. Outside of work, it was a fairly open secret, and I was almost casual in my confidence that the two worlds wouldn't meet. I gave copies of the pieces to cop friends from before I went on the Job, like Mike Shea and Brian McCabe, though I'd caution them not to mention my real name or where I worked if they showed them to other cops. I was supposed to fill out an "off-duty employment" form, but that had to be signed by the commanding officer of the precinct, which was a little close to home.

And home was where the first breach took place. John, who lived with his family some sixty miles outside of the city, had begun to stay over at the Vanity Court apartment one or two nights a week by the end of the summer. I never quite understood how cops like John—or PK, who lived seventy miles away—could manage three or sometimes four hours a day commuting to and from work, where they might spend another eight hours in a car. It seemed contradictory to the whole point of being a New Yorker. But after John had been staying there a few weeks, it seemed polite to explain why the floor was littered with manuscript. It may have been the least of the peculiarities of the place, with its perpetual back-alley twilight, the mysterious leaks and smells, the sounds of roosters and neighbors crowing from all sides; and the fact that he didn't question it may have reflected generally lowered expectations. But I told him, and as a hidden diversion he thought it was reasonably interesting, and for successive mornings after the revelation, he showily brought copies of the magazine pieces with him into the bathroom. *Ya gotta have a story, don't ya?* It wasn't a glass toilet, but it was there that John became familiar with the idea of one, as our innermost workings ran parallel courses, body and mind.

• • •

THE FRENCH CONNECTION HAD TWO SEQUELS, ONE A DISAP-pointment, one a disgrace. In the movie, Popeye goes to France. In life, no one knows where the drugs went. In 1971, *The French Connection* won the Academy Award, and in 1972, at the height of the Knapp Commission scandals, it was discovered that much of the heroin had been replaced with pancake flour. It had not been a good year for the NYPD. Throughout the nation, there was general upheaval in attitudes and beliefs, and the blind faith with which many supported public institutions was replaced with an equally blind contempt. The Knapp Commission was set in motion by an expose of police corruption in *The New York Times* based primarily on testimony by two cops, David Durk and Frank Serpico. Serpico became *Serpico,* the book and the movie, where the old expression of "good cop, bad cop"—which referred to an interrogation technique, rather than integrity—was reframed as good cop . . . and everyone else. It was a time when history repeated itself, and reversed itself, moving from farce to tragedy to something in between; the shifts in fortune were dizzying, as bit players made it big and the great figures were brought down, and cops negotiated between movie deals and indictments.

Frank Serpico has many admirers and many detractors, but there was no disagreement that he was a very strange man. A chief told me he remembers him with his pet mouse scrambling around his coat collar. Peter Maas, the author of *Serpico,* was infatuated with the idea of the hippie cop in his velour bell-bottoms, leather jerkin, and huge gold Winnie-the-Pooh medallion, with his love of opera and one-night stands. The enthusiasm sometimes takes on an Austin Powers tone, such as when he notes that Serpico's amorous attentions were divided between "a carefree airline stewardess who looks as if she just walked in off the Southern California beach where she was raised on sun and surfing," "a somewhat tense, twenty-six-year-old, blond, hundred-dollar call girl with stupendous breasts," and a "volatile black model." *Yeah, baby!* Next to the poor stiffs who went home every night to their cookie-cutter houses to eat meat loaf with the same old frau, Serpico's superiority is depicted in nearly evolutionary terms.

Serpico was moody, intense, and self-absorbed; from childhood, his admiration for cops ran so deep that he traded a bike for a Cub Scout shirt because it looked like a police uniform, and he'd explain to other kids that he couldn't talk because he was "on a case." Like many who come on the Job with fervid, romantic expectations of police work, he was disappointed with the rule-bound, time-killing nature of patrol, and the tone of cynical self-preservation that prevails when cops talk among themselves. And yet his resistance to cutting corners was hardly absolute: he didn't "coop," which meant to hide somewhere, to sleep or hang out with other cops . . . except when it was really cold. On his post, he accepted free meals . . . until he noticed that cops tended to get leftovers, and so he decided to pay . . . part of the check. That was why the commonplace, small-time "gifts" could spoil cops' relations with the neighborhood, even if there was no great crime being committed— a merchant might well be delighted to offer the local beat cop a free haircut, shoeshine, or lunch, but word of his good nature would spread, and the sector cars might stop by, and the sergeant, and so on, so that the small gesture became a larger burden, resentfully proffered and with greater expectations of payback.

But the long-anticipated thrills were there, too, at Serpico's precinct in Bedford-Stuyvesant: he caught burglars and delivered babies. He shot the balls off a rapist. One collar, after a brutal gang rape, showed that Serpico had both real ability and awful judgment—after catching one perp, he brought him back to the Squad, where a detective beat the man, demanding the names of his accomplices. The perp clammed up, and when Serpico brought him to court the next morning, he stopped, uncuffed the perp, and took him out for breakfast. It's not a technique recommended in the *Patrol Guide,* but Serpico got the names. Where Maas sees the episode as maverick and humane, I see a cup of coffee in the eyes and a perp who'll send you postcards from Florida. Another episode that made me cringe told of how, off-duty, Serpico would dress in shabby clothes and wander alone through the ghetto, hoping to be jumped. He was.

After a few years, he was rewarded with a transfer to Vice, as a plainclothesman, because a new department regulation had mandated assignment there before promotion to the Detective Division. The idea was to circulate as many honest cops as possible through the traditionally rotten detail, to flush it clean. The old characters like Pat Brown would make way for the new generation of Serpicos. At the time, the NYPD made 10,000 arrests for gambling every year; the DAs barely prosecuted them, and the judges barely sentenced them. Though Vice was a charade, Serpico had been assured that the age of the grafter was over, by bosses who were certainly honest themselves, and presumably better informed about the Department as a whole. Serpico accepted the transfer, though he shared his ambivalence with his new friend David Durk, whom he met at a criminal-investigation class.

When Serpico met Durk, it was like meeting Bobby Kennedy and Leonard Bernstein at once. Durk was well connected and well read, living with his wife and child in an Upper West Side apartment that was a salon of like-minded people. Serpico would go to dinner parties there and sit in silence, but he could talk long into the night with Durk. In *Target Blue,* in which Robert Daley tells of his year as a deputy commissioner in 1972, he describes the instant bond between the two, who were in most ways as unlike each other as they were from the rest of the rank-and-file: "There were cops who took gambling graft and cops who didn't. There were those who thought gambling graft amusing, or unimportant, or exaggerated, or negligible, or deplorable; and there were those like Durk and Serpico . . . who were fanatically opposed." They had earnest debates over how to show your badge to a city bus driver, so that you wouldn't "blow your cover," and even whether to do so to the motorcycle mechanic who was ripping off Serpico. (When Durk did, Serpico was furious.)

Though Durk was older than Serpico, he had less time on the Job— in 1966, when they met, he had three years on, to Serpico's six. David Durk was Jewish, a doctor's son who grew up in Manhattan and graduated from Amherst. He was brashly confident and a genuine intellectual, idealistic and dedicated to reform. In the Academy, when the recruits were asked why they had become cops, the first answers were the typical ones—because my father was, for the pension, because the Fire Department wasn't hiring—and Durk made a fiery speech about justice and public service. The next cop asked responded, "What he said." At his midtown precinct, when the desk officer told him to mop the floor, Durk would protest, quoting articles from scholarly journals on effective time-management. Unlike most reformers, however, Durk also enjoyed the daily, hands-on oddity of patrol; he actually liked cops, and saw them as people who, for the most part, wanted to work harder and more honestly than the system permitted. He saw them as the victims of graft as much as its beneficiaries—for example, cops were forbidden to carry lunch with them, but many had posts which were too far from the precinct to eat what they brought from home. On what cops made, the cost of a daily meal in midtown might have been as much as their rent. Durk also had a good perspective on the matter—that a free lunch was often just a free lunch—but he took mischievous pleasure in persuading cops not to go along. In one case, a steak house that gave cops free meals even advertised that it had "free parking" for its customers, who double-parked and blocked hydrants. Durk needled the other cops into enforcement, asking if they liked being ordered around by waiters in exchange for a piece of cheap meat, which they probably spit on anyway. He wrote anonymous letters of complaint to Headquarters, which gave them a pretext for action. The parking problem around the restaurant stopped, and Durk noticed the new pride that the cops took in their work.

That kind of success inspired Durk to believe that things could be changed, in small ways and large, and that he was just the guy to do it. In a chance encounter, he upbraided some hecklers at a speech in the park, and his eloquent explanation of the First Amendment was overheard by Jay Kriegel, a young volunteer for John Lindsay's mayoral campaign who became one of Lindsay's inner circle of advisors. Kriegel stopped to talk to Durk, and in conversation it emerged that he, too, was an Amherst graduate, and a friendship was struck. Durk, while still a rookie, wrote much of a Lindsay policy paper on crime and policing, and opened up a critical line of access to City Hall. When the head of the Department of Investigation—which monitored all city agencies, though in practice it left the police alone—needed a police captain assigned, Durk chose the man, who in turn brought in Durk to work for him.

Six months into his new assignment in plainclothes, in Brooklyn, Serpico was passed an envelope with three hundred dollars in cash. There was no doubt in his mind who could solve the problem. There was no doubt in Durk's mind, either. He took Serpico to his boss at the Department of Investigation, which marked the first of many disappointments and betrayals. The captain's horror at learning of the corruption was matched only by the idea that he might have to do something about it; he told Serpico to forget about it, or he could wind up "face down in the East River." From then on, Serpico became resentful toward Durk as well, though the latter shared his frustration and worked relentlessly to help him. Serpico kept his distance from the other cops, but his arrests complicated arrangements with the gamblers, and the strain increased. The canard that gambling money was "soft" or "clean" was again brought home when Serpico collared a three-hundred-pound mafioso. When Serpico returned to the cells, he found the perp sitting outside, talking happily among the cops, who brought him coffee and saw to his comforts. Serpico exploded; he had checked his record, which showed that the man was a cop killer. The arrest also brought out the vagaries of corruption in the NYPD, which was no more one big happy family than the City was. Paying for police protection was like paying for rain insurance in the desert; it worked most of the time, except for when it didn't. Gamblers could pay the precinct, but then the Division could hit them; they could pay off the Division, but then the Borough could hit them; they could pay off the Borough, but then Headquarters could hit them; and even when everyone was paid off—or was supposed to be—they remained vulnerable to any honest cop.

Together and apart, Durk and Serpico searched for an audience; though Durk's access was extraordinary, his results were lacking. Serpico was transferred to the Bronx, assured by a high-ranking police contact that it was as "clean as a hound's tooth." In the Bronx, however, things were no better. Serpico was persuaded that Headquarters understood and was grateful for his work; for the present, he should sit tight. They would be in touch. They - weren't. For hours, Jay Kriegel listened to Serpico and Durk in rapt attention, taking notes, asking questions, and assuring them of an immediate response from the Mayor. Mayor Lindsay's relations with the NYPD had always been poor, however, and Kriegel, too, had disappointing news: the summer was approaching, and so was riot season, and the Mayor didn't feel that he could further alienate the police. Returning to the Department of Investigation, the commissioner first offered Durk some primitive surveillance equipment, but his aversion to Serpico was so pronounced—again, the Winnie-the-Pooh medallion, but also a hardening attitude of sarcastic disconnection—that he shortly demanded its return, calling Serpico a "psycho."

Serpico grew more combative in his dealings with the honest bosses, adding conditions and demands for his participation: he wouldn't wear a wire, and he didn't want to testify. He didn't want to "get" them as much as change "It"—the worst possible outcome was for the Job to shitcan a couple of cops, declare victory, and move on. Durk was instrumental in this demand for systemic change, in his affection for street cops, and in his belief that they were pawns on the chessboard, the injured parties as much as the injuring. But while this kind of big-picture thinking galvanized Durk, it seemed to overwhelm Serpico, provoking an angry and erratic absolutism. His frustration was more than understandable, after a year of empty promises, but his was a self-defeating position: if you have facts, you have a case; if you have ideas, you have an editorial.

When the Bronx DA, Burton Roberts, indicted eight plainclothesmen, Serpico was largely left out of it. A gruff and flamboyant character, Roberts had been an honest and hardworking prosecutor for a long time, and he found Serpico insufferable as a person and awful as a witness—vast amounts of energy were expended in persuading him to shave his beard. When Serpico's cooperation was finally induced by promising the kind of case he'd hoped for—stretching across the five boroughs, throughout the Department—it went no further than a handful of convictions, though Roberts blamed Serpico's recalcitrance for the limited results. Regardless of who was at fault, Serpico was neither promoted nor protected for his efforts. The gold detective's shield never materialized. Leaks of the investigation made him an outcast, the victim of threats, subtle and otherwise—"I oughta cut your tongue out," said one cop, playing with a switchblade—and when he was transferred, it was to a plainclothes division in Harlem, where his reputation preceded him. On many nights, Durk had to persuade him not to quit.

In Harlem, however, Serpico found an unexpected friend in his commanding officer, Inspector Paul Delise, known as "St. Paul." Delise offered to work as his partner, and together they hit the streets, breaking through doors and chasing people over rooftops. Delise pressed his superiors for assistance in rooting out corruption, but the response was meager. In his own way, Delise provides an oblique counterpoint to Serpico—not to mention *Serpico*—and the sweeping judgments made about the NYPD, which was that the whole system was rotten, perhaps most of all the bosses, who failed to listen, or failed to act, or failed to eradicate corruption in any way. Delise was able to report his suspicions only as such, virtually without details, though in fact he was a highly experienced commander who spent his days on the streets with a veteran plainclothesman who was literally obsessed with corruption. Certainly, there was a lack of will to root it out, but Delise did show that even when there was plenty of will, the way was not always so clear.

Meanwhile, as Serpico suffered, Durk prospered. Though his cases at the DOI were mostly penny-ante—twenty-dollar bribes to building inspectors, stolen gallons of paint—the rest of his waking hours, and many in which he might have been sleeping, were devoted to whatever cause he happened upon, Serpico not least among them. An old partner told him about a building manager who was terrorizing tenants out of his apartment house; when the DOI passed on the information, Durk leaked it to *The New York Times,* whose front-page story prompted an indictment. A friend's cleaning woman forwarded him a tip about narcotics in Harlem, which led to the seizure of two kilos of heroin. He won a Department of Justice grant to tour colleges for a year, making speeches to recruit young people to become police officers. At the height of anti–Vietnam War sentiment, cops were viewed by many as "worse than Dow Chemical"—the manufacturer of napalm—but Durk loved to challenge the complacent and superficial militants of his audience: "If you see social progress as a mass movement with you as the director, this job is not for you. But if individuals count, become a cop." Durk sold the Job as a domestic version of the Peace Corps, where "altruism mixes with fun." He was profiled in *Life* magazine and appeared on talk shows, including *The Tonight Show* with Johnny Carson. Of himself, he wrote, "Modesty is not a flower that grows in my garden."

Though Durk had been in contact with David Burnham, the police reporter for the *Times,* for several years, the relationship was not always firm or fond. Burnham was unwilling to merely take dictation from Durk, while Durk was afraid that Burnham just didn't get it. Burnham wrote a front-page story on cooping, which made a surprisingly big splash, that Durk thought flat-out ridiculous: *Civil Servants Doze Off After Midnight!* Stop the presses! Not only did it pay a great deal of attention to a trivial issue, but in the fallout, Durk felt there was a strong odor of upper-class disdain for the working stiffs. And the story that mattered, that he'd been trying to tell for years now, was about the big shots who were napping, not the little guys.

On February 12, 1970, David Durk, Frank Serpico, Paul Delise, and three other, still-anonymous cops sat down at *The New York Times* with David Burnham. A three-part story led with the headline POLICE GRAFT SAID TO RUN INTO MILLIONS. Lindsay formed a commission, headed by a former federal prosecutor named Whitman Knapp. Commissioner Howard Leary, a dull, pliable man who had been brought in from Philadelphia—and returned there most weekends—didn't resign, but rather simply left the office and - didn't come back. He didn't make an announcement or even leave a note; he took a cruise, and after some days, a puzzled City Hall announced his resignation, with gratitude for his service.

Nine months after the *Times* story broke, in February 1971, Serpico was shot in the face during a drug bust. He had been transferred to Narcotics but otherwise left to languish, and the shield which had been dangled in front of him had never been awarded. He had to keep testifying in the trials of the Bronx plainclothesmen, but he skipped appearances, forgot what he'd said, or contradicted himself. His part in the trials was public, and he had few friends; he had even broken off with Durk. When he was shot, there was widespread dread that a cop had done it, and he received several notes from fellow officers wishing him ill. Months later, the new Commissioner reluctantly gave him his long-sought gold shield. Serpico didn't want it anymore. He got a disability pension and a movie deal, and then he left the country. *Serpico is living in Switzerland,* we are told, as the screen fades to black.

Durk was close to a deal for a movie about himself and Serpico, starring Robert Redford and Paul Newman. Their story might have joined *Butch Cassidy and the Sundance Kid* and *The Sting* as a classic buddy movie of the 1970s. But Serpico pulled back, afraid that he might be treated as a "lame-brained Italian sidekick," a fear that was inflamed by Peter Maas, whose own version was adapted for the screen. It probably didn't help that when Paul Newman bragged about how he charmed his way out of speeding tickets with autographs, Durk called him "a poltroon." Durk had to settle for a supporting role in *Serpico* as a Yalie twit in seersucker named "Bob Blair." He's not even a Jew anymore.

Serpico is not a buddy movie. It is the opposite of a buddy movie, a virtual sermon against buddies in general and cop buddies in particular. Almost no one is honest, and the honest cops offer only a mirage of fraternity, a false hope that working together will be better than working alone. Though its treatment of real-life cops varies in accuracy—the movie is fair to Inspector Delise, unfair to Durk, and profoundly unfair to the cops who worked with Serpico when he was shot—the overall effect is one of dismal distrust. *The French Connection* has a lonely maverick hero, too, but Serpico describes a tragedy so extreme it precludes a sequel. There's no place to go, and no point in trying. And that's what rings false about *Serpico* to many cops, in New York and elsewhere, even more than the implicit rebuke of our fathers being on the wrong side of history. Police work is a buddy movie, and there are always sequels, because you don't do it alone, and it goes on, with or without you.

. . .

AS PARTNERS, CHARLIE AND TOMMY WERE NOT FARING SO well. I had begun to think about signing up Tommy, in the event that I was obliged to surrender Charlie to Narcotics. But with Charlie, I had a nearly ideal informant relationship, in terms of comfort and control: he was loyal as a dog from the pound, and he presented no risk beyond drug-addled inaccuracy. We were not up against kingpins or cartels, and I was not concerned that he would lead us into ambush or otherwise betray us. Charlie wanted drugs now, and freedom from drugs at some point, and I figured prominently in both ambitions. But Tommy remained an unknown commodity, to a degree, and even his sly confidences—that Charlie had stolen a dealer's stash, or was on a worse binge than usual—had a slightly unsavory quality, as if he was reaching for leverage rather than expressing concern. One day I went to see them and found Charlie truly jubilant, the only time I'd ever seen him in that state, whereas Tommy hung back, sheepishly. "I got great news," Charlie announced. "A real miracle!" Both had been tested for AIDS, he explained, and both were negative. I didn't expect Tommy to take an eraser to the bottom third of his HOMELESS, HUNGRY, AIDS sign, but I wondered why he'd told me he had the disease. Maybe he'd just assumed he had it, I thought, having dedicated the last decade and a half of his life to the risk of infection. But the next time I saw Charlie, he said that Tommy had just made the whole thing up.

Tommy had other problems, too, Charlie told me, chief among them that he was a "complete psychopath." Charlie was furious, and surprisingly afraid, wiping his hand through his greasy hair and looking around as he explained the latest complication: "Whenever I panhandle on the ramp, I make decent money. Sometimes I work with Tommy, and sometimes I do it alone, but when I do, he tells me I owe him half. For Chrissake, the guy thinks he invented panhandling! But I gave him the money, since he told me he'd smash my head open with a lead pipe when I was sleeping. And I know he has a pipe!"

"Geez, Charlie, I thought you guys were friends."

"C'mon, Eddie, would a friend smash your head open with a lead pipe when you were sleeping?"

I thought of John.

"Not a good friend, Charlie, no."

"It's just not right, Eddie, I mean, whaddaya think?"

"You're right, Charlie, it's just not right."

And it wasn't, of course, so I decided to keep Charlie in play as long as I could, and let it go from there. We'd developed other sources in the Four-Six, with problems and promise of their own. First, there was the Fat Kid, a portly teenager who was a manager for the West Hell Cartel, which ran dope out of a huge and mostly empty apartment building on University that was undergoing renovations. On the day that we grabbed him, the Fat Kid was pitching, but none of the hand-to-hands were in the open, so we could only charge him with misdemeanor possession, for the single bag of dope he had when we stopped him. For a Bronx dealer, the charge is like a parking ticket, and so his whispered offer of cooperation was unexpected. So too was his entire presentation, when he sat down with us across a table in an interview room, and had he begun the discussions by saying, "Gentlemen, I propose a merger of our interests," it would have been less remarkable than the initial public offering that he subsequently detailed. You forget sometimes that what dealers do is make deals.

The Fat Kid explained it simply and clearly: he sold heroin, and had done so successfully for several years. He had saved seventy thousand dollars, which he had divided among the bank accounts of relatives. For the next phase of his career, he had a government job in mind, preferably in the post office. It - wouldn't do to have a record, so he'd like to work something out. The plan was almost every criminal's—*As soon as I put a little nut together, I'm out of this racket*— and you heard those words in one form or another from three different Al Pacino characters alone: in *Dog Day Afternoon, Carlito's Way,* and *The Godfather Part III.* Whether the idyll of retirement was a honeymoon with a transsexual, a car-rental business in the Caribbean, or control of the Vatican Bank, the plan never quite worked out. But as the Fat Kid negotiated the circumstances in which he found himself, it looked like he was going to make the transition with ease—he had even volunteered as an Auxiliary Police Officer in the Four-O. If his mother had brought him up to be a criminal, she should have been proud.

We had him for a bag of dope, and in return he offered their organization: the time and place of the weekly drop, with the players, the guns, and the thousands of dollars worth of heroin. We were so impressed that we called Mike Donnelly from HIDTA, as it looked like the case might be more than we - could handle. When Mike arrived, he was just as taken by the detail and weight of what was offered, as well as the cheapness of the deal. But his next step was not quite what I would have done, and I was as glad of that as I was amazed by what took place later. I thought I had a knack for talking to perps, for interrogations and debriefings, and maybe I do. I was like a little blind kid who could pick out a tune, the first time he bumped into the piano. When Mike took his seat across the table from the Fat Kid, it was as if he straightened his white tie and tails, cracked his knuckles, and played him like a baby grand. And the song that came out of him was one that I'd never heard before.

We had asked about the operational particulars, the code words— *Mojando!*—the apartments, the stash places and re-up times. He'd told us, with no little pride, that they'd found a new connection, whose high-quality dope would permit them to reintroduce the brand Turbo, which was "the best in this neighborhood, for a long time—ask anybody, they'll tell you about Turbo." We had no relationship with the Four-Six Squad, so we didn't know if they were looking at the West Hell Cartel for any robberies, assaults, or homicides. Inexperience was one reason why we didn't press further; another was that what was offered was already at a fire-sale discount, and to ask for more might have queered the deal. Still another was that to be an informant, which was of necessity confidential, was less life-altering than being a witness, which was, by equally firm definition, public in nature. But we knew that Mike worked for a task force that dealt with violent drug gangs, and the West Hell Cartel seemed to fit the bill. Mike introduced himself, and had the kid repeat what he'd told us already, listening patiently as he explained that "'West' is because we work the west side of the street, on University, and 'Hell' is because of the neighborhood, and 'Cartel' because, well, just because it *goes*."

Mike then talked about how smart the Fat Kid was for making this choice, in that he was getting out early from a life that would end badly, and how he could not only escape from the consequences of what he'd done, but also make a little money from it, if his information was good and we all worked well together. "And the way it's gotta work, for us to work together," Mike said, "is for you to tell me what else these guys have done—not just where the dope is, or what money you make. You know you guys are serious, and you know what makes people serious in this business. So let's be straight with each other, and start out right. Tell me what you guys have done."

And the Fat Kid did: he told us how they—he—stabbed another dealer named Chino, over a turf dispute; how they beat down a Rasta weed dealer, with sticks and bats, over an insult to one of their guys' sisters; how they took another man who owed them money down an alley, into a stairwell, and shot him through the chest. That made for a nice trifecta from a teenage auxiliary cop. I wondered if he was such a smart young gangster after all.

Mike thanked him for his honesty, taking careful notes. He was never not genial, or respectful, or firm. "This is good, this is good that we know this, up front. Basically, you have to tell me this stuff for your protection, because we want to work with you, and I think it could work out great for all of us, I hope we work together for a while. The thing is, we have to know everything, for our sake and yours—we can't go after these guys, and have one of them turn around and say, 'Listen, you got me, but what I can give is this . . . ,' and he's gonna give us *you*. He's gonna say that you're the bad one of the bunch, you're the one that has *bodies*. So let's be serious, let's be real with each other. Now, you can tell me everything, but later on, I can't be surprised. Later on, I don't want to hear about you hopping a turnstile, but now, now is the time to come clean. Now, we can deal with anything. We both know you've done shit with your boys, in the West Hell Cartel, but you gotta tell me about whatever else you've done. Neither of us was born yesterday. You know and I know you didn't just walk in and be a big shot—and you are—so now, now's the time to talk."

And the Fat Kid talked some more. He talked about the springtime, when he got a call from a friend who said to go with him, into Manhattan, to help steal a car. They met up and took the subway down to the Upper West Side, near the Museum of Natural History, on Central Park West. They sat on a bench for a while and watched the traffic. His friend would choose the car, when traffic stopped for a light. He picked a late-model Acura, because it was valuable, and a burgundy one, because he liked it, and a white lady - driver, because she wouldn't fight. They stepped up together, guns drawn, when she was alone in the car, and she surrendered the vehicle without a struggle. He didn't remember much about the lady, except that she had blond-ish hair and wasn't that old.

"Okay," said Mike. "That's good. You want a soda or something?"

I took his order and left. I brought it back, along with the first dissonant note in the melody. I'd checked his rap sheet, and then I looked up the collar. The Fat Kid had been arrested before: he'd gone into a candy store and picked up a pack of cigarettes, and when he was tired of waiting on line, he walked out. When the owner ran after him, he pushed him aside, telling him he was a cop. The owner then called the cops, who arrested him for shoplifting and impersonation, confiscating his badge. The auxiliary coordinator at the Four-O said that the Fat Kid was not permitted in the precinct.

In the peculiar nature of our profession, past violence presented less of a difficulty than ongoing dishonesty. The fact that he had fibbed about his status was more troubling, or at least differently troubling, than his carjacking. If he was a danger, you evaluated the risk of letting him out; if he was a liar, you questioned the reason. Before Mike Donnelly could confront him with the impersonation issue, the Fat Kid owned up to two more carjackings. One had been the year before, and the details were vague: near Penn Station, in the late fall, he thought it was a red car, and probably a Honda, but definitely a white woman. White people have money, you know. The one before that was still more vague. Calls were made to the Four-Six Squad, the Two-O,

Midtown South, Manhattan Robbery. I thought, No, I was wrong, the Fat Kid's mother would not be proud. Maybe he'll get to pass out the mail for his cell block, but he's not going to work for the post office. He's a dead letter.

Confronted with his arrest, the Fat Kid explained himself, not badly. Like a lot of perps, he didn't really consider it an arrest because he got a Desk Appearance Ticket. He said it was basically a misunderstanding—a dispute with the store owner, who didn't speak English, and then a small oversight on his part. I was more concerned with why he was an auxiliary. Auxiliaries are volunteers from the neighborhood, who patrol in uniform similar to their police counterparts, for which they are often mistaken. Though their service is honorable and useful, I never quite got it, since I looked forward to leaving the uniform behind, and I never understood why someone would go on patrol in the South Bronx without a gun to take with them or a paycheck to take home. The Fat Kid offered a vague answer about being interested in police work, which he certainly should have been. In one sense, he was shifty but also shrewd, playing a chess-game of disclosure and omission; he had also miscalculated badly, confessing to six violent felonies in the hope of escaping a day of community service. What hadn't occurred to any of us was the possibility that the game he was playing was entirely different from that in which we were keeping score, or that he wasn't playing a game at all.

For the shooting, the stabbing, and the beating, the Four-Six Squad had nothing, nothing, and nothing. No complaints, no reports, no open cases or closed ones. Since they were all drug-related, uncooperative victims were par for the course, and in order of likelihood, for a drug-dealing Rasta who had a suffered a beating—perhaps not such a bad one as it first appeared—a refusal to report it was quite reasonable; for an addict who was sliced by men who he feared, it was still possible; but for a man to be shot, under any circumstances, it was highly unlikely. The Fat Kid nonetheless held firm, on the first two, at least: for the shooting, he was there when they took him down the hall to the back of the building, but he was keeping watch on the street when the shot was fired. He didn't know if the victim lived or died because he didn't see him afterward, but it could have been, he admitted, that they shot in the air or beside him, just to frighten him, and the guy got the message and high-tailed it out of the neighborhood. The Fat Kid still had a story, I felt, that stretched but held.

And then the word came back from Manhattan, with three more strikes. If your pocket is picked, you might not report it, thinking your wallet might have been left somewhere; some people might not even report a purse-snatching, chalking it up to the risks of city life. But no one is carjacked and says, *Well, there you go, I guess I'll have to get the bus.* We had next to nothing on the earliest robbery, but just about everything on the latest, and the middle one should have been on file as well. Did a rookie screw up one case, and report it as a stolen car? Did another victim, distraught from the offense, race straight from the crime scene to the river and jump in? Not bloody likely. From then on, Mike Donnelly's interrogation was more like a narrative autopsy, as the story was laid out, cut open, and dissected.

"What time did you meet?"

"What train did you take?"

"How long did it take you?"

"Was it above ground or underground?"

"What stop did you get off at?"

"What street was that?"

"And where did you walk to from there?"

"And where did you wait? What street? What did you see? Was it dark out, cold out, windy? Was there a lot of traffic? How long did you wait?"

"And then what happened?"

"And then what?"

"And then?"

"And?"

At the end, he made him retrace his steps, backward, from the robbery to the street to the train to the Bronx, which is an effective trick for testing the integrity of a story, like reciting the alphabet backward when you've had too much to drink—it's something only the honest and the sober can do, with rare enough exceptions. The Fat Kid passed the test, as far as I saw it: when there were details requested, he supplied them, but he also said he didn't know or remember at various natural junctures, which suggested an ordinary memory, vague at times, with some gaps, rather than the vivid completeness of a fantasy. The earlier carjackings diminished in detail, which was appropriate for their perspective in time, especially if such acts were ordinary for him. He could tell the story backward, without any breaks in the chronology. And yet for the robbery in the spring, on a warm weekend, late in the afternoon, by the museum and beside the park, there was no victim, no witnesses, nothing. It was a lie, or so wrong in the particulars that it amounted to one. Had he slapped his head and said, "Did I say Central Park? I meant Prospect Park, in Brooklyn!"—we could have begun again. But he was firm in his commitment to the story, and we did not, we could not believe him. He had confessed and found a kind of absolution.

I took consolation in considering the little miracle of his half-dozen benighted victims suddenly restored, unrobbed, unstabbed, unshot, but the episode continued to irritate me for a couple of reasons. When we had another caper going, later on, a few bosses would bring it up again, saying that we were the ones who fell for that lunatic's story, which was ignorant and cheap. To have said "Bullshit!" and walked away from the Fat Kid—though PK had by then redubbed him "Mother Goose"—would not have been the reaction of a good cop, but of the opposite. What bothered me was not that he'd told a pack of lies, but that he'd made a series of statements that existed along a continuum from the demonstrably true to the inescapably false. On one side of the scale, we knew that he was a mid-level figure in a small but vigorous heroin operation, and had watched him several hours a day for weeks, during which time he committed perhaps thousands of felonies. That was real criminality, which we could not deny him. And at the far end, which we'd discovered to our dismay, there was complete falsehood, because half-truths—even if you conceded that much—are lies nonetheless. There is no such thing as a half-lie: if I said I was Dr. Conlon it would be as much of a lie as if I said I was Dr. Einstein. But there was no clean break along the scale, from black to white, fact to fiction, and I still don't know where the shift took place.

If an informant is working off a case, there is no need to be friendly, and often there's cause not to be—for certain predatory mind-sets, kindness is not only mistaken for weakness, it is transformed into it. I don't know exactly what motivated Mother Goose, but even had we found sufficient facts to move forward with him, it would have been better to do so without pretense of affection or trust. You run these informants with a short leash and a firm grip. So it was with our next informant, Flaco, with whom I found myself taking the hard line.

Flaco was another grab from the Four-Six, a sale collar that I would have thought weak in any borough, but dead in the Bronx. Late one night, I watched from a rooftop as Flaco hit off a strangely storklike woman in a beat-up old Jaguar with Jersey plates, who in turn hit off a man on the corner. She was a regular customer, but the man was a stranger, and so Flaco - wouldn't sell to him. When I gave out the customers, the team was only able to pick up the man, and so when twenty minutes passed without any other buyers, we moved in on Flaco. He was charged with sale, and the man with possession; the stork woman would have been charged with both, but her absence made Flaco's case weak. Nonetheless, he had two prior felony convictions, for burglary and weapons possession, and was eager to cooperate. Stix would handle him, and Tony sat through the debriefing, while I was busy with the paperwork. Afterward, when I talked to Stix and Tony, I was impressed not only with what he had to offer—stash houses, delivery routes from Virginia with young girls bringing up bricks of heroin in cake boxes— but by how taken they were with him. Flaco was a skinny nineteen-year-old whose addict parents had died years before. He'd just found out that his girlfriend was pregnant, and he was desperate to avoid prison.

Tony and Stix looked like they'd just come from a Disney movie, like *Old Yeller,* which ends with the boy having to put his faithful dog down. They - weren't dewy-eyed, exactly, but there was a rich lather of sympathy, a feeling that was broken when I said something like, "Dead folks, knocked-up chick, wants to flip. Check." I then sat down with Flaco and had him write out a statement about the sales we had witnessed. He smiled and did so blithely, while Tony and Stix looked on in discomfort. "You know," they said, "with what he's written, if it doesn't work out with us, he's really fucked, he's done for a long time."

"Umm . . . yeah? So?"

Maybe it was because it was late at night, and fatigue had softened them, or maybe because Flaco knew a great deal, and that intrigued them, or maybe they were simply touched, on human terms, because he'd told his sad story with real feeling. Maybe if I had been there, or he was my CI, I would have felt that way, too, but that inch of distance, that slight remove of proprietary interest, was enough to inoculate me against caring about him in any way beyond the utilitarian. He wasn't mine the way Charlie was, which had become something of a team joke—would he come for Thanksgiving dinner with the family, did I give him clothing or just let him borrow my underwear, was I setting up a CI compound like the Callahan Compound, and would we play them in softball? Homeless junkies were part of the landscape, like pigeons, and the people who spent their days feeding them bread crumbs had a hobby that was kindhearted but maybe a little unhealthy. Charlie was a perp, after all, and an especially bad-smelling one at that, and whatever he signified for me, as a cop's son or street spy, was for my own private contemplation. What more was expected of him, when his own family would have nothing to do with him?

I did like Flaco, for what it was worth: he genuinely wanted to be a father to his son, and he was young enough to make a clean start of things. He was reasonably bright and very funny, and spoke in a ghetto slang of almost hieroglyphic purity: *I be, you be, he, she and it be, na 'mean, B? Yo! We be movin' tha D to tha bundle custies, dogg!* But he also talked about his best friend and cousin with expansive and abiding affection, and they were the first names that he gave up, in his bid for probation. At least the boy in *Old Yeller* put the dog down because he had rabies; Flaco would have done it if the dog pissed on the rug.

As it happened, I became a better friend to Flaco than I would ever have thought necessary. When Stix asked an ADA to release him without bail to work for us, he refused. So did the supervising DA for Narcotics: the offer would be three-to-six. For an observation sale, it was severe; for two-thirds of an observation sale, it seemed unreal. Flaco had money and sixteen glassines of heroin on him, but if he hadn't had the two prior felony convictions, he would most likely have been arraigned on a misdemeanor possession charge, which, for once, would have suited us fine. Because we worked in SNEU, especially, the term "repeat offender" was nearly meaningless: almost every dealer we caught was charged with what they did once, twice, or three times, over a matter of seconds, when they did exactly that, hours a day, for months and years. They committed felonies more often than they ate, and if eating had been illegal, our food collars would have been thrown out or pled out because we didn't have the menu, the fork, the tip, the waiter, and the belch, all at once. We could bring in chain gangs of the morbidly obese, sumo wrestlers and opera singers by the groaning busload, and the ADA would say, "Well, according to the record, this was their first meal." But for predicate felons, they are prosecuted in the Bronx as severely as they would be in Staten Island or even upstate; it was a sensible policy—a second chance may be a good thing, a third might not, and a fourth . . . even in the Bronx, that was pushing it. But Flaco had made a serious offer, and it would be a shame to let it go to waste.

My mother had mentioned to me that she worked with a woman named Friedenthal, whose husband was a bureau chief in the Bronx DA's Office. I stopped by Ed Friedenthal's office and explained who I was and what I wanted. He asked for the particulars of Flaco's record, as well as what he knew. "No problem," he said, and after a twenty-second phone call, it was done. Moments like those made me agnostic whenever someone told me "No" after I felt I'd made a good case; clearly, they hadn't listened, or understood, and I just had to ah-tic-ya-late a little louder, or a little better, or to someone else. And, by the way, thanks Mom.

We also had to work out a deal with another Narcotics team, as some of the apartments Flaco gave us were DECSed by them, showing they had active investigations there. A detective named Nick Ferraro was sent down to see us, and his initial mood was cautious. When he talked to Flaco, it became clear that he knew a great deal about Flaco's gang, and even more about their suppliers than Flaco did; when he talked to us, later on, it was just as clear that he didn't like him. "He knows what he's talking about, definitely," said Nick. "But I doubt he's gonna work out. He's too slick, too street, and he's gonna wind up trying to play you off. It's worth a shot, definitely, and we'll help you guys out, but personally, I don't think we'll be using him when you're through."

Whenever we came into contact with Narcotics, whether it was because we had an informant or because we had to get out of the way for a Buy and Bust operation, there was a colonial aspect to our relations. We were the natives who had rich natural resources, while they were the well-armed foreigners who knew how to mine and sell them: at first, they would sit down with us at our tribal feast, offering conspicuous compliments on our colorful costumes and folk-dancing, as they forced themselves to take bites of our barbaric delicacies. If that didn't work, their warships would gather by the shores as they informed us of what would be required. With Nick, there was no feigned heartiness, no announcement of his hope for a long and fruitful partnership as he asked to speak privately with the informant—when that had happened before, CIs had told us that they'd said, "From now on, if you find out anything, you tell us—only us!" Nick also knew about that gang and that neighborhood far better than we did, which was also atypical. Flaco's gang was *his* case, and the possibility that we might have something valuable to add to it was to be pursued, for what it was worth.

Nick gave Flaco a stern lecture about how and whether he was to remain in play: he would step back from selling drugs, telling his partners that he had to be careful while his case was pending. Only if he found that he was arousing suspicion, or was utterly kept out of operational details, could he lend a hand, and whenever he did so, we had to know. We didn't want to see him pitching, or, if he was collared again, for him to try to explain that he was on a secret mission for us. Though Nick got some decent intelligence out of him, and we got a couple of warrants, it worked out as he predicted: Flaco's mood when he dealt with us shifted from the contrite to the increasingly cocky, and Nick would call Stix to say his team had seen him on the block when they did B&B, and it looked like he was working. Flaco grew lax in returning our calls. He was arrested for possession, and then sale, and then we stopped taking his calls. He was sentenced to the original offer of three-to-six, having talked his way back to the exact spot where we first met.

As we continued to work in the Four-Six, we kept in touch with Nick Ferraro. Charlie's next warrant was for a coke spot, in a semi-vacant building, that dealt in weight and had a significant Jersey trade. The apartment itself was vacant, used only for business, and had we the landlord's permission to enter, we wouldn't even have needed a warrant. But Charlie said that he was in on the deal, or at least the superintendent was, and we couldn't approach them. There was no real tenant there, it was only a workplace, and the absence of kids, dogs, or old people was a relief. Since it was a coke spot, Charlie was happy to visit, several times a day—for research, of course—and though that kind of enthusiasm tended to undercut the accuracy of his reports, I made one of my after-hours excursions to the building, and I found everything as he described. Nick confirmed it, through his informants, and PK set it up for us to do the entry together with Narcotics.

It would be my first warrant since Operation Hindenburg in which we would be the first ones through the door. I had practical objections to using ESU, but my real frustration was that taking the door was the most thrilling part of the warrant, and even of the Job, as far as it can be predicted or planned. The preparations for a warrant had grown familiar: the tac plan, with the layout of the apartment, the building, the block, the assignment of roles for entry, search, security; the scribbled marker-board sketches and hazy photocopies that sought to approximate in crude and static clarity a moment that would be a blur of adrenaline and instinct. In the muster room, at the appointed hour, PK led some fifteen cops from two commands through the arrangements, calm and cheerful but never less than precise and well-prepared. Tony and I only had to look at each other in such moments to communicate the mad elation of it, the unspoken circular conversations that asked and did not answer, *If I like my life, why do I like this so much?* Now, I could look at John for the same conversation. It was his job to knock down the door.

There is something in the way the caravan of cars moves from the precinct to the tac point, a few blocks from the target, that seems designed to build suspense. You drive slowly, in single file, and then you stop; the walk-ons and ghosts drift out to the location, to open the lobby or hold the elevators and watch the door; you wait for them for the "go." At the signal, the caravan moves forward, a little faster but still with restrained haste, until you pull out front and break from the cars into a run. The suddenness makes people on the street stop and stare; in the lobby, passersby have no time to ask questions as we pile into the elevator for the sixth floor, the top floor of the building. Others run straight up the stairs. Someone carries the ram for John so he'll be fresh when we arrive. We step out and step forward, I point out the door, John takes the ram and with one shot sends it clean off the hinges. I charge in, gun out, bellowing, "Get down! Get down! Get down!"

Behind me, the cops fan in, and before me, two men sit at the table, shocked. Between them on the table are a large bag of cocaine and a small tinfoil packet of it, cash and a scale. A naked light bulb dangles from a cord above them. The apartment is otherwise bare and empty. We cuff them up, take them out, bag up the drugs. We are sweating like pigs and smiling like beauty queens. One of the guys from Narcotics says, "This one should be in a textbook." We don't disagree.

· · ·

INSPECTOR MULLEN DIDN'T EITHER. HE DIDN'T GUSH OVER it, of course—that was a once-a-week, pat-on-the-back kind of operation for his cops—but he was impressed when I told him about it, about PK and the team, our warrants and CIs, and our beat-Roger month of August. Skills can be taught, experience comes inevitably, and talent was happily abundant, but motivation like ours was a rare thing. Mullen grew more enthusiastic at the prospect of our coming to Narcotics, and it was contagious.

"Whaddaya think, Eddie? Would you like to come up and work for me?"

"All of us, as a team, with PK?"

"It's been done before, and I don't see why we can't do it again."

All of us knew we had something special with the team, a rare combination of intensity and ease, a balance of abilities, and a depth of trust. Maybe we worked all the harder at it, knowing that it was a gift. There must be something inborn in people, a seasonal instinct, that makes them love the heat of Indian summer, knowing that it will be the last basking sunlight of the year. We had from time to time discussed what we wanted next in our careers, whether it was a detective's shield or a sergeant's, but we had resolved more or less explicitly to stick together unless something great came along, for all of us. It was like the end of high school, where all the crepe-paper decorations and cheesy anthems, the TV clichés of "bittersweet parting" and "coming of age," do nothing to diminish the truth that some of you will go and some of you will stay, and much will be better, but the life you have known together is done and gone.

Not all our recent days had been successful—once, when I was away, Alicia and another cop worked in the prisoner van, while the others were either in OPs or on bikes. When they moved in to catch one perp, Alicia stepped out and he started to fight her; the other cop jumped in, and they eventually subdued him, but when they brought him back to the van, they noticed they were light two perps. Technically, the cop made a mistake by leaving the van; morally and in every street cop's view, she did the right thing. Every procedure was followed: PK put the escape over the radio, a search was commenced, and both perps were recovered within a half-hour. My own impulse might have been to handle it unofficially, and other bosses suggested as much aloud. No disposition had been issued for the incident, as yet, for the "failure to safeguard" the prisoners, or for PK's "failure to supervise" the team in the field. But I was relieved when I told Mullen about it, and his response was to shrug and say, "So? It happens."

All the while, we went out for the daily scrimmage, which I liked, and the long, complicated plays, which I loved. The days grew shorter and cooler, but the diversions and wonders did not change. For a few weeks, as we worked in Melrose-Jackson, our sets were blown up hourly by other cops, responding to complaints about a family of raccoons. They threw people into a panic; the raccoons got more calls than gunfights did—they were always "rabid," which was unlikely but possible, and often "attacking children," which was nonsense—and I was amazed by the fear that they inspired in the neighborhood, where robberies and shootings were daily events. Wiseass cops would ask over the radio: *Do you have a scrip, Central, I'm holding three, but - they're wearing masks. . . .ž*

In the Four-Six, we saw Mother Goose at work from time to time, until he was collared for selling to an undercover. In early October, John and I found Charlie and Tommy and gave them some clothes. I shook Charlie's hand, and asked him, "You know what day it is, Charlie?" He didn't. "It's your birthday." Tommy laughed, slapping his back, and said, "Hey, Charlie, how about that! Who knew?" Charlie smiled weakly and thanked me, before looking away. He was touched but also ashamed, because this most elementary fact of his life was news to him. We didn't dwell on it—as soon as we shut down the sixth-floor apartment from the last warrant, the dealers set back up on the third floor. He made his buys for me and put everything else out of his mind.

A few weeks after our talk with Mullen, PK gave us some disappointing news. "I talked to the CO," he said, "and he won't sign off on the transfer. The inspector at the Borough doesn't want him to—he gave him some speech about us being too inexperienced—but he basically doesn't want to give up the team. And the CO's not going to go against him." It was bullshit, we all agreed: hadn't the Inspector thrown us to the Rape Detail without a second thought? All of a sudden we're rookies he has to look after, when it's to our benefit to make a move? For all that, I wasn't devastated—we were still together, doing what we liked—and Inspector Mullen's response was hugely heartening, because he blew up when I told him.

"Of course you hate to give up your workers!" he said. "But if they're doing the job for you, you can't stand in their way. It's bad faith, and it's bad management. What a jackass!"

The CO's refusal made things difficult but not impossible, he said. The "airlift," as we'd come to call the transfer, was still many weeks away, even by the precarious calendar of the NYPD. We might still get on board. And what meant more to me than that remaining hope was the vindication of Mullen's belief in us, that we were ready and deserving to move up—and that we were being treated with cynical disregard.

We closed ranks and went back to work, but something had changed, I think, even then: we had become embroiled in the politics of the Job, and at best, we would leave the PSA amid some ill will. Increasingly, we would have to think about more than collars and warrants, PK and the team, as the larger machinations of the bureaucracy intruded. The good part of the Job took up enough of my life as it was, for fifty and sixty hours a week. I had been living with my cousin Brian, and when he moved out to get married, John moved in full-time. He had become one of my closest friends, and it was a great thing to have him there, but in retrospect I realize how much more of my time was then given over to shop talk. *Remember, you're a cop twenty-four/seven, three hundred sixty-five days a year. You are never off-duty. . . .* I thought back to the Academy, when it seemed laughable for Sgt. Solosky to warn us not to surrender our civilian lives and friends, and here I was—spending five days a week with a bunch of cops, five nights a week with another cop. What else was left to give? I gave my car already—should I sleep in my uniform?

Not long after that, a day or two before Halloween, we went back to the

Four-Six to collar. Somewhere in the distance, there was gunfire, but otherwise it was a little late, and a little slow. We were working at one of our old standbys, 1678 and 1684 Nelson: Brainstorm, Shotgun, Checkmate, crack. I was in an OP, and I gave out a body to John and OV in a catch car, heading north to Macombs, where he made a right. Another one came up to buy, and I asked over the air:

"You ready, guys? You get him? Anyone ninety-eight?"

There was a pause, and I asked again: "John, OV? Is he a hit?"

More silence, and then John called for PK to come over. There was real fear in his voice when he then called for an ambulance, forthwith. PK said for - everyone to come around the corner, that it was a wrap for the night. It didn't sound good.

The perp was down on the sidewalk, unconscious and twitching. John - didn't look much better. When the ambulance arrived, one of the EMTs lifted his head and said, "I think he's been shot."

I was curious, and leaned in to see the small raised welt. "This looks like a small-caliber round, a twenty-two or a twenty-five, maybe," the EMT continued. "You hear any shots?"

"Yeah," I said. "But they sounded farther off."

As I searched the perp—needles, heroin—I tried to figure out the bizarre scenario the EMT had detailed. Had he been shot just then, as John went for him, or earlier? Could he walk around with a bullet in his head? When Vinnie "the Chin" Gigante shot Frank Costello in the head with a .22, the round went through his scalp and circled his skull like Magellan. What the hell happened here?

The EMTs began to pack him onto the stretcher, and he came to, fighting. It took four of us to hold him down before they could strap him in. The perp's revival lightened John's mood somewhat, and as we followed them down to Lincoln Hospital, he cut me off before I went on any more about what a funny thing it was. "I don't know what the hell that EMT was talking about, but that guy wasn't shot. He ran on me and I knocked him down, Eddie, and I swear, at first I thought I killed him. He ran down that hill, and I chased him, and he started to turn around with something in his hand. . . ." The perp had bounced off a wrought-iron fence before hitting the sidewalk. For a few minutes, John thought it was over, for both of them.

At the hospital, the mood of unease returned when the doctor came out from X-ray: "It's a little weird. He has a skull fracture, but it looks like an old injury."

I turned to John and said, "That's just your luck. Your perp had a pre-broken head."

He laughed, but I wasn't sure if he was kidding when he said, "You want this collar?"

"All yours, big guy."

PK notified the desk at the Four-Six and the PSA of what had happened, and we finished up some paperwork and went home.

Afterward, when we talked about it, I was a little hard on him—John was a strong guy, the junkie was running downhill, and he could have flattened him with a flick of the finger. I grilled him: *How much force was used because you were pissed at him for running? Did you really think he'd stab you with the needle? How well could you see it?* I thought they were questions he should think about, for his own sake, since they were the same ones he'd have to answer—asked less kindly, and not in private—if the perp died. A couple of days before, there'd been a story in the paper about a cop who threw his radio at a junkie he was chasing; it hit him in the head and he died. John said, "I'm not a bad guy, I don't like to hurt people. I became a cop to help people, not to hurt them." He said that he worried now that in the next confrontation, he - wouldn't react naturally, he'd second-guess himself, and he'd get hurt. That was a good point: there's a wall at police headquarters full of names, and some are of cops who hesitated.

And the truth of it was brought home a day later, when we set back up again. It was after sunset when I slipped into a tenement on Courtlandt Avenue, went to the roof, and crouched down by the low parapet with my binoculars. I watched for a while and heard a dog bark inside. It sounded big, and then it sounded closer, running up the stairs. There were dealers on the second floor, and I wondered if they'd sicced the dog on me, though a lot of - people let their dogs out to shit on the roof. I took out my gun, and I took out my mace, reckoning the distance I'd need for either. We'd been taught that your average opponent can cover twenty-one feet in the time it takes an average cop to sight and shoot a target. I didn't have much more than that from the door to the edge of the roof, where I stood. The mace would be effective only within a dozen feet or so, and there was a light wind. I put the mace away. The dog charged through the door and stopped, barking fiercely, and then advanced again, then stopped. It was as big as it sounded, a pit bull mix, sixty pounds. Twenty-five feet, twenty.

I bellowed: "Get your fucking dog off the roof! Get that fucking dog, now!"

Twenty feet, fifteen. We barked at each other, and I thought I should shoot, because it was getting too close, and then I thought about what would happen if I did: a "shooting team" would respond and investigate as if I was a perp; Internal Affairs would interrogate me, PK, and the rest of the team for hours. The bosses would look at PK and say, *Escaped prisoners, injured perp, and now a shooting, is this guy in control out there?* I waited and shouted again: *"Get your fucking dog off this fucking roof!"*

The dog stopped, and then a man called it from the darkness inside the stairwell. It growled, then turned around and went inside. I sat down and rested for a minute before leaving. As I passed the dealers' apartment on the second floor, the dog began to bark again.

I was glad I hadn't shot, but I was troubled by how the white noise of politics had impinged on my thoughts for the four or five seconds of the confrontation. When you make a decision about self-defense, the only thing that should concern you is self-defense—tactics and cover, the possibilities and necessities of threat and response. The dog could well have knocked me over, off the roof. I was not eager to shoot, but if I was obliged to—with intended consequences or unintended ones—there would be a lot of people asking questions, but only my partners and PK would ask, "Are you okay?"

I shook it off, and we set up another OP a few blocks away. Nothing had happened, after all, and I put it aside and went back to work. The threats we faced were real—PK had been shot by a perp. That moment remained with me, and it would weigh in some manner in the decisions I made each day—as it did for John, and PK, and Tony, Stix, Orville, Sammy, and Alicia—not just to shoot or not shoot, but how hard to push. Time would tell the virtue of our choices, and at least we still had time.

So we believed, as a week passed, and another, until we drove up to the Four-Six one afternoon to set up. We were cruising through the blocks—University, Tremont, Popham, Andrews—when we received the summons over the air to return to the precinct, forthwith. DI Cavanagh had retired, and we had a new captain. PK met with him in his office, for fifteen or twenty minutes. We stood in the driveway at the back of the precinct, apart by ourselves, wondering what nonsense was afoot. We were curious, I remember, but not especially concerned. Were we arguing about something? Maybe I don't remember what we were talking about, or how we felt, but I won't forget the sight of PK as he came out of the precinct. His face had fallen, he was pale and stunned. He took us aside.

"I'm out of the unit," he said, and he went on to explain, haltingly, that the new captain told him that relatives of John's perp, who was a homeless junkie, had hired a lawyer. Though the perp didn't remember being arrested, and had in fact fractured his skull in a car accident, some time before, he remained in the hospital. The lawyer called the *Daily News,* announcing that he was representing the victim in the "latest police-brutality case in the Bronx." The *News* called Headquarters for comment, and the comment was "What are you talking about?" The Job does not like to be surprised; Chief Anemone, the Chief of the Department, was said to be furious. An Interim Order had been issued the year before, after the Louima case, which said that if a perp is "seriously injured" during an arrest, the duty captain has to be notified. If necessary, a crime scene will be set up and the matter investigated immediately, to protect the Job from subsequent litigation. We didn't know that, and PK didn't—I believe the order had been issued around the time he was burying his son Paulie, and Interim Orders fell by the wayside.

I don't remember exactly what we said—*"Bullshit!" "No, it can't be!" "That's crazy!" "That's wrong! . . ."* I think I began to protest and scheme—I'd call Mullen, or—better yet—Chief Anemone, I'd go right into his office to tell him what was going on. PK shook his head, stricken, knowing it was done. I thought I'd never seen a sadder face, until I looked over at John. Oh, laddo . . . He said nothing, and then he walked away. I didn't see him for days, and he wouldn't answer the phone. After the futility of it all began to sink in for the rest of us, we all shook hands, and then we went home, too.

EIGHT

For the NYPD, the era that followed the Knapp Commission was as the Civil War was for the United States, bloody but necessary, proudly defining but remembered without joy. The Knapp Commission may have achieved relatively little, on its own terms, and there are not only institutions but individuals who can claim to have done more concrete good. But the Commission took place in an age of extraordinary change, and during its tenure it was the dominant fact with which all the other forces reckoned. Though cops have certainly done wrong since, singly and in groups, even the most bitter critics of the NYPD would concede that the transformation has been radical and enduring. I have seen well over a thousand people arrested, and have witnessed only one offer of a bribe. It may be too much to wish that such reforms could have come more cheaply than they did, with less sacrifice of what was good as well as what was not. The NYPD was denounced not merely for what crooked cops did, or what other cops knew, but what still other cops should have known, and it tore through them all like an accusation of child abuse, too terrible to believe and too important to ignore. Whether innocent or guilty, everyone that it touched was stained.

One of the more bitter paradoxes of the Knapp Commission was that afterward, the NYPD began to truly deserve the respect that was lost to it, it seemed, forever. The epidemic of gambling graft that had bedeviled the police since the beginning ended with Knapp. While the facts of the *Times* story were appalling but not altogether unfamiliar, the theory—that the scandal was in the coverup more than the crime—propelled a great scoop into a new paradigm of investigative journalism. The adversarial posture became a reflex: for the *Times*, the word "police" became primarily an adjective used to modify the noun "corruption" or, later, "brutality"; they got their story thirty years ago, and they've stuck with it ever since. No longer would cops get the benefit of the doubt.

The Knapp Commission might have died on the vine, but for a variety of political alignments and odd chances that were plotted so perfectly as to strain credulity. Mayor Lindsay, who, in the columnist Jack Newfield's phrase, "gave good intentions a bad name," kept a degree of racial peace in the city by sheer bribery. Whoever shouted loudest got a meeting, and often a check; millions of dollars were funneled to self-proclaimed "community activists" whose community ties were most evident in their criminal records; a city job was provided to a man recently released from prison for plotting to blow up the Statue of Liberty. Lindsay had run as a Republican for his first term as mayor and as an independent for his second, and he was gearing up for a presidential run, in 1972, as a Democrat. President Nixon had liked him less in each incarnation: long hostile to the liberal, Eastern wing of the Republican Party, Nixon saw Lindsay shift from an internal rival to an outright opponent. If the Knapp Commission was going to produce evidence that New York City under the Lindsay Administration was a cesspool, it deserved firm federal support.

For six months, the Knapp investigators had virtually nothing—what Durk knew was old, and rarely firsthand, while Serpico was a pariah—until one winter night when they stumbled on eight uniformed cops stealing meat from a warehouse. Whether it was burglary or a theft staged for insurance fraud, the wide-open indifference of the cops was startling to the investigators. The warehouse was owned by none other than James Reardon, ex-cop and ex-con, and likely an acquaintance of my great-grandfather. Reardon was the one-time partner of Harry Gross, the bookie who had brought down the mayoralty of William O'Dwyer. Reardon also wrote an engagingly novelized memoir, *The Sweet Life of Jimmy Riley,* which presents an unusual defense of the life of a cop on the take: *Don't knock it till you've tried it.*

It got worse: a few months later, the law of unintended consequences was bent, if not broken, when the author of *The French Connection* supplied the

Knapp Commission with its star witness. As his next literary endeavor, Robin Moore had chosen the story of Xaviera Hollander, a Dutch prostitute working in midtown, which would be entitled *The Happy Hooker.* Hollander had a problem with getting arrested; it seemed to happen all the time, no matter who she paid, and at least one of the men who took money from her turned out not to be a police officer at all. She decided to remedy the situation in a two-pronged strategy: first, on the advice of a lawyer, she contacted a reliably dirty cop named William Phillips to settle things on a more permanent basis. Second, she had her apartment wired by one Teddy Ratnoff, an otherwise dubious character who was a "genius at electronic listening devices," whom she met through Moore. Hollander claimed that Moore urged her to bug the place to pick up conversations for purposes of "authenticity," while Moore, at least as plausibly, said she hoped to blackmail influential johns into protecting her. Ratnoff was also trying to convince the Knapp Commission to use his equipment, and when he caught Phillips in a shakedown, he had a deal. Soon, Phillips did, too. "You can't make this stuff up," as they say, though plainly, some people did.

Whenever a bad cop is collared, there is a duel of clichés: is he the rotten apple, or the tip of the iceberg? The rottenest apples always work hard on the iceberg story, that they are random samples rather than standouts. When Phillips was taken in by the investigators, he flipped immediately—there was no conscience to wrestle with. As far as bad cops go, Phillips was the real thing—he called his uniform "the money suit," and he even tried to bribe the Knapp investigators. He was dirty early on, with his whole heart and both hands. His own term for his type—which he said was common usage, and later became so—was that he was a "meat-eater," a cop who aggressively pursued a score, rather than a "grass-eater," who took what came his way. In many ways, his profile was iceberg-ish: his father, whom he hated, was also a crooked cop, and his career, which had taken him from patrol to the Squad and back to patrol, was an encyclopedia of corruption. But he was also apple-ish, in that he was a solitary operator who didn't even socialize with other cops, and he had already been flopped from the Squad back to patrol on the slimmest of pretexts, which suggested that he was marked as a problem long before he was caught outright.

When the Knapp Commission televised its hearings, Phillips was the star witness. He told about what he did on patrol, shaking down tow-truck companies for car accidents, funeral homes for DOAs, bars to quash brawls, construction sites for code violations, drivers for everything. As a detective, he'd hit up complainants for their property and perps for their freedom. He made a profound impression, not least on a detective who thought he resembled the face in a sketch for a double homicide, also in a brothel, not far from Hollander's. Phillips was tried and convicted of both murders and sent to prison for life. The prosecution of Phillips was the source of great conflict between the Manhattan DA, Frank Hogan, and Knapp, and whether it proved or impeached the entire thesis of what was rotten in the NYPD, as a last-act twist, it was hard to beat.

Honest cops felt that the Knapp Commission was a hatchet job, long on sound bites and short on substance. They had a point, in that the Commission took credit for the indictment of a mere fourteen cops, not counting Phillips, of course. Citywide, there were sixty-two cops indicted in 1971, which was certainly a result of the scandals, though in 1968—ages, it seemed, before Serpico, Knapp, and the rest—there were twenty-nine. For old-timers like Frank Hogan, an icon in the criminal justice system who had succeeded the legendary racket-buster Thomas Dewey thirty years before, this kind of separate and temporary commission was regarded as a publicity stunt; for newcomers like Commissioner Patrick Murphy, who was largely kept out of the loop, it was a minefield. Knapp himself later said that he expected Murphy would—and should—ask them to disband, though the request never came. But for Murphy, who in his own words "based his program on yesterday's headlines," the additional media pressure helped steer his course.

For New York City in 1970, Patrick Murphy was the perfect commissioner, a "law-and-order liberal." He was from a cop family—one of eight children, where the boys became cops, the girls nuns—and he was the father of eight children himself. He had risen through the ranks of the NYPD, and then taken jobs in Syracuse, Washington, and Detroit. In Washington, after the King assassination, he ordered cops not to shoot looters, and there was little bloodshed. In Detroit, he instituted a firearms-discharge review policy, in which every shot fired by a cop had to be examined by every rank through the Commissioner; police shootings dropped precipitously. According to Robert Daley, his Deputy Commissioner of Public Information, he had no friends, no interests, and no ability to make small talk. In his first career with the NYPD, Murphy had spent two years on patrol before assignments in ESU, Headquarters, and the Academy. As a street cop, he was a rookie, but in time, Daley came to believe, Murphy didn't even care much about cops or crime, but rather management and public relations.

Under Murphy, there was an emphasis on local command, an early version of crime analysis, with a "Precinct Planning Sergeant" working on pin maps; there was computerization, and other technological advances; there were Anti-Crime Units in each precinct, and later a citywide Street Crime Unit, in which plainclothes cops and undercovers were deployed against mugging and violent crime, for the first time, rather than just against gambling and narcotics. These cops, who were about 5 percent of the Department, made almost a third of its arrests. As for internal reform, there was a purge at One Police Plaza: the chiefs were summoned to a conference, in which they found charts with their ages and longevity of service, and they were obliged to fill out a financial questionnaire. Responsibility for anti-corruption efforts was delegated to field commanders: if a scandal broke in their precinct or division, they fell on the sword. Instead of evaluating cops for their arrest records, Murphy looked at their conviction rates, and he flopped hundreds of plainclothesmen from Vice and Narcotics back to the bag. Ultimately, he stopped gambling enforcement almost altogether.

Despite these improvements, Murphy was not a friend to most cops, good, bad, or indifferent. Cops who knew there were grave problems in the Department but were nonetheless proud of what they did were a little stunned to hear him refer to the Job as "this monster . . . with all its pockets of power, its traditions, its mythology, its cynicism." Earnest discussions were conducted in Headquarters as to whether precinct Christmas parties should be banned entirely, or allowed with special permission as long as all receipts were submitted. (The Headquarters party went on as planned, of course.) In public statements, denunciations of corruption had been traditionally accompanied by some expression of support for the rest of the troops, a rote reminder that most cops worked hard and deserved respect; such words were often left unsaid by Murphy. The Job was getting harder: in 1970, major crimes rose more than 12 percent, and cops would make over a quarter of a million arrests that year. They were getting kicked more, bit more, and shot more—forty-five cops were shot and seven were killed in 1970, and another ten would die before the end of Murphy's first year in office. In the street, rich white kids and poor black kids shouted "Pig!" in cops' faces; the headlines proclaimed that they were thieves; and the boss didn't seem to disagree.

All the usual kinds of murders were up—bar fights, robberies, drug deals—but there was a new kind of homicide taking place, more and more often, in Harlem and elsewhere, that had cops terrified not only because they were the victims, but also because a lot of people refused to admit it was happening at all. A splinter group of the Black Panther Party called the Black Liberation Army was taking out cops. In April of 1971, the Panthers themselves had wounded two cops in a shootout in Harlem, as an epic conspiracy case against thirteen of their group was winding down into farce. It had been the longest and most expensive trial in state history, and the outcome depended chiefly on the testimony of two black undercover cops. The jury took minutes to acquit the defendants of plotting to blow things up all over town. The prosecution must have been on to something, though: during the trial, the judge's house was firebombed, and almost a week after the verdict, in May, two cops assigned to stand guard at District Attorney Frank Hogan's apartment house on Riverside Drive were cut down by machine-gun fire.

Two nights later, two cops responded to an Aided case in the Polo Grounds projects in Harlem. One cop, Joseph Piagentini, was white, and his partner, Waverly Jones, was black, and as they were returning to their car, they were followed by two young men. Jones was shot three times in the back and once in the back of the head, and died instantly. After Piagentini went down, the perps flipped both cops over, took their guns, and fired at Piagentini over and over as he tried to swat away the bullets. He was hit thirteen times and died on the way to the hospital. For the next cop killing, there was no political motive—it was in Brownsville, when a lunatic stepped out of an alley and nearly decapitated a cop with a butcher knife—and so too for the one after that, when a cop ran into three armed junkies holding up a candy store. No one knows what happened with the next one, a detective sergeant found in his car by the side of the Belt Parkway in Brooklyn, shot on either side of his head.

As it happened, the BLA hit men had moved west for the summer. In San Francisco, Waverly Jones's pistol was recovered after two men were arrested for shooting at a cop with a machine gun, which fortunately jammed. The next day, three men walked into a precinct and shot the desk officer dead and wounded a clerk. It was learned that these events were the second and third installments of a four-day assault on San Francisco cops—the first, a bazooka attack on a precinct, was a failure because the missile didn't work, while the last, another double assassination of black and white cop partners, was called off for unknown reasons. In the winter, however, the group returned its attentions to New York.

In January, a cop who stopped a car for running a red light was shot clean through with automatic-weapons fire; a day later, a cop was stabbed in the chest as he sat in his squad car. Three days after that, another pair of partners, black and white, named Greg Foster and Rocco Laurie, were walking up-town on Avenue B, near 11th Street, when they passed three men headed in the opposite direction. The three men turned, and one shouted "Shoot them in the balls!" and then opened fire. Laurie was shot six times, three times in the back, twice in the groin, once through his penis. Foster was shot three times in the back and once in the back of the head; then they shot his eyes out with three more rounds. They took the dead cops' guns, and two of them ran away immediately, while the third did a dance in the street. Murphy was in-clined against making any statement about the BLA, though the group sent a letter to a wire service claiming credit.

Within the upper echelons of the Police Department, there was deep skep-ticism of the idea of a conspiracy, and outright opposition to making such a belief public; regardless of its reputation for being crustily reactionary, Head-quarters is acutely sensitive to the political winds, which at this point were blowing hopefully toward the White House. Lindsay's proudest claim was that during his administration, there had been no riots in New York, though through his work on the Kerner Commission, he had defined "riot" as any disturbance larger than those that had happened under his watch. It was in this climate of mistrust and expediency that Daley made public the facts of the case as they were known. The Mayor's Office was furious—for them, in Daley's view, "two dead cops was preferable to Harlem in flames." Two days later, the *Times* received an anonymous call that a cop would be killed at eight the next morning. It proved true, almost: a cop driving alone in his radio car was hailed by a man who called him over to the curb and stabbed him. A week later, two more cops in St. Louis were shot with Laurie's gun.

One spring morning in 1972, in the Two-Five precinct in Harlem, cops called a "10-13," for an officer in need of assistance. The legitimate 10-13 had followed a false one, phoned in to 911 by a man claiming to be a "Detective - Thomas," on the second floor of 102 West 116th Street. When Patrolmen Phillip Cardillo and Vito Navarra arrived, they saw that it was a mosque of the Nation of Islam, which was led by Louis Farrakhan. Although there had been a spate of false 10-13 calls by the BLA to draw cops into ambush, they went inside, where they heard scuffling upstairs on the second floor. Navarra ran up first, where he was met by at least fifteen men, but his retreat was cut off by more men downstairs, who were fighting Cardillo and shut the door. Cardillo was shot. Very quickly, there were more than a thousand people on the block; bottles and bricks rained from the rooftops; a police car was turned over and set on fire; and white reporters were doused with lighter fluid and ignited. Two members of the Nation of Islam were taken into custody, and there was some preliminary collection of evidence before the police acceded to Farrakhan's demand that all white cops be removed from the scene. At the hospital, where the Mayor and the Commissioner had gone to see the mortally wounded cop, Daley remarked that the disturbance was "close to a riot." It was the wrong word for Lindsay: "Riot? What do you mean, riot? There can't be any riot. There won't be any riot. It never came close to being a riot. How can you say such a thing?"

Though Cardillo was not expected to live, he lingered on for a week. On the advice of Deputy Commissioner Ben Ward, the police made no statement whatsoever throughout that time, a silence which seemed to support Farrakhan's claims that it was a reckless, racist, and premeditated assault on a house of worship. Ward was the highest-ranking black member of the Department—he later became Police Commissioner under Mayor Ed Koch—and as such he was acutely sensitive to a crisis in Harlem. He had also spent years in the trial room, dealing with cops accused of corruption and brutality, which may have affected his views. But he was also a lawyer, which made his insistence that it was illegal for the cops to enter the mosque simply bizarre. When Cardillo died, Murphy didn't go to the hospital, claiming he - wasn't feeling well; then he flew to Europe for a conference the next morning. A brief statement was released, saying that Cardillo had died from a gunshot wound after responding in uniform to a call for assistance which later proved unfounded. The Mayor missed the funeral as well, campaigning in Florida. Officially, the Department refused to say that Cardillo had done nothing wrong, or even that it had been wrong to kill him. Ben Ward announced that the police had made mistakes, and apologized to Farrakhan. The commanding officer of the Harlem precinct, DI Jack Haugh, demanded an apology to Cardillo's family, and when it was not forthcoming, he resigned.

At one point, there was a single cop officially assigned to the investigation. The police were not allowed back into the mosque, which left them without much evidence or even a sense of the crime scene. Through his Hollywood contacts, Sonny Grosso was able to have a model of the crime scene built from the few photos taken. Sonny was in Harlem on another BLA murder on the day of the riot; he was at the mosque and worked the Cardillo case, often on his own time. After almost five years and two trials, a Black Muslim named Louis 17X Dupree was acquitted of the Cardillo murder. The judge called the political interference a "disgrace." No movie was ever made of that story, but Louis 17X Dupree found work in Hollywood, playing a police captain in a movie called *Supercops*. Sonny left the Department and took a job on *Kojak*. He also wrote a book called *Murder at the Harlem Mosque*. He told me that when he endorses his pension check, he writes "under protest" on the back.

• • •

"MOONLIGHTING" IS ONE OF THE FEW BITS OF COP SLANG that has worked its way into regular speech. Unlike "collar" or "perp," in which the cop context is plain, "moonlighting" has traveled so widely and well in the language that its police origins have been lost. It comes from the early days of the city, when men were drafted for the night watch. If someone had the inclination to pay a substitute, they were permitted to do so. You - could see it as an aspect of decline in democratic ideals, or a pragmatic adjustment of the market to meet a civic need, but it marked an early separation of the police function from the public as a whole. Then, to moonlight was to work as a cop; now, at least for us, to moonlight is to work as anything else. To be a cop anywhere, you have to be a jack of all trades, but to be a cop in New York, most of us have to be a jack of at least two.

My own moonlighting was about to move on to the next phase, as I'd been encouraged to start thinking about writing a book. I had my doubts: any book would make it harder to remain anonymous, and a good book ought to make it impossible. I was still new—a rookie by some standards—though I was coming up on four years as a cop. But the pieces I'd written had begun to coalesce in my mind into something larger, much as the Job had become both ordinary and nearly all-encompassing for me. The skin on my hip was rough from the gun, and if I went on vacation, it took a couple of days to feel natural without it. I would reach down to pat it, not out of need but for fear that I had lost it, and the weight never left me, like the pain of a phantom limb. With the recent events at SNEU, I'd begun to understand that there was a quality to a cop's life that reminded me—maybe not by coincidence—of Senator Moynihan's observation after the death of JFK, that to be Irish is to know that, in the end, the world will break your heart. Ya gotta have a story, as they said, and I began to believe that I had one.

At first, we were determined to follow PK out of SNEU, to walk out en masse: his removal was so unexpected, so unsound and unkind. The cases of the escaped perps and the injured perp were run-of-the-mill mishaps that had occurred without malice or even real negligence, and they were re-dressed without deception. Wasn't it just a month before that they were fight-ing dirty to keep us? The justice of our cause was so compelling that it seemed that no one of decency would oppose it: PK was a great man and we were a good team. I just had to make them understand that. We went for a sit-down with the new captain.

Despite our crusaders' zeal, we'd all begun to wonder what kind of favor we'd done PK with our high spirits. Why did I think it was such a fine thing to hunt for junkies in the woods, so that we could knock down the doors of felons? Was this what a therapist would recommend for him? I remembered the look on his face when he caught up to me in Manhattan, with the perp over the hood of the car and the big dog in the back seat, or seeing Stix and John speed by on bikes, clutching the bumper of a city bus, or all the crazy chases in my car, with the black snow floating around inside and the red light bouncing off the dash as we vaulted the sidewalks. And yet when he went home with the news of the transfer, PK said, his wife cried for three days.

The Captain had come from another PSA, where the rumors of him were good: the word was that if you worked hard for him, he took care of you. A new commanding officer looks at the numbers and listens to the rumors. Our numbers would have been better than our rumors. The "Manson family" gibe wouldn't have warmed the heart of any manager, and one of the pre-cepts of the new, modern-management NYPD was to create a system where any part was replaceable—and to remind each part of that precept whenever necessary. On the other hand, in a police department where morale seemed to vary between bad and worse, a leader who created a team of cops who looked forward to work each day shouldn't be dismissed lightly. We had a chance, I thought, if we sat down and reasoned together. And if we couldn't, we had all resolved to leave SNEU.

I didn't expect we would settle our differences like rival dons, exchanging flowery tributes and veiled threats over espresso, but the minimum require-ment for a sit-down is a sufficient number of seats. The Captain genially re-ceived us from behind his desk, but the office was too small for our group, and those without chairs withdrew awkwardly back into corners. The Cap-tain didn't look like a cop or talk like one. His lowercase moustache, comb-over, and rumpled-short-sleeved-shirt-and-tie combination gave him the look of a back-office supervisor, familiar with the sales figures for each line of production. It heartened me to think we were both a big seller and a premium brand. If Compstat inspired terror in the upper ranks for its inquisitorial accounting—*You went up three homicides last month, but your felony drug collars are off ten percent?*—it inversely gave hardworking cops a sense of worth. You could think, I may be a number, but the business is numbers now, and all I have to do is add up.

The Captain said that Chief Anemone himself had flopped PK from SNEU, and so there was nothing he could do, even if he wanted to. The finality made all of our protests irrelevant, as if we'd barged into the governor's mansion to beg for a stay of execution, only to be greeted with the news that the electrocution had been yesterday and the governor lived next door. *Alrighty, then!* We could ah-tic-ya-late all we wanted, they'd already flipped the switch. When we said we all wanted to leave SNEU, he told us we couldn't all leave at once, right away. He praised us and soothed us, telling us that he knew how hard we worked; he also told us that it made sense for us to give the new sergeant a chance—we should meet him, at least; it was only fair. He also added that he thought the chief was right: what a boss did was keep you out of trouble, on the street and on paper, and our recent past showed that PK didn't have what it took to run a team. I asked about the last search warrant I'd gotten with Charlie, which would expire in a couple of days.

"I think we're going to have to let that slide. We're going to be looked at closely for a while, so it's a bad time for anything to go wrong. You can always go get another one."

We left the office. I didn't like how it had gone; I felt that we hadn't been persuaded as much as we'd simply been had. The speed of our acquiescence troubled me, and for all that he'd said that was sensible or flattering, other remarks made it clear that he didn't understand things as we did, or he didn't care, or it didn't matter. The Captain had dismissed the search warrant so casually that it seemed he didn't know how much work went into them, and his remarks about PK were insulting and gratuitous. I don't know if we would have been a better team to stay or go, and I wondered how much self-interest figured in our decision, and whether there was anything wrong with that: *Now I can take my kids to school in the morning—what am I going to do if they put me on day tours or midnights? Will I see much of my wife if I lose my steady days off? How will it feel to be back in the bag, to have to think about how many parking tickets I wrote this month instead of plotting clandestine meetings with informants and to work out the signals for the drop? What about our goatees? First they take away PK, now they're coming after our goatees!*

But PK was against our quitting. "You guys have each other," he said, "and I don't think I have much to teach you. To tell you the truth, I never thought I did—I more or less let you run, and it was great. But you shouldn't give up what you have together." He also told us that it sometimes happened on the Job that you had to take a fall, and if you accepted it with good grace, it could be quietly arranged after the passage of time to restore you to a fit position. What he had been offered or promised along those lines, he didn't reveal, but it was plain that he had been given some encouragement that all could be made right in due course. And though the transfer had been a sharp blow, he'd landed softly—the Captain had made him the "Gang Coordinator," a new title that permitted him to make his own schedule. He supervised one cop, Tom Frankenberry, a computer whiz who would compile photographs and other intelligence for a database. For Frankenberry, it wasn't especially heavy lifting, and for PK, it was less. He needed that, and we did: John wanted to leave most, to just disappear, but since the rest of us would be stuck in the unit for a while, he refused to "benefit" by our new situation: *I'm the one who wrecked the team, so I can't be the only one who gets out when it goes bad.* One departure is easy enough to manage, but when an entire unit has to be remade, there's more administrative work—though when Sgt. Clark and the Crime team quit, the summer of the Rape Detail, they were permitted to leave all at once, and without recrimination. That, too, would not be the case in the new regime.

For weeks, we floated, filling in for sector cars or footposts, not knowing what we'd do each day. Sometimes we worked together, sometimes we didn't. "Patrol is the backbone of the Department," the expression went, though cops usually revised the anatomical correspondent to "backside." The midnight platoon commander, a veteran lieutenant, was flopped to day tours as a result of our shake-up—technically, it had been his responsibility to notify higher-ups about the injured perp—which resulted in the loss of "night differential" on his paycheck. When we did our day weeks, he was not inclined to accommodate us. I thought about approaching Chief Anemone, an old-time cop with a fearsome reputation, hard-charging and flinty. Opinion among my teammates was mixed only in that some thought he would show me to the door, while others thought he would throw me out the window.

We wondered who our new boss would be, knowing that each name on our wish list was wished for in vain—O'Hagan would stay with Bike, certainly, and Fackler on midnights, and Clark would not pick up SNEU after leaving Crime. When the SNEU sergeant was finally assigned, it made all our speculation idle: he was new to the rank, and new to the command. He was younger than I was, I thought, and though he had a couple more years on the Job, they had been interrupted by long stretches in the military. There was no presumption or pretense to him, and when it was time for our sit-down, there were enough seats. He told us, "I know you guys have had a rough time lately, and how you feel about PK. I know you've done great work, and you know what you're doing. I don't want to change anything, and I don't plan to. All I'm asking is that you give me a chance." The dewy sincerity of the request—*the request!*—took us by surprise. We'd been punted around and shunted aside, and here was a boss asking for our permission to work with us. Tony laughed, and feigned brushing away a tear: "He's like a puppy!" We'd give it another shot.

To my amazement, two cops from Bike wanted to join us, George "Chicky" Mendez and Scott "Smacky" Mackay. Bike had lost some momentum when Tommy "Stretch" Dolan had left the Job for a better-paying small-town police department upstate, and Chicky and Smacky were motivated cops, eager to go out and make collars. Our setbacks didn't deter them, apparently, and they remained determined to work with us.

Within the team, the debate was brief:

"All right, it might work—there's one of you people, and one white guy."

"Can't we get another Italian?"

"I said, 'white guy.'"

"Fuck you, we don't want another Irishman."

"Smacky's not Irish, he's Scottish. You can tell because his name is 'Scott.'"

"It's as if Tony's parents named him 'Puerto Rican.'"

"Chicky's Puerto Rican."

"He's not Puerto Rican, he's Short-a-Rican, like Sammy."

"Then maybe we should get two of them, they're small."

"That's the thing about you people, you always have to push."

Chicky was the opposite of Sammy: outgoing and emotional, and a shameless comedian. He was the senior man on the team by several years, and he'd been in SNEU before, under Messer. Smacky was from upstate, far enough that his accent was almost Midwestern. In an OP, he gave out a scrip of a man in a "Payne Stewart cap," which left the catch cars wondering exactly what a "paint store cap" might be. If we were a unit in a World War II movie, he'd have been the farm boy, a big white guy, earnest and idealistic, whose small-town decencies were surprisingly disarming. I'd tagged along behind him on my first days on patrol, when my remark about how Melrose-

Jackson was a little on the slow side—during the heyday of Satan and Loochi, in fact—made him laugh. His eye was almost as good as Orville's.

It seemed that SNEU had bottomed out, and now morale began to creep back up again. There was a corner of the PSA basement that seemed ripe for conquest as an office: there were a few boxes of files and a few drums of mysterious chemicals, leaking on the floor. For a week or so, we cleaned it out and fixed it up, sweeping, mopping, scraping, and painting, singing SNEU spirituals as we worked. Frankenberry, who was good with sheetrock, walled off our corner from the rest of the basement, despite constant assaults from the Bike guys, who took the separation personally. PK and Frankenberry would share the office with us. The Sergeant requisitioned a few desks and cabinets from the quartermaster, and we pitched in with whatever else we needed: I brought in a carpet and a television, and a coffeepot and water cooler followed. A phone line was installed. A couch was discussed but it was disapproved, on the grounds that it might make the place too lounge-like and we would find it too irresistible to leave.

That kind of petty restriction had become increasingly common, and increasingly hard to take. The real purpose of the room was not so much to work as to wait: most arrest paperwork had to be done in proximity to the perp, and someone had to stay by the cells at all times when we had prisoners. But on our ten-to-six weeks, we had an hour or two in the morning while we waited for the van, and it was better to be out of sight when we had a cup of coffee and read the papers, or even, in fact, did work. And on four-to-twelve weeks, when you collared you often finished at three or four in the morning, and went back on the clock at eight, at which point you sat for hours until the DA called to write up the complaint. Even in the busiest precincts working at optimal efficiency, there is at least as much waiting as not-waiting in police work, and the arbitrary way they made that harder for us was deeply frustrating.

Elsewhere in the precinct, you could try to sleep in the lunchroom, but the television was on or people were there eating, and in the dorm—a tiny room with three sets of bunks with bare mattresses—cops on the late tours would come in to sleep for their meal hours. The midnight cops amazed me, on the few tours I stayed over, in their ability to fall asleep in an instant, as if a hypnotist had snapped his fingers. The cops would come in serial pairs for the three o'clock, four o'clock, and five o'clock meals, and collapse on a mattress, sometimes without even taking off their gun belts or vests. All of them snored like chain saws, and I swear there was one time when Koesterer began to snore even as he was walking in from the locker room. John brought a beat-up chaise longue into the SNEU room, but when I slept I usually just went facedown on the floor, glad that I'd brought in the rug.

Such were the workaday gripes of every cop, and they filled the conversational spaces when there was little else to talk about. For hairbags and burnouts, there rarely was anything else, and each new indignity was greeted with a measure of satisfaction for proving their resentment to be right. When any new cop first takes in this ambient sound of cynicism, it can be jarring and dispiriting. You think about how you threw your white gloves in the air at graduation, as the Mayor led thousands in cheering for you, or how you tried not to smile the first time you looked at yourself in the mirror in uniform, or how proud you felt the first time someone said, "Thank you, Officer," and the blast of bitterness breaks through like the voice of Tokyo Rose over the airwaves to the fighting men in the Pacific: *Why you fight for, GI Joe? General MacArthur, he no care about you! Your wife, she no wait for you! GI Joe, you be smart, go home!* At first, I tuned it out, but in time, I found myself nodding in agreement, or adding my bit. As long as it was a matter of healthy ventilation, I thought it was fine, and I could complain with the best of them. I had to be careful, though, remembering the comment from the first days on patrol—*The way you're going, you're gonna be burnt out in five years. . . .*Our complaint, however, was that we wanted to work but they wouldn't let us, and it sprung from a still-abundant reservoir of enthusiasm for the Job. We were becoming seasoned, not soured, and it looked like we were going to get back into things. I asked the Sergeant if I could take Charlie back in for another warrant, and he told me to go ahead.

Charlie had decided that he was finally ready to go to rehab, but he couldn't find a treatment slot. Though the DA's Office ran a program for addicted defendants, I made the case that we ought to do at least as much for people who are working for us as we did for those working against us, and they agreed. A representative for an eighteen-month, residential treatment program would be in next week to interview him. I went back to the woods to find Charlie and tell him. He seemed grateful but guarded, and I asked him: "You've been to rehab before?"

"Yeah, couple of times, but not for a while."

"What's the longest you were clean?"

"Nine years."

"When you slipped up, how long was it before you were back in the street?"

"Two weeks."

Charlie had barely been indoors for the last several years; for the past two winters, he'd slept outside, fearful of the shelters. What was it about cocaine and heroin that he loved so much? Did they love him back? For the near-decade that he was sober, it was as if he were hiking across an icy ridge, where any false step could let loose an avalanche, or give way to an abyss. He'd have a few more days to decide if life at the peaks or the valleys was more perilous. I'd take another trip to the woods, to see if there was some enchantment that I'd overlooked—through the hole in the fence with the snake strung through it, over the headless white chicken on the hardening ground, and then scrambling across the slope to the befouled camp beneath the bridge, where they lived like the trolls in the nursery story. Nope, I didn't see it.

When I took him in for the warrant, it went quickly. We'd been in front of this judge before, and she didn't ask Charlie anything. She did ask me, "Weren't you here with this earlier? Didn't I issue this warrant sometime last month?"

"Yes, your Honor."

"Why wasn't it executed?"

"Administrative reasons on our part, your honor. Our sergeant was—"

"All right, then."

"Thank you."

We left the judge's chambers, saying nothing until we were almost outside the building. Charlie would be going into rehab from there. "Listen," he said, "I appreciate all you did for me."

"That's all right, Charlie, you helped me out, too."

"I hope it was worth it for you."

"If it wasn't, I wouldn't have done it."

"And I'm really gonna try to do this right, this time—to clean up and stay clean, and go home."

"You can do it, I believe you."

We stepped from the side exit of the courthouse, out into the public daylight, for the first time without concern for who might be watching. He had his freedom. I shook his hand.

"Good luck to you, Charlie. Don't take this the wrong way, but I hope I never see you again."

That caught him for a moment, until he worked out the meaning, and he smiled. "I gotcha. But you know, if it doesn't work out, you know where to find me. Just come looking for me, under the bridge. . . ."

"Don't even say that, Charlie. Take care now."

I held the door for him and let him walk on.

. . .

THE FIRST BOOK BY A MEMBER OF THE NYPD WAS WRITTEN by the first Chief of Police, George W. Matsell, in 1859, and it was called *Vocabulum; or, The Secret Language of Crime.* While most true-crime writing offers lurid gore in the often thin guise of moral condemnation, Matsell's book is an amazing miscellany of slang, some criminal, some not. The book claims to be both a decryption of a universal underworld code—"The rogue fraternity have a language peculiarly their own . . . no matter what their dialect, or the nation where they were reared. . . . The language of the rogue in New York is the language of the rogue the world over"—as well as a list of funny or foreign words that poor New Yorkers use, which "are being interwoven with our language and many are becoming recognized Anglicisms." He fudges the difference between the secret languages of gypsy racketeers or the thieves' guilds of *The Threepenny Opera,* and the pidgin English of the streets, some of which has become proper, some of which has disappeared, and some of which has become more or less O.K. (from "oll korrect"). Sometimes you get the sense that he believes these words have invaded the language and have to be repelled, and other times he thinks it's pretty neat that we all get to use them now. The mix of censure and allure is further confused by the appendix, which includes glossaries for the terms used by "Gamblers, Billiard Players, Stock Brokers and Pugilists."

Words with which Matsell presumed his audience was unfamiliar included "booze," "bordello," "negligee," and "pimp," which seem to fit as ordinary words for impolite things. In the same vein, he cites "swag" for stolen goods and "scrape" for trouble, not to mention "bilk" and "bluff," which aren't even slang anymore. There is nothing criminal or even off-color in "duds" and "togs" for clothes, unless slang itself is seen as irreverent instead of merely irregular. "Birthday suit" for "naked" we still say, but "wooden coat" and "eternity box" for "coffin" we don't—it's hard to believe this kind of jokey euphemism has much to do with crime. It shows the same kind of wit to refer to pride as "starch," watered-down liquor as "baptized," or a black-clad widow as the "ace of spades." So too to call the tongue the "red rag," although the example is the real prize: "Shut your potato-trap and give the red rag a holiday."

Many words have gone, but some have come again: a "crib" was a house for the Bowery B'hoys of the mid–nineteenth century as it is for the rappers in the late twentieth. (Incidentally, a "rapper," according to Matsell, is a perjurer.) A lot of the technical, criminal terms are obsolete, such as those that describe MOs for thefts with female decoys, or that pertain to using inside men to make wax impressions of keys. I don't know of any recent arrests for "sweating" or "snagling," the first defined as "reducing the weight of gold coin by putting it in a bag and shaking it violently for some time, and then collecting the gold dust which is then worn off." "Snagling," of course, is "stealing poultry by putting a worm on a fish-hook, thereby catching the fowl." To "pork," in those days, was to "inform the coroner of the whereabouts of a corpse." On the other hand, to commit a robbery, then as now, was to "do a job," and to kill someone was to "hush," "stifle," or "silence" him, or to "make him easy"—all of which are clear in meaning, even when - they're not current. To inform was to "peach," "snitch," or "squeal," and a bit of such information was a "tip." Except for "pigs," all of the words for cops are now out of date—"Philistines," "Moabites," "prigger-nappers" (literally, "thief-catchers"), "shadows," "trappers," "traps," and "stops"—but all of the slang terms for arrests are still in use: you could book 'em, collar 'em, pinch 'em, nab 'em, or run 'em in, ideally when you had 'em "dead to rights." Maybe you could infer that who we are has changed, but what we do has not.

The *Vocabulum* is more tourism than counterterrorism, but it makes the characteristic claim of cop books and crime books, before and since, that what is contained within is dangerous to know. It is forbidden knowledge, and a lot of people—*powerful people, you follow me?*—don't want you to know about this thing of ours, whatever it might be. When I talked to various editors about what kind of book I might write, I got a lot of questions that picked up on the whistle-blower theme—"What would you change about . . ." and "How would improve . . ."—which told of a presumption that any bright young cop would find himself locked in battle against the system, à la Durk and Serpico. And there was a moment of mutual epiphany when one asked, "So then, you're . . . *not* a reformer?"

And I said, "No, I guess not."

When the story of the book deal made the news, I took a couple of days off. Though I was able to remain anonymous in the stories, at least at first, since the whistle-blower theme had been sounded, I knew I had to take my team aside and tell them what was happening. They were all surprised, but they seemed to think it was fine and kind of funny. Tony said, "So that's why you type like a bitch!" Not long after, Stix gave out a scrip from an OP, and when I stopped the perp, I recognized him as a junkie we'd talked to about working as a CI. I put him against a wall, not gently, but I wasn't going to take him in. "Hey, it's good to see you again," he said nervously. "I hear - they're writing a book about you." The remark captured perfectly his limitations as an informant, and we didn't use him afterward.

There was graffiti on my locker, the first and only time anyone ever wrote on it. Some guys had silly things written on theirs—"Papi Chulo!" and "Lover-boy," and Orville had "Orville Redenbacher," after the popcorn company—and others had graffiti with an edge to it, accusing them of being rats or suck-ups to the bosses. When one guy failed to qualify on the firing range, someone made an elaborate target out of black tape, with Magic-Markered bullet holes all over the outside, going up to the ceiling, and a little advice: "Try a knife." When I looked at my locker, there was a simple scrawl that said, "Self-Made Millionaire," which was not the worst thing I'd ever been called. A lot of people joked about it, and a lot of people slapped me on the back, and a lot of people said they wanted free copies, and a few said they didn't want to be mentioned in it. Some of them asked me how to write a book, and I told them I'd let them know when I wrote mine. I never heard a cross word from cops, and I began to wonder if the years of caution were a little paranoid. I trusted the cops I worked with, and they trusted me.

Not for the first time, not for the last, I had it all backward. I thought cops would give me a hard time, but the bosses would like it, if only for the enjoyment of having a Harvard guy to order around. I'd passed on earlier offers from Inspector Mullen to work at Headquarters, at the Office of Management and Planning—"the NYPD think tank," as Mullen called it—because it wasn't the kind of police work that interested me. But the fact that my chief concern was that the upper echelons would find me irresistible showed how wildly misguided I was—to the extent that cops cared, they seemed to think it was fine, but word came early and often that I made the Captain uncomfortable. A dozen cops approached me to pass on his comments: "I don't get that guy. . . ."

"I don't trust that guy. . . ."

"I'd watch my step around that guy. . . ."

"What's he think he is, some kind of Serpico?"

The Serpico remark was especially perplexing, because my idea of a scandal at PSA-7 had to do with the couch ban in the SNEU room, and if there were any deep, dark secrets at the precinct, they were secrets to me as well. Moreover, if I was Serpico, what did that make him? I went into his office and asked him if he had a problem with me or my side job, and if there was anything I could do about it. He amiably denied that there was anything wrong.

The search warrant was due to expire in a few days, and I'd set up a date and time with the Sergeant to execute it, arranging with EMS, ESU, and all the rest. The Sergeant was pleased with the work, and how our continuing efforts showed we'd accepted him as our boss. He'd neglected to tell the Captain about the warrant, however, and when the Captain heard, he called us into the office and asked me why he hadn't been told about it. The Sergeant sat there like a wooden Indian as I apologized for the lack of communication and fielded his questions about the CI and the apartment, which varied between the astute and the simply bewildering:

How can you trust this CI? Aren't they all addicts and liars?

If he's established as a CI, why hasn't he been turned over to Narcotics?

Why are you paying him out of pocket? He can turn around and make all kinds of allegations against you. . . .ž

I explained that it was a vacant apartment, used only for sales, so that there was no risk of running into kids or old people; that we wouldn't need a warrant if we spoke to the landlord, but we'd heard the super was in with the gang; that Charlie was reliable, and Narcotics didn't want him, and he was finished as a CI now, hopefully for good. The money issue wasn't addressed—as PK said later, if you don't understand that you have to throw these people a couple of bucks now and then, you don't understand anything. But the Captain's opposition seemed to stem mainly from not being told about it, and in fairness, if his cops were going to smash a door down, he ought to know. And since he didn't, we wouldn't. Another warrant went down the drain: a dealer would keep his money, addicts would get their drugs, and all would be free to do as they pleased.

The Sergeant didn't seem to know much about SNEU operations in general, and he knew nothing about warrants in particular. That didn't matter much, I thought, because we did. We didn't need guidance in the street from him, we needed cover in the precinct, but the loss of another warrant suggested that that might not be his strength, either. We began to have Team Meetings—or "group hugs" as Tony called them—in which our shortcomings would be somberly addressed and our successes generously praised. The praise had a kindergarten quality, as if he were handing out gold stars for us to stick in our coloring books, and the reprimands were also jarring, in part because we were unused to them, but also because the rebukes persisted long after the infractions had passed. Each meeting had to have an upside topic and a downside, and if there was no occasion for the latter, the reprimand from the week before was recycled. There was some motivational formula at work there, a military or management-seminar prescription for How to Maximize Employee Performance, but we'd been marching to our own music for a long time by then, and his speeches came to sound like a broken record from a radio station that never quite came in.

In December, I went to a funeral out on Long Island, calling in to say that I'd be a couple of hours late, and then calling again to say I'd be a couple of hours later. I should have just taken the day, but we'd taken off a lot since PK was gone, and we were all short on time. Though I got back to the precinct in the afternoon, that single day's lateness continued as a subject at Team Meetings through the next summer. One day around that time, I called in from Headquarters at the start of the tour, where I'd gone to pick up Uncle Eddie's personnel records. I got the Sergeant on the phone and said I'd be an hour late, but if he put me down as present for duty at HQ, I could stay to get the rap sheets for a new informant. He said it was fine, and he'd see me later, but for the next four or five Team Meetings he'd say, "And another thing—Ed, this concerns you—from now on, we start our tours here."

The nagging unease—literally, now that I think of it—that our little family was becoming a corporate subdivision didn't go away, but we were getting back to work, which took our minds off everything else for hours at a time. And though the Captain had canceled the last two warrants, he asked me to see what I could do with a would-be informant who had approached another cop in the command. The informant, whom we named Christmas in the seasonal spirit, was a frumpy, middle-aged crack addict who wanted a respite from her frequent arrests for trespass and possession. She was an easy number for a team of cops who worked where she lived, as they watched her dawdle from crack spot to dope spot the way another woman might browse from the bakery to the greengrocer. She knew most dealers, and no one paid much attention to her, which made her nearly ideal as an informant. She'd also run errands for other addicts, picking up drugs for them because the dealers didn't know them, or because they were afraid of being arrested themselves. I talked to the sergeant who ran that team, and he said they'd lay off her; I told Christmas that if she went somewhere or bought something for us, she'd be fine, but she didn't have a license to buy drugs, let alone sell them. Essentially, the law against trespass had been suspended for her.

What Christmas had to offer was a new crack spot opened up by an old dealer, one of the Jefferson brothers, who had been major players in that project for years. Both of the brothers had long rap sheets, and each had been identified by first and last name several times in kites, or drug complaints about the building. Because the spot had just opened, we wouldn't have a problem with the DECS, but there also wouldn't be any kites on that apartment. Steve Carroll, another cop from the command, told me he thought an old woman lived there, but that she hadn't been around in a while; she also had a middle-aged son with diabetes or some other health problem. It was an unexceptional situation, with certain small advantages—known perps—offset by small handicaps, such as an untested informant.

With Christmas, some of the usual problems presented themselves—instructed not to tell anyone that she was working for us, she promptly told her husband, and she changed her mind about coming to court on the day I'd arranged to get the warrant. I changed her mind back again, and John and I took her in to see Sam Ramer, an ADA who worked for Ed Friedenthal, a chief in the Bronx DA's Investigations Division. Eddie Ramirez, a cop from the Four-O, had a CI in as well, a yappy little character who was giving up his friends to save some time. Eddie told him I was writing a book.

"Yo! You won't believe it! Me, too! I'm gonna call it, *Papi, What I Been Through!*"

"There goes another good title, out the window."

After Eddie was finished, Sam wrote up our warrant and took us in to see the judge. Christmas was a bit scatterbrained but performed reasonably well, and we got the warrant. Since the Captain had asked for it, no political difficulties were expected back at the precinct. I was out of the building, a day or two later, when the inspector from the Housing Borough called in John, the Sergeant, and the Captain to explain what we had. I returned to the precinct sometime afterward and saw their faces, and wondered whether I should have been sorry to have missed it. The warrant had been canceled.

By each of their accounts, the meeting was nearly surreal. In the past, when PK had told the Inspector what we had in a warrant, he'd ask him any number of questions, but he liked PK, and PK had all the answers. Though the Captain, the Sergeant, and John knew the Inspector and the warrant less well than PK would have, the meeting was less of an inquisition than an outright repudiation: What nonsense it was, the Inspector said, he couldn't believe it! The DA must be a rookie, to write this up! The judge must be a rookie, too, to sign it! There were no kites in the building, and only a few collars—it was one of the safest, cleanest buildings around, a senior-citizens complex in such-and-such houses! John thought it futile to protest that it wasn't a senior citizens' building, and it wasn't in that project, and you - wouldn't expect the accumulation of kites and collars since it was a new spot. The Inspector announced with vivid finality: "This baby's going right back up the vagina!"

The three of them thought the Inspector had lost his mind. I wondered, too, but since I'd heard a rumor that Narcotics had set up an intensive, long-term undercover operation there, I held out the hope that the Inspector might have been told to keep our people away for a while. I could even understand putting on a show like that to discourage us, and I took no offense at being kept out of his confidence—I'd had some recent experience with trying to get a large number of people to keep a secret. In the end, my guess that he might not be crazy was no better than their guess that he was—my warrant was gone, regardless, and the Captain would be extremely reluctant to attempt another one.

I still saw our street collars as the paycheck work, the daily basics, and if we could make something more of it, it was all for the good. It was as if we were oystermen, and the man who threw out his catch every day because he - didn't find a pearl wouldn't be long for the business. But we were being told to throw away the pearls, too, and even to drop everything that shined a little when you opened it. Two days before Christmas, I got a call from a friend in the FBI, Jeff Drubner, to ask if I could get a couple of cops to ride with his - people, to see where a suspect would take an undercover agent for a drug meeting with a Nigerian. I'd met Jeff a year or two before, at a party after the St. Patrick's Day Parade. I was in my dress uniform, and we were introduced fairly quickly, as we were the only armed people in the room. For a few minutes, we fell into the absurd, movie-cliché cop-versus-Fed standoff, sussing each other out, but we hit it off and stayed in touch. Jeff had once been assigned to investigate a threatening letter sent by a Nigerian national to the head of the New York office. The letter, which turned out to be more of a curse than a threat, had the effect of associating Jeff with Nigeria, where there is a significant heroin-trafficking network, and those barest qualifications made him the New York Bureau's Man for Africans.

Jeff needed a couple of bodies to ride in surveillance cars for the morning of December 24. Their man was to meet the dealer and travel to another place to talk; it was hoped that it was his house, so he could be identified. It would not be difficult, dangerous, or even interesting work, but because of the date, they didn't have the manpower available. It would be a pure favor, since we were working a double shift to leave early on Christmas Eve, starting at four in the afternoon and finishing at eight in the morning. The FBI might need us through noon. John, Stix, Tony, and a couple of others were willing to go, and I was referred up the newly tightened chain of command to ask the Captain if it'd be all right. He didn't seem pleased.

"What if somebody gets shot? How do they know who this guy is? What if it turns out Narcotics has a case going on him already?"

I said I'd have Jeff call him, and I left the office. An hour later, Jeff called me: "You know, if your captain just told me, 'I don't get anything out of this, so I won't let my guys go,' I'd have a lot more respect for him. But this is bull-shit—what do you mean, 'What if somebody gets shot?' Well, it would suck, wouldn't it? Would it suck more than it would the day after, or yester-day? I told him, no one's even getting out of their cars. And how does he think we ID the guy, except by talking to him and following him? And not for nothing, who cares if Narcotics has a case—if it's good enough, they'd try to take it federal anyway. I'm sorry, but your boss doesn't know what he's talk-ing about."

And so we slept in on Christmas Eve, and SNEU got to spend the holiday at home. Though it was hard to tell afterward, I think that the Captain grew more firm in the opinion that I was more of a problem than an asset, and even my zeal for police work was compromised by a dubious private agenda. Four recent efforts—three search warrants and what might have been styled a "Joint Operation with the FBI"—that I'd brought into his office as bouquets somehow turned into stink bombs. The Sergeant forgot to tell him about one warrant, the Inspector might not have told him everything about another, and even if I turned out to be closer to Sgt. Bilko than Frank Serpico, he didn't understand it all, and so he didn't want to try anymore. I asked the Sergeant if he still wanted me to get warrants, and he said he did, and then I asked if he thought the Captain still wanted me to get them, and he assured me it was the case. I didn't quite believe him, but I decided to act as if I did—if I proved to be a fool, they would be proven liars, which was a verdict I could live with. And in the meantime, I could go on working as a cop, which was all I wanted to do anyway.

· · ·

THE NEW YEAR OF 1999 BEGAN WELL—ON NEW YEAR'S EVE, we were assigned to Times Square in plainclothes, and then sent back to the Bronx with loose instructions to "make periodic checks on major landmarks," which I interpreted to mean relatives and friends. PK and Frankenberry were in the SNEU room with us, and so when we were inside the precinct, it seemed like he was our boss again. Early in the month, we had some good collar days, and later in the month, we had some better ones—the Sergeant was away for a week, and PK took us out. While we did want the numbers to jump that week—*Let's make PK look good!*—there was no corresponding effort to diminish the new boss. The fact was, for every sergeant who had us, from Carroll, Carrano, Kelly through the new guy, as well as O'Hagan and everyone else who filled in to cover us, when we hit the street, we thought about the street.

Whether you were watching or catching, you concentrated on the perp: where his hands were, where he could run to, what he had done in the past. It was wearying but also exhilarating, as if you'd run for miles, and then decided to run more, and you were uplifted simply by the will to undertake the farther distance. Chicky and Smacky fit into the team as if they'd always been there, and in fact they'd been doing what we did longer than we had. Chicky would break us up, taking on character roles to slip into the OP, the most disturbing being a kind of spastic, hobbling and twitching his way across playgrounds into projects, arousing pity but not suspicion. One day, he dressed as a mailman, and so many people handed him letters that he truly transformed into a disgruntled postal worker. When Smacky was in the OP, he called out the action in the hushed tones and stop-and-pause rhythms of an announcer at a golf tournament: "The pitcher is a male Hispanic, with blue jeans, white Air Jordans, no belt . . . and he is, he is smoking a cigarette, left hand, no, wait, he's lighting it to give to a girl, looks like, stand by . . . yeah, it looks like a Newport, and he has a shirt that is blue, white, green, and red, the design is . . ."

"Smacky, you on?"

". . . the design is triangular, with a border of . . ."

"Smacky, you on?"

". . . circles and squares, the circles are blue . . ."

"Smacky, you on?"

"Somebody trying to raise me?"

"Yeah, I got a question for you."

"Go ahead."

"Do you get paid by the word?"

One day, Smacky had us take a player who was stepping off—we'd missed a couple of buyers, but he wanted us to take him with whatever he had, which turned out to be sixty-six slabs. He was wanted on a bench warrant, and he had another open Narcotics case. Smacky talked him into turning, and he gave up two apartments with guns and another with drugs; he was a player in the revived Melrose-Jackson gang wars, whose most recent casualty had been a kid who was blasted in the face with a shotgun the day before. Smacky worked through the night, but there were logistical problems from the outset and legal ones soon after; the ADA told him that the perp had a right to an attorney because of the open case, which is simply not true. Though they refused to move in the day after the arrest, I still thought we - could make a deal a week later in the Grand Jury: he had felony weight six times over, he was wanted on a warrant, and he had another open case. But the next week, the ADA in the Grand Jury told Smacky that without buyers, they weren't going to indict, anyway—the offer would be for a misdemeanor plea, with a couple of months in jail. Smacky called me at home to tell me. I thought there might just be a communication problem, and I told him to explain that we already had cooperation, and that all we were asking was to hold back on the offer while we went after the guns, one of which might have been used to shoot that kid in the face. In any county in the state, the perp would have faced years in jail. Smacky told me to wait, they would bring it up to the supervisor. A couple of minutes later, he came back. "They said no. They're making the offer, today."

"Let me talk to her," I said. I started to get steamed.

"I don't think I should," he said. I didn't argue with him. Smacky had a better idea of when to quit than I did.

One of the nights out with PK, we did a double, working through midnight and hitting the crack spots at Mitchell Houses hard. OV and I were in the van, and we rolled back and forth down 138th Street, up and down Alexander, Willis, and Brook, picking up bodies. A scrip came over: *male Hispanic, twenties, black leather jacket with fringes on the sleeves, riding a little-kid bike, east on One-Three-Eight . . .* When we rolled up and grabbed him, he was wild-eyed and damp with sweat. We fired off questions and he fired back lies:

"What were you doing in the building?"

"I didn't go in the building!"

"We saw you in the building."

"I went in the building but no one was there!"

"We saw you talk to the pitcher."

"I went in the building and I saw the pitcher but I changed my mind—"

"Stop it."

"My brother's a cop."

"He must be very proud of you. Listen, tell you what, just give it up, gimme what you got, and I'll get you a Desk Appearance Ticket, you'll be out in a couple of hours."

"I don't got nothin'! My brother's a cop! Don't you have anything better to do?"

"Turn around and give me your hands."

I cuffed him up and threw him in the van: "Tell me the truth now or I'll put you through the system!"

And then he broke down, crying and shouting from the back of the van for another hour as we worked: "I'm a good person! I work across the street! I can help you out! Where's my money? I had money in my pocket! You stole my money! Let me go, my brother's a cop!"

At the precinct, he continued the double-edged harangue of pleas for mercy and threats of litigation. When Sammy put him in a cell, the perp told him that we'd stolen thirty dollars from him, and he was going to make a complaint. At that point, I was still inclined to write a summons for trespass if he came up clean on the search, a Desk Appearance Ticket (DAT) if he didn't, on his brother's account. His brother was supposed to be down the street, and his father had been called to get him, but he never showed up. When he repeated the Internal Affairs threat, I joined in with the "Fuck him!" crowd—which was everyone else—and decided to put him through, regardless. In the cells, he became the shop steward for the angry perps, loudly denouncing cops for being stupid and crooked and mean, then demanding candy, cigarettes, and phone calls. When we searched him, we found a half-smoked joint, with the acrid smell of angel dust. That explained a lot: angel dust is an animal tranquilizer that induces psychosis in humans, and a lot of cops have stories of how it took six large men to subdue a hundred-and-fifteen-pound dusthead. It wasn't as if crack was getting great press in the South Bronx in 1999, but it took a particular kind of idiot to wake up one day and say, "Angel dust is a product I've heard nothing but good about, and it's about time I was involved."

When I pulled him out for debriefing, I told him he was going to jail no matter what I wanted to do with him, or what his brother could do for him, because he had a warrant for an old summons, and he was also on probation. I said that there was no point in lying or crying, because it was just us in the room, and at least one of us didn't feel sorry for him at all. But if he wanted to help me out, I could keep him from being violated on his probation and thrown back in jail. He thought for a moment, and then he told me about dope spots, crack spots, dust spots, and the people he knew who carried guns. What was of unique value was that he worked in a video store, where a number of dealers had memberships, and he could pull out their cards for names and addresses. I told him to come back and talk to me again in a few days, when his head cleared.

The Sergeant congratulated us on our accomplishments while he was away, and he seemed to expend his energy in administration and requisitions for the room—file cabinets from the quartermaster, laminated precinct maps for the walls. Each of us was assigned a precinct map to color in the public housing with blue marker. I told him about the new CI, his possibilities and pitfalls, and he said to go ahead with it. Once, I asked him to sit in on an interview with the CI—in part, because I wanted a witness for each conversation—but he sat there listlessly, saying nothing and looking ill at ease, so afterward I asked PK. I hadn't written the Sergeant off yet, but the past week had rekindled hope that PK might return. When we were in the office together, PK remained the conversational center of gravity, attracting all the jokes and tactical questions. There was no disrespect—the Sergeant's official position was always acknowledged—but there was also no doubt about who we loved. Maybe the new guy would win our affection and trust, and maybe he would not, but we had had a father once, and the stepfather had yet to prove himself.

When the CI came into the precinct, I took him into the muster room with Chicky to start the registration paperwork. He couldn't sit still, couldn't shut up, couldn't concentrate or respond. He didn't want to sign the forms, didn't want his picture taken, and told Chicky, "Stop looking at me like that, you're scaring me!" Now and then, he'd catch himself, realizing that he came off as an eight-cylinder psychotic, and attempt some poor feint at normalcy, like when he looked over at Chicky's Yankee hat and piped up, "So, you like the Yanks? I love the Yanks! Yeah, baseball!" He was like a surrendering German soldier leaping from a trench, hands up and shouting, "Babe Ruth! Bugs Bunny! Betty Grable!"

When I finally got him to sign the forms, he signed in all the wrong places—where I sign, where the captain does—and insisted on "J-5" as a code name, which was a little James Bondish, and prematurely self-congratulatory. He'd done nothing yet but raise my blood pressure, and I didn't want him to get wrapped up in secret-agent fantasies. When he screwed up another set of forms and began to complain again about having his picture taken, I bellowed at him:

"How fucking dare you come into my house fucking high, bugging out, all fucked up, and try to play me like this! You fucking insult me like this, coming here, and expect me to do you favors with probation? Get the fuck out of here!"

And then he started to bawl, Yes, okay, so maybe he'd had a drink—

"YOU ARE LYING! YOU DID NOT HAVE A DRINK!"

Boo, hoo, hoo, it was all the stress, he was afraid to come, he'd been in jail all weekend. His face streamed with snot and tears, and I told him to clean himself up and go home. We'd try again in a couple of days. When we left the room, there was a little crowd by the door. It had been loud, and Chicky said he'd wondered how long I'd let it go before cutting off the interview or punching him in the head.

A few days later, he was back, a little on edge but otherwise of sound enough mind, and he gave excellent, detailed information about three spots where they held or sold dope. When it came time to pick a code name, I decided to make it a kind of Rorschach test, and lead him out into wider fields of self-image. I said I couldn't just let him pick it, because it might reveal specific information about himself—Charlie's code name had been the town he was from, which said too much, so we just called him "Chuckles." I asked him what his favorite animal was, and he said, "I don't know, all of them, dogs." Pushed for a specific, he said, "the little ones, like the kind they have in the Taco Bell commercial." I was deeply satisfied by his choice. "From now on," I solemnly intoned, "you have a new identity, and you will be known to us only as 'Chihuahua.'" He nodded. For days, "*Yo quiero* angel dust!" was the office catchphrase.

Chihuahua was still a loudmouth and an aggravation, but the information was good: there were kites on two apartments out of the three he gave up, and the names he provided, "Tony" and "Jamie M—" were both specified in the kites. Jamie was on parole for drug sales. Chihuahua said the third apartment was where most of the stash was, hidden behind loose bricks in the wall beneath the sink. An old man lived there, but Chihuahua hadn't been inside in a while.

"Can you get in?"

"Yeah, the old man's a little gayish. He'd let me in."

"Well, do what you have to do. If you have to take one for the team, you're authorized. Excellent work, Chihuahua. You may go now."

I walked through the buildings, and all was as described: the odd turns of the stairway, the tile pattern on the floor, the stickers and marks on the doors. There were glassines for the brand of heroin—China White—all over both lobbies. We had Tony identified with a drug arrest; we had Jamie's mug shot, parole record. The old man was still unidentified, but we were at least able to corroborate the door markings, which way the windows faced, what they looked out on; I stopped an old woman going into the building to ask for a young girl in that apartment, and she told me I must be wrong, because an old man lived there who didn't like girls. We didn't expect too much from Tony's place—it was a sale spot, so only a couple of bundles and weed would be on hand, but there should be a good amount at the old man's. And Jamie had volume and a gun, too. I kept on Chihuahua to get into each apartment several times within a ten-day period, and set up a date for him to come into court. I let the Sergeant know where we stood for each apartment, and that I would try for warrants for all three, but that I wouldn't be surprised if a judge held back for the old man's place. He said to go ahead and get the warrants.

Though Chihuahua had become far more manageable—and credible, at least about where he got drugs—I hadn't learned to like him any better. Smacky went with me, the sole volunteer. In the morning, Chihuahua was late, and he hadn't been in one of the spots over the weekend, as I'd told him to do.

"Did you go into Jamie's?"

"I can get in there any time."

"Did you go over the weekend, like we said?"

"Nah, but I can get in, any time."

"I thought I explained to you that we don't get a warrant because you *can* get inside. We get a warrant because you *were* inside, recently, and saw shit there."

"It's no problem."

"Yes, Chihuahua, it is. We were on our way to court. Can you get in now?"

"No problem."

On the way, he blathered, in his usual nails-on-the-blackboard manner, complaining that I never called him enough—though my calls were never returned—and about how he'd like to get involved in the Internet. "Listen, I could find out things for you guys, too. Hey, I got an idea! You know what would be good? If you guys got me a computer! If you all chipped in, it wouldn't be so bad for you. You know, I could find out a lot of things, and I'm really into computers."

I took another breath, and refused to look at Smacky because we would have broken each other up. "We'll see," I said. We drove to a place a few blocks from Jamie's and let him out, crossing our fingers that he'd come back. He did, no worse for wear.

At the CI room, Bea Moore and another cop from Narcotics arrived with their own informant to get a warrant for the old man's house. I don't know who made the mistake in issuing them a DECS number for our apartment— had we gone to court a day later, there might have been a serious problem. As it was, I felt badly for the Narco cop, Ocasio, who'd worked needlessly through the night with his own skell to set up the warrant, but he did provide the corroboration for the third apartment. I was there first, on paper and in fact, so there was no dispute of ownership, and Ocasio told me about another floor trap, with two guns and more dope. A couple of hours later, we returned jubilantly to the precinct, free of Chihuahua and with three warrants.

While a lot of cops go for their entire careers without getting a search warrant, and others might get one a month, it had been almost two years at PSA-7 since anyone had a search warrant before SNEU started up again with PK. They tend to go in runs, when a cop gets hold of a quality informant, and I was proud that I'd gotten three in one day from an informant who was so difficult to manage. I pushed for them because of the other corroborative evidence—I wouldn't have knocked a door down on his say-so alone—and the fact that I disliked him so strongly was a positive; I wasn't spending time with him because I enjoyed the company. I thought nothing of him as a person, and whatever he had to say about anything aside from drugs was of no interest to me. I had an appreciation for the fact that it could appear as if I chose to believe what suited me, but I had evidence to support his statements on the only aspect of his life that mattered to me. He was not a whole person to me, but a key to a door. And he fit.

And then I threw out my back. I'd done it once or twice before, since I'd become a cop, for no apparent reason. The first time, I was leaving for work, and as I locked up my apartment I felt an electric shock through my spine and fell to my knees. I managed to get to my car and I drove to the precinct, where I asked for the day off, and the next, which brought me to my weekend. When I'd been at the command for two months, an older cop had told me, "I wouldn't go sick for at least a year. Your sick record is one of the big things they look at for transfers and so on, and if you go sick more than a couple of times, they bust your balls." At the time, my peculiar reasoning on the subject was that if it turned out to be a serious injury, I wanted to keep it off the record so I could keep working. When my back went out the first time, it took about a week for me to get better, during which I made gradual improvements toward upright posture, like a schoolroom poster of evolution, from all fours to Homo erectus. This time, after I took the day, John came home to tell me that the warrant was off again. Though I was barely in knuckle-scraping Neanderthal phase, I went back for the next tour, where I spent most of it on the floor of the SNEU room. Again, I was glad I'd brought in the rug.

John told me that the Sergeant had called a Team Meeting, during which he announced all the problems the Captain had with me—that I had a tendency to run off and do things on my own, that there was something suspect in how I could call up DAs and ask for favors. John told me the team gave it back to him, and there were fierce arguments, but in another meeting with the Captain, they were grilled on the details on the warrants and didn't have all the answers. It would be a better thing in future, he said, if the whole team knew the warrant inside out.

When I went back in, the Sergeant told me that the Captain was concerned about Chihuahua's brother, the cop. We had an obligation to find out who he was, and to let him know what we were doing. I told him that the cop-brother issue had only come up the night he was arrested, as leverage for release, and that I didn't see it as significant. (I had brought it up with Chihuahua after the arrest, and he almost cried, telling me that he didn't want his brother involved.) Whether the brother gave his blessing—if there was a brother, and if he was a cop—we were past the point of approval: we had the warrants, and the only question was whether we would reap any benefit from them. Few people, cops or otherwise, would be delighted to learn that relatives are working as informants: they don't want to deal with what led to the opportunity, and they don't want to think about the risk. I'd talked to another cop who had a brother with his own legal troubles, and he told me, "I said to him, 'If my job doesn't mean enough to you to keep from fucking up, don't start throwing my name around when you get caught.'" I didn't expect enthusiastic approval from the brother, but it was also troubling to imagine it—what if he wanted to be involved, to have a say in what we did or how we handled Chihuahua? We knew something about the informant; we knew nothing, nothing, nothing about the brother. Moreover, we don't let *anyone* know that someone is working for us.

At the end of the tour, the Sergeant told me we were not going ahead with the warrants without the brother's name. There wouldn't be a problem, he said, the Captain just wanted the name and where he worked; the Captain didn't have to talk to him, but it was a small detail that needed to be cleared up. Even at the time, I thought the conversation had the same quality as my earlier talk with Chihuahua, when he asked me to buy him a computer— "*We'll see . . .*"—in its unreality and inequality, in the attempt to keep a straight face. I called Chihuahua and told him he was giving up the name. He began to whimper and I cut him off. He gave me the name and the precinct. I gave them to the Sergeant and went home.

The next morning, we waited uneasily in the SNEU room, as the Sergeant chose his moment to make his announcement: the warrants were off, this time for good. He had a confidence about him, an assured and superior manner with which he delivered the news that the Captain had talked to Chihuahua's brother the cop, and that he was a cop but not his brother, just a friend of the family. He pronounced it as if it were an investigative coup, that the Captain—the old fox!—had cut through to the truth of the matter, while we were chasing our tails. The warrants would be given to Narcotics to execute. "You guys are going to have to get things a little tighter next time, it wasn't quite there," he went on blithely. "We'll go for the training, search-warrant training, and we'll know what we're doing next time."

Where to begin? To ask why he'd lied to me about talking to the cop brother? To ask why, if he'd thought it was an important issue, they hadn't forced it beforehand? To ask how many warrants he had gotten? Or the Captain? Or merely to ask if the *Pop!* was audible when he pulled his head out of his ass? Instead, I asked him whose decision it was to cancel the warrant.

"It was mine," he said. When I began to challenge his reasons, he backed off, saying he canceled it only because he knew the Captain was going to. And the Captain canceled it only because the Inspector would have. I said I'd talk to either of them, but he forbade it. Chain of command, you know. He said, "I don't know what you guys think about me—think what you want, but I fought for this, and I fought for you, tooth and nail!"

"You canceled the warrant. Is that fighting for it?"

He conceded I had a point, but insisted he had fought, then returned to the circular diversion of chain of command. I don't remember exactly the order of things: Orville left the room yelling that he was quitting the unit; Stix jumped in on the "fighting tooth and nail" remark; Smacky said that he now knew how difficult it could be to get a warrant, and how much work goes into it, and that it was just plain wrong to have this happen. The Sergeant said that any of us could leave SNEU when we wanted, and the unit would go on without them.

I wanted to return to the cross-examination: "Everything about this warrant I told you about as soon as I knew it, and every next step I did was cleared by you. So why is it that the Captain thinks I'm running around and doing things on my own?"

"I don't know . . . he just thinks so. . . ."

"But you straightened him out, right, told him you knew everything and approved everything?"

"Oh, yeah, of course."

"But he just thinks that anyway, despite what you tell him, you don't know why."

"Uh-huh."

That afternoon, I called Bea Moore in Narcotics to say that we had warrants for them, and to ask when we could meet and go over them. There were only a few days left in their ten-day life, and the last one I tried to give them, with Christmas, had come to them too late. The Sergeant was in the office with me, and he began to scream as soon as I hung up the phone: "That's exactly your fucking problem! You're always running off and doing things on your own! This is not your fucking warrant! It's my fucking warrant! I will decide who gets it and who doesn't get it!"

I was floored. We went back and forth some more, but I stayed lock-jawed and lawyerly to keep my temper. Later that day, my back was still killing me, and I said I wanted to leave early. Permission was denied. He made us get in uniform and go out on patrol.

The aftermath was bitter and blurry. Stix asked Sgt. O'Hagan about going to Bike, where there were openings. O'Hagan brought it up with the Captain, who told him that no one was moving from SNEU. I took days off whenever I could. On one of them, John told me that Chief Dunne, the CO of the Housing Bureau, had come in to address the troops. He told everyone about how when he was the CO of a Brooklyn precinct, the SNEU team got warrant after warrant, their investigations were far-reaching, and it was a tremendous success. John said the Captain stood beside him, nodding in agreement. During another Team Meeting, the Sergeant announced that no SNEU business was to be discussed with any supervisor outside the immediate chain of command. The rule meant specifically that we were not to talk to PK.

We ignored the Sergeant and talked to PK all the time. PK could only shake his head. "What a shame," he said. "What a waste." Not long after, Frankenberry was driving him when they hit a truck. John and I were in my car when we heard it over the air, the weakened voice calling for help, the slow recognition that it was PK. We would have preferred to have been hit ourselves, and almost were as we flew to the scene, as John bellowed directions in my ear as we cut through traffic. The front end of their car was mashed in, and they'd broken the windshield with their heads. PK was pale and dazed in his seat, and he didn't move. I turned away for a moment because I could picture him dead. I put my hand on his shoulder and asked him how he was doing. He smiled and said, "Not so good. . . ."

Other cops came, the rest of the SNEU team and sectors from Housing and the Four-O. PK and Frankenberry had been driving down a street that was two-way for most of its length, but one-way for a single block, which was where they were rammed by a beer truck. It was an easy mistake, but they were at fault. The scene had a feel of thwarted force—*What can we do, dammit?*—and messages were sent back and forth over the air: *Ascertain the status . . . advise which hospital . . . close down the streets.* . . . Central asked if the ambulance had left yet, and the Sergeant said, "Not yet, Central—they're still bagging him up." Whoever was listening whipped around to glare at him, then ignored him again. John took PK's shield and put it around his neck, and we divvied up the gun, belt, and the rest of the equipment to safeguard as if they were relics. We followed him into the ambulance and closed the doors. "Don't worry, laddo," I said. "I found a bundle of dope in the back seat, but I threw it out." He almost laughed.

As we were about to leave, the Captain opened the doors to ask two questions, "Is he all right?" and "Who was driving?" It seemed to me that the real concern was in the second. I said PK was fine, and Frankenberry had been driving, and we left.

It is almost a wonderful thing to be hurt as a cop, or rather, there is something majestic in the spectacle of the Job taking care of its own. Highway entrances are shut down all along the hospital route; flashing lights and sirens guard the road as you pass, and escort you to your destination. The world is told that a cop is hurt, and that is all that matters. PK and Frankenberry had concussions and bruises, and they were treated and released in a couple of hours. We drove them home and they had a couple of days off.

Soon after PK returned, the Captain told him he was no longer the Gang Coordinator. He would be issued a Command Discipline for his "failure to supervise" his driver, and be reassigned to patrol on the four-to-twelves. The flexibility to take care of things at home was already strained—PK always used his vacation days early, and rarely had time on the books—and now he'd have none. He went to the Inspector and asked to be transferred to PSA-8, in the north Bronx. "I'm not a fuck-up," he said. "And I'm not going to be treated as one." The Inspector ran the Borough, which covered all of Housing in the Bronx and Queens, and PK was accommodated. The Captain seemed to regard it as a slap in the face, and I was happy to think so. But it was also clear that we were going nowhere ourselves.

NINE

There is so much to the City, so many little worlds on the wax and wane, pulling you in and pushing you out. You might be met by a wary eyeball through the peephole, or with wide-armed welcome, if you have a pretty face, a pocketful of cash, the name of a friend. The dress code could be black tie, or you might have to leave all your clothes at the door, or a simple weapons check would do. There are cafes and clubs where you can speak Amharic, Bulgarian, or Catalan, and next door to each there are others where you can leave the mother tongue and mother country behind. People come here to be dancers, bankers, witches, chefs; to take jobs that have been just invented or long forgotten, union jobs and city jobs. New York maintains civil-service positions for ostlers—they take care of the municipal horses—and may be the only city to do so since the Kaiser left Berlin. If you require other Bulgarian ostlers so as not to feel lonely, you might have a problem, but we have both Bulgarians and ostlers. And there may well be an enclave of Bulgarian ostlers—in Queens, most likely—that I just haven't come across, because I haven't looked. You can never get lost in New York, as long as you keep on moving, but you can get stuck sometimes. It depends on your stamina more than your sense of direction.

After college, I'd sometimes run into people who'd complain about the narrow sameness of New York, which for them meant a Wall Street job, an Upper East Side apartment, and a social life in which they took cabs to restaurants, clubs, and dinner parties where they met other young men and women who had not only gone to the same schools, but studied the same majors. Hasidim mix it up more, I thought. But later, I thought that I was doing the same thing. In the Academy, when Sgt. Solosky warned us against getting lost in the Job, it sounded a little laughable: *Make sure you keep your old, civilian friends. . . .* What was irresistible about this world—the gray polyester uniforms, the hours spent mastering the dogshit-disposal regulations, or the months of obedience-school drills to sit, stay, fetch? *Good boy, gimme a paw. . . .* Though most of my old friends had shamefully low arrest activity, I didn't shun them altogether. But absent the last step of dating another police officer, I was in as deep as you could get.

I kept much the same company, on duty and off. I'd become good friends with two cops who'd left PSA-7, McTigue and Killian—I would be in both of their wedding parties—and we'd catch bands at bars, Shanachie at Rocky Sullivan's, Pat McGuire at Marty O'Brien's. Both bars were dark and smoky, narrow and long, and you could look at pictures of JFK, RFK, Shane McGowan, and Brendan Behan from behind your pint. Chris Byrne played with Shanachie and owned Rocky Sullivan's, and he had been a cop for ten years before quitting to play full-time with his other band, Black 47. Brian McCabe had been his partner in Midtown North, before he became a detective sergeant with Manhattan South Homicide. McCabe's nephew was Pat McGuire, of course, and he played for George Kornienko, owner of Marty's, who had worked for Chris with the band and at his bar before striking out on his own. Both bars were cop-heavy, and the density of off-duty Irishness was Uncle Eddie-ish, but there was a generational irony, as well: "Rocky Sullivan" was the James Cagney character in *Public Enemy*; "Marty O'Brien" was the stage name Frank Sinatra's father had used for his boxing career. Still, you could hear "Danny Boy" on the jukebox, and the pipes, the pipes were calling, for us as they had for Pat Brown.

John broadened the circle still further. He was a joiner and an organizer, a natural coach—he ran the precinct gym and played on our softball and basketball teams. He'd see someone who'd fallen off his weightlifting regimen and snap, "Look at him, the fat fuck. He's swollen up like a blood tick." The cult of fitness was new to me, the calorie- and carb-counting obsessions, the supplements, shakes, and nutrition bars: "I was good today, egg whites and turkey, with pepper and ketchup. All protein, no fat."

"And it gives you a shiny black nose and a fine, glossy coat."

With the gym cops from PSA-7 that John was tight with—Eddie Tibbatts, Andy Bielawski, John Chase, Chris Esposito, Reynaldo "Ray-Ray" Reyes—we'd step out to the nightclubs now and then, tinning the doorman—flashing your badge—to cut the line. *Right this way, guys, how many are you? Where do you work? The South Bronx!* You'd keep an eye on some of the guys, wondering if you'd collared them, and keep an eye out for the girls, too, just to be fair. Sometimes, we'd hit the Copa, but I think I was the only one looking to make a case there. I knew we were going out when I could smell John's cologne from around the corner. Inside the apartment, I'd see him trying on various shirts and expressions in front of the mirror: *What about the blue short-sleeve, and a brooding scowl?* He'd examine his reflection with an air of sober detachment before concluding, "The mirror doesn't lie. I get better-looking - every day."

"It's cold out, John, put on more jewelry."

"Ah, shut up, you prick of misery."

"That's a nice expression. Where's that come from?"

"My grandmother says it, about my grandfather."

Even Mickstat and Wopstat continued after hours: John became a member, and then a delegate, and then a trustee of the Columbia Association, the NYPD Italian fraternal organization. "You finally got your button," I said. "Who'd you have to kill?" He raised his hands, as if it would be wrong for him to say more: "I'm a good earner . . . and you should have tried the *szviadell*!" Though we both marched on St. Patrick's Day, he took no small pleasure casually tossing me an Emerald Society card, saying, "Here you go. I got plenty. If you need anything else from them, let me know. The Irish owe us, big time."

My counterpunch was directed straight to the gut, where he was most vulnerable. A good night out for me would be at a restaurant—a legacy from high school, at the Commuters—and we did eat well, and most often Italian. At my regular places, the waiters took such good care of us that John took to calling me a "closet guinea." "Listen," I told him. "I've been to Italy and I've been to Ireland. What I don't get is why you people left." I said that there were Fitzgeralds in my family, and the Fitzgeralds were once the Gheraldini, who had left Florence before Dante did. Moreover, as I pointed out, one look at him could show that his family had offered a warm welcome to travelers from the North; with his blond hair and blue eyes, a Viking or two had clearly developed a taste for Sicilian cooking. I'd say I could out-guinea him, anytime, as my knowledge of Italian covered most of the menu, whereas the only words he knew were for insults and pastries. Several times, we breached the walls of the fastest redoubt of guineadom, a restaurant in East Harlem called Rao's, which is over a hundred years old and fits eight tables inside. Over the years, its clientele graduated by degrees from gangsters to Sinatra types, who were happy to see gangsters, to people who were happy to see the Sinatra types. Politicians and sports figures often went there, and more often were turned away. *Is Frankie in? Nah? How 'bout Frankie Junior?* Sonny Grosso had a regular table on Monday nights, and he gave it to me once. I went with John, Killian, and McTigue, and as Nicky the Vest took our orders from behind the bar, he said, "You guys like sports?" After three answers in the affirmative, he offered the curt instruction, "Turn around." We did, to witness Hank Aaron. Sonny was the Joe DiMaggio of our business, and I was more than a little proud to know him. He remembered my father and Uncle Eddie from years ago. A few times he invited John and me out, and as the roast peppers with *pignoli* and raisins arrived, he might wave a hand for a friend to come over, and wave again for the waiter to turn off the jukebox, and the friend would shiver the windows with arias from *Pagliacci*.

"Still unsigned, can you believe it?" Sonny said. "I'm taking him to Vegas, to meet people. . . ."

At times like those, I wished that the phrase "Prince of the City" had been unspoiled by irony. We were used to being cops by then, settled in our skins. In all the Irish bars, Italian restaurants, and many other places we went, to be a New York City cop was to be met with gratitude and respect. People knew that if there was trouble we would help, and if there wasn't, we could tell them a funny story they could repeat to all their friends. Because of us, they - could walk around at night, and if they thought about leaving town, it was because New York was becoming too expensive, and not because they were afraid they'd be killed if they stayed. I liked the feel of a shield on my chest, and it began to make sense that you wore it over your heart. So Sgt. Solosky was right, after all, or maybe he should have warned us against being caught up in the Job when it had nothing to do with good guys and bad guys, at least not in the expected way. But probably not, because it wouldn't have made sense at the time to have reached a point in my career where everything was great about work except work.

• • •

I HAD BEGUN TO FEAR THAT WHAT HAD MADE ME MAD AND miserable over those months on the Job was more than a run of bad luck or bad treatment, but signs of a larger and darker disorder. From PK's departure from the team to his escape from the precinct, the Job had been dental-visit dismal, with hours of discomfort broken by jolts of pain, but at the dentist's, at least, you knew that the visit would end. The Captain's talk of Serpico began to take on an ironic resonance, because I certainly began to feel like a lonely crusader in a hostile system, no matter if my cause was nothing greater than to stop my work from being screwed up all the time by a couple of jackasses. Until then, there were bosses I didn't care for, but the general and final alignment had been that I worked for people who were in some way older, wiser, or better than I was, and bore good will to good work. My predicament was vertical: we had the odious Sergeant, and above him, a Lieutenant who avoided us like a train wreck, and then the wretched Captain, and then the enigmatic Inspector, and beyond that, who knew? It began to prompt the belief that I was the part that didn't belong, at least not there. Cops would say, "The Job is not your friend," and I suspected the expression was an old one.

After Knapp, the old heroes were regarded as suspect, at best. Their very success under the old regime was held against them—how could they thrive amid the corruption and compromise, untainted themselves? But the new heroes were treated little better, at least on the Job: Durk had to complain about the Narcotics Division on a talk show—not the preferred format for an interoffice memo—to start an investigation that led to the breakup of a major Mafia heroin operation, with the arrest of more than sixty traffickers, though he was left out of the case. When he shot a mugger off-duty, the *Times* ran a front-page story about it; when he was frustrated with a particular assignment, they ran an editorial about how the NYPD ought to find a position for him that was commensurate with his talents. He continued to work with the DOI, sometimes on interesting cases, sometimes not. With the passing of each administration, he hoped to be brought back for a significant position, and Mayor Koch did bring him back, but that didn't last too long, either. He was hard to place: friends would get him job interviews, and he'd ask his prospective employers what they'd do if he caught them doing wrong. When he retired, six years of his city service were cut out of his pension, in a dispute over whether they counted as NYPD time. As of this writing, it is still being litigated. The Job was not his friend.

Sonny Grosso and Eddie Egan were split up in 1967 and sent to precinct detective squads in Harlem and Brooklyn, respectively. They were celebrities then, and when the movie came out, they were stars. Aside from the predictable jealousies that fame and presumed wealth provoked, the hard-charging, rule-breaking, smack-'em-around-and-figure-it-out-later Popeye Doyle was the exact opposite of the image Commissioner Murphy wanted to project for the NYPD. Egan was as good a street cop as the NYPD ever produced, and Sonny told me, "He was the first through the door and the first to the bar. Perps in the cells used to brag about getting locked up by him."

Eddie and Sonny both began to moonlight in the movie business, one as an actor, the other as a consultant and later a successful producer. On the Job, their paths diverged less sharply, but all the same Sonny moved ahead steadily, while Eddie occasionally stumbled. He still made cases and collars, but the glory days were behind him; moreover, there was far more paperwork in the Detective Bureau than in Narcotics, and Eddie could barely spell. Most aggressive cops find themselves the subject of allegations of wrongdoing, and more than a few such claims surfaced about Egan. None of them was ever substantiated, but when he put in for retirement, he was hit with a slew of paper violations to stall his departure, while Internal Affairs continued to investigate. Chris Borgen, a Narcotics cop who worked with Egan and later became a TV reporter, said of him, "He's crazy, he's a fanatic, but honest he is. He just has no use for the dumb regulations, and no time for them. He nearly broke up Grosso's family because he kept on calling up at three o'-clock in the morning saying, 'Sonny, we got to meet an informant,' and Grosso would go with him. He's a completely gung-ho cop. He loves being a cop. All he cares about is the Police Department."

Egan had been made a first-grade detective with less than four years on the Job, a record-breaking achievement. On the day before his Department hearing, he was summarily flopped to patrolman. He appeared in the trial room in his ill-fitting uniform, backed by supporters who included Roy Scheider, who played Sonny in the movie, and William Friedkin, who directed it. Egan was found guilty of various procedural infractions, as was expected, even though Murphy himself had since abolished some of them as onerous and wasteful. The judge gave him the maximum penalty—twenty days for each of the two sets of charges—and the matter was forwarded to the Commissioner. Murphy tried to fire him. After all, there had to be something, -

didn't there? Wasn't a cop like him who wasn't caught taking money simply too smart to be nabbed? And with all the Hollywood money, how would they be able to tell the clean cash from the dirty? Wasn't it safe to assume he's a bad guy and cut him loose? As it happened, Egan had made a total of $3,900 for all his work on the book and the movie. Though he was eventually reinstated, when he left the Job he owed back rent, owned a seven-year-old car, and had a bank balance of $89.79. Egan found some work as an actor, usually playing a cop, like an old gunslinger who retired to perform in Wild West shows. He ran a detective agency that failed, and a bar in Florida called The Lauderdale Connection. Egan died in 1995, at the end of my first year on the Job. Though he had his pension, he was broke at the end, and pretty much always in between. When he died, his latest wife was going to cremate him, but Sonny brought him back up from Florida and paid for his funeral, and arranged for a Marine Corps color guard to send him off. The Job was not his friend, either.

It was a radical moment for me, the awakening instinct that where I'd arrived was not a detour or a derailment but the intended destination all along. Should I ever have expected to fit in? I was unusual in my education and my side job but typical in my background, and common enough in the enjoyment and drive with which I worked. Only part of my problems had to do with my extracurriculars, and when I look back at the legends of the 1970s, most of them left the Job with the taste of ashes in their mouths. Maybe Sonny came to believe that it was a tragedy how the world had changed, because New York had reached a point in history where cop killers were treated better than cops, and maybe Serpico came to believe that the tragedy was that the world would never change, because the real culprits were not held to account. But both viewpoints as I imagine them sprung from a deep conviction that justice in New York City depended on the political courage of the NYPD, and these men feared that it was lacking.

In February of 1999, that sense of urgency began to awaken again in the city, with a degree of divided passions that had not been seen in decades. I came into work one morning and Angelo Ricci, our union delegate, began to pass the word: "There was a shooting in the Four-Three. Street Crime killed a guy, no gun on him. It doesn't look good." Four cops from the Street Crime Unit, who had been deployed there to search for the same rapist we'd hunted the last summer, had approached a man who was standing by a dark lobby. Many victims had been taken from lobbies, and more assaults had occurred in that neighborhood than in any other area. When the cops told the man to put his hands up, he withdrew into the lobby and reached to his waistband, and one of the cops thought he saw a gun and called out, and another of them tripped and fell as the gunfire began, leading the others to believe he'd been shot. In all, the cops fired forty-one times, and the man they killed, a West African immigrant named Amadou Diallo, was unarmed. He had apparently been reaching for his wallet. The encounter had taken place over a matter of seconds. When the cops realized what they'd done, one of them crouched down by the body and wept.

In the days afterward, the street static was heavy: the punks and the drunks were loudest, as always, but there was a palpable anger among legitimate people as well. The facts as they emerged didn't seem to favor the cops: Diallo had lied about political persecution on his immigration form, but he'd otherwise led a blameless and harmless life, earning a meager living as a street peddler downtown, though his family in his native Guinea were prominent and moneyed. The forty-one shots became a public fixation, cited as proof of the extravagant violence of the NYPD, and the Street Crime Unit in particular. Its motto—"We Own the Night"—was seen as a vigilante boast, though the logo in its entirety centered around a decidedly unmacho picture of an elderly woman walking in safety. (The old woman was an undercover cop, a reference to the decoy work of the unit's early days.) Though cops debated the tactics and the training of the four officers among themselves, there was little doubt that they had acted without malice, in the belief of a hideous necessity, the defense of their own and their partners' lives. Anyone who has had to challenge strangers on the rooftops and in the alleys of this city, who has confronted the furtive or forthright menace of sudden movement by half-seen hands, knows that instant of decision when gunshots can echo through a lifetime—whether that lifetime will last for a moment or decades. And few who had been there rushed to judgment.

Mayor Giuliani cautioned against a quick decision in the matter, which contrasted with his generally established manner. He had never enjoyed significant black support, having lost and then won in two bitter campaigns against David Dinkins, New York's first black mayor. The issues to which his administration was dedicated—crime and public order, welfare reform and cutting taxes—pitted him squarely against the left-liberal political establishment, which encompassed most of the city and almost all of its minority leadership. His style was combative and personal, and he gained enemies even as his support grew, winning a second term decisively as the city enjoyed such peace and prosperity as could barely have been imagined in my lifetime. Though the prosperity was concentrated in white Manhattan, the lion's share of the peace dividend went to nonwhite neighborhoods like the ones where I worked. The homicide rate had peaked at more than two thousand a year during Dinkins's term, and in the year of Diallo it would continue its dive, to about seven hundred.

In the public mind, Giuliani was not just the commander-in-chief of the NYPD, but a kind of incarnation of it—cops were seen as virtual mini-Giulianis. For six years, our successes were such that our association won both parties the reputation as the gold standard in their professions: he was the Big City Mayor, we were the Big City Cops. After Diallo, the next national news story from New York became the expected contest for Senate between the Mayor and First Lady Hillary Rodham Clinton, and Democratic leaders spoke openly of the need to transform his chief political asset into a liability. The theme that the price was too high, that Giuliani had "unleashed" the police, and "condoned" brutality for the sake of order, had been picked up by the opposition, which came to include most Democrats and much of the media, *The New York Times* included. The allegations flew in the face of all evidence: civilian complaints were down, and Commissioner Howard Safir, who succeeded Bratton, had fired more cops than his two predecessors combined. New York City cops shot people less often than in any other big city, and they shot people far less often than they had during the Dinkins Administration, and in the overwhelming majority of cases where they did shoot, there were unambiguous findings of justification. These facts were ignored and belittled, and Giuliani's reliance on them was even held up as evidence of his heartless and penny-wise indifference to the feelings of people of color. The Mayor and the cops never denied that Diallo's death was a tragedy, or that it mattered greatly, in human terms, but what it would come to mean in political ones would astonish everyone in the city.

You might have thought a lot of things by reading the papers then. You might have thought that the Dinkins Administration was a golden age of police-community relations, instead of the culmination of the crack wars and race riots such as those in Crown Heights. You might have thought that demagogues like Reverend Al Sharpton had become thoughtful and credible, when, as recently as 1995, he had made a vitriolic speech outside a Jewish-owned department store in Harlem, in which he used the words "the Jew" and "the enemy" interchangeably, and one man in his audience firebombed the building, killing seven people. And you might have thought that Giuliani's robust embrace of the NYPD would have made cops his most loyal supporters.

Before Diallo, the major police scandal of the Giuliani Administration had been the rape of Abner Louima by PO Justin Volpe, on the midnights in the Seven-O, in Brooklyn. Volpe thought Louima had punched him in the face, following a brawl outside a nightclub. After Louima was arrested, Volpe shoved a stick up his rectum in the precinct bathroom, causing major internal damage. The outcry in the incident's aftermath was fierce but relatively brief: an atrocity was alleged, and decisive action was taken. The assault was an aberration in every sense of the word, as even the harshest critics of the police would likely concede. Cops rightly took issue with certain aspects of the case—from the lies of the victim (his teeth were not knocked out by cops) to the ruthless zeal of the prosecutors, who dragged both the fiancée and father of one of the defendants before the Grand Jury—but on the Job, you heard little protest beyond a weak and wishful hope that it just wasn't so, it wasn't one of us. And cops knew that all was not what it appeared to be when it was claimed that one of Louima's alleged assailants had bragged, "It's Giuliani time!" Such a boast was as likely to come from a crack dealer in Bed-Stuy as a New York City police officer.

For years, the same moment of low comedy was repeated thousands of times in station houses, when a perp spat out his hatred for the Mayor to the cop who'd brought him in, expecting the provocation to be on the order of an insult to motherhood. The perp always had a look of beautiful confusion on his face when the cop shrugged and said, "That much I agree with you—I don't like him either."

The great achievement of the Giuliani Administration was the cut in the crime rate, and its instrument was the NYPD. Public safety laid the foundation for public prosperity, and cops could also be proud of their contribution to the city's recent and abundant wealth. And yet the NYPD didn't share in the reward: they were paid less than their counterparts in almost every large city in the country, though the cost of living was higher here than almost anywhere else. Cops in suburban counties like Nassau and Suffolk made nearly twice what we did, but cops in inarguably poorer jurisdictions, like Newark, New Jersey, also had salaries that were nearly 30 percent higher. We were partly to blame, in that the best that could be said of our union, the PBA, was that it was blind to the appearance of impropriety. One of our lawyers was caught gambling with union money, but when he was disbarred, he returned to work for us as a consultant, at still higher fees. None of the indifference and incompetence of the old union would have mattered much, had they secured for their members a decent raise, but after two years without a contract, the final settlement was a five-year package with small raises for three years, and no raise for two. There was an insurrection among the rank and file, and a new leader named Pat Lynch took over the union, but the damage had already been done. Giuliani had supported the police in every way but one, and for that, cops felt not just disappointed but betrayed. If there was any constituency in New York more alienated from the Administration than blacks, it was cops.

If Giuliani won the Senate race, he would be gone from Gracie Mansion the next year; if he didn't, he would go the year after that. The cops would remain to suffer the consequences of the Diallo furor for years to come. Most viewed the protests as highly dubious, mixing the well-intentioned with the plainly hostile and the occasionally surreal. Many commentators denounced the cops at these demonstrations for being deployed in "riot gear," which meant nightsticks and helmets. But cops always carry nightsticks, and the sole purpose of a helmet is defensive; I still can't figure out why the desire to avoid a head injury is such a grossly provocative act. Sometimes there would be five stories on the news about Diallo before there was mention of our sort-of-war against Serbia. We were daily witnesses to a search for truth led by Reverend Sharpton, whose first stop on his "national tour against police brutality" was at the headquarters of the Nation of Islam, which holds that white people were accidentally created in a laboratory by a pumpkin-headed demon. Diallo's mother joined him on his crusade, which was broadened in theme to denounce the police throughout the United States. Though Mrs. Diallo's loss was profound and her intentions were doubtless sincere, her own nation was a human-rights disaster—Amnesty International reported that an opposition leader was jailed because a police official had a dream that he would try to overthrow the state. Mrs. Diallo's grief was understandable, and Reverend Sharpton's stunts were predictable, but what was new in recent memory was how established figures and organizations were roused as much as the rabble. Politicians and union leaders, celebrities and clergy joined with racial radicals, ex-cons, and gang members for marches and photo-op arrests, as pundits intoned solemnly that the NYPD represented the most profound threat to peace in the city. The most astonishing assertions went unchallenged and unchecked, such as when Mayor David Dinkins blithely announced on a television news interview that the police would have opened fire on the young daughter of Bronx Borough President Fernando Ferrer, had she failed to obey their orders to stop her car. Was this where the healing would begin?

As the Diallo protest movement gathered force, it could still be argued that talk of a "crisis" in race relations in the city was overblown or premature, though the protesters labored long and hard to create one. There certainly was a crisis in the Police Department, in the soft science of morale but also in the hard figures of recruitment and retention. The coming years would see the retirement of one-quarter of the NYPD as the big hires of the early 1980s reached the twenty-year mark; other cops retired earlier, to take jobs in other jurisdictions, or to get out of the business altogether. There was great difficulty in filling the new classes in the Academy, and the valedictorian of one class quit the day after graduation, to take a job in Suffolk. Recently raised standards would be lowered again, and though the quality of recruits was defended by City Hall, one cop at Applicant Investigations told me that they were taking "just about everyone without a felony conviction." The Diallo protesters also blasted the NYPD for its lack of diversity, in that it was roughly two-thirds white in a city that was less than half white. But despite the failure of a ten-million-dollar advertising campaign targeted at non-whites, there was no crisis as such in "minority" hiring, either—Hispanic cops were roughly proportional to the Hispanic population, and I'd guess that officers named Gonzalez will become the kind of cultural cliché in the next century that patrolmen named Murphy were for the last two. The recruiting crisis faced by the NYPD was specifically in hiring black males, who made up less than 10 percent of the Department. But when Mayor Dinkins narrated a TV commercial showing a small black boy living in terror of the police, it was hard to envision how that made a practical contribution to solving the problem.

It may be overreaching to say that this feverish attention to scandal caused physical harm to cops—even when cops were gunned down by the dozens in the early 1970s, there were other forces at work—but it might not be, either. Who knows how many extra cinder blocks flew from rooftops at that time, or how many people watched from their windows as a cop struggled with a perp, and decided not to call 911 for help? When the rhetoric of scandal—rogue cops, racist cops, and so on—becomes the received idea, when we are so engrossed by exceptions that they seem like rules, we still send cops out, in ones and twos, into angry crowds, fighting families, and darkened alleys, though stripped of a measure of defense.

I wondered if Amadou Diallo died because the NYPD thought too little of the South Bronx, or too much. Whenever I heard about the forty-one shots, I thought about the fifty-one women raped. At the time of Diallo, there were just under two murders a day in New York City. Seven years before, there had been more than six. Four killings a day, mostly of men of color—some as blameless as Diallo, some not—were no longer facts of life here. The police tactics that saved these lives, from the "quality of life" crackdown and "stop and frisk" policies to cameras in housing projects to the very existence of the Street Crime Unit, which took in almost a thousand guns the year before—guns that were in play, in waistbands and in cars—had been opposed with shrill vigor by most of the protest leaders. The homicides that occurred around me rarely made the news, and of the hundred-odd murders that took place in the South Bronx that year, I doubt if ten victims were mentioned by name in the papers. In editorials, the debate was framed as a rift between the people who cared about the body count and the people who simply cared.

It is a relief, after all, that you can't care every time someone dies. But it can be chilling to see how people choose between the symbol and the statistic, passing over one death as an incident while elevating another to an issue. The Bronx DA personally arraigned the four cops who shot Diallo on murder charges, stating that his presence was necessary to send a message in the case—his second such act in his ten-year term of office, the first being for the Happy Land social-club killer, whose act of arson led to eighty-seven deaths. But police officers have also been killed in the line of duty in his jurisdiction during his term, and his absence at their killers' arraignments now takes on a symbolic weight.

A month after Diallo, we went to the funeral for Matthew Dziergowski, a cop in Staten Island who was killed when he drove into the path of a vehicle that was speeding toward his partners, who were at the site of a jackknifed truck. When you go to a police funeral, your job is to stand there for hours, at ease and then at attention, then at ease, then at attention again. That day was cold and rainy, which heightened the gloom of the occasion. The thick blue wool of our reefer jackets soaked up the cold water, and our feet went numb in our black patent-leather shoes. And I doubt I was alone in feeling sorry for myself, at times, and then feeling a little ashamed, for dwelling on my small and passing discomforts at such a tragic scene. When the hearse approached us, in our formed ranks, we raised white-gloved hands in salute. As the rest of the cortege filed past, I noticed that in the first cars, the limousines with family and close friends, no one looked out at us. Behind the rain-beaded windows, the faces looked down, or straight ahead, and several held their heads in their hands. Amid the hundreds who had come for the funeral, they remained alone in their loss. But as more and more cars went by, the focus of the passengers' attention seemed to shift outward, and the faces inside gazed at the ranks of blue. Their distance from the death—a matter of a few emotional degrees—let them take in the larger spectacle of mourning and tribute, which can have a power, in time, to comfort and to heal. Perspective is a blessing, and it can be had with a glance through the window.

I don't know much about the family of Matthew Dziergowski, but I'd guess that they cared as much about the color of the man who killed him as the color of his car. There are times it seems to matter, and times it doesn't. Two of the three cops who died in the line of duty the year before were black, Gerard Carter and Sean Carrington. Both were killed by black men, and in Carter's case, his killer was a teenager who had killed two men prior to that, both also black. The Urban League had published a report on cities that stated that one out of every three black men in their twenties was in prison, on parole, or on probation. It is a devastating number, and a national disgrace, and I haven't got the least idea about what to do about it, except for my job—which some would charge is part of the problem. Because the issues of crime and race—when they belong together, and when they do not—draw such awful and vociferous attention, too many people keep a kind of silence on these matters that is not entirely honorable, either.

There is an exercise I have seen a number of times in department training, which the instructor sets up by calling up a number of cops, black and white, from the audience. First, the instructor takes a black cop and makes him put his hands up on a wall, while two white cops flank him. "What do we have here?" the instructor asks. Several in the audience call out, "a collar" or "a stop." The instructor then puts a white cop on the wall, with two black cops holding him there. Laughter breaks out from the crowd, because no one wants to say "a mugging." The first lesson, of course, is of the power and danger of these stereotypes, which is of paramount concern to minority cops who work in plainclothes. But in watching the audience, I also noticed that the reactions tended to be the same across the color line, that black, white, and Hispanic cops tended to have the same reactions, of matter-of-fact nods for the first scenario and chastened laughter for the second. Over time and in the main, cops tend to think like other cops. One of the largely overlooked findings of the Kerner Commission, which studied urban unrest and decay in the late 1960s, was that black people said that black cops treated them no better than white ones did; they supported minority hiring strictly as an employment opportunity, without expectations of improved police-community relations.

We are responsible for our actions, to be sure, but our perceptions are formed in a long and often passive process. In street encounters, you have to remind yourself: *You never know.* But this wariness about exception suggests that there are, if not rules, terribly regular events that you learn to recognize, ever more quickly in time: *You know what you know.*

One day that spring, when we were bossless again, that lesson was repeated for me. The team was split up to fill in with sectors and conditions cars, and I worked with a team of seven other cops—all nonwhite, as it happens. We swept a lobby that was a steady crack spot, without success. As we filed out through the back door, a crackhead approached, a skinny white guy who was almost theatrically dirty, like a chimney sweep in a musical. He froze as he saw us, his relief at avoiding arrest spoiled by the realization that his pipe would remain empty, at least for a while. "The spot's shut down," I said. "If you want crack, come back in an hour, or try a block over." He about-faced and left, joining up with two other white guys, who hovered in the middle of the project grounds. They were not street people: they were younger, cleaner, and bigger, and they could not have stood out more if they were wearing tuxedos or cowboy hats. Because of their race, they could only be cops or criminals—and shabby amateurs, regardless—but they couldn't be just *people*. The three drifted off together. Several of us asked at once, "Are they cops?" I was instantly impressed by the idea of the crackhead as undercover, marveling at his mastery of disguise. I knew that white undercovers were rarely used in this area, but this was an operative of such surpassing skill that he could pick where he worked. The other two spoiled the scenario, however—even if a white undercover was in play, he would never have white "ghosts," deployed to discreetly follow him. But then one of the other cops said that he saw a radio in a back pocket, he was sure they were police. And then I wondered if they were with some other agency, and I shuddered to think of what state or federal group worked with the subtlety of the Bulgarian secret service. We stayed to watch them, more out of curiosity than the expectation of a collar. The two coppish guys began a series of lethargic migrations, back and forth across the grounds, from building to building. When they finally walked off, we rolled up on them, and all visual ambiguity disappeared at around twenty-five yards—and a strong olfactory read became available at ten. They drooled, they stank, their eyes rolled like dice, but in the distance and the dark, most of us had taken them for colleagues.

The history of race, the idea of race, is largely one of irrationality and cruelty, and there is no reason to expect that suddenly to change. When I hear black people complain about historic prejudice that endures in many and often not subtle ways, I tend to agree; and when I hear white people complain about set-asides and preferences intended not so much to keep them out but to bring others in, but having the same effect, I tend to nod along with them as well. I can be one hell of an agreeable guy, so much so that when a black cop said that I was one of the few white people she'd let in her house, I may have been more flattered than I should have been. I have been to see a judge, in plainclothes, with Orville, when he was told by a court officer that informants had to wait outside. And I remember reading about a black cop who was hired in spite of a robbery conviction, during a rushed drive to hire minorities. There is a troubled middle ground that most people occupy, myself included, where you shrug things off in order to be able to sleep at night, even if it means you're signing up for more tomorrow. You pick your battles, take small steps. As a cop, you have to take things day by day, case by case: if you collar a wife-beater or a dope dealer, you think about the household or the corner that is a little safer, for now, without dwelling on whether you've made some lasting contribution to the crusades against drugs or domestic violence—let alone whether these crusades are envisioned and equipped as they should be. And I thank God, or whatever party is responsible, that big-picture policy making on hot-button issues is outside the job description of a New York City police officer. It's easy to forget sometimes.

· · ·

IT MAKES ME LAUGH—A LITTLE BIT, FROM A DISTANCE— that as that miserable winter turned to miserable springtime, the only harmony we had on the SNEU team was racial harmony. If nothing else, it was a reminder that things can always get worse. After my last warrant, I didn't fight anymore. I noted the periodic explosions with scientific detachment, observing that the screaming matches between the Sergeant and one or more of us seemed to happen every six weeks, at first, and then every four. All the little things that bothered us before—the sudden changes of schedule, the increasing demands for collars, the diminishing support—became less bearable because there was nothing more to fight for. We'd begun to process our collars at the PSA again, but with our recent difficulties, we realized we were treated better as guests in other precincts than we were in our own house.

We went out to collar, or we didn't. One day, we had to wait so long for the van that finally we didn't leave the office. The Sergeant later told us that we were almost evicted from the room we'd built, but he'd managed to save us. None of us quite believed him. The remark also reminded us that our little corner of the precinct, which we'd built with our own hands—and our own money—could be taken away on a whim. When our numbers were down, the Sergeant told us that he might be thrown off the team himself, which - didn't exactly spur us into fits of activity. We volunteered for dull errands that would have been insults before, like radio repair, making a day of it. The radio repair shop was in Jamaica, Queens, and if we went, Stix would call his wife, who would call her grandmother, who would walk to the corner poultry market and have a chicken killed. She was a tiny woman who spoke only Italian, and she made everything herself—cheeses, roast peppers—and in the basement of her house, homemade sausage hung from the ceiling and the shelves were stacked with bottles of homemade wine. If something had to go to Headquarters or the Academy, we'd volunteer, driving slowly.

Still, we worked out of self-respect, and we worked because we liked it, not least because it provided a few head-clearing hours in which our opponents were plain and the fight was almost fair. The fact that good work would reflect well on the Sergeant became a bewildering disincentive—it was the only poor power we had.

The Captain told the Sergeant to "do something with the kites"—the complaints of drug sales called in, that patrol could not respond to—since so many were in public housing. The most that might have been accomplished was that had we randomly arrested an individual who happened to live in a kite location, the Narcotics cop assigned—if we knew who he or she was— could have arguably closed that case. I pointed out that the vast majority of the kites were for apartments, which the *Street* Narcotics Enforcement Unit was not even permitted to address. Orders were orders, however, and for a couple of weeks, we were obliged to generate still more pointless paperwork for investigations that we were unable to conduct ourselves. Eventually, we stopped bothering. The wall maps were a source of pride for the new Sergeant, so I took to coloring in lots more public housing—random blocks, at first, but eventually Yankee Stadium, the Bronx Zoo, and even islands in the East River became housing projects, by the stroke of my pen. Maybe it was a way for the world to become ours again.

The dreary Team Meetings continued: "The old man loves the walls. . . ."

"The old man loves the kites. . . ."

"From now on, we start our tour here, okay, Ed?"

"What happened yesterday can never happen again. . . ."

"Our days off are being changed—this is straight from upstairs, my hands are tied. . . ."

"We were this close to losing the room—I fought for you guys, tooth and nail. I can take an ass-chewing with the best of 'em. . . ."

When we did make it out, many of the unexpected moments of amazement or hilarity now took on grim and cautionary tones. Maybe it was because we cared less and let our guard down, or maybe it was that when we did care more, our trust in our judgment was more instinctive and complete. One day, John, Alicia, and I grabbed a crackhead, bent and scrawny but full of manic energy, who pushed away from us, hiding something in his hand. We knew it was probably drugs, but it could have been a razor, and he continued to resist, screaming that he'd just had back surgery even as he demonstrated surprising strength and agility. I held myself in check even when I knocked him down; after Alicia maced him, I cuffed him somewhat loosely, as he shuddered and howled about his ruptured discs. In the van, he began to rub his face against the seat, and I told him to sit still. He shrieked at me, "You shouldn't worry about how I'm sitting! You should worry about what's important! You should worry I got out of my cuffs! You're lucky I'm not a bad guy, I took my pills today, I'm not so crazy!"

And then he showed how he had freed his hands.

"You're right, that is important," I said. He had tiny wrists, bent thumbs, and his arm had been twisted around. This time, he got less slack, and within twenty minutes—one perp later—he began to scream again about his back, slamming his head against the window with his whole weight behind him. I thought the window would break, so we called it a day and took them in. Later, he told Tony that he didn't even have back problems; he just didn't want to ride around in the van for the next couple of hours.

There was one small consolation. When John took each perp's name for the paperwork, he turned away and said, "Oh! No!"

Alicia looked over and smiled brightly: "Another two numbers for Wopstat!"

Another night, we worked in light snow and gale-force winds. I always thought bad-weather work was better, since the perps were sloppy, anxious to unload their stash and head home. John and Chicky took rooftop OPs for the crack strip on Park Avenue, One-Five-Six to One-Five-Eight, the tall red projects of Jackson Houses, the taller concrete ones of Morrisania Air Rights, which were known as "Vietnam." The Sergeant got in my car without asking, which I took as an unwanted peace offering. The small talk we made was small indeed that day, but the set was busy: the first guy I took was on a bike, and the wind almost knocked us both down. When I rode his bike to drop it off at his apartment, two blocks away, I almost sailed there. The seller was in a car, and he hit off another buyer in a car, who drove up to One-Five-Eight before cutting left to Morris, where he was stuck at a light. We came up behind him, out of the line of sight of the seller, and we jumped out of my car, leaving it running. I took the driver out at gunpoint as the Sergeant approached from the passenger side, when the OP called out:

"The seller's moving, he's coming up your way!"

We didn't want the seller to see the stop, but the storm made the visibility poor and we had already committed to the act; beyond that, when the seller leaves, the set's done. The Sergeant yelled out, "We gotta move or the set is blown!" He ordered the driver back in the car and jumped in beside him. My car was still running, twenty feet behind. I wasn't going to get in a car with a crackhead who hadn't been checked for weapons and drive off into the snow. I also didn't want to leave my car. As their car began to move around the corner, I edged forward, keeping a midpoint distance between the two vehicles, watching both. Four facts occurred to me, in such bald clarity that they almost seemed numbered on a list:

1. I like my car.
2. I don't like my sergeant.
3. If I lose my sergeant, the Job will give me another one.
4. If I lose my car, the Job won't. . . .ž

And as I stayed put, I also thought, "What are you gonna say if the Sergeant is hurt? When they ask, 'Why weren't you in the car with him?'" That, too, came easily, and I answered myself as I would have answered them: "Because I'm not an idiot, that's why."

Buyer and seller were both taken without incident, however, and we went back in. The Sergeant went to the SNEU room to study for the lieutenant's test as we got to work. When John asked me where the drugs were, I told him to ask the boss, who held on to the evidence more often than not. John went downstairs and was told, "Ask Eddie." After John said that I didn't have them, the Sergeant began to yell for everyone to report immediately for a Team Meeting, on the subject of lost narcotics. They weren't lost, of course—Alicia had them, but John hadn't asked her yet—we never had and never did lose any product, but the Sergeant made us stop everything to listen to a ten-minute tantrum before he stomped out and went home.

In its way, his leaving was a kindness. Other bosses were forced to consider that SNEU's problems might be with management instead of labor. The desk officer had been barking at us to hurry up and get the perps out, but now he had to sign all our paperwork; two other sergeants were divided as to whether I should voucher the seller's car as evidence used in the commission of a crime or under asset forfeiture. We also had the buyer's car, and I'd locked the keys inside. He was a social worker at a hospital, and his ex-wife, with whom he still lived, was there to pick it up. She brought their four-year-old child along, and she explained that the back seat was loaded with groceries. John sat with her, feeding her lines to catcall to me: "We're waiting, Ed, you could be a little better organized. You didn't lose the keys, did you? Well? Where are they?"

I finally recovered them, and made a mental note to have a laugh at John's expense the next time the shit began to land on him. I didn't have to wait long, but I took no pleasure when it came: I worked through the night and into the next day, writing up the collar and taking the seller's car to the pound on the docks of Brooklyn. As the team came in for the four-to-twelve, I was leaving the precinct. The Sergeant ordered everyone into uniform and out on footposts, in punishment for our misbehavior the night before.

Though nothing bothered me as much as the vicious circus in the precinct, the cracked-out streets were not always a balm for the nerves. One day, when the Sergeant was out, Sgt. Rhoden covered us. We always worked harder then, hoping that someone might notice that we did better without our own boss. Tony and I caught a woman who ate her slabs of crack when we stopped her. Though we would have let her go, she decided to make a scene in the street, drawing a crowd, screaming that we planted drugs on her, that we raped people with broom handles—thanks again, Volpe—that we were racist white crackheads—Tony, too, apparently—and that she'd never been arrested. She finished by bellowing that she was pregnant and that she was going to sue us. That did it for me: I put my life in the hands of God every day, but I would never put a nickel on the table against a pregnant lady before a Bronx jury. As I put the cuffs on her, she screamed at the crowd that I'd stolen her food stamps. When I took her in, it began another twenty-four-hour odyssey that I dubbed Operation Lying Whore.

We filled the van, and took in bodies till we ran out of handcuffs—reasoning that seven would be a respectable number, eight would be a matter of principle, and ten would be a slap in the face. My collar was only the second, so poor Sammy and Orville had to listen to her rant for the next two hours till we came in. The perps were a loopy bunch—I told one to raise his hands while we searched him, and he began to pirouette, spinning around until the crack popped out of his pocket. Another tried to eat it as we approached, and I flattened him.

"Is it a hit?"

"Yeah, it's a hit."

My perp maintained her rage, hitting her high notes of Justin Volpe and stolen food stamps and miscarriage and lawsuits. The name of Volpe made us cringe. "He wasn't a cop," John said. She threatened to piss in the cell and demanded to go to the hospital. She looked me straight in the eye and said, "I never had any drugs. I would never do anything to hurt my baby." If I'd never met her, I'd have believed her.

When she returned from the hospital, hours later, I read the doctor's report: "Patient warned of potentially fatal danger of ingesting cocaine; patient denies ingestion. Patient complains of wrist pain from handcuffs and is given Tylenol. Patient claims to be three months pregnant but states that she plans termination."

I went home in the morning to shower and change before coming back in. As expected, most of the charges were dropped, but the ADA gave me a sympathetic ear on Trespass and False Personation, a relatively new misdemeanor which forbids giving a false name and address when in police custody. My prospects brightened considerably when I saw her rap sheet, which listed twenty-seven priors for prostitution and resisting arrest, with multiple variations on the names Tracy Johnson and Lisa Smith, neither of which was the name she gave me. Still, I reckoned that a Bronx jury might have at least as many whore buffs as cop buffs. And unless I had some kind of conviction for this arrest, I would most assuredly lose in civil court—when the DA declines prosecution, it has the effect of sending a telegram to a civil jury that the cop was flat-out wrong. The DA told me I needed proof that she was trespassing, in the form of an affidavit from the landlord, or I needed to prove who the woman who claimed to be both Lisa Johnson and Tracy Smith really was. At the Four-O, the affidavits were locked in an office, and no one had the key. There was a loose pile of out-of-date affidavits, in no particular order, that could cover a square mile of tenements. A cop who helped me at the Four-O shook his head before giving up, muttering, "If I saw how this place works when I was young, I would have turned to a life of crime, no question."

The search for the Lying Whore's true identity was equally exhausting, though a birth certificate she had used to apply for an apartment was finally obtained. I was relieved but also disgusted, as I might have found Jimmy Hoffa with all the effort it took. That spring, there were cops who made collars for guns and homicides, who took out savage gangs and sophisticated international conspiracies, but I have a feeling that years from now, when I sit down to tell war stories with other old veterans, I can say, "Those cases were all interesting and good in their way, fellas, but let me tell you about Operation Lying Whore. Very few people knew about it at the time, of course. . . ."

I'd had a trial for a minor but aggravating case, in which a drunk was having an argument with his wife, and she called the cops, but he wouldn't let us in. When we finally forced our way in, he fought us and gave one cop a lump on the head. The perp had screamed nonstop for six hours after his arrest: every white cop was a racist, every Hispanic cop was really white, and every black cop was a faggot. He spat at us in the cell and banged his head against the wall, yelling, "I want bruises!" He filed a complaint with the Civilian Complaint Review Board prior to his criminal trial, and after it, a civil lawsuit would doubtless follow, again in front of a Bronx jury. We had acted properly and the perp was on parole for armed robbery; nonetheless, everyone seemed confident of defeat.

The DA had already reduced the charges to Attempted Assault 3, the lowest level of misdemeanor, punishable by up to thirty days in jail. My ADA explained that even though the charges were less, at this level the defendant was not entitled to a jury trial, and they had greater hope for a fair hearing from a judge. In the Bronx, the conviction rate had dipped below 50 percent, and for misdemeanors it was even worse, as juries often didn't take the accusations seriously. I asked the ADA, "Do you ever prosecute jurors for perjury? Because it seems that every day, people swear under oath that they will listen to the evidence, and then they set out to sabotage these cases that can take years to put together."

"Well," she said, "we did prosecute the forewoman of one jury, not long ago. She was in the middle of a trial, and she asked the judge for a day off, because she said she had a doctor's appointment. A court officer noticed her in the building—she was a defendant in another case, and her trial started that day."

"That's a good one," I said.

During voir dire, the interviews for jury selection, each person is asked under oath about their experience with the criminal justice system, as defendant or victim, but usually not even the most elementary effort is made to corroborate those claims. One ADA told me about inheriting a murder case, after the first jury deadlocked. He checked the raps for the jurors and found that four had criminal records. None of those jurors were prosecuted. Nor was it policy to prosecute defense witnesses who were demonstrably lying— by providing false alibis, for example—because, as another ADA told me, if they win the case, they don't bother, and if they lose, "it looks like sour grapes." A cop told me about a brawl at court one day, when he saw court officers tackle a man who tried to escape from the Grand Jury. An undercover was testifying about a buy when the juror recognized him as someone he had sold to. Another cop told me about locking up a woman for buying crack, who begged for a Desk Appearance Ticket, because she had to get back to court, for jury duty—she was the forewoman on a Narcotics case, of course. The worst part about these stories is that when I told them to various ADAs, none were at all surprised; most of those I'd worked with I respected, but the institutionalized expectations were abysmal. They were too used to losing, and it showed in how they played the game.

At the trial of the drunken cop-puncher, however, the ADA surprised me on the stand by asking me where I went to college. As it would have been perjury to answer "Howard," I told the truth, and the perp took a plea. I'd have to tell my mother that my Harvard diploma had not been earned in vain, but in fact had proved essential to winning a conviction for Disorderly Conduct in the Bronx.

The lunacy reached such levels that you had no choice but to enjoy it sometimes, and maybe to add your bit now and then. When you went sick, you had two choices. You could go Regular Sick, which meant you had to see the District Surgeon on the next tour, who would determine when you had to come back, either for limited assignment or full duty. If you'd broken a leg, you'd get a couple of weeks off and a couple of weeks limited, working behind the desk or handing out radios. You could go Administrative Sick, for one or two days, without asking anyone, more or less, if you hadn't gone sick more than four times in a year. You called the precinct to notify a sergeant, and then you called the Sick Desk for a log number. But for some reason, when you called the Sick Desk, you couldn't say "I have a cold." The first time I called in with a cold, I was corrected: "You can't have a cold."

"But I have a cold. Why can't I have one?"

"We're not allowed to put that down. You have to say you have 'flu-like symptoms.'"

"Fine, I'll take it, put me down for a set of flu-like symptoms."

I didn't know what other diseases you were allowed to have, so for my next non-colds I tried out a variety of exotic ailments. The first one was Space Dementia, which Steve Buscemi had when his spaceship circled the comet in *Armageddon*. I think I identified with his inability to feel especially useful in saving the world from destruction. That got a laugh from a cop named Tommy Casey at the precinct, but it was recorded without irony at the Sick Desk. Maybe there was more of it going around than I thought. The next time, I went with Dutch elm disease, which, together with the gypsy moth, has wiped out many magnificent trees across the country. At the time, Dutch elm disease seemed a reasonable diagnosis because I certainly didn't feel like moving much. That one got by at the precinct, but I met unexpected resistance at the Sick Desk.

"I can't put it down that you have Dutch elm disease."

"Why can't you say I have Dutch elm disease?"

"You can't go Admin Sick with Dutch elm disease. You have to go Regular Sick."

"Right, I forgot. I guess I'll have 'flu-like symptoms.'"

"Okay, you got it. Hope you feel better."

And when my friend McTigue put in his papers to quit the NYPD to move to California, I advised him on his final illness. We'd had a few beers, and a death with dignity for him was not my highest concern, so I suggested that he call in with autoerotic asphyxia, a condition that results when self-pleasure and self-strangulation are combined, in the belief that oxygen debt heightens the climax. He called it in and got the days off, and he must have had a very bad case, because he never went back to work here again. Still, I talk to him often and he claims to feel fine.

• • •

OUR PERSONAL LIVES BEGAN TO TAKE CENTER PLACE AGAIN, as maybe they always should have. Stix was getting married, Orville's and Chicky's wives were having kids, Tony's mom was sick. I broke up with the girl I'd dated since the summer, when the Rape Detail had seemed an intolerable burden. Smacky left for Narcotics, finally, with the group that we all might have been a part of, when we were with PK. Alicia was thrown out of SNEU, after another Team Meeting was devoted to our shortcomings. She blew up at the Sergeant, yelling, "I do my job but I don't give a damn! I got my kids and my family! But these guys work too hard to be treated this way!" She had to be held back by us, and I don't doubt who would have won the fight. We began to talk about getting out.

Our career ambitions came to appear as not just a means of advancement, but a way of escape. But the sergeant's exam was given only every other year or so, and it might be another year or more before promotion; a transfer to a detective assignment, in the Squad or Narcotics, required them to need people and to want you, circumstances that often took years to coincide. John, Smacky, and Orville were determined to take the test; Tony, Stix, and I were determined not to, aspiring only for the detective's shield. I was determined not to step back: SNEU was our unit, not his, and he should go, not us. Sometimes, that seemed to be the likelihood, and that's why we stuck it out. Other times, I resolved that I would only accept being pushed up-and-out, but not back to patrol. I liked walking better than driving, but to walk again in the Village held no allure. And though the Village remained the biggest and busiest footpost, it had slowed down somewhat of late, which was good for - everyone there, but not for me: I'd be running between domestic disputes and "stuck-occupied" elevator jobs, with fewer guns and robberies to make it worthwhile. We'd missed the boat for Narcotics, and no other specialized unit was picking up cops, with one exception.

I decided to go to Street Crime. Tony and Orville had gone for two weeks, earlier in the fall, and they made a gun collar on their second or third night. Tony especially liked the gun hunt, the nocturnal and freestyle prowl, but he felt that he could not in conscience join full-time. His reasons were the same for his refusal to become an undercover—the work could be exhilarating, but the risks were too high for a man with a wife and child. Kevin Gillespie, a cop from Street Crime, had been killed during a carjacking in the Four-Six two years before; Chicky had been one of the first cops at the scene, and he didn't sleep well afterward. Tony knew Sean Carrington, another former Housing cop who'd gone to Narcotics, who had also been killed in the Four-Six. Tony was inclined against Street Crime before Diallo, and afterward it seemed ridiculous. John, too, had been drawn to the unit—his brother-in-law, Rob Reed, was assigned there, and he loved it. But he still blamed himself for PK's transfer from SNEU—and maybe he always would—and he was reluctant to expose himself to more risk. The four cops from Street Crime would go on trial for the murder of Diallo, and the unit was under investigation by Internal Affairs, the New York State Attorney General, and the Department of Justice, while politicians still clamored that they were "not being held accountable."

Even so, John agonized for a month over whether to apply with me, tilting one way and then the other before asking for more time, and then more, before finally declining. I began to have a deepening sympathy for his poor girlfriend, Julie, whom he'd dated for five years. John's reasons for not going were better than mine for going—he had a modest appreciation for how a split-second decision on the street can change things—but Street Crime worked for me in a number of ways: you had steady days off, and you worked from six at night to two in the morning. In my career so far, I'd worked a couple of years on a beat, a couple of years in SNEU, and so a couple of years on the gun hunt seemed to fit. As long as I had good partners, it offered far more fun and games than SNEU, with even bigger prizes: you wouldn't sit on a roof, looking for slabs and bundles, but instead drive all night, chasing guns. Search warrants would not be thrown away. Street Crime was not classified as an investigative assignment, and there would be no gold shield at the end of eighteen months. Whether or not that was well-planned or even fair, the result was that it drew cops for whom the work was its own reward. It was a guts-and-glory unit, and within the Job, some cops muttered the same complaints about them that police critics at large leveled against the NYPD. I thought it would suit me fine.

When I asked the Captain to sign my recommendation for transfer, he reacted as my mother might have if I told her I was joining the Foreign Legion. Now, it seemed, he wanted me to stay at PSA-7. But as usual, he packed his argument with as much stupidity as sense, claiming at one moment that the unit would be disbanded, and the next that I'd be stuck there for ten years with nothing to show for it—"And then you'll be sent back here." Throughout the speech, I'd interrupt, "But will you sign it?" He fumfered and told me to think about it over the weekend. When I pursued him again the next week, he signed the recommendation with a terse smile, but he omitted the section for the evaluation. When I dropped off the application at Street Crime, on

Randall's Island, they sent me back to the Captain, who referred me to the Admin lieutenant for a few lines of modest praise.

That day, I also got my first Command Discipline, for having "unauthorized off-duty employment." Though the magazine pieces had been approved by a Commissioner, I hadn't filled out forms at the command level. My punishment was the lightest possible—"warn and admonish"—but I was also perturbed at the thought that this could be considered a fortunate resolution. I'd told people how much I loved the NYPD, of its wonders and dangers, and I got off with a slap on the wrist.

You have to talk to people about these things. I had Tony, Orville, Stix, Sammy, Chicky, and John to talk to at work, and John even afterward. Aside from Inspector Mullen, my chief consigliere on the Job was Mike Shea, a friend and neighbor who was then a newly appointed captain. Mike was a distinctive figure, military in bearing, with a crew cut and wire-rimmed glasses, and even off duty, he wore a coat and tie. He had an MBA and a law degree, and had turned down a free year of graduate school at Harvard to study for the captain's test. In the event that working at, living with, and writing about the NYPD somehow wasn't enough, I'd have dinner with Mike for a little cop talk. Mike thought that Street Crime was an excellent idea—that I'd like the unit, and that I'd work well there. He also knew the CO and would make a call for me.

Cops explain a lot of things by saying, "He had a phone call," and the "hook" is a long-standing feature of Department lore. The comment was most often made when it looked like a cop was about to get in a lot of trouble but didn't, or got a prize assignment without working very long or hard for it. But being called a "son of a chief" wasn't the same as being called a "son of a bitch," and it was rarely held against a cop who was liked or respected. There was so much unfairness on the Job, so much undeserved aggravation, that an unearned break was accepted by most fair-minded cops, if only because they would accept such breaks themselves. I had a more nuanced view of the value of a real phone call—not a casual "Let me know if I can do anything for you," from a captain at a racket, or a "My uncle's old partner was best friends with the Commissioner's nephew"—but a true "contract," a deal. I thought of them as resembling Internet stocks more than blue chips, in that their worth varied wildly from one moment to the next and depended on circumstances which were largely out of your control.

My father was a master of the phone call. He met every Police Commissioner from the fifties through the eighties, but an entire generation had come and gone since he'd retired himself—the rookies of his last days had already packed for Florida. My uncle Joe would often mention how he just went to Ireland or Atlantic City with this Chief of Detectives or that Chief of Patrol, since retired, always ending the story with the line, "And he knew your father very well." My father was liked and respected, and he was around for a long time. Various friends had risen high: one friend, Andy Maloney, had become U.S. Attorney at the Eastern District, and he put John Gotti away for life; two others, John Sprizzo and Kevin Duffy, had become federal judges. And because my father had little ambition—at least of the conventional kind, preferring to remain a field agent for the entirety of his three-decade career—his influence was thus increased because he was not in competition with anyone at the FBI, and certainly not in the NYPD. He could take people to dinner at the Commuters and arrange for summer jobs for cops' kids at Con Edison, where he would work himself after retirement. But my father knew clearly the difference between influence and power, and understood the limitations of each. He'd tell me the story of a chief who had a favorite seat at a steak house, and when he'd arrive, the maitre d' would evict whoever sat there, and though my father never mentioned it, I assume that the chief didn't pay the full freight when the check came. "Only a couple of days after the chief retired," my father went on, "he went back to the steak house, and instead of going straight to the table, the waiter says, 'It's great to see you again, I'll let you know as soon as something opens up.'" The chief could have had a heart attack right there. But when you play that game, you're in it or you're out, and when you're gone, you're gone. People don't care who you used to be.'"

I wasn't anyone, really, and the fear of what I might become was a part of my problem at the precinct. The Serpico stuff was ludicrous—there would be no Conlon Commission to succeed Knapp. I would not testify in the halls of the Congress, answering questions before the cameras, as lawyers whispered in my ears and aides scribbled notes.

"Officer Conlon, is it your statement, under oath, that the Captain is a weasel?"

"Yes, Senator, a very big weasel."

"And the Sergeant as well?"

Whisper, whisper . . .ž

"More of a rodent, I'd say, Senator."

"Very well, then. Let's now address the matter of the couch in the SNEU room. . . ."

"With all due respect, Senator, there is no couch in the SNEU room."

Resounding laughter and applause . . .ž

At Street Crime, there was a push for minority recruitment, since one of the many criticisms of the unit was that it was mostly white. A new black executive officer—or XO, meaning second in command—had been brought in, DI Wheeler, who had been the XO at PSA-7. Wheeler had not been at the PSA long, but he was highly regarded, seen as someone who would remain a street cop at heart, regardless of how high in the Department he rose. When he stopped by the precinct, he saw Tony and Orville and made a beeline to them, asking if they were interested in coming over. They knew Wheeler and I didn't, and I hung back at the side like a homely girl at a dance. Tony had decided against it, but Orville seemed tempted, and I think if he'd demanded a chauffeur and a three-day week, Wheeler might have said, "Let me see what I can do." As it was, when Wheeler asked, "So, do you want to come?" Orville just laughed and said, "Where, from the frying pan to the fire?"

Not long into my Street Crime interview, it became clear that I'd remain in the frying pan for a while longer. I showed up in a new suit on my day off, and I was a little surprised to see that there were only black guys there. I knew a couple of them, including one friend, Crosby, from my Academy company, and we gathered in a little huddle, wondering about what questions they'd ask. Whenever a cop came out from his interview, he told us what they wanted to know, and we pored over the words like schoolboys with half the answers to a test. When I was sent for, a white cop approached me on the sly and whispered that he was glad to see a guy like me there. A passing sergeant looked at me and observed, "You must be Conlon, the white guy." The interview was conducted by a captain, a lieutenant, and two sergeants, who asked questions as they looked over my application, in which I'd written where I went to college in the same scribble that two out of three of my Academy teachers took, happily, for Howard. Other questions such as off-duty employment were finessed with understated generalities ("self-employed"). At first, I enjoyed the interview, breezing through the law questions and debating the tactical ones, asking as many questions back as were answered. Then the sergeant asked, "Where did you go to school?" I told him, and there was a pause, and the captain asked, "Did you write a book?"

"No, but I'm writing one."

There was another pause, and then he said, "I know who you are."

The subject went no further. That was my mistake. It would have been faster if the lieutenant had just pushed the button for my ejector seat, but instead he thought a moment and asked, "What if you were with a team that just worked out for half the tour, and spent the other half hanging out in a diner? What would you do?"

"I'd have to get off that team. I'm here to work, and besides, I'd be new here—if I didn't produce, I'd be gone."

The next question was ratcheted up a notch: "What if they worked out and hung out for six hours a day, but managed to make their collars in the remaining two?"

"I wouldn't want to work like that. But if they're good enough to grab gun collars in two hours, who am I to tell them how things are going to be different?"

It was an honest answer and a fair one, although utterly naive to the direction we were going. I got some sourpuss looks, and then it was on to the next level. "What if you found out that when they went out," said the captain, "they were taking money from stores?"

"That would be completely different."

"How is stealing money different from stealing time from the City?"

"One is a crime, one isn't."

From that, it should have been clear that I was finished. A few hours later, I was told that the board had given me the lowest possible rating. I'd failed on my responses to the "integrity questions." There were echoes of Orwell in the interview, from the suggestion that laziness was a crime against the state to the way that my failure to tell them the lies they wanted to hear reflected a lack of integrity. I was informed that I could appeal, or request another interview, but I decided I'd let it go for now.

Later on, John's brother-in-law, Rob Reed, said he was there when I was discussed at a supervisors' meeting, and the prospect of bringing a reporter into the unit, so to speak, at that point in history was a nonstarter. I could hardly hold it against them, but I wish they hadn't wasted my day off. The Captain approached John and remarked with an amused air that he heard about how my integrity sank me in the interview. It made me wonder who the Captain had spoken to, and when. I had a hard time believing he'd be any happier about me staying than I was, but he threw up roadblocks every time I tried to leave.

Our old CIs didn't seem to prosper any more than we did. Stix saw Chihuahua on the street holding a live earthworm in his hand, with which he was engaged in earnest conversation. A few months after I'd last seen Charlie, I ran his name and saw that he'd been collared again in Washington Heights, for drugs, and in the spring, John and I went back to look for him under the bridge. With Charlie and Tommy, the little camp looked like a dump hit by a hurricane. Now, it was clean and orderly, enclosed by a windbreak of trash bags wrapped around broom handles. A mattress had blankets folded on it, and the collection of books and clothes in a shopping cart was piled up more or less evenly. New tenants, I thought—the idea that Charlie and Tommy had become house-proud made me laugh. There was movement behind the enclosure: another white junkie, with long hair and tattoos. We - couldn't ask about Charlie directly, but as we drew him out, he said that he used to have a friend who stayed there, and for a while there was an old man, who wasn't a junkie but a recent widower who couldn't bear to sleep at home. I gave him a cigarette, and he relaxed. "Can you believe it?" he asked. "I've only been on junk for two years. I was a machinist. . . .ž

"We help out the cops here, look around if somebody's robbing or beating people or whatever. We don't steal. I help out, you know, but I won't inform. You guys did a great job here with dope, I mean, I gotta go to Jerome Avenue to score. It's a hike. But crack's still all over the place on University. I stay away from crack, though. Crack killed my sister."

Though we were not in the market for informants, sometimes they turned up regardless, like postcards sent to the wrong address. And since it's not against the law to read someone else's postcard, we tended to take a peek. John signed up a CI who named himself Gallo, which is Spanish for "rooster," when he stopped by the precinct to say he wanted to work. When we talked to him, all he had to offer was a stash spot in a tenement mailbox for the crack dealers down the street. I thanked him and sent him on his way. A couple of days later, when I was stricken with Dutch elm disease, he came back and found John, telling him about how he knew a guy who had seven guns to sell. John and I talked a dozen times on the phone, going over new facts and old omissions in the story, and again when he got home, but for that day and the next, John had to pull the whole load alone. I think I felt more sick from being out of the game than from Dutch elm, but we also decided that it would be better for John to run with it by himself. Gallo was his CI, and he had to to learn how to handle an informant and an investigation on his own. And we didn't need to dwell on it, but the fact that my mere presence might shitcan whatever developed was a risk to be avoided as well.

I wouldn't have wished Gallo as a "starter CI" on anyone. When he first came in with news of the man with seven guns, he only had a first name and no address for the perp. When told to find out more about him, he returned the next day, brimming with excitement about another guy he'd met, again with no address and not even a first name, who had a quarter kilo and a .38. A few days later, he was back with a story about a third guy in the Heights, with half a kilo and two guns; the first two perps were forgotten. Each day was entirely new, and in subsequent appearances, he told of a local guy who had a .38 for sale, and of the twice-weekly drug pick-up, in which four guys, all with guns, made the trip from One-Five-Three and Melrose to 175 Alexander and back. I thought there was something to each of his stories, but for all they were worth in terms of evidentiary or even investigative value, he might as well have told us to quit our jobs because he knew there was gold in California.

Gallo himself was a strange bird who cooperated for the double thrill of playing cop and criminal at once. He was awful about staying in touch, rarely calling when he said he would, with excuses that were sometimes plausible—"One of the dealers was with me by the phone!"—and sometimes just aggravating—"It turned out to be a great party!" Despite constant instructions, he would stroll right in the front door of the precinct, when the perps he was giving up were two blocks away. John was the good guy ("When you don't call, I'm afraid you got killed") and I was the bad ("If you do that again, don't bother coming back"). I took a stronger dislike to him when I found out he was a rich kid, the son of two doctors who owned a laboratory in Puerto Rico. He had gone to college in Arizona on a baseball scholarship, where he majored in business. Afterward, he came to New York and looked for a job.

"What kind of job did you find?"

"Counting money at a dope spot."

Though he was sentenced to probation when his dope spot was raided, Gallo got tired of the city and went back to the Puerto, where his fun-loving ways continued. He worked for the police, and he claimed that they almost let him make arrests himself. He wore a wire that helped catch a bank robber, and he testified at the trial. He asked us for a vest, and made it clear that if we wanted to give him a gun, he wouldn't complain. After a brief, bad marriage, his wife had him arrested for assault and burglary, but he nonetheless won custody of his kid, whom he handed off to his parents. He hadn't seen the kid in years. After bouncing around the island for a while, he decided to return to New York. He was looking for work, and he could use a little money.

At first, John had casino eyes: he wanted the seven guns and the two guns and the one and the four, plus the drugs—why not?—while we were at it. Shortly after, he calmed down a little, and even though we didn't expect to go all the way through with a warrant, we began to look at it, to begin to verify the information just to ascertain his credibility. Gallo had gone back to the spot in the Heights, and we schooled him on the importance of addresses and apartment numbers. He gave us a building on the southeast corner of Audubon and 180th Street, apartment #6C, and a perp named Tony who worked for the phone company. We went there late one night: the building had five stories, and there were no six-story buildings in the area. Sorry, sorry, the next day, he corrected himself: it was Amsterdam and 180th. Later that night, we found a six-story apartment building where the apartments were numbered 61, 62, 63, and so on, rather than 6A, 6B, 6C. It was after midnight, but I told John to call him. Gallo said it was too late to talk, but he would take us there tomorrow. He hung up the phone. "This guy isn't splitting atoms on his day off," said John.

"Give me the number," I said.

When he answered, he was surly: "Do you know what time it is?"

"Yeah, I know exactly what time it is, because I just wasted the last two hours chasing your bullshit information. I told you how this is gonna work. You don't get three fucking tries to get a fucking address right."

"I'm sorry, I'll take you there tomorrow."

"That's not good enough," I said, and I hung up on him.

We let him alone for a few weeks, and then John called him up again. Gallo apologized, and explained that his aunt, with whom he was staying, had a habit of listening in on his calls from the other extension. That was not a bad excuse, in fact, but his credibility—at least in terms of elementary accuracy of detail—was so poor that I would not bring him before a judge, let alone take a door on his say-so. But we always saw him on the corner with the dealers, and bit by bit, he gave up plausible information about the weekly trip to Alexander Avenue. We watched it informally for a while, and we identified the two regular travelers; Gallo sometimes went as one of the two extra men. If a warrant was out, a car stop was definitely possible.

The problem was how to set it up for maximum effect—perps, guns, and drugs—without getting anyone hurt or exposing Gallo as an informant. We thought about telling Gallo to just run away, without the gun, but Orville pointed out that you just shouldn't program that kind of chaos into an already volatile situation. We talked to a number of DAs and detectives for ideas, though nothing seemed to fit, until John and I went to talk it over with Sam Ramer. Sam happened to be having lunch with his boss, Ed Frieden-thal, the bureau chief, as well as two other DAs I'd written warrants with, Frank Randazzo and Tina Petrillo. We had a little brainstorming session, - everyone arguing upsides and down, legal and tactical, and it was a thrill to be with people who knew what they were talking about and were deter-mined to make it work. If we took the two in the building, we'd lose the two in the car; if we took the car before the visit, we'd lose the drugs, and we still needed a pretext for the stop. I thought of it: when the car parked outside of 175 Alex, we would wait for the two to go in and out of the building, and just as they were about to get back in their car, we would grab them. We would take them for trespass, and their proximity to the other two men and the car would give us grounds to toss them, too. Gallo told us that he and the fourth man always waited outside the car, and Gallo would leave his gun on the car floor, in plain view. We would get four guns, all the drugs, and four bodies, but with a terminally weak case against Gallo and the other, less culpable perp. And two cases dying a natural death would halve the suspicion on Gallo.

We tacced it like a warrant, with diagrams of both locations, and all the as-signments for OPs and tails, roadblocks and hospital cars. We must have had eighteen cops involved; it was to be the D-day of car stops. John presented it to the pack of bosses, and he defended it with far more diplomacy than I would have when the predictable objections were raised.

The Captain said he wanted everyone taken in the car: "I don't care if he's killed, I don't care if he has to go through the system, I don't want any cops hurt." John pointed out that Gallo was a volunteer, and that while he was willing to spend a night in jail for the case, and even to risk his life, we were in no position to tell him he faced real jail time by helping us. When that made no impression, John said that the plan was Bureau Chief Friedenthal's, and he was adamant that we adhere to it. It was precisely the right pitch. There was more give and take—

"We don't want a gun battle in a moving car."

"We don't want a gun battle in a foot pursuit, either."

"What if he doesn't show up?"

"What if there are more guys?"

What if the building collapses or the cars explode? Finally, the plan was approved, and we waited for Gallo to tell us when they'd be going. A few days later, he called: it would take place tonight, no earlier than ten, no later than ten-thirty. We took our places half an hour before and waited. Ten passed, and ten-thirty, and at ten-forty, orders were given to quit. After eleven, Gallo called to say it had been postponed. On another night, we planned it again, but Gallo again failed to appear. We would not get another chance, with the full manpower it required, and we debated uneasily among ourselves whether we should run with it alone, if we suddenly got word. It was a damn good plan, I thought.

Gallo continued to blithely drop by the precinct. He would ask random cops at the desk to borrow money, or for a ride somewhere. Once, he was stopped on his way downstairs to the SNEU office. His long-lost kid came to visit him at his aunt's, and he brought her to the precinct, too. I was disinclined to have anything more to do with him, but he told John that he'd run into the local kid with the .38, who was anxious to sell it to him. He could set it up whenever we wanted. John was against shutting him down completely—he couldn't give up the guns—and he decided to play it by ear.

I heard how it went at home, when he called me. Orville and I had done a day tour for court, and the rest of the team was out, too, leaving John and Sammy alone on the four-to-twelve. Gallo called and said the kid was meeting him in an hour; John picked the place, around the corner from the precinct, and sat in an unmarked van with Sammy to watch. He told Gallo to scratch his head like he had lice to signal when the kid was there with the gun. Gallo showed, the kid showed, the head was scratched, and John and Sammy moved in and took him. "It turned out perfect," he said.

Again, I felt like the ugly girl at the dance, but John was right when he said that there are times when you have to move at the moment or forget it forever. I was disappointed that I hadn't been there, though I understood why it had happened. But in a later, fuller account from both John and Sammy, I was even more frustrated, because "perfect" might have described the ending, but nothing else before it. From the start, Gallo called to say that the meeting was set, again ignoring instructions that we were to choose the time. And when the seller showed up, he wasn't alone, but with his brother, who also had a gun. John and Sammy watched them talk from the van, and then the brothers stepped off for a moment. Gallo then took the opportunity to stroll over to the van to let them know the play-by-play. When I heard that, I was horrified: had the brothers returned a moment too soon, it would have told them to prepare for an ambush. Gallo had put everyone's lives at risk because he couldn't wait to tell John how well he was doing. A minute after he returned to his place, the brothers came back. He scratched his head, and

John and Sammy rolled in; the kid dropped one gun, and they took him; the brother ran and got away.

Gallo had another gun in the works, from a guy who lived in the Village, in one of my old buildings. John said, "This collar's yours, if you want it." I didn't want to lose the gun, but I wasn't going to let Gallo run rampant. I talked to Smacky in Narcotics, who was working for Sgt. Poplaski from the PSA, and both of them now worked for Lt. Zerbo. I figured that if anyone could lay down the law to Gallo, Zerbo could. It was the classic dilemma: whenever you asked for help, you risked losing control. I told John to decide whether we should keep him. His decision was that it was my decision. I thought about what I could live with and what I could not, about the collar and the possibility of casualties. Some of my partners had children and the rest of us would like to. I called Smacky and said, "He's all yours. Be careful." Gallo made one dope buy for them and then he disappeared.

• • •

THE WARM WEATHER CAME BACK AGAIN. WE HUNG IN AND hung out, worked and waited. Sometimes weeks would pass between blowups with the Sergeant, and after a few peaceful weeks, the chill silences would give way to jokes and casual conversation between one of us and him. Stix invited him to his wedding, which annoyed me. But he explained that since everyone else was invited, and we joked about it—how the sheriff would have to be notified that minorities were coming to town, or that Orville would park the cars and Sammy would do the dishes—it would be disrespectful not to invite him.

"But you don't respect him."

"I know I don't respect him, but he's the boss—and it's a slap in the face if I don't invite him. It'd be too awkward, too weird."

I didn't have to say that things were plenty awkward and weird as they were. The Sergeant sometimes rode in his own car in the field, which did minimize the fights over who would get stuck driving him. On occasion, it emerged that his separation from us was more than physical. He didn't really know the precinct, and once, when we charged a lobby to hit a set, he ran in a building half a block away. Another time, we looked at 550 East 147th Street for an hour before concluding that nothing much was happening and moving on. The Sergeant stopped at the precinct as we set up for another spot, and a few minutes later, he called us all back.

"I have a new spot, it's working, it's hot," he said, with excitement.

"Where is it?"

"Five fifty East One-Four-Seven."

"Um, Sarge, that's where we just were."

As our respect eroded still further, his assertions of authority became more frequent and desperate. Since the drug game was clearly not his forte, he lunged into any other kind of police activity that came over the air. All cops raced to 10-13s—"Officer in need of assistance"—wherever they were, but for robberies and gun runs, only cops in the immediate area should respond. The Sergeant would have us fly two precincts away for those jobs, driving at breakneck speed, and he'd bark orders at the scene even if lieutenants and captains who actually belonged there were present. The team took to calling him "Captain Chaos," and Orville resolved, "I am not going to drive with him again until my child is born."

Another time, he sent us out in the field, saying he'd catch up with us later. That day, John and I fought a guy I almost shot—hand in pocket, pointed at me, repeated refusal to remove it—and when the Sergeant arrived, he announced it on the air like a conquering hero: "Hey guys, I'm back! And I got the van!" John said, "I gotta say something to this dope," and picked up the radio: "Who gives a fuck where you are? Do us a favor and stay home!" I yelled, "Holy shit! No!" and tried to grab the radio from him. John laughed his head off—he hadn't keyed the mike—"You were afraid! You really were afraid!"

The Sergeant would complain about the numbers, and then he'd announce that we'd spend one day a week cleaning the office: "We'll call it Clean Day." He went away for a week, after telling us that he'd arranged for Sgt. Rhoden to cover us. On the first day, we told the four-to-twelve lieutenant—a new transfer—about the situation, and he smiled and said, "You're not going anywhere. I have other plans for you." He sent us back to get into uniform, and then he pulled cops who had regular sectors into conditions cars, and we filled in the sectors. Sgt. Rhoden asked, "What does he have against you guys?"

"I have no clue. The guy just got here, he hasn't even had a chance to hate us yet."

So it went for the week, and when the Sergeant returned, we told him what had happened.

"Maybe he needed to cover patrol," he said.

I said that wasn't the case.

"Yeah, he told me he was fucking with you," he admitted.

What was there to say? I remembered the line that went, "Hollywood is high school with money," and wondered, "Is the Police Department high school with guns?" I thought of my father trying to make me the messenger to Mike Kelly, saying that he had no idea what awaited him on the Job. That June was my father's eighth anniversary. My family went to eight o'clock mass in the morning, and then we all went to work. The family got together again for dinner later on, and my sister Marianne asked me how my day was. I said, "I grabbed a guy by the neck until he spat out his heroin." She covered her ears, and I don't think she's asked me how my day went since.

Still, there were little things at work that made us laugh. The way we talked, the way perps talked, the way the Penal Law and the *Patrol Guide* failed to describe the realities we knew. One cop was yelled at by his wife when she found a note in his pocket that said "ADA Smith" and a phone number: "Who is this Ada Smith, and what does she want with you?" One night when we were watching *Jeopardy!* on TV, a couple of the guys challenged me to call out the answers. I got them right, and Sammy nodded in approval as he remarked, "You're a regular Rogue Scholar." Sammy had a few other deft slips, my favorite of which was when he referred to the "Verbal Judo" course the NYPD was big on that year as "Gerbil Voodoo." I found a great OP for One-Five-Three and Melrose, from an apartment roof just down the block. John and I went up, and we gave out four bodies in five minutes, crouched down by the low parapet, which reached just above the knees.

"I wish I had a bucket to sit on," John said. Just then we both looked across the roof, at a clean plastic bucket of the perfect height, which we'd failed to notice earlier.

"You idiot!" I said. "What a waste of a wish! You could have had Cindy Crawford, a million dollars—and all you got was an old bucket on a South Bronx tenement rooftop. I'm ashamed to even know you."

"Still," John said, looking down. "It's a good bucket."

Other moments of fun made us think that in the end, we might have the last laugh. There was the bribery collar, which came about one day when Chicky, Tony, John, and I drove up University, in the Four-Six. Since we - hadn't been back much since PK left, and we later took to processing collars at the PSA, our disappearance seemed to have taken on sinister overtones. I saw a Four-Six cop at Central Booking, who said, "I heard you guys killed a perp and got disbanded." I just shook my head. It was a novelty to be back, and when we stopped at a light, John had another surprise, as he looked over at the scrawny white guy in the Camaro next to us, shooting up. Some junkie intuition kicked in on Camaro's part, too, and he peeled out up the street, breaking right on One-Eight-One, down a one-way, against traffic. We didn't chase him, as such, because the streets were narrow and crowded, and our van had only a little dash-top light—there was no siren, and the horn was still busted. But Camaro forced other cars off the road, and he left so many pissed-off people in his wake that the whole neighborhood joined in to help us, standing at the corners to point out where he'd turned, until we found where he'd abandoned his car to flee on foot. Chicky and I jumped out to chase him down an alley while John and Tony rounded the block in the van. At the end of the alley was a six-foot wall with a chain-link fence on top, which the so-called Short-a-Rican vaulted like an Olympian, and then there was another alley, wall, and fence, and by the time we got through the block, we saw Camaro lying on the sidewalk, hyperventilating, twitching, and bleeding from the hands. Chicky and I were spent, too, and we just sat down next to him. Camaro was lucky we caught him—he wasn't even cuffed for fifteen minutes, because we let him breathe into a beer-soaked bag, and the street justice would have been unforgiving. As it was, when we went back to his car, the radio and his jacket were stolen. The neighborhood treated us like conquering heroes, like we were firemen instead of cops. Camaro looked like he might go DOA, and I asked the guys if anyone wanted the collar:

"Nope!"

"Nope!"

"Are you kidding me?"

I wanted to put this guy away for a while; he could have killed kids. At the moment, we had a hundred witnesses, but tomorrow we might have none. If Camaro went into cardiac arrest after his junkie triathlon of shoot, drive, and run, a few months down the line we would face a wrongful-death suit with nothing to show but four Bronx cops saying, "You shoulda been there!" I told John to spread the word that we didn't care about the radio, we just wanted to check the jacket for drugs, and he disappeared in the crowd. Moments later, the jacket was produced, but it was clean of dope and works. Chicky and I drove back in the Camaro, an immaculately restored 1982 model, tricked out with flame decals. One tire was flat from its jump over the sidewalk, but we took off the top and enjoyed the ride, screeching around corners in second gear.

When we got back to the base, John said the perp had cried the whole time. He was going into rehab the next morning, and his fiancée would kill him if she knew that he went back to the Bronx for a last shot. We didn't understand, he *couldn't* go to jail, it would wreck everything. His fiancée would leave him, and he worked for her family—he'd had chances before and he'd blown them. Handcuffed in the back seat, he couldn't help but notice how much Chicky and I seemed to enjoy the car. If we let him go tonight, he said, it was ours. Such was John's summary when we met back at the precinct.

"What do you want to do with it?"

"Let's run with it. Fuck him, for all we know, this is the only charge that'll stick."

Inspections was notified, and a detective, sergeant, and lieutenant arrived to give me a tape recorder and drill us on the niceties of entrapment—we could say, "Remember what we talked about?" but not, "Remember that offer?" I had the recorder in my shirt pocket behind a pack of cigarettes as I went into the cells to get Camaro. As I walked past the desk, a great veteran lieutenant named Brophy followed me and leaned directly over the mike for a confidential whisper: "Careful! IAB's in the house! Make sure that none of the perps dropped anything in the cells!" I tried to kick him and point to my pocket, but we were already inside, and what was said would be there for posterity. We brought Camaro out and talked to him for twenty minutes, but he seemed to have forgotten his offer. Over and over, I tried to look greedy while remarking, "That's some nice car," and finally he got it, offering that car and others, as well as to come over on weekends and paint our houses. I thanked him and we left. The Inspections sergeant took time out from our case to yell at a cop for walking in with his shirt unbuttoned, and the Lieutenant then grilled John on why we had engaged in a "pursuit" in an unmarked vehicle and why we didn't transmit it over the radio. John was disgusted—bribery was supposed to be for major players who manipulated and corrupted the system with real money, not this addled little sap who could barely remember his own name. "This is garbage," he said. "I will never do this again, ever."

I didn't agree. I told him that as I saw it, this might be the only way we could hold him accountable, since the drugs were gone. "Besides," I added, "it's another number for Wopstat."

Within a couple of days, our new lieutenant, Andy Johnson, let us know that the arrest was of some significance. A bribery collar was a big deal in the NYPD, as a hangover from the Knapp Commission days, and it won you a medal, and an entire career point, and an interview with the Integrity Review Board, which could arrange for a transfer to your assignment of choice. To put that in perspective, I'd begun to scramble to put together my "career path" application, for which an excellent annual evaluation could get you two or three points. A medal for a stupendous collar, like a bank robbery, might get you half a point. A college degree would get you two. A year without going sick would get you one. You needed fifteen for a transfer.

I was short of points, since for the first two years on patrol, my sergeant seemed to change monthly; I rarely saw him, her, or whoever it was, and my evaluations were rated a quick "satisfactory," which awarded me a total of zero points. I never thought or cared about those evaluations until I realized that I'd worked my first two years for free. But it appeared that to make a bribery collar—which was, in effect, simply to refuse to commit a crime— would be worth more than two years of work and a couple of bank robberies combined. The only thing that could have made me a more valuable police officer would have been to avoid flu-like symptoms for several years running. It didn't seem very fair—it didn't seem sane, in fact—but a break seemed to be rolling my way, and I wasn't about to dodge it.

A few days later, Orville, Frankenberry, and I grabbed the perps from an armed robbery, I think. It was just before ten in the morning, when the 10-30 came over from a clothing store a couple of blocks away. We'd just finished getting dressed when Chicky came in, saying, "It looks like Columbine High School over there!" ESU and Hostage Negotiations were called in, surrounding the store with armor and guns; civilians fled the block, and neighboring stores lowered their steel gates. The three of us rolled up on the scene as a woman called over to us, in lowered tones: "It's those two guys walking away right now, down the block! They changed their shirts inside!" We jumped from the car and chased them, throwing them against a fence. The cops who caught the job came around the corner, and we handed off the perps. An hour later, they called the precinct for our names for the medal write-up, and Orville said that it was he and I who had done it. I felt bad that he forgot Frankenberry, but he wound up taking a better cop job upstate, and Orville and I were left out of the story, regardless.

So it went that our hopes rose and fell. The months took their toll on us, and the resentments built, and the separate concerns of impending marriages and children, sick relatives and side jobs, made the daily indignities no easier to bear. We didn't always spare each other our frustrations. A lot of our old street antics, the spirited improvisations and crazy chases, seemed needlessly risky for a game that was hardly worth winning. One night, when we dropped off perps at Central Booking, I said that I didn't like how the perps were cuffed—one hand apiece, on a chain, instead of individually rear-cuffed. When you had a lot of bodies, you often ran out of cuffs, and it is difficult to herd ten single perps from the precinct to CB, and often again to another precinct to lodge them, if CB was full. Partners should talk tactics all the time, going over each collar and confrontation like a football team studies videotape of last week's game, win or lose. If the criticism was offered in the right spirit, you were grateful to learn; if not, it could be construed as an insult on the deepest level. Because tactics became paramount in times of crisis, the talk of tactics was talk of much more: a good tactical cop is a good cop, saving lives, and a bad tactical cop is a bad cop, cowardly or dumb or otherwise lacking control. At a moment of crisis, where was your head, and where was your heart? What might begin as a discussion of training could quickly end as a verdict on character.

At the end of one Team Meeting, Tony told the boss: "Um, I don't think what you did the other day—when you went by yourself, and walked ahead of the perp back to the van—I don't think you should do that anymore."

"You're right, okay, that was old school," he admitted, as if the act was one of Shaft-style hyperconfidence. It wasn't old school, it was Special Education—nobody walks alone ahead of a perp, who hadn't been searched and wasn't cuffed—and it amounted to an open invitation to assault or escape. The tactics, and the temperament behind them, summed up the Sergeant for us: all who were supposed to follow him—us no less than that perp—were provided ample occasion to wonder why.

When I told John my thoughts on perp-cuffing, he agreed, and he went on to bring up something that had long been on his mind: "As long as we're talking tactics, Tactics Boy, how about how you ran after each of the three perps yourself earlier today—the first one, even after he was cuffed up, I made run across the street with me after you jumped the fence. And then the other two . . ."

I laughed.

"You don't care, do you?"

John was in his twenties, two hundred pounds of maintained muscle, a star of his high school wrestling team, and he always shot perfect scores at the range. I was none of those things. Seeing a partner hurt or worse was high atop the list of the many bad things any cop could imagine, and when John watched me go after someone bigger than myself, or after a couple of -

people, the thought of my excellent education going to waste didn't just cross his mind, it made him crazy. There might be things on the Job worth dying for, but three slabs of crack was not one of them.

But I'd stopped perps alone for a long time, made arrests alone for a long time—even in SNEU, it was often more practical. In some sets, the dealer would wait until he could unload a bundle at a time, and he might have the buyers wait, for five minutes or forty-five, and then ten people would walk off in ten directions at once. You split the difference—and not in a tough-guy way—between Academy tactics and street needs. If I did stop three at a time, I wouldn't move in to search them, but I'd hold them at gunpoint till backup came. These were not SWAT-team extractions by any stretch of the imagination—we didn't have black helicopters, we had my 1980 Oldsmobile—but to my mind, the risks were not reckless ones. Or they were no more reckless than anything else in the statistic-driven but slapdash enterprise of SNEU, and if we were going to do it at all, we were going to do it with guts. That was part of another give-and-take between John and me that had gone on for months: What do we give to this? Is it worthwhile? Do we quit the team, or quit without leaving, and force the Captain to keep us or him? When John was more despairing, earlier on, I said, "You ought to keep at it, keep collaring and taking things wherever they go. If you do go—when you go—you'll go out on top of your game. When some new sergeant or captain looks at your arrest record, deciding whether to take you in, he sees felonies every month instead of hearing stories about Captain Chaos, which he won't believe anyway." When I'd thrown in the towel, after the sixth warrant was canceled, John gave me the same speech. It was like the movies where escaped convicts are shackled together by the ankles: when one steps forward, the other follows.

John had been in SNEU for a year by then. The first half was beautiful, the second was hardly bearable. Even in the good times, with PK, John would sometimes confide his doubts in what he brought to the team: "It's like - everybody has a gift, a skill, whether it's OV doing OPs, or you running with CIs and warrants. But me, I think that PK has me around because I'm a lot of laughs." He thought for a moment. "Plus, I'm good-looking and can lift heavy things." In the daily decisions of where we should work, who should watch and who should catch, there was a phase of noise in which our collective and single inclinations shifted one way and the next before settling. I told him, "If you want to be in the OP, don't ask, just get up in the OP. And if you want to get better, get better—don't wait to be helped." He did, and he developed his own eye in an OP, and in streets where even slightly dodgy-looking white people, like Stix or me, couldn't get into a building without getting made, he'd put on coveralls or a Con Ed helmet, or pick up a mop or a toolbox, and march in whistling.

Before he came to SNEU, John had driven bosses for months at a time, and he had worked in a Target Team at Mott-Pat, as well as on a solo footpost in Highbridge in the Four-Four. He had three or four gun collars, and had tackled a bank robber who had been featured on *America's Most Wanted*, checking the right building when a vast NYPD–FBI Task Force was fanned out in the area. But for the first years on the Job, he'd been living at home, sixty miles away, and finishing college at St. John's: collars and street action were not foremost in his mind. A chaotic schedule didn't suit him in other ways: he liked to eat, healthy and often, and to get at least an hour in at the gym every day. John was the most natural and least natural athlete I knew. He was great at games—softball, football, basketball—and when he went to the projects by our apartment for pick-up games, "Watch the white boy! Cover Whiteboy!" was the courtside chorus. But without almost constant attention to diet and exercise, he would have turned from Schwarzenegger to the Pillsbury Doughboy in months. John could gain three pounds by taking a long nap. He didn't like the negotiations over where the team would eat, which could take hours and result in a plate of grease and beans instead of grilled chicken and steamed vegetables from the Chinese takeout where they knew how to cook for him. At first, SNEU was worth it for the fun and the experience, and later he felt locked in like the rest of us, only more so, blaming himself for PK. But when the bonds between team members began to tense and fray, even for a short time, the sacrifices that he made to stay in SNEU began to seem pointless.

Because John and I were so close, I didn't want to be seen as his automatic partisan whenever there was some disagreement on the team. Whether we should do a double on the last one, for a longer weekend, or whether we came in early or late on the first one back, was routine debate that usually set the single guys who always wanted as long a weekend as possible against the family men who had other responsibilities and events on the schedule. As it happened, the three white guys were single, and the Puerto Rican, the Short-a-Ricans, and the Jamaican were married with kids. We'd always been able to work things out among ourselves, and when we were in higher favor in the command, we were usually accommodated for shift changes and days off. Patience and goodwill were no longer in such strong supply, however. As I saw it, if we fell out with one another for any reason, it would be a tragedy, but if we fell out with one another amid rancor and racial division, it would be a disgrace. There were no signs that our frustrations with one another and everything else were anything but color-blind, but I knew things could go very bad, very quickly.

At the end of a long night, one of the guys blew up at me for trying to get him to switch collars with John. John wanted a day tour the next day, to get out of the precinct early, but no one listened when he asked. The guy had a seller with unapprehended buyers, which he was going to write up as misdemeanor possession, since it would be dropped anyway and he didn't want to come in early the next day. The switch made sense to me, of course, but it could also be reasonably seen as none of my goddamned business. It was a brief explosion, and we both knew a day later that there was nothing more to it than tiredness and tender nerves. At the beginning of another tour, four of us were in the van, when John brought up my tactics again, in the hope of getting the other guys to urge me to be more careful. One of the other guys disagreed with him on a point. Within moments, the debate on tactics became a personal argument, and then a fusillade of shouted curses—"Fuck you!" "Fuck me? You're the fuck-up!" The other noncombatant and I sat in shocked and horrified silence. For me, a fight between my partners was like a fight between my parents—if they ever fought—and anything I could add would only make it worse. It was awful. The other two guys left the van for an OP, and John and I stayed in the van. We didn't talk much. All the perps were runners or fighters that night, and John was stuck in the van with prisoners while I rolled around in the street with one perp, who was over six-two and 220. It didn't improve his mood. The next week he went sick for a couple of days.

A week or so after he came back, the Sergeant gave us our evaluations. When I looked at mine, I saw that it praised my activity and integrity (the bribery collar gave me my integrity back) but stated that I "needed improvement following instructions and team cohesion." He might have been on to something with the cohesion issue. When John was brought in—his evaluation had the identical praise and reprimands as mine—the Sergeant told him that he'd better talk to me, because I "was on my last legs on this team."

"You can talk to him," John said. "I'm leaving. I'm going back to my old post."

The Sergeant was quiet, and then he asked, "Is it because of me?"

John shook his head and walked out. I didn't know what to think. Minutes later, I couldn't: a cop called over the radio that there was a barricaded perp with a gun, One-Six-Six and Brook. The precinct emptied, as everyone grabbed keys and jumped into cars. The Sergeant took the wheel of the last unmarked car, and Chicky, Tony, and I reluctantly hopped into the back. Racing to the scene, Tony yelled at the Sergeant the whole time: "Follow the marked car! No, the other one! Turn, no! Turn! Keep the siren on 'Yelp!'" Chicky tried to jump out of the car every time it slowed down. It was a spectacle: ESU and K9, scores of cops, taking positions around the garage door, a captain from the Four-Two trying to find a Spanish-speaking cop to talk to the complainant. The adrenaline began to dwindle when the complainant was asked, "Did you actually see the gun?" and the reply was shaky. Maybe it was a knife, and maybe the perp wasn't barricaded in the garage but had walked through it, and maybe he wasn't a perp, really. Maybe it wasn't even a knife. It all arose from a dispute over a parking spot. Maybe it was a really great spot.

A sergeant appeared on the rooftop of the garage, striding across to make sure there was no one hiding there. He looked commanding, despite the loss of urgency for our being there. Our sergeant must have thought so, too, because a few minutes later, another cop told me, "Your boss is hurt—you better go check it out." I saw the Sergeant limp across the street. John and I stood there. "Yeah, I guess." I went over to him, on the side of the building where he sat, wrapping a towel around his bloody calf. "You all right?" He said he was, and he explained that he had stepped through a windshield of a parked car, as he tried to vault onto the roof.

"Another sergeant was with me, he went through the windshield, too. He didn't get hurt, though, I don't know how. I don't know where he went, either."

"Huh."

I walked away to tell the guys—"C'mere! C'mere! You gotta listen to what this guy did now!"—and for the first time in a week, John broke into a smile. Tony and Chicky went on an extended riff on the theme of Captain Chaos.

When the Sergeant got into an ambulance, each of us asked him how he felt, and then walked a hundred yards away to make more jokes, out of earshot. The Sergeant limped over to say that he had to go to the hospital for stitches, and it wouldn't take more than an hour. As he turned, he must have felt the debate, even if he didn't hear it: "*Somebody's* gotta go with him!"

"I'm not!"

"Not me!"

"Fuck that!"

"Fuck him!"

Tony finally volunteered to go, calling out "Boss, hold up!" when he was almost back to the ambulance. I thought about how when PK was hurt, we were stricken, surrounding him like widows at a wake. When we drove back to the precinct, however, the desk told us to get into uniform: there were power outages in the neighborhood, and we were on alert. The news seemed to awaken some charitable instinct in us: "We can't! Our sergeant is hurt, we have to go to hospital. We have to be with him, what if he needs blood?"

It was good to laugh again. It had been a while. I heard that Warrants was picking people up, and I went to the Captain, to ask if he would consider putting my name in. He was with the captain from Vice, which had their office on the second floor of our building. The Vice captain asked if I needed to talk alone. No, I said—fortunately, it seemed—and I stated my business.

"You don't want that," the Captain informed me. He went on, "You're going to stay on the Job? What do you want to do with your career?"

"I want my shield, to be in the Detective Bureau."

He shook his head. "No, what you really want is to be a boss. Do you have enough time on to take the test? Did you file?"

I didn't want to be a boss, I said; I did have the time, I had not filed. The Captain said, "Warrants is a mess, the people there are miserable, they hate it there. You don't know what's going to be happening there." That was news to me, and it would have been news to them, too. Slowly, I said that I knew - people who loved it there, and that it would get me my shield, and he interrupted, "You think a Squad is going to pick you up from Warrants?"

"They're not going to pick me up from SNEU."

There was no answer for that, and so he suggested that I go to Narcotics. I said that I'd go in a second, but there was no movement there, according to Inspector Mullen.

"Go as an undercover, you could work at Columbia," he said.

The Vice captain remarked, "If Mullen said there's no movement, I'd take his word for it." The Captain then suggested that I go to Auto Crime, which is like saying a good way to visit England would be to get a Rhodes scholarship. I said I'd talk to more people about Warrants and get back to him. I left it at that.

A day or two later, I ran into the Vice captain in the parking lot, and he said that I could come work for him if I wanted. "We only take cops as temps, you know. You'll be back here in six months, but you're that much closer to your shield. Besides, you'll wind up back here, and the Captain likes you."

The last part baffled me, but I ran to get John, and we went back to the Vice captain, to see if we could go together. He told us to fill out the applications right there. Vice, or Public Morals, as it had been known, was a far smaller unit than it had been in its inglorious past, and the work—underage and after-hours drinking, gambling, and prostitution—didn't seem so compelling, the success of Operation Lying Whore notwithstanding. But I did like the thought that I'd be taking up in 1999 what Pat Brown had begun in 1915, and that it would move me closer to the gold shield. On many days, had I been offered the chance to dredge the Gowanus Canal with a toothbrush, it would have been more appealing than PSA-7.

So it seemed that as each door closed, another one opened. John went to the Admin lieutenant to ask to go back to his old post, and he was told it would take some time. Weeks passed and nothing happened, and then he was told that he'd have to work with a rookie in a conditions car for a couple of months before it would be arranged. The Captain told him, "The way I see it, I'm doing you a favor, letting you keep your days off." John didn't see it that way, but that didn't matter. When he suggested that he and I go to a conditions car together, in the Four-Four, the Captain said, "Eddie Conlon is not leaving SNEU." It wasn't clear whether it was his decree or his bet that I'd stay, and it didn't matter. For my part, when I went to the Integrity Review Board, I was doubly hopeful that I'd finally get to leave the PSA, and that I could talk them into helping John as well. Though only the arresting officer was to supposed to benefit with the career point and the transfer, John had seen the perp shooting up, and he had been the initial recipient of the bribe offer. I filled out a set of forms for each of us, including the tantalizing section which asked for your dream assignments. At the interview, I gave a quick rendition of the collar to the sergeant who ran the Board, and she said that the arrest met their qualifications. When I began to argue that John's part was at least as important as mine, she thought for a moment before saying, "You're right. You don't belong here, he does. Have him call me to set up an interview."

I hadn't expected to be quite so persuasive. I felt like saying, *Are you kidding? I bet Timpanaro would have taken the car! Look at me, I'm an Irishman, you think I'd drive a Camaro with flame decals? That car is right up his alley!* I went back to the PSA and told him. Maybe I should have said that for each door that opened, another one closed.

• • •

OTHER DOORS SEEMED TO REVOLVE, IN THE MOST SURPRIS-
ing ways. I talked to PK often, and he was doing well at PSA-8, where he was
the SNEU sergeant. For a while, he talked about trying to import the lot of us,
but I doubted that they would permit the wholesale loss of manpower at
PSA-7. Later on, we talked about a few of us coming over—John and me,
maybe—but we were uncomfortable with the idea of splitting up the team.

At PSA-8, PK had taken over their SNEU team, replacing another Sgt.
Kelly, of course, who'd had his own problems with the CO there. The trouble
prompted the other Sgt. Kelly's transfer to PSA-7, where he filled in to cover
us while our sergeant was away, and then he stayed, as he was due for promotion to lieutenant in a few weeks. We had half a boss most of the time, and
now we had two. The rumor was that our captain was angry at theirs for
treating PK well, and so he returned the favor. Was it a Bedouin saying that
the enemy of my enemy is my friend? The local translation was, "If you make
my enemy Sgt. Kelly your SNEU sergeant, I will of course make your enemy
Sgt. Kelly my SNEU sergeant." And so we remained a little people, wandering the desert, with our tents and our feuds.

One feud happened soon after the new Sgt. Kelly arrived, during a Team
Meeting. For most of the month, we were on patrol, and our activity was low.
That was no excuse, we were told: our day-tour weeks would henceforth be
changed to one-to-nines, and no leave would be approved for the rest of the
month. Chicky said he couldn't do one-to-nines, because he had to take care
of his kid. If we changed, he'd have to leave the team. And then he got
heated, telling the Sergeant how he was punishing us for circumstances that
were out of our control, and to have one slow month and get this bullshit was
in fact bullshit. "These are the best cops in the command, and every day we
come in to collar, and every day we get a smack in the face. Nobody wants to
do anything anymore, and we still collar!"

"You guys think you can do whatever you want, come in when you want,
and it's gonna stop—and if anybody wants to leave, they can!"

"You go ahead and replace us, you're losing the best cops in the precinct!"

Chicky walked out of the room, shaking with anger. The Sergeant said we
should have written summonses, even when we were getting punished, and
so last month's low numbers were our own fault. He said that Sgt. Rhoden's
team always had their own van, exclusively for their use, because their num-

bers were always good, regardless of quality. I said when our numbers were great, we still had to fight for a car every day and usually lost. Orville then told the Sergeant that it was because he didn't fight for us.

"You can't say that I don't fight for you, nobody fights for you like I do—"

"I did say it."

"What the fuck did you say, you—?"

"That's my opinion."

As the Sergeant began to scream and curse, Orville walked toward him and said, "I am thirty years old and I have two children. I am not your child. I didn't curse at you and you will not curse at me."

They both got up and approached each other, the Sergeant cursing and Orville dressing him down with pulpit fervor. Tony got up between them, then pushed Orville out of the room so he wouldn't smack him and get fired. Later on, Chicky said that when he went home, his wife wanted to call an ambulance, because he was so mad, she thought he'd have a heart attack.

The other Sgt. Kelly had been amazed by the ferocity of the ill will. He offered to talk to our Sergeant and Captain for us, but he said that we'd need to get some numbers for him, so he'd be in a position to negotiate. Most of the time, when we could work, we did, but there were other occasions when it seemed necessary to make a statement, even if it wasn't completely understood. One day, John took to giving out "phantom" scrips, sending the boss scrambling all over the streets to catch nonexistent buyers. John pushed it a little—"Okay, we got three female whites, in business suits . . . you can't miss 'em!"

"No luck? Huh. Nevermind, now we got a Japanese guy in a convertible. . . ."

"My God, are you blind? Forget it, forget it, this one—please, if you don't get these two, I don't know. This one's a couple, male and female, on a bicycle built for two. . . ."

The Sergeant still asked me to talk to perps, whenever any cop in the command brought in a prisoner who offered information. I wondered why we bothered, but I never said no.

I debriefed one perp, asking, "Would you buy guns?"

"No," he said, "I'd buy clothes."

I liked to think that my interview skills had grown acute with time and experience, and maybe that was the case. When Orville took a guy for a couple of vials, I asked him if he would be willing to work for us. He said, "Okay."

I asked him if he'd ever worked for the police before.

"Yeah, sure," he'd said, and he gave me the cop's name, Jerry Gonzalez, with the Brooklyn DA's Squad. He'd been caught for a sale and a gun, and he'd worked it off: a Jamaican drug ring had been wanted for a number of murders, and though the case was never made against them for the homicides, the CI had put them away for life, arranging buys for half a kilo of coke and twenty pounds of weed. Detective Gonzalez said the CI was energetic and reliable and a bit of a cop buff. The CI took on the code name "Paiton," which was close to the Spanish for "python," and though I never got what he meant by it, he could have called himself anything he wanted.

Paiton was thin and hungry-looking, with the immigrant's mix of deference and drive, anxious to please and determined to succeed. He picked up jobs working with Sheetrock and tile, and his hands always had homemade bandages coming off his cuts. He was struggling with cocaine addiction, buying it a couple of times a week, but he hadn't lapsed on heroin for over a year. Every day, after the methadone clinic, he had two- and three-hour commutes, before dawn and by subway, bus, and train, to his work sites on Long Island and in New Jersey. He'd been arrested a decade earlier for attempted murder, but he hadn't done time for it—"It was a family thing," he said, scowling. He was one of seven children, six of whom had become heroin addicts. He'd been partial to speedballs himself, combined shots of heroin and cocaine. When he inherited his grandfather's sugarcane plantation, one hundred thousand dollars' worth of drugs went into his veins in one year.

Paiton could be hard to find, sometimes. He had a wife and young children in the Four-Six, and elderly parents in the projects by our precinct. He also sometimes stayed out by his work site for a couple of days at a time. The first set he told me about, he gave us the wrong block, and John and I spent several nights walking through apartment buildings and over rooftops, trying to match what we saw with what he'd described, without success. But when we spoke again—whether I'd misheard him, or he'd misspoken, in his heavy accent—he said the coke spot was in his own building. Once we'd locked that in, he became extremely conscientious about calling me, providing all the detail I requested on such aspects of the layout as the door markings, the type and number of locks, and which way the windows faced.

The spot would be the most promising and challenging we'd ever gone after: it was on the top floor—the seventh—of a corner building, and they sold cocaine by the ounce. A customer would ring the bell, which turned on a light inside the apartment; a "doorman" would check the peephole, gun in hand, to see if he knew the face on the other side. If he did, he'd let the buyer in and walk him to the kitchen, where another dealer cut cocaine from the pile, weighed it on a digital scale, and packed it in tinfoil. The dealer also had a gun, on the table or under his leg, on his chair. In addition, one or two men patrolled the sidewalks in front of the building, carrying transmitters like those used for electronic car-door openers; if the cops showed up for a search warrant, an alarm would be set off before they reached the lobby. There was also a "panic button" behind the gum machines, outside the bodega on the corner, but Paiton thought it had been disconnected. It would be tough to crack.

Narcotics had done a search warrant on a sixth-floor apartment in the building earlier in the spring. They had made three arrests, seizing two ounces of cocaine and a .38. Paiton told me they were the same people, who had set up shop again on the seventh floor after the raid. I went to Narcotics and talked to a detective named Danny King, who'd done the earlier warrant. He was about to be transferred to the Intelligence Division, and he handed his case folder over to me, despite being yelled at by his sergeant, "Why don't you check with me before you give away the store—we got a CI who told us they started back up in the building, it was gonna be our case!" Because I'd DECSed the apartment, it was mine, but had Narco claimed that it was part of some investigation, I probably would have been forced to give it up. King gave me the old apartment layout, and he warned that the door had been so heavily fortified that they made it in only by chance—a customer was coming out as they were about to go in. "These are serious, professional - people," he said. "The whole door frame was reinforced steel, with a steel bar across it. We would have had better luck knocking through the wall." He said that the building super was on their payroll, which Paiton had also told us. Paiton said that the seventh-floor apartment hadn't been fortified yet, but everything else looked daunting.

Sgt. Kelly had been encouraging, saying that his good relations with the Captain would allow us to move forward with the warrant. I wasn't so sure. The Captain had reacted to the news of the Vice offer with displeasure, telling John, apropos of one of their conversations about his move to a foot-post: "Neither of you is going to Vice, I put a stop to it. Vice does nothing for Housing." Weeks had passed, and the Vice captain had told us, "Don't worry about it, we just have to process the paperwork, do background checks, and so on. It won't happen overnight, but it will happen." I wasn't going to argue with him in any case, and the prospect of a new warrant discouraged me from bringing up the issue. At each phase of the investigation, the Captain had allowed me to go forward, and when I had enough for a warrant, he let me apply for one. There was no reasonable objection to what we had—the credibility of the informant had been vouched for by the Brooklyn DA's Squad, the perps were identified as known drug dealers, and the apartment was vacant—but in my police career, at least, the Age of Reason had long since passed, and nothing would be as simple as it should be.

When Tony and Sammy went to the Captain to get their applications for Narcotics signed, he hemmed and hawed, telling them it was awful and dangerous. Was the shield really worth it? How did they feel as minorities, knowing that the Job was "using" them for that kind of work? And though he did sign their recommendations, however reluctantly, he left them with the thought: How did they sleep at night, working with me? How could they trust me? What did they think about me, knowing that I was writing about them? Tony called me at home, over the weekend, to tell me: "That guy has a hard-on for you!" I didn't feel any better a couple of days later, when I was walking past the desk, and a sergeant called out, "Hey, I hear Timpanaro's going upstairs."

"Yeah?"

"Yeah, he got transferred to Vice. He must have some kind of hook, to go from Housing to Vice. Does he?"

"Not that I know. Can I see the orders in writing?"

There it was in the Telephone Message Log: PO Timpanaro is transferred for a ninety-day temporary assignment to Bronx Vice, effective 0001 hrs, 8/30/99.

When I went upstairs to ask the Vice captain what had happened, he said that because I wrote on my application that I'd been to Narcotics only for a month, someone downtown wondered if it meant that I'd been thrown out. Because he was on vacation at the time, he couldn't be reached to explain the situation. I asked if he knew when I might be coming, and he said that he - didn't, but he expected it would be soon. When he first asked me to work there, it was with a cheery enthusiasm, but when I'd check in to ask about the status of the transfer, with John at first, and then without, the reception was increasingly cool. John asked me what I thought was going on.

"Well, as I see it, there's two options," I said. "One, it's what he says—it's just one of those things, a little clerical screwup. Or it's part of the ongoing, worldwide plot to drive me out of my mind."

Since the warrant was moving forward, there was less time to speculate. As far as I knew, I'd be joining John soon enough. The next visits I had with the Captain, however, showed that he'd given the matter some thought. As I sat in his office, answering his questions and listening to his suggestions about the warrant, he'd interrupt to remark, "What happened with Timpanaro? How did it happen? He must know somebody. Who does he know?"

I said I didn't know anything, which must have seemed disingenuous. I could lie when I had to, like I could speak Spanish, in a workable pidgin, though I sometimes thought that after years of being a cop in the South Bronx, I'd be better at both. You gotta have a story: *No, sir, you're not in trouble, but why don't you come down to the precinct to tell me your side. . . . Sure, lady, I'm sure your husband will turn up in no time, with a good explanation. . . . No, Lieutenant, I wasn't sleeping, I missed Mass this morning and I was saying a prayer. . . .* What I told the Captain was true, but it felt like a lie, even to me. I did know people—if I thought about it, I knew people who knew people who knew the President, and ditto the Pope, and yet here I was. I didn't trust the Captain, but for all I knew, he was oblivious to what had happened with SNEU, and had he had an inkling of its near-year of travesties, the Sergeant would have been sent to direct traffic on Staten Island. The Sergeant had cut communication between us, and this warrant, along with the accidental reincarnation of Sgt. Kelly, provided a brief resumption of face-to-face talk. But as it was, when we did talk, it reminded me of the movie scenes where two people drink tea, with one poisoned cup switched each time the other's back is turned:

"Is that your money you dropped, over there?"

Switch, switch.

"My mistake, I thought it was money."

"Quite all right—my goodness, I've never seen such a beautiful woman, so naked, right behind you!"

Switch, switch . . .

When the Captain ran into John after his transfer, he said with a smile, "Don't come back." He said a lot of people were mad at John for leaving us, for leaving his team. But he laughed when he said it, so John knew he was joking, there were no hard feelings, none.

The other guys on the team didn't have much to do with the warrant. We were all burnt out, and they were unbeguiled by the dubious possibilities of the moment. It would take time for the new Sgt. Kelly to earn their trust, and he was nothing if not temporary. For a warrant, there is too much work for one person to do, but there really wasn't enough for three people; even after

John went to Vice, he worked with me almost full-time—his new team neither expected him nor expected much from him, as a temp. Paiton also proved useful to John, when the three of us went out to lunch one day. We went to a good restaurant near the apartment, since I didn't want to take the chance that Paiton would run into anyone he knew. The other customers looked at him oddly, especially when a foul smell began to rise from the table. He remarked vaguely on what methadone does to your body, and we ignored the stink the best we could. When we dropped him off later that afternoon, however, John admitted that he'd been responsible for the gas attack, but when Paiton confessed, he kept his mouth shut. John had taken Vice, he'd taken the Integrity Review Board, and now he'd taken my informant as his blame hound. Some partner he'd turned out to be.

We worked on a tac plan: we had to take out lookouts, before they could transmit a signal, and we had to freeze an entire block, so that if there were additional alarms, we could prevent them from being sent. We needed hallway people, lobby people, roof people, OPs from across the street. Paiton told me that they had an apartment on the third floor, with an even larger stash; if the players ran, they'd probably head there, and we could get a bigger hit if we let them run, as long as we kept them in constant view. One of the players lived on the second floor, which could be a second target of flight and opportunity, and another worker lived on the fourth floor. I put together a booklet for the project, a twenty-page handout of assignments, subject photos, lists of hazards and responses, and maps and diagrams of the apartment, building, block, and hospital route.

The Captain wanted Narcotics to be involved. He called Capt. Hoch, who was in charge of the Four-Six modules, and a sergeant named Tommy McPartland was assigned to work with us. Capt. Hoch had been a lieutenant at PSA-7, working midnights when I had my beat in the Village. As soon as I was sent to Narcotics, the complications arose. Paiton told me the big delivery was on Friday evenings, for the weekend customers, and I set up the execution for Friday night, with Narcotics, ESU, EMS, and the dozen or more cops from the PSA. When I told the Captain, he said, "Friday's no good for me. Put it off." After it had been set up again, the Captain announced, "The Inspector wants undercovers to go and make a buy there. I think it's a good idea, too." Again, I was sent back to explain the change of plan. It was a bad idea—if a CI has an established pattern of buys, you don't make sudden changes before you hit the door. In a shop this professional, they wouldn't fall for it, and if they did, they'd figure it out later and kill Paiton.

I told Sgt. McPartland, who was incredulous, who told his lieutenant, Tom Casey, who was amazed, who told Capt. Hoch, who was dumbfounded. Hoch looked at Casey and said, "Tell me again why it is we're working with these people?" I didn't want to suggest that we say we tried and failed—how could I say to one captain, Why don't you jerk my captain around?

Fortunately, Sgt. McPartland had the same idea and no compunctions. He sent me away, saying, "Call me and let me know what time you want us to say we tried."

The next day, I told the Captain, and he said that we at least had to make a "controlled buy" with Paiton, so that even if nothing turned up in the apartment, we could find the dealers and arrest them for sale. Where the first suggestion was unwise, the second was impossible: we don't make arrests for sales to informants, because they would have to testify in open court. I nodded and walked out of the office.

Even Paiton started to call me, angry that we hadn't hadn't taken the place out, "They sell coke to ten-year-olds, twelve-year-olds, you can't believe it!" I did like his indignation—it was why I worked, too—but his expectations were not a factor in the schedule. And then he disappeared on a job for a couple of days. The Captain didn't like that. I didn't either, but I said, "This is not a guy with a secretary—you can't always get him when you want." Another day passed, as the clock ticked on the warrant, and the Captain told me to go to Paiton's house and drag him back here. I didn't. He lived in the same building as the dealers. The Captain demanded that I find him. I did. The Captain said that he and the Inspector would be content if we had Paiton make a pre-warrant buy on Thursday, and we would hit the door on Tuesday, the last day of the warrant.

SNEU had Friday and Saturday off; Sgt. McPartland had Sunday and Monday. I'd already finished work on Thursday when I found Paiton, and I'd been home for hours when I found McPartland. Later that night, we did the controlled buy, and it was quick and easy. It was also of no value. A pre-warrant buy can be made just before a search warrant is executed, to make sure the product is there—it's a kind of embarrassment insurance—but to do it four days ahead was just an embarrassment. So was going back to McPartland and Hoch, sometimes twice a day, to tell them the new demands and the changes of plans. When the Captain told Tony to drive him to the apartment to see it, he was in uniform, and he refused to go in a car with tinted windows. Tony said, "He had me circle the building six times—and when I tried to drive past at regular speed, he had me slow down again."

I delayed telling the Captain about the pre-warrant buy for a couple of days, because I didn't want to give him time for another brainstorm. Not - every idea of his was a bad idea, but the fact that they arose as last-minute, make-or-break contingencies made me wonder if the real motive was to help. It seemed as if he didn't want to deal with it or me, and wished we would all go away. Paiton told me that the weekend drop was the heaviest, but each day, there was another drop, late in the afternoon. I set up the execution for seven, locking in Narco, SNEU, EMS, and ESU. We would tac at five-thirty. On Tuesday at around noon, the Captain told me, "Seven's no good for me. Let's make it around three." I didn't feel like trying anymore.

Back I went to Narcotics, where I promised that they would never, ever see me again. I was able to put it back together, a little later than the Captain wanted, not as late as I did. At our base, I ran the tac meeting for thirty cops, handing out copies of my handsomely produced booklet. As we were about to roll out, the Captain said he'd called the desk at the Four-Six, and they said to hold off for a while, they were doing gun buys in the area. Okay. We waited a while—I was happy to, in the pouring rain, which would make the lookouts dull—and then finally moved out. A few blocks away, we formed up and waited. Chicky and Stix had been in an OP an hour before, and Mc-Partland's guys would be sent in to the floor, then Sammy would go in and hold the elevator. Sgt. Rhoden and his team would take out the lookouts, from scrips provided by the OP. John and I would go in first with ESU, Orville and Tony would cover the roof, another sergeant and his team would watch the windows and the fire escape. More cops would hold the lobby and the other floors. The signal was given: the Narco guys went in, then Sammy, then Rhoden. And then we rolled up, and raced to the door, and we all - couldn't fit in the elevator, so half the entry team took the stairs, beating us there. In the elevator, one ESU cop said, "I'm more nervous than a Polack on *Jeopardy!*"

We ran from the elevator and I pointed out the door, with its *"Somos Católicos"* sticker. A buzzer was going off inside the apartment: there was an alarm we hadn't gotten. ESU took the door in seconds—no fortifications, as Paiton said—then tossed in a percussion grenade, which shook the windows. They went in and cleared the apartment, and I followed. When the smoke dissipated, I saw the scale, a bag of cocaine, and foil on the kitchen table.

There was no one there. Lt. Johnson got on the air: "Window security, is anyone on the fire escape?"

Pause.

"Window security, on the air?"

Pause.

"Window security, is there anyone on the fire escape or the roof?"

A message came back: "There's someone on the fire escape, but he's on the sixth floor."

Well, then. We were on the seventh floor, so a man on the sixth-floor fire escape was probably just there to water his plants. ESU pulled him back in, with machine guns trained on him. He was an older man, and I recognized him from his picture. "He's under," I said, and I cuffed him.

John and Lt. Johnson went out to check the fire escape, and looking down, John saw a silver semiautomatic on the sixth floor: "Gun!"

When he went down to get it, he looked through the window of the apartment where the man had tried to escape, wondering if there was someone else inside. Lt. Johnson called him to come back up, and we began to tear the place apart. We emptied the refrigerator and the pots from the stove; we ripped up loose planking and kicked in patches of new sheetrock to check for traps. There was a Santería shrine, of candles and dishes of liquid, in a closet. No one touched it. Inside the vacuum cleaner, behind the disposable bag, Sammy found a nice brick of cocaine. There were accounting books in the kitchen, four hundred dollars in cash, a strainer and a pestle, a bowl of rice to keep the drugs dry. The Captain was delighted, and he shook my hand several times. Of the sergeant who was supposed to watch the windows, he said, "That's not your fault—there's only so much you can do. It worked out." We continued to search, soaked in sweat. The bosses left. John and I high-fived each other and took polaroids of the catch.

At the precinct, I debriefed the perp. He didn't speak English, and so Tony translated.

"Ask him why he was there."

He answered, and Tony told me that he just wanted to go there.

"He just likes empty apartments? Ask him why he had the key on his ring."

He offered such a nonsensical explanation that Tony didn't bother translating.

"Tell him he insults me with his lies. . . ."

"Tell him he is charged with an A-1 felony, he can go to jail for twenty-five years. . . ."

"Tell him he insults me with his lies. . . ."

I brought in a picture of his boss, the owner of the spot. I told him he worked for him, we knew, we wanted him, tell us. He said he didn't know him, then he knew him from the neighborhood, but that was all, and that he thought he was back in the Dominican Republic.

He clammed up again, so I pulled back. I asked him if he had ever had a real job, where he lived, when he came here, if he was married, had kids. He came here in the eighties, his kids were still in the DR, he had been a super. I asked where he lived and with whom. He said he lived with his sister, across the street. He said he was illegal but his sister was in the process of getting her citizenship.

"Tell him that he just blew his sister's citizenship."

Tony did, and he said that his sister was legal, and she hadn't done anything.

"Ask him to guess what Immigration will think about a woman who's harboring an illegal-alien cocaine dealer."

An ugly bluff, but it half-worked: he took responsibility for everything that damned him, and lied about everything that might have helped diminish his culpability. The drugs were his, he said, but he worked alone, for no one, and he bought the drugs from a guy he met on Fordham Road, who he just met in passing, he didn't know his name but he thought he might live in Jersey. He took the gun with him from the kitchen because he didn't want to be blamed for it if both were found in the apartment, and the cocaine in the vacuum was all he had left. I told him that the next time he found himself fleeing cops with machine guns, it would be wiser to leave the gun behind. I told him to write down what he'd just said, but Tony told me he didn't know how to write, not even how to sign his name. I borrowed a tape recorder from Vice, and we had him go through it all again on tape. What a jerk, I thought. He did a year or so and was deported.

That arrest represented six weeks of work. I was mostly glad and mostly proud, and I tried not to think about all the pointless errands that were required, and how much better we might have done—more perps, more drugs, more guns—had we timed the execution as we should have. There was another panic button inside the bodega downstairs, which is why alarms were going off when ESU took the door. When I talked to Paiton, he asked, "What went wrong?"

"What do you mean, what went wrong?"

Paiton told me that he talked to the other perp in the apartment, the next day. The "doorman" escaped out the window into another, vacant apartment, where the super let him hide. It was on the sixth floor. He had a gun. I was furious—the sergeant who was supposed to watch the windows from the street had cost me a gun. When I told John, he pointed out that it might have cost him a great deal more—he was on the sixth-floor fire escape, trying to peek in the window. The gunman was there, waiting. What would he have done if John had gone in? With that warrant, I'd hoped to go out on the top of my game, to leave for Vice or anywhere else with a taste of victory, to wash away some of the bitterness of the recent past. It wasn't a failure, but I would come to see it as emblematic of many things, good and bad, including my reasons for leaving.

During one of my periodic visits to Inspector Mullen, he told me that Narcotics was picking up investigators again. He didn't have to ask me twice. I - didn't look forward to the conversation with the Captain, and I waited until the day before I was leaving for vacation to have him sign my recommendation. I waited too long; he was out that day. The XO was there, however, and he was new. I got the signature and ran like a rabbit. When I went in for the interview, I had to come in on my own time again, and I was in the same suit, but the experience could not have been more different from the Street Crime fiasco. Inspector Mullen made a phone call for me, and so did Capt. Hoch; the Admin lieutenant at Bronx Narcotics, Brian Nicholson, was my second cousin, I think, but he could easily be promoted to first. At my interview, I went in to talk to a captain, a lieutenant, and a sergeant. We plowed through the routine stuff: I wasn't married, I had no kids, I could—and happily would, yes!—work late tours on Staten Island. The lieutenant was looking through my papers as we went on, remarking favorably on my arrests, then stopped cold: "Where did you go to college?"

I answered, and she asked, "Did you graduate?" I said I had.

The other two looked at me strangely: "What the hell are you doing here?" "What did you study?"

I said English, and then the sergeant said, "You should write a book, I bet you will!"

And I said I planned to. The captain said, "Well, that's about it—you're in. But we have to sit here for another ten minutes or so, or it won't look right." We bullshitted with each other, as if we were old friends at a bar.

As Inspector Mullen told me, I'd be one of the first cops in the door when it opened, but he didn't know when that would happen. It could be weeks, but it might be months; he'd heard it would probably happen before Christmas—the interview was in October—but it was also probable that the rumor would prove false. I went back to SNEU. The other Sgt. Kelly was promoted to lieutenant and left the command. John was upstairs in Vice. The fights went on, and the work went on. One day when I was on vacation, Tony was walking a perp out of a project when someone threw a bottle of some noxious liquid—he later thought it might have been vinegar—from an upper floor, which smashed on the perp. For a moment, both Tony and the perp were blinded. Orville grabbed Tony and threw him in the van, racing to the hospital. Someone watching from a window called Internal Affairs, claiming that they beat up the perp, and all were called down for a GO-15, an official department hearing. I read in the papers about a cop killing himself at his precinct, in the locker room, before the day tour. He was from my Academy class. Someone said that his girlfriend had left him, and I didn't doubt there was some personal crisis, but I wondered why he came in to work to eat his gun. The Bronx motto is *Ne cede malis:* Do not give way to evil.

I hadn't been to the dentist in years, and when I finally went back, he - didn't have good news. My dental chart came back with more red pencil marks than a dopey kid's homework. I would need root-canal and other work done, requiring a dozen visits over the course of the fall.

I told John that the thought of quitting the Job had begun to flash through my mind lately. It was not a decision that I weighed consciously, and I had no plans to quit. But the idea would pop up in my head, unbidden, like a fantasy, and it was a strangely soothing daydream, like thoughts of suicide are said to be for people in deep depression. In the mornings, I would sometimes think, "What would happen if I just didn't go in?" I told John about it, and he said, "Stop it. Don't even talk like that."

The next morning, when I woke up for the ten-to-six, I lay in bed for a while, dreading the impending tour. But as the sleep left my mind and I began to take stock of what lay ahead, I broke into a smile: "I don't have to go in for the ten-to-six, I have a dentist's appointment! I have root canal!" As I got dressed, I realized what had happened, and right then I decided I would quit SNEU, that day. If the Job made having my teeth drilled look like pleasure, it was time to make a career adjustment. At the precinct, I went directly to the Admin lieutenant, and prepared to stay in his office until I was transferred. John had waited almost two months for his footpost, and when he left for Vice, he was still in SNEU. I'd have none of that.

The Admin lieutenant was at his desk when I walked in. Before I even opened my mouth, he said, "Time to move on, hmm? Well, it's all for the best, probably. What do you want? We have spots open on the midnights . . ." And we went over the squad roster, looking at the possibilities. Eddie Wynne needed a partner, and I'd have been glad to work with him, but the midnights would be a big change. He said to think about it, and I said I'd get back to him by the end of the day. I called Eddie at home and left a message, and then I went down to the SNEU office to let everyone know.

My news was not the first of the day, nor the worst. The Sergeant had thrown Stix off the team for "insubordination," a suspendable offense. Stix - hadn't even been around for most of the summer—after his wedding, he'd gone on his honeymoon, and then he'd broken his toe. He'd been back only a few weeks. Stix was stunned, and then he was enraged. The Sergeant had been a guest at his wedding. Stix had asked him a simple question that the Sergeant took as a challenge to his authority, and now even his career was at risk. He said he was going to the Captain, to fight it. I said that he should clear things up with the Captain at some point, but he should be careful what he asked for—did he really want to stay here? Besides, in all likelihood, the Captain already knew and approved. It occurred to me why the Admin lieutenant had expected a visit from one of the SNEU guys that morning, and why he was so accommodating—he thought I was Stix.

Later that day, when I passed the Admin lieutenant and the Sergeant standing by the Desk, I said casually, "I'm leaving too, Sarge."

"Okay," he said, and I kept on walking.

TEN

When I went to work midnights, it was discovered that I didn't have a nickname. You need one, for patrol, to talk casually over the radio: "Stix, you getting coffee?" "Chicky, did you check the roof?" "OV, T, GQ, can you swing by?" Nicknames never stuck to me, for some reason, and I always thought that nicknaming yourself was like talking to yourself, something that made you look foolish if you were overheard. So the Hat, Hawkeye, Hollywood, Gee-Whiz, Big E, the Count, Rollercoaster, and the rest pitched a few:

"Hemingway—nah, they'd know it was you."

"Ernest is better."

"Or Clancy—he'd be a good one to have."

"What about Edgar?"

"What from?"

"Edgar Allan Poe."

"What about Poe?"

Poe it was. As I thought about it, the fit was neat: Poe had worked midnights, too, weak and weary, upon a midnight dreary, in his most famous poem. He moved to New York City in 1844, the same year the legislation that created the New York City Police Department was signed. He wrote the first mystery story ever, called "The Murders in the Rue Morgue." I don't mean to spoil the ending for anyone, but the killer turns out to be a demented orangutan with a straight razor. There is a brilliant detective, an earnest sidekick, a mood of languor and gloom—all the hallmarks of a genre that has endured for a century and a half. No one else has done much with the crazy ape. Poe spent his last years in the Bronx, living and working in a cottage that is midway between where I lived and where I worked. I was a police officer in the Bronx, where some kids called the cops "po-po." Was it all coming together? Give me a minute.

Midnights for Poe seemed less a time than a territory, a place of woefully distant vistas, as if he were stargazing from the bottom of a well. A lot of that has to do with needing sleep, I think. Everyone lacked sleep on the midnights, and it may have been this state of worn-out wakefulness while the rest of the world was dreaming that lent itself to thoughts that meandered roundabout and far. Each precinct has a list of "cooping-prone locations"—out-of-the-way places, under bridges and by rail yards and the like, where bosses are supposed to check to make sure patrol cars haven't stopped in for a nap. The list is posted, and when you look at it when you're tired, it seems like a recommendation, a Zagat's guide for secret sleep, as if it might say: St. Mary's Park, with its rolling hills and abundant trees, offers superb concealment in a pastoral setting—we give it four pillows! On the midnights, we talked about sleep the way frat boys talked about sex. Did you get any last night? How was it? Nah, nah, but this weekend, believe me, I'm gonna go all night long! Though I asked practically everyone on the tour how long it took for your body to adjust to an upside-down life, only three people gave precise answers:

"Two weeks."

"Four months."

"Never."

Nevermore . . . Uncle Eddie finished his thirty-three years as a cop working midnights in the Bronx, and he would have told me, I know, that he liked it because they leave you alone. That's why I went. I would wait until Narcotics called, or Vice, away from the storms of SNEU. Stix would wait with me, until the Captain understood what had happened, or the Sergeant was thrown out, or enough time passed for no one to care anymore. We would have time to think and breathe. I didn't look forward to coming in to work, but I didn't hate it—root canal no longer rated as a relative pleasure. Stix said that his wife, Anna, thought that he seemed better, too.

We would be partners in Squad A, and Sgt. Yolanda Gonzalez was our boss. Sgt. G would be retiring in the spring, and the precious closeness of her departure, coupled with twenty years on the Job, gave her steadiness and perspective. Sgt. G was pretty and proper, sweet-natured as a schoolmarm, and the cops looked up to her and looked out for her, as if they were reform-school boys who'd found a sudden inspiration for homework. Since she was a veteran of the military and also of undercover work, the protective sense that she inspired in her cops might not have been entirely necessary, but it was certainly good to see. Of the handful of cops in the command who were closer to the end of their careers than the beginning, most of them—Linda McLean, Timmy Anderson, Mike Moxom, Harry Thompson—worked the midnights. They looked at us with sympathy and something akin to bemusement—what we'd been through might have been bad, but no one had been indicted or killed, and so tragedy-wise, we were still a little light. Years before, I'd been surprised to see Timmy Anderson, in the daylight and wearing a suit. He was heading to court. "Someone had the bad taste to die while they were wearing my handcuffs," he said wearily, cutting to the nub of a longer story he told me later, of a perp whose cocaine psychosis led to cardiac arrest, and who would haunt Timmy as a litigious ghost for long after. Did we have problems? *Lemme tell ya about problems. . . .* If nothing else, our SNEU saga made us part of the hard-luck fraternity of the NYPD, and the midnight cops welcomed Stix and Poe as the newest old-timers.

Still, it was a difficult adjustment, for Stix especially. He was so fastidious that when he ate a sandwich, he held it in a paper towel. Once, when he was getting dressed, he dropped his uniform shirt on the floor of the locker room, and promptly threw it back into his locker to take it home to wash.

"The floor is covered with toejam," Stix said.

"Your partner, he's a real perfectionist," observed another cop, dressing by his locker.

"That's one word for it."

Stix found it hard to get used to eating and sleeping on our new schedule, and he was often nearly delirious with exhaustion. In the first week, I think he asked me a dozen times: "Do you wake up at night and have breakfast? And do you go home in the morning for dinner? How can you have eggs at night, or pasta when your wife is having eggs?" For me, a perversely ordered life was somewhat better than the old chaos, but it was still hard. Though the schedule was not kind on either of our digestions, I grew weary of his reaction whenever we encountered any foul odor—he would wrinkle his brow, glare, and ask, "Did you fart?" Quite often, I had not.

On our first night, Stix and I guarded an empty apartment. A woman had made a complaint about her ex-boyfriend, and he had come back and fired a couple of shots at her. For an indefinite period, two cops would be stationed outside her apartment, twenty-four hours a day. Though she had been staying with relatives for some time, Stix and I didn't object to the assignment, and we devoted the tour to reading and the discussion of breakfast philosophies. We were assigned there another night, and then another. The silences grew longer and more leaden.

"Did you say something?"

"I didn't even *think* anything."

A cop from the four-to-twelves who was also on the Captain's shitlist had spent a lot of time there, until he got into even more trouble by bringing in a chaise longue. It made sense to me. A lieutenant from the Inspections Unit made periodic checks on us, I suppose to make sure we were doing nothing. On other nights, we were detailed to guard hospitalized prisoners, or to work inside, handing out radios or working the "T/S," the telephone switchboard, behind the desk.

I had never worked inside, and I didn't think much of the cops who chose to—who would want such a dull and easy assignment? I didn't change my mind about the "dull" part, but "easy" was revised after my first tour on the T/S, when I developed my first case of writer's cramp since college. It was well after four when I was able to look up from the "daily summons recap," which consisted of indexing and cross-referencing the five-digit control number for each day's master sheet with each summons. On the master sheet, I'd write the cop's name and six-digit tax number, the date of issue, and then the ten-digit summons number, and then the plate number if it was a parking summons, or the person's name, address, and date of birth, if it was a criminal-court summons, or the plate number, name, address, and date of birth, if it was a moving summons. Seventy-three summonses had been issued in the past twenty-four hours at PSA-7, and I learned each of them intimately. Then I had to count them again and break them down: back copy for us, front for court, each in its own envelope, with separate envelopes for the two summonses that were turned in a day late. When I finished, Sgt. G politely explained that I'd written the control number on the wrong part of the summons, on the tear-off strip on top that would be thrown away. "Forget it, don't worry about it," she said consolingly. "I don't know who looks at this stuff anyway."

One night, when Stix had a hospitalized prisoner—a seventeen-year-old asthmatic crack dealer—he got the perp to give up three spots, one with a gun, which he'd been inside within the last twenty-four hours. When he came in for meal, we ran the checks and IDed all three players—each with felony narco raps, one on parole. Stix talked to Timmy Anderson about it, and Timmy suggested that we take it up with the Lieutenant, who was usually gung-ho for this sort of thing. But when Stix approached the Lieutenant to say that we wanted to look into something, the Lieutenant laughed and shook his head. "It's a waste of time," he said. "They're never gonna let you guys do a warrant. Tell you what—instead of trying for the warrant, why don't you just run into that wall as fast as you can. Maybe that'll get it out of your system."

After a couple of weeks, Harry Thompson, who was the PBA delegate on the late tour, took us aside. "You guys might have noticed you've been getting shitty assignments."

Yes, we had.

"What happened was that your old boss reached out to fuck you guys. But if you guys write some summonses, get some collars, whatever, Sgt. G is gonna be in a better position to tell them that she won't."

"How are we supposed to get collars on a fixed post or T/S?"

"That's the thing."

It was the thing. Sgt. Gonzalez later had a word with us, as well. "Here and now," she said. "This is a clean start. Whatever happened in SNEU is past—I won't hold it against you."

"What did you hear that happened?" I asked. If I had to write a complaint for the "suspicious DOA" of the SNEU team, Stix and I would have been listed as the complainants instead of the perps. It was disquieting to hear that the common understanding might be otherwise.

"I don't know what happened," she said. "I heard it was something about a warrant. . . . I don't know, and it doesn't matter to me."

Stix said, "It wasn't like that, Sarge."

She nodded. "Like I said, this is a fresh start."

I would have liked to think so. Rumors in the precinct buzzed around like microwave signals, in high volume and low quality—various cops had told me, with utter confidence, that the Captain was beloved by the bosses downtown and had a limitless future; that he was hated and was on his way out; that he hated the Job and would leave the instant he was eligible; that he never wanted to leave and was desperate for promotion to deputy inspector; that the promotion was due any minute now; and that it was a flat-out impossibility, because—and this is on the highest authority, so don't tell anyone—no one in Housing would be promoted. Sgt. G's reference to the warrant had an understated accuracy in my case, but it had nothing to do with Stix. It was little wonder that the rumor mill did less to clarify than to confuse.

The degree of confusion became apparent when a cop informed me matter-of-factly that it wasn't the Sergeant who'd thrown Stix out, but the new lieutenant—who had gleefully sent us on patrol when the Sergeant was out, and who now was the precinct Integrity Control officer—on the grounds of "chronic lateness." Stix had been officially late once, when there was a hurricane. The new lieutenant put him in the Minor Violations Log, and the Sergeant wrote "counseled for tardiness" on his evaluation. It was the only recorded infraction in his career, since the Sergeant's later charges of insubordination were bluntly dismissed by Lt. Johnson. But other cops picked up the theme of the story, passing along remarks to the effect that no one liked the new ICO, and that he was bound to cause trouble. Finally, cops from SNEU told us that the Sergeant now claimed that he didn't throw Stix out, to anyone who wasn't in the room when it happened—"I fought to keep him, there was nothing I could do . . ."—which was a rather grand lie. Since Stix and I had eight hours and thirty-five minutes a night to think about it, I came to speculate that the Sergeant and the ICO spun the story together, since it suited one to look like a nicer guy than he was, and the other to look tougher. It deepened our mistrust of the bosses, and made gestures of support from other cops all the more touching.

When Angelo Ricci, one of our PBA delegates, heard that we were both out of SNEU, he marched in to the Captain to confront him. The Captain said that Stix and the Sergeant "had been butting heads for a while," and that I was trying to transfer just about anywhere, but it wasn't happening because "nobody trusts him." Angelo said, "What are you talking about? Everybody loves him—he's a great cop and a great guy, one of the best cops in the command."

"Well, maybe it's the supervisors who don't trust him."

Angelo left the office, saying, "You just flushed two great cops down the toilet."

As part of my escape plan, I wrote up the bribery collar and the last warrant for department recognition, to get the points for the transfer. I was given bars for Meritorious Police Duty and Excellent Police Duty, respectively. An EPD is the most basic police commendation, and an MPD, which was a step above, was the conventional award for a bribery collar. The bribery collar took a couple of hours, and it sidelined a junkie for a couple of months; the warrant took six weeks, and it disabled the operation of serious criminals, even if the effects were more partial and temporary than they should have been. It didn't make sense, but I made nothing of it. And then Sgt. Clark, who headed the precinct awards committee, told me, "I put you in for a Commendation"—one level above an MPD—"but the Captain said you didn't deserve anything. He said it didn't happen the way you wrote it up, and Narcotics did all the work. He didn't want to give you anything—I had to fight with him to get you the EPD."

Though we were free of the Sergeant completely, and I'd rarely see the Captain, their enduring reach rankled nonetheless. It was not right that such small people had such a large influence in our lives, and similar revelations spurred many cops into devoted study for the sergeant's exam and beyond. Things were bad-marriage bad between us, with the kind of intensity that depends on an element of mutuality. Time and distance might provide a better perspective. The Sergeant was eagerly friendly to me again when we saw each other, as he had been on the first days on the team. I was not friendly in return, but I did wonder whether, if he'd been a cop with us, instead of our ostensible leader, his shortcomings would have been so pronounced. He was a bad fit for us, but not a bad man, at least at first; most people have a breaking point, and we were his. He reminded me of certain clients from my defense days, who were decent enough people as long as life treated them decently, but whom three bad weeks in a row would send into coke binges and liquor-store stick-ups. For the Captain, it was harder to guess—if the Inspector hadn't canceled one warrant, or he hadn't canceled three, or my book news had stayed hidden for another week, or he'd been at the command longer . . . Then again, I thought, the hell with both of them. In one year, I'd made more collars than either had made in his career. For the past eleven months, I had done backflips for them; the next jump would be out. Stix and I resolved that if one of us were hurt, the other would keep them both out of the hospital; if it went worse for us, they were to be banned from the church.

The Sergeant and the Captain cost us faith, time, and needless aggravation, but the worst you could say of them—arguably, at the farthest reach—was that certain criminals owed them their freedom, since they had kept us from working as we should. To encounter people who were genuinely evil, we would have to leave the precinct. We didn't have to go far away. When we finally got out on patrol, we were out for an hour before we were called in for another fixed post, at a crime scene. There had been a rape at one of my old buildings on Washington Avenue, on a stairwell in Morris Houses. The scene encompassed three flights of stairs and the elevator that the perp had taken to escape. The victim's clothes had been thrown all over the stairs: a scruffy brown leather jacket and an orange sweater on one landing, tan pants and a pair of aqua-and-blue-striped gym shorts on another. Her shoes were there, too—gray leather ankle-high boots, each still laced up and tied. There was a condom wrapper on my floor and a condom two flights up. I had the bottom of the stairs, Vinnie Commisso had the top, and Stix had the elevator. I asked about what had happened, and a sergeant casually threw out a couple of details. My job was to stand guard over a pair of shorts, and it didn't really matter what I knew. I overheard that there were inconsistencies to the woman's story: she said she was going to the store, but she didn't have any money and never left the building. One detective on the canvass muttered that she must have been hustling on the stairwell: "We're gonna lock this guy up for Theft of Service." I told Stix, "You're gonna wait here for an hour, and then Crime Scene's gonna show up and say, 'We're not gonna get a print off an elevator button,' and walk away." That happened, only it took longer.

I stood next to a door covered with gang graffiti—"031" and "Tre 9 Bloods"—the babel of proclamations of who was a lover, who was a fighter, and who just was. I was careful not to lean on the wall because of the roaches, and then I wondered idly why there were so many flies in the hall, especially near the clothing. Two detectives from the Crime Scene Unit came and asked what we had, and I told them what I knew. Per their request, I called upstairs, "Hey, Vinnie, is the condom full?" They shone UV light on the clothes, which illuminates body fluids, but there was no evidence of semen. They bagged some of the clothes, and then one of them went to pick up the condom wrapper.

"Uggh, there's shit on it. Check the shorts," he said.

"You check 'em," said the other.

He did, and found they were full of excrement. Did it matter if she was a whore? Maybe it had started as a conversation about a deal, and maybe it - hadn't. However it had started, he tried to move her to the roof, and she - didn't want to go. They were in a public area in the middle of a sixteen-story building with eight apartments per floor. She had been stripped naked, and even forced to take off her shoes. Whether she lost control of her bowels out of pure terror, or in a desperate gesture to repel her attacker, she was raped as she sat in her own shit, and she ran home dirty and naked.

Moments like those cleared your mind of office politics, at least for a while. Not every job on the midnights was as heavy as that, but the jobs tended to be substantiated: "shots fired" on the four-to-twelves often meant someone wanted to clear out the kids in the lobby; "shots fired" on the midnights usually meant shots had been fired. At least half of our homicides were on the midnights, but a higher percentage of those were the "misdemeanor murders," the perp-on-perp hits. When Stix and I went to one, in the lobby of 180 Brook, the body had already been removed, but there were blood and brains all over. White feathers were also strewn about, and they began to drift away in the breeze, except for where they were stuck in the red pools and gray piles.

"What happened here, a pillow fight?"

"Nah, he had a down jacket, EMS had to cut it open to work on him. . . ."

In the lobby of a project on Webster Avenue, a member of the Bloods was ambushed by Crips and shot five times: in each hand, the chin, the belly, and the balls. An elaborate shrine had been set up for him, of candles, beer and brandy bottles, wilting flowers, and scribbled notes and pictures. The notes were from adults and teenagers, but the writing—penmanship, spelling, and everything else—were like kids' letters to Santa. One of them said more than the others:

2 guns up
Shawny AKA
Shady AKA
Waterbug
Let me drop some knowledge on you
I'm sure (God) will make sure that they 'pay' 'how' nobody knows he may send
them to 'jail to life' or he may choose to deliver them to his dogs, dogettes,
b-brothers and sisters
Much love Dutchman RIP
13 murders finest

Was God a Blood or a Crip? I wondered. Did they think of Him as the Original Gangsta? Too often in the projects, the knowledge was promised but never dropped. Two buildings away, a night or two later, we had another gun run—"Male black, dark clothes . . ."—in a lobby where there were eight or so guys hanging out. I knew at least two of them as dealers. We approached with holsters cracked, our voices reasonable at first—"Guys, lemme see your hands"—and several complied, and then the voice harsher—"Up, I said. Hands up!"—and the rest followed, except for one. He sat listlessly and stared at me, and Stix covered the rest as I closed the gap between us. He didn't move—*Get your fucking hands up!*—and I grabbed him, flipped him around and pushed him against the fence, twisting an arm behind his back. The guys on the wall began to shout: "Hey! Take it easy on him!"

"Go easy!"

"That's my cousin, he's retarded!"

"Hey, he's retarded, yo!"

I shifted tone, reassuring him that I just had to check, I was sorry, it would be okay. I patted him on the back as I continued to check for the gun. I felt bad for him, but if they knew what they were doing, the gun wouldn't be on the big guy, or even the shooter. It would be in any of the places the cops don't want or think to look: under the colostomy bag of the guy in the wheelchair, or in the baby carriage, or in the young girl's knapsack. You want to know why I roughed up the retarded kid? *Let me drop some knowledge on you. . . .ž*

At the daylit end of one tour, a woman hailed us to point out white smoke billowing from the top window of an old three-story house with a mansard roof on Courtlandt Avenue. We rang the bells and banged on the door, and then we kicked and kicked and kicked. It was a steel door but we were almost through when a man sleepily stuck his head out from the second floor.

"You all right?" we asked.

"Yeah, don't worry about it—it's just the radiator. This is a city building, nobody's here but me and I don't know how to shut it off. The Fire Department knocked the door down last week to get in, that's why there's a nice new strong one. Thanks anyways, guys."

Both Stix and I were downcast. "I was thinking of the Commissioner," Stix said. "Him saying, 'You saved their lives, where do you want to go?'"

"I was thinking the same thing."

Such were our thoughts, and we didn't lack time to think them. There were fewer jobs than during the day tours, and far less than on the four-to-twelves. Even on the weekends, they tended to taper off after two or three in the morning. You had more time on your own than on any other tour. It felt odd to be back in the bag, back on patrol, at this hour and at this time in my career. When I thought about my past and the past of this place, as we drove and the late hours drifted on, I wondered where I was going. It often brought on a terminal feel, which I would sometimes try to cure by looking at the cause.

One night, Stix and I drove to the corner of 132nd Street and Lincoln Avenue—a cooping-prone location, in fact, though it wasn't the intention for the visit—a dead end at the very bottom of the Bronx, with a warehouse on one side and a parking lot on the other. Across the black shimmer of the river, you could see Harlem and the salt piles along the highway. When I was young, my father told me that kids from Harlem had died playing in the piles, and each time I'd see them I'd think of the little black boys drowning in the white salt. The Bronx began here, physically, and it began here in history, too, when Jonas Bronck built his farmhouse. Not much is known about him: he was a Swedish sea captain who was induced to settle the area by the Dutch West India Company. A peace treaty was signed at Bronck's house between the Dutch and the Weckquasgeeks, who lived in what would become the Bronx and upper Manhattan, ending years of sporadic but bloody skirmishes. Bronck didn't have much to do with it, but his house was the only one around.

"When did he move?" Stix asked.

"I don't know, probably when they built the projects."

It was a funny question, anyway, because it made me think that the Bronx is a place people come from, and not where they go to and stay, if luck is on their side. It was also a place of slow beginnings: Bronck came here in 1639 to homestead, and at the beginning of the twentieth century there was still farmland in the South Bronx; it only became citified as they built the subway. A person alive today could have witnessed its entire metropolitan career: two generations as a vibrant, blue-collar boomtown, and one as a slum so ravaged and riotous that when people from outside struggled to describe it, they compared it to Berlin and Hiroshima at war's end, a place so defeated that its enemies felt pity. They also compared it to the moon.

Stix and I cruised up to 142nd Street between Willis and Brook avenues, a block with a row of little houses on one side and a school on the other. We had chased a lot of junkies down that street, when they bought heroin with the brand name "President," among others, from the projects on the corner. One hundred years ago, stonecutters from Pisa named the Piccirilli brothers had a studio there, where they carved the Lincoln Memorial, but I don't suppose the dope was named in any commemorative spirit. Four blocks up and two over, Mother Teresa's order had a mission. The work they did was holy and noble, but there was also something a little embarrassing about it, to have nuns reassigned from leper duty in Calcutta to lend us a hand here. There was a picture in the *Daily News* a few years back of Mother Teresa and Princess Diana, visiting together, and Smacky was there, standing guard, just out of the frame. A little farther out of the frame is the building where Rayvon Evans died. He was a little boy whose parents kept his corpse in the closet until it seeped through to the floor below and the neighbors complained. John had driven the Lieutenant there when the job first came over, and they looked at both apartments, but the family had already thrown Rayvon's body out the window. The parents were never charged with murder because there wasn't enough of Rayvon left to tell how he died. When it was on the news, I saw Sammy and other cops from the PSA in the footage, in the hallway of the apartment and on the street, but I was glad that wasn't my job. There is a garden dedicated to the little boy, but there is no sign of the stonecutters, the princess, or the rest. Memory is short here, but the past is transparent, and you can look back as far as you want, until the present compels you to see what's happening now. It can take time for your eyes to adjust.

Midnights magnify things, sets them in sharp relief against the empty night, like gems on black velvet cloth. You answer jobs for lonely people who seem more lonely at midnight, more solitary and sorrowful, like the chubby little woman who reclined in her armchair like a pasha after attempting suicide by taking three Tylenol PMs. Or the woman whose close-cropped, dye-drowned blond hair was going green, who denied trying to hurt herself, but whose boyfriend confided that she had tried, by slapping herself, hard. Domestic disputes are all the more squalid and small-hearted when they take place at five in the morning: two middle-aged brothers at each other's throats, hours before their mother's funeral. The place stank and the walls seethed with roaches. One brother had a weary and beaten dignity, and he sat on the couch with his overcoat and an attaché case, like a salesman who had just lost a commission. The other brother shouted drunkenly, jerking and flailing like a dervish because of some unknown neurological misfires. They had argued because he had started drinking again, with a friend, who had called to report the sober one for his lack of sympathy. I took the jerky one aside, to let him ventilate a little. In his room, which was littered with cans of malt liquor, certificates from the Army and alcohol rehab were on proud display, taped to the wall. As he punched his honorable discharge to emphasize that his had been a life of accomplishment, a sunburst of roaches shot out from beneath it. I wanted to punch his rehab diploma, to show that he still had some work to do, but I thought better of it. We knew that we would be back if we left them there, and we dreaded the idea of having to lock someone up before the funeral, so we asked the sober one if he would mind leaving for a while. He agreed that it was the best thing to do; we agreed it was deeply unfair. He used to work as a security guard and he had a business card, which he offered to several cops—on the midnights, cops back each other up more often—and I took it without looking at it. "If there's anything I can do for you gentlemen . . ." he said, and then he went out to walk until daybreak.

If some people call because they want someone, anyone, to talk to, there are others for whom we are the last thing they want to see. For them, we arrive the way the Bible says judgment will: like a thief in the night. It felt like that when we took a woman's children away. With Stix, Sgt. G, and her steady driver, Louie Malagon, I escorted two caseworkers from the Administration for Children's Services who had a court order to remove the one-, two-, and three-year-old kids of a crackhead named Pamela into their care. The midnight visit was a sneak attack, as she had dodged the caseworkers during the daylight hours. Our part was to be—not to put too fine a point on it—hired muscle. These jobs are always awful, even when they run smoothly, and this one did not begin well: when we knocked, a woman answered— "Who?"—and then delayed ten minutes, muttering excuses—"Hold on," and, "Let me get something on," and then, "Who is it, again?"—before surrendering to threats to kick the door down. She was just a friend, she said, helping to clean up—probably in anticipation of such a visit. Pamela was out, she said, and there were kids in the back, but they were Pamela's sister's kids, and the sister was out, too. As we went to see the children, another woman came out from a back bedroom. Three kids were there, sleeping, who looked as if they might have been one, two, and three. But the second woman was coolly adamant: "Those are my kids, and I'm not Pamela, I'm her sister, Lorraine! I can show you, you're making a mistake!" I thought, what are the odds, two sisters, each having three kids the same ages? Somewhat high, and then the sexes—girl, girl, boy—and the odds were a little more comforting— a long shot multiplied by eight, to be precise—but I was still glad it was ACS's call, not mine. We grilled both women but they never broke from their story, and we could find no baby pictures or prescription bottles or anything else that would tie these children to the case—there lingered a twinge of doubt. And so when Lorraine said she could prove it, if we'd let her call her mother to get their ID, we agreed, as it would clearly demonstrate whether we were professional public servants doing a difficult job well, or dim-witted repo men hauling off the wrong crackbabies. But Lorraine didn't call for ID, she called for reinforcements, and the apartment was soon flooded with angry women. Lorraine wouldn't give up her kids, clutching the oldest two, while we had the baby boy, and then another neighbor took a girl, and then Lorraine tried to get out with one kid, walking down the hall. More cops came, and one told her to stop, but a neighbor woman blocked him when he went to follow, then blocked him again when he tried to step around. She howled: "Call the cops! Call the cops and have him arrested! He ain't leaving till the cops come and arrest him!" It looked like it was about to boil over, when even more cops came, two of them running up twelve flights of stairs, and one had to lie down when he got there, and the other was rushed to the hospital with chest pains just after. The press of angry bodies made the apartment hot, and some women yelled for everyone to calm down, and some women yelled the opposite, and as we tried to dress the crying kids, some women tried to help, in earnest, finding their jackets and socks, while others were plainly angling to shoplift them. Lorraine had her last child taken, and she took a swing at a cop but one wrist was grabbed, then the other when it followed, and her friends took her aside, and after a few more eruptions of screaming, we got the kids out. One woman yelled, "This is why people hate the cops!" And though I thought very little of her and the rest of them, the Mothers United for Narcotics and Neglect, she had a point, because no one likes people who steal babies in the middle of the night. Although I was confident that we had done right, it felt wretched, and I didn't want to dwell on it. We had just started our tour.

• • •

THE MIDNIGHT TOUR IS ALSO CALLED THE FIRST PLATOON, the second and third being day tours and four-to-twelves. You begin at 2315 hours and end at 0750. There are three squads for each platoon, working five days on, two days off, five days on, three days off, so that there are two squads on patrol every tour. The five days are the "set," the two or three the "swing." If you have Tuesday and Wednesday off one week, say, you have Tuesday, Wednesday, and Thursday the next, and then Wednesday and Thursday the week after that. It takes some getting used to, because if you're working a Friday, you don't come in Friday, you come in Thursday night. Another depressing thing about midnights is that when you finish work, at ten minutes to eight in the morning, you don't say, "See you tomorrow," which would seem soon enough; you say, "See you tonight." Tonight began yesterday and tomorrow begins tonight, and the days become one rolling night.

You lose track of time on this schedule, much more than on any other. I started out on steady four-to-twelves, Sunday to Thursday. You could lead a more normally regimented life. For my first two years at the Morris Houses, I was busier than on the midnights, when I might cover an entire precinct. The crime rate hadn't fallen as far as it later would, and the hours weren't as late. I knew less local history then, and the landmarks I navigated by were of recent relevance: the pawnshop to check after a chain-snatch; the crackhouse where the baby had overdosed; the rooftop where they fought pit bulls, sometimes throwing the loser to the street below. Sometimes Stix and I covered that area on the midnights, but even with a better grasp of the place and more time to think about it, I still wondered why things had turned out as they had.

Morris Houses were named after Gouverneur Morris, a Revolutionary War hero and coauthor of the Constitution who served with Washington at Valley Forge, and who later established the decimal system of U.S. currency, inventing the word "cent." His half-brother, Lewis, was a signer of the Declaration of Independence, and he tried to get the Founding Fathers to establish the Capitol on the family estate, though the idea was more or less a nonstarter. The Morrises owned most of the South Bronx from 1670, and their name is everywhere: the neighborhood called Morrisania, in the Four-Two, where my beat was, and Morris High School, which graduated the industrialist Armand Hammer and Secretary of State Colin Powell, not to mention dance-school impresario Arthur Murray. The neighborhoods of Morris Heights and Port Morris are named for the family, as is Morris Avenue, although Morris Park, which was built over the racetrack where they once held the Belmont Stakes, is named after someone else. Yet I couldn't say they mean much to anyone here; Morris Houses was the place where the kids Bernhard Goetz shot came from—four thugs who approached the wrong lunatic on a subway, in 1986. One remained confined to a wheelchair, and I'd sometimes see him around. I locked up another one's sister for robbery, after a nasty girl-gang fight, and I can't imagine their mother said, upon each of her children's return from jail, "Gouverneur Morris and his half-brother Lewis must be rolling in their graves!" The Morrises made this place and helped make this nation, but they might as well have knocked up some local girls after a one-night stand, leaving nothing but their name.

It's hard to think of how things could have gone worse, though they certainly could have. On a map of what might have been, I could point out the spot where someone planned to shoot Franklin Delano Roosevelt during a campaign visit. It isn't far from where the ransom was paid for the Lindbergh baby, though the child had been dead a month by then. I could show you the spot on Bryant Avenue where Popeye and Sonny recovered eighty-eight pounds of French Connection heroin, though I wish I could drive by and say, "This is where we won the war on drugs." There are other local monuments to lost opportunity that are not all cause for regret, however. A few blocks away, at 1522 Vyse Avenue, Leon Trotsky lived for a year before returning to Russia for the role that fate had assigned him. When the story broke, the headline of *The Bronx Home News* read, "Bronx Man Leads Russian Revolution." Imagine if he had stayed here. John F. Kennedy lived in the Bronx for a year as a child. I wonder what he would have sounded like, if he'd stayed: *Ax not what yiz can do for ya country . . .* Lee Harvey Oswald lived in the Bronx as a young teenager, in Highbridge and Belmont. But JFK returned to Boston, and Oswald was sent to the Youth House, for psychiatric evaluation, and they would not meet for years, and not here, and they would not know that they had the Bronx in common.

When the time dragged, these scraps of fact that jammed my head like a junkshop's clutter tended to pop up more often. The Russian theme reemerged one night, when it was so slow that three patrol cars showed up for a dispute between two crackheads over a lost shopping cart. To pass the time, we conducted a thorough investigation, asking pointed questions: *What color was the cart? Do you have a receipt?* It was cold, and after a while, one of the cops said we should leave. But I was bored enough to want to talk to the crackheads, who relished the attention. I said to the cop, "They have issues, we can help them work through them, the relationship can come out even stronger than it was before." He looked at me and said, "Hey, I'm no Dr. Zhivago, let's get out of here."

On the midnights, there is a risk of drifting within yourself, trailing off on your own weird trains of thought, so that when the even weirder world intrudes, it is hard work not to laugh. In short, you get a little punchy sometimes. I felt bad after one job, for a few reasons. It was a sad case and they seemed like good people, an old man and his sick wife. He had an upright, military bearing, and she was a stick figure, with plum-colored bruises all over, gasping through her nebulizer, *"Ayúdame, ayúdame, ayúdame. . . ."* We made small talk, in broken English and Spanish, while waiting for EMS.

There was a picture of a young man in a police uniform, and the old man said he was his son, a cop in San Juan who had died at the age of thirty-four, from cancer. The entire apartment was a Santería shrine: cigars laid across the tops of glasses of clear liquid; open scissors on dishes of blue liquid; dried black bananas hanging over the threshold; tarot cards, change, and dice before a dozen statues of saints, including a massive Virgin Mary with a triple-headed angel beneath. They struck me as objects of pity and power at once. I wondered if it was the woman or the man who was trying to stack the supernatural deck in their favor, if disaster, past or impending, could be re-negotiated with the spirits and saints. And then I thought, *They keep the place up, but it's more House Voodiful than House Beautiful.* The line wouldn't leave my head, and I started to break up. I had to pretend to cough and walk outside, while Stix gave me a funny look.

You get in the habit of reading these scenes for signs, forensic or sacra-mental, as they both make the same point about sin and struggle in the fallen world. In Santería, shrines of candles and other offerings are often placed in the corner of a room, near the entrance; and in just that spot, in one apart-ment, there was a black-handled butcher knife, and blood that had not just pooled but piled, it lay so thick on the floor. There were dark sedimentary layers, and a clear overlay like varnish, which I was told came from the lungs. The woman whose handiwork it was explained what brought her to this sacrifice at the household altar: "Two years ago, my brother broke my leg in five places. I came in tonight, he sold my couch. He killed my mother. Well, she died from him and all his nonsense." She stopped talking for a mo-ment, and tried to shift her hands in her cuffs, as EMS took him out in a wheelchair, pale and still. "I didn't stab him," she went on. "He stabbed him-self by accident, in the back, in the tussle." Some objects tell simple stories of fierce violence, like the two-by-four, so bloody it looked like it was dipped in the stuff, used to collect a fifty-dollar debt one woman owed another. Others are more subtle and tentative, like the open Bible in the apartment of a woman whose brother, just home from prison, suffered some sort of psy-chotic break. "He sat there reading the Bible for a while, and then he just looked up and said he was going to kill me," she said. The Bible was opened to the first page of Proverbs, which says, in Chapter 1, Verse 18: "These men lie in wait for their own blood, they set a trap for their own lives." Maybe he only read the first part of the sentence. The woman's husband had just died, and beside the Bible was a sympathy card from someone named Vendetta.

As a cop, you look for patterns, for context and connections that tell a fuller truth than a complainant may be willing to tell. But sometimes the patterns themselves are deceptive; there are parts that belong to no whole. So it was with a matched pair of attempted robberies, twenty minutes and four blocks apart. Each perp was a male Hispanic, tall, slim, and young, in dark clothes (all brown in the first case, all black in the other), with a razor blade. In the second robbery, the perp wore a bandanna over his face and a wig, and the victim was cut in the hand with a razor. We packed up the complainants and canvassed the park that lay between the crime scenes, and we stopped a tall, slim, male Hispanic in his twenties, in all-black clothes, and when I searched him, I found a wig, a bandanna, and a razor in his pocket. If there was some doubt that the perps were the same, there was little that I'd found the guy responsible for one of them. Both complainants were sure, however, that he wasn't the perp, and we let him go. Since the weapon was a razor, maybe I should have remembered Poe and gone to look for the orangutan.

That was one kind of mystery, the puzzle of whodunit, which has a solution that is out of sight but within reach, like the winning card in three-card monte. There are other mysteries that raise questions that are far older and more open, and if there is a hint of a game in what unfolds, you feel more like a piece than a player. One night we went to a routine Aided case, an old woman with a history of heart trouble, whose breath was rapid and shallow. She moaned, *"Mami!"* as she sat on a red velvet couch, flanked by her young teenage granddaughters, and as she left with EMS, Stix told me that the old lady took care of the girls. We drove around for a while, and then we had another Aided case, a "heavy bleeder." When we went inside, a woman said, "She's in bed," and, "It's in the tub," and we checked on the teenage girl in the bedroom, who said she was fine, and then looked in the bathtub, where a fetus the size and color of a sprained thumb nestled in the drain. The head was turned upward and the eyes were open and dark. When the EMTs came—they were the same guys as at the last job—they asked for some plastic wrap or tinfoil, and they were provided with a sandwich bag to pick it up. As we helped them put the teenage girl in the ambulance, the EMT told me that the old lady had gone into cardiac arrest and wouldn't make it. Nothing else happened that night, and as we drove I thought about the two jobs, what they asked and answered, and what went through my mind was that for - every one that dies, another one never is born. It was late but not late enough, not yet time to go home.

• • •

OCTOBER PASSED, AND THEN NOVEMBER, AND CHRISTMAS approached. In the beginning, especially, it didn't seem that John and I worked at the same job: I was a security guard, and he might spend a night drinking, going to bars where an underage police cadet would attempt to be served, or to see if he could buy a drink after four a.m. He was getting paid to drink beer. Technically, he was an undercover, but the assignments were not 007 stuff: he'd go to bodegas and try to buy loose cigarettes, or to Yankee games to scalp tickets. They locked up old men in social clubs for having a case of beer in the back room, or old ladies in bodegas for having policy slips or a joker poker machine. At first, I was jealous of the ease of his life, but later on, when I was back in the street, he was jealous of the stories of real police work. When people asked us where we worked, I noticed that he began to say he was in the Organized Crime Control Bureau instead of Vice.

Nonetheless, the time counted for his shield, and there were other perks. John was trained in the use of the "asp," the new, telescoping nightstick, which you'd extend with a flick of the wrist, and perps would run at the sound of it. He was sent to a day-long course on eavesdropping technology, where they gave out tote bags that were emblazoned SECRET SERVICE NYPD ELECTRONIC CRIME SEMINAR. He came home beaming, holding it up.

"How do you like it?"

"The logo's cool. It's just a shame they decided to put in on a purse. You're probably tough enough to get away with carrying it around, but you could also give it to your sister."

As Vice grew less attractive to me, it was becoming clear that the distaste was mutual. John asked the Vice captain about me a couple of times, and then he stopped, as the answer of "Soon, I think" grew testy and cool. More temps came into the office, and I came to suspect that this constant flow of new people was someone's idea of an integrity tactic, so that the cops - wouldn't trust one another enough to steal. John worked often with another temp named Chris Verdejo, and we went out for dinner one night. Chris had just made a case that was featured on the front page of the *Times* sports section, when he took down a major counterfeiter of pro sports tickets. Chris had worked a Yankee game for scalpers, and he picked up a perp who had counterfeit tickets. Even the "legit" scalpers, who after all sold a real ticket, hated the counterfeiters. Chris developed his perp as an informant, and it led to a print shop where tickets for hockey, baseball, and basketball teams all across the country were produced. George Steinbrenner had assisted the police in the investigation, and it got great press. "I'm the flavor of the month!" Chris laughed. The Vice captain told him he could stay permanently, if he wanted, but later on said he couldn't manage it. Some inspector's nephew would be getting the spot. It reminded me to call Inspector Mullen, and offer myself up for adoption. At Central Booking one night, I noticed a cop from the Four-Seven eyeballing me, after which he asked if I knew Mullen. I said I did, but when he scrutinized my name tag, he shook his head and said, "I thought you were his son." If only that cop worked in the personnel office.

And then John received another unexpected notification. He was called up for the Fire Department, from a test he had taken five years before. The rumor was that the old list was resurrected because the son of one of the big bosses was on it. My cousin Brian had also been called. Both of them were the sons of firemen—my cousin Gerald, Brian's brother, was also on FD—and John's father had worked until he had a heart attack in the firehouse, refusing to go to the hospital until he was carried out. Mr. Timpanaro loved his job, as most firefighters did, while John's love of police work was a rarer and more complex commodity. A lot of cops went over to FD, like my friend Tommy Killian, but you never heard of firefighters who switched over to become cops, except for one or two who traveled from PD to FD and back, and were considered oddballs by both departments. Firefighters could arrange their schedules so that they worked two or three days a week; the camaraderie was legendary and the politics were minimal, next to our job; the public loved them. They died more often than we did, but they killed themselves less. For most people, there was no hesitation to transfer; for John, there was. John was not afraid of many things, and to date I was aware of two of them: he dreaded roaches, and he lived in fear that I might use his toothbrush and not tell him. I was *gabbados* and a *stunad,* thickheaded, but more important I was a *gavone,* a slob; he was a *skeevats,* who saw messy things as positively menacing. His skeeve-levels were nearly as high as Stix's, in the avoidance of doorknobs and of handshakes from bums, and once when I told him I was returning a pair of his underwear—washed, of course—he looked at me with unabashed horror and said, "Keep them." But the third thing he was afraid of was fire, I learned.

"If I see a guy with a gun, I chase him. I know the risks but I'm not afraid— I know I'm smarter, stronger, and faster than him, and that I'm a better shot.

I've been trained in tactics, and he hasn't. In my gut, I know I'm gonna win. But with a fire, none of that matters—a fire cares about me less than even the worst perp, and all I have to go against it doesn't matter. As a cop, I work in the worst part of the city, and the part I love best is the gun collars. If I went to FD, I'd go to the quietest corner of Staten Island, where I can work out all day and help cook and get a cat out of a tree once a year. I don't like fire."

And yet he decided he would accept the job. He went through another interview and medical, and was told he'd get a call on a particular Friday or Monday. The days passed, but then he was told the date had been postponed. When the next date passed without a call, he knew that the job wasn't there for him. My cousin Brian became a fireman, and John stayed a cop. I think he was relieved as much he was disappointed, but I was angry that the NYPD was such that even people who loved it would leave for work they hated, because there were so few real or rational reasons to stay.

Stix and I had begun to find our stride on the midnights, becoming a familiar team like Moxom and Parisi, Otero and Garcia, Flower and Thompson. We collared, and learned how to work an odd little cat-and-mouse OP for 175 Alex, handicapped as we were by uniforms and a marked car, available for jobs at any moment. The building had a back door, so we'd have to wait for someone to walk out in order to make a sneak attack on the dealers in the lobby. One night we had an inspiration to send in someone to open it up for us. We drove a few blocks away, to the prostitution strip on Jackson Avenue, and made the acquaintance of two ladies named Melissa and Snake. Snake explained that her boyfriend lived in the building and that she - couldn't go there, but Melissa figured that opening a door for five bucks would be the easiest money she made that night. But we waited in vain— Melissa went to the wrong building, and Snake marched straight to 175 Alex to warn the dealers.

"What's the world coming to, when you can't trust a whore named Snake?"

We sometimes slipped in to work with Eddie Fackler and his conditions team—Eddie Wynne, Dennis Koesterer, Scott Griszcewicz, Chris Barry, and Danny Campagna, who set up like SNEU each night to collar. Eddie Fackler - could "smell a gun," and his team brought them in routinely. I doubted that either of us would be able to join conditions, but to jump in with them to hit a set or chase a gun was exciting and nostalgic at once. We'd forgotten that the Job could be fun. If the midnights were never quite normal, they began to feel a little more familiar—we were in the streets, at least, and that was good.

As the holidays drew near, Sgt. G organized a Christmas party, where each cop had to bring in a dish from where their family came from, and that night we answered jobs from the precinct, like firemen, around tables of pasta, empanadas, and fried chicken.

Two days before Christmas, Stix was out, and I worked with a new guy named Tommy Rendo. We had a job for a smoke condition, from a fire that had been put out on the four-to-twelve, when someone lit up a couch in a project basement. A few people were gathered outside, unable to return to their homes because the building was still choked with smoke, and we sent a couple with a baby to the hospital for smoke inhalation. Though the Fire Department had come and gone, the building still seemed unsettled and unsafe. We propped the front doors open and waded through the ankle-deep sludgy water of the basement to open more doors, and then we walked up ten stories to open the roof doors—the elevators had been shut down—so the building - could ventilate. On the walk up, the smoke was so thick we could barely see in front of us, and we had to wait on the roof for a while to catch our breath, dizzy and coughing. On the way back down, we checked each apartment, but we had to go back to the roof a few more times for air. I was ambivalent about leaving, though the firefighters knew what they were doing and we didn't. After talking to the people outside to find out which elderly tenants might be at risk, we knocked on a few more doors and then we left.

We had to do a "vertical patrol" at a particular building, and we drove there, a little dazed and short of breath, stinking of smoke. The door was locked, and we sat in the car for a while, waiting for someone to come out. There was a recent decision to make verticals "activity," as a formal and quantifiable unit of work, like a summons or an arrest, and now every cop had to perform several each night, in designated buildings, and to notify the dispatcher at the start and finish of each. I suppose it made some cops walk when they would have preferred to sit, but it struck me as still more pointless and wrong-headed bureaucracy—would beat cops have to fill out reports for how many times they said hello to people, and whether they got a pleasant response? Why didn't they just put pedometers on our feet, and count how many steps we took at the end of the month? At roll calls, a lieutenant said, "Listen, the most important thing is to just put them over the air, so we get credit for them," with the plain message that seeming to do them was more important than anything else.

Finally, a woman walked out of the building and said hello to us—for a point maybe, on the new scale—but we didn't feel like moving just then.

Tommy and I had a cigarette, to get the old smoke out of our lungs, and then we waited awhile longer. Finally, I said, "The hell with this," and we drove off. A few minutes later, the ICO raised us for a scratch, and twenty minutes later, we were called back to the command—he had been watching us, with binoculars, and had seen that and we hadn't gone into the building. He called me into his office, and gave me a speech about how shocked and disappointed he was: "I can't believe this! People say good things about you here! How could you do it, when you've got a rookie with you, who doesn't know any better? If Inspections caught you instead of me, this would have been a serious hit! What if there was a homicide in that building, and you put over the air that it was OK? I'm thinking about just writing the CD and getting it over with!"

As he spoke, he huffed up his sense of indignation, until he almost believed it himself. I knew it didn't matter, and I knew that neither of us really cared. I was on midnights in the South Bronx, on punishment posts more often than not, and there was little else that could be done to me. I also knew that he had me, dead to rights. I'd radioed that we'd gone into a building, and we hadn't.

I said, "What can I say? It won't happen again." Tommy and I went back out on patrol and checked the building, which of course was empty. Though I wasn't much concerned about the ICO, I told Tommy about a recent experience Stix and I had with him, when we were called in for a GO-15—an official department hearing, with union representatives—over a dent in the car. When we were assigned the car, Stix inspected it—checking the back seat for contraband, looking at the fluid levels, and so on—and he noticed a crimp on the passenger side, where the door hinge met the front panel. Every time you opened the door, the crimp got bigger, and after trying a few times, the two-inch gap became a three-inch gap. Cars pick up all kinds of nicks and scratches, and sometimes if cops dent the car more seriously, they'll pay a body shop to pound it out, rather than going through the fuss of the paperwork, or losing the car for weeks to the police mechanics. Once the accident is reported, the last cops to use the car are responsible for the damage; in this case, Comparetto and Clifford might catch a little grief, since someone gave it a kick on their watch. We were reluctant to report it, but we'd had enough trouble for ourselves, and the senior cops we talked to said we had no choice. The lieutenant at the desk said he'd have a look at it, as the ICO was walking by.

Had you seen the ICO look at the car door, you might have thought that he'd found a murder weapon; had you heard him, you might have thought that the homicide was of his twin brother. "I bet they were in a hit-and-run!" he said, as Stix and I stood by, unable to share in his mounting excitement. "There was a pursuit in the Four-O on the four-to-twelve, I bet they were in it and hit somebody! Let me see if they put it over the air that they were there!" and he raced back to pull up the printout of the job, certain that he was closing in on the culprits. Comparetto and Clifford, who each lived more than an hour away from the precinct, were summoned back at two in the morning. If they weren't so tired and enraged, they might have felt sorry for the ICO. As it was, they were informed of their rights to union and legal representation. The Accident and Investigation Section of the Highway Unit was called in, to photograph the dent and dust it for prints; the District Attorney's Office was notified of the possibility of criminal prosecution; a team from Inspections arrived to conduct the formal interrogation.

Lt. Mahoney, who had the desk that night, said, "Leave it to the Police Department to turn a hundred-dollar dent into a ten-thousand-dollar investigation."

And so it was with a mix of false confidence and real indifference that I put my thoughts of the ICO aside, when we went back in for meal at five. When we left, an hour later, Tommy told me that the ICO had decided to write us up for Command Disciplines. I said, "Turn around, I'm gonna talk to him, we'll say we didn't go in on my account." Tommy began to protest that whatever we did, we did together, but I said forget about it, let's just settle this, and we headed back. As soon as I walked into the ICO's office, he said, "Where were you? You stink!"

If anything, we smelled better than the first time around, and I told him about the fire. I said that we could have gone to the hospital and gone sick for the next couple of days, but we were the only Housing car covering the Four-Two, and that wasn't the kind of cops we were. My diplomacy was not what it might have been, but he'd left me with the clear impression the reprimand would be man-to-man. He hemmed and hawed, saying that he had to write me up because he'd talked about it in front of another cop, whom he *really* wanted to get—and eventually would, for taking days off while claiming to be in the military. Finally, he told me, "Don't worry, you're one of the Captain's best guys, you won't lose any time."

"I don't think it's right," I said, and I walked out. It was the morning before Christmas Eve, and I'd have the holiday off for the swing. When I went back in, the day after Christmas, our PBA delegate Harry Thompson told me that the Captain wanted to take three days, and it was non-negotiable. The

CD, for "improper patrol," would remain on my permanent record. My great-grandchildren would be able to look at the citation, much as I had been able to look at Pat Brown's. At the roll call, the lieutenant bellowed about what a fuck-up I was, and he sent Stix and me on another fixed post, for another threatened witness who wasn't home. It was more than a mile away, near Hunts Point, and the rest of the cops were ordered explicitly not to drive us there—we would take the bus. As we waited at the bus stop, for fifteen minutes, twenty, half an hour, the other guys kept driving up to us and saying, "C'mon, get in." "Forget about it," we said. "If they want us to take an hour to get there, it'll take us an hour to get there. If somebody gets killed, we'll be glad to explain why."

That would be my post for the next two weeks, sometimes with Stix, and sometimes with Parisi, who also had run afoul of one of the bosses. I sat there and read. One night, Eddie Fackler, Eddie Wynne, Chris Barry, and Dennis Koesterer got a gun, from a pistol-whip cab robbery. The perp hid in the bushes, reaching down to his ankle as they saw him. At the precinct, Koesterer yelled at him: "What the hell is wrong with you! I could have killed you!" "I had to straighten my sock," said the perp. Louie Malagon and Sgt. G got a gun, from a robbery at 169 and Cypress. Alex Otero and Louie Garcia got a gun, and Chicky got a gun with Sgt. Toth. Chicky had also come to midnights, a month after we did. He was tired of the fighting, too.

I called Inspector Mullen, and he said that Narcotics should come soon, not long after the New Year; I shouldn't worry about the CD, he said, but I had to have it adjudicated before the transfer. Harry Thompson was able to negotiate down so that it would be removed from my record if I stayed out of trouble for six months; my dark secrets would remain hidden from my descendants. I took the three days and signed the CD. The Lieutenant apologized for blowing up at me, and said that it was the Captain's orders. Once the two weeks were up, I could go back to work with Stix again on regular patrol.

On New Year's Eve, I was assigned to guard the PSA parking lot, and it was there that I greeted the new millennium. After five years of hard work in the NYPD, I was sent to stand there, freezing amid the empty cars, as the fireworks erupted somewhere out of sight, and the gunshots rang out, a little closer. I was with a new guy named Ullman—since he'd seen combat in the Israeli Army, "rookie" seemed patronizing—and we bullshitted away the hours. I tried to say what I liked about the Job, but it was hard to come up with anything. I didn't want to come off as a hairbag, though it wasn't far from what I felt. The Captain and the ICO both paid me visits, to make sure I was at my post. I think I said "Happy New Year" to them, but I don't - really recall.

. . .

WHEN MY FATHER'S FBI FILES FINALLY ARRIVED FROM WASH-ington, eighteen months after I'd requested them, there were a lot of little surprises and one larger shock. For the NYPD, Uncle Eddie's career was con-tained in some fifty pages of paper, and Pat Brown's was summed up on an index card. The stack of documents on my father was more than three inches thick, and it comprised his initial application and the exhaustive research into his medical, military, family, educational, vocational, and personal his-tory. His annual evaluations were also comprehensive, and included a med-ical exam. Once, when he was twenty pounds overweight, a pay raise was withheld for several months until he slimmed down, under a doctor's su-pervision. There were congratulatory notes from J. Edgar Hoover on his tenth and twentieth anniversaries with the Bureau, as well as for his mar-riage and on the births of each of his children. For his casework, there were many congratulatory letters from supervisors and outside agencies, but they were distinctly unilluminating: the names of his fellow agents were blacked out, and so were the names of the defendants. Since my father had the origi-nals, I could see which gangsters and agents were involved, but none of the names had any special meaning for me. One did stand out: Robert Morgen-thau, who wrote Hoover to thank him for my father's work on a case of the theft of nearly half a million dollars in American Express traveler's checks, in 1967, when he served as U.S. Attorney for the Southern District. In the letter, Morgenthau noted that the perps were in the Mafia, and he was especially pleased with how my father had been able to secure the testimony of one mobster even after his first cooperating witness was murdered in an unre-lated matter.

Morgenthau had been the District Attorney in Manhattan since the early 1970s, and he was without peer in the country in terms of stature and longevity; in all of American history, only his predecessor, Frank Hogan, had a comparable record of innovation and integrity. I gave him a call and we talked for half an hour. "Sure, I remember your father," he said. "He was a terrific agent, one of the smartest if not the smartest around, an extremely bright guy. Did he go to St. John's Law?"

Fordham, I said. I asked him how he had jurisdiction in the case, since the airports were in the Eastern District, which was the junior partner and occasional rival of the Southern.

"Damned if I know. If they were looking at Manhattan, we had jurisdiction."

Morgenthau reflected on the changes in the U.S. Attorney's Office, which now had seven times as many assistants and produced half as many indictments, and how it was controlled more by Washington—from whom you needed approval for a wiretap application, for example. As a federal and then as a local prosecutor, he had worked with FBI and the NYPD for decades. "We had an extremely close relationship with the agents, to our mutual benefit, I think. With the Police Department, it was very uneven; it depended on the Commissioner and the Chief of Detectives, and it took time to build up confidence. You knew someone trusted you when they didn't ask who an informant was.

"Most of the time, we did very well with the Bureau, except for the time when [X] was there in New York. He was a real turkey. What did the agents call him, Cement Head?"

I did recall references to Cement Head as my father talked to my mother over dinner. Morgenthau went on to ask me what I was doing, and I said I worked midnights now, but I expected to go into Narcotics soon. "Well, if you want to work in Manhattan, let me know, and once you get your shield . . ."

When I hung up the phone, I was a little giddy. I was proud of my father, and proud to be able to talk to the District Attorney. I wasn't especially proud of my professional life in recent months. It wasn't fair to compare my career at that point to either of theirs, I knew, but I was willing to hazard a guess that they never had to put their verticals over the air. I was glad to have learned the Job from the ground up, but at the moment there was an abundance of ground, and up was not in sight. The law-enforcement world of Morgenthau and my father brought serious people to work on important cases; their efforts and methods reflected dignity and thought, and there was a gravity and grandeur to their cause. The return of stolen traveler's checks might not sound so lofty, but the perpetrators were part of a powerful and murderous criminal conspiracy in the most important commercial center in the world. By comparison, I was getting yelled at over parking tickets by bosses who weren't fit to shine Cement Head's shoes.

As I looked over my father's FBI files, I was taken with the differences between the Bureau and the NYPD. There were almost 40,000 cops in the city, which was roughly four times the number of agents in the entire country. Our

evaluations were one double-sided page, mostly of five-point numerical rat-
ings for dozens of qualities, some of which were purely nonsensical—"Spatial
orientation" and "Visualization"—and others which were well-meaning but
essentially moot. For "Integrity," should everyone get the highest score until
proven guilty, or should anyone who doesn't get a 5 be fired? The Bureau's
evaluations were far more detailed and substantive, and they looked at what
each agent brought to the institution, beyond their immediate workload—one
criterion was for how many new FBI employees the agent had recruited. Great
emphasis was placed on how agents secured and developed informants. My
favorite part was a section that praised my father's dictation skills—he was
called a "great dictator," in fact—which in my adolescent years, especially, I
understood.

Each note of congratulation represented a case: weeks and months of stake-
outs, wiretaps and raids, tips and the interrogations, moments of broad comedy and dull fear, and finally—it would seem by the fact of the letter—a
measure of satisfaction. There were no letters for cases that fell apart, of course,
for the non-arrests, the tentative informants who disappeared or clammed up,
the wiretaps where the conversants stuck carefully to talk of girlfriends and the
Yankees and what they ate for lunch. Failure spoke for itself, or rather it didn't:
the absence of reprimand in my father's files—weight-loss notwithstanding—
suggested that even when a case didn't work out, either nothing in particular
had been done wrong, or no one had held it against him.

That seems to have been the case with the great revelation of the files. I remember asking my father when I was young, "Hey Dad, didja ever kill anybody?" I suppose every cop's kid asks that, and since my father was in World
War II and then in law enforcement for thirty years, it was not an altogether
unreasonable question. But his face darkened at my idle enthusiasm, and as
far as I can recall, his response was more of a dismissal than a denial. It was
a rude question, as I know from having been asked it myself, many times,
and children who don't know better need to be taught. So when I came across
documents relating to an incident in the summer of 1961, when my father did
kill someone, the fact of it was as surprising as the form. It was in a traffic accident in the neighborhood, on Broadway at 256th Street. An elderly couple
walked across from east to west. My father was driving northbound on
Broadway. The woman lagged behind, having reached the middle of the
street while her husband was already at the curb; a car sped southbound, and
the woman hesitated, then turned suddenly back into my father's lane,
where he struck and killed her. There were a number of witnesses who of-

fered consistent testimony about the second car, which fled and was never found, and the woman's husband did not pursue a case against my father. Since he was not at fault, I almost wonder why he never told me about it. I think if I'd had a driver's license—I got mine only a week before I went into the Academy—the story might have found its way into a cautionary tale. I asked my mother about it recently, and she paused a moment before she told me, "We were married only a few months then. He came home, and he said—he had a hard time telling me about it—he said it was the kind of thing that was so awful and unreal that he wanted to run away. He couldn't believe it was happening."

What did I know about my father? When he'd come home from work, he'd take off his hat and say, "Traffic was bumpita-bumpa," and for years I thought the phrase must be Italian. He drank Sanka and put Brylcreem in his hair. Every night, he said his prayers on his knees, beside the bed, but when he wanted to sneak into the Fordham gym to go swimming, he would drive past the security guard and bark, "Father Maloney!" Often, he was as direct as a billboard, but there were times when he was a literal sphinx. Once, a college roommate of mine who was visiting asked him three questions in quick succession: *How did Napoleon's army retreat from Russia? How does the Israeli mafia work? How long does it take to become a federal judge?* Though they were odd questions, they matched my father's interests in history, crime, and politics, and he traced the route of retreat, described a typical electronics-store bust-out scheme, and in response to the judicial question, he returned to reading his newspaper and said, "How long is a piece of string?"

I was twenty-six when he died, but we had lived under the same roof for most of those years, and even when I left, it was for his old home. He was a good storyteller and I was a good listener, which acquainted me with much of his biography, the facts and his feelings about them. We were each one of five children who remained close to their siblings, geographically and otherwise, providing an ample if sometimes contradictory pool of recollections. We were in the same line of work, which we seemed to regard with the same complex intensity. Further understanding would come as I grew older, when I would have children of my own to annoy me.

There were no other real surprises in my research, only bits and pieces that were pleasant to read or funny to think about, as when I found letters from his Marine Corps buddy, Nathan Perlmutter, who went on to head B'nai B'rith. I knew he was friends with Perlmutter; I didn't know that Perlmutter called him "Jocko." While it was uplifting to hear from Morgenthau, "Sure I knew him," I wonder what I would have said if I ran into a man who could say, "John Conlon, of course. He killed my wife."

I didn't know what to make of that, or how much. Mostly, I would have liked to know what he made of it—whether he ever forgave himself, or whether he felt he needed forgiving. For me, it pointed up one of the ironies of police work, of how people take dangerous jobs for the security they provide. While my father was at war, his mother died in bed; after almost ten years as a G-man, he killed a woman who was crossing the street. Work isn't as dangerous as life; you could get hurt or killed on the Job, but off-duty, - everybody has to die sometime. Maybe work helps to put that in perspective. If it doesn't lend meaning to your death, it should lend purpose to your life. The NYPD had done that for me, for four years, and then it hadn't, for one. As a percentage, that was adequate; at present, it was not. I wanted to look forward to going to work again. The night was getting old.

. . .

FROM THE SIXTIES THROUGH THE EIGHTIES, THE LANDSCAPE of the Bronx was a record of public failure, high and low, from the powerful, such as Robert Moses, who moved through the Bronx like Sherman through Georgia, evicting thousands to build highways, to the scavengers and predators among ordinary people, who made ordinary life impossible. Since then, the landscape has changed for the better, and the record has been rewritten, often quickly and well. And it was easy to forget how most of the great landmarks of the Bronx remained throughout the burning years. The Yankees continued to play at the House That Ruth Built, no matter the distractions. Crowds still went to the Bronx Zoo, where the American buffalo was saved, a hundred years ago, from a small breeding herd. At Woodlawn Cemetery, people still paid respects to Herman Melville, Duke Ellington, and their own remembered dead. Miles Davis is buried there, too, now, beneath a shiny black headstone that calls him "Sir Miles Davis," with the *i*'s dotted with musical notes. Across the north Bronx, thousands of acres of parkland— from Wave Hill and Van Cortlandt Park, by the Hudson River, to the Botanical Garden, to Pelham Bay Park and Orchard Beach on the Long Island Sound—were enjoyed, though sensibly only in the daylight. Near Hunts Point, there is a cloistered convent where nuns pray in silence behind high stone walls. They lit candles as the neighborhood burned, confident that their fire would endure. The synagogue that was open through the 1990s on

Intervale Avenue was now the Thessalonia Baptist Church for All People. A menorah and two Stars of David are still visible on the cornice, carved in the worn stone. What had they prayed for, when the temple was their own? Maybe the prayer was, *Get out, schmuck, get out!* and their prayers were answered, too.

James Lyons, the borough president in the 1930s who chose the corpse flower for us, hoped that "Borough of Universities" would become the nickname for the Bronx, as Borough of Homes and Borough of Churches were for Queens and Brooklyn. It never stuck. NYU abandoned its Bronx campus, but Fordham stayed. Poe became friendly with the Jesuits there when he lived nearby, and he spent some time in their library and grounds. It was called St. John's then. He wrote his poem "The Bells" about the bell in the University Chapel, because it irritated him. Poe died from politics, it could be argued, or maybe even from democracy. Four years after he moved here, in 1849, he was on a lecture tour to raise money for a magazine when he paid a visit to Baltimore during an election. His health was poor and he had long struggled with alcohol. Somehow, he fell in with a political gang who enlisted him to become a repeat voter, paying him with liquor after each trip to the ballot box. He was found, incoherent, in another man's clothes, and died four days later from the binge-voting and drinking. Poe Cottage remains, just below Fordham Road, though it was moved twice from its original location, a few hundred feet away. There isn't much to it. It is a small and cheerful place, with low ceilings and wide-planked floors. The portraits of Poe show an intense look and a top-heavy head, with a vast brow, as if made for fever, and the small mouth, "which was his only defect, showing weakness," in the view of a family friend.

Poe was buried in Baltimore, and his wife, who had died two years before, was moved from the Bronx and interred with him. If he haunts anyplace, it would more likely be Baltimore. I wonder what he would have thought of the South Bronx, at its worst; what his ghost would have made of our ghost town. He wrote about loves lost to death at an early age, and he set his tales in ancestral houses gone to ruin. He might have easily adapted his castles and crypts to the abandoned factories and the tenements whose graffitied walls fell down, leaving them open like cabinets. He might have said, *Don't change a thing!* Then again, such a landscape might have left little room for the imagination, or offered too much. Poe was a dark romantic, who worked to make something lastingly beautiful out of what went wrong with his life— if he were a convict, he would have been the type who spent his sentence decorating his cell instead of plotting an escape. A great city can't think that way, and here, we have done the opposite, bulldozing over our mistakes, building on top of them and hiding them from view, and we almost expect that in another generation, we'll tear it all down and start again. And so there is another, more dramatic difference: when something came back from the dead in Poe's world, no good came of it: *It is the beating of his hideous heart!* . . . When the Bronx came back, more people wondered how than why, but no one supposed it was purely for revenge. The phrase "with a vengeance" does come to mind, when I look at Charlotte Street—or the next street over, called Suburban Place—the center of several blocks of well-tended ranch houses, reminiscent of Levittown and other postwar developments. There is something a little surreal about the neighborhood, with its fences and lawns, given both its past and its surroundings, which are still plenty rough. You could look at it as a plot twist in a mystery story as unexpected as anything in Poe. *Ne cede malis.* Do not give way to evil. You had to wait for it, and be accepting of surprise.

· · ·

THE FIRST THREE MONTHS OF THE YEAR 2000 WOULD PASS before Narcotics finally called. I went on vacation for almost a month of it, and I went on strike for the rest. I worked as I always had, but I gave my arrests away and I wouldn't write any more tickets. I would do my job, but without benefit to the Captain. The little act of mutiny was liberating, and when I was not preoccupied with rumors that Narcotics would call this Friday, or the next, I enjoyed patrol as I hadn't in a while. As theater, there is no match for it, and even the way you engage the spectacle is like something a kid would invent—you knock on a door and someone has to tell you a story.

We had a domestic dispute, where the female complainant barely spoke English. I asked what her husband had done, and she cried, "He killed me!" Another lady, who ostensibly did speak English, had a fight with her neighbors, because "I don't socialate with Puerto Ricans."

"Why don't you try a little socialating, ma'am? They're not bad people when you get to know them."

We locked up a guy for choking his girlfriend, and as I was filling out his paperwork, I asked what I thought was an employment-related question—"What did you do in Jersey?"

"Six years."

"You shoot somebody?"

"I shot up a place."

"A place?"

"Mostly I shot the stereo."

After another attempted drive-by murder, the miraculously unwounded complainant gave us a strangely unemotional recounting of events, until he noticed that the windows of his own car were shot out: "This is the second time they shot at me tonight. . . .ắHoly shit! Look at my car!" Half an hour before the end of tour, another job came up: *10-34, assault with a weapon, the weapon is a frying pan. . . .*"Jeez, do you think this one could be domestic?" In the hall outside the apartment, a closetful of men's clothes had been strewn on the ground and splashed with bleach. A large woman met us at the door in a nightgown, shuddering with rage: "I want to make a citizen's arrest! It's my husband! For what? Adultery, that's what! No? Of course not—adultery is not a crime, 'cause the men write the laws! I want female cops the next time!"

We asked to talk to the gentleman in question, and she retreated to the back of the apartment. When he emerged from the kitchen, it was clear that he'd been out the whole night, and the fun he'd had might have been worth the trouble. "Look at this!" he said, pointing to the clothes. From the back of the apartment, there must have been half a dozen kids, all young, peeping out of rooms and creeping down to investigate. He brushed them back with the reflexive indifference of a horsetail swatting at flies.

"You see this?" he asked, holding up his eyeglasses, which had been twisted into a scribble of wire.

"Yep," I said. "I see your kids, too."

He shook his head. "I swear, Officer, I did not touch another woman, I was sniffin' coke with my bloods all night, I'm still flying!"

He agreed that it might be a good idea to leave for a while, but he was concerned about what she would do to his aquarium. "I'm like a father to these fish," he said, pointing to the large and well-equipped tank, where three huge black-and-orange oscars gulped in the water with malignant looks. "You know how rough these fish are? Look, they love me!" He dipped his hand in the tank and the fish nibbled his fingers. A few of the children tiptoed down the hall again, and again he waved them away.

On Sunday mornings, as the dawn burned into day, swarms of gulls descended on the uncollected trash, hovering and dropping in the cold clear light. On rainy nights, we might drive for hours, looking for drug dealers who were standing close to puddles. One night, Stix spied an enormous rat nosing around a sewer cap in the middle of the street. He sped up to it and then stopped short. The fat rat scuttled away in safety.

"I couldn't do it," he said.

"Professional courtesy?"

Half an hour later, he turned to me and said, "You're an asshole." I smiled and nodded.

A lot of times, Stix brought in food for me from Anna's deli. His own diet was the subject of intense curiosity on the midnights, and Sgt. G and Louie Malagon always asked him what he was having when they raised us for the scratch. "Just some plain pasta and a little *fanook,*" he'd explain, holding up a plastic bag of what we finally decided was, in English, raw fennel. Tentatively, they tried some, and for a brief period Stix initiated a mini-craze for *fanook,* and some cops took it up with the airy nonchalance of sophomores with clove cigarettes. I wasn't converted to *fanook,* and neither did I take to the tofu heroes that Stix was also partial to. Then again, he didn't sell them very well: "If you don't like it you don't have to eat it—you don't have to be polite. I mean, I gave Chicky one and he threw up—it's not for everyone."

Stix had struck a bargain with the Admin lieutenant—if his numbers were good for a couple of months, he could go back to a beat on the day tours. It was a fresh-out-of-the-Academy assignment, but it would give him his life back. They wanted fifteen tickets a month from him, and thirty tickets could reasonably be seen as the price of his freedom. But as we sighted a car with an expired inspection, Stix went into agonies of indecision over whether to write another ticket, since he had written the same car for the same infraction a week before.

"Should I do it?"

"I don't know."

"Do you think it's cheesy?"

"Do what you want."

So went the first of eight verses. Finally, he seemed to decide against it, and he ran the plate in the hope that he would find further discouragement—"Maybe it's an old lady, an old man . . ."—it proved to be registered to a thirty-four-year old woman who lived half a mile away.

"She's probably living in sin," I said. "Why don't you write her for indecency?"

Still, he wasn't sure. "This has been a real emotional roller coaster for you," I said as we drove away. At the end of the block, he turned around and came back again.

"Would you like me to pray on it with you?"

"Fuck it, somebody else is gonna."

He wrote the ticket.

On the night after the Diallo verdict, we had two encounters with French-speaking, West African Muslims. We recovered a stolen car that belonged to a woman from the Ivory Coast, and we tracked her down at her apartment in Harlem from a phone bill in the back seat. She was grateful for our efforts, despite the hour. And shortly afterward, we stopped a livery cab that blocked traffic to pick up a fare. The cabbie was all manic hands and explanations, and he couldn't come up with any paperwork at all—no hack license, not even a driver's license. I told the fare to get another cab and went back to our car to run the plate as Stix continued to talk with him. Stix returned, and to my surprise he had all the paperwork, which was entirely correct and up to date—the man was just nervous when we stopped him, whether he was afraid he was getting a ticket or the fear ran deeper. Stix said, "When he gave me this stuff, he kind of flashed a twenty with it."

We talked over the rules of engagement for a bribery collar, and what it might mean—though the Integrity Review Board had done nothing for John, after nine months and counting, the possibility of an escape for Stix, not just from the midnights but from the precinct, appeared like a map of buried treasure. We thought for a moment, and then Stix said, "Nah—forget it. It's not like this guy's a drug dealer."

"Yeah, you're right. This guy comes from a country where the cops might beat him up, lock him up, if he doesn't offer money. He's scared, he doesn't know."

We returned his paperwork to him, and I told him that the next time he picked up a fare, he had to pull over to the side of the street. He thanked us and drove off. When we returned to our car, however, neither of us felt that the encounter had gone quite like it should have. We followed him and pulled him over again, and again he was nervous.

"Listen, relax," I said. "You're not in trouble, you're not getting a ticket, you're getting a talking-to. You had money in your hand when you talked to my partner, and we both know what you meant by it. I want to let you know now that we don't do that here—you could have just turned a traffic ticket into a serious crime. I know you're a good guy out trying to make a living, so I just want you to know that—don't do that again, okay?" We shook hands and he drove off again.

When you have time, you have everything, and on the midnights, it can seem you have nothing else. When it's busy, the busyness is strange, the hectic activity out of place for the night, and when it's quiet it's strange, because it strikes me as going against the sleepless nature of the City. It is a contradiction, I know. One night, we raced to the scene of "shots fired" from a subway platform, which EMS had put over when they were driving past. A number of passersby confirmed it, but the shooter was long gone. Four hours later, with little to do in the intermission except for driving around in the dark, we received another job of shots fired, from an apartment right next to the train. Inside, a lovely old couple pointed out the hole in the window, the neat chute the bullet cut through the hanging basket of African violets, littering stems and leaves on the floor. "I love my plants, they're my babies," the woman said, more concerned for what had happened than what might have. She was a kind of grandmother to the neighborhood, and had been for generations. There was a picture on the wall of her with Mayor Lindsay, who had given her a house for a dollar a year to take care of local children. "Give your plants a big drink of water," I said. "And I'll play them some nice soothing music, too," she added. We found where the bullet hit the back wall—not far from Mayor Lindsay—but we had to hunt for the slug for a while, before we found it under the refrigerator. The heat and speed and impact had transformed the sleekly lethal missile into an oddly shaped glob, like a scoop of mashed potato, harmless and pointless. It was a big slug, probably from a .45, and it would have taken her head off had she been watering her plants. It frightened her, to be sure, but she had slept through its arrival and she would sleep again, now that it was gone.

The bullet took less than a second to travel from the barrel into their home, but in my mind—from when it was heard to when it was found—it was a four-hour journey, and I could picture it in slow motion, floating over like a soap bubble on a windless night. Both perspectives were true, the explosive instant and the glacial glide, and I was glad to be able to see each of them, in the luxury of time. The old couple, I'm sure, were glad of it as well. That night passed, as did the long night of the South Bronx. And those who survived that nightmare, even now can sleep through the worst, sure of the morning.

ELEVEN

O n the night I found out I was transferred, I drove home singing in my car. For the next two weeks of Organized Crime Control Bureau training in Brooklyn, I sang on the drive there in the morning and I sang on the way home, and I would have sung in the classroom if it - wouldn't have aroused suspicions about why I'd gone to Narcotics in the first place. Stix had gone to work for Sgt. O'Hagan a week or two before I left, and he'd become used to daylight again. John had come back from Vice, and had finally been reassigned to his old footpost in the Four-Four. One afternoon, I did a tour change and we worked together, idly checking out our old spots in between jobs. The next day, he collared and signed up a perp as a CI. I was at dinner downtown with my new girlfriend, who got to hear me talk on the cell phone about crack and kites and DECS from the appetizers through coffee. Ultimately, he decided to hand the package over to Smacky and Pops in Narcotics, and when he informed the Captain afterward, he was offered semi-grudging congratulations for his work and complaints about having given it away. Stix and John had gotten what they wanted, and it was good enough, for now. "Partners come and go," Mike Moxom, a veteran midnight cop, told me. He also said, "You can put this in your book: What comes around, goes around." I sang it in my car, along with everything else.

For a while, it looked like I was the last happy cop in the NYPD, at least for the moment. It was a strange time to be singing: two weeks before I left for Narcotics, a cop from PSA-8 SNEU killed a man named Malcolm Ferguson in a struggle for the cop's gun during an arrest for drug sales. Ferguson had an extensive criminal record, and he had half a dozen glassines of heroin in his pocket when he died; his death was controversial primarily because it took place in the Four-Three, where Diallo was killed. Nonetheless, the cop received death threats from the Latin Kings, and on my last midnights, I was assigned to guard his house, sitting outside in a marked patrol car. John was assigned there, too, on the four-to-twelves, and he'd go up and visit the cop, partly because it was a better hour and partly because it was in his nature to reach out. In the event of the second-worst-possible outcome from a SNEU op, we knew, a patrol car could have been parked outside our apartment door: we had all been there, struggling alone with perps in project halls, wondering if we could reach the radio before he reached the gun. PK had been that cop's boss, too, though he wasn't working at the time of the shooting. PK told John that the man was an excellent cop, who felt he had no choice: "He said, 'It was him or me. . . .'"

The day after my transfer, an undercover in midtown asked a man named Patrick Dorismond for drugs. Dorismond took offense at the question and began to rough him up. As they struggled, his "ghost"—the cop assigned to tail him from a distance—interceded, and Dorismond was shot fatally by the ghost. Dorismond had several arrests, for a gun, robbery, and marijuana sales, and he had been most recently accused of hitting his girlfriend as she held their child, but he had no convictions for serious offenses. The altercation was difficult to understand, to say the least, in that it ostensibly began with his refusal to commit a crime. Dorismond was also Haitian, as Louima was, and that stirred anger, as did the Mayor's release of his arrest record. Several years before, Giuliani's release of juvenile arrest records had quelled the controversy in the killing of a machete-wielding felon named Kevin Cedeno in Washington Heights, which some politicians had previously styled the execution of an innocent. The cops in the Ferguson and Dorismond cases were nonwhite, which blunted the accusations of racism only somewhat— they expressed institutional rather than individual racism, apparently—and both were cleared. But the reaction against the police from so many quarters had become so vehement and reflexive that morale plunged still further. The

Narcotics team in the Dorismond case was led by a Sgt. Richard Romano, whose brother was the star of the hit sitcom *Everybody Loves Raymond*, and both brothers were featured in a recruiting ad for the NYPD, in which Ray Romano praises his brother for being the real success in the family. The ad had just begun to run when the Dorismond killing occurred, and as the protests began to mount again, Sgt. Romano announced that he'd had it, and quit. The recruitment campaign was not a success.

Still, I was delighted to be there, and I reported to work with an immigrant's zeal: *Your American floors, it is a privilege to scrub them.* The two weeks of training took place in trailers on a fenced-off quarter of the Brooklyn Army Terminal. They trained investigators, undercovers, and supervisors for OCCB, and they also trained dogs. Periodically, an instructor would quit her explanation of buy reports or case management as the sound of canine assault rose from the lot. "I'm not going to kid myself about how interesting I am, next to this," she said. "Take five." We would all rush over to the windows to watch a German shepherd attack a cop, biting at his padded limbs to yank him to the ground.

As with any police training course, it took twice as long as it should have, though the instructors tended to be veteran detectives from Narcotics who knew how to tell a story. One told about the elaborate sting operation designed to catch a wanna-be mafioso named Henry Vega, who had killed an off-duty cop named George Scheu in 1987 when Scheu tried to stop him from stealing a car stereo. A social club was built and populated entirely with undercovers posing as made men. Vega was desperate to be accepted, and he was allowed to insinuate himself, bit by bit, into their midst. When he begged to be allowed to join, he was asked if he could be trusted to carry out a hit. Vega then bragged about killing Scheu, and his statements were recorded.

The lecturers from other specialized units—Asset Forfeiture, Major Case, TARU (Technical Assistance and Response Unit, which did everything from installing wiretaps to installing hidden cameras)—varied more widely. The hours might crawl during a discussion of radio frequencies and UHF signals for the "kels," or transmitters, that undercovers wore, or of "traps," the custom-engineered concealed compartments for carrying drugs or guns in cars: "In a 1989 Ford Taurus, we found a trap in the center console by clicking the headlights twice, turning the radio to AM, and turning on the windshield wipers. In a 1995 Lincoln Continental, the trap was in the trunk, and to activate it you had to turn the engine on, off, and on again, put the car in neutral, and turn the defogger to maximum. For this Ford Explorer . . ."

We field-tested drugs, gathering around a long table in which little heaps of white and beige powder were spread across a dozen sheets of paper. You took a blue plastic scoop like a flattened toothpick to drop a dab of powder in a clear plastic packet with glass ampules inside. For cocaine, there were three ampules of reagent, and you broke them left to right: if the fluid encountered cocaine hydrochloride, it turned pink, and then the next ampule turned it blue, and the final ampule turned it pink and blue, with the blue layer rising thinly to the top. For heroin, there were two ampules, for which the first remained clear and the second flushed green, sometimes with a dramatic suddenness. Some piles tested negative for both, and one tested positive for both, and we dipped in the piles and shook our packets with the earnest studiousness and easy jokes—*Hey, this is good shit!*—of high school biology students dissecting frogs. We did the same for marijuana, which flushed gray, then purple, then purple and gray.

During the breaks, we would step outside and gather in little groups to talk or smoke cigarettes. There were almost forty of us: investigators, undercovers, a few sergeants, one lieutenant. The cops clumped together by borough, either because they knew each other before, or were likely to afterward, as the group would be sent to Brooklyn and Manhattan North. I clumped sometimes with a cop from the Five-Two named Ricky Duggan, and a sergeant named Jimmy Gildea, who had been in Narcotics as a cop and had survived a shooting. Sometimes we went out to lunch together, but more often I disappeared to read the papers in a restaurant by myself, or to meet with my Ryan cousins, Mary and Catherine, who lived in the neighborhood. There was a time-killing aspect to the two weeks, but I didn't object.

On the second-to-last day, Lt. Russo, who ran the program, announced, "Unless you were at dinner last night and had the opportunity to say, 'Howard, pass the salt,' you are going to Brooklyn North and Manhattan North. That's where they need people, and that's where you're going." "Howard" referred to Commissioner Safir, and when they read the list of assignments the next afternoon—

"Alvarez . . .Brooklyn North . . .ž"

"Baker . . .Brooklyn North . . .ž"

"Buono . . .Manhattan North . . .ž"

"Calderon . . .Brooklyn North . . .ž"

"Conlon . . .South Bronx Initiative . . ."

—more than a few people turned around to look. *Howard, pass the salt.* I was a little surprised myself. I'd talked to Inspector Mullen, who'd been transferred to Queens, days before I went to Narcotics, and Lt. Nicholson—my cousin—and Pops, and they said they would try to get me to the Four-O. The idea of Manhattan North wasn't unattractive by any means—I could work uptown, amid the violence and depravity that make cop life worthwhile, and then go to court downtown a couple of times a week, where my girlfriend lived. But the Bronx would remain home and work for awhile longer. I still sang on the last drive back from Brooklyn.

. . .

WHEN I GOT TO THE SOUTH BRONX INITIATIVE, AT THE PRE-cinct which had housed the old Fort Apache, Chief Tiffany called me into his office to welcome me to the command. He told me that he liked one of my pieces, how it reminded him of a Fellini movie. I blinked and thanked him: this was a change. Later on, he told me about a federal agent who had asked him about corruption, and his testy response. "I said to him, 'You recall in the *Inferno,* when Virgil and Dante are about to enter the seventh circle of Hell?'" He looked at me, and I nodded, in vague assent. "The stench was so awful, they had to step aside, to acclimate before going in. But down they went, as we do. Too many of the feds keep bankers' hours, they don't get too dirty or go too deep. That's why corruption happens, I think, and it's part of the risks of the Job." What the chief said about corruption didn't bother me, but what he said about Dante did; would there be a test, or did they ask about it in Compstat? *The Commissioner wants to know why damnations are down for hypocrites and usurers. . . .* Narcotics could be a tricky business, I knew, but I hadn't expected this.

Lt. Nicholson was similarly welcoming, as were Pops and Sgt. Billy Clune, who were the sergeants for the module, and Capt. Mahony, who was in charge of the Four-O teams. When Lt. Zerbo saw me, he said, "Ah, fuck, not you again."

I grinned like an idiot. One of the guys told me, "Don't worry about Zerbo, he just talks like that. He'll never hurt you."

I said, "If Lieutenant Zerbo kicked me in the balls every time I walked in the office, I'd still be happy to be here."

When I worked there two years before, there were ten teams that covered the Four-O; now, there were four. Pops and Billy Clune each had a team, and they reported to Zerbo, but there were other familiar faces: Smacky and Billy Clark had arrived the previous year, joining Hector Nolasco in the PSA-7 contingent, and John Reilly, Rob Richardson, Adam Leibowitz, Abe Garcia, Dexter Powers, and a few others. I was assigned to Billy Clune, but both teams worked together so often and in such combinations that I never quite figured out who was assigned to which.

Billy Clune's father had been a cop, and his brother was a cop, a lieutenant in Midtown South. His was the attitude of the veteran: *Don't go crazy and don't get hurt. Let's take care of business, make our overtime, and go home.* He called everyone "Atlas" or "Slim," even his infant son: "Atlas Junior was up sick all night, poor fella." Clune was even-keeled and easygoing, except for when cops complained about assignments. "Try getting stuck in Internal Affairs for two years, Atlas," he said. "Then you can bitch about having to stand on a corner for a couple of hours. Arright, Slim?"

Most cops found the Internal Affairs Bureau distasteful to some degree, and the unit had first choice of supervisors who put in for OCCB or the Detective Bureau, which made many of them hesitate to leave patrol. At IAB, a routine operation might involve calling in a job of drug sales, where the caller specified that the stash was under the mailbox. An IAB surveillance van would watch the cop respond: if the dealer wasn't around, would the cop mark the job "90-X" and move on, without checking under the mailbox, or if he checked, would he just kick the drugs down a sewer? The appropriate response would be to search for the drugs and find them, and then to raise a boss over the air to apprise him of "found narcotics," and then to return to the precinct to write up a report and voucher them. The result was the same as if the cop had kicked them down the sewer, though the correct procedure might take the cop off the street for two hours. Doubtless there was division and mistrust even within IAB over how to address such situations, where the actions were technically improper but essentially right. The unit had the responsibility of arresting cops whenever it was necessary, and for cops in bad relationships, the vindictive 911 call from a significant other was a conventional weapon. It was no great pleasure to respond to incidents where cops were guilty of domestic violence, either.

Pops had also been stuck in IAB, and while he wasn't glad to be there, he was more forthright in his acknowledgment of its necessity: "We had an uncle try to get done in this place in Harlem, it was both a crackhouse and whorehouse. They had a 'security guy' at the door, who told them not to do the uncle, he could be a cop. Anyway, a couple of days later, the uncle goes to court, and he sees the 'security guy' is a cop, on modified assignment at the courthouse. Turns out he's been on modified for years, he molested his ten-year-old niece or stepdaughter or something, but she wouldn't press charges. The Job wouldn't let him have a gun, but they couldn't fire him, either. Our case against him is in the Trial Room now."

Pops was driven, determined to make collars and cases, to make things happen. His heart was in the Job, and when we did B&B, his mood lightened after each successful set. Pops was close to PK at PSA-7, not least because they had both lost young sons to illness—a heart ailment in Frankie Poplaski's case. But where PK had a sense of kindly quiet about him, with Pops you felt the urgency of his resolve, that he would not let time go to waste. Pops worked federal cases and he worked closely with the Four-O Detective Squad, especially Bobby Addolorado, who was assigned exclusively to homicides. Bobby had a number of superb informants, and he shared them with Pops for Narcotics work. Though the primary responsibility of a Four-O Narcotics module was, not surprisingly, narcotics in the Four-O, Pops would scramble to make cases happen, no matter where they led. As John Reilly, the senior man on his team, liked to point out, "The shield doesn't say, 'Only for use against drugs in the South Bronx,' it says, 'Detective, City of New York. . . .'"

With Lt. Zerbo, we had a man whose experience began in the late 1960s, before Durk, Serpico, and the Knapp Commission, and had continued through the blackout, the financial crisis, and Son of Sam killings of the midseventies; when crack and AIDS first appeared in the early eighties, he was barely midway through his career. In the spring of 2000, he was as physically active as anyone on the team, and mentally, he was on his own level. There was a letter on his wall from a bank president in Yonkers, thanking him for catching a bank robber. Lt. Zerbo had been on line to make a deposit, and he'd chased the perp on foot for blocks through a snowstorm. As I drove him one afternoon when we were doing B&B, he glanced at a man getting into a car, a white Honda with New Jersey plates.

"Pull over," he said, and I did. After a moment of conversation with the would-be driver—he had no license—he told me to check the trunk. I found a bulletproof vest. Lt. Zerbo had recalled that the car was involved in a case they took down six months before.

Lt. Zerbo never failed to surprise you, whether by walking past your desk and taking a handful of your lunch—even if you were eating it, and even if it was pasta—or by passing an offhand remark that began, "That reminds me of when I was in the seminary. . . ." The seminary? There might have been a Father Zerbo, a Monsignor Zerbo, a Bishop Zerbo? *This is a reading from effin' Ephesians, so shut your damn mouths. . . .* But Zerbo also looked out for his cops, and if there was a problem at home or with the Job, he was a trusted advisor and a formidable ally.

Zerbo was hilarious with perps, having heard thirty years of the most dire threats and inventive lies. One perp, who was shouting about how he'd sue us because he knew we were going to beat him, was shut up by the nonchalance of Lt. Zerbo's remark: "Well, we used to beat people up all the time in the old days. Now, we're not allowed to anymore."

Another time when I drove him, he took me down Weiher Court, a block-long street in the Four-Two. Weiher Court is a classic landscape of the old South Bronx, where a little fortlike house stands out like the Alamo over a junk-strewn field of weeds. "They chased Twymon Myers all the way from the subway down to here," he said, pointing to a spot in the field. Twymon Myers was a Black Liberation Army hit man who had taken part in the murders of several police officers; Sonny Grosso had been hunting for him in Harlem when he was called to the Cardillo killing at the Nation of Islam mosque. Zerbo went on, "And he hid under a mattress, with his gun, ready to blast whoever lifted it up. But they never checked underneath it. When they finally did get him, at One-Five-Two and Tinton, there were all these cops with machine guns, shotguns, all this heavy artillery—but what killed him was one regular cop who took him out with his .38. There's still a bullet hole in the streetlight there, I'll have to show you some time. . . ." I did look for it later on. Chief Tiffany had told me, too, and I found it one afternoon: a kidney-shaped hole, some three inches by one inch, where two large rounds had grouped together. It was hard to tell how much wider it had become in time, and it didn't even look like a bullet hole anymore. It was another place where a killer was killed, in a place that had seen a thousand killings since.

Chief Tiffany and Lt. Zerbo both had an appreciation for local history, though each seemed to draw different conclusions from it. I'd given the chief two books that I admired greatly, by an author named Jill Jonnes, *We're Still Here,* a history of the South Bronx, and *Hep-Cats, Narcs, and Pipe Dreams,* which told of drugs and drug enforcement in this country over the last century. The subject matter might be of interest to the Chief of Bronx Narcotics, I figured, and I was correct, as I haven't seen either book since. If he saw me outside having a cigarette, he'd stop and talk about the books.

"This block was tenements, this block burned," he said. "If you've been around this neighborhood as long as I have, the change is nothing short of miraculous. That's because of us—a lot of it is, anyway. What I love best about it is how when the kids play baseball or stickball here on the sidewalk, they play right in front of the precinct, and our stoop—or the front door, or the doorknob sometimes—that's third base for them."

A few weeks later, as we were loading up the equipment for a warrant— the hand-held ballistic bunkers, crowbars and hydraulic door-openers, fire extinguishers and flashlights—the stickball game didn't stop for us, and the ball bounced near Lt. Zerbo's head as he stepped out. As the ball was thrown back near him, he snatched it out of the air and brandished it in front of the eight-year-olds. "I told you kids a thousand times, this is a police station, and you can't get in the way when we're working! Well, the game's over now, be- cause I have the ball!"

. . .

NARCOTICS HAD WHOLESALE AND RETAIL SIDES TO IT: THERE was Buy and Bust, and there were cases, which developed if an uncle got a phone number for a dealer, or a CI made an introduction, and we would buy into the crew, from grams to ounces to kilos, until you were ready to take them down. Cases were labor-intensive and paper-intensive, and months of work could lead to the purchase of a half-kilo of soap flakes, but they were the only way you could rip out a drug crew by the roots. Some teams— bosses and cops alike—lived for cases, the reach and the depth of the game, while others preferred the simple and semi-predictable exercise of Buy and Bust. B&B was Basic Bullshit, and Boring Bullshit, and Bread & Butter, and we did it two or three times a week. The work was half-familiar from SNEU, and half-familiar again from having done it for a month two years earlier, and the procedure was learned in short order. Before we went out, the ar- resting officer would get eighty dollars or so in "buy money"—known as "bim," for short—to photocopy, laying out the tens and twenties on the ma- chine so that each serial number was recorded, and then give it to the uncles. Sometimes you'd mark the bills with an X or a stroke of red pen, so you could recognize the bim in the street. The sergeant would write up a tac plan, list- ing each cop's role for the day—arresting officer, or "A/O," catch cars, the prisoner van, known as the P-van, uncles, and ghosts—the radio and car assigned, and the list of spots to hit. Most spots were steady ones—One-Five-Six and Courtlandt, One-Four-Eight and Willis—though particular addresses would be added if there had been a recent shooting or homicide, or if it was a kite location, an apartment or lobby for which someone had called in a complaint about drugs sales. We would gather up our equipment and head to the cars. The A/O would drive the boss, strapping the receiver in the back seat and sticking the antenna on the roof by its magnetic base.

Outside, the Sergeant would test the radios and the kels:

"Four-O Leader to uncle car, on the air? Okay, Uncle Abe, you're on C Channel? Uncle Dex, you're on B? Abe, gimme a kel check."

"Kel, kel, kel, kel, kel—you read me, Leader?"

"Coming in five-by-five. Uncle Dex, gimme a kel check. . . ."

The kel was a one-way transmitter, which only the sergeant and his - driver could hear, but the ghost wore a regular radio, with extensions that allowed him to transmit and receive without being seen.

"All right, Bobby Rich, can I have a ghost check?"

If the equipment worked, we headed out for the first set, deploying the cars in a rough perimeter for each direction the perp might run, ready to move in case the uncle was steered elsewhere.

When everyone was in position, the sergeant would put it over the air: "Four-O Leader to uncle car, you on? You ready?"

"We're ready, Leader."

"Okay, uncle car, you got the green light, you got the green. Field team, be advised, the uncles are out of the car. Repeat: the uncles have stepped . . ."

In the sergeant's car, you heard the uncles strike up a conversation over the crackle and static of the kel:

"Yo, you working?"

"Wassup, anybody out?"

"Anybody got work?"

They were pick-up lines, of a kind, and each uncle had a style: Dex and Teddy had a suave reserve, while George and Abe tended to be up-tempo and avid, and Curtis and Damian were somewhere in between. As a female, Janet found that sellers often wanted to sell themselves to her. Abe's hustle always sounded like he was in a nightclub: quick and eager, loud enough to be heard above the music, definitely interested but never desperate: "Yo, baby! C'mon! You *know* me! You saw me *last week!* Are you kidding me? *I ain't no cop!* C'mon now, don't be like that. You and me, you and me, let's get them krills and we'll fire 'em up together, we'll go right up to the project roof and *beam up!* No? Arright, if that's the way you wanna be, I'll just go up the block . . .žNo? Arright then, let's do it. Gimme two . . ."

They had to connect, and their hunger for connection sometimes reminded me of guys on the make for women, and sometimes it reminded me of actors at an audition, hungry for a break. While their styles varied, I wondered whether there was a need to convince, or a drive to perform. For some, that inner thrill was plain to see, though for others it was simply how the job was done, and if they had to sing for their supper or scream for it, that's what they did, though not for any special love for song or screaming.

As the uncle talks to a seller or steerer, the ghost watches and reports: "Uncle Curtis is in conversation, female Hispanic, One-Four-Eight and Brook, blue hoodie, black pants, Yankee cap . . .žlooks like we have a positive buy. . . ."

The kel failed constantly, for a couple of seconds at a time or for longer. The uncle never knew, of course, because it was only a transmitter. The uncle would have a visual sign for "positive buy"—pulling up his hood, lighting a cigarette—for the ghost to read and tell the field team, but the ghost often had to pull back, or step inside a store, or look away for a moment, if his scrutiny of the uncle appeared too purposeful.

"Stand by, Leader, I gotta step off a minute, they're getting raised on me, I gotta step off the block and I'm dropping my ears. . . ."

"Catch up to him, ghost, and give him the cut-off sign, give him the cut-off, we're gonna wrap it. . . ."

The kel would cut in and out as the signal bounced through the landscape of twenty-story projects: "Positive buy, Leader, we have—*ssssshhhhhhh*—male, that's repeat—*sssshhhhhhh*—wearing—*sshhhhhhhhhsshhhhhhhhhhsshhhh*—right on the corner of—*ssssshhhhhhsshhshh*. Okay, Leader, you copy?"

If the conversation was in Spanish, the static might be scarcely less intelligible, though the sergeant could read the tone, and pick out *yayo, bomba, sí, no.* The field team would wait in their cars, in dull boredom if the uncle found no one who would talk to him, or in heightening apprehension if we lost contact. Sometimes, we'd have to charge into a building or fan out through project grounds if we lost the uncle for too long; fortunately, none of our uncles was ever in trouble then, and when we'd find them—talking on a bench or in a stairwell—you could run past, as if you were looking for someone else, or you could put them both on the wall, hoping that the uncle hadn't been made. Usually, the uncles worked in pairs, so that if a buy was made, the ghost could remain on the set to watch the seller while the uncles returned to the car. The uncle would fill in over the radio whatever was missed on the kel transmissions. Sellers were "subjects" and buyers were "Ps":

"Okay, Leader, the set has three pieces, the female black who steered me, and the two male Hispanics. The hand-to-hand is the tall one in the red jacket, it says 'Chicago Bulls.' Also, there's three or four Ps, who came all at once, and are heading south on Brook . . ."

"All right, forget the Ps for now—what's the product and how much did you spend?"

"Twenty, and it's D, the brand is 'HBO.'"

"All right, Field Team, let's move in. . . ."

And we'd go, all at once if it was a one-piece set, or a car for each subject at their last known position. There were runners and fighters, as there had been in SNEU, when I worked the same sets, but they ran less and fought less, it seemed. We had better equipment, more cars, more people, and more experience, which together would tend to reduce misadventure, but sometimes I thought that it was just a matter of the perps getting older, too. When we moved in and took the subjects, the uncle car would drive by for a confirmatory identification.

"That's them, Leader, you got 'em both. . . ."

"Ten-four, that's a wrap, everybody—Field Team to the Four-O, uncles, you can take it back to the barn. . . ."

When the undercovers returned to our base, they had to field test and voucher the drugs they'd bought, and write up buy reports: *At T/P/O I UC#123 approached JD Braids (M/B/20, 5'8" 150, blue shirt, blue jeans, short braids) in front of 550 E 147 St. and asked him if he had dope. JD Braids asked "How much do you want?" and I responded "Give me two." I then handed JD Braids $20 USC/PRBM and he approached JD Newport (M/H/40's, 5'5" 130, Newport T-shirt, green shorts) and handed over the USC/PRBM for small objects taken from the rear of his pants. JD Braids then handed me two glassines of heroin stamped E-Z Money. I then left the scene and notified the field team of what transpired.*

Visibility: Clear

Weather: Sunny

USC/PRBM stood for "United States Currency/Pre-Recorded Buy Money." "JD" meant "John Doe," and the uncle could have called JD Braids and JD Newport "JD Blue" and "JD Green," or whatever he saw as a distinguishing characteristic. JD Gap Tooth, JD Bald, JD Stutter would all be fine, JD Heavy would be preferable to JD Fat, but JD Stupid, JD Ripe Shorts, JD Face-

Only-a-Mother-Could-Love—no matter their accuracy—might later suggest to a jury that the undercover was not taking his work entirely seriously.

In the early 1970s, when Narcotics did B&B, they did B& . . .ᴁB, as the field team picked up subjects days and even weeks after the uncle had made a buy. The delay protected the undercover from exposure, as the seller might have to guess the cop from hundreds of buyers, but it also weakened the case, and it's hard to imagine a modern Bronx jury voting to convict. It amazed me how some of our uncles could buy drugs in the same precinct two or three times a week for years—Dex and Abe would do that, and so would Janet and George, though at least their street work would be broken up to monitor Spanish-language wiretaps for months at a time. There were at least thirty steady sets, from individual apartments to the wide-open pill and methadone market of One-Four-Eight and Willis, where the junkies sold "spitback" from little plastic juice bottles. (Methadone must be consumed on site at the clinic, and spitback is just what it sounds like.) There was enough turnover at the steady sets and enough new spots to allow them to work—carefully, and on the move—but all the uncles had stories of being run off a set by perps who recognized them from the last time around. Few of the undercover cops who have been killed died because the perps thought they were cops, but rather because they thought they were attractive victims or fellow criminals—when we were in SNEU, the uncle who killed the perps on 160 was being set up for a robbery, and Sean Carrington's killer thought Carrington was coming to rob him of his stash. Sean Carrington was Rob Richardson's cousin. Rob spoke at Sean's funeral, parts of which were televised, and so his own undercover career ended. After that, Rob only ghosted.

A new uncle was expected to make eight buys a month, give or take; if they couldn't buy, they might be transferred to a different area, but continued failure meant a return to patrol. Uncles who were established were given more slack; they might only work major cases, or in time they, too, might be moved, voluntarily or otherwise. After three years, undercovers "flipped" to investigators. Because Narcotics depended so heavily on undercovers, there were star performers who emerged, and were courted like seven-foot-tall high school juniors by college basketball coaches, with whatever poor perks the sergeants and lieutenants had to offer:

"Listen, if you work for me, we'll do anything you want—we'll go to Manhattan, we'll go federal—anything! And believe me, I'm tight with the chief, if we run with something good—sky's the limit, overtime-wise. . . ."

Some investigators claimed that this encouraged a prima donna attitude among certain undercovers, and you did sometimes wonder when an operation with a dozen cops, planned for weeks or more, was suddenly called off when the uncle said, "I ain't feelin' it, boss." And some of them doubtless scammed on occasion, but I also heard the flip side from other uncle friends, who said that bosses especially, but also cops, tended to change their attitudes about them. In time, they came to be treated more like informants than colleagues—they weren't worked with as much as they were dealt with. I - didn't see that in our office—maybe because I was an investigator—but I heard a lot one night from an undercover who worked in Queens, who told me that the change was profound: "I was a cop for five years before, and so it wasn't as if I was used to being talked to like a human being—but this - really surprised me. You have to get into it a little, whoever you want to be as an uncle—white-trash guy hitting the city, biker guys, local dealer who's not afraid to mix with the ghetto. And you dress up, or grow a beard, or buy different clothes or whatever, and you have to forget about being a cop, how you deal with people as a cop. But what shocked the shit out of me wasn't how I bought into it, but how other cops did. Other cops asked the boss for a day off, it was 'Yes,' or 'No,' but me, I thought every time I asked him for something he looked at me and *wondered*. . . ."

On B&B, you always had to be alert for the runners and fighters, not to mention the shooters, but it became fairly routine for undercovers and investigators alike. Not so the search warrants, though we did several each month: the moments before entry were always heavy with adrenaline, and the people on the street always stopped, jaws agape, as the convoy of cars pulled up in front of a building, and the cops in raid jackets ran out with rams and shields. My first warrant there was through John's CI, just after I got back from training. I rode with John and John Reilly to the tac point, and as we waited for the signal, Reilly turned to me and said, "This is the best part of the job." I nodded. You never knew what waited for you on the other side, whether it was more than you expected or less, or something entirely different. I remember waiting in the car with Rob Richardson, who would ram the door for an apartment where there were supposed to be several submachine guns, as he shook his head. "I got kids," he said. "I ain't feelin' this."

The bigger guys—Reilly, Leibowitz, Smacky, Clark, and Richardson— usually handled the ram, and the number of hits it took to knock in the door was always noted wryly afterward:

"What did that take you, four? Five? Hector says six. Maybe it's time to hit the gym. . . ."

Or, "Yeah, so it went down in one shot, my daughter has a tougher door on her Barbie town house. You could have sneezed on it and got in, so get over yourself. . . ."

Once you were in, another set of worries took over. We took a door one morning for a dope dealer, a man in his mid-thirties, who had a record of armed robberies. When we got in, we found only an old woman, who began to hyperventilate and clutch her chest, chattering rapidly in Spanish about her heart. She lived alone, she said, and she thought she might die. We all felt uneasy, as I had years before, during Operation Hindenburg. The apartment was small but cluttered, as they all seemed to be, and it would take some time to go through it. I was glad to notice several men's coats hanging on a rack outside the closet, and more men's clothing in a back room: it meant that her son stayed there, often enough, if not every night. Her little lie gave me my first hope, and as I went through the coat pockets, I came up with a couple of bags of heroin. The dope made us happier than it would have any junkie—the little glassines were our passports out of lawsuit country—and I handed them to Pops, smiling. The search always played out with the heady, heartless drama of a hand of blackjack, card by card—

Hit me!

Yes!

Hit me!

Yes!

Hit me!

Oh, I shoulda stuck. . . .

Your instinct is like an overeager hunting dog, pulling you in the right direction but sometimes on a trail that has long gone cold: you think to check the watch box for the stash, but it's full of empty glassines; you feel a metal weight in a sock, but it turns out to be a wrench. *Of course, I always keep my wrench in a sock.* You wonder: Does he want his stash close by and convenient, so he can grab it for a quick sale? Or does he keep the weight or the gun hidden in a box under loose floorboards, where no one will find them in a robbery or raid? What looks new, and what looks different? How much can I break?

The dope put us in the game, and when Pops showed it to the old woman, she seemed to recover her composure, and she toned down the silent-movie theatrics to daytime-TV level. After I went through the coats, I checked the closets and found one with more men's clothing. On the top shelf, there were black plastic grocery bags, and I tore them open to find stacks of old phone bills, twenty-year-old report cards, letters to friends in prison. One bag had a box shaped like a stick of butter, only larger, in red and green Christmas wrapping paper. I opened it up and found a brick of heroin, some fifty bundles, neatly double-stacked. "Hey, Pops! Have a look!"

Pops had called for an ambulance for the old woman, as a precaution, but she seemed to feel much better now, after being assured that she would not be arrested. I went back to my closet, through the pockets of coats, pants, and shirts hung up on the rail, and then down below, to the boxes of shoes. There were lighter boxes for dress shoes, and heavier ones for boots, which made me a little excited when I lifted up the first one, thinking that the weight was metal. And then I got to a box that was too heavy for boots, and it felt just right. I opened it to find a new Smith & Wesson nine-millimeter, and boxes of rounds. *Hey, Pops . . .ž*

And Pops was even happier when our subject returned. He'd been out in the neighborhood, but when he spotted the ambulance in front of his building, he rushed home in concern. At the apartment, he hurried to the EMTs, as Pops stepped in beside them.

"What happened? Is she all right?"

"Who are you? Do you live here?" Pops asked.

"I'm her son, I live here, what's going on?"

"Your mother's fine, but you're under arrest. Turn around and face the wall. . . ."

• • •

OUR TEAM TOOK IN HUNDREDS OF PEOPLE EVERY YEAR, AND Narcotics took in thousands, even tens of thousands. You could picture a chow line leading to the massive wooden precinct door, with its green copper lanterns and worn stone steps, a line of young hustlers and old dope fiends, aging players and new fools, reaching down the block and even past the horizon. The size and sameness of the problem could be daunting, or dull, depending on your mood. I was past my disenchantment with work, but not yet truly re-enchanted by it, and maybe the Job for me was like drugs were for Charlie, a cycle of detox and retox, rehab and dehab, a trip through happy hell and back. I needed to find Charlie again, or another Charlie; to find a face in the crowd that was more than a number—five hours of over-time, to be precise—a face with eyes and ears, and a big mouth. Anyone in the chow line could prove to be my underworld guide, or at least have a piece of a map—they knew where the crack was cooked for Brook and One-Three-Eight, or they'd witnessed a murder on a Saturday night in the summer of '95. Everyone knew something, or something that could lead to it, provided you could reach them, and provided you both made the time.

You hoped to make a case, something sustained and substantive. You tried to talk to everyone. Sellers tended to know more than buyers, but that rule was riddled with exceptions: a seller might only know the person he worked for, at one place, whom he met in the lobby when his stash ran out, while a buyer of long experience might know all the major dealers in the neighborhood, at every level of the organization. You could often spot perps who you felt might be receptive. You might have a word as you fingerprinted them, planting a seed of speculation before you put them back in the cell, returning in half an hour to ask, "Didn't you say you had to go to the bathroom? C'mon, I'll take you." Others resisted, and you found yourself in a position of peculiar reversal, as if you were on a Parole Board, and had to beg a contented prisoner to consider life beyond the cell block. *"Naah, on the outside, I hear you have to pay for the gym, I think I'll stay. . . ."* And some you succeeded in persuading proved that their first instincts were right, that it was better for them to remain. Still, you keep on talking.

When I signed up the first informant, no harm came of it, but no good did, either. We had taken three young guys for selling marijuana, and one of them was a marked Blood, with three cigarette burns on his shoulder in a triangle pattern. At the precinct, he surprised me by his extreme discomfort at taking off his clothes when I searched him in the bathroom. Most perps in Narcotics have been arrested many times, and many have spent years in prison, and that kind of self-consciousness falls away soon enough, if it was ever there to begin with. The other two dealers seemed to look up to him, and the combination of gang seniority and criminal-justice novelty marked him as a person of interest. Since we both knew that he faced no more than a night in jail, I couldn't bargain seriously with a reduction in sentence, but it gave me an idea of what I could work with on him. I took him out on the fire escape and gave him a cigarette.

"So what's up? You never been locked up before?"

"Nah, never. . . ."

"Yeah? That means never-never, or you only count convictions?"

"Nah, never—I got a ticket here and there, but I never got taken into the precinct."

"Well, that's 'never,' then. How do you like it?"

He shook his head.

"You're not supposed to. You work?"

"Nah . . ."

"Go to school?"

"Nah . . ."

"What do you do for money, if you don't mind my asking—remember, we're just talking here, I never read you your rights, so nothing goes beyond us. You make enough money selling weed?"

"Nah, that was just—that was just tonight. I got a settlement, my father was killed, run over by a car. My Grams keeps thirty thousand in the bank for me, for when I turn twenty-one. Also, I get Social Security."

Oh. So he'd be out tomorrow, and he had plenty of money. What did I have to offer? I thought a moment, and went on, "Well, that's nice. You turn twenty-one next year, right? You got a girl, you got kids?"

"Yeah, I got a girl, we gotta a little boy."

"Okay, then. Well, listen, Joe—can I call you Joe? My name's Ed—I'll get to the point. I can help you, and you can help me. For now, you're set up pretty good, and I won't lie to you by saying getting locked up for weed in the Bronx is the end of the world. But it is on your record, and some people are very narrow-minded about hiring drug *dealers,* I mean, everybody has their fun when they're young, but this is *dealing,* and a lot of employers, they're still a little funny on the subject. Your check stops after your next birthday, and even though thirty Gs sounds like a lot, you and your girl can live for a week like rich people or live for a year like poor people—believe me, it's not all that much. Cops make thirty a year to start, and everybody knows cops make shit. So you gotta be serious about your future, because you won't have it easy, even if you don't get in trouble again, and you get to take showers with your girl every night instead of thirty other guys. Big guys, and they're winking at you. And you can say no to me, or you can say yes—it's all the same to me, but for your sake, and your kid's sake, you should see if we - could work something out. You wanna talk to me?"

"Yeah, arright."

"The only thing I ask is you gotta be honest. If you lie, it's over, and you got an enemy. If you don't know something, say, 'I don't know.' Don't tell me what you think I want to hear. And if you can't say something, say, 'I can't say,' or 'I won't say'—don't try to play me, 'cause that's a lie, too. Let's start basic. You're Blood, right?"

He shifted uncomfortably, and fingered his red beads.

"Come on! You got the burns, you got the beads, you and me both know that if you wasn't Blood, real gangstas would beat your balls off."

He paused a moment, and then he said, "Yeah, I'm a Blood. They everything to me, they family. Blood up!" He talked about them with the misty-eyed nostalgia of a veteran of Omaha Beach. "I couldn't give up anything on my Bloods."

"Okay," I said. "How about the Crips?"

"I could do that."

After telling me about certain Harlem Crips he knew who carried guns, he gave me his home and cell-phone numbers. He chose "Damu" as his code name, which he told me was Swahili for "blood." I said he wasn't free to commit crimes, and if he saw other Bloods hurt someone, he had to tell me.

"Yeah, but my Bloods, they—"

"Listen, I'm close to cops, they're my friends, they have my back, they mean everything to me. But right is right—if a cop crossed the line, if he was robbing or beating people or hurting girls or whatever, that's on him. And I ain't going to jail for nobody, and neither should you. You understand?"

Slowly, he nodded, and agreed. We shook hands. It was classic jerkology: in ten minutes of conversation, I'd talked him into breaking his most sacred oath, and I was pleased with both of us and with the thought of what we might do together. But I never saw him again—he was wanted for armed robbery and had skipped out on his bail. It hadn't been his first arrest, by a long shot. He had lied to me about his past, of course, but we spoke little of his past and at length of his future, and in his hope for a long and untroubled life, he was as sincere as anyone. I think he believed that his past might not catch up to him, or that he might have an ally on the police before it did, and had the fingerprint system not been computerized, he could have been right. Blood in, blood out. So much for Damu, who resumed his place on the chow line, and sent me back to mine.

My next informant took less persuasion, but more patience. He came over as a buyer, with a perfect scrip for a crowded city street—*Male Hispanic, blue tank top and shorts, with a hat with a big purple-and-yellow umbrella on it, holding a bag of dope*—and he was amenable to work from the beginning. He called himself "Lesty," which was his broken-English version of "Lefty," and I worked with him for months. Lesty wasn't bright, but I was never sure how much was lost in the translation and how much was lost in the heroin. I would ask him how many spots he knew, and he'd think hard and come up with one or two, but whenever I told him of a new spot to try—usually for a kite—he often knew it anyway. Things tended to occur to him quite a bit later, as when I asked him if he knew anyone who had or sold guns.

"Gonz?"

"Yeah, gonz, you know—*pistoles.*"

"Nah, I don't know nobody with gonz."

But he did, he remembered a week later—two brothers were always pestering him about buying guns from a connection they had in the Heights. But they would deal only with him, Lesty said, and he couldn't bring anyone else. Our office wouldn't pay for the guns with an untested informant, even after I'd IDed the subjects—Flaco and Gordo, or "Skinny" and "Fats"—who had several priors, including an arrest for attempted murder. Had Lesty been able to bring someone, he could have brought another CI or an undercover—without being told which it was—and still another introduction could have been made later on, providing another layer of insulation for Lesty. As it was, we would be paying street prices for a gun, without a case against the seller, because we couldn't have Lesty testify in open court. John Reilly suggested I call ATF, and after the call was transferred through a series of indifferent secretaries and desk agents, I met with an agent who sounded so excited he almost dropped the phone:

"When can we meet?"

But when I told my bosses, they told me to go slowly, because one of our chiefs was at odds with one of theirs. The political squabble had imperiled the future of the NYPD-ATF Task Force—it was later disbanded—and the agents I spoke with weren't even part of that. Still, I set up a meeting, and the two agents met with Lesty. Others in the office cautioned me about working with feds, much as cops in SNEU were wary of Narcotics: if the little dog invites a bigger dog into the pack, they might bring down larger game but find that there was less food to go around. As I saw it, the worst that could happen would be for them to cut me out altogether, and though I wouldn't be happy about that, at least they'd be using Lesty properly.

When we met, one of the ATF agents spoke Spanish, and again there were revelations: Lesty had no problem bringing someone else along. I asked the agent to ask Lesty if he didn't understand me the first time, or circumstances had changed, and Lesty smiled and nodded. The agents asked him all the questions I'd asked—make, model, color—as well as one I didn't think to: Did the guns look brand-new or old? They were new, "still in the box," which made them less interesting: new guns would be from a store in Georgia or Virginia, and the case would probably be fairly uncomplicated, as the gun moved north through two or three sets of hands. But if they were older guns, guns with histories, they might have bodies on them, and ballistics could link them to shootings in Brooklyn and murders in Jersey that might otherwise have gone unsolved. The agents were eager to meet again and set up the buy, and they were so friendly that I was a little concerned, as cops or New Yorkers are rarely so cordial. But I handed over my material on Flaco and Gordo, and let them sign up Lesty. And they never screwed me, because I screwed them first, or rather, screws were turned on both of us, from higher levels.

Lt. Zerbo broke the news to me that the politics had doomed this effort, and that we would not be allowed to work together. I called the first agent to apologize, and we both bemoaned the stupidity. A few days later, as I was figuring out how Lesty could make the buy with one of our uncles, I got a call from a lieutenant from one of the other modules:

"Detective Conlon?"

I liked the sound of that, but the warmth of his tone made me suspicious.

"Still a PO, Lou. What's up?"

"You have this address DECSed on One-Three-Nine Street?"

"Yes, I do."

"Well, we're here, we want to get an emergency search warrant. Flaco sold weed to one of our undercovers and ran on us, inside his house."

"I take it you know about the gun under the bed."

"Uh, yeah. But I know it's your spot, and I wanted to make sure it's okay with you."

"If you're there, you're there, Lou, but I should talk to Lieutenant Zerbo first."

"I spoke with him already. It's okay."

"I guess it's okay with me, then, too."

My case fell apart, for the second time. So it went: sometimes the wheels turned and the cogs caught and broke, and sometimes they caught and meshed, sending other wheels turning in the machine. Lesty caught for the guns, and then he spun out, and then the guns caught on another one of our wheels, but then Lesty spun out and caught onto something else, making buys into Bloody Rich's crew. That, too, was a federal case, part of a far more collegial collaboration of the NYPD with the U.S. Attorney's Office.

Bloody Rich was the subject of "Operation Hellbound, Phase Two"—I wondered if Chief Tiffany had come up with the Dantesque name—which would be prosecuted under federal conspiracy statutes. John Reilly would be responsible for the narcotics aspect of the investigation, while Bobby Addolorado of the Four-O Squad took charge of the shootings and homicides. Reilly and Addolorado had handled the first Operation Hellbound, which was directed against another violent drug gang called the "Thief David" crew, which ran crack in and around Millbrook Houses. Thief David had been at war with Bloody Rich, and fortunately a truce had been reached just as the case was taken down, which meant that Thief David's people were in business with Bloody Rich before they were locked up. The prospect of twenty- and thirty-year sentences inspired thoughts of cooperation against their new allies, whose present freedom could be exchanged for their own.

Phase Two was off to a rocky start. Bloody Rich had beaten an attempted murder rap, a year before, for shooting it out with the cops after a Buy and Bust. Bloody Rich's people had begun a shooting war with another crew, and one night one of his lieutenants was shot on a streetcorner in a drive-by. When it happened, John Timpanaro and John Parisi, with whom I'd worked midnights, had filled in a patrol sector, and they headed to the scene. They saw the shooters' car, and gave chase: the perps abandoned the car and fled on foot, and one of them knocked over a kid on a bike and rode away, abandoning the bike when he fled into a project. Timpanaro ran him down and collared him, as both of them gasped for breath in a stairwell. Though the gun wasn't recovered, the perp was charged with the shooting and the robbery of the bicycle. But the bike owner was content to have his bike back and declined to press charges; the shooting victim was uncooperative as well, reasoning that his people would take care of things in their own way.

At that point, the wholesale and retail aspects of police work came into conflict; there were competing demands for immediate results, and for lasting ones. That year, 2000, homicides would rise 50 percent in the Bronx, and though all crimes, murder included, were still a fraction of what they were seven years before, the trend was sharp and ominous. Though Compstat had brought about a greater integration between the separate fiefdoms of the NYPD—in this case, the Four-O Precinct for the Patrol Bureau, the Four-O Squad for the Detective Bureau, the Narcotics modules assigned to Capt. Mahony in the Organized Crime Control Bureau, and of course, the Housing Bureau of PSA-7—the harmony was not quite pitch-perfect. As Bloody Rich's feuds heated up, the CO of the Four-O would be grilled at Compstat for the escalating rate of shootings and homicides, and the bosses downtown demanded arrests. Often, the Squad knew who the perps were but there was no basis for an arrest, or the case would fall apart, as John's shooting-robbery had. Once, Capt. Mahony came back from Compstat fuming that the CO of the Four-O had announced that all of his recent problems were due to Narcotics and Housing, which left him and my old captain holding the bag. Capt. Mahony looked at me tentatively and said, "I know you had your differences, but your old CO doesn't seem to be such a bad guy. . . ."

I laughed. "I'm just happy to be here, Cap."

I was happy enough. Now, I was on the team that played through, one of the big dogs that the little dogs asked for help.

As charges of ignorance and arrogance were traded back and forth, the precinct SNEU and Anti-Crime teams would be sent to the hot spots for quick results, which sometimes conflicted with our investigations. Timpanaro had returned to the PSA from Vice and had moved again from his old footpost to Anti-Crime. Though he still planned to take the sergeant's test, he hoped to get picked up by a detective squad in the meantime. The Captain ordered John to collar a guy who was wanted by the Four-O Squad, despite the fact that a "wanted card" had been issued, which meant that he had been identified in a case, and was unequivocally Squad property. The Squad Commander, Jimmy Ruane, chewed out John for taking the collar. Ruane was a friend of Pops's, and he had been a sergeant with the Four-Four Squad, where John hoped to go. Pops told me to pass along a message to John, and I relayed it: "If you get picked up by the Detective Bureau, let Pops know. His buddy Jimmy Ruane might be able to help you out to get to the Four-Four."

"Uh, yeah—I just met Ruane the other night. . . ."

I had no quarrels with anyone. I kept mostly to myself, eyes open and mouth shut, as I had during my first days as a cop. I didn't miss the fights, but there was a detachment, which I recalled from when I first came to Narcotics, a degree of remove that was a result of the division of labor between undercovers and investigators. If you didn't have an active CI, or it wasn't your turn to "get on" as the arresting officer for B&B, weeks might pass when you didn't even talk to a criminal. There was a disconnection, though I - wasn't sure how much it mattered or what it meant. When you were in the field, a team had to work cohesively, to know their positions and their subjects, when to move out and when to move in. At the same time, there was little need to know much about any given case, and I found that perplexing and somewhat uncomfortable. You could float through Narcotics, and I didn't like floating.

Our office had two major cases that year, Operation Hellbound and Smacky's wiretap case. I knew Hellbound fairly well, as Lesty had made buys for it, but Smacky's case was largely mysterious to me: by the time the wire went up, Smacky had several binders of DD5s, or "fives"—the standard detective memo—as thick as phone books, and it would be almost a year from the first buy until the case takedown. It began as a routine CI buy, and then an introduction was made for an uncle; phone numbers were exchanged as we bought in greater and greater weight. Dex and Teddy were the uncles in that case, and in one of the first major buys, they met one subject in the Bronx and traveled to Manhattan to meet another at a diner to conclude a sale. The second subject had not been identified, and so we didn't know his past or his propensity for violence; the level of transaction had moved up into the range of ounces and thousands of dollars; and traveling always brought an additional degree of risk, whether the subjects spotted the tail or we lost the uncles. When the uncles met the subject in a "flash car"—a Mitsubishi Gallant from the small fleet of rental cars at our disposal, which was not so flashy but deemed a better mid-level dealer vehicle than our stodgy old Mercedes four-door sedan—there was tension in Pops's voice as he called the tail like a horse race:

"Arright, they're off . . . south on Third, east on One-Four-Three . . . north on Morris . . . okay, I'm off—you on 'em, 402? They're probably going across to Manhattan on One-Six-One. . . ."

"On him, Leader, this is 402, he's north on Morris. . . ."

"Everybody, everybody, he's north on Morris, keep on parallelin', keep on parallelin' . . ."

"Okay, Leader, they took the left on One-Six-One, I'm out—368's coming across on One-Six-One, copy?"

"Copy—I can't hear you 368, you on him?"

"On him."

"You gotta tell me, you gotta tell me—everybody still parallelin'?"

"Parallelin'—Pops, we're north on Courtlandt, coming up on Six-One. . . ."

"That you, Eddie? Ten-four. . . ."

I rode with Fran Nugent, one of the senior men on the team, and peppered him with questions about the case.

"Who are the uncles?"

"Dex and Teddy, I think."

"Where are we going?"

"Somewhere in Harlem or the Heights."

"What are we buying? How much?"

"How am I supposed to know?"

"And what about—"

I didn't bother finishing, because Fran began to laugh.

"So basically, when we go out on a case, most of us don't really know what's going on?"

"Pretty much."

"Oh."

What I didn't know didn't matter to the case, but the headiness of that hour was heightened by the uncertainty: the uncles met the subject at a restaurant in Hamilton Heights, and we took positions around the perimeter. You didn't want to double-park with the engine running, because you looked more like cops, but then again you might, so you could move quickly if you had to. The kel faded in and out, and one of the subjects left the restaurant and headed toward me and Fran. Fran's hair was red as a siren, and I wasn't too close to passing as a local, either. Too late to move, Fran cut the engine and we dropped our seats back, so the car looked empty. He passed by, oblivious to us. The uncles made the buy, safely, and went back to the Bronx. We followed soon after, and I didn't think about the case again until the next buy.

• • •

THE SHIFTING AND PROVISIONAL NATURE OF THE WORK WAS inevitable, to a large degree, but other interruptions and adjustments of routine were easily avoidable. That year, apparently as a kind of morale-lowering experiment, our days off rotated three times, from Friday and Saturday in the spring, to Tuesday and Wednesday through the summer, to Sunday and Monday in the fall. Our daily schedules also changed, well, daily—and the next day's tour might be posted and adjusted several times over. With some modules, the tours were changed to fit the schedules of the bosses, and the whole team might come in late one day so the sergeant could see his kid's Little League game, or come in early so the lieutenant could have a night on the town; other modules kept fairly steady tours. For us, Lt. Zerbo changed the tours purely for reasons of professional gain—to do a late buy or an early warrant—and while you had to respect his decision, I never figured out how the cops with families could manage that flexibility. Even without a family, it was a strain, and it was the chief objection that John cited whenever I relayed offers from Pops or Chief Tiffany for him to come over to Narcotics.

In addition, there were the details, a uniformed assignment to a protest, parade, or some other special event. In the spring and early summer, we might have one or two a month, but as the summer turned, they began to pick up to twice a week. From Labor Day through Thanksgiving, New York City would host the playoffs, the World Series, and the U.S. Open. We had the United Nations anniversary, in which hundreds of heads of state were gathered in midtown for a week. That fall saw Hillary Clinton's run for the Senate and Al Gore's run for the Presidency, and the Clintons and Gores were in town constantly, together or apart, to campaign and raise money. We lined the motorcade route for hours beforehand, and froze the blocks before the cars passed, shutting down sections of the city. The Narcotics Division had four thousand cops, a pool that was tapped without hesitation for any of these events. The office joke was that OCCB didn't stand for the Organized Crime Control Bureau but "Other Commands Can Borrow." You might have several days' notice for them, but you might not, and when you came into work you were told to get in uniform and head out. The detail notices said NO DEPARTMENT VEHICLES and NO OVERTIME, but you always took a department car, and you usually did overtime. Your plans for the day—a CI buy, catching up on paperwork, or whatever else—were done. Though I was on vacation for the major disaster that year—the Puerto Rican Day Parade, in which numerous women were sexually assaulted—even the most peaceful details had moments of confusion and ill will, as cops were assigned for the day to a place many had never been before, without radios, and with little information. When I had to work Shea Stadium for a Mets–Braves game—Atlanta pitcher John Rocker had recently given an interview in which he denounced New Yorkers of all colors and preferences—I was assigned to a parking lot, where numerous drivers asked me for directions to various highways. When my first answer—"I have no idea"—seemed to invite denunciation and debate, I revised it to "Take the first left." For all I know, those people are still lost in Queens.

You had to be there hours before: at the precinct an hour and fifteen minutes before the muster, and at the muster hours before the event. On the Fourth of July, we had to be at the precinct at a quarter to four in the morning for a muster in front of the *Intrepid* at five, whereas the events would not begin until after ten. We were a slow-moving, slow-thinking herd, lowing in the dark for coffee, until someone found a bagel store on Forty-fourth Street and we ambled over en masse. The pre-dawn river chill gave way quickly, and the sun was hot and strong. The crowds gathered to watch the great wooden ships of forty nations sail up the river.

The spectacle was majestic, but after I'd stood there for ten hours, twelve, fourteen, in the blazing sun, my appreciation wore thin. We had booklets with the listings of berths for each ship, and schedules for when they sailed, but everything had been changed after the printing, and we had no answers to the questions from Argentine and Japanese and German tourists about the *Esmerelda* or the *Zenob Gramme*. A tidal condition had forced the flotilla to turn back down the river, and the crowds who had gathered above 72nd Street saw the ships only in the distance, and then in retreat. As they moved downtown, the street crossings were closed, and people were shunted to Fifty-seventh Street to cross, and then down to Fiftieth, and then to Forty-eighth, by cops who told them that the next crossing was open, or the past one had been. We had to keep the sidewalks moving, and if your attention lapsed for seconds, the crowds filled in and blocked traffic. No one was supposed to cross the West Side Highway where I stood, but if a man came up to me and said his elderly mother couldn't walk anymore, or his kids were worn out, I'd quietly let them through. And if it seemed safe, I'd let more across, until some captain would shout that the lines had to remain intact, and I'd hold them for a while. And then someone would come up in a wheelchair, and I'd let him through, and then the rest of the crowd would shout, "Why can't we go, too! What's wrong with you!" One woman shouted in my face, "My feet hurt, and you wrecked my day!"

At the Harlem Day Parade, the daylit hours were crowded with families watching the majorettes and marching bands, the Masonic lodges with dapper gents in Sinatra-era suits with gold-embroidered fezzes, calypso bands, and stilt-walkers, strutting and bouncing a dozen feet off the ground. After the sun set, however, there was an edge in the air, and it seemed that the families didn't leave as much as fled. The afternoon had been bright and balmy, and we wore short-sleeved shirts; now, we shivered in the chill and waited for dismissal. Bloods began to move down the streets in packs, in red jerseys and bandannas, and the children who remained alone after dark looked like they were accustomed to running the streets at night. A fat girl of about ten danced in the street to the rap:

Shake your ass
Watch yourself
Shake your ass
Show me what you got
Shake your ass . . .ž

She did a side-split on the pavement and ground to the beat, and a bony little boy of seven or eight hopped up onto her thigh and danced on it.

The parade went on an hour after schedule, and then two, and a last sound truck appeared in the distance, surrounded by a dancing crowd, determined to finish the route. A captain decided to close off the street, and we lifted the wooden barriers to block the passage. When the crowd saw that the street was closing, they raced ahead to the barriers before they shut, and some leaped over them. As the gap closed and the mass of the crowd drew near, they surged and started to stampede. Kids were mashed against the barriers, and the cops were pushed back, and the captain called out, "Stand fast! Hold the line!" The crowd poured through one corner, and I saw a cop stumble; I began to push through toward her, furious at the captain for forcing a confrontation, when he gave the order to pull back the barriers and let the crowd through. "Let 'em stop 'em at 125th Street," he muttered in disgust. The cop was all right, and I stepped back to the side, and I began to wonder why I was more angry at the captain—who had made a stupid decision, certainly—than the crowd, who risked crushing children so they could dance in the street for three more blocks.

The Palestinian "Day of Rage" didn't promise to be such a pleasant afternoon either. I remember watching Lt. Zerbo make up the detail roster in the office, pencil in his mouth, as he said, "Hmmm . . .ž don't think I'll send Leibowitz to this one." The protest was to take place outside the Israeli Embassy, and a few cops noted that it fell on Friday the thirteenth. "It's much worse than that," I added helpfully. "The date's 10-13"—the radio code for "Officer needs assistance." As it happened, the protest was peaceful and uneventful, with one moment of near-catastrophe. I was with Clune, and his brother the lieutenant was there, too, and we amiably passed the time on our side of the barricades. I stood in the sunlight on a corner, my gaze drifting from the crowds in head scarves who carried signs on one side of the barricades, to the crowds in business suits who carried briefcases on the other, when my attention was caught by a middle-aged man who wore an Israeli flag around his shoulders like Superman's cape. He marched with great determination - toward the thick of the protest, followed by an entourage that included half a dozen teenage boys.

"Hey! Hold on a second, there!"

Beautiful, I thought, it's the Palestinian Day of Rage and I'm going to collar a rabbi. The Clune brothers and a few other cops rushed over with me to intercept them. I recognized the man as a controversial rabbi who had last been in the news for denouncing a convent on the grounds of Auschwitz as "an abomination." The rabbi said he was exercising his First Amendment rights, and the boys behind him nodded with wild looks in their eyes, ready to meet their fates on the corner of Forty-second Street and Masada. Another, younger rabbi pressed us with questions, as if trying to trap us into an admission of guilt.

"Can't the rabbi walk up Second Avenue? Isn't this America? Are you saying to me that the rabbi *can't* walk up Second Avenue? Are you *ordering* the rabbi not to walk up Second Avenue?"

"Yes, I am telling you—ordering you—saying to you, asking you, if you want. But the rabbi can't walk up Second Avenue."

Third Avenue, yes. First Avenue, yes. Second Avenue, no. By the way, did you get these boys' parents to sign permission slips for suicide? In the end, Super-Rabbi and his crew were content to march in a little circle on the far corner, well attended by police, and no harm came to anyone. The Day of Rage had become a Day of Mild Annoyance, as so many of them did that fall.

The West Indian Day Parade, over Labor Day weekend, was always dreaded by cops: it would be a twenty-hour day with huge crowds and flatbed trucks piled twenty feet high with speakers that turned out reggae, calypso, and soca at tooth-loosening volume. In the past, drinking had been permitted and cops had turned a blind eye to marijuana, and there had inevitably been violence after sundown. This year, the Mayor banned beer sales, and there was concern that the reaction might be stronger than if - people had been allowed to drink. Just about everyone in the office would work, and I expected to, but the day before it happened I couldn't get out of bed.

My back had gone out again, a little worse than before. I knew what to expect, and I knew I wouldn't be moving the next day, still less standing for twenty hours. I was more concerned with what Lt. Zerbo would say, and how he'd react to the "sudden illness" that kept me from the longest day of the year. It was three or four more days before I returned to work, and as I walked into the office, Lt. Zerbo shook his head, an expression on his face that would curdle cheese.

"Don't even talk to me, I don't even want to hear it."

"But Lou, I—"

"But what—what happened?"

"My back went out."

"Oh. Okay. You all right?"

"I'm better, I think."

I was better, and a few days afterward I hardly felt it at all. And then it came back again, and never really left. For a while, changing posture from sitting to standing hurt, and I had to ease into each, and choose which might be more useful for the next few hours. I tried to be sneaky about it, the way an alcoholic slips into the bathroom and comes out with a mouthful of peppermints. If I couldn't stand up right away, I'd pretend to have an itch or tie my shoe until I could try again. The pain would go away for a few hours, and I was hopeful that it would stay away, as it often had. I just wanted to get better, or at least to get sick and get better, on a clearly defined timetable. What was not possible was to be on restricted duty indefinitely, not quite good enough to be in the field, but not quite bad enough to be allowed to stay home. There just wasn't enough to do in the office—even when my own casework was backed up at its worst, it could be dispatched in a few hours. If restricted-duty status continued for more than a month or so, I would be reassigned, and though working at the front desk at Narcotics would be far better than Central Booking, I didn't want to do either.

The pain drifted down from my lower back to the left kidney, and then to the left hip and leg. The condition is called sciatica, and it comes from the vertebrae compressing a nerve. I tried acupuncture, which felt fine at first, but walking back to my car I thought my leg was being yanked out of its socket. I staggered into a pizza parlor and sat at a table, tearfully ordering a slice. I went back a week later and told the Chinese woman what had happened. "You okay," she said. "Health take time, like beauty."

The way I moved was neither healthy nor beautiful. After a search warrant, Leibowitz told me, "You run like Walter Matthau in *Grumpy Old Men*." One afternoon in early September, I worked in the surveillance van with John Reilly to shoot video of one of Bloody Rich's spots. Reilly had a severe toothache, and I was half doubled over with my back. It was nearly ninety degrees outside, and we had to keep the windows shut, which drove up the interior temperature to well over a hundred. We also had to keep our movements to a minimum, so the van wouldn't rock. We ate handfuls of Advil and drank quarts of water, sweating it out as fast as we consumed it. As each junkie doddered up to the stoop where a dealer named Omar manned the stash, we zoomed in and out on the faces, dripping sweat on the camera, keeping our groans low. I would have liked to have that afternoon listed as a count on the indictment against Bloody Rich—Aggravated Backache, in the First Degree—but less imaginative legal minds prevailed.

We kept at it, as the cases closed and opened, the CIs came and went. Lesty had disappeared. He was going to be evicted, he told me, and he asked me for two thousand dollars to cover his back rent. I said that wouldn't be a problem, if he got me twenty guns or a couple of kilos. He didn't leave a forwarding address. Another informant took his place, sent to Pops by Bobby Addolorado. Sol was scrawny, pocked, and patchy-skinned, and she often seemed near physical extinction from her various drug-related illnesses—hepatitis, shingles—but she made it painfully clear that whatever its condition, her body was available for Ricky Duggan to ravish. I'd gone through OCCB training with Ricky, and he'd come over to the Bronx from Manhattan North that summer. His manner was cheerful and otherwise unflappable, except with regard to Sol. When we took her out for CI buys, she'd return to the car with crack or heroin, and we'd ask her what the seller looked like or where he kept the stash. Sol would gaze dreamily at Ricky and respond, "Ricky, alls I wanna do is lick your ears."

Often, she brought her boyfriend Mike along, who either went with her on the buys or waited with us in the car. It was, I suppose, what you could call an open relationship, because Mike would gleefully tell of having sex with Sol's young niece in the shower the day before, or how he shot a video of Sol with several friends in bed together. "I directed it, I produced it, I even wroted it," he said brightly. "Well, I co-wroted it."

"Aren't you a lucky fella," I said. "So you have no problems with Sol and Ricky being an item?"

"Hell, no. Ricky's the best!"

"You couldn't ask for better, Mike."

We paid them money and took their drugs, and then we dropped them off on a desolate block to return to their own diversions.

"What nice people," I said. "I'd like to see a lot more of them."

We took them out one night, as Ricky and I sat in the front seat, sending Sol off on her little errands. She continued to profess her love for Ricky, which he laughed at, until just before we dropped her off.

"Oh my God," he said, shuddering.

Sol called out cheerfully as she left, "Bye now, Ricky, I think I'm pregnant, and I hope it's yours!"

"What happened?" I asked.

"She hiked her skirt up for me to see," he said.

"Like Sharon Stone, in *Basic Instinct*?"

"She did what Sharon Stone did in *Basic Instinct*, but I couldn't really say it was like *Basic Instinct*. I think I'm going to have to tell Jennifer the engagement's off, indefinitely."

"In *Basic Instinct*, Sharon Stone didn't show her colostomy bag, did she?"

"No, I don't think she did."

"There's no shame in seeking counseling these days, Ricky, the Department has a number of fine services, and confidentiality is assured."

"I might have to take advantage of that."

When we took Sol to court for warrants, she was usually somewhat restrained, at first, in surroundings which had not always been so hospitable or so profitable for her. She was polite to the ADAs, and she often waited until they had elicited some legal information from her before she asked, "Do you like jokes?"

Sometimes they said they did, and sometimes they said they didn't, and neither answer mattered to Sol, who had one performance piece of which she was very proud: "Okay, so there's this guy? So he gets out of jail, and he's so horny he goes to Coney Island and picks up the first hooker he sees. She goes, 'How much money you got, yo?' And he says, 'Five bucks.' And the ho' goes, 'Fuck that!' And he goes, 'C'mon! I just got out, you gotta fuck me, five bucks is all I got!' So she takes the five bucks, and fucks him under the boardwalk. And the next day he's itchin' and scratchin', and the next day and the next, and the doctor says, 'Yo, you got crabs, mothafucka!' So he goes back to the boardwalk to look for the ho', and he says, 'Yo, bitch! What's up with you! You give me crabs!' And she says, 'Whaddaya expect for five bucks— Red Lobster?'"

I always laughed when she came to the part about the doctor. It reminded me of Crazy Larry's notes to his ex-girlfriend, on hospital stationery—*You got the AIDS, Bitch!*—or maybe there was a South Bronx doctor with that exact bedside manner. A few ADAs laughed, but more than one felt it necessary to caution her, "That's a good joke, but you have to promise you won't tell it to the judge."

I don't think Sol would have sold out her own child, but there was no price for him, yet. In one case, she looked through a "set book," which contained photographs of subjects, and as she flipped the pages, she said, "That's my father . . . that's my real father . . . that's my uncle . . . that's my godson. . . ." Once, she gave up her cousin who was wanted for a stabbing when she met him at a family party, calling the Four-O Squad to say, "Hello, can I have a cab at 180 Brook . . . ," as a prearranged signal to the detective who had the case.

A lot of the cops wouldn't deal with Sol, because she operated at several skeeve-levels above their threshold. For some reason, Leibowitz usually chose the moment when I was eating to tell me about her latest endearment:

"And she got out of the car, and she squatted down right there—"

"I'm trying to eat here. . . ."

"And she takes a squirt right there in the street, and—"

"Hey! Adam! Save it!"

"Hey, sorry . . . you gonna finish that sandwich?"

Sol was an unusual young lady, to be sure. She would mention offhandedly how much crack her mother used to sell, or how she used to rob dealers herself, sticking them up at gunpoint and making them strip naked. Though she weighed about eighty-five pounds, she reminisced about how she tipped the scales at over two hundred when she spent a year in Rikers. "Yo, I *really* liked the food there. I'll show you a picture if you promise not to laugh. . . ." But Sol made sense to me, because she was in it for the money, and that single motivation made her more manageable than many less objectionable informants.

In dealing with informants, my pitch had always been rational, to show perps that they had a choice, and why working with us offered better prospects than fighting a charge. I hustled them in the sense that there was a technique to the persuasions, but I never lied or even exaggerated. I could offer money or freedom, on a sliding scale. If the deal was for freedom, I avoided explicit terms to the effect that three buys and a warrant gets you from two-to-six to probation, because I didn't have the authority to adjust a sentence, though I could make my case with most ADAs. If it was a money deal, I told them exactly what they could make—on each set, fifteen dollars a try, thirty dollars a buy, and a hundred for a warrant if it was a hit—and if the office didn't have the money at the moment, I covered it myself. The approach was effective, as far as it went, but it encouraged a tendency to expect perps, or anyone else, to calculate advantage and risk in side-by-side columns. It's what I would do, I supposed, and that was the mistake: we were not the same. And not because I was a cop and they were criminals—though that was a real distinction, in that I didn't wake up wondering where to get my dope, let alone whom I would rob or rape—but because everyone has a percentage of themselves that makes no sense, and there is a percentage of people who never make any sense at all. I had to remind myself that the lines of human thought were neither straight nor clear, but it was a better lesson when the perps took it upon themselves to remind me.

We set up to watch Smacky's wiretap subjects—the still-unidentified JD Red and another man—come from the Heights to meet a Bronx dealer named Mike. JD Red carried a VCR in a cardboard box. They waited outside a pizza place, and we waited in cars around the perimeter of Mott-Pat, with uncles and ghosts floating through the project grounds. They waited and then they walked, and then they waited again, and then Mike met them, and all three walked again, into a building. We waited, tensely, wondering whether to move. We didn't want to take them yet, but the thought of what we might miss lingered like an itch—what if this was the big drop? We wanted to take in JD Red, just to identify him, but we didn't want to let him know that he was being watched, let alone overheard. As they stepped out of the project lobby, JD Red no longer had the VCR box, and we moved in and took them for trespass. We took them to PSA-7, hoping they'd believe they'd been picked up by Housing cops instead of Narcotics, and checked the name that JD Red had given us. If JD Red had a gun or a kilo on him, we would have been glad, but as it was, we had what we needed and hadn't been made. As we walked him out, however—Smacky, Billy Clark, and I, who were all from the PSA—a cop called out jovially, "Hey, what are you guys doing here? You're not in Housing anymore, you're in Narcotics!"

JD Red turned to Smacky and gave him a strange look. Smacky said nothing, and I shuddered. Would he have to write another binder full of fives to explain how the case was destroyed? No, I thought, one page would do. None of us mentioned it to Pops or Zerbo. I was anxious to look at the transcripts from the tap over the next few days, to see what they had taken away from the encounter. I found out when another dealer named Angel called JD Red, and while I was relieved to see that we hadn't been made, I was amazed to see his take on it. JD Red didn't think in circles but circuits, repeating figures of grievance and ego, and could pull facts like taffy. It was classic perp logic:

> "What's up, bro, I heard about what happened to you!"
>
> "Yeah—nah, but I was out quick. They got me only for bullshit trespassing, yo."
>
> "What, coming out of the house?"
>
> "Nah, I was inside the building and shit, in the fucking projects, and I was waiting, you know, for my man . . . in the lobby and shit."
>
> "Yeah, you serious? And they took you?"
>
> "Yeah, man, they took me for the little bullshit, yo. I was telling them, 'Yo man, you know you wasting your time and my time.' And he said, 'Well, I'm not really wasting my time, 'cause I'm getting overtime.' And I said, 'Ain't that a bitch. . . .'"

That part was true—Billy Clark said it. Angel had some questions about Article 140, Section 10 of the Penal Law, which Red explained fairly well:

> "I don't understand, you waiting for a friend, how they have that right just to take you, bro?"
>
> "If you don't live in the project, okay, you not supposed to hang out in the building. I told them, 'Listen man, be honest, it's cold out there. You know it's cold out there. You know, we ain't commit no crime, you know, we just standing here, staying warm. I had told them I went upstairs to my friend's house but there was nobody there.'"
>
> "Right."
>
> "You know what I'm saying? And we're just waiting for a cab to come."
>
> "Right."
>
> "You know? And then he said, 'All right, well what apartment your friend lives in?' And shit, you know, and I couldn't really remember the apartment, you know, so I had told them it's the twelfth floor, the first door to the left, this and that. So he says, 'All right guys, just don't hang out inside the building, y'all could stand outside.' So we stood outside waiting for my man."
>
> "Right."
>
> "And them motherfuckers went and knocked and shit, it was some black lady that opened up the door. And she said, 'Nah, I don't know . . . you-know, you-know, because I had to give them my name, and shit, she said, 'No, I don't know no Eric, this and that.' And ahh, nigger radioed in, yo. The next thing

you know, like four DTs and shit, two vans and two fucking cars, bum-rushed us, man, it was like, 'What the fuck is going on, yo?' And he was saying—you know the cop came, and shit, he said, 'You know, I don't like no fucking liars.'

That part was true, too—Smacky said it, and it was a good line, because it made it seem that we brought him in because one cop was angry about what he said, instead of many who were interested in what he did.

"And I told him, you know, just because we're standing in the fucking building, c'mon man, I could see if we selling drugs . . ."

"You a grown man. . . ."

". . . or robbing people or something, you know. . . ."

"You ain't no kid. . . ."

"I told him, he said, 'But you know, it's the law, you cannot trespass.' I told him, 'Listen, okay, that's the law—it's true, you right about that. But you know that's a bullshit law, yo!'"

"Yeah, no doubt."

"I could see if I'm some young thug and shit, hanging out around the building to mug somebody, or sell drugs, you know. I told him, 'Yo, I'm an older man, you know what I'm saying?'"

"Right!"

"I told him, 'That's not right, man.' I told him, 'Listen, if I bet you anything, if I was an old lady or a man with a cane, y'all guys would never arrest us. But being that we look like we're from the street or whatever, that's the reason why y'all took us in.' You know?"

I was happy to hear that. It meant that even Red thought—his own case aside—that cops enforced the law selectively but sensibly. Angel took a different perspective:

"They were white, right?"

"Yeah, two white cops, and shit. You know . . ."

"Prejudice."

"I told him, 'Yo, I'm too old for that bullshit!' I told him, 'What you think? I'm gonna be an idiot and stand right there selling drugs? You gotta be kidding me!' I told him, 'If I was selling drugs, I woulda been the fuck out of there. . . . I'm forty-one years old, you think I'm an idiot, yo?'"

"I hate white people. . . ."

JD Red was no darker than Dan Quayle, with red-brown hair that gave him his JD name.

But clearly, when he looked in the mirror, he didn't see the same things that we did. There was no realization that we were on to him, but there was also no recognition that we had any right or reason to be. *It's not as if he were selling drugs!* His indignation was sublime, in its way, as he was a drug dealer who was talking to another drug dealer, about having just delivered a quarter-pound of cocaine:

> *"Oh yeah, I knew, I knew I was gonna be out quick, but you know, thank God, man, because, uh . . . Just before that happened and shit, I had a hundred of them things. You know what I'm saying? And I took it to my man."*
>
> *"Thank God, man."*
>
> *"In that building, you know what I'm saying?"*
>
> *"Yeah, yeah."*
>
> *"So I was waiting for my man to come down and shit, 'cause you know, he had to—uh, you know—he had to kick up the cash and shit."*

Red had dropped off a hundred grams of cocaine—almost four ounces—and Mike was going to cook up ten grams into crack, for Red's sister to sell. Angel said that his mother and stepfather also sold drugs, and then went on to say that he had been at Mike's that morning to buy crack but the quality was bad—*"I disapprove, you know—I'm-a get rid of it . . . but it's gonna take me long, niggas ain't feelin' it. I hope he ain't get it from you."*

The two went on to talk about their pride in their families and their business, which appeared to frequently intersect:

> *"And let me tell you, I won't give you no garbage—you know what I'm sayin'?—because to me, what's important is that you make your money, 'cause if you don't make your money, then I can't make no money."*
>
> *"Your word is good. You know what I mean? And my family tells me that."*
>
> *"Uh-huh."*
>
> *"I'm proud of you, and I take that very serious."*
>
> *"I know what's good and what's not good. I've been in this shit like twenty-five years, you know what I'm saying?"*
>
> *"You could teach me, bro. . . ."*
>
> *"Yeah, you know—hey, we all teach each other, you know?"*
>
> *"Yeah."*

"That's how I've learned, and I've taught other people, too . . . whenever I put my foot in the bucket, I make sure I get myself out of it, you know what I'm saying?"

"No doubt."

"'Cause I mean, it's too many years experience in this fucking world, you know what I'm saying? Not that I know it all—'cause I don't—and it's always good to reach out, you know what I'm saying? But whatever I get myself into . . . thank God, knock on wood, you know?"

What struck me was how Red cast himself as an injured party, how his sense of order had been violated, if not, technically, his rights. He sounded like a stockbroker furious at a traffic cop who had ticketed him for speeding, making him late for the 0650 express train. He sounded exactly like the stockbroker, in fact, who might have been expecting agents of the Securities and Exchange Commission, but was positively offended by the lowly flatfoot. And Angel understood completely. Angel's parents were dealers, and maybe his children would be, too; Red's own quarter-century in the trade itself spanned generations. It had been bred into them. Maybe my great-grandchildren would arrest theirs.

I thought about how his sense of the normal was as remote from my own as that of a Berber tribesman or Prussian colonel. But then I considered that I was not an entirely logical creature myself: I was thirty-five years old, with a good education and a bad back, and I spent my days grabbing crack dealers in the South Bronx. What had been bred into me? I had occasion to think about that, a week or two later, when we had a Christmas party at Louie's on East Tremont Avenue, where part of *The Godfather* was filmed. It is a pivotal scene: the Corleones are at war with Sollozzo, Tartaglia, and Barzini; Don Corleone has been shot, and he is threatened further in the hospital; in his first encounter with the law, Michael's jaw is broken by the corrupt police captain, McCluskey, who is on Sollozzo's payroll. At home, Sonny and Tommy Hagen, the consigliere, debate their options, when Michael proposes that they agree to a sit-down with McCluskey and Sollozzo, where he will kill them both.

Sonny laughs at him, impressed at his ambition but dismissive of his ability: "Hey, what are you gonna do? Nice college boy, who didn't want to get mixed up in the family business . . . now you want to gun down a police captain? Why, because he slapped you in the face a little bit? . . ."

"It's not personal, Sonny, it's strictly business."

As I watched the scene again, I wondered which was true: was it for his family's sake, or his own?

McCluskey is old, oafish, crooked, and brutal, and no matter how perfect the character, the role is one that stretches historical reality—a captain might be in the mob's pocket, but he wouldn't be a personal bodyguard for a gangster. His risk of exposure would be too high, and the gangster could certainly do better than a cranky geriatric. But McCluskey's first line as they sit down at Louie's is one of my favorites in the movie: "How's the *Italian* food in this restaurant?"

The emphasis brims with disdain, barely conscious and barely concealed. There is something in the way that line is spoken that reminded me of my older relatives at Italian restaurants, fumbling with a menu before ordering lasagna because it was the only dish with a name they could pronounce.

"Good. Try the veal, it's the best in the city," says Sollozzo.

Wine is brought, but the only glasses are for Michael and Sollozzo—it is their little revenge for his being Irish. They speak Italian, but it is not hard to follow: *Padre . . . rispetto . . . molto difficile . . . ž*

As he's rehearsed with Clemenza, Michael asks permission to go to the bathroom—"You gotta go, you gotta go"—and returns with a .38.

He sits down and listens, barely—*"Tuo padre . . ."*—and then he shoots Sollozzo in the forehead, as McCluskey sits, open-mouthed, a forkful of the best veal in the city suspended in the air. Michael shoots him, too, and drops the gun, as he's been told, and though he was told not to run, he starts to, just as he reaches the door.

When we sat down to dinner at the Christmas party, I said, "How's the *Italian* food in this restaurant?" but I don't recall getting too many laughs. I didn't try the veal. If I was the only one who appreciated a joke, I was happy to laugh alone. It may have made a few people raise their eyebrows, but I didn't much care.

You never really know what your own reputation is, or how your view of yourself conforms with those around you. I was liked, I thought, and I got along with everyone in the office. The occasional jokes about going to Harvard or writing a book were infrequent and good-natured, and when someone was genuinely interested in one or the other, they'd approach me quietly to ask about them. As far as my eccentricities, they were not extreme: I dressed like a bum but I drove an old Cadillac and drank martinis; I could wreck a desk with paperwork; I read all the time—books, newspapers, magazines. Ricky Duggan said I looked like a panicked junkie if didn't have anything to read, tearing around the office for last week's *Post*.

I was quiet in the office and kept a low profile. I didn't have a desk, or even a drawer in one, and so no one was used to looking for me in any particular place. I used my own car again, for the freedom and convenience it brought, and if I had business to take care of that didn't need another cop, I took care of it alone. Early on, before I built up a caseload, I had some free time, and later on, when I didn't, I had a lot of errands like picking up rap sheets at Headquarters, or meetings with ADAs or CIs. I became a PBA delegate, and I got a day off each month for union meetings. Our office went out on most days, for B&B, CI buys, or case buys, but if we weren't doing anything, I'd take off—I did have another job to do. Billy Clark took to calling me "The Phantom."

The tag reminded me of something, and when I looked through my father's scrapbook, I found a poem that his colleagues had written on the occasion of his twentieth anniversary in the FBI:

> *John Matthew Conlon, the Phantom, Will-of-the-Wisp, each day*
> *Reporting to work every morning, folding his tent and fading away.*
> *Oh, Gray Fox, we wonder how you disappear in a Flash.*
> *You can make the elevator in the record time of a hundred-yard dash.*
>
> *However, we know you are working, because it's easy to see*
> *How happy you are when you arrest someone and deprive him of Liberty.*
> *Of all the Agents on 26, there probably is no other.*
> *We bet you would be happy even if you arrested your brother.*

On the opposite page of the scrapbook, there was another poem, and I wondered if it was composed by the same Agent-Poet, or if—God forbid—there were two in the office.

> *He joined the ranks in '51*
> *And sat down to take a rest.*
> *While waiting for his interview*
> *He swallowed the Reader's Digest.*

The magazines piled high and high,
His wife was pressed for space.
John took the kids from the bunk beds,
The books will take their place. . . .ž

And as we sign him in today,
Never fear and be not reticent,
For John will always change his name
To protect the pure and innocent.

My teammates might not have been entirely unfamiliar with the figure of a book-loving cop who drove an odd car—a Volkswagen Beetle, in my father's case—but when I thought about the similarities it was almost embarrassing: a casual attitude toward punctuality, and a penchant for aliases . . . Sometimes I wondered whether I was coming into my own, or merely repeating what had been my father's. In either case, there were worse ways to be.

By the end of the year, I was confident in my new assignment, and comfortable with my bosses and partners. It was not as it was with SNEU, with its intensities of camaraderie and cause, and if I wasn't singing in my car anymore, neither was I looking forward to a root canal. The next year, I would be made a detective, as I'd determined when I first put on a uniform and threw my gloves in the air. But there was no sense of culmination on the horizon, and that troubled me somewhat, as I looked ahead. I didn't want to just collect the gold shield like a paycheck, but there was no particular reason to leave, and no particular place to go. There was little I could do about it, except to keep working and hope for a case that would engage me, that would lead to some kind of Door. I had no expectation of a French Connection, but I needed a renewed sense of purpose and place. And after being shamed by Chief Tiffany into brushing up on Dante, I began to think that the problem might be that work didn't stink enough—I didn't have to pause before descending to the next level of Hell. As you go on in the Job, your career should follow a double arc, down and up at the same time: as you get better, the work should get worse, to graver tasks and tests. For Dante to find his Door, he had to head where it hurt to go: Are you feelin' this? *I ain't feelin' this.* Good, this must be the way.

Only one thing did hurt for me, more and more, and that was my back. I had trouble standing up, or moving very fast or far. My posture was like a question mark, and on B&B, I took to standing outside the car as we waited on a set, so I would be able to run if we moved in. In January, they kept me in the office for a week or two, and then I would go on vacation, and then I would have surgery. I wouldn't work again until May, but on New Year's Eve of 2000—for the true millennium—I worked the Times Square detail for the first time in my life. The crowd swelled up to our post at Fifty-ninth and Seventh, filling up the pens in the center of the street. The New York Athletic Club opened a room for us with a coffee urn and donuts, and we slipped out of the cold now and then. Snow was banked hard and high on the sidewalks, and I helped a little girl clamber up to see over the crowd. Japanese tourists asked me where they could go to the bathroom, and I laughed. All the crowd fell silent as the count wound down, and we had a clear view of the ball as it descended through the neon canyon of Times Square, the first of all the lights, the last of the year.

TWELVE

For five months, I lay down and thought. Often, I felt old. In some ways, I was old: had I gone on the Job when I was twenty, I'd have been a few short years from retirement. It might have been the painkillers, but when I looked back over the six years I'd been a cop and the hundred and fifty that the NYPD had somehow managed without me, there was no clean line between them. I had begun a year after Giuliani and Bratton had been sworn in, but I'd lived in the city and worked in the courts when Koch and Dinkins were in office. As a cop, I would talk to Inspector Mullen, Chief Tiffany, or Sonny Grosso about the major events of the 1960s and 1970s, of Phillips, Serpico, and Leuci, and sometimes I thought that they talked to me no differently than they had with their partners at the time. So, too, it was with my father's friends on the Job, who began work in the 1950s, and even in the 1930s, in Jim Falihee's case. Falihee had been a chemistry major in college and planned to become a doctor, but the Depression intervened, and he spent most of his career in the Bomb Squad and the Police Laboratory. He could reminisce about the World's Fair bombings of 1941, and hunting for Nazi saboteurs. Falihee's time began as Pat Brown's was ending, and in Pat's rookie years, the old-timers doubtless groused about how Teddy Roosevelt had damn near ruined the Job. *The beer pail is empty! And the spittoon is full!*

Mother of God, if my father ever lived to see the day when they let Eye-talians into the New York City Police Department . . .ž

If these generations ever came together, I could tell them about how computers had changed things, how we didn't take fingerprints with ink or photographs with film, and Uncle Eddie and Sonny Grosso could recall when television was invented, and if Pat Brown was still talking to us, he could reminisce about when the automobile made its debut. But all of us could talk about walking footposts on winter nights, and how the sergeant would touch your shield to check if it was cold. All of us, from each end of the century, knew the green lights of the precinct, which hearkened back to centuries before. We could talk about shoe-flies and rackets, roll calls and rounds; we would even know some of the same paperwork—the UF 61s and DD5s. We might even agree that the time of the Irish had passed, but maybe it had always been passing, and always would. And Sonny would likely complain about that less than the rest. We would see eye to eye about many things.

No matter how natural it felt to be a cop, and no matter the pointed weight of heredity and history, it was by no means inevitable that I had gone on the Job. When I was younger, I had never read mysteries, and I had no pronounced interest in crime, true or otherwise, until I happened into a job in criminal defense. Sometimes I wondered what had happened to my old clients from CCJA. I remembered poor Cecil, who cut off his stepson's crack-crazed head, and how he'd look down and mutter, "I would not be able to say," no matter what I asked him. Not long after we'd banished him to Montserrat, I read about the hurricane that wiped out much of the island. I caught another name in the papers a few years later, just after I'd gone on the Job, I think. A one-paragraph item in the *Daily News* told of an off-duty cop who stopped at a gas station as it was being robbed at gunpoint, and he shot the perp in the chest. The perp was Dondre, who had last played with guns with his best friend Kataun. The gas station was in Greenpoint, not far from where his grandmother lived, reading her John le Carré novels. Dondre was twenty-one, and he must have just been released, if he maxed out as a juvenile. He would max back in again; so much for second chances.

For a while, I stayed in touch with Jack, my first client, and his mother, Maria. I wrote to Jack in prison, after Maria told me that he was getting in trouble again with gangs there. He had joined the Five Percenters, which was affiliated with the Nation of Islam. I was concerned for Jack, and angry, not to mention a little confused: Jack was Puerto Rican, and not even dark-skinned, and he had no brighter a future with black supremacists than he would have with the Klan. His fights and gang activities cost him his first chance at parole, and he spent three years in prison. When he came home, I went over to his house for dinner, and the time showed on him. At eighteen, he was bigger and stronger, but he had a nervous quickness to him, as if someone had just turned on the lights. We had fried chicken and rice and beans, and we made polite small talk. Jack handled his knife and fork clumsily; he was unused to metal utensils. When the bell went off on the microwave, he jumped. "I thought it was the panic button," he explained. "You know, for when they do lockdown."

When Jack talked about "up north," it was as if he'd been at college or in the Army. I was uneasy with his nonchalant tone, and how it suggested that further confinement would be less of an adjustment than freedom would be. Nor did I trust the parroted references to "keeping it positive" and "not being a follower." After dinner, when he walked me back to the subway, I had even further misgivings. I watched him watch the street, rapid and roving, combat-ready. In the prison corridors upstate, the high-alert attitude might have been defensive, but on streets of Brooklyn, he looked predatory, on the make. At the subway, we shook hands and assured each other we'd stay in touch.

"You be careful out here, Mr. Conlon."

"I told you, you don't have to call me 'Mister.' "

"All right, but you be careful—there's a lot of knuckleheads out here."

"I always keep an eye out for knuckleheads, Jack. You take care, now."

Ten years passed before I thought to call again. It took some time to remember the name of the Catholic social-services agency where Maria worked. I wondered for a moment if she was still alive, or if Jack was. I talked to a nun at the agency and persuaded her to give me Maria's home number. After the first ring, I almost hoped to get an answering machine, so I could hang up and call again after thinking about what message to leave. But Maria answered, and though I was certain she would remember me, I wasn't prepared for her reaction:

"God has sent you! God has sent you! Oh, thank God, my goodness—it's so good to hear from you. . . ."

Nor did I expect to hear news that would make me as elated as her greeting. Jack had gone to college in Maryland, and he stayed there after graduation. Now, he was married and had two children, and he worked as a counselor for troubled kids. He had a master's degree, and he had nearly completed his Ph.D. I'd been afraid that he'd find his way back to the knuckleheads, but I never expected that it would be on these terms. We talked some more—about her health, which had been uneven—and my own career adjustments, which she was happy to hear about. She gave me Jack's number in Maryland, and I called him.

"Oh, my *Gaaawd*—Mr. Conlon!"

And we talked for a while, about his kids and his wife and his job and his Ph.D. He was as casual about his striving and his hard-won substance as he had been about panic buttons and lockdowns the last time we'd spoken. Was there anything so strange about that, going from life to life? No, I thought, but so few people manage it so well. I thought about his intermediate-school teachers and the people at St. Barbara's who saw such great things for Jack, and how even after he became a criminal, and then a prisoner, and then an ex-con—it had been a short period, but it had not been a long life—they remained undaunted in their hope. For a moment, I felt like an absentee father, and I laughed at myself for the vanity. But I told him, "Jack, I'm proud of you," and I think he was glad to hear it. Anyone can learn from their mistakes, but it takes a savvy or a sanctity beyond ordinary measure—St. Augustine comes to mind—to make those mistakes mean so much, to whomever is willing to listen.

As they told us in high school, the word "vocation" meant a calling: you knew it when you heard it, and you went. To prepare for our freshman year, the Jesuits gave us a book about the history of the order, telling of St. Ignatius Loyola, the founding soldier-saint who devised a form of meditation, and of other missionaries, martyrs, and scholars. The last chapter had been torn out, which we found highly intriguing; what secrets were being withheld from us? In fact, the chapter had been removed because it discussed preparation for the priesthood, and the school feared that it might scare off parents who were hopeful for grandchildren. Three of my classmates entered the priesthood, though all three eventually left. Would there have been more if the last chapter had not been torn out? Would they have stayed? Maybe the voice that called had fallen silent, or other voices called louder.

I had two vocations, cop and writer, which called not only to me but to each other. Much of police work is storytelling, from the journalism of an investigation, to the post-arrest sales pitch to the ADA. I always felt a little superior when a sergeant or an ADA looked at my paperwork and said, "This is very well written, you know." I felt the opposite after my first evaluation for Narcotics, where the marks varied from average to above, until Clune explained that Lt. Zerbo did that for everyone, so that later evaluations would reflect progress. "I'm not sure what to say about this," I said. "But maybe that's because my 'Judgment' is only average, three out of five. I could go one way or another."

"Don't be insulted. He was going to give you a three in 'Communication,' too, but I thought you'd take that a lot more personal."

I thought for a moment. "You're right, I would have." In any case, I was less unhappy than the teammate who wondered whether the purported tribute of being a "well-rounded detective" was a jibe about his weight.

On duty and off, cops are storytellers, but when a group of cops tells stories, there is usually a degree of self-consciousness if a non-cop is around. Sometimes it's because you have to break up the story to explain a bit of slang or procedure, but more often it's out of a wariness that things won't sound right, that the cop will look as rough and rude as the work can be. Even when the purpose of police work is to disclose a secret, to reveal a true mystery—who stole what from where, who killed whom—there is a shifting balance between the unsaid and the said. A patrolman is entitled to use his discretion, and on some days, the D is heavier than others. More is left out because it's too dull to explain rather than because it's dangerous to share, and many omissions really aren't either—in one verse of my father's FBI anniversary poem, there is mention of an extremely valuable and delicate old painting he recovered, which he tossed in the back seat of his Volkswagen, amid the coffee cups and peanut shells. Until he retired—and maybe after— my father would have said of the painting story, "Let's keep that one to ourselves, why don't we?" It is easier to talk your way into trouble than to talk your way out: cases are often solved because criminals talk—bragging to their friends, yapping on a tapped phone—and convictions are more likely after a confession. *How does a fish get caught? He opens his mouth.*

But ya *still* gotta have a story. For cops, despite the Blue Wall of Silence and the Fifth Amendment, the well-founded fear of the media and an adversarial legal system, sooner or later, we are all called to testify. It saddened me to hear a story about a rookie who chased a perp to a rooftop, where the perp fell to his death trying to escape. Though there was the expected street-corner chorus crying *Murder!* the Squad had moved in quickly, finding several witnesses who corroborated the account of an accidental death. Before the rookie could give his statement to Internal Affairs, however, he was taken aside by an old hairbag, who said, *Listen, kid, listen to me, ya hafta say you - weren't there, ya hafta say you never made it into the building, ya can't trust anybody, trust me on this. . . .* The rookie had done nothing wrong until the interview, after which he was fired. No doubt the old-timer is generous with his advice still, enjoying his pension in Florida. *Poor dumb kid, he didn't listen. . . .* Nobody ever says *nothing,* not even a monk. Our silences are as articulate as our stories, are part of them, and they too can be held against us. In *A Man for All Seasons,* Thomas More correctly insisted that under the common law, silence indicates consent. More had refused to take the oath of allegiance to Henry VIII as head of the Church, and hoped to keep his head in spite of it. He did not beat the system, and though Sir Thomas became St. - Thomas, he would have preferred survival to either title. If you don't have a story of your own, one may be supplied, and you may be surprised, not happily, by how well it fits.

• • •

FOR PAT BROWN, I HAVE A COPY OF WHAT IS CALLED A "TEN card," which lists his disciplinary record as well as the barest administrative data: assignments, addresses, and shield numbers. His first six years were spent in the 172nd and 148th precincts, neither of which exists today, and then in June 1914, he was transferred to the 15th Inspection District for a series of ten-day temporary assignments that extended for four years. In 1918 he moved to "BBH," Brooklyn Borough Hall, and then to "HD," Headquarters Division, for two years, with a note that says "200 Ex Com." In 1920, there is a severe-looking note that says "Ex Com Revoked," marking a return to patrol in Brooklyn, with another temporary posting to the Brooklyn DA's Squad before promotion to sergeant in 1926. He had been a cop for twenty-one years, and he spent his remaining twelve between the First Precinct, "the old First," on Old Slip, near the Fulton Street Fish Market, and in the 78th, in Park Slope, in Brooklyn again, from which he retired.

For most people, these notes would be hieroglyphic; for me, the risk is not failing to understand what they say—though I don't understand them completely—but rather reading too much into them. In the spring of 1914, when he was first transferred, the city was consumed with the Becker–Rosenthal scandal, in which a police lieutenant was sent to the electric chair for the murder of a gambler. Such events, then as now, invariably provoke a frenzy of administrative housecleaning. Moreover, it was just after the inauguration of Mayor John Purroy Mitchel, the reform candidate who beat Tammany in the wake of the scandal. Whether Pat Brown was seen as a man who could be trusted not to take a penny, or someone who could keep his mouth shut, ad-

vancement presented itself in a time of political crisis. His move to Headquarters similarly took place during a period of political transition, a month
after John F. Hylan took office as Mayor, ousting the reformer after one term,
as was the pattern. Hylan, a Brooklyn Democrat, was regarded as "honest
but befuddled" and had an obsession with the subways—he had been a railroad conductor until he was fired for nearly running over his boss. His police
commissioner, Richard Enright, was the first former NYPD officer to occupy
that position; he was best remembered for giving out solid-gold shields to
wealthy supporters, known as "Enright's Millionaires." Whether there was a
Brooklyn hook or a cop hook at the changing of the guard, it pulled Pat
Brown to the center of things. The center, as the late Lt. Becker might have
told him, is not always the best place to be.

1920: Ex Com Revoked. It sounds worse than an ordinary transfer, certainly, though there is no mark against him on his disciplinary record. The
78th Precinct was near his home in Brooklyn, and had he seriously crossed
his bosses he would have been sent to the Bronx. Nonetheless, for most cops,
a purely lateral move from the capital to the provinces is rarely a step up. Regardless of whether 1920 was a year of great professional turmoil for Pat
Brown or simply occasioned a routine administrative shift, it was then that
the marriage broke apart. I can guess wildly if not well about what happened: he was caught taking money, or caught not taking money, or he was
taking money and never got caught, but he lost it when he left Headquarters,
after he fought with his boss, or his boss lost a fight, or there was no fight, but
two years was considered to be the proper term for a cop at HQ. Or his boss
was promoted to Brooklyn, and he followed him there. Or he learned the
trade of the shakedown in the city, so when he hit the boondocks, the rubes
were ripe for the picking. The sudden loss of income pushed him into bitterness, or the sudden gain in income made him want to live like a playboy. I
don't know what happened. I do know that most cops bring their work home
with them, when it's going badly; that they carry the smell of the streets on
them even when they change clothes. And even though, as a plainclothesman, he walked better streets than he had on patrol, the smells were often
worse. It might be worth noting that 1920 was also the year that Prohibition
went into effect.

Pat Brown spent the next six years in Brooklyn, as the city came to realize
that the good times didn't end with the Volstead Act. Tammany reached its
heights under Governor Al Smith, who was the first Catholic candidate for
President, and from whom his onetime and ungracious protégé Franklin

Delano Roosevelt lifted much of the New Deal. In 1925, Jimmy Walker convinced Smith that his rakish ways were behind him to secure the nomination for mayor, and for a time he had the city fooled, too. Walker was known as "the Night Mayor" and "Beau James," and he embodied the city far better than he administered it. When a Long Island casino he was visiting was raided, he slipped into the kitchen and put on an apron to watch the cops haul off the other patrons, his girlfriend included, as he ate beans with the dishwashers. He remarked that it wouldn't do for a man in his position to turn up in a "rural hoosegow." Walker was *the* man about town, all wisecracks and diamond stickpins, who co-wrote a hit song, "Will You Love Me in December As You Do in May?"—a question which, if considered political in nature, was answered with a resounding "No!"

Pat Brown was a boss himself by then, having been promoted in 1926. He worked in the 1st Precinct in lower Manhattan through the Walker years, remaining until a few weeks before Fiorello La Guardia appointed his great reformer, Lewis Valentine, as Police Commissioner. It is hard to read the transfer as a coincidence. The 1st was not the Tenderloin—it encompassed the financial district and some of the waterfront—and as such had a relatively tiny permanent population. It was never known as a red-light district, though its bankers and sailors must have had some nearby diversions, but waterfronts were famously useful to organized crime in general and bootleggers in particular. By the length of his stay and the timing of his departure, I would assume that the command had some value for Pat, as well as some risk. The 1st Precinct covered Headquarters and was uncomfortably close. Prohibition had been repealed, and Valentine was about to arrive when he returned to Brooklyn, to the Seven-Eight, in Park Slope, where he finished his career in the NYPD in 1940.

Pat Brown did not leave much of a paper trail I have his ten card and the menu from his retirement dinner; beyond that, there is a clip from *The Brooklyn Eagle* of Wednesday, June 14, 1916, which raises more questions than it answers:

TRIED TO "BUY" POLICEMAN?

Brown Says He Was Offered $10 to Drop Case

Charged with attempting to bribe Patrolman Patrick Brown of the Fifteenth Inspection District, who had arrested his friend, Joseph

Lopoma, 45 years old, of 52 Dooley Street, was held on $1000 bail for a hearing by Magistrate Geismar in the Coney Island Court yesterday afternoon. The officer states that in the corridor of the court yesterday Lopoma offered him $10 to discontinue the complaint of selling liquor without a license, made against Basile Peccelro, 23 years old, of 50 Dooley Street.

Peccelro was arrested by Patrolmen Brown and Daly, charged with distributing and selling to a construction gang boxes of bottled beer. He pleaded not guilty and was held on $500 bail for examination on June 16.

They were indeed different times. If Pat Brown was someone else's relation, what would stand out for me in the story would be the old New York ethnic casting, of Irish cop, German or Jewish judge, and Italian defendants with dubiously spelled names. The bail is extraordinarily high, somewhat understandable for a defendant charged with bribery, but appalling for a man accused of providing beer to laborers. As a Bronx cop, it's somewhat refreshing to see criminal cases treated with firm dispatch, but it is hard to be nostalgic for a system so petty and cruel. My guess is that the bribe was too little, or too late. I wish there was better to say, and more, without offense to ancestral spirits. When a relative came to my father for advice about a newspaper column that he felt was disrespectful to his late brother, my father pointed out that, as a matter of law, you cannot libel the dead. If Pat Brown could not sue, I figured, he was well within his rights to haunt me.

Whenever I find myself in an out-of-the-way part of the city, I like to walk around a bit, or to stop by with relatives or friends whom I haven't seen in a while. If I think about it, I'll know somebody just about anywhere in town. One day I gave John Timpanaro a lift to Kennedy Airport, which put me in the far reaches of Queens on a balmy spring afternoon, so I decided to pay a visit to my great-grandfather. It would be our first meeting. At St. John's Cemetery in Middle Village, I meandered amid groves of marble angels on high pedestals, moneyed and majestic and sentimental, and I could almost feel the cool of the moon-colored stone. I passed a bunkerlike mausoleum that bore the name Profaci, which with some injustice but better luck escaped becoming a brand name of a Mafia branch, now known as Colombo. The brand names are there, too: Colombo, Gambino, and Genovese, and other bosses, like Carmine Galante, who helped organize the French Connection; Salvatore Maranzano, the first "Boss of Bosses," who founded the Commission and the Five Families as Prohibition ended; and Charles "Lucky" Luciano, who became the next and last true Boss of Bosses after killing Maranzano. John Gotti would be buried there, too, in time.

So Paddy the Cop finally got his table at Rao's, I thought, or a spot at the bar at an eternal, underworld Copacabana. I would have gotten along with him, I think, despite myself. New York has always been full of heroes who are hard to like and villains who are hard to hate. My mother and her sisters never spoke with him, in any real sense, but Pat Brown did speak with his daughter-in-law, Marie, by telephone a few times, and she recalls him with some affection. Then again, Marie had a knack for getting along with some very difficult men. My great-aunt Marie Doherty Brown Marcus was a jazz pianist from Boston. While she was still in her teens, her mother brought her down to New York for her first job, at Keen's Chop House, and told her employer, "My daughter is a good Catholic girl, Mister, and if she has any problems here, you'll have me to answer to!"

"Yes, Mrs. Doherty, of course, Mrs. Doherty, she'll be fine here," was the response from Dutch Schultz, perhaps the most murderous gangster of his day. Schultz himself was gunned down not long afterward by his underworld colleagues, after announcing his intention to kill Special Prosecutor - Thomas E. Dewey. Schultz was a fairly dour character, as Marie remembers him, though she was thrilled when he included her in his visits to the Cotton Club in Harlem, where she watched her idols Fats Waller—he had given her piano lessons when she was young—Cab Calloway, and other jazz legends play. From there, she went to work for Frank Costello at his Venetian Palace, where, on one early occasion, there was an apparent misunderstanding between them as to the nature of the entertainment she was to provide. He sent her to play at a private party of mobsters at a hotel room, and she was utterly stunned to see the singers remove their gowns before the first verse. When it appeared that one of the hoods expected her to follow suit, she fled the room and went back to the club, where she hunted down Costello and gave him an earful, much as her mother had done Schultz, and he apologized profusely, saying he had no idea it was that kind of party. Once Costello was straightened out, she told me, she had no more problems. She met Lucky Luciano there, and thought Bugsy Siegel a "very nice man," who called her "the Coca-Cola Kid," because that was all she drank. Her public was thick with Public Enemies.

Marie married Jack Brown, and for a time they had an act together in the clubs and hotels of Manhattan and Brooklyn. She played the piano and Jack sang, and when I asked what "their" song was, she laughed and said, "Melancholy Baby," as if it held some clue as to why their marriage was not to last. Few people now recognize that song except as a punch line, but it seems to have been the national anthem for the underworld in its tender moments. At the Venetian Palace, a gangster requested it, and when Marie told him she'd gladly comply, after playing a prior request, he put his cigarette out on her gown. In turn, she broke a chair on his head. Some capo resolved the matter by giving her a hundred dollars. ("The gown only cost five dollars to have made, plus the fabric!" she recalled, triumphantly.) When asked what Dutch Schultz's favorite song was, she told me, "Melancholy Baby." Asked if she ever met Meyer Lansky, she said, "Yes, I'd see him on the beach in Miami, he was a very nice man. Always wanted to hear 'Melancholy Baby.'"

Lost in the cemetery, I grew melancholy as well. A groundskeeper gave me directions to the office, and then gave me a look of pity when he saw me circle past again, a few minutes later. When I found the office, I waited for a woman behind the counter to stop taking calls, though the phone seemed to ring every ten seconds. She seemed like a new or nearly retired teacher, not quite in control of an unruly class. "No, I'm sorry, but no quotes, no hyphens, no nicknames," she said, as if handing back a homework assignment. "I think so, I'm pretty sure, but let me check," she said, putting the caller on hold to check another aspect of post-mortem etiquette. "The father's Catholic and he's in the grave. The mother isn't either—but she's ready to go. Can they go in the grave together?" The answer was yes, as she thought, and I thought it was an easy question. Even a nostalgic one, harking back to a more defined age, with sharper edges. When she had time for me, I told the woman I was looking for Patrick Brown, that he had lived in Brooklyn and died in January 1946. I didn't say why I was there, and she didn't ask, though there was a moment when we both seemed to expect an explanation. I did feel a little guilty, as I was there to work—though whether to dig up Pat Brown, or to bury him again, I wasn't yet sure. She gave me a map that looked like a place mat and traced a route from the office to the grave, filling out the coordinates for section, range, and plot, "8—G—22," in this case.

I found him easily enough, at a green edge of the cemetery, beneath a sycamore tree. Beyond the fence was Woodhaven Boulevard, and a generic commercial strip: gas station, motel, car wash, auto body. He had a modest gray granite stone, polished and clean, with a cross flanked by two camellias. On the lower left side was his name and dates, and on the lower right was space for another. Mom had told me that his second wife, Margaret Cramer

Brown Sullivan, was buried with him, and the absence, the pointed absence, said either that she was buried elsewhere—against her wishes, as my mother recalled them—or that no one had attended to the inscription. I sat down by the grave and intended to say a prayer, but instead found myself daydreaming about things. Was I the first to visit him in twenty years? Thirty? What would he think? I felt like I was there to serve a subpoena. After a while, I went back to my car, but found I had lost my keys; they must have fallen out of my pocket as I sat by the grave. As I walked back, a woman carrying two bouquets of flowers asked me, "Do you work here? Where can I find some water?" I said I didn't work there, and I didn't know. "But I need it for the flowers," she said, as if I might have been holding out on her. Back at the grave, I found my keys and remembered to say a prayer, a Hail Mary and an Our Father, before I took to daydreaming again, if you could call it that, because the day itself was like a dream, pointless and portentous at once: I got lost while looking for my great-grandfather's grave and found his wife missing, and then I forgot to say prayers and my keys were missing, and a woman asked me for water for her flowers because she thought I worked in a graveyard. I wondered if another piece would make the whole thing clear, and then as I reached the path again I met with another item that carries a certain charge of symbolism in my culture: a dead rat. It was not just dead but flattened and skeletonized, softly gray and almost transparent, like a pencil sketch of itself. It was as if a certain ancestor had slipped me a subtle and coded message, and when I did not rise to the challenge, the telegram would have to be sent. *We can do this the hard way or the easy way. . . .ž*

Back at the office, the woman was surprised to see me again. I explained that my step-great-grandmother was missing, and asked if it was simply a neglected inscription or whether she was with a party named Sullivan, whom I believed to have died in the mid-fifties. At a Catholic cemetery, there is never any shortage of Sullivans, and there was—I won't say digging— some work to do. Two Hispanic women came in, with their place-mat maps, about to ask for directions, and to spare the woman from distraction I took it upon myself to explain how to find the section they were looking for, and how to read the codes on the stones. "You should get a job here," one of them said, and the woman who worked there looked up from her lists of Sullivans to say, "It's yours for the asking." I was glad the woman with the flowers - wasn't around. After a while, the deed to the Brown grave was found, and it showed that Margaret was not there; I called my mother to ask her date of death—she died in the eighties, it turned out, at the age of eighty-five—and we were eventually able to ascertain that she was in fact buried with her second husband, John Sullivan, as well as his first wife. I found them—some two hundred yards from Pat Brown—and saw the three names: wife, husband, wife, on a stone almost exactly like Brown's, with a cross and camellias, but twice the size, with a well-tended bed of begonias in front. I sat down there, too, and began to feel indignant, as if I'd found them out. And I also felt bad for Pat Brown, to have been left out altogether. My mother was certain Margaret had intended to be buried with him. On the back of the gravestone were several different names, probably also relatives, but the words had a sneaky look, like the answers to an exam written on the back of the hand. I thought, *This is how it turned out for you, poor Pat: forever with the knuckleheads, stood up by your date.*

. . .

SUCH WAS MY SICK LEAVE, FROM JANUARY THROUGH MAY IN the year 2001, when I became fit again for duty. I had been back at work for three weeks when it appeared that I was due for another change. A friend of a friend had dinner with Police Commissioner Bernard Kerik, and when I got home from work one night, there was a message on the machine. "I talked you up. Don't be surprised if you get a call from Kerik, sooner rather than later," he said. "And don't be worried if you do." I was glad for the warning, because the call from the PC's office to Bronx Narcotics came the next morning. Admin called me at home, and told me I had to report downtown "forthwith." I had a detail that day—a teachers'-union protest outside of City Hall—where my sister Marianne would be among the demonstrators, and I wanted to arrest her. "Go now," they told me. "Forget about showering and shaving, just get there as soon as possible." I did skip the shave, but I showered, as a favor to both of us.

I had never been to the fourteenth floor of One Police Plaza, which housed the offices of the Police Commissioner. I waited in the oak-paneled foyer and uncertainly told the cop at the Desk that I was Officer Conlon, of Narcotics, to see the Commissioner. We looked at each other for a moment. I wondered whether he thought his seat there was a punishment or a privilege. After ten minutes, I was shown inside, through an open work area of cubicles and computers, modern and dully functional as the building itself, and then into the Commissioner's office. The windows were wide and looked out over lower Manhattan, with its towers and lights, its power and money, and the Commissioner sat at the vast carved wooden desk that had belonged to Theodore Roosevelt. He was eating lunch—tuna on pita bread, Diet Coke, I noted—and I wondered whether I was supposed to salute. I wasn't in uniform, and the Commissioner doesn't wear one. I half-saluted, which seemed like a fair compromise.

He nodded and fired off questions:

"Where do you work?"

"Are you happy there?"

"What do you want to do on this Job?"

Narcotics, yes, to be a detective, I told him. He nodded.

"Do you like being a cop?"

"I love it when it doesn't suck, sir."

He nodded again.

"Loyalty is very important to me," he said. "And I trust you. I'd like you to come and work for me—speechwriting, research, whatever else." His chief of staff, John Picciano, walked me out, and said I could take the weekend to think about it. I would come back in on Monday to tell him what I decided. I thanked him, shook his hand, and fled.

I didn't know what to think. While I was honored to be asked, I had become a cop precisely to avoid work that entailed a suit, a commute, and a cubicle. At the same time, the speed of the offer showed that there was no real definition of my duties, and that offered room to maneuver. I had recently run into an acquaintance who told me he was working in an arson unit out of Headquarters. As far as I knew, only the fire marshals investigated suspicious fires, but it showed that there were all kinds of interesting things happening downtown of which I knew nothing. There were any number of small, specialized details that were created—the Art Squad, Hostage Negotiations, even a one-man team who investigated cases that involved Santería—because the right cop had the right idea, and the right boss listened. That was a possibility, I thought. It was also possible that my duties would primarily consist of licking stamps.

At the office the next day, Chief Tiffany drew me aside on the way in. "C'mere, Eddie," he said, with a puzzled look. When Admin had told me to report to the PC, I wanted to keep it quiet, and so I told them to say that I was called in for a random drug test. In retrospect, it was not a clever story, because it didn't so much cover the real reason as much as mingle with it, and the rumor thus circulated that the Police Commissioner personally wanted to test my urine. After I explained, the chief laughed and said, "I didn't think you were in any trouble. Let me know what you decide, but I don't think it would be good for you to say no."

On Monday morning, on the drive down to Police Headquarters, I happened to look down at my clothing. In my haste, it seemed that I had put on a black suit jacket and a pair of blue pants. On the fourteenth floor, there was the same wary exchange of glances with the cop at the desk—"What is this guy about?"—and I was sent in to see Chief Picciano. I must have had the look on my face of a kid who was sent to the principal, because he spent five minutes reassuring me that I wouldn't be in trouble if I declined the offer. Like a lot of outer-borough street cops, I believed in some inconvertibly primitive place in my heart that there was a catapult on the roof of One Police Plaza, and that if you crossed someone who was influential, they launched you through the air to Staten Island, where you landed on the pavement in a uniform that was too small, and you spent the remainder of your career on a corner, watching empty buses pass.

"Yes, sir," I said.

"You wouldn't actually be working for me or the Commissioner," he said. "You'd work for Deputy Inspector Rising. Let me take you to meet him."

"Yes, sir," I said.

Chief Picciano dropped me off at DI Rising's office, where I glanced around for the catapult as I thanked him.

"Listen, relax!" he said. "Don't worry about it—you're not in trouble!"

"Yes, sir."

But I was in trouble: too much good luck can be the same as bad luck, I knew. When I worked at CCJA, the office had a case of a guy who had his troubles with drugs, did his time, and then cleaned up and went home. For years, he worked as a truck driver, getting by, honestly but barely. One night on his way to work, he stopped at a bank machine and crossed his fingers. He knew that he had just over or just under twenty dollars in his account, and if it was $19.75 he'd be screwed, but if he had $20.25, he could take out the bill, buy some gas and food, and get through the day. He closed his eyes when he punched in the request for the twenty, and felt dizzy with relief when the cash slid out of the machine. When he checked his balance, he could barely stand: a bank error had put more than fifty thousand dollars in his account.

He didn't go to work that day, nor did he for many days afterward, and shortly he met a woman who convinced him that the habit he had abandoned almost a decade before was more than supportable for a man of his newfound means. So it was that through his extraordinary good fortune he became a client of Consultants for Criminal Justice Alternatives.

Deputy Inspector Rising was friendly and polite, but I'd been deposited in his office like an extra filing cabinet; in time, he'd find a place for me, but at the moment I was taking up space. I said that I'd always been a street cop, and that I had my reservations about working in an office. I said that I was due for my detective shield in a couple of months, and that I didn't want to derail my investigative time for this assignment, no matter what.

"As a matter of civil-service law," he explained kindly, "the PC can make you a detective tomorrow. It's purely discretionary.

"Another thing you should know is that the Commissioner doesn't really speak from prepared text. He happens to be a good speaker. At a funeral, he'll stick close to a written speech, but he's good off the cuff, and what I try to do for him is to set out five or six talking points he should make, and he takes it from there."

"Oh."

I had never heard the Commissioner speak. On the news, commissioners only seemed to say, "There will be a thorough investigation," which I'd never written before, but I supposed I was up to the task.

"So offhand, I thought of a couple of things you might do. You're in Narcotics, and the PC worked in Narcotics, and so whatever you might be able to bring to the table in terms of policy, we'd be happy to hear. In terms of more concrete things, one is that when a cop gets a Letter of Commendation, you could personalize it—make the cop know that we really understood and appreciated what they did, instead of just sending a thank-you card for stopping a bank robbery. The other is that you could write letters to the Parole Board, when cop killers are up for parole. That happens a lot more than you think, and it's an important thing that these cops who gave their lives are not forgotten or overlooked."

These were valid points, and important tasks, and my heart sank to hear them. I doubted that a real policy role would emerge, not least because I - didn't have any big new ideas, which left letter-writing in the portfolio of tasks. But I liked DI Rising, and I thought that maybe there was space to improvise. I said, "I don't know if this work is going to take three hours a week, or sixty. But in my gut—and this is why I do this, why I am a cop—I have to have the opportunity to do some kind of enforcement work, so that if there's some down time—one day a week, four and a half days a week, however it works out—I get to go outside. It's an honor to work for the Commissioner, and I would never say no to him, but it just wouldn't work for anybody if I stopped being a cop."

DI Rising said that he had worked for Chief Tiffany, too, and he understood why I would be reluctant to leave. I trusted Rising, but I didn't want to work at Headquarters. It might be important, but it just didn't sound like police work.

And so I talked to my consiglieri: Inspector Mullen first, who told me, "Did you ever hear the expression, 'This is an offer you can't refuse?' This is that offer. Don't say no. Even though they say there won't be recriminations, there may be recriminations, just because someone else is pissed off that you had the PC's ear for ten seconds. More importantly, this is an opportunity—go have a look at Headquarters, at the largest and most important department in the world. Do it. Why not? If you're on the Job for life, this is an opportunity that might not come around again. Go ahead. And did I say that this is an offer that you can't refuse?"

Chief Tiffany agreed, and Capt. Mahony put it even more bluntly: "Listen, Timothy McVeigh is gonna have a longer shelf life than this guy. Go there, suck it up no matter what, and in six months, you work wherever you want to." As it happened, Kerik did survive McVeigh, but the point was taken. If you were a soldier, you were a soldier, and whether you were told to stand at attention for twenty hours or to write love letters for the PC, you did what you were told. Rising had left open the possibility that I could find some enforcement work, my other duties permitting. In my head, a jingle began to ring:

Commissioner Kerik is the mightiest of men,
If you do a push-up, he will do ten . . .ž

And I put it out of my mind. When I told Lt. Zerbo, he thought for a moment and said, "You're a douche bag."

I laughed. I hadn't quite expected to hear that, but time would tell if it was true.

"A douche bag. Look at you, and look at him. He should be working for you."

It was one of the more roundabout compliments I'd received, but I'd take it.

My first day of work would be the next Tuesday, after Memorial Day, when I would accompany Rising and the Commissioner to the Police Academy graduation to get a sense of Kerik's speaking style. Friday would be my last day of B&B, and on Thursday night, we all went out for a farewell dinner. Most of the people who had left the team did so without even a handshake—Leibowitz went to Queens, Nugent to midnights—but I liked my teammates and bosses, and I was determined to commemorate the occasion. I had been happy there, and I took my reluctance to leave as a sign that I was destined to, because if I'd been as desperate to go as I had been at the PSA, the departure would have been postponed for months.

It was not a late night, but B&B began the next morning at seven, and we all felt it a little. A foot pursuit into a project on One-Four-Six helped get the blood running, and I was almost feeling normal again when the base raised Clune on the radio, telling him that I had to call the Commissioner's office, forthwith. I was driving him, and he gave me a worried look as he relayed the message. When I called DI Rising, his tone was grim.

"You better get down here right away," he said.

"Uh, we're in the middle of B&B," I said. I wondered if it was the wrong thing to say; maybe at One Police Plaza, they considered the wishes of the Commissioner to have priority over the next three crack vials from Courtlandt Avenue.

"All right," he said. "Get down as soon as you finish up."

I didn't want to leave it at that, as the conspiracy theories ricocheted in my skull.

"Can you tell me what's going on?"

"I don't think this is going to work out."

I thought again: What had I done? I didn't have a dead hooker in the trunk of my car, did I? Maybe they reviewed the file footage of my second interview, and noticed the mismatched pants and jacket. What had happened in the two days since we'd last shaken hands?

"Is there anything I should know?"

There was a pause, and then he said, "No, it's nothing you did. But I don't think it's gonna work out. Just get down here."

Clune made a remark about a refund for my farewell dinner. We hit a couple more sets and I headed downtown.

DI Rising was mercifully blunt: "I hope you didn't go out and buy a bunch of suits, but this isn't going to happen. I'm sorry, I was looking forward to it, I hope you were too. Basically, down here we don't just have to think about what's right and what's real, but how things look. The PC signed a book deal last week, and for you to come here now makes it look like you're going to write it for him. We can't have it. Believe me, I'm sorry, I'm embarrassed and the Commissioner feels bad about it too. I hope you didn't make any big arrangements."

"Well, we did have my farewell dinner last night."

"The Commissioner wants to make it up to you. Do you want to go anywhere? I can't promise the Joint Terrorism Task Force, but . . ."

He left it hanging like that, and I said, "Can I think about it over the weekend?"

"Sure."

I shook his hand and left. I was ecstatic: I was getting alimony, and I never even had to kiss the guy. I called Clune to say we'd have to set up a welcome-back dinner, and then another farewell right afterward. I also called Timpanaro and told him to start thinking about what we should ask for—we'd talked about working together again, but the opportunity never seemed to arise. Now, it might: Rising had offered a big favor, but maybe I could make it two slightly smaller ones. Or two big ones.

My friend Brian McCabe was a sergeant at Manhattan South Homicide, and he had told me that after I got my shield, I should think about coming to work for him. Compared to the Bronx, Manhattan South had relatively few homicides, but whatever they had tended to be high-profile. You would catch glimpses of Brian on the news for the perp-walk in cases like the Carnegie Deli murders, where five people were shot, three fatally, during the robbery of a marijuana dealer. Manhattan South Homicide also worked like the old Confidential Squads for the Chief of Detectives, in that they filled in and helped out whenever some situation presented itself—the theft of an antique Torah, the escape of a dangerous prisoner—and the chief wanted special attention to be paid.

But I had to wonder: if I was murdered, would I want someone like me to catch the case? Maybe they could start me off with something easy, a practice murder, in which the victim wasn't quite dead, or the killer hadn't quite left. They could wean me on easy manslaughters until I cut my teeth. In answer to my question, I thought, Yes, if I was killed, I would be content to have someone like me assigned to the case, even now. But how much better would it be later? When I called Brian, he was a little cool to the idea, explaining that the rumor was that his Squad was going to be cut, and that for me to arrive—with a white shield, no less—while others were facing eviction could be complicated. Now was not the time. I thought again, and asked him what he thought about Manhattan Robbery. He said that it was a fine idea.

The Manhattan Robbery office was on 12th Street, but it covered the entire borough from the Battery to Inwood. Homicide was an "assist" squad, working in collaboration with the precinct detective who caught the case, whereas Robbery took over cases themselves, usually if a pattern was established where crimes crossed precinct lines. If a liquor store on East Eighty-sixth Street was held up, the case went to a 19th Precinct detective, but if the same perps hit a liquor store on West Eighty-sixth Street, in the 20th Precinct, and a bar on Thirty-eighth, in Midtown South, it was designated a pattern and assigned to Manhattan Robbery. "You'll get real bad guys, real good cases," said Brian. "And you'll get to be in Manhattan. How many years have you been in the South Bronx now? Maybe it's time for a change."

Though it seemed that John planned a different career every week—he had in mind the boss route, through the sergeant's exam, but also a detective's shield, and law school, but also maybe the Fire Department, or a better-paid cop job on Long Island—there was one thing of which he was certain: he was tired of PSA-7. Anti-Crime had made a number of gun collars through the winter, largely though his work, but they'd been dry for months. He cast about for some outlet for his competitive drive, and one day, he announced a victory in a field that I am sure no one had ever thought to view as a contest: the Adopt-A-Senior program, in which cops volunteered to help the elderly. "I kicked ass!" he crowed. "You shoulda seen these old ladies, there was a busload of 'em. Most of 'em, forget about it—they whined, or they smelled, or they just sat there, like nothing. But there was one great one, Mrs. B, and I snapped her right up. What a nice lady! And so clean! You shoulda seen the other guys, they were so mad!"

John wanted to go to a precinct Robbery Squad—a RAM, or Robbery Apprehension Module, which the busier squads maintained as a separate unit—specifically, in the Four-Four, which had always been among the busiest in the city. The Integrity Review Board continued to assure him that something was in the works, but two years had passed since that promise had been made. More important, the Police Commissioner had recently revived the "upstairs route" to the Squads, telling each precinct CO to select three cops for the Detective Bureau. It had been a traditional means of ascent for the hardest-working cops to move from patrol to a team like SNEU or Anti-Crime, and then upstairs to the Squad, where a shield was awarded after eighteen months. It was a sensible progression, in that the cop knew the terrain, and I never understood why it had been discontinued. For all my problems with the CO of PSA-7, I respected his choices for the Detective Bureau: Tony Marcano was the first, and he went to the Four-Two Squad in the fall. Timpanaro and Eddie Wynne were the next two names, though the rumors placed one first, then the next, but neither moved as winter turned to spring. Mike Shea—then a precinct commander on the Upper West Side—told me that all three of the cops he'd recommended were already gone. We didn't know whether it was because the Housing Bureau was given second-class status, or because PSA-7 was, or if there was some other complication, but after eight months, there had been no movement for either John or Eddie Wynne. John didn't take long to say that Manhattan Robbery sounded fine to him.

At the same time, I reminded him that we had been made offers before, and they hadn't come through. A year and a half before, just before John had gone to Vice, we went out to a party in Manhattan, where I saw a man at the edge of the crowd with a familiarly watchful manner. I whispered to John, "Look at him—I bet he's a cop."

John said, "Good eye you got there. He happens to be Joe Dunne, the Chief of the Department."

"Well, I was right, then, wasn't I?"

As it happened, John was friends with someone Dunne knew, and he went over to say hello. Ordinarily, I wouldn't have followed, but as this was my root-canal phase, I walked so closely behind him that he poked me in the eye when he pointed back to introduce me.

We wound up having a few drinks together, and Chief Dunne asked us where we worked, and we explained that we were partners, but there had been an administrative mishap with my transfer to Vice. He offered to take care of it, and wrote down my name. I felt lottery-ticket lucky, and wondered why I was wasting such a great favor on such a small matter. But when that night ended, I worked in SNEU for another month, and on midnights for six, and another five in Narcotics before I got a call from his office, asking me if everything was all right. "Now it is, yeah," I said. Chief Dunne was a highly respected thirty-year veteran, and since he was responsible for the safety of eight million people, my temporary transfer should have been on page 5000 of his "To do" list. Still, the offer was made, and I was disappointed.

A few weeks after the party, on a midnight, Stix and I guarded an empty apartment for eight hours again, watching the roaches on the walls and discussing the unnatural aspects of breakfast at night. When we finished talking about that, Stix decided we ought to talk some more, to pass the time. "It's all who you know," he ventured. "That's the lousiest thing about the politics on this job."

I spat on the wall at a cockroach. "If only that was true!"

And so with the new offer from the PC, I told John that it looked as good as these things got, but you never really knew until it happened. When I wrote to DI Rising to say that I wanted Manhattan Robbery for both of us, he wrote back to say that he hadn't expected it to be a "two-fer," but that he'd do what he could.

• • •

IN THE MEANTIME, WE WAITED, ME IN NARCOTICS AND John at the PSA. He had run into our old CI, Christmas, in the holding cells. He took her phone number and passed it along to me, and Pops spoke with Sgt. Rhoden about giving her a pass if his team only saw her trespassing. She was not much the worse for wear after the two years since I'd last seen her. She was housewifey, in an odd, rundown way, and it was easier to picture her in a bathrobe, rye and soda in hand, dusting the knickknack shelf as she wept at the soap opera, than it was to imagine her scoring crack in the projects. Nonetheless, Christmas began to work again with enthusiasm, making buys every week. The first warrant she gave us was for a 350-pound woman who sold heroin. "She's a big woman, in a dress like a tent."

"JD Tent she is, then."

When we hit the door, she lay sprawled in her bed, bare naked with her legs spread, and the team nearly turned around without searching the apartment. Other warrants followed: Christmas was working on crack spots, weed spots, and dope spots for me, and she could hardly keep track of them. Christmas was ditzily affectionate and absentminded, like an elderly aunt who kept looking for the handkerchief she kept in her hand. Her voice was nasal and Noo-Yawky, and her thoughts left her mouth as soon as they entered her head.

One Saturday afternoon, we sent her out on a few routine buys. Clune and I sat off in the middle of a quiet block of warehouses, in a car with tinted windows, waiting for her to return. As she emptied her bra of crack and heroin, a thought occurred to her.

"Oh, yeah! Ah, I meant to ask you guys but it slipped my mind. Are you interested in guns and shootings and stuff, or only drugs?"

Clune and I looked at each other.

"Sure, we cover guns and all kinds of things. Why do you ask?"

"Well, you remember how I told you about Shaka?"

"Yeah, he sells crack, green tops over on One-Five-Three."

"Right, so anyway, I went over to his place the other morning, and he was out of 'work,' but he said that he was having a fight with his mother over his girlfriend, because she was staying there and anyway, he says he can't keep his gun in the house anymore, and he wants *me* to keep it. So anyway, I say my husband, Louie, he's very old-fashioned, and he wouldn't want the gun in the house, especially because my mother-in-law is so nosy, you know? I mean, she's a very nice lady, but—"

"Christmas?"

"I mean, she is my mother-in-law, and Louie is very straitlaced, and—"

"Christmas?"

"You know, I hope she doesn't stay so long this time. I mean, the apartment's in her name, but still—"

"Christmas?"

"Yes, Eddie?"

"Where's the gun?"

"Oh, the gun, it's in the bedroom closet, but I can't keep it there. If Louie knew, oh my God, I bet he'd throw me out!"

"You're right, Christmas, you can't keep it there. You have to give us the gun."

"All right, I'll go get it."

"Hold on a second."

Clune and I thought for a moment, and asked, "What's Shaka gonna say when he comes back for the gun?"

"Oh, that's no problem, I'll just tell him Louie threw it out."

We thought again.

"That's not a good story, Christmas. Tell us a little more about Shaka, why don't you?"

"Oh, he's all right. I mean, I don't think I have to worry about him."

"Well, he does sell crack for a living, and we know at least that he used to carry a gun. What's to keep him from getting another one and using it on you?"

"I guess."

"Tell you what—the best way to do it is, you come out of the building and we stop you and pretend to lock you up. There'll be a crowd, they'll see everything, Shaka is gonna hear. That way, he owes you a favor, instead of you owing him a gun, you follow? You have to lie low for a day, maybe stay at your daughter's or somewhere, and then it's all over."

She pursed her lips and frowned.

"I don't think so, Eddie. You know, I don't *like* getting locked up."

"That's the thing, Christmas, I'm not sure you heard me. We wouldn't *actually* lock you up, we'd just take you away so it *looked* like you got locked up. I know it might be a pain in the ass to have to disappear for a day, but in the long term, it's a lot less aggravation."

She shook her head. "No, my mother-in-law, she would not want to hear about my getting locked up, and Louie—forget about it. I'm not gonna do that, I can't. I'll just tell Shaka I lost it."

For Christmas, an arrest was a routine occurrence. It had happened to her fifty times in her life, two or three times a year in the last twenty years, and it was a waiting-in-line kind of aggravation, like other people experience in holiday traffic. You don't like it but you deal with it, and if you can't, you should skip the beach trip on the Fourth of July, or the in-laws in Jersey on Christmas, or the crack dealer's every day. And though I saw that she was being childishly stubborn, petulant in her refusal to accept a small inconvenience to avoid a threat to her life, I didn't have it in me at the moment to push her hard. She looked like a little old lady, and I didn't want to make her cry.

"How about this, then. You tell Shaka that Louie found out, or he was about to, and you had to get the gun out of the house right away. You were taking it over to his place, and you saw cops in the building, so you had to ditch it."

"I'll say I threw it out the window."

"No, you won't say you threw it out the window. Do those projects have windows in the stairwells? You threw it down the trash-compactor chute, that way it's gone for good, and it's still on him, if you tell the story right—you did him a favor, and you almost got jammed up for it."

"Oh, okay!"

And then we let her out of the car to go home to collect the gun. She returned in fifteen minutes with a little black knapsack, slipping into the back seat of the van. She handed the pack forward and Clune took it, gingerly, and handed it to me. I opened it and there was a .45 pistol and a box of ammunition, each wrapped in a bandanna. We gave her money and sent her home. We had a crime but no case, and while getting the gun off the street was the primary task, I wasn't content to leave it at that.

Nor was Christmas, however, and she took it upon herself to open up new avenues of prosecution. The next week, she called me, hysterical:

"He's going to kill me!"

"Who?"

"Shaka!"

"What happened?"

"I was sitting in front of my building with my girlfriend, and he came up to me and said, 'Yo, I need that thing back.' And I said, 'All right, lets go up-stairs and get it.'"

As far as I recalled, that was not what she had been instructed to say. I was interested in hearing her improvisation, and I didn't doubt that, as she walked Shaka through the graffiti-covered and trash-strewn lobby and rode the elevator upstairs, she might surprise herself. They entered the apartment and she led him to the bedroom, where she made a show of searching the closet.

"Oh my God! I can't believe it! It's gone!"

I bet she clapped both hands to her cheeks. "What did he say?" I asked.

"Oh, it was bad! He was cursing and he said he was gonna kill me! 'I got no problems taking out a woman,' he said, and he demanded to know what happened to the gun, I had to get it back. I said my brother was here over the weekend, he musta taken it."

"Do you have a brother?"

"Yeah."

"Does Shaka know where he lives?"

"No, that's no problem, he's straight, never in trouble, and he lives in Virginia. But Shaka told me I better come up with the gun, or I have to come up with six hundred dollars to pay him for it. Can you get me the money?"

"What I gotta do is think. What you gotta do is what I tell you. Remember last week, I told you we'd pretend to lock you up, and that would have solved the problem? And you wouldn't do it? And then we came up with an-other story, and you said you'd do that, and you didn't? And now we got a big fucking mess to deal with. You know what I'm saying?"

She agreed with me, weeping. What a dingbat, I thought. And she was my guide into the criminal underworld. If she'd been leading Dante, he'd be lucky to get into Hell, let alone out of it. I told my bosses, and the consensus was that we'd just have to move her: we weren't going to pay for a gun that we already owned.

I had a few ideas: What if we have Christmas call Shaka to say her brother gave her the gun back? We set up an exchange, she gives him the gun, empty, and we jump Shaka when he takes it?

What if he has ammunition?

"Okay, what if we take the gun to the range and disable it, take out the firing pin?"

What if we lose him during the takedown? And then, what if he gets the gun fixed?

"Okay, how about . . ."

Capt. Mahony said, "So this shemp wants his gun back? What do you suppose he wants it for? And with the six hundred, don't you suppose he's gonna pick up another piece? I haven't looked this rule up lately, but I don't think the Police Department is supposed to be in the business of buying guns for crack dealers. Nah, the only thing to do is to move her."

If a witness or an informant is threatened, we can put someone up in a motel for a few days or a few weeks, but more permanent accommodations are arranged through the DA. I thought Christmas's viability as an informant was coming to an end, and that we would have to eventually relocate her, but I didn't want to go through all that effort without a collar to show for it. I had an idea: Why didn't we supply her with the felonious brother she'd fabricated? There was an undercover who worked in another precinct, who could arguably pass for a relative of Christmas—though I wouldn't stress that aspect when I told him about the case—couldn't we send him in as her brother, wearing a wire?

Capt. Mahony was averse to that, too: it wasn't an ordinary gun buy, Shaka was coming in angry, feeling like he got ripped off, and the risk was too high. If he escaped, or if something went wrong, there would be too much to explain. The objections were all valid, and I couldn't override them. I did like the idea of fabricating a character to fit my addled informant's offhand lie, and I suppose it was a good thing she didn't claim the .45 was taken by the Gun Fairy.

And so I went to see Sam Ramer. He liked the case, and he said he'd run it by Ed Friedenthal to see if they'd take it. Ed Friedenthal said, "So you want us to pay for a gun we already own, huh? Well, why not?" He set up a meeting with the DA's investigators.

There were two DA's Squads, one of which comprised active NYPD officers assigned to the office, and another of investigators employed by the DA, many of whom were retired cops. We would work primarily with Frank Viggiano and Rocco Galasso, both of whom were retired NYPD. Rocco had worked as an undercover in the 1980s, and he volunteered to become Christmas's brother. I didn't know Rocco well enough to make any jokes about the family resemblance, but his colleagues were kind enough to pick up the slack.

We sat down with Inspector Nasta, who had just retired from Bronx Narcotics, Viggiano, Galasso, Ramer, and a few others, and went over the scenario. Shaka had priors for robbery and drug sales, and there had been a lot of shootings recently in the project where Shaka lived, and while he was not known as a major player, he sold crack in a competitive market, and he felt the need for a gun. A .45 had been used in a recent homicide there. It was proposed that Rocco try to buy crack from Shaka, as the gun sale was only a D felony, while drug sales were a B. I also said that I thought we had Grand Larceny, a C felony, as Shaka had threatened to kill her when he demanded money, which was the legal definition of extortion. It was decided that Rocco would call Shaka first, and we'd tape the conversation.

"So that's the setup," I said. "I don't know what you'd call it, exactly."

Several voices in the room said, "It's a reverse sting."

At least I wouldn't be in the pawn shop like my father, with my finger in my pocket, pretending to have a gun. But as soon as the plans were in place, Christmas began to make changes.

I brought her in to Sam's office, and we were going over the story when she corrected me on a detail: "No, Shaka didn't say he'd kill me, Eddie, he said he'd beat me up."

That was relevant, and at a certain level, I was glad to hear it. I pointed out, "You told me he'd kill you, when you called me the first time. You remember, 'I got no problems taking out a woman. . . .' What did you think he meant, dinner and a movie?"

"Did I say that? Well, you know, I was very upset. I think all he meant was he'd beat me up. Also, he'd tell Louie, which would be real, real bad—he'd throw me out, I know it, and—"

"Okay, we gotcha."

We looked up the statute. Threat of death was downgraded to threat of physical injury, a class C to a class D, no worse than the gun possession or sale. But for the final charges, we'd have to see what Shaka said on the tape, and what he did if he agreed to meet with Rocco.

And then the process of arranging a new life for Christmas began, setting up a new apartment, reapplying for welfare, and arranging for a treatment program, which didn't interest her at all. In fact, she didn't think there was much wrong with her old life, aside from the business with Shaka. It suited me, too, in its way. When I first signed her up, I told her that she didn't have permission to do anything with drugs, other than what she did for us—if she was caught for anything on her own time, it was her problem. Often, she'd run to pick up heroin or crack for a neighbor, sometimes as much as two or three hundred dollars' worth, for which she'd be given a couple of vials. She made no effort to conceal these activities, but I'd learn of them only as absentminded afterthoughts, and she broadly construed this kind of thing as field work, which of course it was. OCCB guidelines took an altogether narrower view, but if addicts quit just because I told them to, I could eliminate half the crime in this country without getting up from my couch. I didn't worry about Christmas hurting anyone but herself, but that was an abiding concern.

A few days later, she called me again, in tears. "I can't move, I don't want to, I don't care. . . ." The prospect of leaving husband and home now seemed unbearable. Her safety was my concern; her happiness was not, especially since it seemed to depend on the freedom to buy drugs in the neighborhood she knew best. She met Shaka on the street, she said, and he hadn't threatened her: "As a matter of fact, he was real friendly, real nice to me. Like before."

I asked her, "Why? What did you tell him?"

"I told him I'd give him the six hundred dollars on Friday."

"Do you have six hundred dollars to give him on Friday?"

"No."

"So what are you going to do on Friday?"

"I thought I'd go to my daughter's in Jersey for the weekend."

I didn't argue with her. Christmas was a quintessential crackhead: the next ten minutes were the only ones that counted. She had bought herself a weekend of peace, and she would deal with Monday when Monday came. And when it did, I knew that Shaka would persuade her to cooperate far more effectively than I could have.

On Monday night, she called me again, crying. Shaka had seen her when she returned from her daughter's house. They were no longer friends, it seemed. Christmas had told him that her brother from Virginia would be coming back, and they could work it out with each other. We were back in play.

We set up the phone call in a small room at the DA's Squad, with Christmas, Sam, and Rocco. Rocco had been an extraordinary undercover, and more than a few cops told me stories about times when dealers had held guns to Rocco's head. Not all of the dealers had survived, but Rocco clearly had. For Rocco, this caper was light exercise, and all the more fun because it had been a while since he'd had a chance to stretch. We all felt an exhilaration, reminded of how much like play our work could be, that even when it was life-threatening, it could have the goofy freedom of summer camp.

I turned on the recorder and headed the tape, "The time is fifteen hundred hours on July 12, 2001. This is Police Officer Conlon, shield number 9786, of Bronx Narcotics, along with Lieutenant Rocco Galasso of the Bronx DA's Squad, and a confidential informant, dialing number . . .for the purposes of a monitored conversation."

The number for the cellular customer you have called is no longer in service. . . .

"The time now is fifteen-oh-two hours, on July . . ."

I handed the phone to Christmas, but a little girl answered. "Nah, Shaka's not here now. Maaaa? Do you know when he's getting home?"

Another call, not long after: "The time now is fifteen thirty hours . . ."

When they spoke, Shaka wasn't happy. I listened on another extension, with the mouthpiece off, so he couldn't hear me breathe. Shaka took a tough stance:

"We got a problem, me and you, and bad things are gonna happen if you don't fix it. There's gonna be big problems, if you don't get me the gun, or the money. . . ."

It was a good beginning, but he hadn't talked himself into the charges yet: "my gun," or "the gun I gave you to hold," would determine possession more clearly, and while "bad things" was better than "big problems," the threats were vague. Christmas said that her brother was here, and that the two of them had to deal with each other now; Shaka refused, but he didn't hang up when Rocco got on the phone: "Hey, Shaka, what's up? What's going on with you and my sister?"

And so began a strange conversation. Shaka was a lot less tough. Rocco sounded as Virginian as Sonny Corleone. Rocco told Shaka that he had no business getting his sister involved with guns; Shaka said that no one had forced Christmas to do anything, and now someone owed him the gun or the money. Rocco said the price was too high—he was from Virginia, and guns were cheap there. Shaka asked why he took his gun, then, if he could get them so easily—good point, that—and Rocco said that a friend had sudden need of it. Shaka got scared: "What if he does something with it, and it gets back to me! What if he does something with my gun?"

That worked. Rocco turned it around: "Don't worry about it, I wiped it clean, nothing can get back to you. What about my friend, though—is anything you did with it gonna get back to him?"

Shaka said it wouldn't, which was disappointing but not conclusive. He said he wanted his money, now. Rocco said he couldn't do that, just yet. Shaka seemed to find a measure of courage as he thought about the money, and we wanted to get him stoked up, to make threats on tape, without putting Christmas in further danger.

Rocco went on. "Listen, Shaka, I'm gonna get you the money, but six hundred's too much. And besides, I got things to do for a couple of days, things to do with people, but I gotta know if my sister's gonna be okay—this is between you and me now, and we'll straighten things out—but I can't worry about her. Shaka, you gotta tell me if I got anything to worry about."

"We got problems. She owes me money. I ain't gonna say what's gonna happen if you don't set things straight."

"C'mon, Shaka, don't play games with me. Me and you gonna have problems, you threaten my sister, arright?"

There was a pause, and Shaka sounded like a sly and nasty ten-year-old brat. "I might have to tell Louie. . . ." Rocco and I made the same face: what a pussy, what a loser, what a piece of shit. That's the threat the crack dealer makes when you take away his .45: *I'm telling on your sister, she's gonna get in trouble. . . .ž*

And he even backed off that threat, as Rocco alluded to the people he had to see, the things he had to do, that would delay the payment for a few days.

"What people?"

"Shaka—*people,* you know?"

"What things?"

"You know—*things.* Things . . . *with friends* . . ."

It did sound ominous. We all were impressed. Shaka gradually warmed to Rocco—he was excited by him and afraid of him, and it looked like he was finally going to see some money. An hour before, he didn't even believe that this bizarre redneck-mafioso character even existed, and now they were in business together. They made an appointment to meet in two days, with four hundred dollars. Even Christmas was delighted with the show, and took to referring to Rocco as her brother so naturally that I felt compelled to ask, "You do realize, Christmas, that Rocco is not your brother?"

"Oh yeah, I know . . .but I want to get used to talking like he is."

"That's fine, I just have to make sure that we're on the same page."

We worked through lunch, and Sam ordered from a nearby diner for us, where the DA's Office had an account. He asked Christmas what she wanted to drink.

"That's okay, Sam, she brought a beer," I said. The bottle cap had set off the metal detector downstairs when I'd brought her in. Sam suggested that she save the beer for later.

I could have used one, too. No matter how it concluded, I would be stuck with Christmas afterward, and I still thought we'd have to move her. Even if Shaka didn't have her killed, there would be others happy to rid the neighborhood of an informant. And I knew that Christmas would feel the pull of home again, once Shaka was behind bars. We couldn't force her to go anywhere, or to stay away. I'm still not sure if it was for my benefit or Christmas's, but I worked out a twist for the last act.

We set up a tac plan, readying our radios, cars, kels, binoculars, and vests. We drove out to the projects and set up in position. There was apprehension as Rocco waited, and we listened to the OP narrate Shaka's approach.

"Okay, he's coming down the block, he sees Rock, he's up to him—it's okay."

"Okay? Does he look pissed?"

"Nah, he hugged him."

Viggiano reported the next conversation from over the kel: "He didn't bring him any crack, the lazy bastard! I could come up with ten vials in fifteen minutes in this neighborhood!"

Rocco handed him the money, and we swept in. Shaka looked stunned, and betrayed—*Holy shit! What the fuck!*—but as he was cuffed and thrown over the hood of the car, he saw that Rocco was in cuffs, too. And Rocco seemed to be getting worse treatment than he was—*It's over, now, scumbag! We gotcha!*—as they were whisked away, in separate cars.

Shaka was taken to a room at the DA's Squad, and left to imagine what great conspiracy he had stumbled into. When we confronted him, it was less of an interrogation than a kind of guided meditation on La Cracker Nostra:

"Do you have any idea who you've been dealing with?"

"This is big-time! Interstate! Federal! You're not in a precinct, are you?"

"This goes way beyond you! This goes deep!"

"We've been on to this guy for a long time, Shaka."

"The Virginia Mafia! Nobody fucks with them!"

"We got him in a room down the hall—this guy gave up his own sister! You're lucky you got out alive!"

Shaka didn't know what to believe, and held his head in his hands. We staged another, highly visible arrest of Christmas later that afternoon, so word would leak back to him in jail. I tried to imagine Shaka's conversation with his lawyer, as he tried to explain the garbled cabal. The lawyer must have considered an insanity defense; she had a highly puzzled expression when she approached Sam Ramer to ask what had happened. Sam rolled his eyes in a bored, heard-that-before dismissal and offered eighteen months. The lawyer went back to Shaka and gave him her advice. He took the plea, and Christmas went home to Louie.

• • •

THE WEEKS PASSED, AND I BEGAN TO WONDER ABOUT THE delay at Headquarters. Now and then, I'd check in with DI Rising, and he'd allude to the political complexities of the placement. The PC could put me anywhere, I knew, but I also knew there was more to it, and the last thing I wanted was to be dropped in a place where I wasn't wanted. I'd landed softly at Narcotics because people knew me there, from cops to the chief, and I hadn't forgotten the last miserable year at the PSA. It didn't take much to make things hard, and I could wait until things were right.

John's frustrations rose and fell, and we were soon reminded that a job change was not always for the better. My cousin Brian was a firefighter now, and that June, on Father's Day, his house in Queens lost three men fighting a conflagration at a hardware store, started by two kids who knocked over drums of gas in an alley. The scope of the loss seemed unimaginable—three men in one day, from one house—and firefighters from all over the country attended the funeral. John didn't talk much about his lost opportunity to go to FD, and eventually he wouldn't count it among his regrets. I had to laugh when he was passed over for a job in a Long Island police department, if only because his sister was offered a position. His sister Barbara is a wonderful person, the mother of three children, but prone to announcements such as, "I could never arrest an Italian, and besides, if I saw any criminal, I'd run the other way." Like most departments, the NYPD sets a minimal academic standard, after which they try to weed out the demonstrably unfit through a psychological exam and background checks. The Long Island department had instead hired consultants to develop a hodgepodge profile for their ideal candidate, who would be married instead of single and preferred math to reading; the New Haven police had adopted a similar strategy and made headlines for their refusal to hire a candidate on the grounds of excessive intelligence. I laughed a lot less when John told me that the Long Island job would have effectively doubled his salary. But in mid-July, as I was in the thick of my Christmas carol, John got his own present: he was picked for the RAM, and was assigned to the Four-Four. That could work out, we figured—he'd know what he was doing with a robbery case, and he could teach me when we got to Manhattan Robbery.

That was a hard summer at Narcotics. There were no public controversies, as there had been with Dorismond and Ferguson the year before, but two cops died in a private horror. A male undercover had dated a female undercover on his team, and when she broke it off, he went to her house and killed her before turning the gun on himself. We'd all known the male undercover from PSA-7, and liked him—he'd been a good cop, effective on the street, cool and low-key in person. Sammy had worked with him at Narcotics. Pop told me that IAB would be watching the funeral, and anyone who went to his wake on job time or in uniform would be written up—he wasn't a cop anymore, he was a cop killer, and no official tribute could be paid. But another cop from the PSA lost his father within days of the murder-suicide, and both wakes would be held at the same funeral home, at the same time, and it was customary to send a van of cops in uniform to pay respects. Would they make the cops change before going from one room to the other? I spread word to the PSA to watch themselves, but I'd miss the funerals, as I had to go to a wedding out of town. When I got home, I found I'd missed a third—Mike Shea's mother had died as well.

We had Sundays and Mondays off, but through July and August, we worked late every Saturday, sometimes until six or seven the next morning, and began again early on Tuesdays. The weekends felt like a brief overnight, and if I had a personal life—my girfriend and I had broken up, and I had another job—I might have resented it. For a time, it seemed as if it rained every B&B Saturday, and that we had a pursuit that led to a car crash, but even on cloudless days, the chases could go awry. Once, a seller disappeared into the middle of the projects, and we spread out along the perimeter as he was sighted again, and we closed in, walking slow, then walking fast. When he saw us, he broke into a run. I saw the perp cross the street as a civilian's car drove up, unable to stop, and he tried to vault the hood one-handed like a stunt man, but the moving car threw him. I watched him land on the street, bouncing off his shoulder, stand unsteadily and run again; I watched the horrified woman in the car, who thought she'd hit an innocent pedestrian; seconds later, she saw him get up, and then the cops follow, and she broke out laughing. As I ran past her, I gave her the thumbs-up, and she nodded and drove on. The perp cut down the block, and though he'd slowed, he was still running. I stepped into the street and stopped two Spanish guys in an old Toyota, opened the door, and jumped in the back: "Turn around! Follow him!"

They screeched a U-turn and barreled down the street, delighted to be deputized. I don't think they understood English, but they knew exactly what was going on. Two cops on foot had already caught the perp and put him against the fence, and all three were winded and gasping for air. I stepped out and thanked my drivers, and they drove off, grinning. For all I knew, they had three kilos and a machine gun under the seat, but we were all happy with the spontaneous moment of cooperation.

On another day, an uncle went to an apartment to buy heroin. The dealer said that she was out, but she could get some more. "Stay right here, and would you keep an eye on my kids?" There were two of them, both under five. The dealer was gone for fifteen minutes, half an hour, forty-five . . . the field team grew apprehensive. "Anything on the kel, Leader?"

"Stand by, Field Team, the uncle is baby-sitting. . . ."

Maybe when the dealer later realized that she'd left her children with a police officer instead of a random junkie, she'd feel a little better. Maybe one day the kids would appreciate that, too.

Every other Saturday, we did a late tour for B&B, and on the off weeks, we worked a case at a nightclub, where at long last I got to be an undercover. The club put on "raves," all-night dances with techno music and designer drugs. Alcohol wasn't sold, and the crowd was as young as thirteen and fourteen. There had been overdoses and a report of an unconscious girl dumped in a back alley by the bouncers. White teenagers would flock in from the subway, and parents in station wagons would drop off the kids at the club, as the local felons cruised around the edges, almost disbelieving of their good fortune. There was a strong underground culture to the raves, which I couldn't begin to describe without feeling old, or sounding like my father might. Some of the drugs, such as Ecstasy, we knew about, while others were entirely strange—GHB, ketamine, and other chemical combinations that I forgot as soon as I heard them. What was with these kids? Was there anything wrong with good old-fashioned heroin? At the briefings, we were like G-men in the Eisenhower days, trying to pronounce "beatnik" and "hashish" after the manner of the in-house hipster:

"Gentlemen, repeat after me: 'Lay some of that mary jane on me, Daddy-O. . . .' Got it? Together, now! *Lay some of that mary jane . . .*"

I intended to ask Clune if I could file a line-of-duty report for the loss of dignity when I found out that infant pacifiers and glow-in-the-dark wands were mandatory costumes—the former reduced teeth-grinding and the latter supplied hours of fun, waving slowly in the dark, to the properly medicated. Ricky Duggan and I would go for our team, and Pops brought in two other white uncles who worked the north Bronx. They studied a video and said, "We'll need parachute pants." Parachute pants were funded. Everything was: bribe money to skip the line, admission, money for candy, non-alcoholic drinks, glow sticks and pacifiers, of course, and lots of drugs. I would have a video camera with a night-vision lens, and all of us would have "fireflies," pins to put on a hat or shirt that flashed an infrared strobe light, so I could find them with the night vision in the darkened club.

The subjects of the operation were the security guards, whom we had been told by an informant were selling the drugs. The club had a vast open dance space and smaller rooms, and a section like a bazaar, with a table where drug-free rave literature was handed out—I picked up leaflets, to figure out what to buy—and booths for candy, gum, water, and CDs. In the smaller rooms, groups of kids would huddle on the floor to hug each other, or just to collapse, panting and gasping like runners at the end of a race. We were told to keep an eye out for open sex acts, and we were indeed vigilant. Ricky and I spent some time at the piercing booth, watching the young girls line up for punctured eyebrows and bellybuttons. "Go for it, Ricky—surprise your fiancée, Jennifer, with a nice tongue stud," I said.

"I really want one, but I think it would be wrong to spend taxpayer dollars on it."

I nodded and we bought more glow sticks instead.

At first, we had a lot of laughs: the scene was novel and bizarre, and after all, we were getting paid to spend a Saturday night at a club. But after a few hours, we had headaches from the relentless and barely changing beat of the music. You'd see a beautiful girl, but when you got a closer look, you'd realize she might be fifteen years old. The night wore on, and fights broke out: I watched an enormous bouncer argue with a teenager, and then pick him up and shot-put him: he sailed ten feet through the air, smashed through a door, and landed on the sidewalk. As an undercover, I had no gun or shield, and the music was too loud to call for help; an arrest would have ended the investigation, and we had planned to develop the drug case into a larger tax case against the club. But if the teenager had a broken neck, I had no choice. I strolled over a few paces to get a look at him on the sidewalk. The kid popped up from the gutter and danced like a marionette, screaming that he had to get back inside.

One of the other uncles handed me a couple of bags of weed, which I pocketed. "They said they had something called 'Special K,' too, but I didn't know what it was, so I said forget about it." I checked my drug-free rave pamphlets and said, "Go back and buy the Special K."

At first, we bought from whoever offered, but then we concentrated on the bouncers. One of the freelance dealers confided that the bouncers sometimes took them into back rooms and stole their stashes. *Thank you, sir, I'll be sure to add that to the report.* We worked our way in to the bouncers, who were deft as dealers, well organized and well supplied. I shot footage of sales until one of them approached me and said that I couldn't film anymore. After witnessing the shot-putting incident, I thought his politeness suspect, but he didn't demand the tape. I would have been happy to add on a robbery charge to the eventual indictment, but I would have preferred to skip the assault. I called Pops on the cell phone and met him around the corner, to hand off the camera and the drugs. "You look sharp," he said. I took the pacifier out of my mouth and told him where he could go.

When we worked the raves, we'd stay till six or seven in the morning, arriving back at the base in sunlight, exhausted, to voucher the drugs. We bought liquids, powders, and pills from large men in security shirts and headsets, as the cars with out-of-state plates pulled on to the block to drop off their children. The nights seemed to go on as long as the midnights had, with the same strangeness, the daylight bedtimes and breakfast in the dark, and a different strangeness, as we worked while pretending to play. The case would continue as we IDed subjects and ran checks, copying down plates and investigating business records. But the party would go on without me.

In mid-August, I got an e-mail from DI Rising, telling me to call him right away. He said, "Here's what I can do for now—you and your partner can go to any Squad in the city, tomorrow, and by the end of the year we can look at Manhattan Robbery. Where do you want to go?"

I told him that John had been at the Four-Four Squad for a couple of weeks now, and that I'd like to run things by him first, but it sounded good to me. I would call him back tomorrow. In fact, I wanted to stall for time. I had a few cases that I wanted to clear, and I also had four free days off for the PBA convention, which would lead into Labor Day weekend. I could use the break. When I called him back, I asked if we could delay it through Labor Day, and he said, "I don't think you should. You never know what's gonna happen." He was right. There could be an incident or a scandal—if a Four-Four cop got in trouble, or someone from Narcotics did, it could be suddenly impolitic to make changes at either place. I thought of all the near-certain non-events of my career—the SNEU team going to Narcotics, Street Crime, Vice, Manhattan North Narcotics, Headquarters, even Manhattan Robbery, maybe—and how differently things had turned out despite all my effort, luck, hustle, and hooks. When the door opens, you go. I said, "Okay, then. Let's do it." I'd finally be going to the Detective Bureau, to the Four-Four Squad. Effective midnight, I was gone.

THIRTEEN

The word "investigate" comes from the Latin *vestigium,* for footprint, and came to mean "to follow a trail." I arrived at the Squad before the news of my arrival did, and when I introduced myself to the bosses, the truth of my announcement had to be checked downtown, as if I might be an impostor. After I said hello to whoever else was in the office, I went back to Narcotics to pack up my things. Though the drive was no more than fifteen minutes, my investigators had beaten me back on the return trip. When I saw Ricky Duggan, he said, "Geez, the phone's been ringing off the hook about you, they want to know what the deal is."

"What did you tell 'em?"

"Great guy, hard worker, all that."

"Good, throw them off the scent."

So too at Admin, when I went to say my good-byes up there—"We've had a bunch of calls from the Four-Four. . . ." It hadn't been an hour since I'd set foot in there, and my footprints had been tracked back to Narcotics, Housing, and beyond, to my off-duty work. I came clean with them right away. They were detectives, after all, and it was their job to find out.

When I started out on my beat in the Village, I'd take my collars to the Four-Two, where I was a guest twice over. I was a new cop amid older ones, a Housing cop in the NYPD. The PSA was less than two years old, an air-conditioned and freshly painted cinder-block box, while the Four-Two had been built just after the turn of the century, cobbled together from pieces of dungeon and saloon: a high oak promontory of a desk with a brass rail, behind which an old Irishman decided who was served and how; in the back was a dank row of iron-barred cells, foul-smelling, dark, and covered with graffiti that could have been scrawled by the Birdman of Alcatraz. When I went upstairs to the Squad to have my perps debriefed, I was a three-time outsider, and I sometimes hesitated before I crossed the threshold, half expecting that they'd release the perp I'd brought in for trespassing and charge me with trespass myself.

There was nothing distinctive about the Squad, built on the cheap and badly maintained, with scuffed floors that looked like they were mopped once a week with the same bucket of dirty water. Detectives doubled up on desks beneath fluorescent lights; wanted posters papered the walls over the layers of peeling, military-surplus paint; rows of file cabinets broke the rooms into alcoves. Sometimes there was nothing distinctive about the men there—they were all men—who seemed to have taken on the worn-out look of their surroundings. But they had a way of looking at you, especially if you walked in without knocking, that reminded you that first impressions can be deceiving: there was more to them, and more to this place. If you took the time, you began to notice why. Detectives were unencumbered by the vests, belts, and sticks of patrol cops, and their movements were lighter and looser; it also made them more individual, more themselves. Their shields were on their belts, exhibited with the casual undraping of the suit jacket, a brief movement of the left hand that showed a flash of gold. Some wore their ties unknotted, with the ends crossed over in the center of their shirts, secured with a tie tack; it had an aura of old custom, like a homburg or a monocle.

Cops were standardized and general-purpose, dressed alike and designed to react to everything—disputes, traffic, broken elevators, loose dogs. Patrol had the most immediate part of the Job, and the most important. But while this immediacy was a great thrill, it was also the limitation: even if you got the first look, you rarely heard the last word, or even the middle of the story. The arrival of detectives at a crime scene signaled the end of patrol's responsibilities beyond the preservation of evidence. If there was a body on an apartment floor, they would slip in to draw a weeping woman aside, offering condolences while aiming questions. On the street, they might fan out into the crowd that had gathered, drawing out people there, too, for a quiet word, or to conceal a card in a handshake to speak in private later on. Their purpose was to inspire confidences, and their manner reflected confidences won, and a self-confidence; they carried themselves with a Broadway swagger even on streets that had never seen bright lights.

For almost a century, the Detective Bureau was its own separate kingdom within the Department, beginning with Inspector Thomas Byrnes in the 1870s and ending a century later. Byrnes, an Irish immigrant and Civil War veteran, was made Chief of Detectives after solving a three-million-dollar robbery from Chase Manhattan Bank. He instituted a high degree of professionalism in the Bureau: the mug shot and line-up were his inventions, and the police began to be known as "the Finest" at this time. He created a "dead line" at Fulton Street, the northern border of the Financial District, below which known criminals were summarily arrested if they happened to venture. Byrnes himself was a master detective, with an encyclopedic knowledge of the MOs and territories of individual perpetrators. He collaborated on several books, including *Professional Criminals of 1886*. The state legislature made the Detective Bureau a separate division of the NYPD at his request. His unquestioned honesty led to promotions after Boss Tweed fell in the 1870s, and then to Byrnes's becoming Superintendent after the Reverend Charles Parkhurst's sensational denunciations of vice and police corruption in the early 1890s. In 1892, after Congress assigned federal marshals to the polls, a Tammany district leader issued orders for police to arrest them if they committed "breaches of the peace." Byrnes told each of his captains he would "take the buttons off him" if he did so, and none did. Reformers like Lincoln Steffens and Jacob Riis, who generally had little praise for the police, admired him personally. For Steffens, he was "simple, no complications at all—a man who would buy you or beat you, as you might choose, but get you he would." And Riis mourned his retirement, musing that "chained as he was in the meanness and smallness of it all, he was yet cast in a different mold. Compared with his successor, he was a giant in every way. Byrnes was a 'big policeman.' We shall not soon have another like him."

But many detectives followed who would become nearly as well regarded and well known, and for many decades, New York knew its good guys as well as its bad guys by name. Joseph Petrosino, the first Italian-American in the NYPD and the founder of the "Italian Squad," put more than five hundred mafiosi in prison, and he was killed in revenge while on assignment in Palermo in 1909. More than a quarter of a million people, mostly Italian immigrants, turned out for his funeral on the Lower East Side. Broadway

Johnny Broderick, also known as the "One-Man Riot Squad," once tossed Legs Diamond into a dumpster. Johnny Cordes was a two-time Medal of Honor winner who didn't carry a gun, and who found jobs for two perps who had shot him when they were later released from prison. The bank robber Willie Sutton provided an admiring blurb for a biography of Frank Phillips, the detective who captured him: "He's just about the best there is. You never felt safe if you knew Phillips was after you. If Mike Hammer ever read the record of Frank Phillips's accomplishments as a detective, he would undoubtedly pass a few snide remarks about Mickey Spillane's ability to create a super-sleuth." In the 1950s, the Detectives Endowment Association would have annual parties at the Waldorf and the Plaza, where the likes of Frank Sinatra and Dean Martin would perform. Though the independence of the Detective Bureau was curbed by Commissioner Patrick Murphy as part of his modernization of the NYPD—Murphy had strong ideas about preventing crimes, but little experience in solving them—it retained a measure of its old autonomy and character.

Then as now, cops with ambition became bosses or detectives, and the former was not an option for those without a talent for politics or test-taking. The Bureau also drew cops whose view of the Job was essentially romantic, an evergreen game of tag with the bad guys, profoundly boyish in its excitement but adult in its consequences. More than anything else, what a detective does is talk—to witnesses, victims, perps—and talk them into talking; you chose your own words as you chose your own clothes, and you rose or fell on your style. When I'd talk to friends like Brian McCabe, he'd say things like, "The Squad is the Job. Hurry up and come here."

The Four-Four was one of the busiest squads in the city, closely knit and conscious of tradition. The Three-Four in Washington Heights and the Seven-Five in East New York, Brooklyn, had traditionally dueled for first place in homicides during the crack wars, racking up eighty or a hundred bodies a year, but the Four-Four, which was a fraction of their size, was always close behind. And while the Three-Four and Seven-Five had seen reductions in crime as dramatic as any in the city in recent years, the Four-Four began the year 2001 with a homicide on each of the first four days of January. Within blocks of East 161st Street and the Grand Concourse, the Four-Four contained Yankee Stadium, the courts, the DA's and Borough President's offices, and the Bronx County Building, which had housed the Democratic machine that had put FDR and JFK into the White House. In *The Bonfire of the Vanities*, Tom Wolfe called this corridor of influence "Gibraltar":

All over Gibraltar, at this moment, from lowest to the highest, the represen-
tatives of the Power in the Bronx were holed up in their offices, shell-backed,
hunched over deli sandwiches, ordered in. . . .žYou could ascend to the very top
of the criminal justice system in the Bronx and eat deli sandwiches until the
day you retired or died.

And why? Because they, the Power, the Power that ran the Bronx, were ter-
rified! And they ran the place, the Bronx, a borough of 1.1 million souls! The
heart of the Bronx was now such a slum that there was nothing even resem-
bling a businessman's sit-down restaurant. But even if there were, what judge
or DA or assistant DA, what court officer, even packing a .38, would leave
Gibraltar at lunchtime to get to it? . . .žYou were an alien in the 44th Precinct,
and you knew at once, every time Fate led you into their territory . . .ž

After six years in the South Bronx, the Four-Four was a small adjustment,
but the Squad would be a true change. I felt like I was holding my breath a
little, not from a Seventh Circle stench—though Dante and Virgil began their
transit to Lower Hell there, the realm of the violent, where I was headed,
too—but so that I would not be heard as I crept in. Housing had had its own
Squads, before the merge, but since leaving my beat, my contact with
precinct detectives had been sporadic. I didn't know many of them, and I -
didn't know all that much about what they did or how they did it. It was as
if I was peering over the edge, readying for the jump, and I was glad to have
Timpanaro there with me. I felt like giving him a little poolside shove—*Let me*
know how the water is—but he leaped in first, and he loved it.

When John arrived the month before, in July, he attended a seven-day Detective Bureau orientation. For several of those nights, I was out for dinner
with friends downtown, and John would join us on his break, beaming and
dressed in new suits, telling us how various bosses had welcomed them, including the Chief of Detectives himself, and the tone seemed to be that of an
awards ceremony or an initiation to a secret society. He carried himself with a
sense of delight, of having arrived, and by the last day, I almost expected him
to produce a key to the city. He told a joke from the orientation: "They set up a
weekend down south, in Virginia, for the best investigators in the country.
They have cookouts, lectures, softball games—all that—and everybody has a
good time. In the end, on the last day, they say, 'We're gonna have a demon-
stration, see what everybody's got.' They go out to the woods, with two guys
from the CIA, two guys from the FBI, two guys from Bronx Homicide. They

have a little white rabbit in a cage. They let it go, and it scampers off into the woods. The guy waits a little bit and says, 'Okay, first up is the CIA—go out and find that rabbit!' The two CIA guys run off and disappear, and in ten minutes they come back with the rabbit. Everybody claps—'Great work! Look at these guys!' And then they let another rabbit loose, and they wait, and the guy says, 'FBI—you're next! Go get 'em!' And the two FBI guys go off in the woods, and everybody waits, but in an hour, they come back with the rabbit. 'Good job, guys, good job!' Finally, Bronx Homicide is up. The rabbit goes, and they go out after it. An hour passes, and another hour, and another. It's starting to get dark, and everybody's getting worried—they're gonna have to send out a search party for the Bronx guys, forget about the rabbit. As the sun goes down, they get ready to head into the woods. Just then, Bronx Homicide comes out of the woods with a bear. One guy has it by the neck, and the other guy is kicking it in the balls, and the bear is saying, 'Okay! Okay! I'm a rabbit!' "

A month later, I heard the joke, too, at my orientation, and though the Chief of Detectives did welcome us, there appeared to be far less fanfare. We were on day tours instead of four-to-twelves, as an apparent hedge against us enjoying our dinner breaks too thoroughly: a cop in Brooklyn had worked a midnight, drank through the day at a strip joint, and returned for another midnight when he ran over a pregnant woman and two children, killing them all. It was a gross tragedy, and the Job reacted grossly in turn: any cop who had been near him that day was punished, it seemed, and a rookie who had gone to the strip joint was fired. It was the way the Job offers an apology, and the mood was sorrowful and sour. The move to the Detective Bureau was a lateral one for me, moving over rather than up, and though I was content that I'd made the right decision, I wasn't singing in my car.

In Narcotics, at its best, you are an entrepreneur, with the freedom to choose cases or even invent them, as I had with Christmas, and follow wherever they led. Just before I'd gone, in August, I had the beginnings of a case with great potential. That month, my sister Regina had married a man named Michael Pacicco, who ran a family jewelry store on 47th Street, in the Diamond District, who called to tell me that a vendor of his, a Russian, had been sold fifty thousand dollars' worth of fake gold. When I talked to the Russian, he said the sellers were connected both to his in-laws and to organized crime, but he said that he was fed up with their stalling, and he wanted the police to help. It was a bit of a tricky situation: for the crime of Grand Larceny to have been committed, it would have to be shown that he was knowingly sold false goods, and it would have required him to wear a wire. It took a dozen phone calls to shop the case around, and it was only after I heard that Morgenthau loved cases with the Diamond District and the Russian Mob that I was able to find a receptive audience with the Manhattan DA's Squad. As it happened, the Russian ruined the case—he told the perps he had gone to the police—but the two men were taken down a year later, as part of a multi-million-dollar stolen-property ring. Manhattan gold fraud didn't have much to do with Bronx Narcotics, but I thought that Pops would be able to smell the overtime all the way to Forty-seventh Street. As John Reilly would say, "The shield says City of New York. . . ." The open-ended nature of the work was the best part of Narcotics: you went out to see what the stories were.

In the Squad, you were a historian, and the stories came to you. You - couldn't get just any bad guy, you had to get a particular one, who had done a specific thing to a distinct individual. It seemed narrow at first, and later it felt oppressive, not least because of the shift in the audience. In Narcotics, a collar brought some relief to a building, a block, a neighborhood; even with one less dealer or one less gun on the street, the benefit you provided was an environmental one, and as such it was to some degree abstract. For gun and drug cases, the complainant is the People of the State of New York, and they - didn't call to tell you to hurry up while you worked a case, or to thank you when you finished. In the Squad, they did: you had victims, living or otherwise. It had been a while since I'd worked for real human beings, and the shift was refreshing at times, and at others it was a burden.

The Detective Bureau would be as novel and challenging as my first days on patrol, when the Academy, at least, had provided six months of theory before the practice. You began the day with the 60 sheet—the list of complaints for the previous day, which someone from the Squad would skim each morning, through reports of nuisances and crimes, lost property and missing persons, to see what would become a case. The 494 sheet determined who "caught" the case, from the catching order: there were three two-man Robbery teams, A, B, and C, each working from four in the afternoon through one in the morning for two days, from eight in the morning through four in the afternoon the next two, followed by two days off. The cops on each team alternated catching for the tours they worked, and the day-tour team caught from midnights as well. The case folders were assembled by hand, folding the cardboard, punching, stapling, and clipping the 61 and the fives on the right side, and all other documents—computer checks, vouchers, pictures—on the left. Most of the fives you typed were pink, but you typed blue ones for arrests. There were the case-closing classifications, amenable and non-amenable, from A-1, for an arrest by the Detective Squad; D-1, arrest by patrol; B-5, transfer to another office, like Transit for subway robberies or Bronx Robbery for patterns; B-7, inaccurate facts; C-2, when a witness can no longer identify a perp; C-3, uncooperative complainant; C-4, all leads exhausted. B-15 also meant that a complainant couldn't ID, or an arrest by patrol, but only sometimes. There were procedures for issuing wanted cards, conducting line-ups and showing photo arrays. Most of it was brand-new to me, and much of what I did know I hadn't done in years.

There was a feel of age to the place, a consciousness of legacy. Unlike most of the Job, there were men who were not bosses who had gray hair. When I looked at the old Homicide logs, leather-bound ledgers that were older than the building that housed them, I saw how we averaged about fifty murders a year in the early 1980s, crested to over eighty in the crack years, and had come down to the thirties more recently. The logs were yellowed and the pages were crisp, divided into columns that listed location, weapon, motive, and the name, age, and race of victim and perp. In the 1980 log, there were a fair number of elderly Irish and Jewish ladies in their seventies and eighties, strangled or bludgeoned at home during burglaries; the race of one victim was listed as "Y," which stumped me for a moment, until I saw the victim was Chinese, and the detective meant "Yellow." Other motives were set down simply as "Homosexual," and child-abuse cases were categorized as "Discipline." Some of the detectives in that log had come on the Job soon after World War II, and men they taught had retired just before my arrival. They were men who could have worked with my father, and to be there felt like I was closer to him than ever, in type and time.

The Squad was run by Lt. George Corbiere, with two sergeants, Larry Sheehan and Tom Rice, while the RAM was headed by Sgt. Scott Adler. From Corbiere, especially, I began to understand some of the intensity of pride that John had felt at the orientation. There were few precincts as dangerous and few Squads as dedicated and driven. Sgt. Adler talked about the "adult-hood" of the Squad: he was here to help with anything I asked for, on duty or off, and he should know about any major developments in the former, but I was my own man. I liked that. I certainly liked it more than when he said that he valued neatness and he didn't want smoking in the office. As I tapped the pack of cigarettes in my pocket, I thought of how Capt. Mahony would sometimes stop by my desk just to stare at the alp of paperwork. I told Adler my preference for the B Team, of Danny Scanlon and John Timpanaro, and he said that it sounded fine.

I slowly began to understand the layout of the Squad, the roles and rotations: the separate five-day chart for the two-man Burglary team and the three detectives assigned to Domestic Violence. The RAM took robberies and grand larcenies from persons, which generally meant chain snatches or purse snatches. Ron Kress and Steve DeSalvo were the A Team, and Keith Clinton and Jimmy Reilly made up the C. Most cops in the Squad began in the RAM, as there was an average of upper-middle seriousness to the cases, from the kid-who-punched-the-other-kid-and-took-his-jacket stuff, to commercial robberies and stick-ups in which the victim was shot. The Squad took everything else, from homicides to cases of aggravated harassment, which required nothing more than a phone call to the threatening phone-caller, telling him to come to the office. The A, B, and C teams on the Squad worked on the same rolling chart as the RAM—two nights, two days, two off—and in the event of homicides, shootings, or other heavy cases, the entire office responded to the scene. The senior men were Mike Rodriguez, his brother Steve, and Eddie McDonald for the A team, Bobby Nardi and Bobby D'Amico for the B, and Bobby Colten, Al Rosario, and JR Carter for the C. On my first day there, I listened to JR talk casually about his recent trip to Florida to collect the hit man a woman had hired to kill her husband. There was no need to point out that I was the new guy, because I was well aware of it myself; I respected all of them a great deal and I showed it, I hoped, without servility. Billy Coakley introduced himself by asking jovially, "Are you a dump job or an IAB plant?" I thought before answering. "A little of both."

As I grappled with the new faces and forms, further investigations were conducted: I had worked with Jose Morales's sister, Janet, in Narcotics; Capt. Hoch knew Scott Adler, and Larry Sheehan knew my brother John—his daughter and my niece Elizabeth went to kindergarten together. When Corbiere asked how I'd gotten here, Larry Sheehan said, "Clearly, this is a transfer by osmosis." His nickname was Vocabu-Larry. That was easy to remember, but it was harder to tell Glynn from Flynn, and Flynn from Flood. John Flynn had worked with Uncle Eddie in the Four-Seven: "He was a barrel of fun. . . ." And John Flood must have had some Jesuit training, as was shown when a perp called to him from the cells, "Where's D'Amico at?"

"Listen, guy, I'm gonna tell you two things," he barked. "First, D'Amico's not in, and second, in this Squad we never, *ever* end a sentence with a preposition. You got me?"

For the first few days, there was little to do with me, and I listened and watched. One morning, a midnight cop named McNamee told Danny Scanlon about a collar he'd made the night before, of gang members at a prostitution area the cops called "Pickle Park." A group of Bloods had set upon a gay teenage boy working the area, but they were driven off by another teen prostitute, a transvestite with a bullwhip. Another morning, the Squad was crowded with chiefs; I slipped into my desk and pretended I had work to do. Someone knocked from the interview room, which was a few feet away, and when I opened it, an eight-year-old boy stood before me and said, "I have to go to the bathroom." He had killed a four-year-old boy, stabbing him in the neck with a pen. They lived in the same building, and the eight-year-old had bullied the smaller boy for a year. He stabbed him when the four-year-old was sent out to the garbage disposal in the hall to throw away a diaper. I led him out to the bathroom, and then I took him back, and locked the door again.

I stuck with John, picking up bits and pieces from him. While he had only been there a month, he'd worked in the precinct on and off for years. He wanted the Four-Four to work with Scanlon and Jose Morales—he had known them from his old footpost, when they were on Four-Four SNEU. Danny and Jose were the young turks of the precinct, aggressive cops who came to be known as Batman and Robin on the busier corners. Jose had come upstairs just before Danny, and he was on the B Team, on the Squad side. John and Danny were all hustle and heat, and they called each other on their days off to talk about how they could finagle the next gun collar. John had been on a hot streak from the moment he arrived: there were a couple of good collars after canvasses, and a gun collar after a foot pursuit in the park; he had also caught a few great cases, including a cab robbery where the perps shot up the car. On my first day back from orientation, I came in as John and Danny were setting up a gun rip for the next day, with a guy they'd stopped the night before for a traffic violation.

Danny was as hard-charging as Popeye Doyle. He'd worked for eight years in the Four-Four, and he couldn't drive down a block without an old complainant stopping the car to say hello on one side, and an old collar calling out, "Hey, Batman!" from the other. And Danny would stop and talk to each. Once he'd collared a perp, Danny treated him like an old schoolmate, joking about past times and planning to meet again: "Tell me for real—you got a gun at home? Who does? You know who's carrying? Let's help each other out. . . ."

If it felt like I lived in a police state sometimes, Danny made my world look relatively civilian. Though he was a first-generation cop—his mother was from Mayo, as my grandmother Delia was—one of his brothers, John, was a sergeant in Street Crime, and his other brother, Brian, was applying to the FBI. He met his wife, Lily Roque, when they were partners in SNEU, and she still worked at the Four-Four, in Community Policing. They had two children, Nina and Danny Jr., and while the little ones had not yet expressed any job preferences, there was an easy bet to be made on what they'd do. Danny had begun as a cop in the Four-Four and fully expected to end his career there, in the Squad, and to stay past his twenty years.

At first, Danny was welcoming but wary with me; John's endorsement counted for something, but you never knew how you'd work out as partners, balancing rhythms and personalities for fifty hours a week. Taking on a partner was more like an arranged marriage than a blind date, and in our business especially, you didn't just take someone's word for things. Compared to OCCB, detectives in the Bureau operated with tremendous independence: they came and went from the office without asking permission from a boss, and they decided the course of an investigation as they saw fit. Because no one thought for you, you and your partner had to think alike, or at least to disagree with respect. With Danny, I deferred to his experience in most matters, and with John, the combination of an old partner and a new assignment was the perfect balance of the familiar and the strange.

When the prospect of living and working together suddenly presented itself, John and I looked at each other and wondered if it was such a good idea. It had been two years since we were steady partners in SNEU, and at first, work was so much fun that we were happy to talk about it at home, and then it was so miserable that the bond formed a natural defense. We'd planned to partner up again, but as the time passed, the plan became almost a figure of speech—"Next year in Jerusalem!"—as John didn't want to go to Narcotics and it didn't look like I was going anywhere else. Over the summer, it seemed that things would work out: John would learn the robbery trade at the Four-Four, and then he could teach me at Manhattan Robbery, maybe at the end of the year. Maybe then, too, he would stun his longtime girlfriend, Julie, with a proposal. She was in the third year of her medical residency, and I advised him to do it at the hospital, where she could receive necessary treatment. From the time he'd moved in, he'd planned to propose to Julie the next Christmas, or the next Valentine's Day, and then on vacation in the spring, but the signs were never quite right. Three years of holidays and trips had passed, and it had even been a year since he'd asked me to be his best man. I was honored, and I asked him to be my pallbearer in return:

"Just you—not five other guys. I want you to carry the coffin yourself, on your back, and give me five squat-thrusts coming and going from the church."

"No problem. That gives me, what—a good three, maybe four years to get in shape."

"Four years, easy. Here's my rough draft of the best-man speech: 'Good riddance.' How's that sound?"

John thought for a moment. "You know, I've heard worse."

We decided to give it a try—John was on the Island on his days off, and with the detective's chart, it felt like you lived with your team: you went in late on the first day and left early on the last, and the middle two ran together for the "turnaround"—the night tour ended at one a.m. and the next day began at eight, and half the Squad slept over in the precinct. On work days, life was work.

One afternoon, I went with John to Lincoln Hospital to interview Alfonzo, his complainant for a stabbing-robbery from the night before. Alfonzo had been waiting to hail a cab for his girlfriend when two men approached from either side and cut him in the leg and chest. Other detectives had interviewed him that night, and he was hostile and uncooperative, and when we looked up his record—the "victimology," conducted in every case—we saw his prior arrest for robbery. Often, these victims feel a sense of professional courtesy - toward their colleagues, and they prefer to shoot them instead of having them arrested. It was an unpromising beginning and an unprepossessing setting, but for me it was a pure thrill. Patients and doctors alike looked at us, and someone called out from the waiting room, "Ooh, FBI!" It was like on my first day of patrol, when the drunk in the blue styrofoam cowboy hat had called out, "There's a new sheriff in town!" And though no one had their facts quite right, then or now, I was flattered nonetheless. When you wear a suit in a room full of suits, you look, at best, like you belong there; when you wear a suit in a place full of sweatshirts, everyone else wonders if they do. When we stopped to announce our visit to the woman at the information desk, John dropped his voice half an octave to the finest Squad-guy tone, grave and confidential, but willing to share in the secret, just this once, for you: "Timpanaro and Conlon, Four-Four Squad," he said, as he pulled his jacket half-aside to show the shield. "We're here to see . . ."

The suave and serious mood was broken when we stepped into Alfonzo's room. He seemed to be playing with himself. I said, "Ahem . . . hey, Alfonzo, how are you feeling? My name is Conlon and this is my partner, Timpanaro, and—"

John gave me a little shove, and I looked at him, and followed his nod. "We'll give you a minute, excuse us," I said, as we withdrew.

Outside, John said, "You couldn't see he's pissing in a bedpan?"

I shook my head sadly: "Sometimes you have to look past the obvious, to get to the truth. Frankly, I'm not sure if you have much of a future in this business, John."

Alfonzo had suffered a deep cut to the side, requiring fifty stitches to close; he was both heavily sedated and in pain. He didn't know why he had been attacked, he said, but he thought he knew one of his attackers, who didn't live too far from him. We asked what he looked like, and he gave a description so detailed he might have dressed him that morning: twenty-year-old male Hispanic, hair in three thick braids, a tattoo of a Chinese character on his neck, wearing a Cincinnati Reds cap over a black do-rag, a gold chain without any ornament; a black jacket with red piping down the sleeves, black Air Jordans with red laces. Most people couldn't provide such a description if they'd studied a photograph for ten minutes, and Alfonzo had a split second before the stabbing. John asked if the perp sold drugs, and Alfonzo said that he did, on One-Five-Seven and Gerard. When I asked what he sold, he responded without hesitation, "Red tops."

Alfonzo's portrait of his attacker was a self-portrait as well. Though he didn't have any drug collars on his sheet, his familiarity with the product and perp was not that of a spectator. It didn't mean that we didn't want the case or wouldn't work the case, but we had to establish whether Alfonzo wanted us to—he could be our complainant now, or the perp in next month's homicide, and while it wasn't quite all the same to us, there was only so much we could do to gain his cooperation. When I looked at the 61, I saw that today was Alfonzo's birthday, and I offered congratulations. He began to cry a little, saying that he never had any luck, how he tried and tried. . . . We let him go on for a moment, and then John said, "Do you want to work with us on this, Alfonzo? I mean, we want to get this guy for you, but do you want us to help? Some people don't want to deal with cops, for whatever reason, they've been in trouble before, whatever. You ever been in trouble before?"

Alfonzo's hiccuppy whimper opened up into a full-throated sob: "The only time I really got locked up was on my birthday, two years ago! I got drunk and took a TV . . .a birthday present . . .one birthday in jail, another in the hospital . . ."

Whether it was the kind words, the birthday coincidence, or the morphine, when we walked away, it felt like we'd rescued the case. The other detectives had been discouraging before we went in, and maybe we made an additional effort to draw Alfonzo out, just to defy expectations. It was a good feeling to be able to shift the circumstances, to make Alfonzo someone you were glad to help, and to take off running. It also felt good to work with John again, to tag-team an interview to draw out facts or feelings, and to talk it over afterward, noticing details, pointing out problems and possibilities.

It felt right, the rhythm of the place, the professionalism and the pride. There was far more paperwork than I expected, and more time spent in the office, where the phones could ring without rest. One afternoon, after a series of calls that asked, "Is this Crown Donut?" I picked up with the intention of taking their order, but it was the sergeant at the desk, downstairs.

"There's somebody here, wants to see one of you guys."

"Who? You got a name?"

"Nah, but from who they describe, I think they want that skinny new detective."

"Conlon?"

"Yeah, maybe."

"Send 'em up."

When the skinny new detective caught his first case, John, Danny, and I made another hospital visit, to talk to Ethan Prescott. Ethan had been walking home from a family party late one night, when a man followed him from the subway and asked for change. Ethan knew what was coming next, and so he walked faster, when the man stepped up to him and cracked him in the head with a pipe. Hours later, he came to, and someone helped him to his apartment, a few blocks away. For the next two days, he was in and out of consciousness, and it was not until a social worker came to visit him that help was sought. Ethan had AIDS, and his injuries would have been severe under any circumstances, but here they might have been lethal. His jaw was broken, and he had developed an infection. He would be happy to work with us, he said, but we had to understand that there were other things on his mind.

As a case, it was not altogether lost: Ethan thought he could recognize the man, but it was unknown when he'd be able to get in to view pictures, and by that time, his memory might have faded. He did remember getting a phone call when he lay delirious in his apartment: a credit-card company asked whether a particular charge was authorized, after someone had signed the slip "Evan Prescott," and the merchant had become suspicious. He had two credit cards, and he wasn't sure which company had called, but when he got home, he'd look at his bills and know which. There might be a problem finding the bill, however, as he was preparing to move, and his belongings were all in boxes. It was a slim chance, but someone at the store should remember him, and might have a videotape, and if we were extremely lucky, the perp might have been arrested at the scene. We went back to the office and I typed my first DD5 for my first case, on the long pink sheet. It felt strange to write my new command, "44 Robbery Apprehension Module," and I tried to remember how long it had felt strange to write "Narcotics," and wondered how it would feel to write "Detective Conlon" in a few months. But when I look at that five now, by far the strangest thing about it is the date, which presaged a change far greater than any from Housing to Narcotics to the Detective Bureau. The date was September 10, 2001.

. . .

IT WAS IMPOSSIBLE TO THINK THAT THE TWIN TOWERS WERE now a part of "old New York," lost like the Third Avenue El, Ebbets Field, or the Polo Grounds, of a piece with the age of pushcarts and cobblestone streets. Their stratospheric, clean-lined reach defined the modern skyline: they had an utter simplicity and a vague symbolism, like an equal sign or a number—two? eleven?—that didn't demand to be understood, and were at once truly awesome and a little dull. My sister Regina and her husband, Michael, returned from their honeymoon two days before, on a cruise ship that entered New York harbor at dawn. Regina took pictures of the Statue of Liberty. She didn't think she'd want a picture of the Twin Towers, any more than she'd take a picture of my mother's house. We'd been there so often there was no need.

We had gone to the World Trade Center since it had opened, to my uncles' restaurant at the underground level of the PATH trains to New Jersey. There were three uncles—Joe, Herman, and Victor—and three businesses, a bar called the Trade Inn, a coffee shop, and the Commuter's Cafe. My family had gone since the 1970s, and my friends had gone since the 1980s; the tradition ended in 1993, after the first bombing. Herman was at the coffee shop when the bomb went off in the underground garage, and there was chaos and near-disaster in his escape. Afterward, the restaurant and coffee shop didn't re-open, and in the years since, Victor and Joe had died. Only Herman and the bar were left by the year 2001, and I thought of them an hour after I arrived at work on the morning of September 11.

I'd caught a case the night before, and at 0848 hours I was looking at the report for a commercial robbery—gun, bodega, two males, one with a prominent gap in his teeth, I was glad to learn—when a shout went up from the lunchroom. It wasn't so loud or extreme, only slightly more than you might have heard at a tie-breaking touchdown. And like a football game, there was instant replay, over and over. I walked in and watched the plane hit. It looked small, like a private plane, for a hobbyist or a local charter. If I hadn't been new in the office, I might have expressed my opinion, which would have been that there was room for accident and coincidence, that we shouldn't jump to conclusions. I might have pointed out that a plane had struck the Empire State Building once, and there had been nothing sinister about it. Our TV flickered a little, but the image of orange flame and black smoke, silver skyscraper and blue sky came in unbroken in my mind. I watched it play over and over, and then I stepped out of the room again, and then there was a greater shout, and I went back in. Another plane, another tower, banking in from the south, and striking with such force that it left an exit wound.

"We're at war," said Sgt. Adler. "Let's suit up. Everybody in the bag."

I don't know if I was especially collected or a bit numb. I called my mother to tell her I was all right, and I called a few others, to spread the word. Whenever a cop is shot in the city, everyone who had a relative or friend on the Job feels a jolt of dread. I felt *too* safe, and I ran through my own potential casualty list: Herman probably wasn't in yet to open the bar, but his son, Steve, was a cop in the First Precinct, which covered the World Trade Center. He worked the midnights, which finished at 0750; had he left yet, and had he gone there? The Fire Department had gone down en masse, and I had two cousins, Brian and his brother Gerald, and Tommy Killian, and a list of other names, less close, that ran longer than I could count. I wasn't even sure where my brothers worked—one a lawyer, the other at a bank, somewhere downtown. Steve Rodriguez had talked to his wife, who worked in the south tower, after the first plane hit the north. "They're telling us not to evacuate," she told Steve. "Get the fuck out, now," he said. Steve grabbed a car with his brother Mike and two other guys from the Squad, Bobby Colten and Rocco

Farella, and they sped downtown. People in the towers began to leap to their deaths. Some of them were on fire.

My uniform was at home; I didn't have a locker yet and was sharing John's. Another plane struck the Pentagon, and another had been hijacked and was somewhere over Pennsylvania. Most cops were grim, but now and then someone made a forced, whistling-in-the-dark joke about Arabs or war. One cop was in a state of high agitation, nearly yelling, "My aunt works there! My aunt works right there! Fuck that! Man, fuck that!" I wanted to tell him to calm down, but I also wanted to smack him. One tower fell, trembling and blazing, and the black smoke shot up as if released from the core of the earth. A column of steel and glass became a column of ash, rising ever higher. As we watched, it was as if the air had been sucked out of us. The second tower fell, with the same haunting motion, the same stop-action descent, floor by floor, from something to nothing, like a magician's top hat, disappearing with a snap. I thought how everything was landing on my last uncle's last bar. I went home to get my uniform.

As I raced home on local streets, a flashing light on the dash, John called from Long Island. "Should I come in?" he asked. "I don't know how you'll be able to," I said. "Everything's shut—bridges, tunnels, trains." I said I'd call him back. Just after noon, we all mustered outside our new Headquarters on Simpson Street; Detective Borough Bronx had taken over the building from Narcotics over the summer. We awaited our assignments, and some wondered whether we would guard bridges or airports or the perimeter of the Trade Center, but others speculated that we would go to the morgues. Forty thousand people worked in the two towers, and though it was early in the morning, and many had left after the first plane hit, there were estimates of five and six thousand dead. We milled about in the street for hours. A city bus came to pick up detectives and went downtown; a captain sent out a few carloads to collect water and flashlight batteries from supermarkets. I struggled to think of something useful to do, and then I went to a diner and ordered dozens of sandwiches. They didn't take a dime off, not even for the coffee. It's a slippery slope, I suppose. Danny came in, and I called John again, who was already on his way; the bridges had been opened for emergency workers. When he got to Simpson Street, he said that he was the only one on the Throgs Neck Bridge coming into the city, and he stopped his car for a moment and stepped outside. The day was perfect, a balmy, windless moment of Indian summer, and he looked at the empty gray span and the empty blue sky and then downtown, at the geysers of smoke on the skyline. And then he thought, "Maybe this isn't the smartest place to be," and he sped off the bridge.

Someone said, "The whole first platoon at the First Precinct was wiped out." That didn't make sense: the first platoon is the midnights, but the plane had hit fifty-eight minutes after end of tour. Maybe they meant the second platoon. That meant that my cousin Steve would be all right, but a lot more cops would be dead—three times as many would be at work during the day. I calculated odds, as if it mattered. Someone said that there was a separate morgue being set up just for cops and firemen. A detective named O'Hagan from the Four-O Squad was called off the line; his brother was a fireman. I knew the family: I'd gone to high school with one brother, Joe, and another was a lieutenant in Narcotics. Ron Kress said that someone saw Steve Rodriguez on TV, running into the south tower just before it fell.

The hours passed, and the sun set, and we stood idle on Simpson Street. Sometimes we'd drift into the building to watch TV, to hear more rumors and wonder why we were kept on what seemed like the quietest street in the city. I don't think there were many robberies or assaults that day, but anyone who called 911 didn't get an answer. At ten o'clock at night, half of us were dismissed until four in the morning, the other half until four in the afternoon: we would be on seven-day, twelve-hour shifts until further notice. John, Danny, and I would be back at four in the morning. We went home and tried to make calls. My brother Steve had flown to England the night before, and we hadn't heard from him. I wasn't worried; he wasn't here. My firefighter cousins were alive, and so were the Tretters. We didn't sleep much before we went back in.

Another twelve hours passed, milling about in uniform on Simpson Street. I kept my wallet full of cash and brought back more food. More rumors circulated: carloads of uniformed city cops were being turned away from the site; one story, which was more than a rumor, told of twenty cops from the Four-Four who had gone down in uniform during their twelve hours off, only to be cursed at and sent home by some captain. Not everyone was desperate to play a part: the agitated cop who worried for his aunt later called in sick. His locker was broken into, and a yellow stripe was painted down the back of his uniform. I heard that he later resigned. When volunteers from Massachusetts and Pennsylvania were interviewed on TV at Ground Zero—though it wasn't called that yet—the mood became belligerent. They wore hard hats and were covered in ash, and said how they just got in their cars and came over to help. People shouted at the TV: "What the fuck's up with that?"

"We got dead brothers there, and they turn us away?"

"We got NYPD ID cards, uniforms, and shields, and it's get-the-fuck-out, but this guy shows up with a shovel and it's 'Welcome, brother!'"

I thought about how the President would arrive in a day or two, and I wondered how secure the perimeter might be. Would there be a Phase Two of attacks, or a Phase Three? New York had changed its driver's licenses not too long before, and the first time I saw one, I looked at the guy who handed it to me like he was trying to pull a fast one. How well would any other NYPD cop, or FBI agent, let alone a National Guardsman, recognize a legitimate license from Indiana or even from New Jersey? And yet Ground Zero was teeming with out-of-state cops, firefighters, volunteer firefighters, and paramedics, not to mention freelance volunteers who offered food, counseling, clean socks, water, Bibles, and everything else that could conceivably be of use. They came with truckloads of things, from rescue dogs to homemade lasagna. It was a scene of improvised nobility that may have been commensurate to the evil that provoked it, and yet in terms of security, it was a travesty, at least from my TV set. By the end of the day on Simpson Street, fewer cops were watching TV, and more were scheming how to get down there to work.

John had talked to a cop at PSA-7 named Bobby Tucker who had managed to get in at Ground Zero the day before. After a twelve-hour shift, we met him at four in the morning and drove down to the site. Bobby had brought hard hats, and we put on respirators, raid jackets, and dusty boots, and we marched past the National Guardsmen at the perimeter as if we'd just stepped out for a break. There was an uncanniness to it all: the sight of soldiers on Canal Street; the movement and noise in the predawn hours; the air acrid from smoke, with a sour, chemical tang. I passed restaurants where I'd eaten, offices where friends worked, the apartment of an old girlfriend. It was still dark, but there was a kind of anticipatory underglow, of light waiting in the wings, though we would not be glad for the sunrise. We turned a corner and saw what had been Seven World Trade Center, and stopped. What had been fifty stories was now five or six. It didn't look like it had fallen down. It looked shattered, broken apart by hammer blows. It stank like it was rotting and burning at once, as if the next of kin couldn't decide on burial or cremation. It was gone.

We passed on wordlessly to Ground Zero. There were hordes of cops, firemen, construction workers, many collapsed along the sidelines, exhausted, or staring blankly at the piles. There were steel I-beams stuck like darts in the towers that surrounded the site, and on a row of old buildings, cloth and paper hung like confetti from the fire escapes, flattened back from the blast. Cranes lifted up sixty-foot girders made of four-inch-thick steel, twisted like shoelaces. There was a mountain of broken things, and pits that led to still more devastation below. It didn't look like war, or even a war movie. It looked like a monster movie, where some great beast had punched holes in buildings and battered down the city. You found yourself standing, staring, forgetting about time. The sun rose, and it was another beautiful day.

We made our way into the piles and fell in line on the bucket brigade. A hundred cops passed five-gallon drums full of rubble from the center of the pile to the perimeter, and passed back the buckets, empty. Teams from FEMA in blue jumpsuits followed their dogs to pick a spot to dig, and the line fell back from where the dogs thought there might be life, moving toward each false hope, a bucket at a time. A hundred feet before us, a six-story section of facade from the North Tower stood, undulating double columns of steel that meshed like a screen. It gleamed silver in the new daylight, regal as a tiara. Fires blazed behind it and black smoke plumed. We passed back buckets, and larger pieces of plank and rebar by hand, and now and then there was an explosion, as air rushed into a new void and fed the fire. You would stop and stare, and then someone would tap you on the shoulder and pass back another bucket. The hours passed, and the hundred million tons of wreckage began to shift to the side, handful by handful.

There was a great blast, and the ground shook, and the facade trembled and nearly fell as the flames roared behind it. Some people broke from the line and ran back—John scrambled a few steps back—but I just stood there. It would have crushed us if it fell, but the facade shook and held. The line reformed, but then the FEMA team told us to break for a while. We joined the others off to the side, to sit and stare at the pile. I saw Billy Clune's brother, the lieutenant, and he told me that a Corrections officer had stolen watches from a jewelry store. I saw another fireman I knew, who told me that Tommy Killian was all right. We waited and watched, wondering when the bucket brigade would form up again. The cranes and cherry pickers and earth movers rumbled on; it seemed like there would be fewer opportunities for the digging to go on by hand, and still less point to it. No one had been rescued from the collapse, but some had been hurt in the recovery. We'd been at work nearly twenty-four hours. The bucket brigade fell into line again, but we went home.

At work, we stayed in the office, in uniform, awaiting the summons. As the hours passed, we pulled out cases and began to type up fives from our notes. If we couldn't work, we might as well work. It was fitful and half-hearted, but it had to be done. If you had a gun stuck in your face in August, it was going to wait a while, but not forever, and doing anything was better than nothing.

There were no casualties among my family or closest friends. Steve Rodriguez had made it: his wife had left the building, which had collapsed before he was able to get inside; he was knocked back by the collapse to wander blindly in the blizzard of ash. Mike Rodriguez had injured his knee, and he would be eventually forced to retire. Rocco Farella, who had gone with them, said that you could only recognize cops by the silhouette of gunbelt and nightstick. My brother Steve's best friend, Dave McGovern, had gone from the NYPD to the FDNY, as many cops had. As he struggled out of the rubble, a falling body killed the fireman next to him, a partner from his house. That's what we heard; Dave didn't talk about it.

People I'd known for twenty years had died, like Mike Armstrong. Mike had given me a job as a doorman the summer after my father died—his father was the super of a building on Fifth Avenue—and the Armstrongs had a St. Patrick's Day party every year. Mike worked at Cantor Fitzgerald, the company that had the largest number of casualties that day—their offices were just above where the first plane hit. There were guys from my high school, Matt Leonard, Greg Trocchi. And others I'd known less long but fairly well, like Dennis Mulligan. Mulligan was a cop who became a fire-fighter, and he'd gone out for years with McTigue's twin sister, Kerry. At his wake, my old Narcotics team had shown up—I hadn't known that Mulligan's brother was a sergeant in Narcotics as well. My sister Marianne called me in tears about Mulligan; she had dated a fireman in his house, and they were friends. There was Bronco and Tom Foley, firemen I'd met through Tommy Killian. Of the other three hundred forty-three firemen, I'd look at their faces in the thumbnail-sized newspaper ID photos and wonder how many I'd recognize instantly in life. I did recognize the O'Hagan brother; I'd met him. Among the cops, I knew their faces better—Driscoll and Coughlin and the other Bronx ESU cops, and Mike Curtin, a sergeant in ESU in Brooklyn. My cousin Mark, an emergency-room doctor at Bellevue, had worked with Curtin as part of the FEMA Rescue and Recovery team in Oklahoma City, and he told me about how Curtin searched through the voids, making sure that all the bodies were removed with ceremony and dignity.

You heard the rumors: there might be six thousand dead, seven. Three Arabs in a van filled with explosives had been stopped by the NYPD on the West Side Highway, or on the New Jersey Turnpike by troopers, or just before they made the George Washington Bridge by the FBI. My friend Cahill's wife, Renee, called me, overjoyed, to say that she heard that cops trapped in a pocket had shot their guns to summon aid, and then she called me in tears to say that they had committed suicide. What had happened—if anything, I guessed—was that the rounds went off in the heat. Letters laced with anthrax began to arrive in offices, killing more, and you heard rumors about that, too.

You began to hear the stories about the near-misses and the hideous coincidences: one woman who was fired the Friday before, another who had quit, but had come in that day to clean out her desk. The man who had the week off because his wife had just had twins, but he needed to collect some papers to work from home. The other man who worked where the plane struck, but who was in the lobby when it hit, cursing at an obnoxious security guard who made him come down and sign for a delivery. Every casualty seemed to have a cruel twist: they had just gotten engaged or married, their wives had just gotten pregnant or given birth, they had finally gotten a promotion, or a dream job in a company on an upper floor.

The days were still beautiful and limpid, but the F-16s made the air shudder as they circled the city, and the smoke still rose from downtown. We waited and watched, and our part was not long in coming. We were to go to the Fresh Kills landfill in Staten Island, which had been the city dump until it was shut down two years before. "Kills" is from a Dutch word for "stream," but no one needed to point out the irony. It was a man-made mountain of trash, foul-smelling and besieged by thousands of gulls. The refuse would be trucked in from Ground Zero to the landfill, and we would pick through it for body parts, the black boxes, and other evidence. A city bus brought us from Simpson Street in the late afternoon, and as we went out over the George Washington Bridge, I gasped to see planes flying, commercial jets taking off from Newark. They were big and slow and close, and I hadn't seen one since before the eleventh, when I might not have noticed. I gasped again on the bridge, where a vast American flag was draped between spans. It was larger than the sails of the largest tall ship from the summer, and it moved weightily in the wind, and when it snapped it sounded like a cannon. As we drove south down the turnpike, whoever wasn't facing east got a soft elbow in the ribs, and a nod, a tilt of the head—no one said anything—to take in the sight of the new skyline, the city that had been remade. Manhattan itself is like a skyscraper, tall and narrow and ascending to a point. The Twin Towers seemed to pin down the toe of the island, to fasten it to the earth when it might lift off altogether, out of carelessness or pride. As we looked out the window, a pillar of smoke and fire had replaced them on the horizon, a terrible and temporary monument.

The bus driver was from the Bronx and didn't know the area, but one cop was from Staten Island and he directed us to the dump. We crossed back over the bridge to New York and left the highway on a gravel road that led up to the great plateau of trash, which loomed like a fortress in the declining afternoon light. The bus ground through the gravel and lumbered through the potholes, and at the entrance to the landfill, a gray-haired woman in a raincoat held up a sign that said GOD BLESS YOU. Our bus followed a dump truck up the hill and over the plateau, which had lots the size of football fields for the debris, and lights on stanchions, and, at the far end, a scattering of trailers and windblown olive drab tents. The wind was constant and the air was rank. We got out of the bus by the trailers, one an NYPD command post, the other for the FBI. To the left was the Statue of Liberty, unchanging in its pose of vigilance and welcome; ahead of us, across the harbor, was the Battery and the tragic aspect of lower Manhattan; above us was a sky that to the east was a deepening violet and in the west, orange as fire. A tattered flag that had been recovered from the rubble was strung between tents, lashing in the wind.

This was history, I knew, as much history as my home had seen since the Civil War. I had a disposable camera and I snapped a picture. A captain approached me and whispered not to do that again—"A chief saw a cop do that, and he almost fired him on the spot. This is a crime scene." I waited till he left and snapped another, though the light had gone. A group of FBI agents posed in front of the flag, and an official photographer took some shots of them. The gulls whirled and called raucously overhead. One tent was for recovered FDNY equipment, and it housed a loose array of helmets and boots, tools and bunker gear; in another were a few damp cardboard boxes, marked VALUABLES and IDENTIFIABLES, with a few wet twenties in one and a growing heap of credit cards and licenses in the other. There was a supply tent and a mess tent and a trailer for the Medical Examiner. Sometimes it looked like a military outpost and sometimes it looked like a mining camp.

We wore white Tyvek suits—a thin plasticized-paper coverall—along with hard hats, goggles, surgical masks, work gloves, and rubber boots. We looked otherwise, like men from space, or men who were going there. Were there a hundred of us, or two hundred? It was hard to tell. Most of us were NYPD detectives, since the chief was correct, at least, in calling it a crime scene, and as such it was the responsibility of the Detective Bureau. There were also FBI and Customs agents, Port Authority police, and a variety of volunteers; some had their commands written on the back of their suits in magic marker. There were racks of picks, rakes, hoes, and shovels, and we grabbed our tools of choice and spread out over the piles.

At first, there appeared to be little order. The fields were long and broad, and there weren't enough lights. The well-lit areas were searched over and over, while the dark areas went unexamined. Dump trucks rolled in and unloaded more wreckage, and bulldozers scraped the fields clean, and the little people in white suits scampered out of the way of the monstrous machines, sometimes with seconds to spare. Goggles blocked our view, and the grinding roar of the engines was deafening; we could hardly see or hear anything coming, as we picked through the rubble like gulls. Sometimes you were picking away when you felt a slap on the shoulder, and a figure in white, masked and goggled and helmeted, shouted something you couldn't understand. And then more shouting, and a hand was pointed at an oncoming earth mover, thirty feet high, and you ran off to the side. You didn't know if they saw you; they didn't seem to slow down. Sometimes you were that figure, shouting, slapping, pointing, to someone else on their knees in the debris fields, and they ran off behind you. I stuck with John and Bobby Nardi, and there was a lot of that, watching your back as you picked through the rubble, as the convoys rolled in from the city, with what once had been the city on their backs. In a few hours, a loose sense of organization took hold, and instead of drifting across fields like migrant workers, teams of a dozen formed around each new load as it was spilled out on the ground. A bulldozer would spread it out, clearing the larger pieces of metal and concrete, and then we would clamber into the pile and pick through it by hand.

There was everything there, and nothing. The dirt wasn't even dirt; not earth, but a blend of ash and dust—concrete walls, wooden desks, the people who sat behind them—broken, burnt and hosed down. The largest pieces of structural steel were deposited off to the side, but twenty-foot sections of I-beams and concrete boulders the size of cars arrived on the trucks. There were little things that had survived and big things that hadn't, and there was a sense of the miraculous and the—what? the counter-miraculous? The steel head of a hammer seemed to be attached to a head of human hair, wavy, greasy, and gray, fanning out like an old-fashioned feather duster. What was this? I lifted it to show the mutant next to me, in the practiced pantomime of the deafening, silent piles: shoulder shrug—*What?*—pointing—*This?* It was a freakish crossbreed, half-hammer, half-wig. The goggle-man lifted his mask to yell, "Fiberglass handle! Heat on fiberglass handle!"

There were a lot of bones. There were yards and yards of fire hose. There was white metal from the hulls of the planes. There was a Toyota, mashed flat. A lot of single shoes. There were all kinds of documents, some in perfect condition, from Cantor Fitzgerald, Blue Cross Blue Shield, Aon. I found the personnel file for an Irish Williams, with a reprimand for being late in June 1992. I hoped Irish Williams was late on September 11. All the warranties and guarantees, limited liabilities, risk assessments—had they been voided? All the projections, conditions, and contracts, the paper that is to the corporation what coral is to the reef, just as monumental, just as fragile. For a while, I came across a lot of little yellow pebbles, and I'd always stop when I saw them, because they looked like teeth. We had white plastic five-gallon drums, and we filled them with bones. You got a feel for them, and after a while you - could tell them from plastic molding or wooden sticks, but to be certain, you would break them. They had a certain give, unlike cable or a dowel. It felt sacrilegious at first, but it saved time.

When we broke for meal, we were starving, and we stripped off our muddied Tyveks. We were soaked to the skin with sweat. There was another tent full of T-shirts, sweatshirts, and socks, and I changed clothes several times that night. At first, the only supplies they had were hard candies, packets of butter cookies, and Salvation Army coffee, which required faith to drink. Firemen arrived, with vanloads of hot food—pizza, lasagna, sandwiches— and we looked at each other with gratitude and pity: they were sorry for us, because we had to dig, and we were sorry for them, because of what we dug out. The firemen laid out the food for us and left for the tent with their gear, tenderly cradling recovered boots and helmets as if they were infants. We went back into the fields.

At the end of the night, we filed back into the buses, exhausted. I looked out over the fields, with the pole lights and the convoys, the cranes and bull-dozers shifting and spreading the remains of sixteen acres of city across the foul, muddy ground. I thought, this is where the world goes, after the world ends. We all fell asleep, and woke to find that the bus driver had gotten lost.

We slept again, and woke in the Bronx. At home, John and I spent half an hour trying to yank our rubber boots off, falling back like stooges. I boiled myself in the shower for half an hour, but I could still smell the dump.

• • •

THAT DAY BLENDED WITH MANY AFTER, ARRIVING JUST before sunrise or dawn, for brilliant twilight hours of purple and golden skies before they turned bright or dark. F-16s in pairs and trios patrolled from the air. The Statue of Liberty held a torch, and the city still burned. I stopped to watch a single silver hearse creep down the road, wondering why there was only one. Helicopters descended from the air, and the roar of the rotors as they set down outmatched the roar of the trucks. For one helicopter, we were called in to hear a speech. A captain spoke with a bullhorn that barked and squealed, but when he turned it off, most of us couldn't hear him. There were cynical grumbles from some people—*I don't need the "Attaboy," let me work or send me home*—but I wanted to hear what was said, and I pushed to the front. The Captain introduced Barry Mawn, head of the New York office of the FBI, and Mary Jo White, U.S. Attorney from the Southern District. Barry Mawn had a heavy Boston accent, and he looked a little like my father, silver-haired and solid. He said that the casualty count was now estimated to be seven thousand eight hundred people, and that he had worked airplane crashes before—it might have been Flight 007, but the bullhorn brayed again—yet this would be much harder, very different, and mostly ours. I couldn't catch much of what Mary Jo White said, but the theme seemed to be "Thank you." Others came to the site, in SUVs—this commissioner, that chief—sometimes to speak, and sometimes just to see it, and the reception was always polite but mixed; there was always something awkward about them. Sometimes we had to stop when they came, and sometimes we didn't, but they would drive away or fly, clean and warm, and we would return to the mud to dig for corpses. *Next time, bring a six-pack. . . .*

You might go to the landfill with one or two guys from the Squad, or you fell in with a group of eight or ten other detectives, to join a sergeant's detail roster. You looked around for people you knew. I worked one day with Mike Donnelly, whom I'd met when I was in SNEU and he was in HIDTA, an NYPD-Federal task force. He was in Bronx Homicide now. He'd known Uncle Eddie at the Four-Seven and was nearing retirement himself. He was with his sergeant, named Duggan, and I jumped on their roster. I asked Sgt. Duggan if he had a brother named Kevin who went to Regis High School. He said that he did. I'd seen Kevin last at a steak house, where I was out with friends, and Kevin had proposed to his wife.

"How's he doing now? Still working in construction?"

"No, he went on the Fire Department a couple of years ago."

I waited a second. "Is he okay?"

"Yeah, he's okay."

The Homicide guys talked about the smell, which was sour from the methane bubbling up from the ground, as well as from the carnage that had been trucked over from Manhattan.

"It's bad here, but not too bad," said one.

"Not as bad as it gets," another agreed.

Mike looked at me and said, "The really bad smell you get from a body, the real putrescence, is from the gas buildup, which makes the body swell. When it pops, it's real bad. But these bodies, well, most of 'em aren't going to be whole, so at least you won't get that. At least mostly, I think."

We watched as the gulls circled like vultures and dropped down on a spot on the ground, fiercely picking. One guy stepped forward, and another, and we broke into a run, waving our arms, to chase them away. The birds had descended on what could only be described as a hemisphere of meat, wet and gray. We stood over it and peered down, speculating. It wasn't a brain: it was smooth tissue, unpatterned, and it was too big, almost the size of half a volleyball.

"I think it's an ass cheek," I said.

"I think you're right."

Someone flipped it onto a piece of cardboard with a stick and carried it over to the Medical Examiner's trailer. When the gulls descended again in another spot, fifty yards away, we ran after them again, waving, but as they alit they tore apart a strip of cloth, and there was no body to be seen. We - couldn't have them there, eating people, but they had their uses, too, like pointers on a hunt. A few days later, Danny Mullarkey, who was on the B Team, told me that a falcon had been brought to the landfill, perched in its hood on the falconer's gloved hand. The falconer walked out toward where the gulls whirled and dipped, and then he unleashed the leather hood from the bird and released it. It shot out in a long, low, and direct line of flight, scattering the flock like a shot. From there, it ascended in a widening arc and circled the sky above the landfill, like a guardian spirit. The gulls fled and - didn't return, and we never saw them again in such numbers.

The night with Mike Donnelly, I found novelty dice, the kind of jokey knickknack that someone had kept on his desk. Each side bore a line—"Go out with friends," "Work out," "See a movie"—with advice to stop and enjoy life, to seize the day. I tapped Mike on the shoulder and showed it to him. He looked through his goggles and nodded. And then I rolled it on the ground, and the side that came up said, "Take the day off." Mike and I pulled off our masks and stepped aside, and we sat down on the generator for a cigarette. We looked at it again: *Take the day off.*

"Poor bastard," said Mike.

"Maybe he did take the day off."

Mike smiled and slapped me on the shoulder.

The cadaver dogs began to move through the piles, young German shepherds, light-footed over the scrap metal, almost dancing as they sniffed. One had a hit beneath a sheet of white metal that I realized was part of the hull of a plane. The dog lay flat and barked. I lifted it up, hesitating. Would I find a face there? One had just been found thirty yards over, hanging like a rind on half a skull. I didn't want to and yet I did, because it meant that part of someone would go home. I lifted the metal up and the dog sniffed below, and the handler pulled it back. I threw the metal away and got on my knees with a flashlight, sifting through the rubble. Rags, sticks, rocks, twisted little broken things, but no one, or nothing that had been part of anyone, that could be seen. We looked at the dog accusingly, as if she'd lied, and she whined. And then I realized that there might not be any body part to see, but that there were people everywhere, or a broad effluent of humanity that permeated the fields. A while later, another dog hit on me, pointing and barking. I waved it away: *Get out of here! I'm not dead yet, I only smell like it.*

As time went on, the landfill developed into a more permanent encampment, with long tents shaped like onion domes built over steel frames, and trailers and sheds for the mess tent and the decontamination station. The tents were covered inside with cards from schoolchildren, mostly decorated with hearts, stars, and flags, though some drew crying faces, or figures leaping from an inferno. In addition to the piles, there were details for the grapplers and the sifters. The grappler was a crane with a claw appendage, which would pick out large pieces of metal and strew them on a field, and then we would look through them. The grappler took almost an hour to lay out the pieces, and it took ten minutes to walk through them. I didn't like that; I was bored, and I froze standing there. I huddled by the light generator, and burned a hole in the ass of my Tyvek suit. The sifter was better: you stood along one of two belts that ran from a central funnel, which dumped debris through two grades of screen. Each belt carried out rubble, and we stood at the sides like an assembly line, snatching out items as they rolled past. It was hypnotic at first, and then it was dizzying.

The operation became more regimented and efficient, week by week, even as the first wave of emotion passed, and the unison of shock and rage and sorrow was tempered by cold and exhaustion. Though most of us worked with little rest and less complaint, pettiness inspired pettiness, in thought if not in act. You did notice that some people didn't seem to leave the mess tent for the entire tour, and there were rumors that some had snuck away early. We drove our own cars to the site at first, but after a few weeks we had to park in a lot down below, where we were taken up in Department of Corrections buses. The top of the site was a sea of rock and mud, and it was terrible for your car, but I'd also heard that the bosses were concerned that people were stealing rakes. Bobby Nardi said that one boss gave a speech before the tour, berating people for taking pictures, and suggesting that it wasn't cops who took rakes, but volunteers. Bobby was disgusted: "These people had come on their own time, from Ohio or Florida, to spend their vacations digging for the dead. What harm would come from a picture? Would the word get out that the towers came down?" For me, the no-car rule was exasperating—you didn't know whether you'd sweat in the piles or freeze at the grappler, and if I brought my car, I could change clothes, bring my own food, and read on the breaks. I wasn't going to ride like an inmate on the prison bus, and I just drove past the cops who guarded the entrance. Sometimes they yelled or hit the siren, but I just kept going; I figured they wouldn't chase me, and they didn't. I always felt elated when I went past, in my petty, private rebellion, a guilty thrill as if I'd robbed a bank. I found a teddy bear in the pile, wearing a red T-shirt from the International Organization of Operation Engineers, with the slogan *Labor Omnia Vincit*. Labor conquers all.

· · ·

WHEN WE DIDN'T WORK, WE SLEPT, AND FOR WEEKS IT seemed we did not sleep. But the sleeplessness accounted for a small part of the bewildering loss of proportion, the confusion of purpose: Was our duty to the dead, or the living? Which victims would we tend to? Aside from the landfill, there were other details: traffic posts, Yankee games for the playoffs and then the World Series. Sometimes we had one day a week to work on our cases, and the cases kept coming in. It was not long before the perps tired of watching patriotic television and returned to the business of stick-ups and muggings. Within days of 9/11, we had a triple shooting, the classic warm-weather ghetto bullshit, which now seemed an affront to history, or a bitter resumption of it: *If we don't get back to thug life, the terrorists will have won!* The victims were no better than the perp, who had let off rounds over drugs, or a girl, or a look, and no one was talking. Relatives raced to the hospital to remove the victims' contraband before we arrived. One victim's mother had witnessed the shooting from a window, but during the interview, the only firm opinion she expressed was that she did not want us to look in his room. I wanted to collar them all for treason. Four days after the Towers fell, I caught my first commercial robbery.

John and Danny had gone to Queens on another case that Saturday afternoon, and I went to the scene with Matt Crowley. Fifteen minutes before, a man walked into a travel agency off the Grand Concourse, where a woman worked alone behind the counter. It was the kind of Dominican place that provided every service that could fit into a hundred square feet: they booked flights, sold cell phones, handled money orders and wire transfers—there was even a barber chair in the back. She didn't speak English, and the perp - didn't speak Spanish, but he made himself clear, holding a gun in his waistband and stepping behind the counter. Though there was more than a thousand dollars in the cash box, he pulled the gun on her and said, "Is that all there is?" He seemed uncertain, confused; he stepped back from the counter to try to close the roll-down gate, trapping them both inside, and then he stood there for a moment, with an apologetic air, and left. Ordinarily, there would have been plenty of Spanish-speaking cops around, but we had to piece together phrases of two broken languages to try to put together a story—

"*Qué color?*"

"*Blanco.*"

"He was white?"

"No, *como,* like white."

"Light-skinned?"

"*Sí,* I think you say."

"Was he Spanish? Dominican? Boricua? *Habla él español o inglés?*"

"*No, blanco.*"

"He spoke white?"

"*Sí.*"

No one on the street had seen him leave, and we canvassed with her, without success. There were no cameras in the store, and the patrol sector would wait until Evidence Collection came, to see if there were fingerprints to lift. She couldn't come with us to view pictures, she said, but she would make an appointment later on. The woman was twenty years old, months in the country and weeks at the job, terrified by the robbery and frustrated by us— by the language barrier, and the dunning dullness of investigative procedure, the waiting, watching, testing, the same questions, over and over, five different ways, when all she wanted to do was go home and collapse. In Saudi Arabia, they cut off the hands of thieves, and at moments I felt the policy had merit.

There were times when the "old Job" and the new circumstances did touch upon each other, albeit obliquely. At John's cab shooting from August, a beeper was left at the scene. He tracked it down to a particular store, and we went to interview the owner, who was from Yemen. He looked nervous when we entered. We asked him if he'd had any problems with people since 9/11, and he said that he hadn't. We showed him the beeper and he looked it up on the computer. There could be a problem, he said. Ordinarily, when a customer buys a cell phone, they deal directly with the company, filling out an application with pedigree and credit information. But he bought beepers in bulk, and he took in monthly fees from customers who might only have a first name, and no phone number—the computer might show only whether the account was current. This beeper had belonged to an Arlene, with no last name, and it had been deactivated. But that beeper was one of eight bought for different women by a certain "Don Q." The store owner didn't even want to say the name, but rather pointed out all of Don Q's girls on the computer screen. "He's a pimp?" Looking around nervously, he told us all he remembered about Don Q—an approximate last name, his brother's name, and so on.

When we left, we wondered how we had benefitted from recent events in that interview. In uniform and out, I'd made a point of buying newspapers and cigarettes from Arab stores, and asked if they'd been given any trouble; all had said no. The owner had been exceptionally helpful, perhaps at some risk to himself—Don Q, we later found out, sold guns as well as girls—but there was also something suspect in how much he knew. When I last bought a beeper, the store owner might have guessed I was a cop, but he certainly - didn't know my brothers' names. Regardless, we now had a solid lead for the shooting, and the Yemenite store owner, along with all of our Arab concerns, receded for a moment beside the new and eager hope for a collar.

For me, at least, one benefit of the endlessness of the days was that I soon felt as if I'd worked with my new partners for years. In the beginning, Eddie McDonald, John Swift, and Chris Perino had been unfailingly helpful, hovering over John and me to look over our paperwork and answer our countless questions. Steve Rodriguez would say, "Don't think like a cop, think like a defense lawyer." For shootings and homicides, the whole team went out, Norbie Tirado and Matt Crowley, who had come from Street Crime, Danny Mullarkey and Jose Morales, Bobby D'Amico and Bobby Nardi. Morales and Mullarkey were a study in contrast: Jose was coolly disciplined, a former Marine sniper and Gulf War veteran, whose heavy-lidded eyes and deep voice added to his sense of watchful reserve; Mullarkey was a firecracker and the office troublemaker. His caffeine intake was closely monitored, as was his spit cup for his chewing tobacco, which often looked dangerously full. When someone slept over in the dorm, Mullarkey liked to pose them with the teddy bear from Domestic Violence and snap a picture. Bobby D'Amico was so meticulous and professional that the joke was that when he closed a case, the perp's whole family pleaded guilty. D'Amico, who had spent his entire career in the Four-Four, served as almost another sergeant in the office. Bobby Nardi had just reached his twenty-year mark that fall, but he had no intention of retiring. He saw being a detective as a vocation. "I think being an astronaut would be a better job, maybe," he said. "But other than that, I can't think of anything. Is there a greater responsibility than catching a killer?" Sometimes, Bobby said he wouldn't retire until all of his homicides were closed. He talked about movies a lot, which many cops seem to, maybe because they have to picture things and figure out a story. He said to me, "Do you remember Al Pacino in *Heat,* when he says he dreams at night of a dinner party full of all his unsolved homicides, and they stare and him, eyes black from eight-ball hemorrhages? It's not like that, at least not for me, but you could tell he talked to homicide detectives. You do sleep better after a collar, and you sleep really well after a conviction. It's like, 'Rest in peace,' for both of you."

Everyone had a useful story, whose moral seemed to be to stick to it, and ask questions, and don't be surprised because you'll always be surprised. There were things you could do, and things you couldn't, and things you - could try, where time would tell. Bobby Nardi had worked for Jack Maple, the architect of Compstat and much else, when they were in Transit; in tough spots, he said, he often asked himself, "What would Jack do?" Maple would bring a chaise longue to a perp's door, so he could wait him out; he also devised a chain-snatch trap for decoys, so the "sleeping drunk" cop had his chain attached by fishing line to a wig, and the cops could follow the chain-snatcher through the crowd, once they stopped laughing. Bobby D'Amico explained that you could lie during interrogations—"We have your fingerprints on the knife!"—but you couldn't lie with a prop; you couldn't type up a report that said, "Positive identification of fingerprints to Joe Perp." In a case that had been overturned on appeal, he said, detectives had invented a "lying machine," assembled from a salad bowl attached by wires to a photocopier, which had a piece of paper with the word "LIE" on it. When the suspect was brought in for interrogation, the salad bowl was placed on his head, for the machine to read his thoughts: "Okay, Joe, say your name is John."

"My name is John . . ."

A detective pressed the COPY button. *Click:* LIE.

"See? This machine never fails. Say your name is Jim."

"My name is—" *Click:* LIE.

"Okay. When I ask your name, tell the truth . . ."

After the response, the detective at the copier simply didn't press the button. Joe saw the futility of fighting the system, and confessed to the murder. But the higher courts felt that he was taken advantage of, and I see the wisdom of their decision. *Click:* LIE.

Early in his career, D'Amico caught a suicide, a young man who hanged himself, which appeared to be a routine tragedy until he received a call from the Four-Seven saying that the girlfriend was missing, too. There was a downpour, and as he and his partner waited in the car, reluctant to re-invade a house in mourning, a young man rode up on a bicycle and said that the suicide had said to him last week, "What if I told you I killed my girlfriend and buried her under my bedroom floor?" They returned to the house and the devastated family to check the bedroom. A rug covered a plywood floor, which had one section fastened with new screws. After calling a captain and ESU, they broke apart the plywood and the oak floor underneath, and then they dug down two feet through dirt. The captain was embarrassed, the family was horrified, and the room looked like a coal mine. "Are you sure you want to go on?" asked the captain. "Just a little further," Bobby said, and after another foot, they hit concrete. It was the body of the girl, entombed. The boy believed that she had given him AIDS, and as he had sex with her one last time, he strangled her. Then he buried her in his room. The next day, he took his own life.

Bobby Nardi caught a homicide when a young white drug addict from the suburbs named Guy was dumped at a hospital with a fatal stab wound. A hospital cop caught the license plate, and it was traced back to another white junkie, who said that they had come into the city to buy drugs. Though they - didn't have any money, Guy knew a dealer named Snake who he thought would give them credit. At Snake's place, Guy patted him on the head to show his friend how cool he was with his ghetto dealer. "I ain't no fucking cat," said Snake, stating the obvious. Guy continued, and Snake stabbed him with a broken broomstick, and both junkies staggered out. Bobby and Danny Mullarkey made their way to Snake's house and asked him if he knew Guy. Snake said matter-of-factly that they'd recently had a fight, and agreed to accompany them to the precinct. As they left, Bobby noticed something odd about how Snake walked, and he asked politely, "Are you blind?" When Snake said yes, Bobby said, "You could hear the air leak out of Mullarkey's body. It was the only time I ever saw him speechless. Snake said it was self-defense, I wrote a statement for him and he signed it. I've never heard of a blind man charged with murder, let alone one who signed a confession. When he testified at the Grand Jury, the jurors' mouths dropped open the minute he walked in, and they stayed open as they sent him right back home."

D'Amico and Nardi had decades of experience; for Scanlon and Morales, the Four-Four was their backyard; and though Mullarkey had come from Street Crime only two years before, he knew it almost as well as they did, through sheer drive. The three of them knew every major case in the office, and they ping-ponged names and theories with headachy speed:

"Rocco's hommie, I hear it's T-Money, he's lucky the Jamaicans didn't find him."

"I heard Baby Blood was involved, he had some kind of grudge."

"Nah, Baby Blood's all about the West Side."

"Didn't he have a beef with Mike Murder?"

"Nah, not Mike Murder, just 'Murder,' a guy from the West Side."

"What about West Side? He's in or out?"

"He's in for a hommie, but in Pennsylvania . . ."

They knew the people, and they knew the job, and when a case broke, they fell to it with the avid and total, face-to-the-ground focus of a pack of bloodhounds. At times I felt like a happy mutt who had fallen in with them, believing we were chasing a Frisbee. I barked gamely and ran alongside, wondering when the "fetch" part would begin. But ignorance is not bliss for a detective, and there were cases in which I chased my tail so fiercely that had I caught it, I would have torn it out by the root.

In October, John and I responded to a robbery at a parking lot in a mall. A twenty-one-year-old gofer named Jasper had been sent to the bank with eleven thousand dollars in receipts and had been jumped. Or so he claimed. When I asked him what had happened, he blinked and moaned, as if he were unable to speak, unable even to understand the questions, and he retreated hastily to the hospital. Prior to his case of the vapors, his story was that as he walked through a hallway, an unseen assailant snuck up on him, punched him in the head, grabbed the money, and ran off. The hallway was twenty paces from the office, but instead of returning, he proceeded to the end of the hallway, up a long flight of stairs to the street-level lot, and then all the way to the back of the mall to report the theft to the security office. He acted like he'd gone ten rounds with Mike Tyson but looked as if he'd overslept on a hard pillow: he had the faintest swelling on the cheek, and a half-inch scratch on the jaw. Jasper had been arrested twice for robbery, and he'd recently finished parole. It was a plain lie and a bad story, but up to a point, it was the perfect crime.

And Jasper's story was only the first negative to disprove. The "robbery" had taken place in a hallway between two video cameras, but there was no tape. The guard who monitored the cameras was a woman named Keisha, who happened to be Jasper's close friend. She made a great show of pressing buttons and pulling tapes, first handing us a cassette of month-old footage, before trying to insist the recorder was broken, when it was working perfectly. Ray, the manager of the parking lot, was equivocal: after telling us that Jasper was lazy, dishonest, and about to be fired, he realized it looked bad for him to hand so much cash to a criminal, and became guarded in his statements. Another employee, Caroline, later whispered to me that Ray had told everyone not to talk to the cops, and that Jasper had talked about stealing the money for weeks. Caroline was a complainant in another case at the parking lot, in which a couple in a car had robbed her, she said, because she was too slow in changing a hundred-dollar bill. That video was of terrible quality, and the camera was pointed too high to catch the plate; several other employees even suggested that Caroline had concocted that story. We knew it was Jasper, but did he do it with Keisha? Or even Ray, or Caroline? Or with someone else? I could have asked them, I suppose. I did try.

I asked the management company not to fire Jasper or Ray, but they said they had to fire Jasper, not least because he'd lied about his criminal record. The security company laid off Keisha, for unrelated reasons. When Jasper came into the precinct the next day, he couldn't even tell a straight story about where he'd slept the night before: he was at his house, but really at his girlfriend's, but not really at his girlfriend's, because he'd left before going to sleep . . . but I didn't get to ask him about much else, because I was sent out to man a vehicle checkpoint at Yankee Stadium twenty minutes later. And I never got another shot at him: a lawyer called to say he wouldn't answer any more questions. The first time I brought Keisha into the office, I had to take her right back to work, as a threatening letter closed down the precinct with an anthrax scare. The next time we talked, we spoke for hours, and against all expectations, I came away convinced of her innocence; she agreed to tape a phone call to Jasper, though he wasn't home. It occurred to me that Jasper might have set up the robbery between the cameras anticipating that his actions would be recorded, and the absence of videotape was an accidental benefit. The more we talked with Caroline, the more we doubted her sanity: on one occasion, she said that a woman had written down the plate number of the car in her earlier robbery, and that she had it on a scrap of paper at home. She'd had it for weeks, but she'd forgotten to tell us. When we drove her to Manhattan to get it, her daughter said, "Oh, *that* piece of paper, Mommy? I threw it out last night, when I cleaned the kitchen. . . ."

On the day I left Jasper's interview for a vehicle checkpoint, I thought about how to handle things. I wanted to throttle him for his mock-innocent pose and his pissy little fibs, and for the fact that as most of the city wept and helped and prayed, he was plotting a phony stick-up. But mostly I hated him because he was a second-rate hoodlum with a second-rate scam, and it looked in all likelihood as if he'd outsmart me. I wanted time to work this one, and time was the last thing I had. How long ago had it been, when I was brooding about the lack of intensity at work? Two months before, a collar might require ten words for charges to be brought: "At T/P/O defendant was in possession of a controlled substance." *The Squad is the Job, Eddie, hurry up and come here.* Thanks, McCabe. With all these details, we couldn't do cases; the perps didn't wait for us, the complainants didn't understand, and the Job didn't care.

• • •

THE CASES KEPT COMING IN, SOMETIMES THREE AND FOUR a day. You read through the complaint, hoping that the facts offered imme- diate promise—a named or known perp, a distinctive description, a plate number or other viable evidence—or that they foreclosed on effort from the outset: an arrest had been made by patrol, or the complainant couldn't ID. Every robbery complaint, open or closed, became a case in the RAM. Some - could be closed by simply reiterating the facts on the complaint, but the stan- dards were constantly being raised before a case could be closed: reinterview the complainant to make sure he can't ID, recanvass the area to make sure there were no witnesses. The worst were the complainants who said they wanted to pursue the case but didn't; they made appointments to come in but never showed, and then they assured you they would come in the next time. When you called them, you found their phones had been disconnected, if they even had phones, and then you had to go to their homes to try to talk to them, repeatedly, before you could send a case-closing letter, C-3, uncoop- erative complainant. If they moved without telling you, you had to call the post office to try to get a forwarding address. You couldn't make the visits alone, and the B Team was fortunate to have the extra man, so that if one of us needed a few hours to type up paperwork, we could still go out in the field. I had to agree with the ex-boyfriend of one crackhead complainant who'd gone missing, when he told me with disdain, "This is a whole big bunch of unbelievable!"

"If it isn't on a five, it didn't happen," we were told. Everything had to be documented, and if you interviewed three different people at the scene of a robbery, you had to type three different fives, each headed by names, dates, and numbers. And I do mean type, on a long pink triplicate form, with carbon- paper backs. Errors were not correctable on the back two copies, one of which went into the case file, and few were not marred with typos. If you closed your eyes when you walked into the Squad, it sounded like a 1940s movie set in a newsroom—*tap-tap, tap-tap-tap . . . Get me the City Desk, Lepke Buchalter just broke out of Sing Sing!* We may have been the only police department north of Tijuana that still ran on carbon paper and typewriters. The air con- ditioning never worked, and on hot days, the fans sent unattended fives flut- tering like autumn leaves. When we got days off again, I didn't have a day off that I didn't work on cases at home, because there was so little time for work at work.

The lousy cases swamped the good ones, and both were both swamped by details, and John and Danny might have theirs on different days from mine, and I might not have anyone to go out with, as the Squad was equally swamped. The volume of work was overwhelming—we would have more than a thousand robberies that year—and I was brand-new, and we were at war. Robberies were often harder to solve than homicides, the Squad guys told me, because most killers know their victims, whereas the large majority of robberies occur between utter strangers. The administrative epilepsy of the Job added to the chaos: Sgt. Adler was informed one day that he had been transferred to Special Victims, as Sex Crimes was now known; he was not particularly worried, as he had been transferred four times in the last year, and each time it had been rescinded, but this time it stuck. He was replaced by Sgt. Mike Guedas, who had been in the Four-O. Guedas was similarly surprised by the move, as he'd been transferred from Narcotics a few weeks before.

In spite of everything, I learned how a case broke: someone said something, someone left something, someone saw something. None of these occurred at the behest of the detective. Few perps were as accommodating as the man who choked and robbed a woman on the street and was trying to drag her into an alley when a Good Samaritan intervened, driving him off. The perp dropped some papers, which included a snapshot of himself, and a note with his address that said, "Directions to my house." It was Danny's case, and he was pleased with it.

"Get over yourself," I told him, "Scooby-Doo could have solved this one."

Information often did surface, over time, when another perp hoped to trade his way out of trouble, but you couldn't clear your desk and wait for it. You evaluated each scene for video, fingerprints, or DNA, in descending order of likelihood, and asked about traceable items taken, most often a cell phone or credit card. Though more and more stores have security cameras installed, perhaps one in five provided usable footage. Some of them never worked, and the merchants hoped the mere sight of them would deter thieves, like a "Beware of Dog" sign; others didn't have recorders and were used only to watch for shoplifters in the back aisles. Many reused the same tape every day for months, so that the faces were like the image on the Shroud of Turin, and were just as haunting, and just as unhelpful. For one bodega robbery, I had what appeared to be a tape of excellent quality, until one overexcited worker ran back for the video and mixed up the buttons on the recorder, leaving me with two seconds of robbery footage and a longer sequence of Danny, Matt Crowley, and me entering the store. Absent these possibilities—and they were absent, mostly—you showed the victim pictures. A photo hit was sufficient for arrest, but the ID had to be confirmed in a line-up. A positive identification was the most emotionally compelling evidence you could provide in a case, and if those two words—*That's him!*—were delivered with steadiness and passion, they trumped all the science in China.

We showed the victims photos on a computer, which contained pictures of all defendants arrested since 1997, when the system was introduced. Though the computer was a great improvement over the mug books, it was temperamental and glitch-ridden, but the viewers could be, too. You'd tell them to clear their mind and think back, and remind them to concentrate only on the faces, and not to focus on clothing, hairstyle, or facial hair, which could change. I had one complainant who said, "That looks like him, but no . . .the man who robbed me, he was wearing a hat." I patiently explained that when the perps were photographed in Central Booking, they had to remove their hats, and that in life, also, even the most devoted hat-wearers take them off sometimes.

"Look at the face and remember. If you want to, imagine him in a hat."

"Oh, that's him!"

If you had a specific perp in mind, you would print out a photo array, with the perp and five "fillers." If the perp had something distinctive about him— a scar on the cheek, say—you had to either find scarred fillers, or do a little cosmetology with white-out on each cheek, which might well obliterate the only thing about the perp that the victim remembered. But if you had only a general description, say, of a twenty-year-old male "white-Hispanic" who was five-eight and weighed a hundred and fifty pounds, complainants would have thousands of pictures to look through, and their eyes would grow so dull from watching that the perp could literally melt into the crowd of faces. The more you knew or could guess about a robbery, the better you could narrow it down. Wolf-pack street robberies tended to be semi-spontaneous and local, and you would run everyone of that description in the precinct, knowing that some of them had been arrested for drugs or assaults but not necessarily robberies; solo and commercial robbers were a different, more dedicated breed, and you might run everyone of the scrip who had been arrested for robbery in the borough. Transracial identifications through photos were often troublesome. If a Chinese delivery boy looked at a computer screen with six black faces, he might say, "That's them!"

If the complainant saw a resemblance to the perp in several pictures on the computer, you might print them out and have the complainant look again.

One detective suggested I have the complainant rate each on a scale of one to ten. I felt terrible for one elderly woman who didn't seem to grasp the concept. The perp had followed her to the door of her house, and as she looked for her keys, he punched her in the head and took her purse. Out of the dozens of photos I showed on the computer, she picked out ten possibles. I printed them and told her to rate them.

"Mmm . . . six."

"Okay, looks kinda like him. How about him?"

"Seven."

"A little better. This one, now."

"Nine."

"Really? You're almost definitely sure?"

She shrugged. At the next picture, she said, "Ten!"

"Ten! It's definitely him?"

"Oh, no, not at all."

"Are you more sure of the ten than the nine?"

"I wouldn't say that."

It was like she was calling out bingo; I stopped the rating system shortly thereafter.

For most robberies, a line-up had to be conducted, and it is a peculiar institution, beloved by cartoonists and screenwriters but by neither the police nor the defense. Line-ups often took hours of work, and some ADAs demanded them even when the victim couldn't ID, or the perp and victim knew each other well enough that it wasn't necessary. You got the feeling that if these ADAs were prosecutors at Nuremberg, they would have wanted six million line-ups conducted. The suspect sits with four or five fillers, who are safe from prosecution, though a detective named Brian Walsh told me that a complainant of his once picked out a filler as the perp from another mugging a week before. Line-ups were conducted at Bronx Homicide, on Simpson Street, and a man named Robert was the exclusive subcontractor for line-up filler in the borough. You would page him and say what you needed—male blacks, male Hispanics, dark-skinned or light, bearded or not—and then he'd call back in fifteen or twenty minutes with a little posse assembled, who were willing to sit for ten minutes to make ten bucks. While the arrangement was more convenient than scouring the streets, there was still a class-trip chaos in putting it together: you had only one car, and Robert and the fillers needed a ride, and the complainant usually did, and the perp always did. Robert often joined the line-up as filler—he was medium-everything, height, weight, skin—and could write a far longer book than this one about the murderers, robbers, and rapists he's sat beside, the miracle sextuplets of Simpson Street.

A detective from Bronx Homicide helped run the viewing, and Mike Donnelly, who was also on the B Team, was usually there when I went in. He led me through the procedure, which, like a lot of police paperwork, seemed tough as taxes the first time I did it, and like signing your name by the third or fourth try. Our line-ups were conducted with the subjects sitting down, with a sheet of black plastic pulled up to the chin, and wearing either baseball or ski caps, so that differences in clothing, height, and hairstyle were irrelevant. Mike told me to stand beside complainants at the glass, and to reassure them that they couldn't be seen. "It's obvious when they're afraid," Mike said. "They look from face to face, and when they see the perp, their eyes pop out of their head. You can't tell them which one to pick, obviously, but you can tell them to tell the truth, and that everything will be okay."

In the first line-ups I helped conduct, there were immediate identifications, there were thoughtful negatives, where the complainant scrutinized each face, one by one, and shook her head no, saying this one looked a little like him and that one looked a little more like him, but her perp was not there. False negatives, however, were profoundly frustrating to watch. At my first one, the complainant was so afraid that he could barely look at the photo arrays, as if the face in the picture would yell at him, *Your money or your life!* When I stood behind him for the viewing, as the blinds were raised over the mirrored window, I watched his head as he looked down the line. He paused for two or three seconds at filler one, filler two, filler three, and when he reached the suspect in position four, his head almost twisted off his neck.

"No, I don't see him."

"Take your time, look at everyone."

He glanced at one, then six before turning away again.

Other complainants were uncanny in their visual acuity. One victim, named Alec, picked out a perp in a photo array even though his identical twin brother was positioned, by chance, right next to him—they had been arrested together earlier in the summer on a drug charge. The sole difference between these genetic doubles was that one brother weighed fifteen pounds more than the other. Alec's eye was such that it properly trumped science, which could not have told the perp from his brother. In the line-up, Robert's fillers all had facial hair, while the perp was clean-shaven, and I had to cover them from the nose down. Alec could essentially see five pairs of eyes, but he chose without hesitation. There was something medieval in a line-up, like a witch-trial, but there were moments where guilt was as manifest as if the perp turned green and floated up into the air, praising Satan. "Okay, that's a positive ID."

I kept at my first case, Ethan Prescott, for weeks: he was in and out of the hospital, and I had trouble obtaining his new address from his social worker. When I finally visited him, he opened the door and looked at me without recognition.

"Ethan? How are you feeling? I'm Conlon, the cop who has your robbery case."

He thought for a moment, and said, "Sorry, I didn't . . . come in."

I wondered if he was losing his memory, and he might have been, but that didn't explain the hesitation at the door. As I followed him inside, he said, "I don't know if you knew, but I was blind in one eye before, and now, well, since I got hit, I lost eighty percent of the vision in the other eye. I have infections, I'm at the hospital all the time, I'm getting registered with the Guild for the Blind. I want to thank you for your help, but I haven't found the credit-card statement . . . you can see I'm not unpacked, and I might not be. I do appreciate you trying, but it's not the first thing on my mind right now, or the second. . . ."

When he did call me with a credit-card number, the company told me it was incomplete, thirteen digits out of the seventeen required; by the time I spoke with Ethan again, it was lost. In the meantime, the credit-card company was taken over by another, and the bank had merged as well, and I was bounced between dozens of account representatives, customer representatives, legal departments, and law-enforcement contacts. I had his name, date of birth, and Social Security number, and no one could find his account. It infuriated me because I suspected that if Ethan called asking for a hundred-dollar credit extension, every bit of information would be at hand in seconds. It was only after writing a true tearjerker of a letter to the latest company that I received an attentive response, but by that time, the account had been long canceled, and any information on where the card had last been used was gone. I checked every arrest for possession or use of a stolen credit card in New York City, but none had any relation to Ethan.

Pity and pique, they were what drove you in a case. I worked for Ethan out of compassion, and against Jasper out of pride, and a third case fell somewhere in between them, a double motive to help and to hunt. A young Dominican immigrant named Luis delivered two large pizzas (one plain, one pepperoni), a lasagna, and a large bottle of soda to an apartment where no one answered. The order had been called in by cell phone, which the pizzeria usually didn't accept, but it was a fairly large order, and it was sent out. After waiting at the apartment, Luis went back downstairs, where he was approached by five or six teenagers, one of whom had a knife. Luis remembered the biggest one, who had dark skin and cornrows and stood over six feet tall. They surrounded him and knocked him down, punching him and kicking him, and took the food. They also took his gold chain and bracelet and a walkie-talkie. When Luis returned to the pizzeria, bloody and bruised, the news of his robbery had already reached them—the perps had called on the walkie-talkie to tell them, laughing, and they called with more clever comments until closing time.

The pizzeria was the best in the neighborhood, and I'd eaten there for years. Whenever I stopped by, I asked for Luis, and we wound up talking often. He was a good guy, a hardworking immigrant who had never been in trouble, and I could see that he came to believe I would catch the people who had hurt and humiliated him. If the kids had just looked to scam a free meal, neither of us would have been especially put out, but they beat him, and took his jewelry, and called the pizzeria to cackle about it through the night. I had a decent complainant, gratuitously nasty perps, and a phone number, and I was confident I could make a collar.

I called Sam Ramer for a subpoena for the cell phone, and it came back to a Kevin Wilson, whose billing address was a small apartment building two blocks from the robbery. When I drove up with Danny, he said, "Oh God, not this building. I don't think there's anyone here who I haven't arrested. And the lady on the third floor, where we're going? The mother of all skells." I had run the building, and there were only three skells that I knew of, three brothers, Khaleed, collared for sodomizing a twelve-year-old boy and menacing a man with a shotgun; Saleem, aka Abdool, car thief and gunman; and Abdul, aka John, armed robbery. We went upstairs and knocked on the door, setting off a stampede of footsteps inside.

"You check the fire escape, I'll wait here," said Danny.

Whatever dignity a suit adds to your bearing when you enter a courtroom, it is subtracted several times over when you wear it dangling from a fire escape. But I scrambled up, ducking past the windows on the lower floors, whose residents might have been within their rights to take a shot at me. Peeking into the apartment, it was empty, as far as I could see. Eventually, a young woman answered, letting Danny in, and me after, through the window. Astonishingly, Kevin Wilson was in a back bedroom, sleeping, and his lack of flight provided some small testimony of innocence. Luis had told me that he remembered best the tall one, with dark skin and cornrows, and Kevin was that; he was also thirty-three years old, twice the estimated age of the perps. Still, it had been dark out, and Kevin looked younger than thirty-three, and no matter what, he was coming in to talk to us. We spoke sweetly and he agreed.

While Kevin might have been a first-class liar, I believed him when he professed ignorance of everything I discussed with him, including ownership of the cell phone. He was staying in the apartment as part of a large and shifting network of young men who knocked up the Mother-of-Skells' daughters, or young women who had been knocked up by her sons. Kevin hadn't even knocked up a skell-daughter himself, but he had begun to date one midway through her pregnancy. He wasn't dumb, but he was a little soft, and while he had done time for drugs, he had stayed out of trouble for more than eight years. He had stayed out of most things—jobs, permanent addresses—and the idea that he had a cell phone was flattering but unreal, as if I'd asked him where he'd parked his Porsche. As I continued to talk to him, Danny Scanlon began to call numbers from the phone records.

"Hello, this is Detective Mullarkey from the Forty-fourth Precinct," he'd say, "and we have a real situation here. We have a young man who's hurt, he's unconscious, and we need to identify him to tell his family. I'm calling numbers on his cell phone, hoping someone can tell me his name. Do you recognize this number?"

After a few tries, Danny got a fifteen-year-old girl named Jasmine, who recently got knocked up herself by the owner of the phone, whom she identified as "Sincere." And though neither Jasmine nor her mother thought highly of Sincere, who had recently dropped out of sight, they saw through the ruse and would not provide his real name. Danny did confirm that he lived at the address in question, and that he was about eighteen years old, and he seemed to get a reaction to the name Abdul. I took Kevin's picture and let him go.

When I put Kevin's picture in a photo array, Luis didn't pick him out, and I didn't expect him to. But he also didn't pick out Khaleed, Saleem aka Abdool, or Abdul aka John. Kevin was tall and dark-skinned, and Khaleed was tall and light-skinned, and the aka's were short and dark-skinned, like the other five perps that Luis said he couldn't identify. The aka's were there, I was sure, and though I could bring them in, I couldn't arrest them unless they confessed. Danny and I dropped in on Mother Skell, who claimed that her boys were traveling in various southern states. We told her we had to talk to Sincere about Jasmine, and if we could work it out, maybe her family wouldn't press charges. Mother Skell spluttered with indignation, "Why, every boy in the neighborhood was into her, dirty thing! My son had *nothin'* to do with that." She seemed relieved that we were only interested in a trifle like statutory rape, and as we left, she shook her head and said, "Some people just don't know how to raise kids. . . ."

Of the three cases, Jasper might well go down the drain, and Ethan definitely would—it was effectively over—and I was at a loss for what to do with Luis. Whether Sincere was Abdool or Abdul, I knew he was a part of it, and maybe both were, but the tall one with cornrows was the only one who stood a chance of conviction. But things turn up, unexpectedly. Some time later, I helped Ron Kress with a line-up for one of two perps who had robbed and beaten a retarded eleven-year-old, savagely, for a dollar. It took place in an apartment lobby with a video camera, and we all flinched when we watched the tape. Since I'd spent a day on the case, I knew it, and when a tip was called in saying that the other perp was in front of his building, right now, Danny and I ran out and scooped him up.

It was not a difficult interrogation. Before we could even mention the videotape, he said, "I'm sorry, I know I shouldna done it." He blamed his friend, though he was the one who had broken the kid's nose, pounding away as the kid staggered in the lobby. He was sixteen, and this would be his first adult arrest, though he admitted that he had spent three years in juvenile detention after he stabbed someone at the age of twelve. He didn't know the kid was retarded, and he became frightened, knowing that the crime was more serious than he thought.

"I'll be honest with you, this could go either way," I said. "It's your first real arrest, but the kid was beaten bad, and it's on videotape—we'll get into that later—and with a retarded kid, all bets are off. That's gonna make people mad. Maybe the judge had a retarded niece or son or brother. Maybe the judge is a retard himself! There's a lot of them!"

He nodded gravely, but the remark seemed to slip past Danny as well. The perp confided that he had a friend named Marquise who had several guns in the house. Danny had him call to say he had a job set up, the robbery of a crackhouse, and Marquise agreed without hesitation to meet with a pair of

.9s. We got a scrip of Marquise: sixteen years old, six feet tall, dark skin, corn-rows. Danny, Keith Clinton, and I staked out the location, but Marquise never showed up. I took the first perp in for a search warrant, and before dawn the next day, we took the door, but Marquise wasn't home, and neither were his guns. His room was a shrine of Bloods graffiti, and there were .38 rounds and a speed-loader in the hamper where he said the guns would be. I pressed the first perp, one last time: *C'mon, what else you got? What else did Marquise do?*

"Well, lemme see . . . there was this pizza guy, Marquise and a couple others called in an order and jumped him. . . ."

Here was my first true hunt as a bloodhound, a long pursuit over hard ground, and I'd found my man. But when I put a picture of Marquise in a photo array and took it to the pizzeria, I was told that Luis had moved back to the Dominican Republic. I should have stuck to chasing Frisbees.

Those were hard collars to lose. The easiest ones to make were the domestics, like the squirmy man whose children's mother put a razor to his neck and emptied his pockets, for "child support," she later explained, though her children had been taken away long before. Or cases that were essentially assaults, like the man whose neighbor led a crowd who stomped him and took his wallet. Both parties were Guyanese, and once I picked up the perp, I thought about letting him go—he said that the complainant had started the fight by smashing him in the face with a bottle, and he had two dozen stitches to back up the story. The complainant admitted to drinking five shots of vodka before the argument, the perp to fifteen of rum. But the complainant had five children and no arrests, while the perp had no children and several felonies. Finally, the perp lied about his arrest record to me and continued to insist that he and the complainant were great friends, regardless of the stitches, so I decided to go ahead with the arrest. But as the ADA took the complainant through the story again in minute detail, he mentioned that the mob that took his money was considerate enough to return the wallet to his pocket afterward, without his noticing. The ADA turned to me and asked, "Have you ever heard a story like that before, Officer? How long have you been on the Job?"

I shook my head. "Not long enough."

The easiest collar was one that was made for me, by Jose, Danny Mullarkey, and Bobby Nardi. A complainant named Michael Monroe had been brought into the station by patrol after he hailed down a car: he had been taking pictures by the Bronx Terminal Market, on the river, when a man approached him with a knife and demanded money. Michael had only twenty dollars, and the perp made him walk to a bank and withdraw another sixty. I was out with Danny Scanlon on another case, and so I arranged to have someone from the Squad show him pictures. That was all that there was to be done—a couple of rounds of pictures and canvasses—and I would pick up the security video from the bank later, to see if the perp appeared on camera. An hour later, we heard Danny Mullarkey on the radio, calling for another car where the robbery had taken place. We raced over to them, and they were cuffing up the perp.

When Bobby Nardi heard about the robbery, he took Michael out on another canvass. He'd caught a homicide in the area earlier that year, of a man stabbed as he walked over the bridge from Manhattan, an apparent robbery. There were no solid leads, but something was bound to break from the crew of whores and thieves who hung around the Market after dark. Michael thought he spotted the perp but said he wasn't sure. "Tell you what," Bobby said. "Why don't you get out of the car and call to him, 'Why'd you do that? Why'd you rob me?'" Michael gamely did as asked, and the response was, "I didn't rob you! You gave me the money!"

The answer was funny, but the story was a little funny, too. The walk to the bank was over twelve blocks, into a crowded and well-patrolled area. The perp waited outside the bank, and Michael could have stayed there, or notified the guard. And the perp didn't take the camera equipment, which was worth ten times as much as the cash he received. On the canvass, Mullarkey asked Michael, "Was there anything sexual happening there? If there was, it - doesn't matter, but we should know about it going in."

Michael didn't react defensively to the suggestion, saying that he was there to take pictures, nothing else. In our car, the perp protested loudly on the ride back: "I didn't rob nobody! Motherfucker wanted to suck my dick, and he only had twenty bucks! He got more, I took the money and split!"

It was a good story, and on the face of it, it was a great deal simpler and more logical than Michael's. Michael had a slightly nebbishy quality, kind-hearted and absentminded, like a bird-watcher stumbling into a battlefield, his binoculars trained on the hummingbird as the bullets whistled past. But his explanations had their own logic: the perp had taken his wallet before they left for the bank, and his license showed where he lived; if he gave the perp the money, he could get the wallet back, and it would be a fair price for peace of mind; if he didn't take any sudden action, no one would get hurt. Once the perp ran, Michael had called the cops immediately. He also asked to call his girlfriend, saying she'd want to wait with him for the next few hours.

I left him in the interview room and hashed over the story with Nardi and Mullarkey. The perp repeated his claims, with vehemence. We tilted one way, then the other.

"What about the cameras? Why didn't he take them?"

"He's a crackhead. Cash-and-carry, he gets money and he's out."

"Okay, let's look at the blowjob. First, this Michael guy doesn't blink when I bring it up. A guy who begs crackheads to let him blow 'em, who pays them for it, is probably not real proud of himself. He gets beat for a couple of bucks, he goes home, he doesn't make a big stink about it. This guy calls the cops, then his girlfriend."

"And not for nothing, but a hundred bucks for a crackhead blowjob seems a little . . . above market."

"Oh, yeah, what do you usually pay?"

"It's not what I pay, it's what I charge."

Maybe that wasn't such a smart comeback after all. I ran both of them, and that cinched it: while the perp had a long sheet, including half a dozen robberies, Michael had never even made a police report. At the complaint room, the ADA listened to the story and said, "That's exactly what happened to another ADA last week! He's walking through the park by the courthouse after lunch, and a guy comes up to him and says, 'Gimme ten bucks.' The ADA says get lost, and the guy says, 'Gimme ten bucks, or I'll call the cops and say you wanted to suck my dick!'" The ADA knew better and didn't care—no cop would take out his handcuffs, even if he believed the beggar—but there was probably a small but reliable percentage of men who would spend ten dollars to spare themselves the indignity of the accusation. You gotta have a story, and the perp stuck with his.

Within the Squad, that kind of collaboration was necessary and expected, but the responsibilities to other cases was a strain, when you had so little time for your own. Danny might have visits to make when John wanted to catch up on typing, and I might have to help with a line-up from the C Team if Reilly or Clinton had a collar. We also had to cover the home invasions and carjackings that would be assigned to Bronx Robbery, if they weren't available. There were only eight or ten detectives there, and they were stretched as thin as we were; we'd often have to respond, examining the scene and conducting interviews, writing up fives and other reports. The job might take the entire tour, and the case would be handed off at the end of it. If the case looked like a loser, it was a relief, but more often there was some promising, playable angle, and it was frustrating to let it go.

A successful debriefing could also take up an entire tour, though if it went that long, it tended to be productive. Two cops named Kevin Costello and Bobby Nugent made a great collar, taking three perps with two guns after the robbery of a laundromat. The first perp stuck by his ridiculous story: he - didn't know his co-defendants, who lived around the corner from him in a distant part of the Bronx; he had found the gun in the street, moments before; he had stopped by the laundromat on a sudden urge to wash his coat and gloves. But the second perp gave it up without hesitation.

"It's a mistake, we all make them, God knows," said Danny.

"When you write down what happened," I said, "be sure to say how sorry you are about it. That's important for the judge to see."

When he finished writing, Danny said, "That's good. It's obvious you're a good guy, come from good people. Who do you live with, your Moms?"

His mother, his twin brother, a younger brother, and a cousin from Boston.

"That sounds good. There's another thing. With all the guns involved in this, we can get a search warrant for your house. We don't want that, and you don't want that."

"We come crashing through in the middle of the night, and everybody gets locked up. Everybody. Is there something there that shouldn't be, a gun? Where's the gun?"

"Arright, there is a gun, but you sure my Moms won't get in trouble?"

"Not your Moms, not your brothers, not even your cousin from Boston. What kind of gun, where is it?"

The sawed-off shotgun was exactly where it was said to be, over the closet in his room. We told him how well he had done, how he'd started to turn his life around, to make things right. But we knew he wasn't being completely honest: no one's first mistake is a three-man commercial robbery with two guns. We pushed harder, and he gave up two more commercial robberies, for a barber shop and a parking lot, and of numerous Mexican delivery boys. And Chinese delivery boys, there were more than he could begin to remember. *That's the problem with robbing Chinese delivery boys, you're hungry half an hour later.* With the second perp's confession, we were able to break the third, though the first stuck to his story.

Danny said that he felt he could talk anybody into talking, with enough time. He once broke a perp in eight words. A crackhead beat his girlfriend bloody and took her gold chain. He didn't remember most of it, he claimed. Danny asked, "When's the last time you saw her alive?" In general, both he and John had a buddy-buddy style of interrogation: *You got a girl? You got a picture? Lemme see. . . . Nice. She got a sister? I'm gonna tell the judge, no bail for you, I should pay her a visit and keep her company. Nah, I'm foolin'. . . . But serious, I wouldn't leave that piece of ass alone too long, you know what I mean? I can help you. . . .* John and Danny were better actors than I was, or at least different kinds of actors. They could muster up an instant intimacy, a brotherly bond, improvised on the quick. I was wary of the we-have-your-fingerprints kind of chicanery, if only because these gambits locked you into a factual stance, and if the perp didn't buy it, it was hard to recover a position of authenticity or authority. While I could conceal my disdain for a subject, I could never pretend affection. Maybe I was more of a method actor, who had to work from a place of conviction. I had to range around to find a point of connection, to spitball and think, and to make the silences weigh on the perp rather than me: *Do you have children? Do you love them? Do you want to see them? Do you believe in God? Do you believe in luck? How about yours, do you believe it's good, even today?* For one perp, I read his horoscope: "When's your birthday, wait . . . Look at this, 'Everyone will understand if you concentrate on your closest loved ones.' And in the other paper, 'Don't wait for others to come to you—approach them first and make things happen.' Is this a sign, or is this a sign?"

I needed a sign, too. Or rather the opposite, a case of substance, that I could use to show I could do this, not least to myself. Though John and even Danny did not have a great deal more time here than I did, they had both proven themselves, collaring on serious cases. Even when a case was closed with a big break—the mask came off during the home invasion, or the perp called home on the stolen cell phone—the very luck of the break seemed a token of justice, of fortune favoring the brave. Though we were trained to be skeptical of coincidence, over time, luck felt like talent, and it was.

Livery-cab robberies in the Bronx had been high-profile for two years, since a slew of cab robbery-homicides had raised the issue in the press. I caught a cab robbery—and a break—in which one perp put a gun to the -

driver's head, and the other grabbed his neck, and said, "Give him the money!" The driver, a Rwandan immigrant, could identify only the man with the gun. I could identify them both, however, almost immediately, from a digital security camera in the car. Though the robbery itself was not on film, a series of pictures showed them getting into the cab, after which one of them put on a mask. It was such a good picture that it ran in the *Daily News,* and two days later, a neighbor of one perp called, and we picked him up, and he gave up the other, whom we grabbed a week later. The first perp, the gunman, who went by the name K-Lo, had just finished parole after doing two years for the robbery of a ten-year-old boy; the other, Diba, had just come out of prison after doing nearly six years for several armed robberies. K-Lo was wearing the same coat he wore in the photo—a mustard-yellow snorkel jacket with a fur-trimmed hood—and he carried the newspaper clip with his picture in his pocket. K-Lo and Diba both made extensive statements in which they admitted to being there but professed innocence of wrongdoing, blaming each other for everything. Diba was the more persuasive, and the one without the gun, but his knowledge of the take—"It was about two hundred and seventy-three dollars"—was impressive for a bystander.

But in some cases, luck was not enough, nor was talent, let alone truth. I didn't know what else you could bring to bear, but I was still new. I was glad it was Danny's case, and I wasn't even in the office the night a man named Tareek robbed one Arab deli, then went down the block and robbed another one. For Danny, the second robbery was beautiful because they had a video in the store, which captured everything, including the counterman hitting him in the head with a hammer, and the first one was beautiful because patrol caught Tareek on the street, as he ran from the second one. The first victim identified him right there, but Tareek was already back at the precinct, bloody-headed, before the second report was made, and the law required that for that complainant, a line-up had to be conducted, at least a day later. Tareek was picked out in a photo array, but when Danny went to get the second merchant for the line-up, he was told that the man had returned to Yemen. Tareek was only charged with the first robbery, and he testified at the Grand Jury that the cops had always hated him, and framed him, and beat him terribly—*Look at what they did to my head!* All evidence of the second robbery was inadmissible, including the videotape of how the injuries were actually incurred. The ADA was also unable to question him about his twenty prior arrests. The first victim testified, as did the cops, but the Grand Jury believed Tareek. Danny was investigated by IAB, however, and though he seems to have been cleared as well, he was told that the videotape was "inconclusive."

But Danny was at least as happy as I was when the Latent Print Unit called to say that the prints lifted from the cash box in my first commercial robbery, at the all-purpose Dominican store, matched the left middle and index fingers of Tareek. I picked him up at court—he had a case for assaulting a Corrections officer after being jailed for domestic violence, though he was at liberty, again, for both cases—and did not try to interrogate him; he was too seasoned a perp to fall for anything I might have tried. When I brought him into the precinct, he said, "Who'd they say I robbed now?" I put it down on a five. While he matched the description—large, light-skinned, in his thirties—the victim couldn't remember his face anymore, and she did not pick him out. But on the way to Central Booking, I drove past the store, and he said, "I've never been inside there." I put that down on a five, too—it eliminated any alternative explanation for the prints.

In the Grand Jury, the victim testified about the robbery, of her terror and the gun, and the perp's strange behavior, trying to close the gate on them. She hadn't been able to pick him out of a line-up, but the description matched. She was young, pretty, and sincere, all you could ask for in a witness. Tareek was not young or pretty, but he seemed to have mustered some sincerity when he testified that the cops had always hated him and framed him, and though he didn't remember what he was doing on that day, he was never in the store. And he was a Muslim, and he loved his children, and he was probably taking care of them at the time. Or maybe he was partying, but he wasn't in the store. He had no idea how his fingerprints had gotten there, but I had a vendetta against him, after a confrontation we'd had when his uncle was shot in 1996. He presently had a lawsuit against me, he said. I had never set eyes on him before the arrest. And the Grand Jury again set him free. The ADA told me that a woman called out as he left, "Give your baby a big kiss good night tonight!"

The ADA called me to tell me, but I didn't call Danny, who had already left for the day. At least one of us should have a decent night's sleep. What did I lack here? Something was seen, something was left, something was said. I'd even been lucky. And I could not credit the loss to mere luck, because it was not the first time it had happened. K-Lo and Diba were also set free by the Grand Jury, by two different panels. K-Lo said the entire case was a conspiracy, that he had never been in the cab, and the picture had been fabricated by the police, probably on some kind of super-computer. The jacket had been planted on him, and the *Daily News* clip had been planted in the jacket, and he signed the confession only because I put a gun to his head. He made me sound like one of the elders of Zion. Diba said that the robbery had happened, all right, but he was simply a passenger: when K-Lo pulled the gun, he was as surprised as anyone. I didn't have the heart to tell the cab driver, who had come to America from Rwanda to escape unreason and hatred. When I told Sam Ramer, he offered condolences, as if I'd told him about a death in the family; he understood. He said that if it made me feel any better, he thought these runaway decisions represented a kind of addled optimism, that the jurors wanted desperately to believe that these perps were not as bad as we said. As a gesture of faith in human nature, however, it was not what I needed at the time.

FOURTEEN

One night before working at the landfill, I didn't sleep; I couldn't, moving from couch to bed, TV to book, looking at the clock to see if I could get five hours, three, two . . . There was an old cop adage, said of perps in the cells: *Only the guilty sleep.* I was guilty of plenty of things; why couldn't I sleep? I packed a kit of aspirin, matches, and disinfectant, and I put on coffee. By the time I arrived in Staten Island, I was ready to pass out, maybe from the guilt of driving past the guards. I had the sifter that day, watching the channeled rubble roll by, steadily brown, with bits of glass that shone pale green, like new shoots in the spring loam. If I looked at the ground, it swam, not with the steady run of the sifter belt but with a seasick, heaving flow. I couldn't look at the ground, I had to watch the belt. There had been fewer bones the last few tours, but still plenty of plastic, credit cards, and the like. Today, there was the head of a putter, a full bottle of perfume, three twisted spoons. A city map rolled past, and I picked it up: the page was open to Staten Island and Fresh Kills. A bike seat, the air bag of a car, two purple bras, still with store security tags, thank God. On breaks, I stepped through the seething, creamy mud, and the wind was putrid and white with dust, the gusts skimming like pale riders over the fields. I dozed off in my car and Danny called. I went back to the sifter. A poster for Excalibur Extravaganza Limousine Service: a jumbo jet over lower Manhattan, the plane head-ing right for the Twin Towers. I was looking for bodies and finding only ironies, and as the belt moved the rubble, the ironies were gone, too.

For a while, there was no rubble, either, and the belt passed by, empty. We stood there, watching it. A baseball-sized steel sphere popped up from be-low, and a cop rolled it back against the direction of the belt. It rolled of its own momentum, but as it slowed, the belt kept it rolling forward, even as it came back to the cop who threw it, its force never fully spent. The ball was tossed again, spinning forward as it rolled back. We all watched, mesmer-ized, as the ball was thrown. What is the physics term? Inertia? Bodies in motion tend to stay in motion, bodies at rest tend to stay at rest. The phrase rolled through my head each time the ball rolled on the belt, forward and back, in motion and at rest. I don't remember much else.

Other duties and details required more than sleep to endure without de-spairing. The city had barely begun to recover from 9/11 when another plane crash brought more devastation. American Airlines Flight 587 was bound for the Dominican Republic when it went down in Rockaway shortly after take-off, killing 265 people. There were no survivors. Most of the dead were Dominicans, and while the Dominicans in New York are concentrated in Washington Heights, there were significant numbers in the Four-Four. De-tectives are obliged to make official death notifications, and I went with John Flood to tell a man that his son had died.

While it is no pleasure to surprise anyone with news of this kind, our re-dundancy made the task seem pathetic, even cruel. But what if the family was estranged, and we brought fresh sorrow instead of stale? What if they - didn't care? We knocked on the door and the house was full: relatives milled about, and a heavyset man sat at a table, a bottle of rum in front of him. There were grief counselors from American Airlines. We both stood there for a mo-ment, and John Flood began, "I'm sorry to have to tell you this, sir, but the body of your son Miguel has been found."

The heavy man wept and looked down, and several arms were thrown over his shoulders. And then he looked up, staring at us through his tears, and asked, "What about the other three?"

The other three? His wife, his daughter, and another son had gone down with the plane.

There was too much of this. This was far harder than it should be. New miseries seemed not only beyond bearing but beyond imagining, rolling up like rubble on the sifter. Keith Clinton told me that the body of a flight attendant was found, still hogtied. By the luck of the draw, I never had the Medical Examiner's detail, which was generally preferred to the landfill, since it was indoors. But when Danny had the ME, he told me that seven firefighters were brought in. The first time John had it, he said, it was so easy that when he got it again, he felt twice as lucky to be spared the elements in Staten Island, natural and otherwise. After, he didn't feel lucky at all:

"It was the worst, my worst day on this job. I start at 0400, get there half an hour early to get on a decent roster. There's one sergeant who looks like he knows everybody—'Hey Tony, hey Phil!'—like he was there every day. I decide to go to him, he'll have it good. Turns out, he wasn't there much at all, or maybe nobody likes him. He gets 'escort.' Next thing you know, you gotta get in all this gear—hospital scrubs, masks, booties, long gloves, short gloves, the whole nine, bundled up worse than a surgeon. Turns out, the job of an escort is for when a cop or a fireman comes in, or any part of a cop or a fireman comes in, they get a cop to walk them in. We get on line, ten a.m., we wait outside. I'm like, 'Hey, this detail's a bunt!' Then we all gotta go out, get to attention, an ambulance comes. We stop, dead silence. The ambulance has two or three cop cars in front of it, two or three behind. The lieutenant who runs the detail yells, 'Preee-sent arms!'

"We salute, and a body bag comes out, with a flag on it, and they put him on a regular rollaway stretcher. They take the flag off, they fold it up by triangles till it's a little package and put it under the stretcher. Then they put another little American flag on top of him, like what a kid would wave at a parade. So there's always a flag.

"They take it inside. It's a full body bag, a full one. 'Present arms,' again, and they open it up. It's bunker gear, a fireman's jacket, a boot—the rest if it, you couldn't make out. It stunk like all hell. A guy in front of me got that. The next one comes in—same thing, salute, walk it in from the ambulance, salute. It's a foot. I'm up next. It's like eleven-thirty when it comes in. This time, the body bag looks real full. There's five or six tables, this one goes to the main table. The medical examiners open it up, and it's a full body, full uniform, it's a cop. He's got Hi-Tec boots, cargo pants, uniform top, shield, nameplate, gun on the side in the belt. All the everyday cop things you see—extra magazines, belt keepers. The body's intact. He was burnt a little but he was mostly dirty. He was buried. That's why he came in as a whole body, but the firemen were smelly soup in bunker gear. They had air, they burnt.

"Stunk like all hell. The body was like the Crypt Keeper in *Tales from the Crypt,* shrunken. It was like the fat in the skin was sucked out, it was around the bone. The cheeks were sunken, the eyeballs were sunken. The face, the face was frozen, and it looked like it was screaming. The 'I'm gonna die!' look, preserved. Like he saw the I-beam hit him, and the face stopped there.

"The guys get to work, like it was nothing. This is what they do. One hand has a leather glove, they take that off. They cut the clothes off, the gun belt, he's naked. The stink is worse. One of them cuts off his pinkie toe for DNA, they sliced it off right there in front of me and put it in a tube. They take measurements, height and weight, head to toe. They put him back in the bag, back on the stretcher. I couldn't believe how they picked him up, no mask, no gloves.

"Next, they yell, 'Escort!' I'm there, I never left. They had two PBA delegates, union delegates, to take his stuff back at the end. Some people are looking, gawking a little, and for the MEs it's like nothing, but the whole thing's so respectful. You know?

"Okay, there's three different stations. First, there's fingerprints. There's an FBI guy there, two NYPD. One's a white shield, I think his family has a funeral home, he's a mortician. They lift up the hand, they feel it for the texture. They got incense burning, but it still stinks, when they open up the bag again, it's like a ton of bricks. The two of them are playing with the skin on the hand, it moves more than yours or mine. One says to me, 'Do me a favor, hold his hand up.' They got me holding up his dead arm. They play with the finger and they inject something in it, it swells up, and then they try to roll a print. It's no good. They try another finger, they inject that. Negative. Another guy grabs a scalpel, he cuts around the finger, all around the tip, he wiggles it so it gets real loose, and he starts pulling up the skin. It gets caught on the nail. I don't know if he took off the nail, I think he took it off over the nail. Then he takes the skin and he slips it over his own finger, rolls it in ink. He gets a perfect print. He cuts off maybe eight of the fingertips, the skins, and he rolls for prints. I was a little too involved. I'm moving body parts, holding hands. All in the stench, looking at the corpse.

"The whole thing takes forty-five minutes, and we zip him back up. Next stop is dental. Oral surgeons, dentists, whoever else. Four guys. They tell us to take a seat. Again, they unzip, and the smell hits you. . . . They gave us the option to wait outside, but I figure I'm the escort, I gotta stay with him, he's a cop. They hacked his face up. They cut his face open and cut his whole jaw out, they cut the fucking jaw right out of the face. They analyzed each tooth, all the molars, eye-one, eye-two, all of them. We were there an hour an a half. That was the worst one.

"The last stop, X-ray. Unzip, board underneath, the chest X-ray, torso. We had to stand outside for that. Finally, there's checkout. They hand over the property to the PBA guys, check off the list. ID card, shield and gun. They zip him up again right there, and the Lieutenant takes the little flag from the top of the body bag. 'This poor sap deserves better than this.' The big flag goes back on top. The Lieutenant yells out, everybody comes to attention, the meat wagon's out front. We snap a salute. I was overwhelmed by how respectful and courteous the Job was for this.

"I stood outside the rest of the day. I didn't want nothing to do with nothing after that. I smelled him and held the rail of his stretcher for two hours, I held his hand for almost an hour. I didn't want nothing to do with nothing after that. The face sucked in, like he was screaming. The look. That was the only full body that day. Noreen O'Shea was working with me. She got off easy, she got a little finger or something.

"I couldn't eat for a long time after. You have it in your system, that DOA smell, you feel it in your clothes, you feel it on your breath, even in the fresh air. That's fucked up. They got me holding up his dead arm. The shitty part was that I'd be standing beside him, and there was a poster on the wall with all the dead cops' pictures, and I'm looking at his live face on the wall, and his dead face in front of me."

As the weeks passed, I saw John's mood darken, his teeth clench more and more. He didn't see Julie because of the schedule, didn't eat right, didn't work out, couldn't study for the sergeant's test, which was a few weeks away. His streak of good collars and even good cases ended, and his desk piled up with fives on complainants who didn't show up or changed their stories, who couldn't ID but wouldn't admit it, of visits to empty houses. "I feel like a secretary," he said. "I haven't done police work in months." Scott Adler called to ask him if he wanted to work on a special task force for a pattern rapist who had assaulted a dozen women in the Bronx and Queens, ranging in age from eight to fifty-eight. He would have steady days off, and a flexible schedule, and he would be exempt from details. Instead of two dozen cases, most of them petty, at least in what was required of him, he would have one tremendously important one, and he would have the rest of his life back. I loved working with John, and he was welcome to live with me as long as he liked, but especially in the weeks after September 11, we were together twenty-four hours a day, seven days a week.

"Do you want to come?" John asked me. "There's more spots open. . . ."

It would be a temporary assignment, he said, for a few weeks or maybe months. But Eddie McDonald, from the A Team, had been on the task force for Isaac Jones and his fifty-one rapes—Eddie had obtained the confession, in fact, with Bobby Dellano from Homicide—and that temporary assignment had lasted two and a half years. At the Four-Four, I was exhausted, but I was exhilarated, too. I was finding my stride in robberies, in the Squad, and with Danny. We'd call each other on our days off to figure out cases, or talk shop over dinner. Maybe it would be three months or six before I felt comfortable and competent enough to think about going over to the Squad and catch homicides. I'd know it when the time came, when to make the move. I told John that I'd stay. I called DI Rising, too, to say that I was going take a pass on Manhattan Robbery. This was the place for me. I told John there were no hard feelings, and I taped a sign to his bedroom door that said "For Rent." He looked at it and shook his head, laughing. "*Gabbados.*"

"*Stunad.*"

"*Gavone!*"

"*Prick of misery!*"

"You hungry?"

"I could eat."

"Let's go out . . ."

We'd partner up again, in time—it was a twenty-year road, and we weren't half done. *Next year in Jerusalem . . .ž*

It was one of the smaller coincidences, I thought, that he left as we had started in SNEU, for a pattern rape detail. Of the old SNEU team, Tony was in the Squad, in the Four-Two, and Orville had never left, though he was now on the list for sergeant. Chicky and Stix had returned, from the midnights and from Sgt. O'Hagan's team. Eileen Brown had been the boss, and then Tommy Clark, and they said that things got better again, almost as good as they had been with PK. My old antagonists—the Captain, the ICO, and the Sergeant—were all gone. Alicia had gone to PSA-8, and Sammy was still in Narcotics. Smacky was a SNEU sergeant himself, in the Four-Seven. PK had left PSA-8 for the Medical Division, which gave him a car to take home, and flexible hours. His boys were getting bigger, and walking better. Though he was now and then tempted to return to "real" police work, the temptation passed; he had done his share, and he'd keep what he had. I talked to him every month or so, and his voice always brought me back: *Laddo!*

I'd run into other cops from PSA-7, sometimes at crime scenes, where I'd be the Squad guy in the suit, asking the questions: *Whaddaya got, kid?* Some were impressed and some weren't; at one commercial robbery, Eddie Tibbatts interviewed me as I interviewed the victim:

"Eddie C! How ya doin'!"

"Eddie T! It's good, good. Hang on—so your hands were taped like this, you said? Did he bring the tape or find it in the store?"

"That's a nice suit. Sharp! The dry cleaning must add up, though, huh?"

"Thanks, yeah, it does—sorry, you said the three guys had masks and gloves. Did they take them off ever, did they touch anything?"

"Didja hear, John Chase is in FD now?"

"Yeah, I heard—and you said you have an alarm? Did you call the company?"

"Thursday night, the Copa, whaddaya say, me, you, and Johnny T, we hit it!"

"Absolutely!"

Eddie T could always put things in perspective. A night out, a night in, a breath, a break: any of them, all of them, were all I needed, and they came, in time. We were all struggling, I knew, even the most veteran detectives, and I wondered what perversity it was to take comfort in the idea that it would get no easier with experience. And to think there were brand-new investigators, like me, with their own cases and details, who couldn't even type. At Fresh Kills, the wasted landscape was infernal, but we would leave it after twelve hours, alive. The damned that Dante stuck in the mud were those who made themselves miserable in life: "Once we were sullen in the sweet air . . . Now we have this blackened mire to be sullen in." I was ready for my next run-in with Chief Tiffany, but when we met again, the lesson was not from literature. He said, "What we're doing at the landfill is unique in human history, I think. At a certain point, you would have expected us to give up. Was it the Battle of Stalingrad, where they bulldozed over it and planted trees? There's never been anything like this, looking through a hundred million tons of wreckage by hand, looking for each individual person," he said. I kept my complaints to myself, nodding. Maybe this war would end, as the Trojan War did, when the bodies of the fallen came home.

In the supply tent, the pictures of people identified from the landfill began to accumulate, firefighters and businessmen, IDed by fingerprints, bones, DNA. The next time I had the detail, I saw Billy Clune and a few guys from the team—Abe Garcia, Jimmy Donovan—and he told me, "They got a foot the other day, and I think they got a pelvis in Area D." His department van was parked next to my car. "How'd you get up here? Never mind, I don't want to know." For our meal, we stripped off our Tyveks, washed our boots, and entered the chow line, as Salvation Army volunteers from Kentucky and Texas ladled out bratwurst, potato casserole, and Salisbury steak, items that had disappeared from Manhattan restaurants before La Guardia left City Hall. In acknowledgment of the cultural divide, they put up a cardboard menu: FRIED POSSUM, BOILED POSSUM, AGED POSSUM, FRESH POSSUM. DESSERT: SQUIRREL PIE. Their kindness and cheer made it hard to complain; they didn't have to be there. As I ate in my car, I read *The Thin Man,* with Nick and Nora Charles, the elegant couple who solved elegant crimes amid wry dialogue and many cocktails. On a visit to Manhattan, the Charleses have become embroiled in the disappearance of a wealthy and eccentric inventor. Nick gives some shrewd interrogation advice to NYPD detectives on how to approach the inventor's venomous ex-wife:

"The chief thing," I advised them, "is not to let her tire you out. When you catch her in a lie, she admits it and gives you another lie to take its place and, when you catch her in that one, admits it and gives you still another, and so on. Most people—even women—get discouraged after you've caught them in the third or fourth straight lie and fall back on either the truth or silence, but not Mimi. She keeps trying and you've got to be careful or you'll find yourself believing her, not because she seems to be telling the truth, but simply because you're tired of disbelieving her."

I made a note of that and returned to the sifter. The observation startled me with its acuity, given the book's breezy style. The value of an interrogation was not always that you arrived at a truthful statement, but that you drew out a story, a character, a line, and kept them coming, and wrote them down. You had testimony, and testimony has its own truth, if not about what witnesses did or know, then about who they are. If I could remember that, I might get along in this business. *The Thin Man* became a movie with many sequels: *After the Thin Man, Another Thin Man, Shadow of the Thin Man, The Thin Man Goes Home,* and *Song of the Thin Man.* Though the series declined in quality, the characters remain irresistible: they had fun and found things out. The "Thin Man" figures only in the first book—he's the missing inventor, not Nick Charles—but it worked, so they kept it, and few people seemed to notice and fewer seemed to mind. If I could remember that, too, maybe the skinny new detective had a place here, after all.

• • •

AT THE SQUAD, THERE WAS MUCH MOVEMENT: LT. GEORGE Corbiere would retire and Lt. George Tagliaferri would replace him, followed by Richie Vasquez, before Jimmy Ruane returned to the Four-Four; Larry Sheehan would retire also; Mike Guedas would be reshuffled to the Four-One, and then the Four-Three, and Timmy McCormack would fill his spot; Tommy Rice would be sent to the Four-Two, and back, and then to the Four-Seven. In the RAM, Ron Bolte would come and go, and Jimmy Mangan and Owen Clifford would come upstairs from patrol, and then Rachel Silva and Barry Jones. They asked me how to do things; I wasn't the new guy anymore, or at least not the newest. One of Owen's first collars was of an armless man, and Owen had to ink his feet to take footprints for identification. I asked Owen what he got him for, and he paused a moment before responding, "Forgery."

"Eddie, you wouldn't believe it," he went on. "He could do everything, he could smoke a cigarette, he could write, he had better penmanship than you or me. He could do everything but wipe his ass." Realizing the next question, Owen added quickly, "I called his wife to come in."

It began to feel as if I'd worked with Danny, Jose, and the others for ages, and it felt good. And detective work began to resume the balance of our attentions, bit by bit—and maybe not by chance, my cases seemed to get better, even as I got better at them.

In the last century, the jails in New York were run by the Department of Charities and Corrections, and these dual motives applied for us today. Charities and Corrections, pity and pique: the victims looked to us for justice, for a compassion that was larger and longer-lasting than the contempt with which they had been treated. We rarely got their money back, and certainly - couldn't unspill their blood, but even when we didn't get the perp, we could help them move on by showing our sympathy and perseverance. There was the two-year-old boy who was picking a flower for his grandmother when a crackhead knocked him down and snatched his chain. That case will never close for me, though I may not get the crackhead, but the father and grandmother were heartened to see the neighborhood covered with bilingual posters advertising a two-thousand-dollar reward. There was the case of the fifteen-year-old whose face was set on fire in a Puerto Rican–Dominican drug-gang war (last score: Puerto Ricans up, four shootings to two), in which Mullarkey scammed the perp into surrender, telling his mother we'd heard of threats to his life. If there was charity in the baby-robbery and face burning, my Dominican counter-abductions were pure correction: the first victim was taken from the street into a vacant apartment, duct-taped, and pistol-whipped. In a moment of Clouseau-like inspiration, he decided the acquaintance who unexpectedly called an hour before must have been responsible, and the next day, he and a friend took the acquaintance for a ride at gunpoint. They demanded the address of his family in the Dominican Republic and told him they would all be killed if he didn't supply the names of his accomplices. It was all drug-related, I was sure: I collared the first victim, and his friend fled the country. That case will always be closed for me. Another correction case was for the Bloods who stomped a little African kid for a few dollars. As I drove one perp to the line-up, he boasted, "You watch, I'm gonna be out for New Year's, see the ball drop in Times Square."

"The only balls that are gonna drop for you are your cell mate's on your chin," I replied.

Danny almost drove off the road.

The Squad is the Job, Eddie, hurry up and come here. . . .ž

If an investigation followed a trail to one person, or one place, offering the satisfaction of hard-won arrival, there were detours and diversions that were horrific, or hilarious, or haunting, or all of them at once. You felt like you stepped into a comedy sketch sometimes, or even a fairy tale. Jose caught a kidnapping, in which a teenage mother had met a friend from school at a laundromat; the other girl offered to take the baby for a while, and even to go out and get some Chinese food for them. An hour passed, and then two, and then eight before the mother finally called the police. The perp lived in the Heights, and Danny and I canvassed there in vain all night, checking in on the corners and at the hospitals. In the morning, the baby was returned, safely, but it was the interval that fascinated me, when Jose told me what had happened: the perp had taken the baby to the house of a boy she had slept with, a year before, knocking on the door at midnight.

"This is your daughter," she told him. "We had twins, but the boy died."

I wonder if she expected to be rebuffed or embraced, presenting her changeling, the true lost child with the imagined one, and I wonder if the embrace was what she wanted, because the boy woke his mother, and she summoned relatives, who brought presents and made food and admired the new baby until nearly sunrise, when she excused herself for a moment and left. She went home to sleep, abandoning the baby in a carriage on the sidewalk in front of her parents' house, where it was discovered by a news crew. The boy and his mother waited awhile, trying to take it all in, before they left for their own local precinct.

"My wife and child are missing!" he said.

I still feel for that boy, who lived a lifetime in those hours, and all of it a lie.

Another evening, I spent a few hours with Bobby Nardi in New Jersey on computer searches for a car involved with one of my cases; a friend named Jimmy Abrams was a cop at a small, prosperous, sleepy town in that state, and he was of great help. On the drive back, Bobby and I talked about how different our jobs were from his, though we were cops, a few miles apart.

"God bless these guys. They make nearly twice our salary, and what do they have to deal with?"

"Traffic, sometimes."

"Exactly. And us, here? What we gotta do . . ."

As we pulled into the precinct, a man staggered down the street and collapsed over the hood of a patrol car, spouting blood from three holes in his chest and one in his face.

"I've been shot!" he screamed.

But wait, it's even funnier: a woman had just pulled up to the cops to ask for directions to the highway; she had gotten lost on her way back from a Mets game.

"Is this a dangerous neighborhood?" she asked, as the near-corpse stumbled over, howling, as if on cue. The man lived, of course—as the cop adage goes, the perps survive machine guns, while we die from paper cuts. The victim had just been released from prison, and he was beating his girlfriend in his car when one of the drunks from the corner told him to lay off. The drunk wasn't a perfect gentleman—he'd been hitting on the girlfriend every time he saw her, drunk or sober—and the girlfriend ultimately chose the beater over the shooter. *Ah, love.*

I began to play a larger part in other cases in the office, to earn my keep in the Squad. Jose caught a homicide, when a man named Gio argued with his girlfriend's nephew over returning a videotape—*Bait,* starring Jamie Foxx— and shot him in the chest. Danny and I searched his apartment, and I came up with his grandmother's address on his parole discharge papers, beneath a couch cushion. We trapped a call to her phone, and an hour later, he leapt from his friends' closet into the waiting arms of Jose, Timmy McCormack, and Brendan Mallon from Homicide. The next day, Danny and I transported him to Central Booking, and we pushed him for the gun:

"Listen, Gio, I know you made a statement last night, and it's one of two stories—it was an accident, or it was self-defense. You can take a plea or take your chances with the jury, and they're gonna think it's your fault or the other guy's. But either way, the gun was there—you didn't throw the bullet at him. Now, if some kid finds that gun and plays with it, and something bad happens, that's all on you—that's your fault, because you played cute with us, now."

At first, Gio told Danny that he'd thrown the gun in the woods by Van Cortlandt Park, but now he told me that he'd put it in a tar bucket on the roof of his apartment. Often, the mood tipped back and forth between the adversarial and the almost amiable—Gio had come into the precinct fighting, and he left it making deals; the gun admission had won him a plate of steak and eggs. He and I began to get along.

"Man, I shoulda come out shooting the other day when you guys got me. . . ."

"C'mon Gio, would you rather be dead? Or full of holes, pissing in a bag the rest of your life, in prison? Now, who knows? Maybe you beat this, you're out in a year. . . ."

"Yeah, you're right."

"What you should have done is run. The apartment you were in? The roof of a church is right out the window. Me and another guy were waiting for you on the street, but who knows, maybe you could have beat us. . . ."

"Yeah? Shit! No kidding!"

He said he wanted to go to the hospital, because his arms hurt a little. At the hospital, rear-cuffed and in leg irons, Gio tried to pick up girls. When an aide walked past, he ran his game on her—"Mmmm, look at you, what a fine woman . . ."—and I laughed at him.

"C'mon, how does that work for you, on the outside?"

"I can't complain, Conlon."

"Well, I bet this lady's looking for somebody with gold chains, not steel ones."

The aide started laughing. "It's a little more my style!"

When a young blonde walked past, he nudged me and said, "That's all you, Conlon, that's all you!" The blonde was a medical student, who stood beside us with two or three others when the attending doctor examined Gio. Danny made sure they saw where the medical-treatment form said MURDER as well as "complaint of ache in wrists." Gio ignored the doctor as he extended his arms for the examination, staring at the blonde.

"Yo, what's your name?" he asked her, abruptly.

She was surprised, but didn't betray any nervousness: "My name is Laura."

He paused a moment, and then cocked his head back and forth for the introduction: "Laura, meet Conlon. Conlon, this is Laura."

He smiled and winked at me. Danny informed me later that I did in fact blush.

The doctor attempted to continue his examination with all seriousness. He asked about past illnesses and medications, if Gio used drugs, drank, or smoked. For the last, Gio stammered, "I smoke a cigarette or two, now and then, but do you mean . . . I mean, the last two days, it's like nonstop, two packs, three . . ."

I offered my assistance: "What I think the doctor means, Gio, is how much do you smoke when you don't shoot people."

"Aww, man, Conlon, you blew me up! And I just hooked you up!"

I was starting to feel hooked up. Or unhooked, in truth. As Sgt. Adler said on my first day, there was an "adulthood" to the Squad, which I didn't fully appreciate at the time. Though the supervisors ensured that certain things were done, or done on time, in a narrow sense, we did what the case required, not what the boss did. I wasn't sure if it was a trait of Irishmen or second sons, but the history of my relations with authority, at least on the Job, tended to split sharply between strong admiration and near-mutiny. Here, I was my own man, fatherless, as it were, and if I was free to succeed, I was also deprived of an explanation for failure. I hadn't expected to be unready for it. The word "perp" itself is a kind of misbegotten son, lost in the law: at the root of "perpetrate" is "father," in *pater*, which extended to a sense of mastery or accomplishment. At first, to perpetrate meant only to do or achieve, for neither good nor ill, but its early usage by lawyers led it to mean "to do wrong." There was a lesson there, somewhere.

It was an interesting thought, of the kind that I tried to keep to myself, though more must have escaped than I remembered. When Danny and I passed an apartment building on the Grand Concourse, Danny jabbed a thumb at it and said, "You know who that was named after? The guy who invented the nickel." I looked quizzically, at him and then it, before I saw the building was named The Lewis Morris. All right, it was his half-brother, Gouverneur, who came up with the word "cent," but close enough. Another time Danny and I were out with Bobby Nardi when I noticed we were passing 1455 Sheridan, and we pulled over. We went to look at the building, an old prewar apartment house. As I explained our purpose, Bobby was excited but Danny just shook his head.

"This is where Lee Harvey Oswald lived, when he was a teenager," I said.

We fanned out into the lobby, a half-century late for the canvass.

"Across the street, it's Taft High School. Do you think he looked out and thought about presidents?"

"Where did he live? What apartment?" Bobby asked.

"A basement apartment is all I know."

"Maybe he carved his name in the wall."

There had to be something here that meant something, at least to us. I scanned the mailboxes; the names were almost all Spanish, but none, alas, was Castro. The walls were stucco, painted a mustard-yellow color, tediously free of graffiti. As we walked out, I noticed decals on the front door, and one stood out, rather dramatically, for a livery-cab company: KENNEDY RADIO DISPATCH.

"Sometimes, it all fits. . . ."

Danny was relentless, approaching each encounter, each interview, with the belief that someone always knew something: if you didn't have a gun, you knew someone who did, or knew someone who was wanted, or someone who should be. You never had nothing. On a day that I was out, patrol made a robbery arrest; Danny debriefed the perps, who admitted that their intended victim was a drug dealer. Danny took the dealer and eleven kilos of cocaine. But outside of the Four-Four, I was happy to tell him, he was clueless as a tourist. When we had to pick up a perp at his job, as a concessionaire at the Midtown theater where *Sweet Smell of Success* was playing, I had to urge him to slow down, to time our arrival. We got there just after the curtain opened, and the manager asked if we could wait until after intermission to make the arrest. "In the meantime, why don't you enjoy the show . . ." At last, we'd made it to Broadway . . . ž

But the real mark of a detective is the interrogation, which at its deepest level is a matter of convincing a perp to trust you more than he trusts himself, and then betraying that trust. *Trust me, trust me, it's my mother's maiden name. . . .* žTo go in, get it, and get out without looking back had not been the way I'd lived my life, and I was uncomfortable with the thought that I might become comfortable so doing. I wasn't sure I had it in me. As Sonny Corleone tells Michael, *You gotta get up close like this, and bada-bing! You blow their brains all over your nice Ivy League suit. . . .* žAnd then I remembered a time when my father returned home from a garage sale with a tent. He was in an abstract and slightly melancholy mood. "It's a sad story, really," he said. "The lady who had the sale, her son was on a camping trip. They had a gas heater in the tent, and it leaked, and the kid died. His best friend, too. Tragic, absolutely tragic. That's why I tell you kids to be careful about gas. . . . Wonderful woman, the mother. Catholic. Anyway, the tent was brand-new—used once—and cost three hundred dollars. The woman wanted two."

"How much did you get it for, Dad?"

Without a beat or even a break in the mood, he said, "I walked away three or four times, got her down to twenty. Now, what's for dinner?"

Alas, I thought, I had it in me, and I might as well use it. I caught a case after two new cops named Calamari and Mattison made an outstanding collar of a vicious assault on a nurse. The perp had slipped into the hospital and happened upon his victim in a storeroom; when he tried to rob her, she started to scream, and he jammed his fist so far down her throat that he ruptured her tonsils. The cops were in the emergency room on an unrelated stabbing when the perp ran through, bloody-handed, yelling, "A lady back there needs a doctor!"

The crime had taken place at about six in the morning, and the perp was asleep in the cell—still cuffed, his hands in paper bags to preserve the evidence—when I came in at eight. I let him sleep a few more hours before taking him upstairs. Although a confession might not be essential in this case—he had been IDed at the scene by the nurse, and her DNA would be collected from his hands—we wanted the case to be Bronx jury–proof, and for him to go away for a long time. I brought him coffee, candy, water, and soda, and I read him his rights. He didn't give me much in return. His name was Jerry Mapes, he said, and he didn't remember anything. He said it was his birthday, and he'd been celebrating with an eighteen-hour angel-dust binge. He said he'd never been arrested, but he'd neither worked nor gone to school for ten years. He wanted to go back to sleep. Only the last statement was true. But one of the real difficulties of interrogation was not telling truth from lies, but rather telling the relevant lies from the reflexive ones. As former prosecutor Thomas Puccio said of Robert Leuci, the crooked cop hero of *Prince of the City,* "You'd have to completely replace his blood with sodium pentothal in the hopes of getting the truth."

I wondered if he was wanted for something else, something worse. Without a real name, we'd have to wait for his fingerprints to find his history. No one does nothing in the Bronx for a decade with neither a pay stub nor an arrest record to show for it, and certainly no one with a taste for angel dust fails to leave a mark. And though I knew he was lying, I knew that there could well be vast gaps in what he remembered.

"Is there anything you want to ask me, Jerry? I mean, you wake up on your birthday in a jail cell with blood on your hands, literally. Me, I'd want to know how the party went. You haven't asked. Sit up when I talk to you. Matter of fact, stand up."

Jimmy Mangan was watching through the window, and he told me later that he thought I was going to hit the perp. But I was doing what they told us to do in the Academy when we thought we'd fall asleep in class. We stood together for the lesson. I asked him how he got money, and he said his mother gave it to him. We talked about his mother for a while.

"So you tell me she's on her knees scrubbing floors six days a week, on her knees in church the seventh. Works for you, prays for you, gives you money, you spend it on angel dust. Does she say that when she gives you the money, does she say, 'Here, Jerry, go out and hurt somebody, anybody, especially yourself? There's always more floors I can scrub, Jerry, don't worry, the back, the knees are fine'? Does she say that to you? Does she say that, Jerry? Answer me!"

"No, she don't say that. . . ."

"Is your name really Jerry? Is that your goverment name? It don't matter what I call you, what you say, you know—I don't know if this is the first time you ever did something, or if you're on the run from killing nuns in Hawaii—we got these fingerprint computers now, they'll say who you are in an hour. . . ."

"Can I sit down?"

"Sure you can sit down, if you don't fall asleep. You can't sleep now, Jerry, this is the most important hour of your life. You made a mistake, there's no way around that. But now—only now—you get a chance to tell me what happened, what really happened, to show your side, to put a human face on it. So the judge don't say, 'This is an animal, he's gonna die in jail!' So the judge says, maybe, 'Look, this guy made a mistake, but he owns it, he takes responsibility, he's a man. Drugs fuck you up, he knows it now, let's get him in a program and move on. He's a man, let's move on.' You understand me?"

"Yeah, I understand."

"So what happened in the hospital?"

"I don't remember."

"C'mon, Jerry, I thought we were talking here."

"It's Antoine, Jeffrey Antoine. That's my name."

"Arright, that's good, Jeffrey. So what's going on here, why you hiding your name?"

"I just got out of prison, I did eight years for robbery."

There it was, the first opening, and if there was one, there would be more. It showed a low-grade con cool: his first instinct was to admit nothing, but he was beginning to realize that his instincts would not help. He was starting to give in to me; we were at the tipping point. At the same time, I realized with a chill that if Calamari and Mattison hadn't caught him at the hospital, we might not have caught him at all: his arrest photo predated the computer, and I would have shown the nurse hundreds of useless pictures. He'd gone to prison just before I'd come on the Job, and all that had happened since was new for him. Maybe he knew about DNA from television, but he knew nothing about digital fingerprints or much else. In terms of the modern criminal-justice system, he was like Rip Van Winkle, awake in a later world. I'd try to work that, as well as some old tricks. He'd probably fallen for them before.

We began inching closer to the crime scene, as he conceded memory after memory: he remembered the afternoon before, and then the night, and then the hospital, which door he had entered, how no one had stopped him. He remembered wandering around to look for the bathroom, and finding the linen room instead, where the nurse told him to leave. And then he didn't remember anything else.

We had run his past arrests, and several of his robbery victims had been female, which I felt was telling. A robbery is rarely just about money. As St. Augustine wrote, when he was a child, he used to steal pears from an orchard, and they were sweeter because they were stolen. Even when he wasn't hungry, he found himself back in the orchard. "I stole them simply that I might steal, for, having stolen them, I threw them away." Perps who repeatedly choose women in their twenties and thirties, as Jeffrey Antoine had done, had to be attracted by more than the paycheck. Although Jeffrey had no sex crimes in his history, there was a sexual element to his predatory patterns, and in the wanton excess of his assault on the nurse. I wondered if he realized it himself.

"Jeffrey, this is good, this is good so far, but it isn't enough. I know you've been away for a while, a lot of what we do now, how we do it, it's all changed. Did you ever hear of Megan's Law?"

"No."

"It's named after a little girl that was raped and murdered. It makes - everybody register who does any sex crimes, it puts 'em on a list, and it tells the whole block. The neighbors know, everybody, that their wives, their mothers, their kids aren't safe. And people have got killed over it, even - people who didn't deserve it, people who got mistaken for somebody on the list. You sure you haven't heard about it?"

"Nah . . ."

"Well, I can show it to you, you can look it up. Because what I'm saying is—and I'm not saying it, she is, the nurse is—that you tried to rape her. You tried to get in her pants. And her pants are ripped, we have 'em."

"Nah!"

We did have the pants, and they were ripped, but even the nurse had said that Jeffrey wanted only her wallet.

"Now I'm not gonna try to tell you what it's like upstate, you know better than me, I can't tell you anything about prison you don't know. But you know time goes by different for a straight-up robber than it does for a rapist. You know how it goes for them. A stick-up guy, he gets his respect. A rapist, forget about it."

Jeffrey shook his head. "I have never, ever laid my hand on a woman like that. Never. All I wanted was her wallet, and I covered her mouth to stop her screaming. . . ."

"That's right, Jeffrey, that's good. You were fucked up on dust, but all you wanted was to keep the party going. You didn't want to hurt nobody. You even tried to get help, running through the emergency room, calling out the lady needs a doctor, right? Why'd you say that?"

"I didn't want her to get hurt. I tried to get a doctor for her."

"That's right, Jeffrey, that's important to bring out. Now, the DA's here with a video camera, and when we talk to her, you gotta be sure to say how you tried to get her help. . . ."

Months later, I testified at a hearing on the admissibility of the confession. As we watched the video, I watched Jeffrey Antoine, and he covered his mouth with his hand the whole time. *How does a fish get caught?* Good instinct there, Jeffrey, you should have stuck with it.

Danny and I talked about going to the Squad often enough. Robbery had been good to us. Many cases took on an assembly-line sameness, and we made factory decisions for their disposal: kid with a new jacket, lady with a chain, Chinese delivery, bodega; IDable or not, evidence or not, pattern or not, even lying or not, for the repeat customers on the first of the month, "robbed" of the rent on the way to the landlord, wouldn't you know! Home invasion, carjacking: let me give you the number for Bronx Robbery. . . . You'd look across at the Squad, and see a room full of typists as they moped between homicides, tapping out fives for Aggravated Harassments and teenage Missings. But then you'd catch a good case, something live and moving, with victims and perps each spurring you on, and it got you hot-blooded and hungry. "It's got meat on it," we'd say, and meat was made for eating.

I caught one case with so much meat on it I still haven't finished the meal. A simple bodega stick-up—man with gun, a thousand in cash, two packs of Newports ("I guess he's trying to cut down," Danny noted)—became a pattern the next day, when he hit the same place again, with a partner. In the week that followed, the case didn't break as much as it shattered. Even the bad leads paid off—a tip led us to knock at the wrong apartment door in Queens, where a terrified Moroccan threw two pounds of hashish out the window— but the leads were mostly good: a nickname surfaced from the streets, Igor, which turned out to be a real name. We tracked down his mother—*Did you really name him Igor?*—who said was staying in Connecticut; the Connecticut cops said that he was wanted for nine robberies there, and a shooting. He was on the run with a woman, Sharlene, who had taken her two-year-old son with her, and when I talked to her father—*You gotta help me, Detective, you gotta, I don't know if my grandson's alive, I don't know what to do, you gotta help, you gotta, I work so hard, I haven't slept*—he gave me the license plate of their car. On the day we got Sharlene's picture on TV—whether she was a hostage or helpmate, she'd brought a baby on a crime spree—the car was spotted at two more robberies in Manhattan. In one, Igor put a gun to the head of a six-year-old boy, threatening to kill him if he didn't get the money. The next day, I got a call from Sharlene's father—*God bless you, God bless you, you saved my grandson*—telling us that she had surrendered to the cops in Connecticut, and that she had agreed to return with us to help find Igor. When we picked her up she was the picture of flustered innocence and mild apology, as if she knew she shouldn't have taken a ride with a friend who'd been drinking. She asked permission to go to the bathroom before we drove back, and when she returned, she flashed a quick smile and said, "Sorry for the hold-up!"

"You'd oughta be," said Danny.

Though Igor had sworn bloody oaths to die before he'd go to jail, when we found him, he peeped out from under his blanket like a kid playing peekaboo and meekly raised his hands. He was dope-sick, and I kept him going on a junkie's banquet of grape soda and Pop-Tarts, aspirin, antihistamines, and Newports. At the line-ups I had trouble finding male Hispanics without moustaches, and a cop from the Four-Four named Eddie Perez sat in as filler. He slumped in his chair with an absent look, but duly noted each of Igor's boasts about the crime spree. I put them down on a five. The Manhattan cops connected Igor to another bodega stick-up, and fingerprints put him at another, and Sharlene told us about a pizza place—again, he put a gun to a child's head—and when I thought we were finally done—we got his accomplice, too—I got a call from a cell mate of Igor's at Rikers Island, saying he'd told him about more robberies, three convenience stores in Massachusetts, a seventy-five-thousand-dollar payroll heist in Puerto Rico. . . . No, I thought, I'd stay at the Four-Four for a while. Maybe we'd have to make a trip to Puerto Rico, when the weather got colder, combing the beaches and bars with my case folder. Maybe a good case never ends, if you keep on investigating, as every trail leads to another trail, and the footprints meet other feet. The case can go as long as you can go, as long as you keep on walking, as long as the world is round. I'd recently run into George again, my old hit man and armed robber from my days on patrol, and he was back on the streets: Ray-Ray Reyes from PSA-7 had picked him up for a blunt collar. No, I'd stay at the Four-Four for a while.

And though I'd passed on the offer to go to Manhattan Robbery, I did take a trip downtown. If I didn't follow the Bronx motto myself—*Get out, schmuck, get out!*—I could at least send my cases to a friendlier venue. New York is, after all, the capital of second chances. Mike Rodriguez had been working on a triple homicide that would be prosecuted by the U.S. Attorney's Office, and I asked him to see if they might be interested in a few robberies. Mike told me that they were definitely interested, and after we hammered out the details— yes, the cab made trips to Newark Airport, which fell under the Hobbes Act, which regulates interstate trade—I testified in the federal Grand Jury and obtained an indictment. K-Lo and Diba, who had robbed the Rwandan cabbie, had a cute act that played in the Bronx, but I doubted it would make it on the main stage downtown.

"What are they looking at, in terms of sentence?" I asked one of the U.S. Attorneys.

"Let's see . . . offhand, I'd say at least twenty-five for this robbery, but maybe with their records, both of them could be looking at mandatory life."

I winced. For a moment, I felt bad for them, but it passed. I knew I would not have to arrest K-Lo, who was already back in jail. After he'd been emancipated by the Grand Jury, I was looking through old cases, and I found a carjacking that he might fit. I called the detective who had the case from Bronx Robbery, Maria Roman, and suggested she show her victim his picture. It was a hit. When I saw K-Lo in the cells, I walked over to him.

"You don't got nothin' on me," he sneered.

"You have no idea. You are done."

When I reached out to Diba's parole officer to tell him that I'd be lightening his caseload, he told me that I was too late; Diba had been locked up a week before, for the armed robbery of a convenience store on Staten Island. The offer there was fifteen years, but Diba could now add a zero to the figure.

I thought about sending Tareek a card, telling him to enjoy his freedom while he could. Instead, I called downtown again, and suggested that the robbery of a Dominican wire-transfer/travel agency was the definition of a crime against interstate trade.

"We're interested," the U.S. Attorney told me. "Let's get this going—can you fax me down his rap sheet?"

"No problem, but you better make sure there's enough paper in your machine."

You guys, you poor guys, I thought, you shouldn't have beaten me the first time. You gotta have a story, pals, and I got yours.

. . .

BECAUSE OF ADMINISTRATIVE MYSTERIES THAT I HAVE YET TO comprehend, my promotion date was on, then off, then scheduled with me, then without, and I wasn't sure of it or myself until the day before it happened. My dress uniform hadn't been dry-cleaned since St. Patrick's Day, but it seemed serviceable enough. I got a tie clip from Bobby Nardi, and swiped white gloves from John. My wallet was on the dog's choke chain that Uncle Eddie had always used; I reported to Police Headquarters in a Cadillac, as Pat Brown would have. I carried other tokens and tributes, and the day itself was a testament to my father, of advice heeded and ignored, all for the good. We had to arrive a few hours early to hear some speeches and fill out forms, for dental plans and next-of-kin. An hour before promotion, we practiced mounting the stage, stopping at the edge for a salute, and then stepping to the center to rehearse an odd cross-armed gesture, the point of which I didn't understand. As we took our seats, I scanned the back for faces: family and friends, old partners and new. There was John, and Mom, trying to get the camera to flash; there was Mike Kelly's father . . . there . . . Inspector Mullen; there—my high school buddy and old codefendant, Eddie. Why hadn't I thought to invite any informants?

It felt too good to be true, and so it was fitting that the promotion ceremony began with a movie, projected on three screens. A montage of cops in action—walking and running, helping people and holding them—it was a powerful and professional piece, beautifully shot and edited, narrated by James Earl Jones, who began by saying, "This is the NYPD . . ." in the sweet but cellar-deep baritone with which he once said, *Luke, I am your father.* If it went a little heavy on the daredeviltry—ESU rappelling from rooftops, helicopters rising over the skyline, boats charging through whitecaps of the harbor—no one complained. There was footage of 9/11, the Towers burning and falling, and ash-dusted cops at work at rescue and recovery. Then came the faces of the twenty-three cops killed. Everyone was glad that a break for speeches followed, so we wouldn't take the stage red-eyed and sniffling.

No one could not think about the dead, the three thousand gone. My sister Regina had just told me about my uncles' bar, the Trade Inn, and how the workers had recently dug down to that level. A camera crew had followed them, and Regina saw it on TV. Commuter's was set against the foundation wall, and it was untouched, intact, with the napkins folded on the bar beside bowls for peanuts and pretzels, the glasses hanging from the racks, undisturbed except for a film of ash. If anyone had been inside when the planes struck, they could have remained until the rescue workers arrived, lacking nothing but ice for their drinks. I could have told the customers that we - didn't pay there, because of my father, because the owners were family, and they could put the drinks on me. My tab would still have been good.

And maybe you couldn't call it a miracle, because no one had been spared by its survival. But you could take it as a sign, even a sacrament—that's what they taught us in high school, that a sacrament was a sign—that showed there is always some refuge, even in the depths of the fire. I cleaned up my face with my white gloves, and I was glad when I remembered they were Timpanaro's. Moments from now, there would be another sign, not a sacrament but a little act of alchemy, when my tin shield would be turned to gold.

The Commissioner couldn't be there, and the First Deputy Commissioner, Joe Dunne, would preside. I'd met him three years before, when he was Chief of the Department and I was trying to hustle my way into Vice. Now, I was glad I hadn't gone, and he was giving me what I wanted most. Dunne would retire at the end of the year, and his speech was often halting and heavy with emotion. Oaths of office were administered for detectives, sergeants, and lieutenants. He had a few words about each position, but for detectives, he had the least: "The gold shield of the New York City detective is the most prestigious in the world." They began calling names, and we filed out, and I mounted the side of the stage and saluted, and when I reached Dunne at the center, I understood the cross-armed gesture—he shook your hand as he gave you a certificate. I felt as golden as my shield. Dunne laughed as I shook his hand.

"Good for you, Eddie, so far you're the only one who's come up smiling. . . ."

An odd thing had happened to my cop shield a few weeks before. My number was 9786, and the seven had fallen off, for no reason I could fathom. Was it because I'd been there seven years? When I handed in the shield, they looked at me oddly; I was handing in damaged police property, which should have been reported earlier. *What if a perp had found the seven, and built a new shield around it?* The cop shrugged and tossed it in the box. The Department would take my old shield and fix it, and maybe next year, a new cop would pin it to his uniform. After so many years of inheritance, it would be my first bequest: an old shield that was broken and remade, and that I'd carried for a time.

ACKNOWLEDGMENTS

Years of thanks to my agent, Owen Laster, at the William Morris Agency; to my editors at Riverhead, Chris Knutsen, who brought the book in, and Julie Grau, who brought it home; at *The New Yorker,* where the pieces began with Amanda Weil and David Kuhn, under Tina Brown and David Remnick, through Susan Morrison and Alice Truax, whom I still owe dinner. I walk upright today because of Dr. Michael Platzman, Dr. Frank Petito, Joan Durcan, Dr. Patrick O'Leary, who operated on my back, and especially Dr. Kevin Cahill, whose family has offered steadfast friendship. Much of the book was written while enjoying the hospitality of John, Duff, and the late Lambros Lambros. My teachers from high school and college, most notably John Connelly and the late William Alfred, have my abiding gratitude.

Among friends from the Job and around it, I thank here whoever isn't mentioned in the text, and apologize in advance for omissions. Good looking out: Peaches McGillicuddy, Scott Hungreder, George Stevens, George Shannon, Jimmy Sullivan, Lynn Awe, Tony Ingui, Bobby Gerardi, Dave Sin, Alroy Scott, Lisa Bartolomeo, Mike Burke, Tony Stendardo, Mike Lowery, Tommy Sileo, Tabitha Bronstein, Greg Bundza, Angelo Polite, Bobby "Cheech" Perez, Jimmy Cronin, Rob Knapp, Chris Lynch, and Chris Murphy from PSA-7; Nefti Gomez and Lt. Manente from Narcotics; Lt. Truta from the Academy; Lt. Brian Burke of DCPI; Brian Monahan, for his early encouragement; Carl Cespedes, Glenn Bresnan, Timmy Nichols, Kenny Sparks, Vic Cipullo, Paul and Kim Morrison, from the unions; Scott Nicholson and Conor McCourt at TARU; Chief Daniel

Mullin, Counselor Eddie Hayes, and Special Agent Elizabeth Gaine Callender, who helped plot my escape; Pete Tarsnane, Jimmy Conneely, Augie Paese, Nicky Ciuffi, Bobby Grant, Ray Byrne, Izzy Hernandez, John Schwartz, and Lt. O'Toole at Bronx Homicide; Scopac and Carson for transport; from the Four-Four Squad, PAA's Leland Chase and Jackie Green, Inspector James O'Neill, Mike O'Brien, John Hennessy, John McCarthy, Moe Acevedo, Lenny Crawley, Jimmy Hanvey, and Billy Polotaye; at the Bronx DA's Office, Meredith Holtzman, Tom O'Hanlon, Christiana Stover, Licet Tineo, Michelle Rodney, Dana Roth, Dan DeFillippi, Lisa Mattaway, Honey Cohen, and Odalys Alonso; at the U.S. Attorney's Office, Dan Gitner, Mike Scudder, and Bill Craco; Judge John Keenan and Commissioner Nicholas Scoppetta, for their time; for various acts of aiding and abetting: the Deiters; the Kusners; the McTigues; the Timpanaros; all Boas, Drakes, Duffies, Evers, Horans, Lawsons, Lillies, Mailers, Marshalls, Patons, Paynes, Rushes, and Stones; the Kellys of 35th Street; the McGraths of Bay Ridge; Lynn and the Flying Fishers; the Phillipses of Charleston; the McCabes of Woodhaven; the Castells, Princes of Havana; the Ryans of Point Breeze; the Driscolls of Beara and Boston; Adam Stern; Keith Kelly of the *Post*; Meg O'Rourke; Aida Turturro; Liz Phelps; Colin Callender; the late Mike McAlary; Mrs. James Draddy; Giovanni Porcelli; Tommy Shaw; Gus and Che; and everyone at Park Place, especially Helen. You are now all deputized. *Sláinte.*

ABOUT THE AUTHOR

Edward Conlon is a detective with the New York City Police Department. A graduate of Regis High School in New York City and of Harvard, he has published articles in *The New Yorker* and has been included in *The Best American Essays 2001*. He lives and works in the Bronx.